Curriculum Studies Handbook – The Next Moment

Through an incredibly eclectic mix of junior and established scholars, this volume represents a uniquely current and diverse presentation of curriculum studies inquiry. The focus on emergent/junior scholars anticipates evolving lines of inquiry in the field, and brings those inquiries into direct dialogue with experts in the field/s. In this sense, this volume is current, progressive, and in some sense revolutionary.

Michael P. O'Malley, Texas State University

What comes after the reconceptualization of curriculum studies? What is the contribution of the next wave of curriculum scholars? Comprehensive and on the cutting edge, this Handbook speaks to these questions and extends the conversation on present and future directions in curriculum studies through the work of twenty-seven newer scholars who explore, each in their own unique way, the present moment in curriculum studies. To contextualize the work of this up-and-coming generation, each chapter is paired with a shorter response by a well-known scholar in the field, provoking an intra-/inter-generational exchange that illuminates both historical trajectories and upcoming moments. From theorizing at the crossroads of feminist thought and postcolonialism to new perspectives that include critical race *currere*, queer Southern studies, Black feminist cultural analysis, poststructural policy studies, spiritual ecology, and East–West international philosophies, present and future directions in the U.S. field are revealed.

Erik Malewski is Assistant Professor of Curriculum Studies at Purdue University.

Studies in Curriculum Theory
William F. Pinar, Series Editor

For additional information on titles in the Studies in Curriculum Theory series visit
www.routledge.com/education

Curriculum Studies Handbook – The Next Moment

Edited by

Erik Malewski
Purdue University

NEW YORK AND LONDON

First published 2010
by Routledge
270 Madison Ave, New York, NY 10016

Simultaneously published in the UK
by Routledge
2 Park Square, Milton Park, Abingdon, Oxon OX14 4RN

Routledge is an imprint of the Taylor & Francis Group, an informa business

© 2010 Taylor & Francis

Typeset in Baskerville by EvS Communication Networx, Inc.
Printed and bound in the United States of America on acid-free paper by Sheridan Books, Inc.

Library of Congress Cataloging in Publication Data
Curriculum studies handbook—the next moment / edited by Erik L. Malewski.
p. cm.
1. Curriculum planning—Philosophy. 2. Critical pedagogy. I. Malewski, Erik L.
LB2806.15.C6965 2009
375'.001--dc22
2008048805

ISBN10: 0-415-98948-5 (hbk)
ISBN 10: 0-415-98949-3 (pbk)
ISBN 10: 0-203-87779-9 (ebk)

ISBN13: 978-0-415-98948-0 (hbk)
ISBN 13: 978-0-415-98949-7 (pbk)
ISBN 13: 978-0-203-87779-1 (ebk)

Contents

v

Preface

This Handbook addresses the question, What is the work of the post-reconceptualization generation(s) in curriculum studies? It marks the first deliberate effort to delineate the shift toward the post-reconceptualization of curriculum studies using inter- and intragenerational conversations to un(map) the next moments in the field. Showcasing the work of newer scholars to provide understanding of where the field is currently and where it might be heading, across the arch of the Handbook is the juxtaposition of the work of newer academicians who offer fresh perspectives on the field positioned in relation to essays from longtime scholars who reveal the historic and current motivations for their intellectual work.

The idea for this volume originated at the 2006 Purdue conference, *Articulating (Present) Next Moments in Curriculum Studies: The Post-Reconceptualization Generation(s)*. The aim of this conference was to engender intellection on the state of the field through 10 keynotes from scholars newer to curriculum studies (mostly assistant professors) and intra- and intergenerational conversations through an equal number of response essays (one per keynote) given by scholars with a longer history in the field. As the reader might already recognize, to speak of inter- and intragenerational dialogues is not to imply agreement or synthesis. Response essays both inspired and troubled keynote speakers.[1] Similarly, break-out sessions sprinkled throughout the conference schedule to encourage informal discussions and inform those who were new to the field about historical debates and intellectual traditions that underwrite keynote papers, facilitated by key scholars in the field, were interpreted differently. Graduate students and newer faculty found them particularly effective while attendees with a longer history in the field wished for more detailed and challenging discussions. By far the most memorable event for many in attendance was the third day of the conference when concerns over race, representation, knowledge production, and ethical commitments were brought to the surface by a number of attendees. The conference program gave way to impromptu discussions, debates, and arguments over what constituted legitimate work in curriculum studies, as well as issues of academic elitism, cultural alienation, and language differences. While few in attendance will forget some of the heated exchanges and accusations of failure brought against the field, what was most unsettling was the incommensurability of viewpoints that became increasingly evident the longer discussions ensued. It would be safe to say that while eventually the original program was reinstated, the breakdown not only changed the tone for the rest of the conference but, along with other breakdowns like it, became a source of debate over the extent to which the field is open to historically subjugated perspectives, ideas, and people.

While it might be hard to determine whether the highlight was one of the intellectually engaging papers, informal conversations with colleagues, or the opportunity to gather with other curriculum scholars to speculate on how the field might change in the future, what has become most fascinating for me in the intervening 2 years involves the range of interpretations that have been offered by attendees on the breakdown that occurred that third day. Some scholars felt that starting the conference with an introduction to the history of curriculum studies, including key scholarship on race, class, and gender issues, might have helped avoid the breakdown. Others saw the breakdown as further evidence of identity politics and the sorts of debates that—lodged in the authenticity of group experience—result in infighting among progressive scholars and balkanization of the field. Still others saw it as evidence that reconceptualization scholarship has yet to make it into the schools or that the field has yet to adequately address the theory–practice divide. In contrast, some found the breakdown a fruitful site for producing and learning differently without necessarily overcoming differences and dissensus on the way toward a reductionist, common sensibility about next moments in the field. This last group seemed to find promise in letting differences surface, engaging in debates over the merits of different viewpoints and theoretical frameworks, and letting those differences stand without a rush toward a conclusion so as to advance the field. Instead, they found the challenges to the character of the scholarship and the conference program to be expected in terms of the myriad of theoretical clusters that make up the field, each operating with different assumptions, outlooks, and histories. Equally telling, after analyzing these different interpretations of the breakdown, I came away with a sense of how the very question of the status of the field illuminates how words and phrases such as *curriculum* and *post-reconceptualization* are less established sites of shared understanding than contested sites in which politics play out and struggles over meaning occur. To borrow an idea from Snaza's chapter in this volume, when it comes to attempts to capture the status of the field, we are only beginning to learn how to pose the question of the state.

After the conference was over I quickly went to work on putting together a collection of essays that kept with the original theme, what is the work of the post-reconceptualization generation(s)? More specifically, a question that I first asked in 2004 after noticing a series of presentations, articles, and book chapters speculating on the direction of the field after reconceptualization, which turned into the 2006 Purdue conference, then became the impetus for inviting 17 scholars to join the 10 scholars who presented at the conference in authoring chapters and inviting 13 additional scholars to craft the additional response essays. I recognized putting together a collection of essays that spoke to the state of the field was going to be tricky, possibly trickier than acting as chair of the conference. In soliciting contributions, I tried to attend to issues of intellectual diversity as well as diversity in scholarly backgrounds and identities, from the usual issues one might consider in terms of race, class, gender, sexual identity, and so on, to less usual issues of intellectual and organizational affiliations and region while not losing sight of the purpose of the text.

Certainly the intention of this volume is not a comprehensive survey of the field, as was the aim with Pinar, Reynolds, Slattery, and Taubman's (1995) *Understanding Curriculum: An Introduction of Historical and Contemporary Curricular Discourses.* Neither is this collection an effort to represent the entire field as it is (without our own agendas) as opposed to how those associated with this collection wish it to be. Rather, the aim here is to offer tentative orientations toward the next moment in the field for scholars and scholarship that comes after the reconceptualization movement. Our agendas and desires are evident in every chapter and response essay. As something less than polemical and more than an exchange of ideas, this collection proceeds with the conviction that the continued dominance of neoliberal, neoconservative, and developmental discourses is a bad thing. What constitutes these discourses, however, is a source of debate and contention. That its effects upon schools, the public's concept of curriculum, and notions of credible educational research must be challenged is not. This is not a choice contributors to this collection made just prior to its publication. Instead, it is work at the dynamic, tension-ridden site of post-reconceptualization that is our inheritance; it is what becomes us and what we struggle toward. Out of our ethical commitments the range of possibilities follow: That there be spaces for traditionalists, empiricists, and developmentalist discourses regardless of the extent to which such ideas need to be challenged, but that such work be displaced so as to break up sedimentary conjunctions, epistemological dominance, to open spaces where a thousand theories and stories are made and unmade, where alternative feasible readings proliferate.

Why focus upon inter- and intragenerational conversations? First, my aim here in presenting curriculum studies in general and post-reconceptualization in particular as contested sites involves moving away from traditional representations of the field and toward juxtapositions of perspectives in order to incite a multiplicity of possible readings, ones that allow for moving along different registers of thought and against grand unifying theories. Here the work of chapter authors sits in conversation with response essays in ways that might offer openings to a broader range of viewpoints than if chapters where not juxtaposed with responses. Second, in referencing inter- and intragenerational conversations the hope is to destabilize the notion of generations of curriculum scholars either wholly rebelling against the previous generation or wholly writing in their shadows. One will notice that many scholars newer to the field are chapter authors while many scholars with longer histories in the field respond to and contextualize their orientations and theories. Also, some chapter authors are set in intragenerational dialogue with response essay writers who have unique perspectives but are possibly of the same generation or closely linked in terms of length of time working in curriculum studies respectively. As something other than repudiating history or continuing on state unchanged, the idea behind the structure of this text is to disrupt the notion that next moments in the field belong to a single generation or that post-reconceptualization necessarily be interpreted as that which comes after reconceptualization, that such terms be locked in hierarchical relationships rather than opened up to play, contestations, and as of yet unknown meanings.[2] As I hope to illustrate in the introduction, delineating what is inside and outside curriculum and the field of curriculum studies is not only difficult business, fraught with problems, but it might not be as useful in assessing the field along two key registers of thought: (1) whether we are responsible and accountable only to the issues and concerns of powerful epistemological forces or those marginalized, subjugated, and distorted, and (2) whether we are committed to only circulating new languages, concepts, and ideas within the field or out, across, and along various lines of discourse to reach variously situated publics, educators, and intellectuals.

Lastly, situating scholars newer to the field as the majority of chapter authors and scholars with longer histories in the field as response essayists is not an attempt to upstage more established scholars or lay claim to post-reconceptualization as the terrain of a younger generation. Instead, what might be a standard convention of the academy to seek the input of longstanding members of a field on important themes and issues is troubled by the effort to highlight the orientations and ideas of scholars who are for the most part earlier in their careers. And, in continuing this vein of thought, to ask senior scholars who might be thought of as experts in the field to read and reflect upon the ideas and perspectives of newer scholars. While the reader can judge the effectiveness of this inversion, this is an attempt to theorize in the organization of this text the qualities of difficult knowledge, those ideas and concepts which evoke surprise, curiosity, and wonder. This is in contrast to what might be termed easy knowledge, or structures for organizing texts that register as expectations met and conventions fulfilled.

The former confronts the reader with something different from what they think they want from a text while the latter functions only to fulfill what has been in terms of what the reader believes they will find in the organization of a state of the field handbook. In this sense, the hope is to extend beyond restrictive representations toward a sort of vacillation between a range of traditions, perspectives, and ideas brought to the reader for consideration. Here irony, juxtaposition, and not knowing as a way of knowing become the very force of learning. It is my desire that in this differently organized text what one knows when easy knowledge is no longer possible becomes the promise of thinking with and through curriculum studies in a different state.

What does all this mean for students reading this book? For students who are new to the curriculum field this might seem like an unruly text, a chaotic collection that offers few guideposts by which to find one's way. This is the reality of contemporary curriculum studies, an interdisciplinary field less continuous and coherent than discontinuous and fractured. Fifteen years ago it might have been appropriate to identify discourses by way of gender, race, political, poststructural, aesthetics, autobiography, theology, and so on, in the field. Since then much has changed. Cultural studies, critical race theory, and critical geography have entered the field. Discourses that might in the past have been distinguishable have made their way into hybrid spaces that make their unique characteristics indeterminable. Queer theory, place, autobiography, and Southern studies combine to make the work of Ugena Whitlock, for example. Similarly, Denise Taliaferro-Baszile brings together autobiography, critical race theory, and postpositivism to carve out a unique onto-epistemological space within the field. Others have shifted theoretical lenses to shed new light on familiar topics. Howard and Tappan move from a focus on poverty within political curriculum theory to highlight the nature of privilege and identity, effectively challenging cultural deficit theories focused on the poor by highlighting the pathologies of the elite. McKnight employs Kierkegaard's notions of despair and passionate inwardness to reconfigure a space within critical pedagogy to deal with the contradictions between existential becoming and restrictive educational environments. Still others have illustrated that there remains many understudied and unstudied topics within curriculum history. Ann Winfield employs eugenic ideology to examine a difficult past, Bernadette Baker illustrates how mesmeric studies informed the concepts that have come to matter so much to the curriculum field, and LaVada Brandon offers an alternate reading of Carter G. Woodson.

I could continue on with descriptions of how the field has changed but the work of these scholars is explored in more depth in the introduction. The point is that the scholarship of the contemporary field represents an increasingly complex and eclectic range of backgrounds and interests with scholars producing knowledge that combines ethical commitments with various theories to take up unique positions in the field. Furthermore, few scholars in the contemporary field seek to identify the traditions that inform their work or seek out consolidation or consensus in ways that easily allow for insertion into a broader typography. This is not to suggest there are no through-lines that might draw dimensions of different scholars' work into relationship (seven are offered in the introduction). Rather, it means for new curriculum students that studying historical movements, debates, and theories has become even more paramount to understanding the contemporary state of the field. The rapid rate of change and increasingly complex nature of curriculum studies also requires giving up on knowledge we can grab hold of in any complete sense to embrace proliferations, tensions, and discontinuities. As new students become more familiar with the field and all of its dimensions, they might do well to trace their own course of study through crafting personal, conceptual montages at the crossroads of the scholarship they study and their personal experiences with it.

Note

1. While many examples might be given, Ellen Brantlinger's response to Guillory's keynote was particularly memorable for the ways it troubled audience members, as well as the keynoter. Largely unchanged from the chapter here, Guillory presented a paper that examined Black female rap as pedagogy, with particular attention to issues of sexuality, power, and same and opposite gender relationships. Brantlinger's response focused on, among other topics, the trouble she had with the notion that explicit sexual lyrics become a part of school curriculum or topics of discussion between teachers and high school students. Audience members at different points interrupted Brantlinger's talk and challenged her positions. Their remarks highlighted concern for Brantlinger's categorical distinctions between acceptable and unacceptable topics of discussion, that the ideas and concepts reflected in the lyrics were already a part of the language, repertoire, and life world of the students regardless of whether Brantlinger felt comfortable or willing to acknowledge it. At moments like these, one might suggest evidence of a generational divide became evident during the conference.

2. Rubén Gaztambide-Fernández, in his article entitled "Representing Curriculum" in a special issue of the *Journal of Curriculum Inquiry* (2009) focused on *The Sage Handbook of Curriculum and Instruction* (Connelly, He, and Phillion), contrasts that handbook with this one. He finds that while both produce curriculum and pedagogy as expanding and changing, Connelly and colleagues portray those changes as continuing past traditions and as bounded or coherent. In this collection, he suggests different assumptions are made. That is, the curriculum field is represented as chaotic, layered, and discontinuous, as more of a mosaic than a linear line of progression. I find his assessment insightful.

References

Connelly, M., He, M. F., & Phillion, J. (2008). *The Sage handbook of curriculum and instruction.* Thousand Oaks, CA: Sage.

Gaztambide-Fernández, R. (2009). Representing curriculum. *Curriculum Inquiry, 39*(1), 235–253.

Acknowledgments

There are many scholars to whom I owe immense gratitude for assistance in turning the vision for this edited collection into a reality. I owe a special thanks to Janet Miller for her guidance and support. I will always remember her thoughtful responses to my inquiries and our conversations about the challenges of organizing a conference. I owe a special thanks to Madeleine Grumet for inspiring me with an amazing recollection of her experiences writing *Bitter Milk: Women and Teaching*. Similarly, I wish to thank Patti Lather for providing feedback on organizing this text and turning me toward additional readings that helped me make sense of the events that led up to this handbook. Your intellectual efforts shaped the conditions of possibility for much of the work included here. Many thanks also to Bernadette Baker, Alexandra Fidyk, Rubén Gaztambide-Fernández, Karen Ferneding, Adam Howard, Bill Schubert, and Patrick Slattery who offered advice and feedback at various stages of assembling this collection. And, of course, I owe a great deal of thanks to the chapter contributors and response essayists who made this handbook possible. Without question, chapter authors showed excitement about the project, gladly accepted constructive criticism through the peer review process and revised their chapters accordingly, and made it easier to make adjustments to the book with their flexibility. Response essayists were equally excited about project and I felt honored by their willingness to contribute and their sense that this is a worthy endeavor. Most of all, I am thankful for the friendships that became possible as the result of this work; I was able to get to know many of the chapter authors and response essayists much better in the process of chairing the conference and assembling this collection. It is those friendships that make the work of editing a collection like this worthwhile.

I also wish to thank many former and present Purdue University graduate students who have provided editorial assistance and help with administrative tasks that ranged from organizing paperwork and sending e-mails to taping the keynotes and staffing the book table at the conference where the idea for this book first took shape. Suniti Sharma, thank you so much for our editorial assistance and literary insights. Who would have thought the multiculturalism course that was required for your teacher certification would turn into a lifelong collegial and professional relationship. Bruce Parker and Tony Kariotis, thank you so much for helping with the conference and initial stages of this book. Similarly, I owe a great deal of thanks to my staff assistant, Kim Deardorff, who worked tirelessly throughout this entire process to keep track of chapters, biographic statements, and contracts. Last, I owe a great deal of thanks to George Hynd, Dean of the Purdue College of Education at the time, for finding worth in this project and agreeing to its financial support, and the Purdue University College of Education for similar forms of assistance.

With special thanks, I want to acknowledge the friendship and mentorship of Bill Pinar. Already familiar with his work in phenomenology, autobiography, and place, I first met Bill and his partner Jeff many years ago in New Orleans over a dinner meeting held during an AERA annual conference. The only graduate student at the dinner and expecting to observe (and not speak), I was taken back at his interest in my research and the sincerity with which he engaged me in intellectual conversation. Over the years we kept in touch and his work on Ida B. Wells inspired my research into the biography of Mahatma Gandhi, the motivation for a research trip to India. For this collection, I want to acknowledge the ways in which he offered his support and guidance from 2004 to the present, from crafting and promoting the conference to feedback on the design and layout of this edited text. During that time, Pinar's enthusiasm for this project seemed boundless; he gladly took my late night phone calls when a crisis arose and sent kind supportive e-mails that always seemed to arrive just when I needed them. Most important, he offered his ideas and advice without apology but remained supportive and unfazed when I decided to go a different way. For example, he has never seemed as interested in the postdiscourses as I have been and wished that I were more declarative in the introduction and my portion of the epilogue for this book. Despite our differing perspectives, Pinar continues to be an influential figure for me both professionally and personally, and I know my scholarship is better because of it. It only seems appropriate that this edited collection on post-reconceptualization be dedicated to him.

Also, I must thank my mother, Janet Adler, and special friend, Gregory Black, for asking, sometimes daily, if I had finished editing "that book." While they feigned interest in all that I was doing, they never lacked concern for my well-being and if I had a productive day doing it. If it was not for your support and constant prodding, it might have taken even longer.

Finally, I wish to thank the editors associated with this process. Naomi Silverman, you have been such a pleasure to work with and I appreciate your spiritedness, knowledge, and dedication. I also wish to thank the editorial board members who took part in the review process, allowing each chapter author to receive confidential feedback from two or more reviewers. Without failure, by means I had most often not pinpointed, they identified ways to strengthen the submissions. When revised chapters came back in and I needed additional insight into whether the changes addressed reviewers' concerns, the members of the editorial board were most helpful. Most of all, it was the spirit with which members of the editorial board engaged in the review process that was inspiring. Almost always, they possessed deep knowledge of the work of chapter authors prior to submission, and were able to offer valuable feedback because of it. And, that feedback was always within the realm of constructive guidance and criticism that comes with deep dedication to a field. I owe all of the editorial board members listed below a great deal of thanks.

Editorial Board

Kathryn Benson, Alan Block, Jeanne Brady, Joshua Brown, Patti Bullock, Terry Carson, Omari Dyson, Jacob Easley, Susan Edgerton, Leah Fowler, Ming Fang He, Bryant Griffith, Kent den Heyer, Jon Kelland, Deborah Keller, Gregory Keller, Michael O'Malley, Susan Mayer, Rich Milner, Nicholas Ng-A-Fook, Patrick Roberts, Suniti Sharma, Kris Sloan, Peter Taubman, Yu Tianlong, Tammy Turner-Vorbeck, William Reynolds, Encarna Rodriguez, Teresa Strong-Wilson, Tony Whitson

1 Introduction
Proliferating Curriculum

Erik Malewski

For Lyotard, the aim of philosophy is not to resolve differends but rather to detect (a cognitive task) and bear witness to them (an ethical obligation) this is precisely what the millennial generation of curriculum works may do. (Sears & Marshall, 2000, p. 210)

An interpretation does what it says. It may pretend to simply state, show, and inform, but it actually produces. It is already performative in a way.... The political vigilance that this calls for on our part obviously consists in organizing a critical examination of all the mechanisms that hold out the appearance of *saying* the event when they are in fact making it, interpreting and producing it. (Derrida, quoted in Mitchell & Davison, 2007, p. 229)

Our Inheritance and the Conditions of Possibility

Huebner, in his 1976 essay, "The Moribund Curriculum Field: Its Wake and Our Work" made an incisive, if less frequently referenced intervention into the debates over the state of the curriculum field. He asserted, about what was termed the field's dying status,

> The curriculum field no longer serves to unify us. The dispersing forces are too great, the attraction of new associations and the possibilities of new households too compelling. The people need our diverse capabilities; but if our own energies continue to be applied to holding ourselves together, we will not have the energies left to serve them. If the diverse interests and collectivities that have been gathering over the past seventy years are cleared away, we might be able to see the original conception of curriculum and to do and describe our work more effectively. (p. 155)

He then went on to claim, "our problem is to explore the nature of the course of study—the content—and to eliminate the interests which do not bear directly upon this content" (p. 156).

Of course, the assumptions that underwrite this take on the status of curriculum studies—and others like it—have in the past and continue in the present to incite debate. There might be reasons to contest the empirical investments in some of Huebner's work, for example. Or, one might dispute the notion that unification is a necessary precondition for effectively examining courses of study. One might even contest his notion that an original conception of curriculum exists and therefore might be discovered by clearing away other seemingly nonrelevant interests. One might also challenge Huebner's emphasis on synthesis and transcendence over multiplicity and difference. Attributable to the effect postdiscourses have had on the field, there is much in this statement that contemporary curriculum scholars might find problematic. Yet—to be certain—to a curriculum scholar who emphasizes evolving spirituality, self-definition, and the critical examination of language and discourse—and asserted in no uncertain terms that relying upon developmental and instrumental concepts would not get either the field or schooling where it needed to go—Huebner's scholarship might function as a comforting text for the present day field. His body of work attests to the belief that curriculum's objects and concepts should not—indeed cannot—function to separate technique from politics, artistry, and temporality, to name only a few domains within the curriculum field to which he made a contribution. Huebner's call to examine democratic ideology, media representations, and issues of power and access might seem prophetic as we look back at the first signs of reconceptualization, an indicator of a field that was yet to come.

To read both with and against Huebner, then, might be contradictory and therefore an unreasonable thing to do. Why, someone might ask, read such work as profoundly central to the contemporary field and also as both limited and limiting? What is the purpose in starting off an introduction in such a way? Part of the argument I offer in this introduction is that in order to have complicated conversations about "next moments" in curriculum studies we must begin to illustrate how historical works, such as Huebner's, give us the concepts and objects that enable dialogue while at the same time those objects and concepts give us the very horizon of intelligibility. To do otherwise, to simply read in concert as a way to honor the past or in dissent as a way to rebel against the work of a previous generation, one subscribes to a quite dangerous dogmatism; in either celebration or denigration there is the very refusal to work with difference. Derrida describes this denial as the inability to see the relationship between mechanical repeatability and irreplaceable singularity as neither a relation of homogeneity or externality (Derrida, 1978; see also Gasché, 1994; Wood & Bernasconi, 1988). That is, an inability to see a relation from past to present in which the elements of each are internal to one another and yet remain heterogeneous. That said, let me acknowledge Huebner's contribution to curriculum studies and the conditions that made possible reconceptualization and, the focus of this text, explorations of post-reconceptualization. His work represents a lifetime commitment to developing political, theological, and phenomenological discourses within the curriculum field, focused not just on the academy, but also on the relationship between curriculum theory and school contexts, as well as the elements of the world that shape educational experiences. Also, it is important to acknowledge, as frequent references in the chapters included here attest, that these pages aimed at getting some sort of grasp on post-reconceptualization owe a great deal to William Pinar's intellect, guidance, foresight, courage, and, above all, his example, much more than they might reveal, as the same should be said for those scholars associated with the reconceptualization movement, ones that make up the editorial board, response essay writers, and arguably select chapters of this collection.

Recognizing that, and that unlike Schwab who focused much of his career on scientific principles, Huebner was working on concepts and metaphors that became more central to a field indebted to the arts and humanities (see Pinar 1999, 2008), the first point that should be taken away from Huebner's contributions to the field is that he made the case for understanding what might be termed postprogressive era politics of curriculum studies, framed not as merely a historical but also an epistemological moment. Content development and instructional strategies were no longer the primary questions curriculum scholars had to address with this changed state of affairs, this shift in outlooks in the field, questions of understanding subsumed greater urgency. The challenge before the field, therefore, was not to employ the "conceptual or empirical in the sense social scientists typically employ them" (Pinar, 1978) or "prescriptive evaluation instruments with an emphasis on curriculum as an object or a noun" (Slattery, 1997) but to focus upon "[t]he intellectual labor of understanding" whereby through "self-reflexive and dialogic labor one can contribute to the field's intellectual advancement and to one's own" (Pinar, 2007, p. xii). The most important element of this movement, its aim, would be the study of "the subjective experience of history and society, the inextricable relationships among which structural educational experience" (Pinar, 2004, p. 25).

Others besides Huebner are cited at the beginning of this introduction because he, the other contributors to this book, and I have been inspired by—one might say enamored with the study of educational experiences—although not from a dogmatic position but rather one inspired by a series of thinkers, ones that range from Heidegger and Foucault to hooks and Sedgwick. Also, it is not the aim here, by provoking the name of one of the less often referenced and yet central figures to reconceptualization, to imply that what follows, while an intellectual endeavor, signals a second reconceptualization, or, to be more specific, a contemporary redirection of the field with the qualities of the reconceptualization movement that occurred in the 1970s. Like Huebner, the concern of the contemporary field continues to involve a rejection (reconfiguration?) of traditional curriculum development in favor of the pursuit of politically inspired scholarship with the capacity to meet the promise of a democracy yet to come, one that engenders imagination, deliberation, and creativity. And also, it focuses upon curriculum-in-the-making, a continuous process of reflexivity, rather than what Schubert (1992) describes as "the necessity of producing theory, which carries a more brittle and dusty image of something finished and on a shelf" (p. 236). Unlike Huebner, the lines between development and understanding in the present day field are a lot less clear. Accordingly, this collection is an intervention in that it seeks to explicitly intervene within academic debates, while contemporary issues in education evidently influence the scholarship included here, and seeks to learn from and influence those issues. In the same vein, it is important to differentiate between interventionist academic work and activist work, a differentiation that became more clear after the breakdown at the 2006 Purdue conference (where the idea for this collection originated) over what scholarly efforts and intellectual practices were appropriate to the field.[1] This collection without a doubt represents a shift in knowledge production in the curriculum field but forgoes what has become an accepted belief in arenas such as cultural studies and critical pedagogy that interventionist scholarship is also activist, collapsing an important distinction between those who produce and circulate knowledge on a subject and those who often take great risks, sometimes involving their livelihood and, even more important, their lives.

Preferring a more modest conception, I begin this edited collection by invoking the name of Huebner and others, such as Pinar, to acknowledge a certain inheritance, a field passing through the hands of generations where each generation is indebted to the forbearers whose efforts to some extent set the conditions for their contributions. To state it simply, this collection would not be possible without the work of innumerable scholars both within and outside curriculum studies. But this begs the question, with the varied scholarship that makes up the history of the field, why choose this particular essay of Huebner's? "The Moribund Curriculum: Its Wake and Our Work" is a relevant essay, or accomplice for establishing through-lines that draw these divergent essays into a collective intervention because, for a start, it too is interventionist and situated between the diagnosis (moribund) and the cure (a shift in the field). Second, and most important when it comes to "next moments" in the curriculum field, Huebner's response to a preoccupation (obsession?) with questions of a technical nature, ones that have confused quick fixes and educational slogans with authentic efforts to change the educational world, is to call for theoretical reflection infused with political engagement and pedagogical work in the field and in schools. Huebner was teaching us that curriculum theorizing must lead to changes in the ways that our intellectual practices are conceptualized and actualized to be considered knowledge of most worth; next moments must focus on creating a more just and equitable world by way of offering alternative language and readings to those focused on developmentalism and technique. Otherwise, he aptly warns us, we risk being "school people…the silent majority who embrace conservatism" (Huebner, 1999, p. 239).

Key to this edited collection, as the scholarship included here shapes the conditions of possibility for present and future scholarship, just as Huebner's does for this collection, what he believes the field needs is not simply a reactionary in the streets activism but theory with the capacity to incite reflection alongside pedagogical and political engagement. To paraphrase Pinar's reading of Huebner's contributions to curriculum studies, the strength of Huebner's theoretical formations is that he refuses to separate educational change from theory, without making the all too common error in the curriculum field of conflating the two (Pinar, 1999). What Huebner characterized as exhausted scholarship that neglected all but the developmental and technical aspects of curriculum (Huebner emphasized, for example, aesthetic language, curriculum history, and praxis as three unique but interrelated areas where curriculum theorists might conduct their work) called for interrogating the conditions that made such a narrow outlook possible and the careful crafting of alternative readings and understandings of the world. Pinar and others of the reconceptualist movement replied; new concepts were offered as a response.

This is exactly the claim being offered here too. Post-reconceptualization in all its as of yet indeterminability will arise from what Pinar and others of the reconceptualist movement have offered, how it shapes and is shaped by those who inherit the field, and also how it is imagined and reimagined in unforeseen ways to produce a different state, a post-reconceptual state. Or, to offer a slightly different viewpoint, that not just the next political moment confronting school curriculum, in the form of questions over what content will and will not be taught, but the next disciplinary or epistemological moment (and what that will bring to bear upon teaching, learning, and studying inside as well as outside schools)—which is referred to here as post-reconceptualization—requires careful attention be paid to theoretical shifts in the field. And, most importantly, that these shifts be read thematically as well as singularly, but not taken lightly or glossed over as regurgitations of existing theories or theories imported unchanged from other fields. As Grumet so aptly reminds us in her response essay to chapter 19 in this collection, some questions might remain the same across generations while the responses of each generation are unique. For doubled readings to occur—those that neglect neither through-lines nor particularities—epistemological and disciplinary next moments will be of paramount importance. Similarly, readers of post-reconceptualization must make discourse on curriculum account for its complicity in naturalizing what are ultimately developmental and technical understandings of contemporary and future educational moments, as well as naturalizing conventional readings of our present context and the implausibility (and impracticality) of imagining a different future.

Our work does not stop here, however. It must also provide insight into the historical conditions that allowed for the objects and concepts that have come to matter so much to the contemporary field and the practice of curriculum (see Baker, Brandon, and Winfield, this collection). In other words, even as the state of public education seems particularly bleak after 8 years of the Bush administration; the dismantling of whatever slight gains in racial equality have been allowed by affirmative action; and national education policies, such as Goals 2000 and No Child Left Behind, ones that make it clear that the educational experiences of the public do not matter, the state of curriculum is not merely a matter of politics, or one to be managed exclusively through a reconfiguration of institutional discourses (It should be noted, however, as evidenced by the establishment of accreditation and professional standards by the American Association for the Advancement of Curriculum Studies and the Commission on the Status of Curriculum Studies, there is a return to institutional discourses in ways that should be of benefit to the field). Questions over studying, teaching, and learning, as well as understanding, reading, and intervening, are profoundly ontological, epistemological, and political. As I argue in my contribution to the tripartite epilogue at the conclusion of this collection, after reading (and rereading) all the chapters and essays that constitute this text, curriculum demands, perhaps with even more urgency, the production and circulation of new concepts. Huebner foreshadowed such claims with his assertion that the field needs "two threads of investigation." The first, he teaches us, involves identifying the knowledge that might constitute a course of study. The second, he shares with his readers, requires mechanisms that make that knowledge present to the public (Huebner, 1976, p. 160). As this collection illustrates, debates over the relationship between theory and practice, Marxism and existentialism, and principles and proliferation are being interwoven, extended across multiple registers, and compelled along various lines of discourse (academic language, lay language, and so on), so as to reach variously situated publics and intellectuals. This is the burden (I hope, one that is welcomed) facing the post-reconceptualization generation(s), those who must work the ruins left by the post-discourses into what Lather (2001), as one of the field's key poststructural scholars, terms "a fruitful site" (p. 200), one that can make use of "the concept of doubled practices" (p. 199).

What, then, is meant by *post-reconceptualization*? In some sense, the term is misleading. While it certainly envelops the postdiscourses and the uncertainty they have brought to bear upon the field in terms of transparency of language, self-presence, and tendencies toward dominance in spite of libratory intentions, this ambivalence is not the interpretive whole of an increasingly complex and interdisciplinary field. It has also been used to refer to a generational shift among scholars working in the field (Malewski, 2006; Morris, 2005); a new phase in curriculum theorizing (Wright, 2005); the move to see a lack of definition and proliferation not as balkanization but as a healthy state (Lather, this collection); the pursuit of translations across difference (Wang, this collection); and the reconceptualization of existing theories of curriculum and pedagogy (Appelbaum, in press). Therefore, by deploying post-reconceptualization, I want to signal less a field at a particular juncture or in a particular state than a site of debate, of contention and struggle. Displacing a paradigmatic take that the "post" indicates a break, the "post" in post-reconceptualization signifies scholarship that is trying to come to terms with reconceptualization through counterdiscourses that challenge concepts and objects that have come to matter so much to the field and the field of practice, and coadunate-discourses that so intermingled "provoke existing terminology into doing new work" (Rolleston, 1996).

The reading practices so evident in this collection—and therefore associated with post-reconceptualization—have been made possible by way of larger struggles with empiricism and its grounding in the empirical. That is, post-reconceptualization is not the equivalent of postempiricism but becomes possible out of the condition it makes— struggles not so much with the idea of structure itself but instead an intellectual practice that involves confronting, attempting to displace, and also admitting complicity with empiricism. As Derrida (1978) teaches us, in his now infamous response to Lévi-Strauss, the system-dream of philosophy could not deliver on its promise of a break with empiricism. Instead, he refers to structuralism's failure as "the empirical endeavor of either a subject or a finite richness which it can never master" (p. 289). So within curriculum studies postempiricism becomes a method for critical persuasion at the site of post-reconceptualization (not one that begins with post-reconceptualization, if such a demarcation is even possible, but one that is put to work with increasing frequency in both conventional and innovative ways) that assumes the following: that reading practices and textual analyses are a point of departure toward new and different understandings. Empiricism, of course, assumes that language is transparent, that it has the capacity to function efficiently and neutrally as a vehicle for representation and can therefore capture the real, the social, the event. Those operating under empiricism assume what Fustel de Coulanges (cited in Barthes, 1989, p. 132) termed the chastity of history, that an objective persona can be adopted by the utter so that the referent might speak all on it own. Via the empiricist lens, language is a vehicle and has no signatory function of its own. Even with attempts to account for the effects of postdiscourses, as seems to be the trend in contemporary educational research, what has been termed the "interpretive" turn in the social sciences, empiricism remains and the object under study is assumed transparent, the "real," on the other side of language, discourse, and the play of signification, waiting to be brought into understanding. Postempiricism, at least as it informs the site of debate over post-reconceptualization, does not assume the subject as autonomous or the complete source for agency; it does assume object as subject and subject as object. In short, the process of reading so evident in the chapters and response essays that makes up this collection works toward the discomposition of the divide between the two.

You might question, what is the relationship between Huebner's assertions, empiricism, and next moments in the field of curriculum studies? What do debates in literary and social science circles have to do with educational research in general and curriculum studies in particular? To offer a response, a series of other questions might illuminate for the reader what is at stake in terms of what postempiricism makes possible within post-reconceptualization: what is this object, this concept, this thing called curriculum in the first place? How might the features of this object be characterized? Why? How have educators come to know this object? This concept? How has the "state" of this object or concept changed over time? Has it changed? Do educators claim to see it, read about it, hear about it? In what contexts? Do educators find what they learned intelligible? What would have made what they learned more or less recognizable? In an interdisciplinary field, such as curriculum studies, do educators give consideration to how different clusters of theorizing within the field might produce and promulgate curriculum differently? That those who work in autobiography might see one thing in curriculum while those who work in phenomenology or poststructuralism, or at the crossroads of two or more clusters, might see another? Does curriculum reproduce inequity and incite resistance among those already disenfranchised as political curriculum scholars might claim? And, if so, should social reconstruction be addressed through material redistribution, cultural resignification, or both? Or, following the Pinarian tradition, is democratization of one's interiority a precondition for social reconstruction? By what criteria might we make our ethical commitments to certain positions and what is at stake in such decisions? And, to pose a more interesting question: do those positions that fail to account for complicity and unintended effects become the eventual barriers toward justice in spite of claims to emancipation? If so, what are the implications for curriculum theorizing? Is it possible that patient, careful reading can make a difference that matters in what has come to matter in curriculum studies? Along the same lines, might whatever transpires in post-reconceptualization function not as a supplement to developmentalism and proceduralism but really, actually, open a site for reconceptualizing how we read and intervene upon experiences in education and in the public?

Of course, these questions are not quite the same as those posed by Huebner. Yet, in an important way they can be found to be parallel. The questions held by curriculum scholars across generations, one might say, harmonize. That is, together they constitute an interwoven network; they are the threads that bind us across time and space. He too asked of curriculum scholars, how do you understand empiricism? You say the concern is with the empirical and proving a relationship between content delivered and learning acquired. For me, it is not so simple; for me it is of utmost importance that we critically examine the concepts used for organizing the data, for giving curriculum meaning. The reader familiar with hermeneutics might grasp, in so saying, that from a careful, patient reading of Huebner's body of work what emerges are postempirical texts. What I am suggesting is that Huebner was not attempting merely a different interpretation *of* curriculum but an intervention *within* curriculum itself. That is, in his work he yearns to produce a different object when educational scholars and practitioners alike think about curriculum. In the work he did to change the status of this object, he also imagines it as a subject; instead of a focus on his own subjectivity, his agency in relation to his scholarship, how he would like his career to advance while on faculty, or how he would like to be remembered, he is seized by the question of how concepts shape the very meaning given to curriculum when curriculum is given meaning. That is, the question is granted primacy as it makes possible an intervention into the object so as to change it.

So too is this the aim of this edited collection, and in so doing, the chapters and response essays included here produce a different object not only for the academy but for those educators working inside as well as outside schools, and those writing within post-reconceptualization as a contested site, a site of vitality and exchange. For readers of this collection, we have produced curriculum as an object that cannot be struggled with empirically, one that when read patiently and carefully will not be conceptualized simply as object and therefore beyond the inquiring subject, but also as living in language and therefore as a subject. For those who think of post-reconceptualization as a break away from reconceptualization—a paradigm shift—this might sound like a rehearsal of existing terminology, a return to a prior period or an extension of an existing one. These conceptions of curriculum as object and change through paradigm shifts date back between three to four decades, if not further.[2] Yet, it seems the stakes are high, particularly when paradigmatic language is inadequate to the changes that have taken place in the field and epistemological conditions have made it possible to assert that we have reached the end of theory. A notion that although challenged by feminist scholar Judith Butler (2004) with the declaration, there is no "'livable' life for the individual or the public without theorizing these existences" (p. 1), resonates with education scholars who find prior language exhausted with no new discourse-systems to replace it. Taking the insights from the critique of developmentalism and instrumentalism interpreted as a creative political–intellectual movement and applying them to the study of not just curriculum but to technical notions of study, which is another term for the critique of teacher education, what the authors seek here is to finish the critique of developmentalism initiated by the reconceptualization movement and added to by way of the tools offered by the postdiscourses.

In our contemporary disciplinary moment, we have come to a difficult crossroads. We assume that because we have achieved certain intellectual advances they are permanent—an enduring strike against those forces that reduce education to instrumental, calculative concepts. The recent turn toward professional and accreditation standards, reinventing the canon, and a commission to assess the status of the field leave one less than certain that this is the case. We cannot risk such assumptions. This edited collection makes a statement that in exploring post-reconceptualization—and postdiscourses, including postempiricism—there remains much work to do despite assertions that reconceptualization is no longer valuable because the movement abandoned schools or has been eclipsed by internationalization. Missing from such assertions, of course, is the work that must be done to translate across the global and local, national and international, school and field of study. Those who have a deep commitment to the reconceptualization movement within the U.S. field should welcome internationalization's emergence. For if the trend is toward what Morrison (2004) terms "conservative foundationalism" (p. 492), let those academics motivated by a "uniform and narrow renaissance" (p. 493) follow the pathway toward a different design; those of us who make up this collection have a lot of work ahead of us, for post-reconceptualization brings with it many questions, and many questions that are as of yet unknown; many new political positions to craft; and many understudied and unstudied histories to investigate. Thus, it might be that the field will bring forward not merely new theories but the reconceptualization of existing theories in new, unique, and unforeseen ways, surprising us with new understandings, new stances on existing ideas; their indispensability for articulating present and next moments in the field and, when feasible, reconceptualized to meet recursive problems, as well as new ones.

Clearly, the fundamental enterprise of reexamining, from the position of the subjugated and from the limits of representation and critique of developmentalism, the question of education, of justice, underwrites this collection; of considering whether the education of the public understood not merely as the study of individual experiences, how knowledge gets produced, or the posthuman condition but as innumerable relations of dominance, enables subjugation, the making of unworthy knowledge, the insignificant experience or perspective. Reading the curriculum debates since the late 1970s leads almost invariably to asking questions about not merely the practicality or necessity but the ethicality of what is undoubtedly the key structural principle at the origins of public education: a curriculum of consensus (or, a common curriculum). This collection, then, aims to displace the concepts that undergird calls to commonality, those that demand synthesis; it attempts to produce a different object when curriculum comes to mind, an object also conceptualized as a subject. This displacement—that also calls for new translations—leads not only to reconceptualizing curriculum in this text but to addressing a significant challenge, one that should concern progressive educators across the globe, quite possibly with a sense of great urgency; this is a concern that curriculum developers, given the emphasis on proceduralism over the study of educational experiences and conditions that elicit such experiences, are not able to see. This question is addressed in part in Quinn's chapter and from a different angle, in Snaza's chapter. That is, the question of hospitality in the former, and love in the latter. Ultimately, it is a question to be grappled with in next moments in the field. I can only gesture toward concerns over openness, otherness, and loving the other, and ourselves and their centrality to educating the public. Since the question was raised when exploring post-reconceptualization, it must be brought to the surface, offered for discussion, and the questions that came to mind shared with those working in the field.

Outsider—In and Insider—Out, Reading Proliferation

This edited collection, then, is a cacophony of voices responding to an impulse among educators: to address the status of curriculum, to enter into that debate in the present moment from an unapologetic justice-driven, post-reconceptualist, praxis-oriented, subjectivity-focused perspective. Crafted in such a way, or as the problem of knowledge and the problem of learning, this question—and others that surround it—are topics of everyday conversation in what departments and ministries of education, education think tanks, research institutes, parents and teachers in conferences, and students in bedrooms and dorm rooms identify and authorize as this concept called curriculum and deliberated less frequently in locales curriculum developers and others deem as beyond its boundaries. *Curriculum Studies Handbook: The Next Moment,* while it is not unrelated to these discussions and aims unabashedly to influence them and be influenced by them, and while the text is not only possible because there are these discussions on this concept called curriculum, and thus this text is a part of them and they are a part of this text, it is not directed toward them. This collection does not represent an attempt at relevance within this particular cultural milieu—of performance, accountability, and choice—only to become irrelevant when the next new set of educational issues arise.

Instead, this collection attempts to intervene on conceptual, academic terrain, not from the position of teacher-insider, asserting the onto-epistemological position of the one in the know about curriculum issues; curriculum scholars, even those who have been teachers in the public schools, might no longer speak intrinsically from the grounds of "conventional practice." Yet, neither do we speak from a viewpoint similar to those of historical figures, such as Bobbitt and others, objective and neutral, attempting to understand and interpret educational experiences at a distance, as outsiders looking in. To readers working at the crossroads of reconceptualization and post-reconceptual-ization—and thinking postempirically—the marriage of objectivity and truthfulness featured prominently in developmental discourse is not defendable. Instead, self, sub-jectivity, and subject positions must be addressed. As curriculum scholars, can we avoid advancing a field that is so distant from traditional thoughts on curriculum that it is conceptually out of touch or so entrenched in school issues that it cannot imagine oth-erwise: feasible alternate readings and interventions into curriculum to reconceive it as curriculum in the making? Does a position in the academy make us outsiders to how curriculum is conceived in schools, politics, and living rooms? Or, worse yet, does a posi-tion from within the academy make us complicit with forms of cultural and material elitism, aiding and abetting bourgeois efforts even with our transformative ambitions? Are our claims as contributors to this collection, to the study of educational experiences in pursuit of social reconstruction, warranted and by what measure? Is it possible to be in the academy and also be for or with those who are subjugated, oppressed, or on the other side of justice? What are the implications when some curriculum scholars assess the advancement of the field by its intellectual vitality while others assess advancement by way of the ability of the field to impact schools, a difference in ideas on what makes "good" knowledge that incited the breakdown at the 2006 Purdue state of the field conference?

More urgent than the above questions, however, what we must ask concerns the pro-duction and authorization of curriculum through two interrelated movements that offer a markedly different outlook from those included in this collection: neoliberal/develop-mental discourse on teaching and learning. Rather than ignore or fall into what Lyotard (1984) describes as "reactionary countermoves" (p. 16), it seems we should index these two interrelated movements' shortcomings, demarcate their contours, highlight their assumptions, and identify their categories. Its dominant strand concerns the problem of transmission—as opposed to what this collection represents, which involves reading and intervening in the discourse on and practices related to educational experiences in order to produce a different object, a different curriculum—from outside self, subjectivities, and subject position, via the routine, mechanized protocols of curriculum techniques. This discourse is set to work via predictable channels, from scope and evaluation to realignment of outcomes to match purposes set by corporate leaders and government officials far removed from the classroom context or the intellectual context of the curriculum field. Justice is achieved, from this perspective, through the absence of difference. This can be found, to offer a recent example, in the 2008 report "Tough Choices or Tough Times," which focuses on school and curriculum reform and is produced by the National Center on Education and the Economy (NCEE), under the leadership of Charles B. Knapp, professor of economics and president emeritus at the University of Georgia. This is just the type of vague text that produces and authorizes neoliberal/developmental curricular discourse and makes declarative statements about motivation, achievement, accountability, and competitiveness—those that must be intervened upon, disarticulated, analyzed, deauthorized, and reinterpreted so that spaces are opened up for alternate readings and curriculum theorizing.

As evident in this collection and among the scholarship of other curriculum theorists (Cary, 2006; Gabbard, 2007) the importance of this argument cannot be underestimated: the neoliberal/developmental take on curriculum (and education) must be discomposed, displaced, and deauthorized—that is, reread and intervened upon—so that readers of post-reconceptualization can identify, produce, and circulate their ideas. For the type of learning that Knapp and the NCEE put forth, in my conception, is the *differánce* of proliferation. That is, it gestures toward the varied attributes that shape the production of textual meaning. Words, such as *curriculum*, offer meaning in relation to other words with which they differ (*lessons, evaluation, tracking, performance, outcomes*). Certain meaning is postponed as the term can only take on meaning in relation to other words—it remains contested and therefore must be continuously repeated—highlighting the importance of textual analysis. But such attributes are differentiated from each other differently, according to the forces of distinction, and therefore generate binary oppositions and dominate and subjugate meanings (and in the current moment, transmission dominates over experience in all its multiplicities and repetitious forms). Hence, curriculum becomes content knowledge organized as necessary to help students compete locally, nationally, and globally, not inquiry into the course of study, self-understanding, and educational encounters. *Tough Choice or Tough Times* (Knapp & NCEE, 2008) is an ideal illustration of a neoliberal/developmental position, generated from both within and outside the academy, one that sees in disciplinarity nothing more than a set of techniques; it makes known the sorts of concerns that routinely come forward from the political/discursive position of an outsider, not just to reconceptualization scholarship, but to self, subjectivity, and subject positions, as well as inquiry into individual experiences in education and the conditions that elicit such experiences:

> World economic leadership would belong to the nations that were technological leaders in field after field and were able to translate that technological prowess into an endless stream of products and services that were the most creative, distinctive, and irresistible products and services available from anyone anywhere. From the boardroom to the factory floor, workers would have to be among the best educated, flexible, most creative, and most innovative in the world. In a nutshell, that seemed to mean that the United States would have to learn how to build schools for all of its children that provided a kind and quality of education that only the very best public and independent schools had ever provided before. (pp. 50–51)

To create such schools, the New Commission on the Skills of the American Workforce (within the National Center on Education and the Economy), chaired by Charles

B. Knapp (2008), advocates the following: "the curriculum would be pretty much the same for all students" for the first 10 years of schooling (p. 52); state board qualifying examinations "intended to measure the extent to which the students had mastered a particular curriculum" (p. 51); and implementation of a rigid tracking system by way of the examinations where "there are passing scores set for two possible destinations" (p. 52): community and technical colleges, on the one hand, and advance placement and International Baccalaureate (IB) programs, on the other hand.

Here it is important to emphasize that, to Huebner, the elevation of economic instrumentalism is nothing new (it marks the history of education and the beginnings of the curriculum field). The reality, of what happens when education and curriculum scholars abstain from responsibility for "making a more just public world," while knowledge produced and circulated about "the political and economic nature of education" continues on relentlessly, is abundantly clear (1999, p. 235). But these might be special insights available to an educator seized by the question of curriculum, one that makes him an insider, changed by the ways he imagines curriculum as both object to be studied and subject alive in culture and language. Knapp and his colleagues are not insiders. They are not seized by curriculum questions nearly so much as they aim to put philosophies of control to work on curriculum, producing knowledge as outsiders looking in. They are not attempting to intervene within curriculum so as to make a more equitable public sphere.

If Knapp's and his colleagues' corresponding claims are the outgrowth of traditional economics, the reader can also find influence of conventional political science and neoliberalism with a hint of neoconservative politics in their description of the object: curriculum. First, they produce curriculum empirically, as that hardline map that underwrites learning that verifies itself in state examinations, which is how people unlike them (their life experiences and subjectivities are not included in this research, a referent without its source) learn. That is, 10 years of a rigid, prescribed course of study (reminiscent of the assumptions that undergirded the curricular recommendations of the Yale report of 1828), are followed by testing that functions as a gateway to two narrow tracks that determine the future of every student. This is by definition a course of study set by empiricists, by outsiders. Second, he and his colleagues interpret worthy knowledge through the protocols endorsed within the fields of business, economics, and cognitive psychology: they make generalizations about students, their needs and desires, and how they interpret the world. Students are not motivated from continuous self-exploration, locating their desires within, or by conditions that incite their commitments (or not) to a more just society. Instead, a course of study is produced according to instrumental, behavioral objectives—when learning is forced from the outside "[students] are working much harder... to succeed on their State Board Qualifying Exams" (p. 55). And therefore, efforts not at "building communities of difference," to borrow from William Tierney (1993), but at "there are no second chances" high stakes sorting processes that dramatically impact the possibilities for the rest of these relatively young lives, "make it easier for teachers, who find their students more motivated to learn" (p. 55). The logic of Knapp and colleagues (2008) is metonymical, reductionist. Complexity, ambivalences, and breakdowns in experience are renounced and the focus is on one element of a much more complicated picture; raising to the surface one thread of discussion in a much more complicated conversation, they make declarative statements about student behavior and human nature, about the right conditions for learning; one size fits all proclamations about curriculum that fit nicely within a society that has lost the capacity for self-reflection and the study of the conditions that shape experience, one that with increasing prescription tracks students into a narrow futures.

As Pinar, Reynolds, Slattery, and Taubman (1995) declare, this is just the sort of knowledge production that perpetuates the "traditional curriculum field," which has functioned in ways "notoriously ahistorical and atheoretical" (p. 12). The critiques of developmentalism and its range of assumptions are simply ignored, or perhaps they are just plain ignorant of them, but in the perspective put forth by Knapp and colleagues there is not the least bit of attention to the infinite variations of experiences, lived histories, or subject positions made available to students. Equally telling, what is produced to account for diversity involves a hierarchy of students over "minority" students; and it is not accounted for in a synthetic course of study, one that identifies difference and then defers its place in the curriculum. Entrapped in developmentalism, it cannot conceive that there are other ways of representing difference, other ways of reading culture and context, other ways of reading incommensurability, ones that highlight singularity and disjunction, ways of reading that might account for subjugated knowledge without fusing divergence. In addition, beneath the call for a common curriculum through which all must pass, with its emphasis on a common history and knowledge, is one of developmentalism's most troubling features; a sort of Lacanian splitting (see Fink, 1995), curriculum's authorizing reach sanctioning insiders and outsiders. It must other, in the spirit of neoliberal/developmentalism, those toward whom it shows benevolence. Demographics aside, once inside the curriculum, students are a single group, "taking [the success of the U.S.] for granted" and also "putting in time in the successive stages of the system" while if there were a series of examinations that were "the only way they could achieve their aims…they might take tougher courses and study harder" (p. 51). The Tyler curriculum is sufficient; all that students need are externally imposed disciplinary procedures.

If an undergraduate student in an economics course wrote this, it might serve as an adequate position paper for a mix of free market capitalism and invasive policies, an argument for external incentives undergirded by a belief that if students are not prepared to compete, the U.S. standard of living will fall dramatically. Produced developmentally, Knapp and colleagues cannot see the worth of subjugated knowledge. That is, they cannot account for what scholars in this collection account for; the subaltern cannot speak. As Guillory teaches us in chapter 10, they do not have "eyes to see" knowledge that distorts the images and contributions of people whose symbols and cultural attributes have occupied the underside of the binary and the violence, intellectual and otherwise, that they incur. They also do not account for the performative and knowledge positioned not in the mind but in the intervening spaces of bodies—the constitutive interstices of bodies and bodies and objects, as Springgay and Freedman, do in chapter 11. Similarly, they cannot see the values in Helfenbein's work in chapter 15, where he illustrates the changing nature of space and the spatial relationship between teacher perceptions of place and global forces that help shape it. Those who are produced as "in need" and require "support and assistance" in order to assimilate to a "curriculum of mastery," as framed by Knapp and colleagues, have much to teach about place making. If Knapp and colleagues had "ears to hear" and "eyes to see" they might learn about students who "see no exit, only the dead-end that a curriculum severed from lived experience so often seems" (Pinar, this volume, p. 318). Quite unfortunate, in contrast to the contributors to this collection who read and intervene within educational experiences and the conditions that make such experiences possible, Knapp and his colleagues see little promise in public education; they see it as if afflicted with a disease only developmentalism can remedy. Here the cure is a prescribed curriculum and a more disciplined and disciplining course of study, one underwritten by images of students driven not by deeper self-understanding and studies of how worthy knowledge has become so, but by institutional gates, and imposed pathways.

What is it exactly that makes this an example of neoliberal/developmental discourse on curriculum? Knapp and colleagues do not claim a neoliberal or developmental orientation, so is it right to offer such a characterization of their work? By what measure are such claims made? Would the inclusion of curriculum developers on the Commission make it neoliberal/developmental discourse on curriculum? Would a publication or two out of their research in curriculum journals make it neoliberal/developmental discourse on curriculum? Certainly, curriculum scholars would find the last assertion quite humorous. The focus of curriculum studies scholars has never been defined by the topics that have made it into curriculum journals. Yet, and this is the point, the developmental and neoliberal character of their work must be identified through patient, careful reading. From my reading, I have identified two interrelated strands of thought. First, Knapp and colleagues (2008) present economic and educational shifts of the past two decades, those that involve dismantling federal and state infrastructures—including remedial education, social welfare programs, and economic safety nets—as inevitable. Corporations will move professional and nonprofessional jobs around the globe according to who will work for the least money; strapped with debt there will be no new funds in state and federal coffers for education; students will have to be flexible, creative, self-sustaining, and willing to change careers on the "turn of a dime" (p. 44) or face unemployment; the United States will face "the dustbin of history" if students do not possess the "hunger for education" (p. 46) evident among students in other countries; and discontinuous courses of study that allow multiple opportunities for failing students to find new pathways must be replaced by continuous courses of study focused on marking winners and losers at an ever younger age or the United States will rank lower globally.

Of course, what is missing are discussions of the role of citizens in shaping government and businesses, entitlements programs as a national right, and policy changes that have spurred undesirable economic and educational situations, and how the very nature of the changes the United States has experienced since the late 1980s means they are not inevitable, can be contested, and offer the promise of change. In other words, it is significant that Knapp and colleagues rely upon conventional economic and political theory, the primary disciplines they use to develop their ideas in curriculum, in this epistemological and disciplinary moment. These are the disciplines that make their writing possible and as something other than curriculum studies make their respective outlooks for public education inexorable. If they read in curriculum studies, they might fall upon Lather's (2004) scholarship on postdiscourses, policy, and research and her call for an "'unnatural science' that leads to greater health by fostering ways of knowing that escape normativity" (p. 27). Or, they might be seized by Pinar's (2004) assertion that curriculum theory is a "public and political commitment that requires autobiographical excavation and the self-reflexive articulation of one's subjectivity in society" (p. 22). Regrettably they did not. Such perspectives might be too messy for them anyways. Knapp and colleagues' theoretical approach necessarily produces sanitized discourse, outsiders looking in, dissecting, and measuring so as to interpret, without ever venturing into the subject, the ways curriculum is felt, experienced, and how those experiences are made possible and live dynamically in language, in the discourse that conditions educational experiences.

Is this scholarship, then, unquestionably a neoliberal/developmental way of producing knowledge, extracted from knowing and being? Clearly the answer is yes. This is particularly true if the reader understands both neoliberal and developmental positions not as economic, political, and cultural, but conceives it as a producer and circulator of curriculum knowledge, shaping an epistemological site and its horizon of intelligibility. Second, in all its developmentalism and neoliberalism, following from the first point, is its resoluteness, its inability to see how to work out of novelty, surprise, failure, and uncertainty to produce and understand differently curriculum, schooling, and education necessarily a problem? Again the answer is yes. It might claim the desire to solve education's challenges but works from a position without the capacity to address the effects of innumerable interactions or outcomes that are unknown or different than intended. It cannot attend to educational experiences? Instead, it generates declarative statements grounded in financial exigency, proposes unshakable agendas for educational reformation, and promulgates the future we will behold if we follow the right path (salvation narrative?), all the while producing the foci of the study—education and curriculum reform—as merely a design to achieve such aims.

At this point I could go on with more examples. I could Google curriculum in a search for writing on developmentalism and educational reform and find nearly a million hits, from blogs and message boards to newspapers and Web pages. After documenting contemporary representations of curriculum, I could write a grant to support research into the basis for this discourse, "the discursive thresholds that had to be crossed for such objects to come into view" (p. 362), as Baker states it in chapter 17. Possibly I could visit archives and examine some of the oldest remaining plans of study for Harvard University or the Boston Latin School. And, if I was lucky enough to have my grant fully funded, I could travel to Europe and study curriculum artifacts in countries with documented histories much longer than that of my own nation. Then, to come full circle, I might return to the United States and study and conduct research into teachers' perceptions of curriculum and how they changed as the result of graduate study. I might then compare my findings with those of McKnight's in his study, which forms the basis for chapter 24 in this collection. I hope it will suffice for my argument here, that I am reading Knapp and colleagues as an indicative, representative text. The point being that the elements of their discourse on curriculum can be named, even if tentatively, within forms of knowledge production that while clearly academic, operate at the crossroads of educational policy and global economics, as well as schooling and curriculum.

This research that helped shape the No Child Left Behind Act produces itself as benevolent, an advocate for the good—progress and change—but as also outside of the debates and contestations over curriculum and sees itself composed of three strands of reasoning: an enlarging private sphere is interpreted as necessitating that a weakening public sphere be put in service to the former (and not a call to restore balance); the intensifying of advanced global capitalism is interpreted as requiring ingenuity and creativity be used to jockey for favorable economic positions (and not transforming the conditions that call for such jockeying); and an increasing pace of everyday life and demands on schooling is interpreted as demanding dissolution of democratic governing structures and installation of performance systems (and not increasing the strength and vitality of democratic, deliberative governance to mitigate these challenges). This dumbs down the complicated nature of the educational situation. A lack of recognition of what de Man (1983) termed the blindness of insight, that the flashes that come with understanding necessarily veil alternative readings, appears to be a common omission for the outsider–empirical perspective. Evidently, for Knapp and colleagues the issue is not developing schools that connect the social to the subjective, a citizenry that sees the inextricable interrelationships between subjectivity, history, and society and therefore demands entitlements from the public sphere of which it is a part (which it socially reconstructs through "truth telling"; see Huebner, 1999) but engendering discourses that Huebner warned us against over 30 years ago: controlling language, legitimating language, and prescriptive language (1999, pp. 216–217), a tripartite that underwrites a "curriculum for individuality" (p. 233) and hides our ethical commitments and intentions in the incongruence that thrives in the spaces between our claims and practices. It would seem at this point that the post-reconceptualization generation(s) has work to do.

Now a turn toward contemporary curriculum studies: How do curriculum scholars conceive of curriculum? Schooling? Do they maintain excessive use of binaries or is there evidence of multiplicity or proliferation? Rather than rely upon Huebner's scholarship—while it is arguably postempirical it is no longer contemporary—and to turn to an author that is not a part of this collection—Kaustav Roy's (2003) *Teachers in Nomadic Spaces: Deleuze and Curriculum* seems like an appropriate place to begin to address these questions, not only for his focus on curriculum but also for the attention he gives to educational reform. Roy notes immediately in his preface that "the inability to *think* difference in most institutional settings" makes attempts at doing so that much more important (p. i) and therefore describes his book as "an experiment toward such change, invoking Deleuze in the midst of an empirical series to open up a new conversation" (p. 1), to which I would add "more complicated" after new. Key here, what Roy is concerned with "is not wholly or even largely empirical" (p. i) but the question of how "to employ empirical work" so as to stage philosophy and theory. That is, he is interested in discourse, "category constructs" (p. 2) in language, how they represent taken for granted knowledge of which the empirical is a part, and the implications of those constructs for the challenges teachers face in diverse school settings. His scholarship, different from that of Knapp and colleagues, for whom words are mere vehicles for expression, offering transparent understanding without signifying complications, represents the getting to work of postempiricism. Or, in Roy's case, as well as the case with some chapters in this collection, employing elements of empiricism to produce postempirical perspectives. A significant text, for reasons that involve ethical commitments and political agendas involving not a process of more of the same in terms of representation, but a focus upon "re-becoming," "emergent relations of force," and a "new set of subjective acts" (p. 3), this is an effort at involved theory. Situating himself as invested, he rejects "all transcendent or idealist grounds of experience" and asserts "all explanation can only come from within *experience*, that is, from immanence, and not from an a priori transcendental ground" (p. 10).

Here, a key difference from Knapp and colleagues (2008) must be regarded even as both Knapp and colleagues and Roy are interested in curriculum and educational reform. Whereas Knapp and colleagues never question developmentalism and empiricism, Roy (2003) is very much concerned about "regimes of signifiers" in education, ones that he deems "fall out from an earlier era of development in the so-called human sciences" (p. 11). This is a cardinally profound difference. Where Knapp and colleagues use terms such as *innovation* and *creativity* they see the meaning of these words as self-evident, simply a matter of fact or arithmetic, curriculum mastery plus originality and ingenuity equals a justification for global dominance and higher standards of living for the United States. To postempiricists, such as Roy, language is neither transparent nor innocent. Instead, Roy's theorizing echoes the thoughts of Lather when she states, "clear speech [and writing] is part of a discursive system, a network of power that has material effects" (Lather, 1996, p. 528). He employs a nonhumanist mode of thought to challenge "excessive categorical thinking" (p. 11) that "fixed reference points of school subjects" and bound learning situations (p. 12). His work suggests that indeterminacy is not a deficit but a "perfectly objective learning structure," one that acts as a fresh "horizon" within perception (p. 13). Roy troubles arenas where Knapp and colleagues cannot see to go.

Without the benefit of Roy's criticality, unwittingly or not, Knapp and colleagues place students, curriculum, and language on the underside of a binary in relation to neoliberalism, developmentalism, and economies. Their claims to have the United States and its future leader's interests at the forefront, show their work as representing an unrelenting partiality toward free market economics and material distribution processes that are unchallengeable, based in rock solid foundations or, equally accurate, they see curriculum in neoconservative, neoliberal, and free market terms. Here reading and intervening to offer alternative possibilities is stymied through phrases, such as "[we searched for] curriculum of the kind that drives...the best-performing nations in the world" that naturalize current conditions. Roy (2003), in contrast, accounts for empiricism and developmentalism but attempts to extend beyond them into what is not measurable but palpable, what exists at "in-between sites" (p. 13). That is, to break away from conventions that limit to attend to what students learned that is significant to their becoming—their endless flux, nomadic experiences, and potential transformations—in as well as out of school sites, sites of family and peer exchanges, and the spaces between experiences and language that give the contours to such expressions. Roy does not simply seek to interpret or repeat prevalent wisdom in ways that isolate groups of signs and unify them into an event or category, as Knapp and colleagues do when they uphold a series of ideas—those that include increasing the coherency of curricula, putting arts and humanities in service to economics, focusing on employability, and tightening the relationship between the idea of high quality teachers and students' scores on board examinations. Is it possible, then, to surmise from this single example of work from a contemporary curriculum scholar, that those who work outside and inside curriculum studies are notably different? Should we therefore assume that the scholarship of the post-reconceptualization generation(s) is notably different from those who produce curriculum from the outside?

This question too is a bit misleading. The above discussion reflects something that scholars working out of the ruins of the postdiscourses already had awareness of: that the borders between development and understanding, between empiricism and postempiricism are more difficult to locate, and possibly too contested to identify with any certainty, a line drawn in the sand washed over with the next wave of counterinsights, the borders more porous than sealed. Knapp and his colleagues might produce a text that positions authors on the outside—less seized by curriculum than attempting to control it—but on at least one level they see curriculum through the lens of historic and contemporary exclusion.[3] This confluence of Knapp and colleagues with Roy's focus on exclusionary practices and the tyranny of the normative suggest that the former cannot be produced as simply outsiders looking in on curriculum. Or, that to draw a clear distinction between insiders and outsiders would negate the notion that curriculum studies are significant and inherently political because the site is contested. To have such a view would forgo discursive and subjective conceptions of sites of understanding, those very conceptions not accounted for by economists and policy analysts. Whereas if curriculum in particular and disciplinary sites in general are conceptualized as texts, as they are in this collection, then no production and circulation of knowledge about curriculum can be deemed as beyond contestation, as above the influence of and influencing curriculum. From this perspective, Knapp, his colleagues, and all the others who, situated as experts, produce knowledge on curriculum, are inside curriculum, for they spin off discourse that shapes what it means to think about "knowledge of most worth"—which also constitutes their texts as educational texts. Yet, we must not let go of the fact that Knapp and colleagues (2008) are deeply invested in developmentalism and neoliberalism. Take, for example, how they characterize teachers' intelligence and abilities:

> Imagine for a moment a dimension line of all the people who graduate from our four-year colleges in a given year. At the left end of the dimension line are the young people who entered with the lowest measured ability. At the right end are those who entered with the highest. One hundred years ago we thought it would be reasonable to set policy in such a way that we were most likely to recruit our teachers from the

left side of this line… [This will have to change.] If we want students graduating from our high schools with the skills we have described, we will have to have teachers who can write well, who read a lot and well, and who themselves are good at mathematical reasoning. (pp. 35–36)

From this perspective, knowledge is easily assessed through objective measures. One can: "evaluate" situations without rewriting them through their discourse and method; make declarations without accounting for their partiality and situatedness; separate knowledge produced from power relations; and indeed claim objectivity, that such practices do not affect the concept under study. In fact, the logic of the text pivots on a clear and unquestioned separation between the object under study and its conception, that how curriculum is conceptualized does not shape what is thought about when thinking curriculum. This division between knowledge production and conception of the object under study is a key characteristic of empiricism; its object is not living in language, but outside, as an entity elsewhere, to be understood always and only as a thing.

Are the texts of the post-reconceptualization generation(s) any different? They certainly refrain from making the claims of Knapp and colleagues, and others who build their arguments upon neoliberalism, neoconservatism, empiricism, and developmentalism, which is why this collection is getting the in-depth introduction it deserves here. But how are they different? And, most important, does it sidestep the temptation to speak from the position of an outsider looking in? Take, as one example, chapter 16 by Howard and Tappan. They argue that social class is not merely a condition inflicted upon others or a lack of culture (a cultural deficit model, a perspective they critique) but that social class is lived in relation within particular conditions and habits. They implore us to move scholarly foci "toward the lived experiences of social class rather than only economic factors" to better understand the symbolic forces at work in reproducing unequal social relations (p. 330). Note that Howard and Tappan are critical of economic analyses that fail to account for symbolism and culture, as well as cultural analyses steeped in deficit-laden perspectives. This embrace of subjectivity, still rare in educational research on social class, is extremely refreshing and sets a context for producing the writers as inside social class and curriculum, seeing the issues as alive and fluid in language and experience. Indeed, if we can look elsewhere, in Howard's (2007) book, *Learning Privilege: Lessons of Power and Identity in Affluent Schooling*, he goes to great lengths to let readers know the extent to which social class is not just object but also subject, sharing his lived history: "Before my research, I knew virtually nothing about privileged schools. I grew up in a different world and attended schools in poor communities in Kentucky" (p. 12). And, although he might be a bit too focused on his teaching successes and ascent through the academy, he speaks intimately of feeling like an outsider among the privileged, a "history of the present" shaped by childhood experiences situated in under- and unemployment, the South, and poverty—not as deficit but difference—one predicated on unequal material and symbolic relations but not anything that resembles an absence of cultural rituals, values, and beliefs, of worthy knowledge. Thus, before Howard begins to engage in the fieldwork that underwrites his text, he shares: "I acknowledged that I had a lot to learn about affluent schooling and much to examine about my own *sense of self* before I could begin forming critical understandings of that which I planned to study" (p. 13). In other words, he attempts to intervene at the crossroads of social class and privilege (his objects of study) as the subjects of intervention, to bring them to life in new and different ways, to recognize how they live in the discourse of privileged students and the discourse of others, not merely to interpret and then represent these concepts to the broader world.

Take also, Guillory's work in chapter 10, which starts off with a description of how students who "belong to the hip-hop generation" use storylines, images, and characters from rap to make sense of less familiar (read White and European) texts from the English canon: "students have represented Victor Frankenstein's monster with a gold tooth… drawn a platinum grille on their illustration of the Pardoner during their study of Chaucer's *Canterbury Tales*" (p. 209). She describes how for educators wedded to developmentalism hip-hop is not a site of knowledge from which to work but a barrier to mastery over appropriate (read official) curriculum content. Guillory imagines differently and wants to work through and with students' lived histories. As a researcher, she reads the lyrics of Black female rappers for the ways they might enable (and also constrain) African-American women to "talk back" to patriarchy, sexism, and capitalism. As something other than attempting the role of interpreter, one who enters into the "exotic" lives and lyrics of Black female rappers to return to the world of a largely White European academy to share stories of what she has learned, she offers a mode of thought that implicates herself as well as her readers in our reading strategies. The Black female rappers represented in Guillory's chapter waver between portrayals of male-centered discourse and pleasure and a female-centered politics that positions them as the center of their own desires and in control of negotiations within heterosexual relationships. The unsettling tension between images of the Black female rapper as "the gold-digging ho" (p. 217) and an empowered woman who controls her own body and representations of it, as well as controls her own wealth, gives life to the very terms under which the curricular possibilities of hip-hop are made and unmade. As something less weighty than attempts to tell the whole story—an objectivist empiricist grand unified theory—she oscillates between reading the ways black female rappers construct knowledge about sexuality in public discourses, ones "sometimes complicit in perpetuating the production of demeaning representations and sometimes resistant to their continuance" (p. 220). Guillory extends beyond empiricism and developmentalism to offer postempirical textual analysis, to see text as discursive; this is the object under study is also the subject of intervention, one that sees hip-hop at the site of curriculum. She wants to forgo developmentalism and work through and with the knowledge of her students

As a last example, see chapter 8 by Ferneding and chapter 9 by Weaver. Are their readings of technology different from Knapp and colleagues? Same question, does it escape the trap of speaking from the outside looking in? Ferneding and Weaver both write about the posthuman condition, specifically a mode or state of being that reclaims the artistry of technology and a doubling phenomenon involving the mechanization of humans and the humanization of mechanisms. Both scholars illustrate concern for the ways in which technology, particularly its representation in scientific discourses, has lost its capacity to account for its place within the sacred and its connection to poesis. Ferneding begins her chapter by reflecting upon a childhood overshadowed by the atomic bomb, "I peered at its unfathomable power crouched beneath a desk in a classroom with small windows—its reality marked a lifelong quest to understand the nature of humanity's relationship to its technological inventions" (p. 171), Weaver aptly suggests that many curriculum scholars have approached technology in ways too literal and rigid, "fearful that technology has and will attack their subjectivity" (p. 192). It is not that the merging of humans and machine has yet to become our way of life; the coalescence has already taken place: "humanity has merged with, or emerged from, technology" (Weaver, p. 192). The problem, one that both Weaver and Ferneding address, is that what is inorganic and organic is no longer clear. Producing technology as a tool and a "standing reserve" that separates it, and humans, from nature is the issue at hand. What is missing are capacities for translating across differences, seeing the poetic in technology, and digital conversions in art. Both Weaver and Ferneding question discourse that produces technology as a neutral mechanism—a tool of developmentalism—unable to reveal its essence and limits. They admit the biases and agendas as writers who are very much insiders, ones who "claim their voice in the biomedical world" (Weaver, p. 190), at the intersection of curriculum theory and technology. They value technology simultaneously as technique, skill, and art.

Compare this to the ways Knapp and colleagues (2008) produce technology. Their explorations include phrases of inevitability, ones where technology encroaches on humanity, such as the following: "digitization of work," "modularization of industry," and "automation of human jobs." Equally important and continuing with the same themes, they manifest technology as the universal driver of the economy and industry: "the application of information technology has by no means run its course" (p. 21), noting that while technologies that include nanotechnology and biotechnology are posed to make a tremendous positive impact, "these technologies have the potential to destroy not just existing products and services but entire industries" (p. 21). They do not attempt to read and intervene upon technology, to see technology as alive in language, discourse, and literally and figuratively in bodies; rather they further naturalize "the ordering of the machine" (Ferneding, p. 174) and its effects. And what is more, this is the discourse that circulates from them to policy makers and government officials. Knapp and colleagues understand curriculum empirically, not discursively, as outsiders who maintain their object of study as an object.

It might be feasible, then, to suggest that a plethora of examples of work inside curriculum studies—both in this collection and in the broader field—operate postempirically, read and intervene to rewrite the object under study. Also, there is clear evidence that those outside curriculum studies produce curriculum as objective, empirical, and nondiscursive. The question remains, however, what about inside curriculum studies? Or, to be more exact are there examples of curriculum scholarship that produce knowledge as outside power? Make claims to knowledge as objective? Investigate curriculum at a distance? Seek not intervention but neutrality? That is, are there instances where curriculum scholarship attempts to interpret curriculum without rewriting it? This can be found, to cite a convenient example (convenient because it is one of the articles I have recently reread as I examined the last 6 years of the *Journal of Curriculum Studies*), in Wraga's and Hlebowitsh's (2003), "Toward a Renaissance in Curriculum Theory and Development in the U.S.A." This is the type of text that reinforces a series of problematic binaries: ideas against ideology, pure knowledge against contaminated (situated) knowledge, dominant against alternative feasible readings of history, and so on. In fact, Wraga and Hlebowitsh (2003) suggest, "advancing any political ideology or doctrine is incompatible with sound scholarship" (p. 431) and then go on to assert a problematic correlation: "If personal biases are largely inescapable [then] political ideologies are largely a matter of choice" (p. 432). Of course, admission of bias for postpositivists is more than an issue of "choice," which retains the idea that knowledge can be produced outside power and claims about an object will have no impact on that object, it is an issue of being "violently troubled" by the knowledge produced and confronted with questions over the ethical commitments embedded in our work. Lather (2000) teaches us an important lesson on bias, difference, and rewriting the objects we study: that to present an object as the real thing is not equivalent to producing it through language. To cultivate her ideas, reading Walter Benjamin as less interested in either a recovery of an original truth or a renunciation of knowing given discrepancies between language and experience, she implores us "to pay attention to the ways the stories are told, to the presentation of the object that is a performative registration of how history courses through us in the scene of writing" (p. 154). That is, a text is always already contaminated by language and to shed light on what has been romanticized, commoditized, and canonized, writing must attempt to account for the contingency of interpretation, knowing all the while it will fall short of its aim. But we learn little of this from Wraga and Hlebowitsh. While inside curriculum studies they seem to share with Knapp and colleagues a distance from their object and a belief in the neutrality of language.

Let us take this analysis a little further. While Wraga and Hlebowitsh (2003) are far outside of accounting for the ways that academic categories can consolidate subaltern narratives, heterogeneity of multiple readings defy easy typographies (or pillars), and decontextualization of knowledge reinscribes the knowing subject, they go to great lengths to use terms and phrases that let the reader know they are insiders to the curriculum field. Wraga and Hlebowitsh advocate for "constructive conversation," "democratic forms of living and learning," and interplay of curriculum theory and practice (p. 433). As evidence of their insider status, they build their argument around Schwab and other key historical figures to the curriculum field, including Taba and Tyler, and, by way of a "corrected" reading, position scholars such as Pinar, Slattery, and Taubman as outside the boundaries of the "accepted" historic field, all in an attempt to produce a traditionalist perspective on the unhealthy state of curriculum studies. Accordingly, when moving the contemporary field into the future, revisionist accounts of the past are paramount; the ideas of previous generations must be excavated from the depths of history, studied for their authentic meanings, and employed in a "historically accurate sense" (p. 434) to current circumstances. Relying solely on "fixed" readings to correct a field in "disarray" (p. 426) there are no counterhegemonic, autobiographical, poststructural, or what Tierney (2000) constructs in his work, an alternative feasible reading to traditionalist history, but rather "correct," transhistorical, essentialist readings. Insiders to the field, but keeping its object at a sanitized distance, Wraga and Hlebowitsh have access, through the legitimating scholarship of the big names in curriculum history, to the full (read official and verifiable) curriculum story. Of course, this presupposes that one can pull together a handful of curriculum scholars from the past that can represent the whole of history. The work of Baker, Brandon, Taliaferro-Baszile, and Winfield in this collection suggests otherwise. That is, that the understudied and unstudied dimensions of curriculum's past render traditionalist interpretations of curriculum history, such as those of Wraga and Hlebowitsh, suspect.

Wraga and Hlebowitsh might be insiders to the field, they might even admit that they have commitments and investments, but both are justified based on their efforts to return curriculum to the centers of the historical field, and allegiances to "correct" readings that neutralize differences and transparent language that assumes words can adequately reflect events and realities of the world. Their racial and ethnic background, nationality, gender, sexual orientation, and position in the academy—their subjectivities—are not brought into relationship with their knowledge production, to the ways they view history, which is produced as a resolute unbending foundation of events and ideas. Here the reader must ask, even as historical events and ideas might be empirically verifiable, are their significance and meaning open to interpretation? Are there multiple interpretations that might conflict and converge? What are the politics of the text? Is it possible to work from empirical evidence to come up with alternate novel readings generated through new and divergent theoretical lenses? By way of patient, careful reading the reader might have noticed that the authors are attempting to produce a comprehensive, singular, conformist narrative of the history of curriculum, one that has made it through the traditional "time-tested" protocols of the academy to become conventional truth. Forsaking all the complications that have been linked with interpreting and understanding over the last two decades, they work in rationalism and empiricism to develop four pillars of the field as a sort of call to order. That is, they have offered four centers that have the effect of marginalizing or all together excluding other interpretations of the status of the curriculum field and alternate accounts of the role of key historical figures. With this endorsement of a traditional narrative of curriculum history, multiplicity within next moments in the field is read negatively, in contrast to what other curriculum scholars might view as a healthy state of proliferation, a state of flux and nonmastery.

William Reynolds (2003), in his rejoinder to Wraga's and Hlebowitsh's article had this to say:

> There must be villains (others) who can be responsible and can be perpetually accused of (blamed for) sending the field into this "so-called" perpetual crisis. Just as a conservative political agenda needs an enemy, an evil empire, or a mad monarch, a renaissance needs an evil to combat…. Although Wraga and Hlebowitsh would never use the term "evil", the logic is implicit. The reconceptualization is evil, therefore, the renaissance is good—this is ressentiment. (p. 448)

What Reynolds is responding to are sanctions for which making insiders and outsiders is essential: the scholar who is (often self-anointed) beholder of tradition observes that left on their own (without outside regulation) another group of scholars have grown, moved, and proliferated the field beyond its boundaries. Unable to see promise in "wild profusion" and admire these features as acts of hope and determination, the beholder of tradition seeks to blame the group for the breach of protocols, its prodding toward advancing complexity, and extension beyond historical frameworks. Accordingly, after applying blame, the beholden scholar responds with an effort to contain experimentation and limit the field, to discipline scholars who violate prior borders and return it to an imagined prereconceptualized state, a correction toward what is an acceptable history of curriculum. Most important, Wraga and Hlebowitsh reproduce some of the most rudimentary *structural* components of imperialist curriculum studies without informing the reader that their argument is steeped in irony or put forth in an effort to amplify the diversity of readings on curriculum history, opening the past to divergent translations and interpretations. They distinguish the inside (traditionalist interpretations of White middle class—mostly male—scholars) from the outside (scholars who are not compelled to traditionalist interpretations of White middle class—mostly male—scholars or turn toward other marginalized figures or figures who are not traditionally viewed as a part of curriculum history), informing a broader, predominately White, middle class audience about this scholarship on subjugated, marginalized, and unconventional perspectives and the risk they pose for corrupting the field of curriculum studies. And, most incriminating, they do not "have eyes to see" that curriculum studies has become less about traditionalism's obsessive focus on correct linkages to the past than extant and new clusters of theories and reflective practices about ethics, concepts, languages, ideas, and experiences. These perspectives, when looking toward history, offer alternate and often unforeseen readings (Brandon, for example, in chapter 6, offers a powerful alternate feasible reading of Dewey). Unfortunately, the scholarship they have put forth here reinforces the epistemological dominance of the dominant and produces knowledge that shuts out counternarratives on the history of the field.

Wraga and Hlebowitsh have taken responsibility for telling a broader audience about the "one true history" of curriculum and how reconceptualization is to blame for the perpetual crisis. In short, they seek to restore the object of study to its prior (unquestioned) position. Wraga and Hlebowitsh, then, do not seem all that different from

Knapp and colleagues. Indeed, by producing the claim that by way of reconceptualization curriculum studies fell into confusion and disarray, they make the field sound as if it is stricken and unhealthy in ways that harmonize with Knapp and colleagues' description of public school curriculum. As the story goes, both the schools and field need to be urged away from experimentation and eclecticism and toward definition and constraint. Wraga and Hlebowitsh might indeed be insiders on one level but with their work on defining, blaming, and accusing they are outside forms of dwelling—creativity and multiplicity—that characterize the contemporary U.S. field. The most important element of Wraga's and Hlebowitsh's article, that which enables me to place it in the same category as the scholarship produced by Knapp and colleagues and not with the scholarship included in this collection, is not that their expertise is outside the curriculum field or that they argue for a "corrective" reading based on historical figures who are outside curriculum history. Neither is the case here. Instead, what is at issue is that Wraga and Hlebowitsh do not intervene into the myriad of complicated conversations attributed to reconceptualization; rather, from a safe distance, belying the complexity and disjunctive character of the work they place under the reconceptualization banner, they move to interpret the field—particularly its failures—to a broader audience, positioning themselves in the process as safely outside responsibility and therefore as something other than subjects making an intervention.

The debate Wraga and Hlebowitsh want to have is certainly about curriculum but it is not an account of curriculum studies, about reading those varied epistemic spaces. They might be curriculum studies scholars but it is those who are outside reconceptualization, as Wraga and Hlebowitsh define it, whom they seek to convince (those associated with reconceptualization already know the field is too complex and varied to capture in simple assertions). Furthermore, it is not just traditionalists who they hope will recognize the value of their arguments—but those such as Knapp and colleagues with whom they share certain political and intellectual space. That is, they might acknowledge historically subjugated knowledge and their concordant groups but both are positioned outside the question of worthy knowledge; Wraga and Hlebowitsh continue to occupy the dominant epistemic space of history. Compare this with Pinar's tremendous efforts to bring raced, classed, gendered, and sexed historical perspectives into the curriculum field even when doing so requires that he read against his own scholarship; that is, even when it requires a reconfiguration of prior work.[4] Wraga and Hlebowitsh only seek to rewrite the past to the extent it buttresses the traditionalist story of curriculum history. That is, they only seek to interpret differently what is already there, not intervene, get involved with alternate readings that have been hidden, erased, or marginalized within the curriculum field (this is in stark contrast to the chapters that make up this collection). These reconfigurations to further support the traditional centers of the field produce knowledge intellectual activity as a sanitizing practice. Whereas, in comparison to Wraga and Hlebowitsh who attempt to produce curriculum (ideas) outside of politics (ideologies), to Huebner the very idea of knowledge production involves something more than interpretation—understanding what is—that is, it requires involvement, to risk an intervention, to challenge the very concepts that organize meaning, to get involved.

As it stands, with the outsiders-in and the insiders-out, the terms *inside* and *outside* might confound as much as clarify when it comes to "rendering unto curriculum studies the things that belong to it" (Reid cited in Morrison, 2004, p. 490). If this binary is too simplistic and its use brings a host of new concerns, possibly more than it clears up, then new language is needed to read and intervene upon the myriad of differences that confront the field. That is, when we read the differences found in the work of Knapp and colleagues and Wraga and Hlebowitsh on the one hand and the work of Roy and contributors to this collection on the other hand, what meaning making strategies might be employed to better capture their subtleties? The differences and corresponding questions they bring to the surface are paramount. They include scholarly activity that produces itself as empirical and objective, as about neutral interpretations of objects under study at a distance; as empirical and subjective, as about accounting for bias in interpreting objects under study; and the sort of scholarship that is characteristically similar to Huebner's, a direct intervention in curriculum that multiplies the opportunities to think teaching and learning through a growing number of perspectives: politics, phenomenology, spirituality, existentialism, developmentalism, and so on. The stakes are colossal when one discerns between producing knowledge aligned with advancing a discipline but not the object under study, to concepts that have implications that are as much political and ethical as they are ontological and epistemological. To be succinct, this is the difference between ideas that uphold the historical canon and those which attempt to intervene within it (see the work of Brandon and Winfield in this collection for examples of work that attempts to intervene within the canon).

This is particularly the case when we recognize that the historical canon shapes how those who are marginalized, erased, and subjugated see themselves and their knowledge (distorted) and academic discourse shapes interventions, intellectual work more accurately described as involved theory than activism. To return to Huebner, he recognized long before his writing career was winding down that making interventions in curriculum in order to highlight its political nature and how it is made available to youth was a key responsibility of curriculum scholars; he also was astute in that he recognized studying the political nature of curriculum and dominate–subjugate knowledge as the product of unequal relations did not come with guarantees, that according to the interests served, political curriculum studies might be poison and remedy to justice. And so Huebner's felt need to speak both to those in the curriculum in particular and education field more broadly about ethical commitments and political perspectives on teaching and learning. Knapp and colleagues and Wraga and Hlebowitsh are unlikely to cite Huebner, whose discussions of politics, the arts, spirituality, imagination, and social justice are too contrary to their points aimed at establishing principles and mastery. So, then, if we have turned outsider-in and insider-out and the terms are too stark to be helpful, it might be helpful to explore a more subtle term: *proliferating.* It captures the nuances of what was described by more than one reviewer as a "chaotic collection."

According to the *Oxford English Dictionary* to proliferate is "to grow or multiply"; "to increase or spread at a rapid rate"; "to cause to grow or increase rapidly"; Proliferation within a field of study, then, cannot mean to stay within a particular form, structure, or constitution. Even if curriculum studies reaches a state of vigor and animation or turmoil and crisis, it is only so because it has been in another state. That is, it has grown and multiplied or diminished and become fruitless. At a time when education scholars intent on curriculum mastery and successor theories are writing off curriculum theorists intent on new ideas for theorizing extant or new curriculum worlds as advancing "political doctrine" (Wraga & Hlebowitsh, 2003, p. 432), my assertion as I head toward the last section of this introduction is that multiplicity might characterize the emerging field in terms of the need for epistemological spaces where knowledge has more to account for in regards to the increasing complexities of everyday realities and the world. Proliferation does not require that we see the field develop in a mode of debate and synthesis where one cluster of theories overtakes another on the way toward "one right way" approaches. Rather, it means to maintain a commitment to a field that celebrates the growth of its theories and stories—and to be seized by its vigor and intensity—and to assert our human inventiveness so as to personalize our theorizing regardless of how unsettling and unwieldy that makes the U.S. curriculum field. It means to remain determined (if not hopeful) in the face of calls for consolidating and totalizing theories with continued affirmation of disjunctive scholarship that necessarily brings together seemingly incompatible ideas without collapsing them into each other (examples here include the work of McKnight, Taliaferro, and Whitlock, as well as others, in this collection). For those of us who have endured government intrusion into both public and higher education and sanction of evidence-based practices and assessments despite resounding evidence that it does not work, this has been an extremely frustrating state of affairs. Accordingly, remaining committed to advancing the significance and sophistication of the field also means taking risks, "to struggle towards a new language which champions the disenfranchised" (p. 468), as Dimitriadis explains in reference to Said in chapter 22 of this collection, without great regard for the repercussions. It means maintaining a commitment to proliferation despite pressures from within and outside the academy toward consolidation.

Of course, Wraga and Hlebowitsh have a different position. They do not seek to grow and multiply curricular perspectives, and with good reason. They aim to bolster a traditionalist curriculum narrative; from the contemplative safety of the academy, "they would have us test or apply our theories in the same world as that which gave rise to the theory" (Morrison, 2004, p. 488). Similarly, Knapp and colleagues also have a different position. Whereas these writers discuss the need for creativity and ingenuity, and even recommend students study the arts and humanities to engender innovative, critical thinking, at the end of the day they equate worthy knowledge to what can be reduced to a test and therefore the empirical. They are not interested in reading emergent theorizing against the limits of existing theoretical frameworks or criticality that cannot easily submit to impartial assessment or evidence-based practices. Proliferating curriculum—that is, multiplying the perspectives and practices of teaching and learning—necessitates risk taking and seeing the unknown as a way of knowing. Accordingly, it requires we avoid a closed system of curriculum scholarship whereby the quest for the unfamiliar and unknown is eclipsed by demands that we assess the fields advancement using extant conceptual tools and intellectual practices. It must draw on extant ideas, texts, and scholars but it also must extend beyond these concepts and figures so as to move the field toward a different, more robust state. The more discussions of curriculum theory proliferate, the more these ideas should spill over into realms that are beyond those of curriculum scholars. Curriculum theory, then, must proceed along multiple discourse registers outside of the academy to engage multiple publics. To return to the theme of this introduction, texts committed to multiplicity and growth see curriculum at the same time as an object of study and subject of intervention. These texts do not merely speculate on curriculum—that is on teaching and learning—they are also, in no uncertain terms, involved in making it. Morrison (2004) offers some help here. In contrast to Wraga's and Hlebowitsh's narrow, structuralist prescription, he offers a prolific, expansive position on what is fitting for study in next moments in the field: "The 'things that belong to' the curriculum are everything that can be learned, how they can be learned, why they are being learned, with what justifications, by whom and with what consequences" (p. 490).

From all of this, one might be compelled to ask, that scholarship can attend to dispersions and scatterings without losing an identifiable field of study or that a field continuously decentered by operations that produce and sustain differences can generate identifiable scholarship. The response, it seems, has to do with examining how discursive formations in their infinite variety are unavoidably contained once they enter into an epistemological space. Unpacking this process necessitates looking at the specificity of the work at hand, at texts, to examine thinking in the hybrid spaces that are so much a part of the contemporary field. More exact, this involves the study of what research designs and analytic practices are retained for the purposes of intelligibility—the speaking positions from which an argument is made—and what is being worked through and against in terms of disciplinary structures. If we are aware that intelligibility produces an outside, an other, the unspeakable, that which cannot be easily turned over to narrative without undercutting our research practices, then we are confronted with the need to continually subvert the coherence of our discourse. That is, we must struggle with the question of our ethical commitments in terms of conceptual strategies and the essential features of our scholarship, as well as what is being discomposed in terms of stable knowledge and intellectual practices in the process of doing our work. Quite simply, what is at hand concerns whether our texts within curriculum studies address, embody responsibility, and accountability to, only the issues and concerns of powerful epistemological forces at play at the site of curriculum or to those marginalized and subjugated events and discourses. If "discursive formations are constantly becoming epistemologized" (Foucault, 1972, p. 195), that is "shot through…with the positivity of knowledge" (p. 194), and we are experiencing a resurgence of neoliberal/developmental discourse on curriculum, then when it comes to proliferation there remains for the post-reconceptualization generation(s) a lot of work to do. And indeed, as description in the next and last section of this introduction attest, that work is being done.

Present Moments: Reading Seven Through-Lines in the "State" of the Field

In a field marked as proliferating curriculum is it possible to locate particular through-lines that mark some commonality in this "chaotic collection"? Is it possible to theorize a post-reconceptualization movement based not on an overly unifying analysis but on a diversity of multiple, irreducible, and yet overlapping analyses? It seems that the answer has to be a tentative yes. I say tentative because an attempt to name characteristics that capture work as expansive and protean as the 23 chapters (not to mention associated response essays) included here runs a lot of risks. It is, of course, helpful to offer some markers that explain the status of various aspects of the field. At the same time, there is the very real danger of working at a level of high abstraction so as to say very little beyond the obvious or at a low level of detail so as capture singularities but very little of the network crisscrossing the various clusters of theorizing within the contemporary field. And, to add to that, there is my own personal concern that I might present too static an image of the field and fail to shed light on post-reconceptualization and curriculum as contested sites, continuously being made and unmade. A review of the section headings and titles of the chapters included here only attests to profound differences in the work that marks the field, and effort that would have to be put forth to name through-lines with any confidence.

To help give me the tools to think through-lines with proliferation, I turned to Lather (2006), which in turn brought me to Spivak (1999) and a form of postcolonial reason I transferred to the scene of curriculum. What Spivak advocates that is helpful here is a sort of uncertain middle passage that is the other to the other of correct, an irreducible "mistake" that gets us through academic identity politics toward more fruitful sites of learning. Taking seriously Spivak's push to think performance over formation and determined effort without reward over a cure, I decided to work from new and existing concepts to the field as a way to ground my analysis within contemporary curriculum theorizing. Rather than unifying themes, I decided to present seven interrelated through-lines that are neither fully present to nor absent of the work included in this collection. That is, they do not provide a comprehensive survey of the scholarship that makes up this text, but rather seven "lines through texts" that provide one of many possible representations of the "next moments" in the contemporary field. The reader will notice that these through-lines are intentionally different from the sections that make up this collection. The aim is to work half in and half out of what is at hand toward a sort of intermediate that wavers between the specificity of chapters and the wide-range of the section headings to offer an alternate reading, a hovering middle ground. As something other than correct readings, when read parallel to the section headings these through-lines offer a doubled take on the field that necessarily informs and misfires. It is my hope that they will spark discussion that extends the analysis presented here.

Flux and Change

The first notable through-line is that the scholarship presented here is something more than a composite of heterogeneous curriculum discourses or a static collection of alternate feasible readings. Instead, as an exploration of post-reconceptualization they illustrate a field undergoing continuous changes, some that might have been predicted (such as increasing evidence of internationalization) and others that might be a surprise (such as relatively new imports from other fields and readings, oppositional discourses together in disjunctive affirmation). Epitomizing the proliferating nature of the field are the contrasts between the work included here and the work presented in Pinar, Reynolds, Slattery, and Taubman's synoptic text, *Understanding Curriculum: An Introduction to the Study of Historical and Contemporary Curriculum Discourses*. Published in 1995, it offered the first comprehensive analysis of the various discourses that make up the contemporary field (after reconceptualization): historical; political; racial; gender; phenomenological; poststructuralist, deconstructed, postmodern; autobiographical, biographical; aesthetic; theological; institutional; and international. Fifteen years ago it was possible to delineate the field according to which "discourse domain" was most prominently featured in a scholar's work. Sure there was overlap and many scholars fell into more than one category, but the framework for *Understanding Curriculum* was extremely insightful and certainly reveals more about the field than it masks through its organization. In the present moment, the demarcations are not nearly as clear and it has become, with increasing frequency, impossible to distinguish a dominant discourse from a secondary discourse within individual essays as well as the developing bodies of work of scholars newer to the field (an example would be Whitlock's chapter that threads together the South, place, autobiography, and queer theory). When the contemporary discourses that helped map the field 15 years ago are compared with through-lines that are offered here, what does become clear is how diverse and varied conceptualizations of curriculum have become over the past decade and a half.

Hybrid Spaces

The second notable through-line of the present moment is that multiple discourses which might have held a circuitous relationship, related to each other in an occasional example from the literature or not at all, are being drawn into new and distinct hybrid relationships. Ugena Whitlock's, "Jesus Died for NASCAR Fans: The Significance of Rural Formations of Queerness to Curriculum Studies," is one example of these relationships as it marks continued work in Southern studies, place, and autobiography while drawing all three into relationship with queer theory in ways unique to the author's scholarship (see also Whitlock, 2007). Topics such as place-making, taboo desires, and sexual identities shed light on the ways in which attempts to gain insight into the lives of gays and lesbians, focused on traditional urban areas, has blinded us to the lived histories and present day realities of same gender loving individuals who live and (attempt to) prosper in more traditional, rural areas of the country. By way of interrelating what many would see as disjunctive theories (dominant fundamentalist narratives and queer theory's efforts to discompose those fundamentalist dominant narratives), Whitlock illustrates the disjunctive nature of her own life, the contradictions and complexities of growing up as a Christian with fundamentalist beliefs and also a rural Southern lesbian.

Another chapter that holds the characteristics of this second through-line (and also the sixth), "Intimate Revolt and Third Possibilities: Cocreating a Creative Curriculum," written by Hongyu Wang, aims to bring Western European psychoanalysis into relationship with Eastern philosophy. Wang reads Kristeva's intimate revolt parallel to Laozi's yin and yang interrelationship to craft a third site for curricular ingenuity, one that is characterized by translations and identifying the spaces between intelligible concepts and the other (read as the unintelligible). It is in this intimate mode of revolt where she sees promise, concerned about the transgressive mode of revolt more common within Western societies. In the transgressive, the self-organizing process of the network is disrupted by an atomized mode of creativity, one where the conflict caused by the singular invention is not generative but fragmentive. Accordingly, Wang creates a hybrid site, drawing Kristeva's work with its roots in feminism, psychoanalysis, and literary criticism into relationship with the ideas of Laozi, a philosopher of ancient China who is a central figure of Taoism. The juxtaposition allows Wang to look in more complicated ways at the question of generational change within curriculum studies, one that might allow for building connections across fragmentation to build something new without envisioning it as breaking with the old.

Other contributors, such as Elaine Riley-Taylor, also offer hybrid theorizing at the juncture of autobiography and place. In her chapter, "Reconceiving Ecology: Diversity, Language, and Horizons of the Possible," she focuses upon how spiritual and ecological discourses can be examined via autobiographical readings of our natural surroundings. Working at the crossroads of indigenous ways of knowing, Huebner's notion of evolving spirituality, and the idea of an earthly commons, she employs an interwoven, blended onto-epistemological position that sets the terms by which to rethink developmentalism and its insistence on compartmentalizing all the elements of human life. Riley-Taylor weaves "being in the world" with "knowledge of the world" to conceive of ecological ways of knowing that are contingent, place-based, interrelationship-focused, and challenge anthropocentrism and developmentalism.

Denise Taliaferro-Baszile's contribution, "In Ellisonian Eyes, What is Curriculum Theory?" also exhibits characteristics of this second through-line. She explores the implications of autobiography for curriculum history and public memory, stating her concern that curriculum studies has been shaped primarily by the desires and interests of the white male psyche. With the lack of Black selves represented in both the historical and contemporary field, Taliaferro-Baszile links raced and gendered subjectivities and postpositivist perspectives with critical race theory to invert "understanding curriculum as racial text" to read as the "racial subject as a curriculum construction," offering a substantially different take on the field's history and highlighting the complicity within. That is, through this inversion she highlights that the curriculum field has always already been implicated in the formation of racial subjectivities. Through neglect, as opposed to concerted efforts to construct all education's beings as racial, what we have had historically is a deracialized curriculum that by way of reconceptualization has come to be understood as having a racial component, one requiring a racial textual analysis. What Taliaferro-Baszile asserts through the study of the racial subject as curriculum construction is that there was never a nonracial curriculum and that by way of a doubled invisibility/hypervisibility racial subjects have historically been formed in both absence of Blackness and the presence of Whiteness. More than a component of the field ("curriculum as racial text"), by way of a disjunctive reading, the entire field is racialized. Her response to this predicament is a hybrid of autobiography and critical legal counterdiscourses, critical race *currere*. This marriage of voice and critical theory functions to intervene within deracialized rationalist academic discourse to illustrate how race—along with gender, class, sexuality, and other subaltern subjectivities—shapes selfhood, as well as educational experience and experiences of the public.

In the last chapter to hold characteristics of this through-line,"Understanding Curriculum Studies in the Space of Technological Flow," Karen Ferneding illustrates the usefulness and limitations of instrumental positions in technology, ones that highlight the characteristics of the tool but fail to account for all the complicated issues involved with how they are operationalized by humans and given meaning through knowledge production. Crafting tentative orientations toward technology and societal change, she draws from curriculum scholar James Macdonald, as well as Marxism, phenomenology, hermeneutics, and postdiscourses to examine humanity's continuously shifting relationship with technology, one of increased subjugation, and its consequences for the organization of time and space. She operates as a bricoleur, linking elements of various social–intellectual visionaries into hybrid curriculum theorizing in an effort to dismantle dominant technical rationalist structures so as to open up new spaces where it is possible to reimagine human potential within the technical. That is, to reconceptualize technology as not just instrumental, she reads it as also poetic, so that technology might enhance rather than denigrate the spiritual and moral dimensions of human life.

Reading Differently

The third notable through-line in the present moment has to do with rereading concepts and objects within curriculum studies (most often relying on scholarship imported from other fields to do so) to think those educational concepts and practices differently. Douglas McKnight's "Critical Pedagogy and Despair: A Move toward Kierkegaard's Passionate Inwardness," is an example of such rereading as it offers an alternative perspective on critical pedagogy by way of an existential condition of despair. In a style of argument reminiscent of Ellsworth's groundbreaking 1989 *Harvard Educational Review* article, "Why Doesn't This Feel Empowering?: Working Through the Repressive Myths of Critical Pedagogy," McKnight describes his graduate students' interest in critical pedagogy and their inability to live a critical existence given the technical demands educational institutions place upon teachers. Upon learning the precepts of critical pedagogy these graduate students, he teaches us, want to craft themselves as critical pedagogues in the classroom. They recognize, however, awareness of the external forces that govern teachers' practices does not change the conditions in which they operate; with the "rage for accountability" there are few opportunities to employ the tenets of critical pedagogy and not do their students harm in terms of their ability to perform on standardized tests. By way of Kierkegaard's notion of passionate inwardness, McKnight illustrates that the "despair of necessity" (practicing in a way that contradicts one's existential becoming after the study of critical pedagogy) is less a burden to be lifted than a necessary condition of teachers' becoming critical pedagogues. He rereads existential becoming as internal to critical pedagogy (not a burden) and a turn toward the construction of the self as a precondition for seeing and hearing the other. Lastly, McKnight illustrates how the self might be set in proper relation with one's own sphere of existence.

Dimitriadis', "Edward Said and Jean-Paul Sartre: Critical Modes of Intellectual Life" is another chapter that carries the characteristics of the third through-line. Whereas McKnight rereads critical pedagogy in light of philosopher–scholar Kierkegaard, Dimitriadis rereads the scholarship of Edward Said and Jean-Paul Sartre to shed light on what can be done within educational settings given the rise of academic capitalism and concordant shift in the character of intellectual life. His effort is to highlight the ways both Said and Sartre offer strategies for thinking counter to the lure of academic careerism, to work from the academy to engage the world. As something other than seeing consumer politics in colleges of education as inevitable, Dimitriadis offers an alternate feasible reading of how we might face the next moment in curriculum by challenging orthodoxy and extreme forms of specialization that draw the modern intellectual away from public spheres. Here the aim is to think differently about the relationships between progressive academics and social change movements; to think through Said to interrupt official discourse to craft new languages that champion the oppressed; and Sartre to attend authentically to our existential freedoms and choices in a world that is becoming as interdependent as it is complex.

Other contributors, such as Robert Helfenbein, read curriculum differently by taking up theoretical frameworks from critical geography and interrelating them with curriculum studies' notions of place to offer new insights into education. In his chapter, "Thinking Through Scale: Critical Geography and Curriculum Spaces," he focuses upon the implications of three geographical concepts—spaces that speak, spaces that leak, and spaces of possibility—for extending the analytical possibilities of curriculum theorizing. Helfenbein finds promise in what critical geography offers for reading differently the relationships between space, place, and identity under the conditions of advanced capitalism and globalization. Via spatial analysis he employs a sensibility to location to counter assumptions of the neutrality and emptiness of space, one that inhibits multiple levels of inquiry and analysis. He reads place differently to open a space for the notion of the shifting scale, beneficial in that it allows for elastic inquiry, interrelating seemingly disparate elements that shape the conditions for education, from the specificities of the local to the broad-ranging forces of the global. Expanding the notion of place to include spatial relations, he contends, highlights the complexity of forces at work on schooling.

Finally, in the last chapter to exhibit the characteristics of this through-line, "Sleeping with Cake and Other Touchable Encounters: Performing a Bodied Curriculum," Stephanie Springgay and Debra Freedman demonstrate how performance art, particularly the work of Diane Borsato, might help us read differently curriculum—conventionally thought of as an issue of an active mind and an idle body. That is, when traditionally framed curriculum and therefore learning as bodied means the mind is active through what the body experiences of the world. Similar to Helfenbein, they reconceptualize the exhausted notion that space is empty, a void. Drawing feminist and poststructural scholars to the stage of curriculum, their aim is to reconfigure spacing as not the mere distance between entities but the very opening where becoming happens, where things happen between bodies. Concerned with scholars who stage the body as present to itself and learning as an isolated event, a perspective that neglects a body ontology, their work emphasizes the performative over the formative, and relational knowing as difference over conceptions of embodiment as universal and not-within context. Movements and forces fill space, to think of a bodied curriculum is to heed the experience of space unfolding, spatial–temporal events that while they are not tangible—an object of study— open bodies to other bodies and objects. A bodied curriculum, they teach us, engenders an ethic of being-with and invites a certain risk that living in the relations between bodies' knowledge is reread as corporeal, as produced with and through touch and proximal relationships with others. Unlike productions of curriculum as content to be acquired or retained, within a bodied curriculum we cannot know beforehand because it fosters our becoming and indeed, in being-with others we are rendered vulnerable, uncertain of the effects our dynamic interactions will have on others.

Divergent Perspectives

The fourth notable through-line in the present moment relates to divergent perspectives that surface when reimagining existing curriculum theorizing (often in ways that could not have been imagined or were different than intended) to offer new lenses of analysis. Adam Howard's and Mark Tappan's "Complicating the Social and Cultural Aspects of Social Class: Toward a Conception of Social Class as Identity" offers an example of the divergent perspectives that become possible when the concept of social class, one with a rich history in the curriculum literature, is reconceptualized as an issue of identity and privilege. The authors dismiss economic, Marxist, and functionalist justifications as incapable of attending to the complexities of social class as an identity that is culturally and ideologically produced and reproduced within specific contexts. Rehearsing scholarship between the 1970s and the present, they refute cultural deficit and social reproduction theories as reifying stereotypes and neglecting agency. Their interest is in reconceiving the relationship between social class and schooling so as to revive political curriculum conversations. To do so, they focus upon social class identity. That is, without dismissing that social class is an economic concept where people occupy strata, they offer an alternate perspective by reimagining social class as lived experience, one formed by social knowledge and also self-understanding.

In addition to Howard and Tappan, another chapter that exhibits the characteristics of this fourth through-line is "(A) Troubling Curriculum: Public Pedagogies of Black Women Rappers," written by Nichole Guillory. Reimaging Pinar's description of Ida B. Wells as a teacher of the American public within the space of contemporary rap music, Guillory introduces hip-hop as the pedagogical medium of the newest generation of Black women who talk back (or fall prey) to stereotypical images of Black women. Guillory notes that while these women work in spaces shot through with capitalist impulses, they remain contested and contradictory. Black female rappers participate in "curricular acts of representation" that simultaneously discompose and reaffirm stereotypes around race, class, gender, and sexuality. Mobilizing transfer of lessons from the classroom to hip-hop artists who school their audiences on sexual desire, heterosexual politics, and Black lesbian identity, the aim is to employ the sorts of critical discourse analysis that have become a hallmark of the contemporary field to complicate a conversation that much too often, stuck in binaries, demonizes or celebrates these artists. In regard to the cultural scripts and subjectivities Black female hip-hop artists make available, divergent perspectives are grounded in efforts to recoup and extend beyond racialized sexualized images to contextualize representations of Black female rappers in a history of self-expression that defies easy categorization. Guillory reframes the curriculum question—what knowledge is of most worth?—for the hip-hop generation.

Asher too focuses on reimagining extant curriculum theorizing to offer new lenses of analysis via decolonization and the notion of implicatedness. In her chapter entitled, quite simply, "Decolonizing Curriculum," she focuses upon the question of what it means for people seemingly untouched by colonization to examine the ways they have been historically and are in the present connected—psychically and intellectually—to the colonizer–colonized relationship. Drawing extensively from Pinar's scholarship on the South and race, standardization and commercialization, and internationalization of the field,

Asher explores her experiences teaching in Louisiana. Here she finds that a colonial history shapes both the lives of her students as well as the meaning she attributes to her own life. Speaking as a woman of color from a former British colony who now teaches in the U.S. South, she highlights how imperialist impulses can be found in the forces of capitalism and globalization, and continued intolerances among U.S. citizens for race, class, and gender differences. Her student teachers struggle to be creative under the weight of a state-mandated curriculum that distorts their history and leaves little wriggle room for self-exploration and reflection; forcing soon-to-be teachers into gracious submission, Asher asserts, is one of many examples of how colonialism continues in the present day. Decolonization requires that we examine how it lives on under many different guises. She recommends that what education needs is critical study of contemporary constructions of identity, culture, and nation in relation to the field of curriculum, as well as teacher education.

John Weaver's chapter, "The Posthuman Condition: A Complicated Conversation," also carries the features of the third through-line. Similar to Ferneding, Weaver is concerned that technology has lost its capacity to unconceal itself. That is, that technology is no longer able to unleash the creative passions and desires of humanity. Drawing from philosopher-scholars Heidegger and Hölderlin, Weaver focuses on how in the biomedical age technology has shown some promise of reclaiming its poetic roots in Greek Techné and also made possible deepening abuses of the human body. Whereas Ferneding continues in her chapter to work in hybrid spaces toward explorations of concepts such as historical rupture and real virtuality, Weaver turns toward the curriculum field itself as a potentially fertile site for further (and future) conversation. He notes that while a handful of curriculum scholars have examined how bodies and subjectivities have been reconceived symbolically and materially, there has been relative silence on the posthuman condition. He attributes this lack of discussion to fears that technology will encroach upon subjectivities and a lack of digital art in the lives of curriculum scholars. Describing how the work of Mary Doll illustrates the power of curriculum theorizing, he implores curriculum scholars to reimagine curriculum theorizing to intervene in biomedical discussions, ones where what is at stake is the very meaning of democracy.

Lastly, Erik Malewski's and Teresa Rishel's chapter, "Difficult Thoughts, Unspeakable Practices: A Tentative Position Toward Suicide, Policy, and Culture in Contemporary Curriculum Theory," demonstrates the characteristics of this fourth through-line. They ask what can be done when suicide prevention practices established through empirical studies and policy analysis have not by their own measure shown that they help reduce suicide. They draw from culture studies to explore the changing nature of adolescence. Finding dramatic shifts in the construction of adolescence attributable to neoliberalism and a certain postmodern reality, they engage in critical discourse analysis and investigate the assumptions that guide two State of Colorado reports on suicide and then make cross-cultural international comparisons with England's report on suicide prevention. Finding a markedly different analysis based in social class in England's report, but a similar set of recommendations, they then explore what was described as an effective grassroots response by a Canadian school district to a suicide attempt. Here, rather than the imposition of new structures recommended in all three reports, they found the Canadian school district had emphasized a dissolution of structure. Dialogue and personalization in excess of formal roles were used to create new spaces to shape children's realities. Excited by the prospects, they turn to three counterdiscourses in curriculum studies to shed light on a difficult topic. They suggest that autobiography, Foucauldian power/knowledge analysis, and queer studies might provide alternative feasible perspectives to those offered through empirical studies and instrumental policy analysis, ones that fail to account for the innumerable variables and plethora of unknowns that come with attempting to intervene within this difficult topic.

Different Contexts

Less frequent in my reading of the chapters in this collection but equally important, the fifth through-line in the present moment relates to reinventing curriculum theories and events in different contexts to allow for new perspectives. Carpenter and Tavin focus on the reconceptualization of art education in their chapter, "Art Education Beyond Reconceptualization: Enacting Curriculum Through/With/By/For/Of/In/Beyond/As Visual Culture, Community, and Public Pedagogy." The authors suggest that unlike curriculum studies, which can now reflect on the reconceptualization of the field and its effects, art education finds that it is currently in a state of redirection and rearticulate. After describing the creative self-expression movement of the 1920s and discipline-oriented movement of the 1960s as two key redirections that shaped contemporary art education curricula, the authors suggest studies of visual culture will shape the future of the field. As something other than an exclusive focus on best practices, discipline building, or a limited range of classroom productions, visual culture is focused on people, a movement toward the study of the ways images shape human consciousness and identity, as well as the creation of knowledge. Most important, the movement toward visual culture has surfaced a series of tensions that resemble the tensions that arose during the reconceptualization of the curriculum field: between development and understanding and schooling and the study of experiences in the broader world. Their interest is in how the shift toward arts-based research, community pedagogy, and environmental and eco-art education might be understood by reimagining the concepts and events of the reconceptualization of the curriculum field within art education.

Alberto Rodriguez, another contributor, also reinvents curriculum theories (particularly political curriculum discourses) at the site of science education to bring new perspectives to teacher education. In his chapter, "How the Politics of Domestication Contribute to the Self-Deintellectualization of Teachers," he focuses upon an autobiographical–ethnographic examination of how the politics of deintellectualization have played out over in his methods courses since the late 1990s. He notes that although curriculum studies has experienced an intellectual breakthrough by way of postmodern and poststructuralist theorizing, Ralph Tyler's four basic principles still dominate teacher education curriculum and inform corresponding instructional practices. Baffled by the disconnect, he turns toward his own journey as a teacher educator to examine the factors that have constrained his ability to promote intellectually robust professional development. He finds a number of factors that include a small but vocal group of teacher education students that resist critical perspectives, student evaluations processes that cause instructors to conform to traditional expectations of teacher educators, and tenure and promotion practices that require faculty to acculturate to institutional and disciplinary standards. The author suggests that by working at the crossroads of curriculum studies and other disciplines, it might be possible to come up with strategies to counter the deintellectualization of educational professions.

Status Questions

A sixth through-line, one that might be expected in a collection focused on next moments in the field, has to do with the use of theories from a broad range of scholarly sources to shed some light on the question of the state of curriculum studies. While it would be quite feasible to argue that all the chapters in this collection concern themselves with the status of the field, the ones associated with this through-line are notable for their preoccupation with where the field stands in these new and unsettling times. Molly Quinn's "'No Room in the Inn'?: The Question of Hospitality in the Post(Partum)-Labors of Curriculum Studies" is an example of a chapter that raises such questions as she invites readers to consider in exploring post-reconceptualization what has been (re-)conceived, given birth to already, and what we might do in next moments with this legacy. Drawing from the work of Derrida on hospitality, Quinn entertains what it might mean to receive a visit from a stranger when in an era of shifting terms for higher education our home might not be ours to live within. Will there be, to borrow Quinn's phrase, room at the inn? Will we remain at the inn? Recounting that for Huebner it was with the call of the other that we might reach out beyond ourselves and with Greene it was making the familiar strange that awakens us to education, Quinn asks us to consider what people and concepts will we be willing to risk inviting in and who and what ideas might be shut out in the future of curriculum studies. Her aim is to illustrate that in asking the question of the state of the field we are also asking whether we are ready to make room for, truly come to know, who the other is. She also questions if we will continue to find homes in the academy.

For other contributors, such as Gaztambide-Fernández, questions over the state of the field have less to do with labels ("post-reconceptualization") than moving forward together, in relation to one another, forging a journey in solidarity. In his chapter, "Toward Creative Solidarity in the 'Next' Moment of Curriculum Work," he outlines the discursive, structural, and personal challenges the field faces and advocates that we confront them through forms of relationality that assume being and action happen in collective movement. Drawing extensively from the work of Huebner and his call for careful attention to the language curriculum scholars employ to frame their ideas, the author suggests that in the next moments workers in the field discompose the false binary between theory and practice, artistic and scientific (the latter related to the work of Ferneding and Weaver in this collection). To engage such work together, he analyzes discourse on the history of the word *solidarity*. Dissatisfied with the functionalist and conflict theories of Durkheim and Weber, he outlines the attributes of a more likeable creative solidarity, one characterized by a language of imagination and political project that is not predicated on sameness but contingency, a field continuously in the making and operating without guarantees.

Jennifer Gilbert's chapter, "Reading Histories: Curriculum Theory, Psychoanalysis, and Generational Violence," also carries features of the sixth through-line. Gilbert argues that conflict and struggle—far from something to be overcome—is necessary in the movement between generations of scholars. Citing philosopher-scholar Hannah Arendt, she describes that the newness of the stranger—the rise of a visible next generation in a field—can surface feelings of mortality and ambivalence and therefore newcomers might be viewed as both a promise and a threat. Whereas Gaztambide-Fernandez focuses on the promise of solidarity across generations as a political project, Gilbert is less sanguine about the state of affairs. She notes psychoanalytic explorations of learning are based in assumptions that the will to know is related to a will to power, to dominate by way of reaching out to know the world. Gilbert, then, explores what reading practices mean to the formation of generations, that through reading one not only extends beyond the family for knowledge but also is implicated in the ideas and concepts available at the historical moment of reading. She wonders in the attempt of curriculum theorists newer to the field to have their own mind what risks are there to toward inflicting trauma upon their intellectual parents. Or, the opposite, if attempts by the newer generation to have their own thoughts are not made what does compliance and deferment mean for the next generation. Gilbert assures her readers that it is in the ambivalence between the two that post-reconceptualization will emerge.

Lastly, Nathan Snaza's chapter, "Thirteen Theses on the Question of the State in Curriculum Studies," demonstrates the characteristics of this sixth through-line. Snaza starts by asking what would make it possible to ask questions over the state of the field and finds that if one is too young, too interested in controlling it might not be possible; one must be involved in patient, careful reading, be seized by the question. In other words, the curriculum scholar does not ask the question; the question must ask the curriculum scholar. Also, this question of the state within curriculum studies in particular and education in general is made more difficult, he teaches us, if one abides by Dewey's and Kliebard's assertion that education wavers somewhere between responsibility for passing on tradition ("what is") and preparing the next generation for what has not yet come ("what might be"). The question of the state then is not only an ambivalent one given that it is about current conditions and their transformation, but also because the state has two forms. That is, in a Derridian sense, we have a language state and a state apparatus, both related to each other but also indeterminate. While Snaza points out all the issues with the question, he is certain of a few things. Warning us that crisis rhetoric is not helpful, he asks what it might mean to engage in careful readings of our founders. He also finds little promise in the concept of man and the focus on discipline building, focusing instead on the centrality of ethical commitments and being in relation with one another. What he hopes for in the next moments for the field are posthumanistic concepts and the capacity to love, both working together against the state.

Understudied Histories

The seventh and last through-line suggests that even with all the work that has been done on subjugated knowledge and events, to produce readings that challenge traditional interpretations and capture what had previously escaped knowledge, there remains more to be done in terms of understudied and unstudied histories. Bernadette Baker's "The Unconscious of History? Mesmerism and the Production of Scientific Objects for Curriculum Historical Research" is an example of scholarship that addresses historical events and their importance to the formation of the educational field and scientific objects that have been the repeated focus of curriculum history. Baker traces hypnosis, mesmerism, and animal magnetism in the mid-19th to early 20th century literature and finds a series of telling equivocations, from whether seeing was to be reduced to the eye or a more organic event and how objective sensory portals are to questions over appropriate ways to distinguish between waking, dreaming, and sleeping states. After reviewing numerous moments of debate, the author notes that historical perceptions of mesmerism are a sort of history of the present. That is, they have shaped educational activities in four ways that include behavior management, expertise, and authority in educational research, the place of willfulness in intelligence testing and child development, and the divide between private and public realms. Mesmerism not only made its way into schools in the 1830s, but also was associated with the fabrication of types of children, from gifted to degenerate, and treatments for children with behavioral disorders. Tracing the history of mesmerism and hypnosis, Baker describes its academic roots in the work of James and Binet, and how their scholarship informed psychoanalysis and what would become acceptable institutional interventions into the life and mind of the child. Most telling, she connects this understudied history to unquestioned values and beliefs about curriculum and pedagogy. That is, she highlights what became permissible in terms of behavior management and contouring of desires in the classroom, and what has become unacceptable practice, such as hypnotizing our students, as historically grounded in mesmerism and specific to the present historical period.

LaVada Brandon's chapter, "Remembering Carter Goodwin Woodson (1875–1950)," also carries the features of this seventh through-line. Brandon argues that Woodson is a reconceptualist, educational philosopher, and a figure of curriculum history. Tracing the history of his life as a son, coalminer, college student, and educator in the Philippines, the author notes that Woodson learned a great deal in out-of-school locations. That is, in the living rooms of African-American intellectuals, the roadway shop where his father was employed, and as a schoolteacher in another country who found miseducation of indigenous people was a prominent feature of colonial curriculum, Woodson began to formulate his ideas on *real education* based on what was excluded from the formal curriculum. Confronted with distorted knowledge of African Americans at the highest levels of education (while pursuing his PhD), Brandon teaches us that Woodson challenged African Americans to be self-serving and not subservient to White economic, political, and educational systems that perpetuated distortions and negative images of people of color. Most telling, when Brandon compares Woodson's notion of experience to Dewey's she comes upon some unsettling conclusions, that Dewey's emphasis on shared interests, social change without disorder, and education as a force against barbarism and savagery implicated him in the ongoing efforts to transmit the cultural dispositions of colonizers. By highlighting the racial dimensions of experience and the colonial dimensions of Dewey's work, Brandon asks readers to reexamine key figures of curriculum history for its understudied elements, to craft alternate feasible readings in the effort toward decolonization.

Finally, Ann Winfield's chapter "Eugenic Ideology and Historical Osmosis," demonstrates the characteristics of this seventh and final through-line. Winfield begins by asking what it means that—half a century after Brown v. Board of Education of 1954—we have apartheid schooling and so little national dialogue on the ways eugenics ideology frames historical consciousness and public memory. She asks how schools can remain as entrenched as ever in spite of the decades of research that have followed from reconceptualization and now the post-reconceptualization movement. Winfield answers that not merely liberal change agents, curriculum scholars have been and are currently deeply implicated in the character of the present situation. It was not merely the socially marginalized hate groups but also the progressives of history that were involved in efforts to wipe out entire ethnicities and control the lives of the disenfranchised. Drawing connections between the contemporary state of the field and its past, she notes that the field's origination was intricately tied not just to the social efficiency movement but also to policy in the service of eugenics principles. Tracing the history of eugenics through Auguste Comte's positivism and Frances Galton's and Karl Pearson's evolution and heredity studies, to Herrnstein's and Murray's (1996) *The Bell Curve* and the recent Ruby Payne phenomenon (see also Howard and Tappan this collection), the author illustrates how curriculum scholars have been and continue to be implicated in classifying and sorting students according to perceptions of their social worth. Testing, tracking, vocational and gifted programs, biology, civics, and life adjustment education are just some of the current formations made possible by a eugenics past. Noting that figures such as G. Stanley Hall, Edward Thorndike, and John Franklin Bobbitt have been central figures of curriculum history, Winfield documents with great care what has been understudied in their work; that is, how it is steeped in eugenics and shapes the conditions for contemporary educational discourse.

Conclusion

After acknowledging our inheritance, reading proliferation, marking through-lines, what more can be said that has not been said already? How does one end an introduction like this one when we are just getting started? Michael Apple (2004) notes that a new conservatism has surfaced in the form of "standardized national curriculum" as if the tensions between subjugate-dominate knowledge, culturally situated and unified theories, national language and linguistic differences, and the infinite variation in educational experiences and attempts to represent them did not exist. Albeit he points out that the rise of this hegemonic, orthodox discourse is best characterized as a "residual form." That is, a reaction to the dissolution of any foundations and its attendant anxiety is met with "a romantic appraisal of the past" where essential truths were unquestioned, a shared morality guided everyday practice, and people knew their proper place in society (p. 8). This nationally mandated curriculum and its empirically based assessment strategies produces itself as offering "a return to higher standards, a revivification of the Western tradition, patriotism, and conservative variants of character education" (p. 8).

In contrast to this orthodoxy, reductionist guidelines for theory, this collection is about proliferating curriculum, a multiplicity of novel and creative ways for going about studies in teaching and learning in terms of finding our way within a field alive with complications and challenging philosophical questions regarding onto-epistemological and political tensions. As something other than turf wars or reconciliation narratives, this collection represents efforts at thinking difference in a field of study differently, of necessarily holding together disjunctive narratives to open new sites of learning, alternative locations for reading and intervening, being and becoming. If the scholarship included here is any indication, in the next moments curriculum studies scholars will not merely be advancing subjugated discourses, events, and perspectives but attending to the specificity of their scholarship in terms of what they regard as its essential features while working within and against stable disciplinary structures and apparatuses.

Within these new sites of learning, the task as represented in the chapters included here, is to find a new way to continue on with curriculum work in the face of a loss of traditional centers to the field and, quite ironically, the rise of new orthodoxies. Already aware that we are inside-out and outside-in by the way of despotic systems that seek legitimacy in their own self-image, the larger effect of which has been that of boxing up difference—a loss of capacity for alternative ways of thinking—feeling, and doing, the reader might sense the work of mourning but not melancholy, the loss of innocence but not determination. This collection, ultimately, is about those alternative ways; about how the changing concept of curriculum is shaped across the proliferation of texts that so characterizes the contentious site of post-reconceptualization. Here new curriculum theories get produced by way of reconfiguring, extending, and translating across traditions positioned as conjectural (as made up of assertions but not foundations) as we pursue intellectual tactics toward the "radical call to make room for that which is, in truth, foreign—other" (Quinn, p. 101). Confronted with the challenge of curriculum work in this historical moment, positioned between what is no longer (reconceptualization as a contested site regarding what was) and what might be (post-reconceptualization as a contested site regarding what is not yet), the task this collection takes on is to produce difference in the curriculum field differently. Across the shifting clusters of theorizing that so characterize the present day, scholars well versed in the onto-epistemological and political positions that shape knowledge production might be better prepared to cope with the ever changing and contested landscape of curriculum studies, far beyond contemporary forces that produce curriculum as techniques, protocols, and principles. Flux and change, hybrid spaces, reading differently, divergent perspectives, different contexts, status questions, and unstudied histories, the intent is to move the curriculum field in multiple directions with the hope that more compelling and beneficial ways of knowing will begin to appear.

Notes

1. While there are many interpretations of the "original truth" in regards to causes of the breakdown at the 2006 Purdue University conference, "Articulating Present (Next) Moments in the Field: The Post-reconceptualization Generation(s)," my take on it has focused on two contrasting interpretations of advancement in the field. On the one hand, there were those who measure advancement by way of the development of rich, comprehensive, robust literature within the field. On the other, there were those who assess the field's current worth by way of its ability to intervene within and improve schools. While a gross reduction of the innumerable variables at play, my sense was that what incited the breakdown has to do with vastly different interpretations of progress and impact by many of the keynoters, speakers, and attendees. Other interpretations can be found, for example in Ruben Gaztambide-Fernandez's discussion of the conference in his 2006 publication, "Regarding Race: The Necessary Browning of Our Curriculum and Pedagogy Public Project," in the *Journal of Curriculum and Pedagogy* and Pinar's interpretation of the event in his contribution to the epilogue of this collection.
2. When thinking about post-reconceptualization many I have talked with at conferences and scholarly meetings have assumed that the term signifies a paradigm shift similar to the one Pinar, Reynolds, Slattery, and Taubman outline in *Understanding Curriculum* (1995). That is, that there has to be development of new traditions within the field that differentiates it from the past and renders previous work more dated or less applicable to the present moment. Those expectations not only seem limiting, but they also seem to negate other metaphors for organizing and thinking with and through continuously changing moments in the field. After reading and rereading the chapters and response essays of this collection, proliferation seems much more appropriate to post-reconceptualization as a contested site than a word or phrase indicating successor theories.
3. Notable in their report is consideration of students who are and have been disadvantaged within public education and the need to equalize resources and support programs. Unfortunately, it assumes a cultural deficit position in regards to historically oppressed groups and bases success for the underprivileged only on evidence culled from a series of examinations. Driven almost exclusively from empiricism, their assumptions and approaches are problematic.
4. I am reminded here of many personal conversations where Bill Pinar has graciously explained how he felt his prior work might have focused too much here and not enough there. Two particular examples stood out for me in regards to the name change of the subtitle in the reissue of his book from "reconceptualists" to reconceptualization and a later discussion he had with me about why he cringes slightly at the title for the book that originated at the 1972 Rochester conference, *Heightened Consciousness, Curriculum Theory, Cultural Revolution*, feeling it a bit presumptuous when he now looks back.

References

Apple, M. (2004). Doing things the "right" way: Legitimating educational inequalities in conservative times. In J. Satterthwaite, E. Atkinson, & W. Martin (Eds.), *Educational counter-cultures: Confrontations, images, vision* (pp. 3–18). Stoke-on-Trent Staffordshire, England: Trentham Books.

Appelbaum, P. (in press). Education is a haunted house. In E. Malewski & N. Jaramillo (Eds.), *Epistemologies of ignorance in education*. Charlotte, NC: Information Age.

Barthes, R. (1989). *The rustle of language* (R. Howard, Trans.). Berkeley: University of California Press.

Butler, J. (2004). *Undoing gender.* New York: Routledge.

Cary, L. J. (2006). *Curriculum spaces: Discourse, postmodern theory and educational research.* New York: Lang.

de Man, P. (1983). *The blindness of insight: Essays in the rhetoric of contemporary criticism.* Minneapolis: University of Minneapolis.

Derrida, J. (1978). *Writing and difference* (A. Bass, Trans.). Chicago: University of Chicago Press.

Ellsworth, E. (1989). Why doesn't this feel empowering?: Working through the repressive myths of critical pedagogy. *Harvard Educational Review, 59*(3), 297–324.

Fink, B. (1995). *The Lacanian subject: Between language and jouissance.* Princeton, NJ: Princeton University Press.

Foucault, M. (1972). *The archaeology of knowledge and the discourse on language.* New York: Pantheon Books.

Gabbard, D. (2007). *Knowledge and power in the global economy: The effects of school reform in a neoliberal/ neoconservative age.* New York: Routledge.

Gasché, R. (1994). *Inventions of difference: On Jacques Derrida.* Cambridge, MA: Harvard University Press.

Gaztambide-Fernández, R. (2006). Regarding race: The necessary browning of our curriculum and pedagogy public project. *Journal of Curriculum and Pedagogy, 3*(1), 60–64.

Gorski, P. (2006). Savage unrealities: Classism and racism abound in Ruby Payne's Framework. *Rethinking Schools, 21*(2). Retrieved February 17, 2009, from http://www.rethinkingschools.org/ archive/21_02/sava212.shtml

Herrnstein, R. J., & Murray, C. (1996). *The bell curve: Intelligence and class structure in American life.* New York: Simon & Schuster.

Howard, A. (2007). *Learning privilege: Lessons of power and identity in affluent schooling.* New York: Routledge.

Huebner, D. (1976). The moribund field: Its wake and our work. *Curriculum Inquiry, 6*(2), 153–167.

Huebner, D. (1999). Poetry and power: The politics of curricular development. In V. Hillis (Ed.), *The lure of the transcendent: Collected essays by Dwayne E. Huebner* (pp. 231–240). Mahwah, NJ: Erlbaum. (Original work published 1975)

Knapp, C. B., & NCEE. (2008). *Tough choice or tough times: The report of the new commission on the skills of the American workforce.* Washington, DC: National Center on Education and the Economy.

Lather, P. (1996). Troubling clarity: The politics of accessible language. *Harvard Educational Review, 66*(3), 525–545.

Lather, P. (2000). Reading the image of Rigoberta Menchú: Undecidability and language lessons. *Qualitative Studies in Education, 13*(2), 153–162.

Lather, P. (2001). Postbook: Working the ruins of feminist ethnography. *Signs, 27*(1), 199–227.

Lather, P. (2004). This is your father's paradigm: Government intrusion and the case of qualitative research in education. *Qualitative Inquiry, 10*(1), 15–34.

Lather, P. (2006). Paradigm proliferation as a good thing to think with: Teaching research in education as wild profusion. *International Journal of Qualitative Studies in Education, 19*(1), 35–57.

Lyotard, J. F. (1984). *The postmodern condition: A report on knowledge.* Minneapolis: University of Minnesota Press.

Malewski, E. (2006). A reading on four registers: Educational reforms, democratic cultures, research methodologies, and the question of the posts. *The Journal of the American Association for the Advancement of Curriculum Studies, 3.* Retrieved September 23, 2008, from http://www. uwstout.edu/soe/jaaacs/vol3/malewski.htm

Mitchell, W. J. T., & Davison, A. I. (Eds.). (2007). *The late Derrida* . Chicago: University of Chicago Press.

Morris, M. (2005). Back up group: Here comes the (post) reconceptualization. *Journal of Curriculum Theorizing, 21*(4), 3–12.

Morrison, K. (2004). The poverty of curriculum theory: A critique of Wraga and Hlebowitsh. *Journal of Curriculum Studies, 36*(4), 487–494.

Pinar, W. (Ed.). (1974). *Heightened consciousness, cultural revolution, and curriculum theory: The proceedings of the Rochester Conference.* Berkeley, CA: McCutchan.

Pinar, W. F. (1978). The reconceptualization of curriculum studies. *Journal of Curriculum Studies, 10*(3), 205–214.

Pinar, W. F. (1999). Introduction. In V. Hillis (Ed.), *The lure of the transcendent: Collected essays of Dwayne E. Huebner* (pp. xv–xxviii). Mahwah, NJ: Erlbaum.

Pinar, W. F. (2004). *What is curriculum theory?* Mahwah, NJ: Erlbaum.

Pinar, W. F. (2007). Curriculum theory since 1950: Crisis, reconceptualization, internationalization. In F. M. Connelly, M. F. He, & J. Phillion (Eds.), *The Sage handbook of curriculum and instruction* (pp. 491–513). Los Angeles: Sage.

Pinar, W. F. (2008). *Intellectual advancement through disciplinarity: Verticality and horizontality in curriculum studies.* Rotterdam, The Netherlands: Sense.

Pinar, W. F., Reynolds, W. M., Slattery, P., & Taubman, P. M. (1995). *Understanding curriculum: An introduction to the study of historical and contemporary curriculum discourses.* New York: Lang.

Reynolds, W. M. (2003). Rejoinder: Debate, nostalgia, and ressentiment. *Journal of Curriculum Studies, 35*(4), 445–451.

Rolleston, J. (1996). The truth of unemployment: Walter Benjamin reads his own times. *South Atlantic Review, 61*(2), 27–49.

Roy, K. (2003). *Teachers in nomadic spaces: Deleuze and curriculum.* New York: Lang.

Schubert, W. H. (1992). Practitioners influence curriculum theory: Autobiographical reflections. *Theory into Practice, 31*(3), 236–244.

Sears, J. T., & Marshall, J. D. (2000). Generational influences on contemporary curriculum thought. *Journal of Curriculum Studies, 32*(2), 199–214.

Slattery, P. (1997, September). *Postmodern curriculum research and alternative forms of data representation.* Paper presented at The Curriculum and Pedagogy Institute, University of Alberta, Canada.

Spivak, G. (1999). *A critique of postcolonial reason: Toward a history of the vanishing present.* Cambridge, MA: Harvard University Press.

Tierney, W. G. (1993). *Building communities of difference: Higher education in the twenty-first century.* Westport, CT: Bergin & Garvey.

Tierney, W. G. (2000). Undaunted courage: Life history and the postmodern challenge. In N. K. Denzin & Y. S. Lincoln (Eds.), *The handbook of qualitative research* (2nd ed., pp. 537–553). Thousand Oaks, CA: Sage.

Wood, D., & Bernasconi, R. (Eds.). (1988). *Derrida and différance.* Evanston, IL: Northwestern University Press.

Wraga, W. G., & Hlebowitsh, P. S. (2003). Toward a renaissance in curriculum theory and development in the U.S.A. *Journal of Curriculum Studies, 35*(4), 425–437.

Wright, H. K. (2005). Does Hlebowitsh improve on curriculum history? Reading and rereading for its political purpose and implications. *Curriculum Inquiry, 35*(1), 103–117.

Part I

Openness, Otherness, and the State of Things

2　Thirteen Theses on the Question of State in Curriculum Studies

Nathan Snaza

Chapter Overview

This chapter focuses on 13 theses that focus on the state of curriculum studies. The author compares and contrasts and makes declarations that include the following: What it means to do curriculum studies versus be seized by it; the challenge of preparing others to enter the world as compared with envisioning a different one; a language state as opposed to a state apparatus; abandoning era as in pursuit of states exchanging ghostly haunting for a return to the founders of curriculum for guidance in how we think; empirical versus nonempirical philosophy of experience; living versus dwelling; displace the concept of man with something both postempiricist and postsocial science; exchange empirical truth claims for ethical commitments; pursue posthuman understandings of dwelling in the world; allow love to function as an analogy to teaching and learning; theorize concepts in the spirit of an ethical intervention; and conceptualize curriculum in a third space that honors the question of love against the state. The author closes with a turn toward art that allows those in the field to think community without identity and read aesthetically in loving hope of a better future.

For Timothy Lensmire, with Love

> Genuine polemics approach a book as lovingly as a cannibal spices a baby.
>
> —Benjamin, 1928/1996, p. 460)

Introductory Note

In presenting these theses, I wish to call to mind the "Theses on Feuerbach" by Karl Marx (1845/1978), "Twenty Theses on Marx" by Antonio Negri (1996), and especially those brilliant 13-thesis sections of Walter Benjamin's "One-Way Street" (1928/1996).[1] I also want to call to mind the gesture of Martin Luther, nailing his theses to the church door—a gesture that evinced, more than anything, his studied love for the Church, a love so strong he could not remain silent. I will attempt to read certain texts closely, drawing out what I see as important lessons to be learned, even if these are lessons that the authors would not recognize as their own. In doing this, I hope you will understand that I am making arguments strictly about texts.

Thesis One: The Question, "What Is the State of Curriculum Studies?" Cannot Be Answered, For We Are Only Barely On the Way to Learning How to Pose It

I want to begin with a gesture of deference, a gesture that I want to make under the sign of apprenticeship. It seems to me that what we will eventually be asking about is learning how to learn, and I must admit that I'm only just beginning such a process. Thus, I find it helpful to summon those who help me learn. The last book Gilles Deleuze and Félix Guattari wrote together, *What is Philosophy?* (1994), begins this way:

> The question what is philosophy? can perhaps be posed only late in life, with the arrival of old age and the time for speaking concretely…. It is a question posed in a moment of quiet restlessness, at midnight, when there is no longer anything to ask. It was asked before; it was always being asked, but too indirectly or obliquely: the question was too artificial, too abstract. Instead of being seized by it, those who asked the question set it out and controlled it in passing. They were not sober enough. There was too much desire to *do* philosophy to wonder what it was, except as a stylistic exercise. (p. 1)

The question, Deleuze and Guattari teach us, can perhaps not be well posed by those of us who are still young, still trying to do too much. Many of us, and I include myself, are not sober enough yet to ask, "What is curriculum studies?" And I'm not sure we can even ask what the "state" of curriculum studies is, because I'm not sure yet that we are seized *by it*, and not seeking too much to control it.

Edward Said (2002) has proposed an idea he calls "lateness," following Adorno's writings on late Beethoven. Such works arise from "a moment when the artist who is fully in command of his medium nevertheless abandons communication with the bourgeois order of which he is a part and achieves a contradictory, alienated relationship with it" (p. 197). Such "late" works would be characterized by their success-through-failure. Lateness ushers in discontinuity and discord not as madness or delirium, but as sobriety, as the consequence of giving oneself over to the demands of the question.

One work that is guided by such demands is William Pinar's (2004) masterful *What is Curriculum Theory?* Pinar has spent his life *doing* curriculum studies with unsurpassed rigor and care. Thus, when he takes it upon himself to attempt to meet the demands of this question that he gives as the title of his book, we are obliged to listen; that is, if we dare to listen carefully enough, and openly enough. Pinar writes, "Curriculum theory is…about discovering and articulating, for oneself and with others, the educational significance of the school subjects for self and society in the ever-changing historical moment" (p. 16). This definition seems familiar to us. It harkens back at least to Charles W. Eliot, and it seems to understand curriculum as something that happens in a relationship between "school subjects" (which are not quite disciplines) and—but we're anticipating here—human subjects. But this is actually Pinar's second attempt in this book to define curriculum theory. The first, on page 2, is more concise: "The short answer is that *curriculum theory is the interdisciplinary study of educational experience.*" This too seems like a definition to which we could all subscribe. Between these two definitions there seems to me an infinite gap, a caesura. In the movement between the two something happens that transforms "disciplines" into "subjects," and more importantly the institution of the "school" flickers in and out of our view, carrying with it what Pinar calls "self and society" but which I would rewrite as "subjectivities."[2] It is here, in the gap we read only because Pinar is willing to answer this question in full sobriety, that we can begin to pose the question of the "state" of curriculum studies.

Thesis Two: Curriculum Studies Must Address the Fundamental Paradox of Education: What Has Been vis-à-vis What Is to Come

It seems to me, and I learn this from Dewey (1938/1997) and Kliebard (1995), that education has an ambivalent aim. On the one hand, it must pass on the traditions of the culture and society in which any education takes place. On the other hand, education must prepare students for participating in a world that does not yet exist, that is still to come. In a short, and often not closely enough read, passage, Dewey (1938/1997) writes: "A primary responsibility of educators is that they not only be aware of the general principle of the shaping of actual experience by environing conditions, but that they also recognize in the concrete what surroundings are conducive to having experiences that lead to growth" (p. 40). Curious primary responsibility here: educators must teach through an experience of what is, but also through that which, although it is *not yet* in existence, shows itself in what is.[3] This demand for growth—a concept that Dewey spent his career working out—is the fundamental ethical tension between living well in the world as it is and creating a world that is more open, more loving, more human. Education is the process of learning what is and what has been so that we may move past it.

On a lower level of abstraction, this seems to demand that educators conceptualize not only the traditions they teach (whatever they are) but that they also philosophize and conceptualize possibilities for the world yet to come. One example I may give is that every educator needs to know something about the geo-politico-economic shifts occurring under globalization and postcoloniality. Even if we cannot adequately imagine what the world will be in 5 or 10 or 20 years, we must try to educate in such a way that our students can cognitively map their worlds, assess their positions in local and global networks, and make full, sustainable lives for themselves.

Thesis Three: When We Inquire into the "State" of Curriculum Studies, We Cannot Avoid Polyvalence

The title of this paper hinges on a certain ambiguity: when we ask about the "state" of curriculum studies, which "state" do we mean? There are, at a minimum, two. To be reductive in the extreme, they concern "history" and "politics," or perhaps the temporal and the social. I want to turn to structuralist linguist Ferdinand de Saussure to help us make sense of the former. In the *Course in General Linguistics* (1916/1959), Saussure writes:

> One might also say that static linguistics deals with eras. But state is preferable. The beginning and the end of an era are generally characterized by some rather brusque revolution that tends to modify the existing state of affairs. The word state avoids giving the impression that anything similar occurs in language. (p. 102)

Saussure is working toward a definition of what he will call a "language-state," a static picture of a *langue* at any given time. For Saussure, the notion of a state refers strictly to language. The question of the state of curriculum studies then must refer us to the discourse of the field, and asks us, despite the seeming impossibility of such a task in the present moment, to set aside the empirical realities that we impute to the "context" of such discourse.[4]

The second notion of "state" which is at play is that of the state form or the state apparatus. I begin with the latter because its theorization played such an important role in the way a certain curriculum studies conceived of the world, especially in the 1970s. In the seminal essay "Ideology and Ideological State Apparatus (Notes Toward an Investigation)," Louis Althusser (1971), writes: "The State apparatus, which defines the State as a force of repressive execution and intervention 'in the interests of the ruling classes' in the class struggle conducted by the bourgeoisie and its allies against the proletariat, is quite certainly the State, and quite certainly defines its basic 'function'" (p. 137). In this conception, the institutions of church, army, judiciary, and so on, but most importantly for us the school, are organs of class struggle where the ruling classes reproduce the existing social order. In certain ways, this conception of the state is very helpful for us—for instance, it allows us to analyze the stakes of standardized history curricula for subject formation—but it also tends to assume that the school is an organ in the hands of some ruling elite, something that has rightly been questioned by many curriculum scholars, in no small part because most of us have been teachers in the schools and such a concept cannot adequately explain our lived experiences.

Refining this concept in light of global empire, Italian Marxist Antonio Negri's theory (1999a; Hardt & Negri, 1994, 2000, 2004), which follows Deleuze and Guattari's (2002) concept of the "apparatus of capture," figures that State as a parasite or vampire, feeding off the living labor of the multitude, thus making the "state" an opponent of the desires of the multitude. Such a concept of the state demands that we recognize the human creative potential which makes possible any social formation.

One of the tasks for curriculum studies in our moment, as well as the next moment, is to conceptualize what these two concepts of the state have to do with each other. How is the State apparatus bound up with the discourse in the field? How does our discourse, the discourse of curriculum studies, respond to the State form? Provisionally, and this guides the rest of these theses, these two "states" are entirely indeterminate. Our conceptualization of one cannot do without a concept of the other into which it constantly blurs.

Thesis Four: Curriculum Studies Must Cease its Crisis Rhetoric (As Well as the Corollary Attempts to Periodize)

In the Introduction to *Understanding Curriculum* (Pinar, Reynolds, Slattery, & Taubman, 1995) the authors write: "The main concepts today are quite different from those which grew out of an era in which school buildings and populations were growing exponentially, and when keeping the curriculum ordered and organized were the main motives of professional activity. *That was a time of curriculum development.* Curriculum Development: Born 1918. Died: 1969" (p. 6). No matter what one thinks of the accuracy of such an assertion, the rhetoric is remarkable. This new "era" (and I note that the authors use "era" and not "state") is founded upon the "death" of the old one. Paul de Man (1983) reminds us that such authors' "claim to being a new beginning turns out to be the repetition of a claim that has always already been made" (p. 161).

For a quick example, I want to quote from the last paragraph of Kliebard's *The Struggle for the American Curriculum* (1995). He writes,

> Neither the hopes nor the fears [of educational reformers] were fully actualized, and, to be sure, the curriculum reforms that were being proposed were only imperfectly achieved, but the different platforms for restructuring the curriculum became part and parcel of a national morality play in which those hopes and fears were enacted. (p. 251)

Kliebard, as an historian, is working from texts to construct an account of what curriculum discourse *did*. And what he finds is that for all the proclaimed ruptures and crises, curriculum discourse changes very slowly. It seems to me that by abandoning a notion of "eras" and the attendant claims to representing empirical reality, and embracing a notion of "state" that must account for how we communicate, write, and read "curriculum," we can move beyond a need to think our moment as crisis, a need that produces rhetoric that is as fantastical and phantasmagorical as it is scholarly.[5]

Thesis Five: In "The Nightmare that is the Present" (Pinar, 2004),
We Will Have To Contend with Ghosts

Very early in *What is Curriculum Theory?* Pinar writes:

> the present historical moment is, then, for public-school teachers and for those of us
> in the university who work with them, a nightmare. The school has become a skill-
> and-knowledge factory (or corporation); the education professoriate is reduced to
> the status of supervisory personnel. While in the schools, millions live the nightmare
> each day, too few seem to realize they are even asleep. (p. 3)

My concern, again, is not to take issue with whether or not Pinar's description here matches up with how I or anyone else sees life in schools. My concern is with the rhetoric that describes American educational experience as a scene from the sci-fi horror film *They Live!*[6]

It seems to me that *Understanding Curriculum* also trades in ghostly images (Snaza, 2004), and thus we have to ask what is so compelling and, perhaps, productive about such rhetoric. Ghosts and nightmares must be thought as displacements of real, and yet unconscious, traumas: displacements, but also returns—the ghost as *revenant*, the phantasmatic being who returns. Thus these ghosts are figures from the past that haunt our present, and they demand a settling of accounts with the past (this is the lesson of so many recent horror films such as *Sixth Sense, The Ring, The Eye, The Others*, etc.). These ghostly nightmares thus demand that we make up to or for the past, but they do so in displaced form. We never know exactly what we are being asked to atone for or to revenge (as we learn from *The Ring* and *The Ring 2*: the past sometimes only *seems* to demand a service; it can also be a purely negative force stripping us of the ability to live well). One crucial feature then of the state of curriculum studies is that it is haunted (which is a purely textual haunting).[7]

There is an *unheimliche* moment at the end of *Understanding Curriculum* that is instructive here. Pinar et al. begin the "Prologue" with the following declaration: "That's how a textbook might end, is it not? A summary statement in which 3200 references are incorporated, requiring, it is true, notching up the level of abstraction, but summing it up in the process. Doesn't work, does it? Even summoning the grand ghost of John Dewey isn't enough" (p. 867). The authors then provide a set of analogies to explain why Dewey is not the most important voice "in the same room" with us, now, and why we need to take account of what I might recast as the heteroglossia of the field. This is an understandable gesture, and one that might be necessary to authorize the type of view of the field Pinar et al. are seeking to stake out. But why summon a ghost, cast a spell, in order to show its inadequacy? Dewey is here conjured only to be silenced, or, to invoke the other sense of conjuring (see Derrida, 1994), finally laid to rest. Rather than allowing such a conjuring to come off without a hitch, I want to read Dewey without the ghostly rhetoric. Rather than being our "grand ghost," I wonder if we may think of him as what Foucault calls a "founder of discursivity" (1994). Foucault is thinking of discourses that require the patient rereading of their founders, and it seems to me that curriculum studies might benefit from being rethought as a line of inquiry that necessitates the careful, laborious reading of Dewey at every moment.[8] Instead of letting his ghostly presence haunt us, let us always return to him for guidance in "how we think."

Thesis Six: Curriculum Studies Has not Adequately Conceptualized "Curriculum"

In 1975 a volume appeared, edited by Pinar, titled *Curriculum Theorizing: The Reconceptualists*. This book presents "curriculum theorists" as constituting "the final 3 to 5 percent of the curriculum field," after the curriculum developers and those scholars "steeped" in social science. Near the end of the preface, Pinar writes, "At its most ambitious, the field will attempt to become a synthesis of contemporary social science and the humanities. It will attempt a marriage of two cultures: the scientific and the artistic and humanistic" (p. xiv). The field is here defined by a subjunctive marriage of two methodological and epistemological traditions. This wish-fulfillment definition seems to have caused us immense anxiety. If every study must have an object and a method, it's important to remember that different methods will not only make different sense of their objects, but will produce fundamentally different objects. In Pinar's description of the field we see a very clear formulation of what I see as our major difficulty: are we empiricists (social scientists) or are we not (humanists)?[9] One cannot be empiricist and not empiricist at the same time. Either one engages in the empiricist study of curricula, defined as some actually existing object in actually existing social situations (like schools), or one engages in the nonempiricist theorizing of curriculum *as a concept*.

I want to propose a misprision of the Reconceptualization as it is presented in *Curriculum Theorizing: The Reconceptualists*. Despite Pinar's subjunctive formulation, what the Reconceptualization has actually ushered forth is the return of "curriculum" to a concept. "Curriculum" can be theorized, "curricula" may be designed or implemented or studied empirically. What Pinar, Apple, Kliebard, Huebner, Greene, McCarthy, jagodzinski, Grumet, and others allow us to do is think curriculum as a nonempirical philosophizing of educational experience.

Thesis Seven: Curriculum Studies Should Be the Nonempiricist Questioning of What the "Human" Means

In the same volume from 1975, Michael Apple provides a very compelling definition of curriculum studies. Apple writes, "Our schools are places where humans confront each other and dwell in the complex situation of being human with others" (p. 128). We need to learn how to read this sentence. First, Apple is pointing to the all-too-unobvious idea that "curriculum" must be conceptualized as what allows us to "be human," or rather *become* human. Education is the process of learning to be human undergone by the human. Second, Apple—consciously or not—introduces the ideas that such a process is difficult (it could presumably fail) and that it concerns "dwelling."

I want to give this word *dwelling* a specifically Heideggerian resonance. In "Building Dwelling Thinking" (1954/1971), Heidegger writes: "We attain to dwelling, so it seems, only by means of building. The latter, building, has the former, dwelling, as its goal" (p. 145). The distinction here, at least the way I want to read it, is that dwelling is fundamentally different from mere living. Schools open themselves then to dwelling, but also to mere living. Dwelling in a school would mean being in it in such a way that one learns how to become human there, and where such dwelling is already to be human. Heidegger again: "The way in which you are and I am, the manner in which we humans *are* on earth, is…dwelling" (p. 147). Heidegger reads Hölderlin to understand *how* man dwells. The answer is "poetically" (*dichterish*) (p. 213). To dwell poetically is to live in the world in a manner of *poiesis* instead of *Ge-stell*, "Enframing." I am now going to risk a certain reductiveness, and I want to point you toward *The Question Concerning Technology* (1977), but I will translate these two terms as "being open to the world in such a way that the world can reveal itself to us," and as "living in the world and thinking the world only as what we can command and order." The difference is between an openness to the world and an attempt at mastery. To be human, in this conception with *poiesis* as its mode of dwelling, is fundamentally at odds with our modern conception of human being, a conception that is the basis of our most prevalent origin myth from the book of Genesis where man is given dominion over all things. There is a lot of thinking to be done here, and it seems to me that what is at stake is ultimately the entire world—all humans, plants, animals, ecosystems, societies, cultures, traditions, and so on.

Thesis Eight: The Concept of the "Man" Must Be Rethought and, Perhaps, Replaced

In *The Order of Things*, Michel Foucault (1970) writes, "It is comforting…and a source of profound relief to think that man is only a recent invention, a figure not yet two centuries old, a new wrinkle in our knowledge, and that we will disappear again as soon as that knowledge has discovered a new form" (p. xxiii). This concept of "man" as Foucault articulates it (rather, as he shows how it has been articulated) is something very specific: an object of social science, which creates "man" as its object in order to measure and classify it. Such a concept of "man" constitutes something like a founding principle of social science; in order to function it has to take "man" as a self-evident object available for empirical study.

It seems to me that there is nothing self-evident about "man" and indeed it is the task of curriculum studies to show what *currere* get run which turn us into human beings. As we have already noted, such a process can fail, and the task of education is to see that it doesn't. But the self-evidence of "man" is breaking down on all levels. Take, for example, the recent work in biology that moves beyond a notion of the "organism" as the basic unit of study (Doyle, 1997, 2003). As Richard Doyle explains, "'life' just isn't what it used to be. The conceptual, rhetorical matrix we used to feel comfortable ascribing to something called 'organisms' has been displaced and retooled" (1997, p. 25).

This does not need to sink into a sort of biological determinism. Rather, it demands a rethinking of how we dwell on earth *with* animals, plants, machines, and information. It is to displace "man" as the privileged center of our ethics and force us to include not only the human other, but every other in our decision making. The hope for such an ethics is education: "Perhaps, ironically, we can learn from our fusions with animals and machines how not to be Man, the embodiment of Western logos" (Haraway, 1991, p. 173).

It is no small task to cast off the thinking of man, and if curriculum studies can begin to address such a problem, it must ally itself quite strongly with the two most powerful theoretical movements now also seeking to cast off "man" and with it empiricism. I am referring to a certain thinking of the postcolonial (Ismail, 2005; Mowitt, 2005) and a certain thinking of globalization (Hardt & Negri, 1994, 2000, 2004). In his book *Abiding by Sri Lanka*, Qadri Ismail (2005) provides an important argument for postempiricism as a necessary postcolonial gesture. One of his examples can be linked directly to Apple's formulation of curriculum studies, and it helps us think what is at stake here: "the place—and place as a concept—is understood not geographically, or though its ally, area studies, but as a debate; not as an object that exists empirically but as a text, or a group of texts, that is/are read" (p. xvii): Getting rid of man means getting rid of empiricism, which means getting rid of social science.

Thesis Nine: The Imperative For Curriculum Studies Is not to Generate Empirical Truth Claims, but Ethical Commitments

If we can learn to set aside empiricism, what are we left with? The clearest answer I know of is with questioning, with reading. Questioning and reading are not methods, they are ethical modes of dwelling. Reading, in the sense that I am going to use it now, is something we don't do much of these days. It requires a lot of time, patience, and humility—things that our modern mode of existing doesn't value very highly. Reading must be set in opposition to both "interpreting" and "understanding." Qadri Ismail (2005) argues that "reading" and "intervening" are in opposition to "understanding" and "interpretation." The former are about ethical commitments and patient attention to an object, understood nonempirically as a collection of texts. The latter are about mastering the world, presumed to exist "out there" in some objective and ultimately knowable form. The former is the realm of the posthumanities. The latter is the realm of social science.

For the social sciences, including much of what goes by the name of curriculum studies, there is always an assumption that something exists which can be accurately described by more-or-less transparent means (language, statistics, etc.). For the humanities, there is an assumption that we live in and through texts, texts in which the precise formulations (in language, music, images) matter—in the double meaning that they are what count, and they are what makes up the "stuff" of our world. Because we live in texts, to make believe we can make accurate truth claims about the world[10] is to miss the more profound calling to us as thinkers: to think as a means of intervening in the world, again through texts. This requires us to give up on truths and to learn to dwell in ethics, in commitments to people and the earth, in readings, which are always imperfect and partial and interested.

It seems to me that we can learn to read and intervene in such a way by learning to question. Heidegger (1977) reminds us that, "Questioning builds a way" (p. 3). Summoning my earlier reading of Heidegger with Apple, we can see that questioning is what builds places (as concepts) for us to dwell, where to dwell is to dwell poetically, together with other beings. This is an ethical task and it is not a question of knowledge. As Marx famously reminds us, "the philosophers have only *interpreted* the world, in various ways; the point, however, is to *change* it" (1978, p. 145).

Thesis Ten: Curriculum Studies Must Have a Concept of the "Community" to Evaluate Its Ethical Statements

I am repeatedly using the word *ethics* here to designate a difference from something like politics. Politics, we might say, is about ethics that are enacted at the level of the state. Politics demands human beings with identities, as we know so well from the multiculturalism debates. One of the tasks of thinking the posthuman and the ethics that correspond will be to think something other than identity. The most advanced attempt to think this difference that I'm aware of is the thought of "singularity" (Deleuze, 1994). Some works (Agamben, 1993; Blanchot, 2001; Nancy, 1991) conceptualize "singularity" against the individual subject and "community" against the State.

An example here will be helpful. The last paragraph of Agamben's book, in a chapter about Tiananmen Square, reads as follows:

> Whatever singularity, which wants to appropriate belonging itself, its own being-in-language, and thus rejects all identity and every condition of belonging, is the principle enemy of the State. (1993, p. 87)

Note here a crucial reversal: not "common being" but "being in common." What links singularities is not a shared identity or essence (nationality, a shared language, a shared gender, a shared race, etc.) but a common being-in-the-world that makes ethical demands. Singularities demand, above all, to be loved. Thinking posthuman dwelling in the world means thinking love and ethics together and evaluating those ethics by the extent to which they allow community to happen to us.

Thesis Eleven: The Primary Ethical Demand for Curriculum Studies Is to Love

I want to put a few questions on the table. First: what does "love" have to do with what we earlier called "interest" which allows us to read instead of interpreting? What does "love" have to do with thinking the object of our inquiry as also subject, that is as something that does not exist apart from us, and which changes us when we interact with it? And, bringing back an earlier discussion, what does "love" have to do with learning to let the ghosts disappear, to put the haunting to rest? A lesson comes from Nietzsche, who writes:

> Just as anyone who acts, in Goethe's words, is always without conscience, so is he also without knowledge: he forgets most things in order to do one thing, he is unjust to whatever lies behind him and recognizes only one right, the right of what is to be. Thus, everyone who acts loves his action infinitely more than it deserves to be loved, and the best deeds occur in such an exuberance of love that, no matter what, they must be unworthy of this love, even if their worth were otherwise incalculably great. (1874/1995, p. 92)

We must forget the past, or parts of the past, in order to be ethically committed to what is to come. Nietzsche here inscribes this ability to forget (also required to be happy) under the sign of love. Thinking love as the ethical commitment of curriculum studies is not a new idea (see hooks, 1994; for a superb account of the importance of love for any political praxis, see Sandoval, 2000). The most important articulation of this thinking I know of is in Susan Huddleston Edgerton's brilliant *Translating the Curriculum*, where she links love not only to the care for students, but also to a rejection of hierarchies that cause us so much sadness (1996, p. 67). Edgerton writes,

> The pedagogical and psychoanalytic risk of love, transference love, is the displacement or deconstruction of hierarchized love.... Henceforth in this writing love functions as an analogy for teaching/learning at the same time that it is often, as in psychoanalysis, more than an analogy; it is a very real and necessary condition for the pedagogical situation. (p. 67; on "transference" in education see de Man, 1986; Felman, 1997; Harper, 2000)

Thesis Twelve: Curriculum Studies Must Be the Posthumanistic Production of Concepts Related to Education

Part and parcel of the movement away from empirical research toward a theorizing or philosophizing of curriculum as posthumanistic labor (of love) is a recognition that what curriculum studies produces is not understanding, or evidence, but concepts, concepts that must intervene in contemporary debates in ethical ways. As Deleuze and Guattari (1994) point out, "philosophy is the discipline that involves *creating* concepts" (p. 5). They link such creation (not discovery!) to the work of pedagogy, the work of learning to dwell in the world. For them, what we require is the

> modest task of a pedagogy of the concept.... If the three ages of the concept are the encyclopedia, pedagogy, and commercial professional training, only the second can safeguard us from falling from the heights of the first into the disaster of the third— an absolute disaster for thought whatever its benefits might be, of course, from the viewpoint of universal capitalism. (p. 12)

Here, we can see that philosophy (the *love* of knowledge) involves pedagogy as resistance to universal capitalism. One of the most profound insights to be gained from globalization theory, postcolonial theory, and the works of Adorno and Benjamin, is that in our moment capitalism is inseparable from the State. To resist capitalism is to be against the State.

Such resistance is indeed "modest." We must intervene in the world through the creation and deployment of concepts. What are our concepts? This is the question that curriculum studies needs to ask itself. To rely on the answers given in that supreme work of late style, Pinar's *What is Curriculum Theory?* I would have to give these: "school," "teaching," "self," and most importantly "curriculum." Our task is to take from the tradition concepts that make demands of us, and to theorize, philosophize them, in the spirit of ethical intervention.

Thesis Thirteen: Curriculum as a Concept Might Be a Third Space of Becoming Posthuman, a Place of Love, a Question of Love Against the State

In the first aphorism of *The Coming Community,* Agamben (1993) conceptualizes the relationship between love and singularity:

> Love is never directed toward this or that property of the loved one (being blond, being small, being tender, being lame), but neither does it neglect the properties in favor of an insipid generality (universal love): The lover wants the loved one *with all of its predicates*, its being such as it is. The lover desires the *as* only insofar as it is *such*—this is the lover's particular fetishism. Thus, whatever singularity (the Loveable) is never the intelligence of some thing, or of this or that quality or essence, but only the intelligence of an intelligibility. (p. 2)

This "intelligence" which is love, is the intelligence of the possibility of intelligibility in the first instance. That is, it is the love of what allows us to be lovable—our being-in-common, let us say—that lets community happen. This love is a matter of attention: For to love neither the qualities nor an "insipid generality" is to give attention to the loved object, attention without reserve. It is to practice what Adorno might call "immanent criticism." This is to say that learning to love, to be posthuman, is to learn to live aesthetically. It is to learn to read and not to interpret. It is to desire ethical intervention and not understanding. It is to wonder and above all to question.

We could benefit immensely from two complimentary and essential texts on aesthetics written in the 20th Century: Dewey's *Art as Experience* (1934/1980) and Adorno's *Aesthetic Theory* (1970/1997). Both of these texts conceptualize aesthetic experience as an ethical relation to the art object as a subject capable of transforming the subject immersing herself in the art object. For Dewey (1934/1980), this opens the possibility of what he calls civilization, but which I would rewrite as "community":

> It is a matter of communication and participation in values of life by means of the imagination, and works of art are the most intimate and energetic means of aiding individuals to share in the arts of living. Civilization is uncivil because human beings are divided into non-communicating sects, races, nations, classes and cliques. (p. 336)

That is, art is what allows us to think community without identity, beyond "common being" of sect, race, nation, class, or clique. Art, living poetically as Heidegger would say, opens us to the possibility of love. And this possibility opens a space for the posthuman dwelling, a dwelling that curriculum studies must conceptualize and study.[11]

As the notion of transference has been worked out in psychoanalysis, it has come to designate a sort of third space, between the analysand and the analyst. It's not uncommon to think this also as teacher and student, given that we understand the pedagogical and analytic situations as both questions of love between (at least) two singularities. I want to end now by asking us to read aesthetically, ethically, in the loving hope of some better world yet to come. And here, perhaps unsatisfactory though it is, I come to the end, and I leave it to an Other, to Hélène Cixous's novel *The Third Body* (1999). I hope we are ready to read this, and to question after it:

> And I had said: Everything will happen to us. And it was the same thing, at least I thought so, it was that thing, love, with its symmetrical faces and its crooked smiles. Between us there was all this Nothing of Everything, the possibility of the impossible that happened, that would happen at one time or another, here or there (which had become homonyms, and I answered to *where are you?* at times with *I am here*, at times with *I am there*, and it was the same place, for the place where he is I am, the place where I am he is in flesh and bones and the spirit of him or me). But today, here, where are my flesh and bones? I want to arrive, but I don't have a body in which to make an appearance. (pp. 24–25)

Notes

1. I want to give special thanks to my friend Matt Hadley here, for sharing his paper "The Form of Thesis" (2005) with me. He writes, "Thesis then, and I want to stress this, is that reduction of form—touching on the very limit of form itself—that exposes, at the same time, both the control and negative enclosure of our lives at the largest scale, and the powerful potential within, asking us to collide with even more intensity against that which bounds us" (p. 3).
2. In rewriting it thus, I am following Pinar. On page 24 of this book, he writes, "We hope to persuade teachers to appreciate the complex and shifting relations between their own self-formation and the school subjects they teach, understood as subject matter and as human subjects." It does seem to me that this formation is slightly messy, however, for it presents teachers as having "selves" while students are "subjects." Despite its importance in contemporary curriculum studies, I think maintaining the concepts of "the self" and of "identity" is not desirable.
3. Although there is no time to work out a full theory here, it seems to me that such experience is what Dewey (1934/1980) and Adorno (1970/1997) mean by "aesthetic." Adorno writes, "Artworks are semblance in that they help what they themselves cannot be to a type of second-order, modified existence; they are appearance because by virtue of aesthetic realization the nonexistence in them, for whose sake they exist, achieves an existence, however refracted" (p. 109).
4. For context explains nothing, as Derrida (1977) has taught us: "by virtue of its essential iterability, a written syntagma can always be detached from the chain in which it is inserted or given without causing it to lose all possibility of functioning, if not all possibility of 'communicating,' precisely. One can perhaps come to recognize other possibilities in it by inscribing it or *grafting* it onto other chains. No context can entirely enclose it" (p. 9).
5. Politically, we should also note that the Right makes great use of crisis language to further their interests. If we allow ourselves to couch our discourse in a language game they already control, we have already lost by virtue of assenting to their rules.
6. Not least troubling to me, but which I can't address in the space allowed, is how such a conception falls easily into the old Marxist ideas of "false consciousness." This description

comes disturbingly close to saying, "We are awake! We know! And we must wake those who cannot see the truths we see!"

7. Of course, curriculum studies is not the only discourse that is haunted in this way. Marxism may be the most obvious other example. Take, in *Capital, Vol. 1* (1867/1990), the following: "The prolongation of the working day beyond the limits of the natural day, into the night, only acts as a palliative. It only slightly quenches the vampire thirst for the living blood of labour" (p. 367). One might also think of the opening lines of the *Communist Manifesto* (2002): "A spectre is haunting Europe—the spectre of Communism" (p. 218), and much of the rhetoric in Hardt and Negri's (2000) *Empire*.

8. This is not the way Dewey is usually read. Dewey is often invoked only to be cheaply dismissed. The kind of reading I'm talking about can only be called the labor of love.

9. In *What Is Curriculum Theory?* Pinar places the weight on the humanities side of his earlier definition, and in proposing that we be posthumanities scholars and not social scientists, I am following his lead. He writes: "The interdisciplinary structure of the field, and especially the strong influence of the humanities and the arts, makes curriculum theory a distinctive specialization within the broad field of education, a fragmented field broadly modeled after the social and behavioral sciences" (p. 2).

10. What I mean by this is that "truth claims" are by definition ethical commitments masquerading as objective claims about the world. Anywhere you find "evidence" you should read "I am ethically committed to...." Fidelity to the accuracy, reliability, and validity of empirical research methods is an ethical commitment, and one that, as a founding exclusion, must bracket the questioning of the self-evidence of the visible.

11. I want to acknowledge here one of my favorite books, a book that brings together aesthetic theory and postcolonial theory to make profound arguments about curriculum: Greg Dimitriadis and Cameron McCarthy's *Reading and Teaching the Postcolonial* (2001).

References

Adorno, T. W. (1997). *Aesthetic theory* (R. Hullot-Kentor, Trans.). Minneapolis: Minnesota University Press. (Original work published 1970)

Agamben, G. (1993). *The coming community* (M. Hardt, Trans.). Minneapolis: Minnesota University Press.

Althusser, L. (1971). Ideology and Ideological state apparatuses (Notes towards an investigation). *In Lenin and philosophy and other essays* (B. Brewster, Trans., pp. 127–186). New York: Monthly Review. (Original work published 1969)

Apple, M. (1975). Scientific interests and the nature of educational institutions. In W. Pinar (Ed.), *Curriculum theorizing: The reconceptualists* (pp. 120–130). Berkeley, CA: McCutchan.

Benjamin, W. (1996). One way street (E. Jephcott, Trans.). In M. Bullock & M.W. Jennings (Eds.), *Walter Benjamin selected writings* (Vol. 1, pp. 444–488). Cambridge, MA: Harvard University Press. (Original work published 1928)

Blanchot, M. (1983). *La Communauté Inavouable* [The unavowable community]. Paris: Les Éditions de Minuit.

Cixous, H. (1999). *The third body* (K. Cohen, Trans.). Evanston, IL: Northwestern University Press.

Deleuze, G. (1994). *Difference and repetition* (P. Patton, Trans.). New York: Columbia University Press.

Deleuze, G., & Guattari, F. (1994). *What is philosophy?* (H. Tomlinson & G. Burchell, Trans.). New York: Columbia University Press.

Deleuze, G., & Guattari, F. (2002). *A thousand plateaus: Capitalism and schizophrenia* (B. Massumi, Trans.). Minneapolis: Minnesota University Press.

de Man, P. (1983). *Blindness and insight: Essays in the rhetoric of contemporary criticism* (2nd ed.). Minneapolis: Minnesota University Press.

de Man, P. (1986). *The resistance to theory*. Minneapolis: Minnesota University Press.

Derrida, J. (1988). *Limited Inc* (S. Weber, Trans.). Evanston, IL: Northwestern University Press.

Derrida, J. (1994). *Specters of Marx: The state of the debt, the work of mourning & the new International* (P. Kamuf, Trans.). New York: Routledge.

Dewey, J. (1980). *Art as experience.* New York: Perigree. (Original work published 1934)

Dewey, J. (1997). *Experience and education.* New York: Free Press. (Original work published 1938)

Dimitriadis, G., & McCarthy, C. (2001). *Reading and teaching the postcolonial: From Baldwin to Basquiat and beyond.* New York: Teachers College.

Doyle, R. (1997). *On beyond living: Rhetorical transformations of the life sciences.* Stanford, CA: Stanford University Press.

Doyle, R. (2003). *Wetwares: Experiments in postvital living.* Minneapolis: Minnesota University Press.

Edgerton, S. H. (1996). *Translating the curriculum: Multiculturalism into cultural studies.* New York: Routledge.

Felman, S. (1997). Psychoanalysis and education: Teaching terminable and interminable. In S. Todd (Ed.), *Learning desire: Perspectives on pedagogy, culture, and the unsaid* (pp. 17–43). New York: Routledge.

Foucault, M. (1970). *The order of things: An archaeology of the human sciences* (A. Sheridan, Trans. [uncredited]). New York: Vintage.

Foucault, M. (1994). What is an author? In J. D. Faubion (Ed.), *Aesthetics, method, and epistemology* (R. Hurley et al., Trans., pp. 205–222). New York: New Press.

Hadley, M. (2005). *The form of thesis.* Paper presented at the Thinking the Present: The Beginnings and Ends of Political Theory Conference, University of California, Berkeley, May 27. Retrieved from http://criticalsense.berkeley.edu/hadley.pdf

Haraway, D. (1991). *Simians, cyborgs, and women: The reinvention of nature.* New York: Routledge.

Hardt, M., & Negri, A. (1994). *The labor of Dionysus: A critique of the state-form.* Minneapolis: Minnesota University Press.

Hardt, M., & Negri, A. (2000). *Empire.* Cambridge, MA: Harvard University Press.

Hardt, M., & Negri, A. (2004). *Multitude: War and democracy in the age of empire.* New York: Penguin.

Harper, H. J. (2000). *Wild words/dangerous desires: High school girls & feminist avant-garde writing.* New York: Lang.

Heidegger, M. (1971). Building dwelling thinking. In M. Heidegger (Ed.), *Poetry, language, thought* (A. Hofstadter, Trans., pp. 143–161). New York: Harper & Row. (Original work published 1954)

Heidegger, M. (1977). *The question concerning technology and other essays* (W. Lovitt, Trans.). New York: Harper & Row.

hooks, b. (1994). *Teaching to transgress: Education as the practice of freedom.* New York: Routledge.

Ismail, Q. (2005). *Abiding by Sri Lanka: On peace, place and postcoloniality.* Minneapolis: Minnesota University Press.

Kliebard, H. M. (1995). *The struggle for the American curriculum: 1893–1958* (2nd ed.). New York: Routledge.

Marx, K. (1978). Theses on Feuerbach. In R. C. Tucker (Ed). *Marx-Engels reader* (pp. 143–145). New York: Norton. (Original work published 1845)

Marx, K. (1990). *Capital* (Vol. 1, B. Fowkes, Trans.). New York: Penguin. (Original work published 1867)

Marx, K., & Engels, F. (2002). *The communist manifesto* (S. Moore, Trans.). New York: Penguin. (Original work published 1848)

Mowitt, J. (2005). *Re-takes: Postcoloniality and foreign film language.* Minneapolis: Minnesota University Press.

Nancy, J. L. (1991). *The inoperative community* (P. Connor, L. Garbus, M. Holland, & S. Sawhney, Trans.). Minneapolis: Minnesota University Press.

Negri, A. (1996). Twenty theses on Marx: Interpretation of the class situation today. In S. Makdisi, C. Casarino, & R. E. Karl (Eds.), *Marxism beyond Marxism* (pp. 149–180). New York: Routledge.

Negri, A. (1999a). *Insurgencies: Constituent power and the modern state* (M. Boscagli, Trans.). Minneapolis: Minnesota University Press.

Negri, A. (1999b). The specter's smile. In M. Sprinker (Ed.), *Ghostly demarcations: A symposium on Jacques Derrida's* Specters of Marx (P. Dailey & C. Costantini, Trans., pp. 5–16). New York: Routledge.

Nietzsche, F. (1995). *Unfashionable observations* (R. T. Gray, Trans.). Stanford, CA: Stanford University Press. (Original work published 1961)

Pinar, W. (Ed.). (1975). *Curriculum theorizing: The reconceptualists.* New York: McCutchan.

Pinar, W. F. (2004). *What is curriculum theory?* Mahwah, NJ: Erlbaum.

Pinar, W. F., Reynolds, W. M., Slattery, P., & Taubman, P. M. (1995). *Understanding curriculum.* New York: Lang.

Said, E. (2002). Adorno as lateness itself. In N. Gibson & A. Rubin (Eds.), *Adorno: A critical reader* (pp. 193–208). Malden, MA: Blackwell.

Sandoval, C. (2000). *Methodology of the oppressed.* Minneapolis: Minnesota University Press.

Saussure, F. D. (1966). *Course in general linguistics* (W. Baskin, Trans.). New York: McGraw-Hill.

Snaza, N. (2004, April 12). *The "death" of curriculum studies and its ghosts.* Paper presented, AERA Division B.

Suggested Reading Questions

1. How might Snaza's being "seized by" an idea, a question, or an experience, in the process of doing curriculum, be a contradiction and an alienation from the very practices and theories that have hitherto sustained the field of education (or curriculum studies)?

2. What might be the implication of State as a apparatus and its relation to State as discourse in curriculum studies be?

3. The author states that while curriculum can be theorized, curriculum must be designed. How might the difference between the two be the key to understanding the author's claim that curriculum is a nonempirical philosophy of educational experience that cannot be both empirical and nonempirical?

4. Snaza refers to the ecopolitics of dwelling as different from living in the world. What are the moral implications of dwelling and how does it give us a deeper understanding of the curriculum crisis that might allow for a poiesis of multiplicity and diversity in understanding curriculum?

Response to Nathan Snaza
Love in Ethical Commitment
A Neglected Curriculum Reading

William H. Schubert

Nathan Snaza has offered 13 theses, the crescendo of which is a call for ethical action immersed in love—a hope for interrelatedness that could issue in a posthumanity. He challenges us to read anew, to wonder without slavery to knowledge, to create concepts that grow in contrast to inert information, and to act on an imperative of ethical commitment guided by aesthetic imagination. I wonder why creators of novels, poems, plays, other stories, movies, and some television programming recognize the need to emphasize love, not just for sales, but for conversion of perspective, emotion, and ethical commitment, but curriculum theorists (especially curriculum developers and designers) have seldom grasped this ingredient as a basis for human possibility?

My transition to Mister Rogers, here, may seem surprising. Fred Rogers had a class size of 8 million for his well-known PBS program, *Mister Rogers' Neighborhood*; yet, each viewer knew he cared about them personally. When some of his former viewers graduated from college, and he was asked to give their commencement address, snickers and raucous demeanor retreated as he approached the microphone. They became his childhood audience again. In his calming manner, instead of the usual kind of address, he simply asked all of the students to stand for a few moments of silence and reflect on those who "loved them into being." Silence prevailed as tears rolled down faces and graduates looked toward the audience where some of those who *loved them into being* proudly watched. Mister Rogers did not look for deficits, as curriculum makers too often do. He liked us "just the way we are," as he so often repeated to children, helping them feel good about who they are.

Indeed, how are we? That is a great educational question, one we pursue for a lifetime. And its subset for this volume is: What is the state of curriculum studies? How *are* we in curriculum studies? To invoke Mister Rogers is in no way to diminish the intellectual tour de force with which Nathan Snaza challenges us—those in curriculum studies, or anyone else who is listening. In fact, my respect for Fred Rogers' accomplishments makes me offer the two together as strengthening the call for love and ethical commitment.

Compelled to Reflect

Together, Snaza and Rogers compel me to reflect on those who loved me into being: my parents, grandparents, other relatives, friends, my children and grandchildren, wonderful colleagues, and most profoundly my loving wife Ann (1952–2006). I think of the pedagogy of my family life in the Midwest, six of us (3 generations) piling in the car for a 3- to 4-week trip each summer for a decade (with the adults encouraging me to plan the curriculum of our journeys). Too, I reflect on sharing of conversations, pretend stories, movies, TV shows, sports, especially Indiana basketball, as a modern chivalry wherein teenage knights defended the honor of their town. I fondly recall the friendships, trying to figure out meanings of life amidst a fundamentalist Christian and small farm town ethos, entering college and falling in love with literature and philosophy as guides that I wanted to emulate.

My parents were highly regarded educators in the small towns in which we lived, and I cannot help but feel a prophetic connection between the early curricula embedded in the life I experienced and what happened next. After completing a master's in philosophy of education at Indiana University in 1967, I became a teacher in the Chicago area. My father, a seasoned administrator and former coach, gave me a dittoed article he thought insightful: "The Greening of Curriculum" (1971) by Paul R. Klohr of the Ohio State University. As an undergraduate, I found that *curriculum* (as is all too typical) was conveyed mostly as lesson planning; however, in graduate studies, it had been suggested that we read *Fundamentals of Curriculum Development* by Smith, Stanley, and Shores (1957), and when I opened the book, it seemed as if I already knew it. I practically assimilated it. The same happened with Bruner's (1960) *The Process of Education*. In contrast, though I felt a similar connectedness, I found that Dewey's (1916) *Democracy and Education* needed a slow read to become part of my emergent repertoire. Under the guidance of A. Stafford Clayton, I discovered that Dewey's *Summary* at each chapter end was really extrapolation, so study of the whole text was necessary! Thus, I had positive inclinations toward both *curriculum*, and also to *greening* from Reich's (1970) *The Greening of America*.

Later, my reading of the Smith, Stanley, and Shores text turned out to be somewhat prophetic, in that I studied with J. Harlan Shores for my PhD at the University of Illinois. Hoping to do doctoral work in philosophy of education, I had been dismayed in surveying college catalogues of the day to learn that philosophy of education had morphed into something called *educational policy studies*, which seemed too connected to the state to be as imaginative and speculative. So, by reading some curriculum theory, along with literature and philosophy, I nourished my imagination as an elementary teacher. From this antidote to the dissonance wrought by the anathema of lesson planning with behavioral objectives, I selected curriculum studies as a practical instantiation of philosophy of education. During doctoral study I looked for curriculum books wherever I could find them, hoping to locate writings that helped me understand what I considered the greatest asset to teaching: the philosophical imagination, especially in the lives of teachers and students. I found far too little in curriculum literature about teachers, students, and their relationships. On my parent's bookshelf, I found Caswell and Campbell (1935), which they had used in graduate school at Indiana University, nearly 30 years before I had been there for my master's degree. Intriguingly, the Caswell and Campbell text has a section on *pupil pursuits*! Sadly, this emphasis seemed to be discarded over the years; something akin to it could only be found in some of the advocates of integrated curriculum (Hopkins, 1937, 1954) and higher levels of the core curriculum (Alberty, 1947, 1953).

To continue the *prophecy*: As many know, Harold Alberty went to the Ohio State University to study with the eminent education philosopher, Boyd H. Bode. What I had not known, and discovered after my father passed away in 1974, was that Harold Alberty, as Superintendent of Schools in Berea, Ohio, signed my father's first and second grade report cards. Paul Klohr was Alberty's student in curriculum, and exemplary mentor of Norm Overly, Bill Pinar, Tim Leonard, Craig Kridel, Janet Miller, Bob Bullough, Paul Shaker, Francine Shuchat-Shaw, and others of my generation of colleagues in the curriculum field—those whose notions of reconceptualization are being considered and built upon here. When I took groups of my doctoral students to present at Bergamo conferences, Paul Klohr often commented (with sentimental eyes) that it reminded him of the ways in which Harold Alberty had taken him and other doctoral students to Association for Supervision and Curriculum Development (ASCD), when ASCD dealt with fundamental curriculum wonderings.

After almost a decade of conferences on the reconceptualization of curriculum, Klohr (1980) reflected on a diversity of themes in the new concepts being advanced. I have found it interesting to ponder Snaza's 13 theses in light of Klohr's nine themes:

- Organic view of nature
- Individuals as creators of knowledge and culture
- Experiential base of method
- Preconscious experience
- New sources of literature for curriculum
- Liberty and higher levels of consciousness
- Means and ends that include diversity and pluralism
- Political and social reconceptualization
- New language forms[1]

In the brief space afforded, I will wonder about these themes as I ponder possibilities for curriculum studies relative to Snaza's theses.[2] Perhaps incorrectly interpreted, I think Klohr, pedagogue and mentor that he was (now a mentor of a field), was not only summarizing, but looking ahead for us all.

Thesis One

Snaza's contention that we cannot determine the state of curriculum studies because we are barely able to pose the question to do so strikes a chord with fact that Klohr simply put his nine dimensions out there for consideration, for wonder, and did not attempt to explicate their meaning—as *topic sentences* for texts yet to come. How, I wonder, does (should) curriculum studies itself as a subject relate to Snaza's discussion of the transformation from discipline to subject, from a schooled subject to a human subject? How do we understand curriculum or curriculum studies, relative to Pinar's (2004, p. 2) observation that "curriculum theory is the interdisciplinary study of educational experience," unless we embrace far more venues of experience than institutionalized schooling (Schubert, 2007)?

Thesis Two

The educational paradox of reconciling (or not) *what has been* with *what is to come*, relates to my observation that Klohr was not merely summarizing but hoping, being pedagogical. The ambiguity of passing on that which does not yet exist, the Deweyan tension between living well in the world and making it better, is kindred to the admonition in an early characterization of *currere* by Pinar and Grumet (1976):

> I work to get a handle on what I've been and what I imagine myself to be, so that I can wield this information, rather than it wielding me.... I choose what of it to honor, what of it to let go. I choose again who it is I aspire to be, how I wish my life history to read. I determine my social commitments; I devise my strategies: whom to work with, for what, how. (p. ix)

Thesis Three

Snaza's query (*what state?*) clearly explores Klohr's political and social reconceptualiza-tion, as he wonders about the state of history or that of politics; that is, the temporal or the social. Multifarious images of corporate state influence, through school, as ruling class sponsored *parasite* or *vampire* vividly capture the damage.

Thesis Four

Snaza's caveat to cease crisis rhetoric and periodization of curriculum history is one that weighs heavy on a mind that has spent a career doing this (Marshall, Sears, Allen, Roberts, & Schubert, 2007; Schubert, Lopez Schubert, Thomas, & Carroll, 2002). Fortu-nately, I've done other things, too! Surely, with Snaza, we should strive for state account-ability to new language forms (Klohr) that move beyond momentary crisis and express the *fantastical* and *phantasmagorical* in tandem with the scholarly.

Thesis Five

Clearly, Snaza is convincing in his call to search for what haunts us, reminiscent of *Cur-riculum Visions* of Doll and Gough (2002). My sense of wonder is accentuated as Snaza draws upon Foucault to suggest that Dewey be a *founder of discursivity* more than a *grand ghost*, illustrative of Klohr's emphasis on both new sources of literature and preconscious experience.

Theses Six and Seven

The possibility, already exemplified, of allowing "us to think a nonempirical philosophiz-ing of educational experience," revives the depth of Klohr's experiential base of method. Further, Snaza's reading a glimpse (via Michael Apple) of Heideggerian *dwelling* evoked in the process of striving to be human with others, within the possibility of failure, rein-vigorates Klohr's image of humans as creators of knowledge and culture. Still more, Snaza's introduction of *poiesis* as a mode of dwelling brings to mind Klohr's liberty and higher levels of consciousness that could exorcise the origin myth of human domination over the world. Let us hope it could, at least.

Theses Eight and Nine

Reconceiving, even replacing the concept of *Man*, with solace from Foucault that *Man* is not as time-honored a concept as many would think, opens the possibility of mov-ing from organism to multifarious fusions among living and nonliving aspects of the world (though all may be alive, or all not). There is much of relevance here to be con-nected with Eastern thought (e.g., Lao Tzu,[3] later expressed in the poetry of Li Po, Tu Fu). This need resonates powerfully with Klohr's means and ends that include diversity and pluralism, giving necessary import to Snaza's call for *education* as a resistive force to impediments that prevent failure of *curreres* that make us more fully human. Two such impediments, identified by Snaza that are in the spirit of Klohr's call for higher levels of consciousness, are postcolonialism and globalization, though my colleague Bill Watkins has taught me to suspect that there is no postcolonialism, only neocolonialism. Klohr's political and social reconceptualization is pushed in novel directions by Snaza's call (inspired by Qadri Ismail) to a reading and intervention that constitute ethical com-mitments that supplant the kinds of knowledge that guide world mastery.

Theses Ten and Eleven

Snaza contends that dwelling in ethics, not accumulating knowledge, is an impetus to enactment—action or praxis derived from pondering, wondering, and speculating on (in) texts—a posthumanities orientation rather than a social science one. Klohr's emphasis on new language forms, is clearly related to his friend and contemporary, Dwayne Huebner (1966), who called for languages of curriculum that transcend the technical and scientific (especially scientistic): political, ethical, and aesthetic, and doubtless we should add spiritual (see Huebner, 1999). Intervention of ethical commitment, is guided by aesthetic perception and educational imagination (as Snaza appreciates in Dewey, 1934/1980) through a Deleuzian *singularity* (ponder connections again to note 3). This relates, I feel, to both Klohr's organic view of nature and his praise of new sources of literature that are not part of institutionalized curriculum development. Could such singularity be microcosmic in the history of solidarity, not of one faction in opposition to another; rather, solidarity (singularity) of being-in-the-world? In any case, Snaza is insightful in seeing singularity as the enemy of the state. I wonder what makes ethical commitment and love embrace. Could it be otherwise? Do we need to watch out for that? Sanza asks well that we ponder the connection between interest and love, to consider how love might help the ghosts disappear. Are there ghosts that should remain and be augmented within us, as well as those that should disappear? How do we guard against, noting Nietzsche's warning (drawing upon Goethe), forgetting the parts of the past we need.

What *is* clear is that we need to consider that place of love in curriculum studies, in curriculum theorizing, in pedagogical relationship, in currere—something that Snaza reminds us well. While he reminds us that this been addressed by bell hooks, Susan Edgerton (1995), and a few others, why has it been neglected by so many curricularists?

Theses Twelve and Thirteen

Continuing to explore this ethical commitment embedded in love, Snaza advocates the posthumanistic production of concepts related to education, as contrasted with social science knowledge. The careful (care-filled) reading he recommends brings creation more than discovery, and wonder at least as much as creation. As I ponder Snaza's mention of "three ages of the concept," derived from Deleuze and Guattari (1994), I wonder how to be *pedagogic*, prevent falling from the heights of *encyclopedia* as I develop an *Encyclopedia of Curriculum Studies*,[4] so that I will not land in the abyss of *commercial professional training*. Clearly, I want to remain in the realm of the pedagogy of love in ethical commitment. Meanwhile, I worry: Who has created universal capitalism that is the state of today? Are we all complicit, or some of us only? Who are those capable of theorizing concepts of *school, self, teaching*, and *curriculum* in the spirit of ethical intervention. Or, at best, can we only write and talk about these matters? As I look at the inhumanity of the world, I wonder if a post-Deweyan faith in democracy is warranted? Can we even form meaningful community, let alone participatory democracy? Can we love greed and imperialism out of the state? I hope so, and I doubt, too. Despite this doubt, what else is worth a try?

I learned to love with family and friends (through family trips, shared stories and arts, sports and discussions, study and teaching, relationships and theorizing, farm town and big city, gain and loss). Therein reside *curricula* of my ethical commitments. So, in response to Fred Rogers's simple admonition to remember those who have loved us into being, and to Nathan Snaza's theorizing of the need for love-based ethical commitment and intervention guided by careful, imaginative, aesthetic reading of the texts of our lives, I appreciate and applaud. Again, what else is worth a try?

Notes

1. Klohr's list makes it clear that there was great diversity, even in the early years of reconceptualization, that there were no *card carrying reconceptualists*!
2. To prevent redundancy, when referring to sources cited by Snaza, the reader should refer back to his reference list. Phrases from Klohr's list and Snaza's paper are integrated without citation in the discussion that follows to enhance flow.
3. Clearly this is related to the paper for this volume by Hongyu Wang, who unites aspects of the *Tao Te Ching* by Lao Tsu (Lao Tzu, Lao Zhi), to psychoanalysis, and has cofounded a new AERA SIG on Confucianism, Taoism, and Education, and especially portrayed by the unity of the river image that runs through Ming Fang He's (2003) autobiographical and fictionalized narrative, *A River Forever Flowing*.
4. This project, to be published by Sage, is one I am consulting on as a senior editor, to be edited by Craig Kridel.

References

Alberty, H. (1947). *Reorganizing the high school curriculum*. New York: Macmillan.
Alberty, H. (1953). Designing curriculum to meet the common needs of youth. In N. B. Henry (Ed.), *Adapting the secondary school program to the needs of youth: The 52nd Yearbook of the National Society for the Study of Education* (Part I, pp. 118–140). Chicago: University of Chicago Press.
Bruner, J. (1960). *The process of education*. New York: Vintage.
Caswell, H. L., & Campbell, D. S. (1935). *Curriculum development*. New York: American Book.
Deleuze, G., & Guattari, F. (1994). *What is philosophy?* (H. Tomlinson & G. Burchell, Trans.). New York: Columbia University Press.
Dewey, J. (1980). *Art as experience*. New York: Perigee. (Original work published 1934)
Dewey, J. (1997). *Experience and education*. New York: Macmillan. (Original work published 1938)
Dewey, J. (2000). *Democracy and education*. New York: Macmillan. (Original work published 1916)
Doll, Jr., W. E., & Gough, N. (Eds.). (2002). *Curriculum visions*. New York: Lang.
Edgerton, S. H. (1995). *Translating the curriculum*. New York: Rutledge.
He, M. F. (2003). *A river forever flowing*. Greenwich, CT: Information Age.
Hopkins, L. T. (Ed.). (1937). *Integration*. New York: Appleton-Century.
Hopkins, L. T. (1954). *The emerging self in school and home*. New York: Harper.
Huebner, D. (1966). Curricular language and classroom meanings. In J. Macdonald & R. Leeper (Eds.), *Language and meaning* (pp. 8–26). Washington, DC: Association for Supervision and Curriculum Development.
Huebner, D. (1999). *The lure of the transcendent*. Mahwah, NJ: Erlbaum.
Klohr, P. R. (1971). The greening of curriculum [editorial]. *Educational Leadership, 28*(5), 455–457.
Klohr, P. R. (1980). The curriculum field—Gritty and ragged. *Curriculum Perspectives, 1*(1), 1–7.
Marshall, J. D., Sears, J. T., Allen, L., Roberts, P., & Schubert, W. H. (2007). *Turning points in curriculum: A contemporary curriculum memoir* (2nd ed.). Upper Saddle River, NJ: Prentice-Hall.
Pinar, W. F. (2004). *What is curriculum theory?* Mahwah, NJ: Erlbaum.
Pinar, W. F., & Grumet, M. R. (1976). *Toward a poor curriculum*. Dubuque, IA: Kendall/Hunt.
Reich, C. A. (1970). *The greening of America*. New York: Random House.
Schubert, W.H. (2007). Curriculum inquiry. In F. M. Connelly, M. F. He, & J. Phillion (Eds.), *Handbook of curriculum and instruction* (pp. 399–417). Thousand Oaks, CA: Sage.
Schubert, W. H., Lopez Schubert, A. L., Thomas, T. P., & Carroll, W. M. (2002). *Curriculum books: The first hundred years*. New York: Lang.
Smith, B. O., Stanley, W. O., & Shores, J. H. (1957). *Fundamentals of curriculum development* (Rev. ed.). New York: Harcourt, Brace, & World.

3 Reading Histories
Curriculum Theory, Psychoanalysis, and Generational Violence

Jennifer Gilbert

Chapter Overview

The author discusses generational conflict as an important site for imagining the future of curriculum theory. Accordingly, the author explains the notion that conflict is a necessity to the formation of intellectual generations or a fact of birth and death with life and within the field. Focused upon the effect generational conflict has on the scholarly activity of reading, she illustrates that the entrance of a new generation into the history of a discipline might result in splitting, or a repudiation of the past in order to differentiate a contemporary generation from the previous one. The author suggests a response to what surfaces as an ahistorical attitude toward efforts in the field to make anew, those working in the field might become aware of our reading practices. This awareness, she suggests, might allow us to work through splitting that makes possible but soon hinders the relationship between generations. The author concludes with call for reparative reading practices.

Introduction

At the conference on the futures of curriculum theory where this chapter had its first life, junior scholars were invited to speak about their research and how that research borrowed from and transformed the work of "reconceptualist" curriculum theory.[1] In response, senior scholars read this work and offered questions, provocations, compliments, and complaints. The conference was structured to create a conversation across generations and to highlight what is new in the field of curriculum theory. Over lunch, in hallways, at receptions, and indeed in the conference room, conversations across and within intellectual generations inspired feelings of recognition and affirmation, but just as often, conflicts over theoretical and political commitments erupted, and feelings of being misunderstood, badly interpreted, or misread circulated. These conflicts, in part, help constitute what may come to be called "post-reconceptualist" curriculum theory just as earlier conflicts ignited the field of reconceptualist curriculum theory. Conflict, however, does not ruin thinking. The kinds of learning we might value when imagining the future of curriculum theory emerge from contested debates over interpretation and unsettle the pervasive if debunked fantasy that education, as both a discipline and a process of learning, should transcend conflict and reach toward consensus. It is the reconceptualists who have insisted that curriculum theory must consider the ways learning is caught up in the conflicts of subjectivity and intimately tied to experiences of belonging and exclusion. Yet while we may theorize these dynamics in curriculum theory, it may be more difficult to tolerate that these dynamics also structure the field of curriculum studies.

This chapter takes up these debates over interpretation and argues that conflict is necessary to the formation of intellectual generations. We are grappling here with the difficulty of both being a newcomer and greeting the newly arrived. It is a condition Hannah Arendt (1958/1997) calls "the fact of natality." "We are born into the world as strangers," Arendt argues, and yet despite the uncertainty the strange ushers in, it is "the fact of natality" that makes possible a new beginning—"the newcomer possesses the capacity of beginning something anew" (p. 9). In conflict with the promise of newness, we must face our own mortal finiteness and the difficulty of this realization can manifest itself as a fear of newness. While suspicious of psychoanalysis herself, Arendt's observations on the human condition echo descriptions of generational conflict in psychoanalysis. The ambivalence that marks the space of the familial, an ambivalence psychoanalysis described as Oedipal, makes the relations between generations fraught with conflict and a psychical violence. The child is received by her parents and the wider community as both a promise and a threat—and the child, for her part, enters the world caught between love and hate. What can it mean for the field of curriculum theory that the love of learning has such violent beginnings? And why might this violence be so difficult to tolerate for those just arriving and those already here? I want to say something about these psychical conflicts and the ambivalence that attends the fact of natality, in order to comment upon the formation of intellectual generations. How do we understand and respond to the violence of newness in intellectual communities? In what ways is newness received as both a promise for the future and a threat to history?

In this chapter, I bring these questions to bear on that most scholarly activity of intellectual communities: reading. In charting of the field of curriculum theory, these histories we are attempting to narrate are themselves an effect of reading. This chapter insists that our reading of history is marked by the "promises and threats" that the new introduces. How do our practices of reading constitute the generations between which conflicts will emerge? At the same time, when newcomers enter into a history that can seem already overpopulated, the repudiation of influence results in a splitting, what Passerini (1996) will call an antihistorical attitude. What happens to practices of reading when history feels like a burden and an insult? And yet, as I suggest toward the end of the chapter, noticing our practices of reading offers the best chance for working through the profound splitting that may initiate but then hamper relations between intellectual generations. Psychoanalysis, with its attention to the ways our reading of the outside world mirrors interior conflicts, offers an ideal framework for thinking through these difficult relations.

Generational Conflict

In his discussion of generational conflict, psychoanalyst Christopher Bollas (1997) observes:

> each generation violently destroys the previous generation's ideals and objects; it is through this process of destruction, then, that each generation constitutes its own objects, through which to envision its own future. And it is in this respect that a generation gets hold of its future and uses it as an object. (p. 31)

According to Bollas, generations are inaugurated through acts of violence. Something of the past must be repudiated or destroyed in order for a future to be made or found. Similarly, Luisa Passerini (1996), in her history of the 1968 student movement in Italy, *Autobiography of a Generation*, links the formation of generations to a refusal of continuity. She explores how the biographical narratives of her subjects record an ambivalence toward fathers and a refusal to regard mothers as significant; in effect, she argues, the generation of '68 "chose to be orphans." For a generation to constitute itself, parents must be forgotten: the generation grows from the illusion that it erupted through a break with the past. "To become history," Passerini writes, "this [new] subjectivity must assert itself as antihistorical. It must nullify, distance, destroy. And even where it finds continuity—with revolts of the past—it must manifest that as discontinuity" (p. 24). At first glance, both of these descriptions of generations conflict with the more common understanding of generation as procreation and creativity—literally, to generate. What can it mean to see the formation of generations as requiring a repudiation of history, an act of violence against one's parents (or parental substitutes), and the illusion of originality?

Consider next this claim by Madeline Grumet (1988), who casts the making of generations in a somewhat different light, as our shared human endeavor: *what is most fundamental to our lives as men and women sharing a moment on this planet is the process and experience of reproducing ourselves*" (emphasis in original, p. 4). This view of generations extends beyond the act of parenting. Whatever one's relation to the raising of actual children, we are all engaged in a process of making or finding ourselves in others: "Even if we choose not to be a parent we are not exempt from the reproductive process, for we have each been a child of our parents" (p. 6). That is, even as we desire to reproduce ourselves, we live that desire through the experience of having been someone's child. Bollas and Passerini locate violence in this relation: becoming a "generation" may require the repudiation of the parent as a defense against, or forgetting of, one's helplessness and dependency. However, in coming to see oneself as part of a generation, one also identifies with the parents' generative power. Reproduction becomes the compensation for having survived childhood.

The ironic logic of these psychical relations means that it may be difficult to tell the difference between parents and children; a fragile distinction Paula Heimann (1989) renders as "children and children-no-longer." If the adult, in "the experience of reproducing [herself]," is always also someone's child, and therefore continues to live the conflicts of early life, the formation of a generation—the construction of a break with the continuity of history—must defend against the return of one's infantile past: the extreme dependency, the impotent rages, and the passionate loves and hates.

What then can it mean to speak of a new generation of curriculum theorists? Through what acts of repudiation, forgetting, and violence will this generation constitute itself? What concepts, ideas, and texts must be destroyed in order to create new objects of inquiry and avenues for thought? How will these objects and ideas, forgotten and disavowed, return to haunt our intellectual acts? And importantly, what might it mean to see intellectual work and curriculum theory in particular as emerging from acts of destruction? Do we require a theory of aggression to imagine curriculum theory as a site of innovation and transformative practices? And, how will we tell the difference between innovation or newness and cloning?[2] Psychoanalysis opens some directions to pursue these questions of how violence, once banished to the outside, returns to threaten phantasies of origin and originality.

Psychoanalytic explorations of learning begin from the premise that the pursuit of knowledge is animated through the desire to dominate. In each act of knowing there inheres a violence. In the many versions of psychoanalysis, this relationship takes different forms. In his book on curiosity, Adam Phillips (1998) connects learning with a ravenous appetite, describing the infant as "the beast in the nursery" (p. 1). Melanie Klein's (1928/1965) early theory of the "epistemophilic instinct" explores how aggression pushes the child out toward the world of ideas. D. W. Winnicott (1989) connects the adolescent's idealism and intellectual asceticism with the phantastical murder of the parents. And Betty Joseph describes the adolescent girl's difficulty in finding her own interests, in having what Robert Caper calls, a "mind of one's own" (as cited in Joseph, 2000, p. 642), as an unconscious attempt to protect the mother from her overwhelming rage.

In each of these examples, the subject's own aggression precedes and shapes her encounters with the world outside. It is one of the significant contributions of psychoanalysis that aggression and violence is understood to exist not only in the external world, but also and originally inside the subject. Indeed, psychoanalysis casts suspicion on attempts to cleanly differentiate internal reality, including the violence inside, from external reality, or the violence outside. Our relationship with knowledge is formed amidst this confusion and defense of boundaries. Yet, that learning includes and even requires aggression pushes against more comfortable ideas in curriculum theory, including that education itself is a violent institution, or that education is a salve against violence and therefore protects students from the cruelty of the social. In this etiology of aggression, there is a clear delineation between violence in the social and the ways that violence comes to affect the self: aggression originates in the external world and comes from the outside to harm or injure the subject. The institution of education, bad social practices, and oppressive ideologies, for instance, are all assumed to inflict a violence on the subject.

Rather than search for signs of violence in the external world only, psychoanalysis asks us to notice the stirrings of rage in our everyday relations with objects, both loved and hated. And, crucially, psychoanalysis asks us to notice how our splitting of the world—badness being projected into the external world, the previous generation, or history and an idealized goodness being protected inside the self, the cohort, or the present—is itself a paranoid interpretation of reality. More difficult for our theories of curriculum and subjectivity is the possibility that we are constituted through and amidst aggression. If we all start life as "beasts in the nursery," we might ask what becomes of that beast as we grow up, enter school, encounter the curriculum, learn to read, and perhaps even go on to become teachers, scholars, or parents.

Reading Histories

In order to think about the problem of generations against the backdrop of violence and learning, I now turn to the problem of reading. There is, I think, an intimate connection between the formation of intellectual generations and practices of reading. A generation of thinkers will dismiss an author, a text, or a theory as irrelevant or outdated. At the same time, other texts will become that generation's favored objects. As generations discover new texts and reread forgotten or despised authors, certain modes of interpretation, theoretical frameworks, and concepts will offer new ways of reading. For instance, the reconceptualists' break with Tylerism and the technical and instrumental models of curriculum was made possible, in part, by a rebellious engagement with phenomenology, certain versions of psychoanalysis, literary fiction, and Marxist and neo-Marxist theory (Pinar, Reynolds, Slattery, & Taubman, 1995). Out of these novel readings, a new orientation to curriculum was mapped that focused largely on practices of interpretation and modes of subjectivity. What matters now, because of that generation's conceptualization of curriculum as an open-ended text, is not only *what* one reads, but *how* one reads. As Deborah Britzman (1996) explains, "Reading might then be one of theorizing reading as always about risking the self, about confronting one's own theory of reading, and about theorizing difference without gathering the grounds of subjection" (p. 163). If we follow Britzman and speculate on the emergence of a *post*-reconceptualist generation of curriculum scholars, we are asking, implicitly, about theories of reading and subjectivity; about how we read the world of curriculum today and how thinking about curriculum helps us read the world today.

This focus on reading is amplified by the privileged status assigned to reading in compulsory education. If education and educational theory have a primal scene, it may be the act of learning to read. As Grumet (1998) argues, reading—and not reading—are invested with all of the passionate dynamics that characterize family life. She writes:

> Just as we are learning to look at family life to understand the way intimate relations of parents to each other and to children involve patterns of identification and differentiation, domination, submission, and negotiation and transformation, we need to look at pedagogy, the relationship of teachers and students, and the relationships among teachers and students and texts if we are to understand how those relationships generate the behavior and attitudes and values that we call literacy. (p. 24)

This makes learning to read more than a problem of acquiring a skill or mastering a technique. Reading has an intimate connection to the conflicts and pleasures that animate family life. What then can it mean to say that one falls in love with a book? Or that one is a voracious reader? Conversely, how can we make sense of the refusal to read, the refusal to find meaning in or to fall in love with a text? How can we make sense of our splitting of texts into good, useful, and relevant or bad, outdated, and persecutory? Here again, I turn to psychoanalysis.

It is one of the most significant contributions of reconceptualist curriculum theory that we now notice both how the family insinuates itself into school, charging the teacher–student–curriculum relationship with the dynamics of domestic life, and how family relations and the student's own sense of self are changed by her encounters with the world of ideas outside of the home. The curriculum, which Grumet sees as a mechanism that pulls children out of the limitations and pleasures of family life, affects the child's relationship with her parents. Reading allows one to imagine worlds beyond the confines of the known. The psychoanalyst, André Green (1986), names this possibility in starker terms: "To read is to incorporate power of a destructive nature; to read is to feed upon the corpses of the parents, whom one kills through reading, through the possession of knowledge" (pp. 126–127).

Through reading—through the acquisition of an extrafamilial knowledge—one can exceed one's family. But this venture out into the world also acts as a violent repudiation of history. Through reading, one can claim, "I am not from here." The aggression of this refusal is felt in phantasy—but, as Alice Pitt (2006) argues, the act "is no less violently felt than if an actual murder had taken place" (p. 87). For Pitt, practices of reading enact unconscious phantasies of murder and reparation. Thinking about matricide, she explores how, in their dismissive readings of mothers in women's autobiographies, students forget their own mothers. The mother, subject to a splitting, must either be idealized or demonized, and for Pitt, both possibilities evidence a matricide—a radical murder that refuses to even grant the mother status as a subject. But this is also ambivalent terrain since, as both Pitt and Grumet will note, the phantastical killing and survival of the mother is both an obstacle to and the precondition for entering symbolization. Again, there is a slippery tautology when the problem of origins is obfuscated beneath an infantile prehistory of splitting, anxiety, and loss: does one read in order to kill, or kill in order to read? As both Green and Pitt notice, this intimate relation between reading and aggression means reading requires taking a risk. Can the child risk damaging the parent in her exploration of the world of ideas? Can parents survive their child's adventures in reading? Or as Pitt puts it: "why must the mother be destroyed and what remains after such a terrifying act?" (p. 1).

It is no surprise, then, that an unconscious fear of injuring the parents can inhibit the act of reading. Klein writes (1931/1988):

> reading has the unconscious significance of taking knowledge out of the mother's body, and…the fear of robbing her is an important factor for inhibitions in reading. I should like to add that it is essential for a favorable development of the desire for knowledge that the mother's body should be felt to be well and unharmed. It represents in the unconscious the treasure-house of everything desirable which can only be got from there; therefore if it is not destroyed, not so much in danger and therefore not so dangerous itself, the wish to take food for the mind from it can be more easily carried out. (p. 241)

There are, perhaps, two difficulties at play here. The child must have confidence that the loved object—originally the mother—can withstand the force of her aggression, that her violence has not harmed the mother, and that, therefore, the mother is not herself a dangerous object. But equally, the mother must receive the child's aggression with love, must not respond with vindictiveness, must be durable and act as a container for the child's terrifying and inchoate feelings. Pitt (2006) notes that if the mother can survive matricide then she will be available for what Winnicott calls "object usage":

> If the object (read now as the mother) survives the destruction and does not retaliate, the subject forms a relation with her. The subject too begins to tolerate and even enjoy living in a world where words do not mean what you want them to and where people exist whose desires oppose your own. (p. 99)

In this scenario, the mother paradoxically facilitates her own (failed) destruction, so that the child might take the risk of speaking, thinking, and leaving. If the mother can survive, the splitting that had previously organized the child's interpretations of the world can give way to thinking. It is a delicate balance.

In this theory of learning, we are asked to notice the ways reading begins in the hostile and loving relations within the family, and how reading creates a psychical space to repeat and then perhaps work through the conflicts that come from being a child and having parents. Britzman (2006) will notice how contemporary readings inevitably reenact old interpretations, worries, and phantasies: "Even when we read external reality we cannot help drawing upon what is unresolved in our own reading archive, yet in so doing the labor of reading reality follows the lines created by the transference" (p. 308). So in reading, we always encounter a disguised version of our own history of reading reality.

Surviving Interpretations

Teachers and the curriculum inherit this conflicted history. While it can be difficult to have one's cherished text, favorite interpretation, or beloved theory subjected to an aggressive "deconstruction," like the parent, the teacher must receive the student's critique without vindictiveness, acting as a container for the student's rage against an unjust world. Such containment might also offer students an opportunity to notice their own use of objects—how affective investments in texts, teachers, and theories gesture elsewhere, to an infantile prehistory of love and hate. Adam Phillips (1997) offers an example of this dynamic. Although it is from the analytic setting, there is an analogy to be drawn to education and the problem of generations:

I think the risk is that if the analyst needs to be believed or agreed with, the analysis recreates a certain kind of childhood trauma, of a relationship in which if you don't comply or agree then you're abandoned or rejected or punished. That, to me, seems a bad sadomasochistic model of a relationship. But, there is, of course, a problem here that psychoanalysis makes very vivid: if there are such things as resistances, and it seems to me that there are, then the analyst doesn't merely capitulate when the patient disagrees. That is to say, the analyst has to be tenacious without being authoritarian, and there might have to come a point, at times, where you as the analyst say, "We disagree about this. I think this is what it means." Or, "I think it's about you and you think differently. I don't need you, however, to agree with me." The analysis then continues despite the disagreement, but we do need to put the difference on the table, without having to decide now, or necessarily ever, which one of us is right. In fact, the question of right and wrong is exactly the problem. What we have to see is who can produce a story, or a version, that we can make something of that we want. (p. 138)

What version, or versions, of curriculum theory will be and are being produced from a new generation's readings of the theories, texts, and methods of the reconceptualists? What will it mean for the reconceptualists to meet this generational challenge without "merely capitulating"? Can reconceptualist curriculum theory act as a container for the enthusiastic critiques of a new generation? How will we distinguish between debates over interpretation that repeat a "bad sadomasochistic model" of an infantile relationship, and those in which the reconceptualists are appropriately "tenacious"? And, what happens when the post-reconceptualists risk having a mind of their own?

It is because of the reconceptualists that these questions can even be asked in curriculum theory. Their work has opened up theories of curriculum to questions of subjectivity, power dynamics, social and psychical conflict, social difference, and questions of culture. If it is not merely difficult to follow in such auspicious footsteps, it is almost impossible to tolerate the destruction required in the development of new theories, questions, and preoccupations. How to have a mind of one's own when such a confidence runs the risk of injuring one's intellectual parents? The other option, fealty, does not escape this problem either. What Betty Joseph (2000, p. 641) calls "excessive agreeableness" is a compliance that masks a fragile and defensive aggressiveness. One need only consider the antagonism with which adherents to particular theories defend the legacies of their teachers to witness the violence mobilized to defend the status quo.

From this ambivalence, the post-reconceptualist moment will emerge. We, in curriculum theory, must be brave enough to murder, and then persistent enough to survive these attacks. If we are to read the relations between generations in ways that work to tolerate the ambivalence of having been someone's child even as one begins to invent one's own children, we must resist the defensive splitting into before/after, traditional/innovative, and even teacher/student. How can we recognize and work through these dynamics, even as we acknowledge them as necessary to the work of making generations?

Citing Derrida, Patti Lather (1997) calls attention to the loss that marks any "post-proclamations and suggests that to live the history of the present is to learn to live with ghosts" (p. 6). Our work is haunted by the specter of past and yet-to-come generations and our responsibility, as people who think about learning, is to let our thinking be crowded with the cacophony of these influences. Perhaps this is what Lather means when she summons us to "work the ruins" (p. 135). Curriculum theory must be affected by its own history; we must notice how historical preoccupations, fights, and disavowals come to structure present concerns so that any rigid delineation between reconceptualist and post-reconceptualist theory will inevitably repeat this history.

Indeed, the talk of generations can come to feel claustrophobic, especially for those who in many ways live outside the expectation of generational continuity. Is there a way to conceptualize generations, and thus history, that does not draw upon hetero-normative metaphors? We are not all part of "the family." As Eve Sedgwick (1997) suggests "isn't it a feature of queer possibility…that our generational relations don't always proceed in this lockstep?" (p. 26). If queers have been kept out of the family, or are those who don't count as family, then what would a queer reading of generations and history offer to curriculum theory? Speaking of Proust and the shock of old age, Sedgwick writes:

> …isn't it worth pointing out that the complete temporal disorientation that initiates him into this revelatory space would have been impossible in a heterosexual *pere de famille*, in one who had meanwhile been embodying, in the form of inexorably "progressing" identities and roles, the regular arrival of children and grandchildren? (p. 26)

For Sedgwick, interrupting the inevitable march of generations requires what she calls "a reparative reading practice." In contrast to what Sedgwick, echoing Klein, calls a paranoid reading practice that demands texts speak the truth, when interpretations are either good or bad, a reparative reading practice rests on the possibility of surprise—including the surprise of generational continuity:

> She [the reparative reader] has room to realize that the future may be different from the present, it is also possible for her to entertain such profoundly painful, profoundly relieving, ethically crucial possibilities as that the past, in turn, could have happened differently from the way it actually did. (pp. 24–25)

The source of this pain and relief is, I think, the realization that one's interpretations of the past are marked by one's desires in the present, but simultaneously, one's present desires are made from "our own reading archive." In contrast to the "antihistorical" attitude of the paranoid reading position, a reparative reading position is forever implicated in its interpretations; it is always already ruined and marked by that loss. The present is always remaking the past, and indeed, this present—itself contingent, multiple, and crowded—will be remade, forgotten, idealized, or otherwise manipulated in the future presents. This is Arendt's "fact of natality," and perhaps what Grumet, citing Woolf, means by "thinking back through our mothers." The complication here, for education and the field of curriculum theory, is that one may have to destroy one's mother, and she in turn will have to survive this destruction, in order that we may think through and with her.

Notes

1. Many thanks to Erik Malewski and the two reviewers for their helpful suggestions. As well, Deborah Britzman and Patti Lather were both generous readers and responded thoughtfully to earlier drafts of this paper.
2. Britzman (2006), in her discussion of Kazuo Ishiguro's dystopic novel *Never Let Me Go*, names the risk of generational violence boldly:

   > Here, then, are a few novel questions: suppose we could create a copy of ourselves and that our affects are the copy. More difficult, suppose these copies are emissaries of our

object relations, phantasies sent out into the world to do our own biddings. What can we make of our psychical constructions—our affects and desires—who then return to read us? Would we need to destroy them? (p. 309)

References

Arendt, H. (1997). *The human condition*. Chicago: University of Chicago Press. (Original work published 1958)

Bollas, C. (1997). Interview. In A. Molino (Ed.), *Freely associated: Encounters in psychoanalysis* (pp. 5–52). New York: Free Association.

Britzman, D. (1996). Is there a queer pedagogy? Or, stop reading straight. *Educational Theory*, *45*(2), 151–165.

Britzman, D. (2006). On being a slow reader: Psychoanalytic reading problems in Ishiguro's *Never let me go*. *Changing English*, *13*(3), 307–318.

Green, A. (1986). *On private madness*. London: Hogarth.

Grumet, M. (1988). *Bitter milk: Women and teaching*. Amherst: University of Massachusetts Press.

Grumet, M. (1998). Why read books with other people? *Journal of Curriculum Theorizing*, *14*(2), 237–249.

Heimann, P. (1989). *About children and children-no-longer: Collected papers 1942–80*. London: Routledge.

Joseph, B. (2000). Agreeableness as obstacle. *International Journal of Psychoanalysis*, *81*(4), 641–649.

Klein, M. (1965). Early stages of the Oedipus conflict. In J. D. Sutherland (Ed.), *Contributions to psycho-analysis 1921–1945* (pp. 202–214). London: Hogarth Press. (Original work published 1928)

Klein, M. (1988). A contribution to the theory of intellectual inhibition. In E. Bott Spillius (Ed.), *Love, guilt and reparation* (pp. 236–247). London: Virago. (Original work published 1931)

Lather, P. (2007). *Getting lost: Feminist efforts towards a double(d) science*. Albany, NY: SUNY Press.

Passerini, L. (1996). *Autobiography of a generation: Italy, 1968*. Hanover, NH: Wesleyan University Press.

Phillips, A. (1997) Interview. In A. Molino (Ed.), *Freely associated: Encounters in psychoanalysis* (pp. 127–164). New York: Free Association.

Phillips, A. (1998). *The beast in the nursery: On curiosity and other appetites*. New York: Pantheon Books.

Pinar, W. F., Reynolds, W. M., Slattery, P., & Taubman, P. M. (1995). *Understanding curriculum: An introduction to the study of historical and contemporary curriculum discourses*. New York: Lang.

Pitt, A. (2004). Reading women's autobiography: On losing and refinding the mother. *Changing English*, *11*(2), 267–277.

Pitt, A. (2006). Mother love's education. In G. Boldt & P. Salvio (Eds.), *Love's return: Psychoanalytic essays on childhood, teaching and learning* (pp. 87–106). New York: Routledge.

Sedgwick, E. K. (Ed.). (1997). Paranoid reading and reparative reading; or, you're so paranoid, you probably think this introduction is about you. In E. K. Sedgwick (Ed.), *Novel gazing: Queer readings in fiction* (pp. 1–40). Durham, NC: Duke University Press.

Winnicott, D. W. (1989). Contemporary concepts of adolescent development and their implications for higher education. In D. W. Winnicott (Ed.), *Playing and reality* (pp. 138–150). New York: Routledge.

Suggested Reading Questions

1. How might the author's notion of generational conflict be an important and necessary site for imagining the future of curriculum theory?
2. The author suggests that the scholarly act of reading by new generations of curriculum scholars produces a "splitting." How might splitting, as a form of rejection of existing interpretations of history, serve as a rupture that differentiates the contemporary generation of scholarship from the previous one?

3. According to the author, splitting addresses the constructed nature of reading in the field. How might working through splitting make possible an ahistorical awareness as well as hinder the relationships between generations?
4. The author suggests that the act of reading is also about risking the self and interrogating our own understanding of subjectivity and difference. How can reading be intimately connected to family life and yet exceed family through a rejection of history and historical knowledge?
5. According to the author, curriculum scholars must be aware of a historical consciousness and then perhaps "work the ruins." In this context how might a queer reading be a form of generational conflict or splitting that leads to reparative reading practices in curriculum theory?

Response to Jennifer Gilbert
The Double Trouble of Passing on Curriculum Studies

Patti Lather

> One repays a teacher badly if one remains nothing but a pupil.
>
> —Zarathustra

By "passing on," I refer to the "doubling," intersecting, and competing meanings encoded in comments by a group of Canadian authors writing about generational shifts in women's studies: "to hand over, to refuse or ignore, to be over, to die" (Braithwaite, Heald, Luhmann, & Rosenberg, 2004, p. 29). By "curriculum studies," addressing what this might mean in the context of curriculum studies, in what follows I will first situate my own work in the field and then comment on Jennifer Gilbert's chapter.

What Is My Field?

I locate my work in some amalgamation of curriculum studies, cultural studies in education, qualitative research, feminist science studies, and poststructural feminism. "Curriculum studies," at least the Bergamo version, is a big enough tent to include all of that. This raises the question of what curriculum studies is not and, if health can be defined by a lack of definition, then curriculum studies is healthy indeed. It is perhaps here that I can best enter and address why my work has taken the direction that it has.

My early focus was on gender and teacher education. I remember Janet Miller as my only audience at my first Bergamo in 1981 and Madeline Grumet at an early 1980s National Women's Studies Association (NWSA) conference where hardly anyone came to my session but there were huge audiences at feminist methodology sessions, so I decided to switch. From titles like "Feminist Curricular Change Efforts in Teacher Education" and "Female Empowerment and the Restructuring of Public School Teaching," I shifted to "Research as Praxis" and "Feminist Perspectives on Empowering Research Methodologies."

Feminist methodology, with a short detour into feminist pedagogy, has remained my interest. I locate my work in curriculum studies because that is what my degree is in. Even when I was teaching in women's studies, I returned to Bergamo each fall as I found it conducive to my work and life. From my beginnings in feminist and neo-Marxist theory to my exposures to deconstruction, I was able to "get smart" about theory at Bergamo. Now for 20 years I have taught qualitative research in a college of education and I continue to locate that work in some mix of curriculum studies/cultural studies/women's studies.

Of late, my interest has turned to the politics/policy/research nexus mostly, I think, out of concern for the implications of the "rage for accountability" movement for the teaching of research methods. So, unexpectedly, I am back to pedagogy but in a detour sort of way, given my central focus on feminist methodology, always and forever (Lather, 2007).

At the American Education Research Association meeting (AERA), AERA 98, I think it was, I was part of a group that assessed the field of curriculum studies, my decade being the 1980s (Lather, 1999). If, as Walter Benjamin says, every era must attempt "anew to wrest tradition from a conformism that is about to overpower it" (1940/1968, p. 255), what was my generation's agenda and what do I see as the post-reconceptualist agenda addressed in this collection of essays? What was the state of curriculum studies when I walked in the door and what does it look like as I think more and more of walking out the door into some retirement heaven by some lovely, inexpensive, and hurricane proof ocean-side villa?

Let me evoke the places in which we thought then: struggles over getting critical and feminist work on the program; the formation of the Critical Curriculum and Race, Sex and Class SIGs at AERA; the "homecoming" of Bergamo each fall. What got multiplied, intensified, and circulated during these times is a long list, but in terms of my own work, the shift from structural determinism and reproduction to cultural resistance was big, as was the proliferating growth of curriculum theory, the early and sustained focus on qualitative research, and the move from ideology critique to deconstruction so evident in beginning to question our own investment in the "good story" and the "innocent story" of emancipatory efforts. The sort of "call to unmaking or undoing" we see in such recent books as Judith Butler's *Undoing Gender* (2004) was evident at Bergamo since at least Ellsworth's (1989) "Why Doesn't This Feel Empowering?" All of this was in the midst of a resurgent right and a fragmentary left and an explosion of competing knowledges within and against empire, in the belly of the beast as we used to say in the 1960s, "complicated and implicated" as John Willinsky puts it (1998, p. 247), in our moment of now.

My contribution to this proliferation has been a particular sense that *not* resolving differences is a good thing. In helping to shape what could and could not be said about my topics of interest, being accountable to complexity, the big fish, I am seeing more clearly now is something along the lines of making an edge toward the development of democratic processes more attuned to differences that cannot be managed by the deliberative, rational, and consensual.

Some of the breakdowns at the 2006 Purdue conference around inclusion/exclusion shed light on such a statement. Bergamo has operated historically as a precious little space in both the good sense of the term (homecoming and comfort) and bad sense (navel gazing and exclusion). Perhaps the "Bergamo at Purdue" nature of the conference could have dealt more productively with in-group/out-group dimensions in terms of what frameworks might help in understanding such issues. What does it mean to theorize the field under shifting conditions? Is the generational focus part of the solution to such tensions or part of the problem, particularly in addressing racial tensions? What happens if the "impossible tensions" of work across differences are seen as the "signs of life of precisely what it is we are trying to help flourish" (Hoare, in press)?

Response to Gilbert Chapter

As Jen knows having a mind of one's own shares aspects of the material conditions of having a room of one's own in terms of the material support that both does and does not go against normative social patterns. I often think of Virginia Woolf's husband, Leonard, his willingness to take on a somewhat "wifely" role, but also his social privilege, his editorship connections, his husbandly "caretaking" of her physical and mental health.

This has parallels with the transference evident in Jen's chapter in terms of her advisors, Alice Pitt and Deborah Britzman, and their psychoanalytic commitments. The Oedipal organization into "father" and "mother," Jen notes, is interrupted by Sedgwick's queer family. Acts of repudiation, forgetting, and violence: what must be destroyed and exceeded, Jen asks. Is a theory of aggression the same thing as a theory of transference I ask after reading Judith Butler's *Giving an Account of Oneself* (2005).

According to Butler, Nietzsche too thought aggression was coextensive with life. For Foucault (1970/1998) it is the norm that inaugurates the freedom of struggle toward a reflexive self that takes into account what psychoanalysis teaches us in regards to the lie of the self-grounding subject: a history, an unconscious, a set of structures, the history of reason. Their focus was the limits of the phenomenological conception of the subject and its assumptions of founding acts of consciousness.

With an interesting twist on transference, neither the Freudian nor the Foucauldian/ Nietzschean kind, Butler suggests, pays enough attention to the other, especially the opacity of the other, the not fully knowable as a grounding for ethics. We all belong to a sociality that exceeds us where there are limits on what we can know of self and other. What would it mean to affirm this "partial transparency [as] an indispensable resource for ethics?" (Butler, 2005, p. 40). This sort of rethinking the cultural terms of ethics might unleash humility and generosity rather than violence. Psychoanalysis teaches us that transference is "the recreation of a primary relationality" (p. 50) where we learn to school our capacity for connection.

In the scene of pedagogy, as teachers, our job is to not overwhelm our students with our need so that they can work through how we are both more and less than what students think we are. What do they become under our tutelage is their main question. According to Butler (2005), they use us toward finding the limits of their knowing through "thematizing" the very broken form of communication they establish with us as they move from a "default scene of address" to something more connected (p. 57). For this to work, we who are teachers must become somewhat mad and survive and remain intact, offering not so much official versions of the truth as interpretations to be played with. Here we use relations of dependency and impressionability toward not mastery but an "emergence, individuation, and survivability" (p. 59) in the face of a necessary limit of coherence, a discontinuity that accepts "the limits of knowability in oneself and others" (p. 63). This is a sort of "necessary grief" form of pedagogy that inaugurates the student into "a certain knowingness about the limits of what there is to know" (p. 69). The goal is a sustainable way of being capable of good judgment in a toxic world. Who are you that demand of me what I cannot give is the inaugurating question (p. 72).

Jen's chapter raises questions of evolution or displacement in the formation of new structures of knowledge. Given such work so firmly situated in the cultural turn, with a psychoanalytic inflection, I ask what is the something historical that is happening in this chapter in terms of movement toward a greater amplitude and range in the name of curriculum studies? The answer I detect has something to do with: Let's be a queer family with a different relation to generations. Let's look closely at Sedgwick's (1997) "reparative reading practice" versus the hegemonic "paranoid reading practice" in terms of the surprise of a continuity that is not so much a "thinking back through our mothers" instead of our fathers, as a move into a space where it is seen as a "good thing" to no longer have credible idealizations.

Sedgwick's compares "reparative reading" with the "paranoid model" typical of critical theory which is about exposing and demystifying. Termed "a hermeneutics of suspicion" by Paul Ricoeur (1970) in writing of Marx, Nietzsche, and Freud, such a practice situates the theorist as "the one who knows," a master of revealing the false consciousness of others. In contrast, Sedgwick calls for a more generous critical practice, a practice that is more about love than suspicion and that draws on rich phenomenological accounts of embodied experiences, feeling, and intimacy. This is about difference without opposition, differences that are expanded rather than policed or repressed or judged. Perhaps here we do not need to kill the mother or the father, as the case may be. Sedgwick associates such a critical practice with the work of consolation and making whole, of love and political hope, an ethic of giving up authority to the otherness of the wholly other, a more "slip-slidy" sort of effect than the confident mastery of the more typical paranoid model of critique. The goal is not cure so much as undertaking a different range of affects, ambitions, and risks. The hope is an escape from the exhaustions of the hermeneutics of suspicion and, instead, using "the violating yet perversely enabling epistemic configuration" (Barber, 1997, p. 403) that is the ground of queer theory toward different practices of knowing and doing.

This is a critical practice that is generous and pleasurable in the risks it takes and provides a different sort of reading of the relation between generations in the field of curriculum studies. This queer family appeals to me much more than the Oedipal family, particularly as I don't have to be killed in either the Harold Bloom or Freudian sense, both enormously patriarchal in my reading. But there is still something about the "family romance," even of the queer variant that seems limiting to me. More interesting in terms of locating the "passing on" of curriculum studies might be the communities of dissensus of Derrida's *Politics of Friendship* (1997) or the inoperative communities of Jean Luc Nancy (1998) or Foucault's (1970/1998) reading of Lyotard's efforts to bring Freud and Marx together not in reconciliation but in "disjunctive affirmation." Here what Foucault terms the tyranny of good will and the obligation to think in common with others shifts toward a "perverting" of common sense where philosophy itself is disoriented by uncontainable difference and distress is produced in order to think difference differently, outside our categories of containment.

Given this, my particular investment in the "passing on" of curriculum studies appears to be that as Jen and her generation move in, up, and on in this field that is home to so many of us in colleges and departments of education infamous for their instrumentalism, they do so in a doubled sort of way that troubles their own interventions as about something other than cure for what ails the field. This is "a project of many and multiple narratives and endeavors—often at odds with each other" but all attempting to be accountable, "open-ended, complicated, situated and always changing" (Braithwaite, 2004, p. 136).

Such a doubling/troubling is brought home to teacher education in Deborah Britzman's (in press) work on the "constitutive impossibility of education." Here Britzman writes of how teacher education is a hated field, including how many teachers hate their own teacher education. She asks what it is to ruin people's knowledge, for example to ruin "the sublime of critical theory" and embrace our discomfort and do the adult work of mourning our losses of the promises of progress, education, and cure. Can we tell ourselves the truth without idealization, she asks, stressing that our educational responsibility may be more difficult than we have ever imagined. We can grow so sick of the order of things, so numb in our work, raising questions of what kind of accountability for what kind of teacher education.

How do we explore the ambivalences and stuck places of teaching for social justice, the "love/hate" relationship that is usually treated as a dirty secret, the messy, troubled, and troubling aspects of it? What does it mean to trouble the Grand Narratives of teacher education, from experience to critical pedagogy, in a way that is responsible in attending to who can live here in this less heroic space where we are disabused of much? What is it to choose uncertainty in our teaching, to insist on limits, to hold up doubt and not knowing as ways of knowing? How might such work address the thought that has been unthinkable for some time and make visible in the name of responsibility an accountability to complexity, multiplicity, becoming, difference, the yes that comes from working the stuck places, the beyond that is what haunts us?

References

Barber, S. (1997). Lip-reading: Woolf's secret encounters. In E. Sedgwick (Ed.), *Novel gazing: Queer readings in fiction* (pp. 401–443) Durham, NC: Duke University Press.

Benjamin, W. (1968). Theses on the philosophy of history. In H. Arendt (Ed.), *Illuminations* (pp. 253–264). New York: Schocken Books. (Original work published 1940)

Braithwaite, A. (2004). "Where we've been" and "Where we're going"; Reflecting on reflections of women's studies and "The women's movement." In A. Braithwaite, S. Heald, S. Luhmann, & S. Rosenberg (Eds.), *Troubling women's studies: Pasts, presents and possibilities* (pp. 91–146). Toronto: Sumach Press.

Braithwaite, A., Heald, S., Luhmann, S., & Rosenberg, S. (Eds.). (2004). *Troubling women's studies: Pasts, presents and possibilities.* Toronto: Sumach Press.

Britzman, D. (in press). *The very thought of education: Psychoanalysis and learning.* Albany, NY: SUNY Press.

Butler, J. (2004) *Undoing gender.* New York: Routledge.

Butler, J. (2005). *Giving an account of oneself: A critique of ethical violence.* New York: Fordham University Press.

Derrida, J. (1997). *Politics of friendship* (G. Collins, Trans.). London: Verso.

Ellsworth, E. (1989). Why doesn't this feel empowering? Working through the repressive myths of critical pedagogy. *Harvard Educational Review, 59*(3), 297–325.

Foucault, M. (1998). Theatrum philosophicum. In *Aesthetics, method, and epistemology* (D. Faubion, Ed., R. Hurley et al., Trans.) (pp. 343–368). New York: New Press. (Original work published 1970)

Houre, D. (in press). Harding and Derrida on making strange. *Feminist Frontiers.*

Lather, P. (1999). The places in which we thought then. *Journal of Curriculum Theorizing, 15*(2), 133–138.

Lather, P. (2007). *Getting lost: Feminist efforts toward a double(d) science.* Albany, NY: SUNY Press.

Nancy, J.-L. (1998). *The inoperative community.* Malden MA: Blackwell.

Ricoeur, P. (1970). *Freud and philosophy: An essay on interpretation* (Denis Savage, Trans.). New Haven, CT: Yale University Press.

Sedgwick, E. (1997). Paranoid reading and reparative reading: Or, you're so paranoid, you probably think this introduction is about you. In E. Sedgwick (Ed.), *Novel gazing: Queer readings in fiction* (pp. 1–40). Durham, NC: Duke University Press.

Willinsky, J. (1998). *Learning to divide the world: Education at empire's end.* Minneapolis: University of Minnesota Press.

4 Toward Creative Solidarity in the "Next" Moment of Curriculum Work

Rubén A. Gaztambide-Fernández

Chapter Overview

The author explores what it might mean if the next moment in curriculum studies were to proceed in creative solidarity. To move toward such a future, he explores three premises that include power, discourse, and politics. Next, the author discusses the ways that the binaries between theory and practice and science and art are problematic and inhibit as yet unknown concepts and discourses within the field. After exploring an example of creative practices, he further outlines three challenges that curriculum workers need to address: the discursive, structural, and personal. Finally, the author attempts to articulate an emerging vision of creative solidarity adequate to current and future curriculum work. Exploring conflict and functionalist theories of solidarity in search of a political concept that might yield a language of imagination—the author emphasizes processes of becoming that are contingent and work against normalcy and coherence. This is dissatisfied solidarity or solidarity without guarantees.

Introduction

Caminante, son tus huellas el camino, y nada mas;
caminante, no hay camino, se hace camino al andar.
Al andar se hace camino,
y al volver la vista atrás,
se ve la senda que nunca se ha de volver a pisar.
Caminante no hay camino,
sino estelas en la mar. (Machado, 2007, p. 146)

We think only in relation. We think only in process and in the constant movement across the boundaries between our inner and outer realities, and that movement, in its very crossing, reconfigures those boundaries and what they make of our selves and of others. (Ellsworth, 2005, p. 61)

For creativity and social self-creation are both known and unknown events, and it is still from grasping the known that the unknown—the next step, the next work—is conceived. (Williams, 1977, p. 212)

What trail will our footsteps make?

In the well-traveled poem by Robert Frost (1920), the walker takes the road apparently less traveled, but a road already made, even if the grass is in need of wear, the road exists, begging to be walked. Spanish poet Antonio Machado is more ambitious. He tells the walker:

Traveler, the trail is your footprints, and nothing more;
Traveler, there is no trail, you make the trail as you walk.
As you walk you make the trail,
and when you turn to look back,
you see the path that you will never tread again.
Traveler, there is no trail,
only your wake in the sea.[1]

What trail will our footsteps make?

Keith Morrison (2004) invites curriculum theorists to "celebrate a hundred thousand theories and stories." In response to persistent attacks against reconceptualist curriculum theory (e.g., Wraga, 1999; Wraga & Hlebowitsh, 2003), Morrison declares; "If there is to be a prescription for a curriculum theory, authenticity, discovery, diversity, novelty, multiplicity, fecundity, and creativity should be the hallmarks of the refashioned field" (pp. 487–488). This chapter takes this vision of curriculum theorizing as a starting point. Whether this constitutes a "post-reconceptualization" or not is far less important than the idea that the footprints we leave in this refashioned field will constitute a trail; not a road less traveled, but a new trail altogether. Perhaps this particular trail will not "shape the direction of the field in the decades to come," as the invitation to the conference that engendered this edited collection suggested, but it will ripple nonetheless. My hopes for this trail are less presumptuous, but no less optimistic. Indeed, in this chapter I will suggest that where the trail leads is less important than the fact that we are on it in relationship with each other, and that, as Morrison (2004) suggests, "curriculum theory must build in people, in all their diversity, humanity, and flesh-and-blood immanence" (p. 488).

Being together and forging new trails is at the heart of this "next" moment in curriculum studies, wherever it is going; and rest assured, it is *going*. The field is neither dead nor moribund; we, whomever *we* are, are walking and continuing to forge a trail. But what trail are we forging? What will the wake of our footsteps look like? This is not a trail we walk alone; "we think only in relation," as Elizabeth Ellsworth (2005) reminds us in the quote above, and therefore we should consider how we can continue to forge a trail being more aware of and more committed to those that forge the trail with us—our colleagues, our students, our families, our ecosystem. However intrepid we are as travelers, the journey will not proceed long on a new trail without joining the old unless we reflect on the solidarities we build with others and engage those solidarities with a creative sense of the possible. Toward this next moment we should proceed in a state of *creative solidarity*.

Before continuing, I must attempt to clarify who is the "we" that I am speaking about and to whom I imagine I am speaking. The profile and content of this collection does some of this boundary work for me, but I want to be more explicit. "We," I assume, are engaged in some way or another in a branch of curriculum studies that, while amorphous, ambiguous, and poly-vocal, shares at least a commitment to maintaining rather than overcoming such pluralism of ideas and conceptions of our work (Morrison, 2004). I assume that even as we welcome pluralism, we reject or at least share a deep skepticism for the dominant scientistic discourse that overdetermines the conditions of our work. Lastly, *we*, I imagine, are at least deeply troubled by the rise in the United States of policies like those found in the No Child Left Behind Act and their mixed-bag of implications for the mostly poor communities of color already brutally battered by a system that has proven unmatched in its recalcitrant ability to withstand any and all attempts to redefine its logic, regardless of the soundness of the empirical evidence, the elegance of the conceptual logic, or the generative richness of the metaphors anyone in the field can produce.

This reflection on the challenges of contemporary curriculum studies begins with two related and familiar assumptions: one about power and another about discourse. I begin from the premise that power is ubiquitous and that relations of domination pervade everything we do, from the most intimate to the most mundane, from the most immediate to the most removed. These relations of domination manifest themselves discursively, specifically through the discursive regimes that organize our experience and our relationships with all others and the earth. I begin from these two premises without offering justifications, in part because there is an abundance of work related to them, but also because to justify such an ontological and epistemological position almost invariably assumes a defensive stance against a hegemonic discourse that never requires justification. Starting with these assumptions, I am also taking a position about the political nature of the work we do and about the urgency of this work.

There is a third premise from which I begin to forge this trail, which I will articulate in some depth and to which I will return throughout. While discourse is both the vehicle through which power and domination are exerted and reinforced, it is also the method through which those very relations can be transformed. This idea is not new either, and I will draw on the work of others to present my argument here (e.g., Gablick, 1991; Huebner, 1975; Sandoval, 2000; Williams, 1977). It is also crucial to remember that just as a critical stance toward discourse can reveal how it operates and suggest alternatives, the process can also produce new regimes that can become just as oppressive and simply replace previous power dynamics for new ones (e.g., Ellsworth, 1989; Weiler, 2001). This may be a fourth premise of my argument, but for the moment I want to avoid the "emptiness and disenchantment" of what Suzy Gablick calls "the seduction and sadness of nihilism" (1991, p. 40). Why get so depressed before I even start?

Searching for a place to begin my reflection, I turned to the classic collection of essays that marked the period of conceptual explosion known in curriculum studies as the *reconceptualization* (Pinar, 1975/2000). In the essay "The Task of the Curriculum Theorist," Dwayne Huebner (1975) states: "to be aware of our historical nature is to be on top of our past, so we can use it as a base for projection into the future" (p. 257). As I revisited Huebner's essay, I found that the invitation I want to put forth here has clear antecedents in his work. Huebner was one of those thinkers who realized the potency of language to both reify and transform social relations (e.g., Huebner, 1999). While some of Huebner's observations about the field have been outgrown since the 1970s, his invitation to pay close attention to language remains imperative. The language we use to do our work (and to talk about what we do), argues Huebner:

> is never a complete or finished system, [and] it is always in the process of being recreated, which means that it is criticized and scrutinized in a variety of ways, parts of it are dropped from usage, and new usages and terminologies are introduced. (p. 257)

Huebner describes three areas of engagement for curricularists: practice, research, and language (talking and writing), but he is quick to note that these are not separate or "distinct occupations" and that any one person usually engages in more than one. The central issue for Huebner is not to make distinctions between these areas, but rather to "untangle the relationship among them" (p. 252). He begins by describing language— which he connects to the task of theorizing, or talking and writing about curriculum— and argues that a primary task of curriculum theorizing is to identify when, how, and through what languages we choose to speak (or write) ideas. The task is to stand in critical attention for the instances when language traps our thinking by becoming stale and unproductive. "Man and his language," he says—and I think he means woman,[2] too—"form a paradoxical relationship. [S]He is inevitably caught in it, yet as its creator [s]he can seek to transcend its confines, but in so doing [s]he builds new snares which are equally confining" (p. 252). Since the source of all language "is the creative efforts of people" (p. 257), it becomes our task to unravel these trappings and generate a new language.

Bogus Distinctions

Consider two dichotomies we use to talk about what we do and that have become confining and bogus distinctions. The oppositions between theory and practice and between the artistic and the scientific permeate how many curriculum scholars talk about what we do.

Despite persistent challenges over the years, the theory/practice dichotomy is one that continues to pervade our discourse. Huebner (1975) addresses this dichotomy in his essay, and he suggests that the distinction is at least distracting and at worst oppressive. For Huebner, theory and practice are not nor have they ever been conceptually "separated" by some unnamed distance that needs bridging. The *bridge* metaphor implies a connection between two entities separated by a chasm. It suggests that there is an actual distance that marks the two opposing sides, in this instance the theoretical and the practical, as distinct and discreetly differentiated. Appealing to this proverbial bridge ignores the reality that theory and practice are closely intertwined in the work we do. Indeed, I would be surprised to learn that there are curriculum scholars who are engaged purely in talking and the production of theory. Huebner's description of practice, research, and talk as areas of practice that we all engage is helpful here. This is not to neglect the monumental physical and symbolic distance in the lived reality of teachers and university-based curriculum workers. Rather, it is to draw attention to the fact that most, if not all, of us are invariably engaged in some kind of practice. While perhaps not as relevant at the levels of policy and national dialogue as we would like, our practice is (hopefully) relevant to our students, in our classrooms, whether those students are learning to become future teachers, or future educational researchers, or future "talkers."

The other distinction that has become pervasive within the discourse of curriculum theory is that between the artistic and the scientific. In the 1970s, "it was hard to tell whether the search for something called theory [was] the curricularist's attempt to establish prestige in academic circles" by establishing a parallel with the behavioral sciences (Huebner, 1975, p. 250). There has been a long tradition of strong critique verging on the obsessive exclusion of the language of science as a way to engage in the field of curriculum studies. Today, some strands of scholarship within curriculum theory have become fixated with artistic metaphors and arts-based-just-about-everything in a similar attempt to claim a different "language of legitimacy," as Huebner calls it; an attempt to establish prestige in other kinds of academic circles and to unlink curriculum from the positivistic state of mind that overwhelms educational thinking. This fixation is most problematic within those strands of curriculum scholarship that mobilize artistic metaphors and models as a way to reconceptualize curriculum work (Gaztambide-Fernández, 2002).

I used to call myself an artist, and I remain passionate about the work that what most people call "the arts" entails. Yet, I concur with Raymond Williams (1977) when he points out that discussions and appeals to the discourse of the arts and the aesthetic, even the best and most compelling of them, "rely to an extraordinary extent on predicated selection, yielding conveniently selective answers" (p. 206). Arguments about the arts tend largely to ignore the role that cultural activity plays in social reproduction (e.g. Bourdieu, 1984, 1993), and rarely consider the complexities of what it means to be an artist (Gaztambide-Fernández, in press). Instead, metaphoric references to the arts mobilize a narrative of discovery, self-realization, freedom, and consciousness as the guaranteed outcomes of any encounter with and through the arts. They become a shortcut to a taken-for-granted notion that, if it is artistic or arts-like, then it must be good, and it must appeal to our emotions and to some sort of human essence that we all share (or ought to share).

Consider for instance the eloquent language that Patrick Slattery and Dana Rapp (2003) use to describe the work of artists: "Artists offer explanations that can serve as windows into the haunting nature of unfulfilled promises and destinies that affect each one of us" (p. 269). Perhaps the work of some artists can be used to accomplish this lofty goal for at least those of us who enjoy the privileges implicit in the encounters presumed in such a statement. But I can attest that the training of artists seldom presumes such goals—quite the opposite (Gaztambide-Fernández, 2002). Most artistic education carries the same problems that we are often quick to identify in all general education and remain squarely grounded in a technical rational paradigm. While the arts can be instrumental in the process of "releasing the imagination" (Greene, 1995), they can be just as instrumental in extending subjugation as scientific rationality (see also Jagodzinski, 1997; Tavin, 2003).

In a defense of the presumed synergy that the arts supposedly "inspire" in curriculum and pedagogy, Eliot Eisner (2004) lambastes schools in a familiar language: "Too much of what we do in school caters to routine. Too much of what we do is mired in tradition and stale habit; too much is formulaic and prescriptive. There is a paucity of genuine invention in education" (p. 16). The same, unfortunately, can be said of the education of young artists in conservatories and art schools everywhere, and thus of the work deemed worthy of the label "art." Eisner proposes a twist in the language that seems to implicitly recognize that it is not artists or the arts that by definition can bring about a paradigm shift. Eisner says:

> Artistry is precisely what we ought to be pursuing in education. Artistry as an icon of excellence can serve as a regulative ideal to guide our decisions about how curricula can be designed, how teaching might occur and how it ought to be appraised. (p. 15)

Thus, artistry comes to replace scientific rigor as the "regulative ideal" that is to guide what we do. In doing so, it replaces the arbitrary yet explicit criteria of science with just as arbitrary but unarticulated notions of the unconscious, of affect, and of a presumed emotional response that remain colonizing, particularly if you are the one that doesn't "get it," or who lacks "connoisseurship," or can speak "artistically." "Artistry" replaces one regime of truth for another by leveling a clearly warranted critique of scientistic discourse without doing the same for itself. Like science, the arts have been an important tool for social distinction and for the sedimentation of a dominant patriarchal culture that uses science as much as art to claim its right to supremacy and imperial colonization (e.g., Bourdieu, 1993; Fanon, 1967). To be sure, artistic disciplines have also been the site of cultural work that challenges and undermines dominant cultural practices by yielding emergent forms (e.g., C. Becker, 1994b; Gablick, 1991; West, 1990). Yet, engaging the language of the arts without a critical stance is to assume notions of "true creativity" and "timeless permanence" (Williams, 1977, p. 206), notions that are drawn from the same humanistic philosophy of the Enlightenment on which the technical rational paradigm we have so vehemently critiqued is historically grounded (Gaztambide-Fernández, in press).

What we do as curriculum workers, whether related to the arts or not, is no less and no more art or artistic than it is science or scientific; whether we frame what we do as artistic or scientific depends mostly on the audience we are trying to convince that what we do is worthwhile and that we are entitled to do it. In this sense, Huebner's (1975) observation about curricularists' concern with the theoretical can be made of how some curriculum scholars engage the language of the arts and the artistic. To put it in Williams's (1977) terms, the problem is that we are challenging a dominant discourse by drawing on a language that has the *potential* to generate new emergent practices. However, by engaging language ahistorically and uncritically, we mobilize its residual elements as well and undermine its subversive potential (C. Becker, 1994a). In this sense, we make the same mistake that Huebner (1975) observed 30 years ago:

> Curricularists have tended to be ahistorical in the awareness of the various forms and institutions that make up their professional gear. Too frequently our tendency has been messianic. The search is often for the new and permanent vehicles of salvation, and thus we fall prey to bandwagons and the bandwagon mentality...we fail to operate as historical beings and shirk our responsibility for the continual criticism and creation of new language forms and new ways of speaking. (p. 257)

I do not mean to dismiss the impetus behind such a shift in our discursive repertoires. On the contrary, I recognize that when Eisner first developed the ideas that came to ground contemporary arts-based curriculum work, he was engaged in the kind of creative solidarity that I want to advocate here. More recently, Jim Henderson (2001) has developed the notion of artistry in relation to curriculum development and to the daily work of teachers and school administrators in ways that I find inspiring in its deep awareness and critical stance toward itself and its own potential short-comings. His work holds great promise for fomenting what he and Kathleen Kesson (Kesson & Henderson, 2005) call a "public disciplinary community" that invites:

> curriculum workers to enact practical and eclectic artistry in the service of democratic emancipation...and encourage educators to cultivate their capacities to shift between and among various "modes of inquiry" in a Deweyan, pragmatic spirit. (p. 7)

Indeed, it was Dewey (1934/1980) who cautioned against "easy beauty," and alerted us to the possibility that just because someone calls it art or artistic, it does not mean it is good, and certainly not liberating. I suggest that the language of the arts, which was once an emergent part of our discourse, has become so pervasive and dominant in the culture of our field as to allow for just that, "easy beauty."

I am not saying that the conceptual elaboration of the arts metaphor lacks a unique exactitude, or that arts-based approaches to curriculum theorizing and research are simply capricious or fickle. On the contrary, I find what we have been calling arts-based work to be by-and-large provocative and valuable to our curriculum work (e.g., Rolling, 2007; Springgay & Carpenter, 2007). Yet, if "virtually anything that is made well," as Eisner (2004) puts it, is about artistry, then the distinction between artistry and scientific rigor becomes an arbitrary and bogus distinction that, more than anything else, draws a boundary that is no longer tenable. Rather than worrying about whether what we do is this-based or that-based, I would invite us to be precise—while contingent—regarding our aims, thorough—while critical—regarding our methods, and persistent—while reflective—regarding the excellence of what we do. Regardless of what we call what we do, I invite us to do it at least while being aware of the fact that we do it with others, for others, and because of others.

Take for instance the masterful work of Anna Deavere Smith, which Ellsworth (2005) uses to exemplify her own vision of a localized pedagogy and the pedagogical concept of a "transitional space." Ellsworth describes Smith's work this way, without ever once calling it art, or artistic, or artistry:

> Her performances center on the gaps that are opened up by the failures of words. If and when we accept her invitation to meet her in the spaces of difference between self and other, we find ourselves in empty spaces of hesitation, stuttering, and identities in the making, but not quite yet.... The power of Smith's performance as pedagogy lies in the way that it *simultaneously fills and empties its pedagogical pivot place.* Her performance becomes pedagogical at the paradoxical moment when the force (the "teacher") that "springs" transitional space simultaneously appears and disappears. Here, pedagogy takes place as the space and time of pure relationality. Here, the teacher's place is a powerful non-place that a teacher both actualizes and vacates. (p. 65)

Deavere Smith's work involves interviewing individuals about their experiences of particular events or about their lives in general. Based on these in-depth narrative interviews, she develops performances in which she seeks to capture what Williams (1977) calls the "structures of feeling" that organize contemporary experience. Deavere Smith's (2000) interview process involves searching for those instances when language appears to fail the speaker, when they must reach deep into their experience to find a new way of articulating what is ultimately an emerging self. In the "creation" of these characters, Deavere Smith exemplifies the kind of creative practice that Williams (1977) advocates, in that it not only seeks to represent the lived experiences of actual people in actual relations, but pushes the edge of what is real and lived toward an emergent form of what might be, "new articulations, new formations of character and relationship" (p. 209).

The Challenge That Is Our Present

Within our field of curriculum studies, the kind of creative activity that Williams (1977) advocates and Deavere Smith (2000) exemplifies is both constrained and potentially fueled by three intricately related challenges that curriculum workers must address. These challenges are the discursive, the structural, and the personal, not necessarily in order of importance (Gaztambide-Fernández, 2004). Facing these challenges may open up possibilities and point in new unexpected directions in which to forge trails and to strengthen and enliven the field of curriculum studies in the "post-reconceptualization."

The discursive challenge involves thinking about what we say, how we say it, and, more importantly, what are the relations that are perpetuated or disrupted by what we say and how we say it. This parallels the tasks around language that Huebner (1975) articulates and the kind of analysis I have sought to present thus far and, therefore, will not reelaborate here.

There are, most certainly, distances and physical structures that constrain what we do, how we do it, and certainly how we talk about it; these constraints constitute our structural challenge. While directly related, this challenge is not to be confused with notions of social structure associated with structuralism (e.g., Bowles & Gintis, 1976; Collins, 1971). Rather, it refers to the actual physical spaces we inhabit, and how these limit not only what we do, but how we think about it—even how we think about ourselves. The physical structures we inhabit and the discourses that produce those structures directly shape who we think we are and what we think we are supposed to do. Thus, the structural challenge lies in rethinking how we relate to each other in space and how we become self-conscious about how the spaces we inhabit and the rules of those spaces delimit what we are able to imagine as possibilities.

Ellsworth (2005) draws our attention to the centrality of time and space in defining the pedagogic moment and the encounters between knowledge and knower. Drawing on the work of D. W. Winnicott on play, Ellsworth argues that the design of spaces is crucial for providing "hinges" or "pivoting points" between what is and what might be through a "transitional space" of discovery. She offers many examples of what she calls "anomalous places of learning" designed with pedagogical intent to illustrate her pedagogic conception. For Ellsworth, pedagogy is a form of:

> address to a self who is in the process of withdrawing from that self, someone who is in a dissolve out of what she or he is just ceasing to be and into what she or he will already have become by the time she or he registers something has happened. (p. 34)

Last and just as important is the personal challenge. We invest a great deal of personal meaning in the discourses we engage, the spaces we inhabit, and the person we are convinced we are. Challenging these means challenging our own selves and risking the safe zone of the language we know and the spaces we call our own. If we are to engage in curriculum work that has significance, we have to be willing to put a lot of who we are— or rather, who we believe ourselves to be—at stake. As Gablick (1991) puts it, "the way to prepare the ground for a new paradigm is to make changes in one's own life" (p. 8).

When I think of myself as a father I need to confront the discourse of fatherhood and masculinity that defines me as such. At the most superficial level, this involves thinking about the space I inhabit with my family; how that space reifies the role of the father in a heterosexist patriarchal society. If I am going to do something about challenging these discourses, I have to be willing to put on the line the privileges and to redefine the responsibilities I attach to my role as father. It also means rethinking my relationship with my daughter and my son, who I imagine them to be, and challenging my own conceptions of what it means to be a father.

This personal work requires deep autobiographical reflection, but it also requires a redefinition of how we go about relating to others and how we choose to engage others in an attempt to, on the one hand, recognize their difference from ourselves, while on the other, build bonds that transgress the very boundaries that such a recognition of difference crystallizes.

Toward Creative Solidarity

The concept of solidarity is not without its problem, and it has a history that is worth exploring and highlighting if we are not to make the mistake of proceeding ahistorically. To that end, this section offers a brief discussion of how solidarity has been conceptualized by specific authors in the social sciences and in philosophy. I will contrast these approaches and make connections to the work of feminist scholars that develop a notion of solidarity as political strategy. Based on this, I will attempt to articulate an emerging vision for "creative solidarity" as an orientation for curriculum work.

Emile Durkheim (1893/1933) is the social theorist most often associated with considering the question of social solidarity in his classic *The Division of Labor in Society*, where he formulated the distinction between organic and mechanical solidarity. Contrary to what Gramscian minds would assume, by organic Durkheim doesn't mean a solidarity that arises from the members of a particular class in order to secure its particular interests, which is closer to Karl Marx's notion of class solidarity, and which follows a different analytic plan from that of Durkheim. Durkheim was, after all, a functionalist, and he didn't only see the division of labor as natural and necessary, but he argued:

> Social harmony comes essentially from the division of labor. It is characterized by a cooperation which is automatically produced through the pursuit by each individual of his own interests. It suffices that each individual consecrate himself to a special function in order, by the force of events, to make himself solidary with others. (1893/1933, p. 200)

For Durkheim (1893/1933), solidarity binds the members of a society to one another and to the social structure that enables them to live together, shaping "the mass of individuals into a cohesive aggregate" and regulating "[man's] actions by something other than his own egoism" (p. 331). Organic solidarity, explains Durkheim, develops along with the division of labor, as individuals assume more and more differentiated tasks and come to increasingly depend on each other's roles and abilities. While a mechanical solidarity characterized preindustrial societies where most individuals performed similar tasks, organic solidarity is necessary for complex societies to evolve and sustain their coherence because it involves the realization of interdependence between individuals constitutive of a social whole (Crow, 2002).

In contrast to Durkheim's functionalist account of solidarity as a source of social coherence, and moral and economic order, social theorists from Karl Marx to Max Weber and George Simmel, deal with solidarity from the assumption that society is not a coherent whole that operates to the benefit of all members, but rather a composite of discrete groups or classes that compete for status, scarce resources, or social space. While Durkheim interpreted solidarity as a source of cohesion between individuals and society as a whole, these "conflict" theorists viewed it as a source of collective action for groups in competition with each other. For Marx and Engels, class solidarity is a prerequisite in class struggle, as "shared interests" provide the cohesion necessary for the resolution of class struggle through the unification of the proletariat against the bourgeoisie (e.g. Marx & Engels, 1848/1888, 1845/1967).

Weber, on the other hand, noted that *class interest* was an ambiguous term, and "suggested that what Marx and Engels observed about solidarity among class members being strengthened by the identification of a recognizable opponent may be a feature of interest groups more generally" (Crow, 2002, p. 26). For Weber all kinds of interest groups, or "status groups" (Weber, 1946, pp. 186–187), seek "closure" in an attempt to monopolize and restrict resources and opportunities from outsiders. Status groups build arbitrary boundaries around "externally identifiable characteristic[s]" such as "race, language, religion, local of social origin, descent, residence, etc.—as a pretext for attempting [another group's] exclusion" (Weber, 1978, p. 342).

This analysis from the perspective of conflict theorists is crucial because it warns us that solidarity can also "pose a threat to individuals' autonomy, creativity and scope of being different" (Crow, 2002, p. 3). As Graham Crow points out:

How people come to distinguish between those with whom they have solidarity and others to whom they have no such obligations is a complex process of classification that has serious consequences.… Questioning the desirability of solidarity may arise out of recognition that a tension exists between the solidarity of a group and the individualism of its members, or it may be prompted by the existence of tensions between the solidarities of competing groups. (pp. 3–4)

While functionalist and conflict theories of solidarity diverge fundamentally in their conception of society, they share a common understanding of what it means to be human and a modernist conception of human progress. As such, both frameworks rely on assumptions about a presumed "human nature" that have been fundamentally challenged by postmodern philosophy (e.g., Haraway, 1991). In his own political and philosophical exploration of solidarity, Richard Rorty (1989) puts it this way:

The traditional philosophical way of spelling out what we mean by "human solidarity" is to say that there is something within each of us—our essential humanity—which resonates to the presence of this same thing in other human beings. (p. 189)

Like the conceptualization of the arts that I critiqued earlier, this traditional way of understanding solidarity assumes that those unable to connect with such an essence at any given moment, according to Rorty, are considered "inhuman." Creative solidarity cannot begin from the notion of a core humanity, as such a view by default excludes and operates on a rejection of difference a priori of all encounters. Like Rorty, I believe that "what counts as being a decent human being is relative to historical circumstances, a matter of transient consensus about what attitudes are normal and what practices are just or unjust" (p. 189).

By solidarity I don't mean the notion that people have things in common "that make it possible and desirable for them to act in unison" (Crow, 2002, p. 11). This approach to solidarity as an explanatory concept, whether seen from the perspective of individual group behavior or as a source of social cohesion, is an important starting point. The former because it points toward the arbitrary and political nature of social boundaries; the latter because it warns us against a modernist "essentialism" that would limit the possibilities we might imagine through a more contingent view. However, I am thinking of solidarity as a political project, not as a social force that would yield explanations, but as a political concept that might yield visions of what is possible; a language of imagination.

Ellen Gorsevsky (2004) writes about the rhetorical dimensions of nonviolent activism, and she describes what she calls "informed and empathic solidarity" that emanates "from the grassroots level and [moves] upwards" (p. 143). She offers the following example:

The case of…a ten year-old boy in Oceanside, California who was diagnosed with cancer. The doctors prescribed ten weeks of chemotherapy, during which, they warned him, all his hair would fall out. To avoid the anxiety and pain of watching his hair gradually disappear, the youngster had his entire head shaved. One can only imagine [his] feelings a few days later when he returned to school, prematurely bald, and found that the thirteen other boys in his fifth grade class, and their teacher as well, greeted him with their heads completely shaved. (Telushkin cited in Gorsevski, 2004, p. 225)

Indeed, I can only *imagine* what this 10-year-old felt when he encountered such expressions of solidarity. I imagine, to use Williams's (1977) language, that such an encounter must have generated a "change of presence" that did not have to "await definition, clas-sification, or rationalization" (p. 132), before he *felt* a "latent, momentary, and newly possible consciousness" (p. 212), whatever its consequence. Such emergent "structures of feeling" can only result from a "creative process" that takes an inherently collectivist definition of human experience and that confronts "hegemony in the fibres of the self and in the hard practical substance of effective and continuing relationships" (p. 212). Such is the grist of creative solidarity.

Solidarity and creativity come together as concepts within the discourse of "process philosophy," particularly through Alfred North Whitehead. Whitehead expert Jorge Luis Nobo is the author of *Whitehead's Metaphysics of Extension and Solidarity*, in which he argues that "the solidarity of the universe is the fundamental thesis of Whitehead's metaphysi-cal philosophy" (1986, p. xiv).[3] In order to comprehend the ambiguities in Whitehead's cosmology, argues Nobo, it is necessary to understand his "vision of universal solidarity: that the entire universe is somehow to be found within each of its ultimate concrete com-ponents or, equivalently, that the final real actualities of which the universe is composed are each in all and all in each" (p. xiv).

Nobo (1997) extends his analysis by building a connection between Whitehead's con-cept of universal solidarity and his work on creativity through what he calls the "meta-physics of creative solidarity." Nobo's work is dense with metaphysical arguments that I am not equipped to summarize here.[4] Nonetheless, I gleaned ideas from his discussion that I found inspiring and affirming of the possibility that there is a way of thinking about solidarity besides describing and understanding social behavior.

Creativity, says Nobo (1997), is the underlying substance of the universe in White-head's cosmology. Since all actualities are in a constant process of becoming, their sub-stance can only be known as a function of that process. Experience is not a manifestation of self-consciousness (or "entension"), but a manifestation of "eternal creativity," mean-ing a constant process of creation. At the same time "the final actualities of the universe cannot be abstracted from one another because each actuality, though individual and discreet, is internally related to all other actualities"; all actualities "are at once mutu-ally transcendent…and mutually immanent" (Nobo, 1986, p. 1). In order to resolve this paradox, Nobo suggests that by extension all actualities exist through a process of *cre-ative solidarity*, which means "that individual realities can contribute their own natures to the creation or nature of another individual reality without losing their identities and while enhancing, enriching, or renewing their own natures" (Nobo, 1997, p. 171). The outcome of the process Nobo describes is neither predetermined nor inevitable. "In the metaphysics of creative solidarity," he concludes, "the eternal is necessary but insufficient for the particularity, individuality, and uniqueness of what in fact does become (p. 183).

Nobo's elaboration of Whitehead's cosmology provides a philosophical basis about human experience from which to theorize a conception of creative solidarity that has political consequence. However, there is a degree of essentialism in Nobo's notion that "actualities" have a certain inviolable "nature," even as that nature is in a constant pro-cess of becoming. Perhaps more importantly, Nobo's language is decidedly grounded on speculative philosophy and metaphysics, and—at the risk of sounding like a pragma-tist—it lacks a direct engagement with the politics of daily life that ought to concern us as we contemplate our own immanence and transcendence of the social universe that surrounds us.

By contrast to the depoliticized language of speculative philosophy, third-world mul-ticultural feminists have theorized solidarity as a political project in a language that is grounded in the daily lives and struggles of women across social locations (Sandoval, 2000). Their work places difference rather than commonality at the center of a redefinition of solidarity stemming from the need to build a political strategy that assumes the intersection of social categories of race, class, gender, and sexuality as a source of strength.[5] For example, Chandra Mohanty (2003) offers an approach to solidarity "as the basis for relationships among diverse communities" in which "diversity and difference are central values" (p. 7). Drawing on Jodi Dean's (1996) notion of "reflective solidarity,"[6] Mohanty (2003) argues that this way of redefining feminist solidarity "constitutes the most principled way to cross borders—to decolonize knowledge and practice anticapitalist critique" (p. 7).

Feminist political theorist and law scholar Iris Marion Young (2002) offers the concept of "differentiated solidarity" as a way to approach political inclusion. The norms of this differentiated solidarity "oppose actions and structures that exclude and segregate groups or categories of persons [and] assumes respect and mutual obligation" (p. 221). Young also rejects a definition of solidarity that assumes common group bonds and loyalties based on sameness in favor of an approach that "aims to balance values of generalized inclusion and respect with more particularist and local self-affirmation and expression" (p. 221). In seeking to resolve this precarious balance, Young retains notions of human essence, particularly around a limited conception of space relying on notions of "togetherness" that I find simplistic and that in many ways echo Durkheim's conception of organic solidarity.

Thus, what do *I* mean by creative solidarity? I mean a solidarity that underscores a way of being with each other that contingently presents itself against a sense of normalcy and coherence. I mean a solidarity that operates under the assumption that we are incomplete, in the process of becoming, a future anterior,[7] as Ellsworth (2005) invites us to consider. Not a solidarity that assumes commonness and sameness, but one that assumes difference (Sandoval, 2000); not a solidarity that builds boundaries to protect resources, but one that enters an interstitial space between boundaries (Bhabha, 1997), that creates a "third space" (Soja, 1996); not a solidarity that stands on the notion that a core identity will be retained, as Nobo suggests, but rather one that assumes that identity is not only in flux, but that it is an impression, a delusion, a falsity (Nancy, 2000).

Homi Bhabha (1997) notes that it is in the "in between" spaces where we can develop new "strategies of selfhood—singular or communal—that initiate new signs of identity, and innovative sites of collaboration, and contestation, in the act of defining the idea of society itself" (pp. 1–2). Entering into such a contested terrain involves a grand leap of faith. Precisely because we have been coerced into giving too much importance to our material conditions, both in our talk and in our practice, we are afraid to enter a space that gives primacy to spirit, to uncertainty, and to instability. It is inside the boundaries that culture "emerges"; this is a place where discourse is unstable and language is highly polysemic, where meanings are negotiated, and discursive practice is contested.

Conclusion

Solidarity without creativity remains static and contemplative, it is like consciousness without conscientization (Freire, 1970). Creativity without solidarity only reproduces structures of power and generates an emergent culture that is either assimilated into the dominant culture or it becomes residual (Williams, 1977). In this next moment that is yet to come, curriculum workers might engage their work with a different ethic, an ethic of creative solidarity. While there may be many examples of creative solidarity already in what we do, I do not think that this is an explicit aim, or one to which we hold ourselves generally accountable. Huebner (1975) describes the task of research in curriculum as:

the use of the unformed to create form; as a focusing on the unconditioned in order to develop new conditions; as attention to human events in order that human institutions can be created or evolve; as the dialectical relationship between criticism and creation. (p. 267)

Our task is to engage within our spheres of influence in political projects that are about much more than just theorizing, designing, or generating pages.

The verb form of solidarity, rarely used in English, is both a transitive and a reflexive verb. It assumes relationship; it assumes a state of being as well as an action, or a state of being toward another being (Gaztambide-Fernández, 2007). To be in solidarity is something akin to being in love (Sandoval, 2000). It means to be in relationships that recognize interdependence and the realization that our lives and our work cannot carry on without others. Indeed, it is not really our work, but the work of an enormous web of collaborators, whose contributions to what we might label our work are often assumed and misrecognized. In this sense, curriculum work is actually very much like cultural work in general and the arts in particular. Contrary to the individualism presumed in the mythology of the artist (Gaztambide-Fernández, in press), artistic work is never—not even mostly—the result of individual effort, talent, or inspiration (H. Becker, 1982). Rather, the arts are the material concretization of complex cultural processes involving multiple webs of cultural producers, each contributing critical elements, materials, and ideas without which artistic work is not fathomable. Creative solidarity underscores that curriculum work, like the arts, is fundamentally collaborative and communal.

Creative solidarity is also solidarity in a constant flux of invention and reinvention. It is a persistently dissatisfied solidarity, one that is always imagining things differently, maybe even a bit better. I return to Williams (1977) here; by a creative process, I mean a process by which we engage in the production of emergent cultural forms. I mean that curriculum work is cultural work, as it is symbolic and narrative, and that it faces the structures of feeling that it encounters with a sense of curiosity and awe that is transformational and that does not take those structures as final but, as Williams argues, as ever changing, seeking to crystallize boundaries and attenuate them. In this sense, creative solidarity is also solidarity without guarantees.

Indeed, creative solidarity insists against the presumption that curriculum work can ever guarantee an outcome any more than works of art can guarantee extra-ordinary experiences. Creative solidarity is neither theory nor practice, but both at once, interweaved in the act of making. Like a story, it awaits to be told in the telling, and "it neither wraps itself in a cloud of oratorical precautions, nor cocoons itself in realist illusions that make language the simple medium of thought" (Minh-ha, 1990, p. 327). Trinh T. Minh-ha warns that such a view of the story "never fails either to baffle or to awaken profound intolerance and anxieties" (p. 329). Yet, to be in creative solidarity is to have little choice but to abandon certainty and leap into what Chela Sandoval (2000) calls "the abyss of absolute difference" (p. 121). If the limits of creative solidarity lie at the edges of our own fears, intolerances, and anxieties, its possibilities lie in our commitment to infinite possibilities. As such, creative solidarity demands a curriculum with "a hundred thousand voices, a hundred thousand theories, a hundred thousand curriculum development approaches," and to paraphrase Morrison (2004), "it rules out nothing, and it rules in spirit" (p. 493).

This "commitment to infinite progress," as Minh-ha (1990) explains,

is also a realization that the infinite is what undermines the very notion of (rational) progress. *Tale, told, to be told.* The to-and-fro movement between advancement and regression necessarily leads to a situation where every step taken is at once the first (a step back) and the last step (a step forward)—the only step, in a precise circumstance, at a precise moment of (one's) history. (p. 329, italics in original)

Creative solidarity is the necessary act of forward motion, in collective movement. At this precise moment in *our* history, it demands of us that we search for new and emerging structures of feeling, for new languages and ideas for doing our work, for new ways of being with each other, for ways of forging new trails, leaving new footprints, new ripples in our wake.

Notes

I would like to thank Erik Malewski, Janet Miller, Polly Attwood, and two anonymous reviewers for their substantive and invaluable feedback. This essay is the product of many conversations and challenging remarks and comments. All its faults and blind-spots are, of course, my own.

1. Translated by the author in collaboration with James Seale-Collazo.
2. Vikki Hillis, editor of Huebner's collected essays, notes that Huebner was well aware of the gendered language in his early work and was inclined to edit the language for the collection. This proved rather difficult and awkward, making the essays feel like "colorized versions of old black and white films," and seemed to remove the work from its historical context (in Huebner, 1999, pp. xiii–xiv).
3. In reading Nobo's philosophically dense work, I was helped tremendously by Aaron Fortune's (2006) essay review.
4. For a helpful discussion of Whitehead and "process philosophy" and its application to curriculum theory, see William Doll (1993; Doll & Gough, 2002)
5. The work of feminists of color like Angela Davis, Audre Lord, Patricia Hill Collins, bell hooks, Gloria Andalzúa, Chandra Mohanty, and Chela Sandoval is of crucial importance here. For a good introduction, see Mohanty (1991). Sandoval (2000) offers a clear elaboration of the theoretical implications of U.S. third-world feminisms through the concept of differential consciousness, which in many ways parallels my conception of creative solidarity.
6. Dean offers a generative typology of solidarity based on feminist theory and heavily informed by the debates over the politics of feminism triggered by the critique of third world women.
7. The term *future anterior* is a literal translation of the French "futur antérieur," which is equivalent to the future perfect tense in English grammar denoting an action that will be completed in a future point (e.g., "this chapter will have been written before you read it"). The term features prominently in the work of Luce Irrigaray, and thus it appears as "future anterior" in English works on literary and film theory informed by her work.

References

Becker, C. (1994a). Herbert Marcuse and the subversive potential of art. In C. Becker (Ed.), *The subversive imagination* (pp. 113–129). New York: London.

Becker, C. (Ed.). (1994b). *The subversive imagination.* New York: Routledge.

Becker, H. (1982). *Art worlds.* Berkeley: University of California Press.

Bhabha, H. (1997). *The location of culture.* London: Routledge.

Bourdieu, P. (1984). *Distinction: A social critique of the judgment of taste.* Cambridge, MA: Harvard University Press.

Bourdieu, P. (1993). *The field of cultural production.* New York: Columbia University Press.

Bowles, S., & Gintis, H. (1976). *Schooling in capitalist America: Educational reform and the contradictions of economic life.* New York: Basic Books.

Collins, R. (1971). Functional and conflict theories of educational stratification. *American Sociological Review, 36*(6), 1002–1019.

Crow, G. (2002). *Social solidarities: Theories, identities, and social change.* Buckingham, England: Open University Press.

Dean, J. (1996). *Solidarity of strangers: Feminism after identity politics.* Berkeley: University of California Press.

Dewey, J. (1980). *Art as experience.* New York: Perigee Books. (Original work published 1934)

Doll, W. (1993). *A post-modern perspective on curriculum.* New York: Teacher's College Press.

Doll, W., & Gough, N. (Eds.). (2002). *Curriculum visions.* New York: Lang.

Durkheim, E. (1933). *The division of labor in society* (G. Simpson, Trans.). New York: Free Press. (Original work published 1893)

Eisner, E. (2004). How the arts inspire curriculum and pedagogy synergy. *Journal of Curriculum & Pedagogy, 1*(2), 15–16.

Ellsworth, E. (1989). Why doesn't this feel empowering? Working through the repressive myths of critical pedagogy. *Harvard Educational Review, 59,* 297–324.

Ellsworth, E. (2005). *Places of learning: Media, architecture, pedagogy.* New York: Routledge.

Fanon, F. (1967). *Black skin, White masks* (C. L. Markman, Trans.). New York: Grove Press.

Fortune, A. (2006). Review of Whitehead's metaphysics of extension and solidarity by Jorge Luis Nobo. Retrieved January 15, 2006, from http://www.hyattcarter.com/whitehead's_metaphysics1.htm

Freire, P. (1970). *Pedagogy of the oppressed.* New York: Continuum.

Frost, R. (1920). The road not taken. In L. Merves (Ed.), *Mountain interval* (p. 1). New York: Henry Holt.

Gablick, S. (1991). *The reenchainment of art.* New York: Thames & Hudson.

Gaztambide-Fernández, R. A. (2002). (De)constructing art as a model/(Re) constructing art as a possibility. In T. Poetter, K. W. Baptist, C. Higgins, C. Haerr, & M. Hayes (Eds.), *(Re)Visioning the democratic ideal* (pp. 84–107). Troy, NY: Educator's International Press.

Gaztambide-Fernández, R. A. (2004). Introduction. In R. A. Gaztambide-Fernández & J. Sears (Eds.), *Curriculum work as a public moral enterprise* (pp. vii–xviii). Lanham, MD: Rowman & Littlefield.

Gaztambide-Fernández, R. A. (2007). *Transitive solidarity and post-culturalism in the age of disaster capitalism.* Paper presented at the Works-in-Progress Series of the Centre for Media and Culture in Education, November 19, Toronto, ON.

Gaztambide-Fernández, R. A. (in press). The artist in society: Understandings, expectations, and curriculum implications. *Curriculum Inquiry.*

Gorsevski, E. W. (2004). *Peaceful persuasion: The geopolitics of nonviolent rhetoric.* Albany, NY: SUNY Press.

Greene, M. (1995). *Releasing the imagination.* San Francisco: Jossey-Bass.

Haraway, D. (1991). A manifesto for cyborgs: Science, technology, and socialist feminism in the 1980s. In *Simians, cyborgs and women: The reinvention of nature* (pp. 149–181). New York: Routledge.

Henderson, J. (2001). *Reflective teaching: Professional artistry through inquiry* (3rd ed.). Upper Saddle River, NJ: Merrill/Prentice-Hall.

Huebner, D. (1975). The tasks of the curricular theorist. In W. Pinar (Ed.), *Curriculum theorizing: The reconceptualists* (pp. 250–271). Berkeley, CA: MacCutchan.

Huebner, D. (1999). *The lure of the transcendent: Collected essays of Dwayne Huebner.* Mahwah, NJ: Erlbaum.

Jagodzinski, J. (1997). The nostalgia of art education: Reinscribing the master's narrative. *Studies in Art Education, 38*(2), 80–94.

Kesson, K., & Henderson, J. (2005, October 4). *Building a public disciplinary community.* Paper presented at the Curriculum & Pedagogy Conference, Oxford, OH.

Machado, A. (2007). *Poesías completas/Complete poetry.* Madrid: Austral.

Marx, K., & Engels, F. (1888). *Manifesto of the communist party* (F. Engels, Trans.). Chicago: Charles H. Kerr. (Original work published 1848)

Marx, K., & Engels, F. (1967). *The German ideology* (R. Pascal, Trans.). New York: International. (Original work published 1845)

Minh-ha, T. T. (1990). Cotton and iron. In R. Ferguson, M. Gever, T. T. Minh-ha, & C. West (Eds.), *Out there: Marginalization and contemporary culture* (pp. 327–336). Cambridge, MA: MIT Press/New Museum of Contemporary Art.

Mohanty, C. T. (1991). Cartographies of struggle: Third world women and the politics of feminism. In C. T. Mohanty, A. Russo & L. Torres (Eds.), *Third world women and the politics of feminism*
(pp. 1–48). Bloomington, IN: Indiana University Press.

Mohanty, C. T. (2003). *Feminism without borders: Decolonizing theory, practicing solidarity.* Durham,
NC: Duke University Press.

Morrison, K. R. B. (2004). The poverty of curriculum theory: A critique of Wraga and Hlebowitsh.
Journal of Curriculum Studies, 36(4), 487–494.

Nancy, J.-L. (2000). *Being singular plural.* Stanford, CA: Stanford University Press.

Nobo, J. L. (1986). *Whitehead's metaphysics of extension and solidarity.* Albany, NY: SUNY Press.

Nobo, J. L. (1997). Experience, eternity, and primordiality: Steps towards a metaphysics of creative solidarity. *Process Studies, 26*(3–4), 171–204.

Pinar, W. (Ed.). (2000). *Curriculum studies: The reconceptualization.* Troy, NY: EIP Press. (Original
work published 1975)

Rolling, J. H. (2007). Exploring Foshay's theorem for curriculum-making in education: An elementary school art studio project. *Journal of Curriculum & Pedagogy, 4*(1), 136–159.

Rorty, R. (1989). *Contingency, irony, and solidarity.* Cambridge, England: Cambridge University
Press.

Sandoval, C. (2000). *Methodology of the oppressed.* Minneapolis: University of Minnesota Press.

Slattery, P., & Rapp, D. (2003). *Ethics and the foundations of education: Teaching convictions in a postmodern world.* Boston, MA: Allyn & Bacon.

Smith, A. D. (2000). *Talk to me: Listening between the lines.* New York: Random House.

Soja, E. (1996). *Thirdspace: Journeys to Los Angeles and other real-and-imagined places.* Malden, MA:
Blackwell.

Springgay, S., & Carpenter, B. S. (2007). "Unframing" arts based research: New directions and
conversations. *Journal of Curriculum & Pedagogy, 4*(1), 9–15.

Tavin, K. (2003). Wrestling with angels, searching for ghosts: Toward a critical pedagogy of visual
culture. *Studies in Art Education, 44*(3), 197–213.

Weber, M. (1946). Class, status, party. In H. H. Gerth & C. W. Mills (Eds.), *From Max Weber: Essays
insociology* (pp. 180–195). New York: Oxford University Press.

Weber, M. (1978). The economic relationships of organized groups. In *Economy and society: An outline of interpretive sociology* (pp. 339–355). Berkeley, CA: University of California Press.

Weiler, K. (Ed.). (2001). *Feminist engagements: Reading, resisting, and revisioning male theorists in education and cultural studies.* New York/London: Routledge.

West, C. (1990). The new cultural politics of difference. In R. Ferguson, M. Gever, T. Minh-ha, &
C. West (Eds.), *Out there: Marginalization and contemporary culture* (pp. 19–36). Cambridge, MA:
MIT Press/New Museum of Contemporary Art.

Williams, R. (1977). *Marxism and literature.* Oxford: Oxford University Press.

Wraga, W. G. (1999). Extracting sun-beams out of cucumbers: The retreat from practice of reconceptualized curriculum studies. *Educational Researcher, 28,* 4–13.

Wraga, W. G., & Hlebowitsh, P. S. (2003). Toward a renaissance in curriculum theory and development in the USA. *Journal of Curriculum Studies, 35*(4), 425–437.

Young, I. M. (2002). *Inclusion and democracy.* Oxford, England: Oxford University Press.

Suggested Reading Questions

1. Given the recent emphasis on dissensus and difference in the field of curriculum
   studies, what new language for discussing solidarity might be necessary to avoid sub-
   suming difference into the same?

2. How might educators enact ways of being with one another that are contingent and
   against normalcy and at the same time substantiate and offer guidance?

3. The author describes a series of false binaries. For those who live on the downside of
   those binaries, or are affected negatively by them (and therefore experience them as
   real), how might we make them aware of such bogus distinctions while at the same
   time honoring their lived realities?

4. Generating new language and taking risks with academic language are two calls put forth by the author. What assumptions might the author be making about the relationship between language and the material realities of those who are assumed to benefit most from creative solidarity?

5. If the individual only thinks in relation, as the author suggests via the work of Ellsworth, what might the implications be for attending to the social contexts within which schooling takes place?

Response to Rubén A. Gaztambide-Fernández
Communities Without Consensus

Janet L. Miller

Not surprisingly, I guess, my invited "response" to Rubén's essay has turned into a form of what Spivak (2008) calls a "familiar essay," where the writer's life-details are always shadowily present, because the familiar essay is neither autobiographical nor impartial analysis, though it courts both. It is certainly not disinterested (p. 9); Obviously, my musings here are not at all disinterested. My "writer's life-details"—or at least how I construe those details in relation to the initial reconceptualization of the U.S. curriculum field and to a possible post-reconceptualization—are more than just shadowily present throughout.

During the Purdue gathering, for example, I worried with/in tensions that the generational as well as "Bergamo-oriented" (and thus perhaps "exclusionary") positionings of "post-reconceptual" presenters and "original reconceptualization" responders generated for me (and for some others, I assume). During that conference as well as in this response, my life-details cast shadows on all my interpretations of what post-reconceptualization might come to mean within current versions of U.S. curriculum studies, and what I might desire it to "mean," especially as juxtaposed with my perceptions of the "original" movement. So, of course, those shadows hover over this response—and I thus worry that readers in part might construe these musings as what could only be considered a fictitious argument for the special-ness or the never-to-be repeated supposed unity among those working within the reconceptual movement within particular historical moments and events of the 1960s and early 1970s in the United States.

Thus, I want to respond here in ways that do not constitute a nostalgic latching onto Rubén's conceptualization of "creative solidarity" as a possibly reconfigured and yet somewhat familiar and comfortable stamp of the "first" reconceptualization onto goals and conceptions of a "post-reconceptualization." I certainly do not want to offer here a patronizing pat of approval for following and enhancing the supposedly similar dreams, desires, and predilections of the elders. My familiar essay is in no way a critique of Rubén's conceptualization of creative solidarity as simply the newest version of what "we elders" already have "experienced" and "accomplished."

So, how can I not be drawn to Rubén's notion of "creative solidarity" in ways that only replicate my initial understandings of and longings for solidarity and community within the move to reconceptualize the U.S. curriculum field? I came of age, so to speak, during the early and mid-1960s in the United States, a time of political ferment, volatile Vietnam war protests, the Women's and Civil Rights movements, and the emergence of a variety of "alternative" and "free" schools that promised enactments of "progressive and democratic ideals and practices" for all students and teachers. I took graduate courses at Columbia University in the summer of 1967, and traveled to San Francisco with my husband and friends in the summer of 1968—cities overblown with flower power, wafts of incense, spontaneous demonstrations of "political/personal" resistances, and "be-ins" in the parks. I really did believe that solidarity was an agreed-upon and similarly defined goal for many of us, a mission, a passion, a dream of race and gender and progressive educator identity-based coalitions and of equality for all.

Some of that fervor fueled, in part, the movement to reconceptualize the field of curriculum in the United States. Or at least, that's how I seem to want to remember it—my initial commitment to reconceptualization as filtered through my resistance, from the mid- and late-1960s through the early 1970s, to teaching prepackaged high school textbook versions of "English curriculum" that stressed behavioral objectives as measured by one true interpretation of the text, for example. And, a bit later, my allegiance to the work of the reconceptualization, from the early 1970s on, interwoven with a visceral sense of possible unity among those of us who wished to move the field from an emphasis on linear, mechanical, and singular versions of curriculum design, development, and content to an examination of the "political and personal" dimensions of "understanding" the nature of one's educational experience.

And so, in attempting to contextualize my understandings of Rubén's call for creative solidarity within my partial memories of the Bergamo curriculum conferences and *JCT: Journal of Curriculum Theorizing,* I could paint these enterprises as those that helped to conjoin scholars, activists, teachers, researchers, theorists, curriculum designers, and developers in a unitary and originary version of Rubén's creative solidarity. My interpretations could embellish a "Bergamo collective" that supposedly functioned through and with visions of creative solidarity. I could posit "us" as a collective united around our experiences as members of a particular generation inflected with 1960s political, social, and cultural demands for social change, as members who declined to transmit our received heritage that framed curriculum as an administrative designation. For, in fact, that was the kind of solidarity that I once envisioned as possible: for a while, at least.

But Rubén disrupts the kind of "solidarity" (and the essentialist and romanticized problems associated with it) that I could conjure here about the work of individuals associated with the original reconceptualization—what Durkheim would term *organic solidarity,* an interdependence that arises from specialization of work and the complementarities among people engaged in that work. Instead, Rubén argues for a form of solidarity that engages a creative process in order to work toward the "production of emergent cultural forms...without guarantees." In so doing, Rubén forces me to again acknowledge cracks in the reconceptual coalition that I initially had imagined, desired into being.[1] At first disturbed by such fissures, and then recognizing the necessary and contingent differences among that loosely organized group of people working toward reconceptualization, I eventually contended that the field needs, and will continue to need what I have called a "riotous array of theoretical stances" that enable curricularists, from differing angles and interests, to analyze, critique, rewrite, and change technologies of curriculum that try to separate pedagogy and learning into discrete, predetermined, and measurable units of content and behavior. And I argued that the ultimate usefulness of such [a riotous array of] frameworks and perspectives depends upon 'ongoing conversations' among curricularists (Miller, 2005a).

At the same time, Rubén's essay in this volume dedicated to "exploring post-reconceptualization" urges me to yet again contend with issues spawned by the fact that I can no longer imagine unitary and singular versions of "communities" or any ease with which those in the field might engage in "ongoing conversations." I now can envision only "communities without consensus"—a construction that marks my active refusal to construct any universal notions of "selves," "collective," or "solidarity" read only as "the same." Instead, I imagine and work toward communities without consensus as composed of "selves" and versions of curriculum work that re-form daily and differently in response to difference and to the unknown. Constructions of communities without consensus thus also refuse any one version of curriculum studies through which one global field and its participants could emerge.

And Rubén's work here indeed reinforces my conviction that "we" in the field now are situated with and in current historical moments, social and cultural contexts, and political imperatives that differ greatly from those that initially framed the reconceptualization of the curriculum field during the 1970s and early 1980s. Thus, the U.S. field, its conditions, its contemporary iterations, and its participants are not and cannot ever be "the same" as during the reconceptual movement (not that "we" were ever "the same" within those moments either, obviously), nor do I think that "we" can aim for one unitary version of "creative solidarity."

For, the field of curriculum studies, writ large, now must contend with and respond to multiple versions and effects of the "unknown" as well as of "difference." The field itself must take into account contemporary and volatile worldly events, including the terrorist attacks of September 11, 2001; the most recent and ongoing wars in Iraq and Afghanistan; the heterogeneity and rapid flux that now characterize global flows of people, languages, technologies, commodities, culture, and capital through and across constantly changing borders, discourses, and subjectivities (Castells, 2000); and embodied effects of transnational flows and mobilities, especially via information and communication technologies, that loosen local populations from geographically constrained communities, thus connecting people and conceptualizing "places" and "spaces" around the globe in new and complex ways (Cresswell, 2002). All of these events, forces, and flows now compel us to consider how the U.S. curriculum field and its implicated "worldliness" (Miller, 2005b) both contribute to and attempt to disrupt Western and especially U.S.-centric versions of knowledge, identities, and their constructions worldwide.

Rubén, in attempting to conceive of a fresh version of coalition politics that would emphasize an ethic of "creative solidarity" in relation to these contemporary conditions, indeed calls attention to our curriculum work as never-ending, never completed, always-in-the-making, always in-relation to others and to varying constructions of difference. And Rubén's notion of "creative solidarity" certainly asserts difference as "a way of being with each other that contingently presents itself against a sense of normalcy and coherence." He thus assumes that identities, solidarities, and curriculum field(s) are always in flux, multiple, and incomplete. These are assumptions with which I agree.

If difference frames the notion of creative solidarity, as Rubén contends, then how might "we" not see ourselves mirrored in reinscriptions of our already familiar, identifiable selves, and versions of the curriculum field? For in difference, we no longer can simply identify with normalized versions of our selves of the field of curriculum studies. Working difference involves making unfamiliar any one version of theory, practice, research, knowledge, selves, the "field," or creative solidarity.

So, how might we take up the challenges of difference, wherein static conceptions of "identity" or isolated cultures and educational practices cannot function as refuge, within a concept of creative solidarity? How might we enact a desire to address and be addressed as in-the-making, without closing down around unitary and static modes of pedagogy, curriculum, or "creative solidarity?" How indeed might curriculum as a field be/come a field comfortable with ambiguity and ambivalence as well as with strategic deployments of political signifiers and discourses that might "congeal at the moment of use," only to be uncongealed and further destabilized in other contexts (Butler, Laclau, & Zizek, 2000)?

These general questions frame my readings of Rubén's conceptualization of creative solidarity as a possible goal and material enactment of "post-reconceptualization," and they form bases for my attraction to as well as further musings about Rubén's contentions.

In his work toward creative solidarity, for example, Rubén draws from Huebner, who posits that the "source of all language 'is the creative efforts of people.'" Rubén extrapolates that it then becomes our task to unravel any potential trappings of language, and to "generate a new language." Rubén identifies three challenges to his conception of creative solidarity and to his desires to "generate a new language": the discursive, the structural, and the personal. As I read and reread Rubén's work, I longed for a more detailed discussion of how he conceptualizes "the discursive, the structural, and the personal." But within his chapter, he does sketch what he considers to be two trappings of language commonly used in the U.S. curriculum field, what he calls *bogus distinctions*, distinctions that he claims keep us from one another, from generating a new language, and from what he names as the political project that is curriculum. These bogus distinctions are:

1. *The opposition between theory and practice.* Here Rubén focuses on the negative consequences of the persistent use of the descriptive phrase, "moribund state of the field" as well as on the apparent recurring need to build that metaphoric bridge between theory and practice. Rubén draws attention to the deleterious effects of this persistent binary construction in the field of curriculum studies as well as in educational theory and research, writ large. And,

2. *The appeal to the opposition between the arts and the sciences.* Here, Rubén questions the focus on arts-based curriculum theorizing currently assuming a primacy that Rubén argues parallels Huebner's analysis of why some in the field might have felt the need to focus on the theoretical. Just as curriculum studies once longed for legitimation as a science, Rubén now wonders if an arts-based focus in curriculum studies simply repeats that longing for recognition, but this time from the humanities disciplines. Rubén argues that the language of the arts should be critically, historically, and discursively interrogated so as to not allow for "easy beauty" with its attendant enlightenment notions of "true" creativity and timeless permanence. And he posits that if virtually anything that is "well-made" is deemed to be artistry, then the distinction between artistry and scientific rigor becomes arbitrary, a bogus distinction.

I would like to hear more about these bogus distinctions and how these work in ways that supposedly keep us from the creative solidarity that Rubén envisions. For example, I wonder: how does claiming a bogus distinction between artistry and scientific rigor advance our work in curriculum studies in an era in the United States where supposedly only random controlled experimental design studies "count" as viable research, and only standardized scores and measurements constitute "strong" evidence of teaching and learning? And while Rubén cautions us not to fall back into an Enlightenment ideal of "creative solidarity" overlaid with an essentialized positivist's claims for "scientific rigor," I wonder about possible essentialist constructions of "creative efforts of people" to transcend the confines of language in order to generate "a new language?"

I instead posit that "we" who compose the U.S. field of curriculum studies need to consider generational/epistemological/methodological/theoretical variations of cultural translation that frame any notion of post-reconceptualization as well as any possible enactments of Rubén's concept of creative solidarity in the "next moments" in and of the field. I gesture toward such possibilities by drawing on Judith Butler's conviction that prior histories are significant in determining the meaning(s) of signs, for "the norms by which I seek to make myself recognizable are not fully mine. They are not born with me; the temporality of their emergence does not coincide with the temporality of my own life" (Butler, 2005, p. 35).

I also grapple, in my emphasis on the necessary worldliness of curriculum studies, with

...the concrete dilemmas of what it is to be local and global at once, to be caught in the necessity of constant translation.... Such an inquiry neither moves us too quickly to assert our commonality, thus effacing our difference, nor seeks to return us to our parochial locations, our ethnic singularities, without showing how the most local struggles are implicated in the processes of globalization. What this also means is that the usual binary oppositions do not hold, and that we must learn to work with one another in our irreducible complexity, bound to one another in many ways, implicated in a process of globalization which works differentially and relentlessly, at the same time that we are irreducible to a collective condition. (Butler, 2001, p. 96)

I thus am drawn to Butler's conceptualization of constant cultural translation, a notion she acknowledges as borrowed from Homi Bhabha (1994), as a way of challenging Rubén's reliance upon Huebner's modernist conceptions of language and "creative efforts of people" as possibly helping to create "a new language" and a collective condition. For example, expanding upon Bhabha's work, Butler argues that cultural translation works at the cultural and social limits of particular conceptions of the universal, exposing what they exclude, and creating space for their reformulation. She assumes that since universality makes its "varied and contending appearances" in different languages, there are differing cultural versions of any posited universal rather than a single transcultural form. Throughout her version of cultural translation, Butler relies on the malleability of language: its amenability to recycling, its inability to always enact what it names (Butler, 1997, 1999; Butler, Laclau, & Zizek, 2000).

For, Butler argues that language is never solely language. It is always and only ever language in its social or cultural operation; language articulated in and as norms, as universals. Butler's work, in general, engages in destabilizations of subject categories as well as the discursive structures within which they are formed. She does so in order to expose limitations, instabilities, and contingencies of existing norms. At the same time, she sees language's potential to engage in the difficult yet necessary labor of constructing, across and within differences, a concept of what it means to be human that can encompass groups with very diverse ideas. Ideas not only about what it means to be human but also about the needs that humans have and the rights that they require. For Butler, the goal is a reconfigured and a more fluid and inclusive form of cultural translation, where "...our fundamental categories can and must be expanded to become more inclusive and more responsive to the full range of cultural populations" (Butler, 2004b, p. 223).

As members of a U.S. field in constant and often contentious flux, I believe that Rubén and I agree that we need to create new possibilities for cultural translation in curriculum studies, possibilities that recognize both our involvement and our implicated status in contemporary worldly events and times. I think a major issue that we both face is how to create such possibilities, such exchanges and translations that are neither contingent on sameness nor reducible to a collective condition. How might we then consider the creative, generative activity that Rubén hopes will lead to a version of "persistently dissatisfied solidarity"—a vision and version that he claims is necessary to restore a sense of collective action in the field of curriculum studies—if we can never be fully identified with any collective "we"? And if we indeed want to work difference in ways that remake as "unfamiliar" theories, practices, knowledges, constructions of norms, and resulting normalized selves?

To address such tensions requires proliferating, in multivariant ways the discourses, practices, and coalitions that comprise and fuel our work in curriculum studies. For me, a notion of "communities without consensus" possibly enables representations of self, other, and the curriculum field to be unfixed, mobilized, destabilized, and released as forces capable of recombining in as yet unimagined and perhaps untraceable ways. In relation to such envisionings, I then can imagine Rubén's version of "creative solidarity" as a potential form of collaborative curriculum theorizing and research that might enable each of us to move (differently) in unforeseen directions that might yield new possibilities for becoming. That is, new possibilities even as we grapple with events, contexts, relationships, and memories that threaten to reify normative and static tellings about others and ourselves as yet another form of a predetermined "curriculum field" and a singular and stationary version of its work.

Rubén's work here, then, reinforces my conviction that those of us who are committed to the field *know that we must remake (differently) the field every day*, in relation to particular worldly events, issues, and peoples; in tension with histories of discursive and material norms that would constrain possibilities of new iterations of "self" and "other;" and in recognition of our irreducibility to a collective "we." I would argue that "we" must do that rethinking of curriculum studies in myriad ways, from a variety of perspectives and cultural translations, and yet always in relation, informed by a conception of the U.S. American curriculum field as situated with/in our encounters with one another (Miller, 2006). Those encounters necessarily embody a "certain agonism and contestation," a certain disorientation and loss (Butler, 2004a), that perhaps will yield Rubén's vision of creative solidarity. But indeed, at the same time I believe, this rethinking will require our field and our selves to come into being, again and again, as that which we have yet to know.

Note

1. For contingent descriptions and "partial histories" of the reconceptualization, see especially the Introduction, Prelude, and chapters 1 and 13 in *Sounds of Silence Breaking: Women, Autobiography, Curriculum* (Miller, 2005a).

References

Bhabha, H. K. (1994). *The location of culture*. London: Routledge.

Butler, J. (1997). *Excitable speech: A politics of the performative*. New York: Routledge.

Butler, J. (1999). *Gender trouble* (2nd ed.). New York: Routledge.

Butler, J. (2001). Transformative encounters. In E. Beck-Gernsheim, J. Butler, & L. Puigvert (Eds.), *Women and social transformation* (pp. 81–98). New York: Lang.

Butler, J. (2004a). *Precarious life: The powers of mourning and violence*. New York: Verso.

Butler, J. (2004b). *Undoing gender*. New York: Routledge.

Butler, J. (2005). *Giving an account of oneself*. New York: Fordham University Press.

Butler, J., Laclau, E., & Zizek, S. (2000). *Contingency, hegemony, universality: Contemporary dialogues on the left*. London: Verso.

Castells, M. (2000). *The rise of the network society: Vol. 1. The information age* (2nd ed.). Oxford: Blackwell.

Cresswell, T. (2002). Theorizing place. *Thamyris/Intersecting*, *9*, 11–32.

Miller, J. L. (2005a). *Sounds of silence breaking: Women, autobiography, curriculum*. New York: Lang.

Miller, J. L. (2005b). The American curriculum field and its worldly encounters. *JCT: Journal of Curriculum Theorizing*, *21*(2), 9–24.

Miller, J. L. (2006). Curriculum studies and transnational flows and mobilities: Feminist autobiographical perspectives. *Transnational Curriculum Inquiry*, *3*(2), 31–50.

Spivak, G. C. (2008). *Other Asias*. Oxford, England: Blackwell.

5 "No Room in the Inn"?
The Question of Hospitality in the Post(Partum)[1]-Labors of Curriculum Studies

Molly Quinn

Chapter Overview

The author discusses what might make it possible to ask the question of hospitality within the post-reconceptualization of curriculum studies. She asks whether our scholarship and institutions respond to the call for hospitality and how a concept such as hospitality might help curriculum scholars rethink, expand, and deepen their work. Pulling from biblical themes, the author asks if at this historical junction there is room for curriculum studies within institutions and within curriculum studies for the other who might make an unexpected visit. Next, she turns to Derrida to ask if we are prepared to receive the other and, more specifically, to risk ourselves before the other and in so doing perhaps to face the stranger in ourselves or be born anew. Here we must be prepared to be haunted by an other than ruptures and proceeds welcoming. Lastly, the author points out, that if we as a field are radically open to an-other, that which becomes possible might be places of pleasure, laughter as critique, and learning from the stranger. This is good enough education learned by living with others as best we can and learning to embrace anew what we have loved to love again within the present moment.

> ...the soul is, in truth, a foreigner on the earth...the step of the stranger resonates through the silver night...."
>
> —Trakl, cited in Derrida, 2002, p. 403

Prelude to the Question (before Conception)

Before and beneath me, before and beneath the "silver night" of our academic labors, lies the "step of the stranger"—thus, the question of hospitality, with its resonant, radical call to make room for that which is, in truth, foreign—*other*. As this question is, then, a living question, one sought to be lived in practice—professionally, pedagogically, personally— here and now and beyond, before me also is a heightened awareness concerning how this query may be most hospitably engaged at the present time. Within this context, perhaps one possibility is but to invite the reader to entertain with me some preliminary queries pertaining to the question.

Do the labors of academia, and here specifically those in curriculum studies, require or lay claim to the call of hospitality, wittingly or unwittingly? If so, how, in what ways? Is there a discourse, and also a practice, of hospitality that is central to the work of education? Our curriculum labors?

1. How hospitable (or not) is the institution of education to its own mission, and to those who participate in it? (Are classrooms places hospitable to learning? Are teacher–student relationships those that welcome the experience of the other— the unknown stranger—in our midst? Does the curriculum invite the child into

a broader and deeper relationship with the world in all its wondrous mystery—its inexorable *otherness*?)

2. (How) might the idea of hospitality help us to rethink, expand, and deepen our understanding of our work in curriculum studies? (How) might considering the question of hospitality serve to impact our praxis—to critically and creatively open up our relationship to the strange otherness we encounter in our work?

Yet, it may be that the call of hospitality, an ethics of the other, asks of me—beyond the open path of questions meant to guide—that I provide a place from which to entertain the reader with the question of hospitality, or rather to entertain the question of hospitality with the reader—an inviting abode. Hospitality itself may require a "home" into which to welcome the other—at the least, an articulation of the space from which I engage the question—professionally, pedagogically, personally. Alas, personally, I have come to this call through the dark night of my own curriculum work, through the haunting longing for home and hospitality all too unlived. Here, I might do well, though, to beckon and greet the reader first from the silver night of our academic labors, to situate our conversation in the field of curriculum studies. Is there, though, a *there* in curriculum studies, one we can know and articulate? Are we even at home, as it were, in our field?

Now, more than ever, curriculum studies has taken up the call to address the ethical questions central to the work of education—the heart of which is the encounter with an other.[2] Turning to the experience of teachers and students who labor daily to understand the world they inhabit, and to engage their work with humanity and hope, scholarship has proliferated, in solidarity with this labor, to both articulate such experience and contribute to its transformation in ways that affirm life and growth. However, now, too, it seems that these so engaged—particularly in the United States where standardized assessments dominate curriculum life—find such labor laden with a difficulty that is umbilically tied to forces that alienate and dehumanize. There is "no room" in the work for being present to or with others fully in "reading [greeting/meeting] the word and the world"[3] of the curriculum, for the educational labor that brings forth life and life together.

Here, I seek to engage this experience of want—want of space, place, and welcome, in our curriculum labors—conceived largely through the poststructuralist studies of Jacques Derrida (1997/2000, 2002) on the question of hospitality, a concept that also speaks in powerful ways to our "post-reconceptualist" work in the present moment. When we bring this question to bear on our work—cradled historically by rich reconceptualist curriculum thought—it represents an attempt to imagine different possibilities for living there, new ways to make room and make welcome, dwellings of fellowship and freedom in the work of curriculum studies.

> Where are we going? What awaits us at the beginning, at the turn…, of this year? You are thinking perhaps that these are questions to laugh about. But perhaps we are going to laugh today. We have not yet encountered this strange possibility, regarding hospitality, the possibility of laughter. (Derrida, 2002, p. 358)

Herein is how Jacques Derrida engages his series of lectures, published in *Acts of Religion*, on the subject of hospitality. He speaks of laughter first, in contrast to hospitality as mourning—a tradition wherein the welcoming is a weeping ritual accompanied with tears, with cries, "the stranger being hailed like a revenant" (p. 359).

Strangely, this ritual is one with which many in the United States have become somewhat poignantly familiar in the aftermath of the hurricane visitations along the Gulf

Coast, which is also my native home. Perhaps I appeal to his words first then, and have given host to his thought on this theme anew, not only because I want to laugh, and embrace the possibility of laughter in my labors—the joy and wonder in engaging and dwelling upon the world with others via the word of scholarship or way of teaching or work of service; but also because I am asking myself anew, too, where we are going in curriculum studies, what awaits us, and that upon which we wait, as for new beginnings.

Thus, for now, I begin with my own beginnings concerning such, the arrival of this question at the door of my mind, the title and topic I was compelled to welcome, in that it took up residence as if at home within—"'No Room in the Inn'? The Question of Hospitality in the Post(Partum)-Labors of Curriculum Studies." I have, as such, taken it to tea, in the manner of all hospitality: sought to read the lines of it, between the lines of it, be read by it as well, partake in conversation together, via a kind of deconstructive/reconstructive hermeneutical homecoming. Freud once asserted in a letter that "theory falls on you from above like an unexpected guest" (1915, cited by Derrida, 1997, personal communication). My own preoccupation with this question—to which I now turn—has fallen upon me similarly, like the gift of a stranger, inviting me to enter into a new relationship with my work. I submit that my own personal (pre-)occupation mirrors a professional one as well: in seeking to understand the present context of curriculum studies, and to entertain or map out the next "post-reconceptualist" moment therein, it seems that as a field we are similarly opening ourselves to the new in relationship to our collective work.

I invite the reader to enter with me into this encounter, as well, giving thought to: (1) "No Room in the Inn"?—the formulation of the problem as the want of hospitality in the experience of our labors, the import of hospitality argued from and established through the reconceptualist tradition in curriculum studies; (2) Derrida and Deconstructive Readings on the Question of Hospitality—the examination of hospitality as radical openness to the other through his work, the remedy and risk implicit in this call considered; and (3) Hospitality in the Post(Partum)-Labors of Curriculum Studies—the exploration of the question as response in the present moment of our own work, the possibilities of a hospitality in education that heals, upholds and hopes for our humanity elucidated.

"No Room in the Inn"?

Welcoming the "Child" in Our Midst: Hospitality and the Labors of "Mary"

> And she brought forth her firstborn son, and wrapped him in swaddling clothes, and laid him in a manger; because there was no room for them in the inn. (The Holy Bible, 1985, Luke 2:7)

This passage from the book of Luke in the New Testament, and no doubt in some way of which my thesis is referential, does not dwell upon the experience of Mary's labor, nor the want of a room in which to give birth to the divine within her. Yet, the experience is there, nonetheless, in the background and as the ground itself, begging the very question of hospitality or the lack thereof. We know from the story that her firstborn arrives in a most inhospitable time and place—secreted away from the dangers of Herod that threaten his life and turned out of the inn at the moment of his coming. Yet, what is celebrated by believers the world over is a tale of glad tidings, a story of welcome, in fact, such that strangers from afar, from the East—shepherds, wise men, and kings—are summoned to the side of this uninvited and unwelcome visitor to joyously receive him.[4]

In "Visitation of the Stranger," Louis Massignon (the Islamic philosopher Derrida claims oriented his entire life, and intellectual testimony, toward the experience of Abrahamic hospitality) enjoins in this event the more profound and abiding hospitality of Mary, as he reports, who "conceived in order to give birth to the immortal," whose whole life and conduct was directed by this "frail Guest [Hôte] that she carries in her womb..., a mysterious Stranger whom she adores...; she devotes herself...; sanctifies herself to protect her Sacred Guest.... waiting for the moment when He suggests to her that she invoke Him, making her progress in experiential knowledge through compassion" (cited in Derrida, 2002, pp. 374–375).

Perhaps, it is because my given name is Mary, and that my life seems ever oriented toward the birth, and rebirth, of the eternal "truth"—or that I live in New York City where "room" is at a premium, but I am not alone in my commentary via experiential knowledge of the labors of academia of late—that one is left with the pervasive feeling that there is: No room in the inn.[5] Had I more compassion, I might make amends along the lines that there is in academia but little room for the living labors, or that it suffers for want of a room with a view. For me this experience has meant personally turning myself away from the inn of academia, for a time, to rethink and know again the very nature of the university itself—of education, and the import of providing "room" to its work. The hospitality of Mary as metaphor for the call of our labors to welcome the child (i.e., student, idea, other—the strange, the new) in our midst, challenging me to (re) open the womb of my own room of/for hospitality, has helped me in this.

I remember reading bell hooks (1994), whose response to receiving tenure was one not unlike my own—disappointment, and even despair. How can one make a home, or settle in as an appointed host(ess), or guest, for that matter—even while enjoying official residence, the lease papers of tenure—in a place where there is not only no room, but where one is still the stranger who is not welcome? How, further, can one welcome students into a home that is no home, and is not one's own? Are we not all visitors, or "host-ages," of the educational institution, subject to mandated curriculum labors unexpected, unprepared for, not our own? William Pinar (2004) identifies our current situation as "the nightmare that is the present" (p. 5) in U.S. education, and speaks of the desperate need for "a room of one's own." Considered with more hope—and even "hospitality" perhaps, however, I might rather ask: How can we welcome students into a home that is only partly a home/our own, where there remains a question as to whose home it is, whether home or hotel as well? How do we engage contemporary struggles around the shifting aims of (higher) education, at least in part ones over who will be owners, visitors, hostages, or other, and to what kind of end or inn?

Within this context, thus, the news of my decision a few years ago to quit a tenured position in the university—without another position in or out of academia, rather than being received incredulously, has been met with understanding from my colleagues in curriculum studies, even "congratulation," and "commendation." I am not alone[6] in the experience and interrogation of the "cabined and cramped existence"—to borrow from Dewey—that academic life seems today to offer to too many.

Curriculum Labors, Difficult Visitations, and Room for Strangers

Yet, what has this—even a religious story about the plight of a pregnant woman in search of a place to conceive (a) god—to do with our academic labors, with curriculum or education? I might appeal with the words Alfred North Whitehead (1967/1929) "that the essence of education is that it should be religious" (p. 14),[7] in the sense that Hongyu Wang (2002) expounds: "listening and responding to the call from the stranger 'with reverence'"—like Mary, education as a spiritual "journey of transforming the given into new forms of life" (pp. 287–288).[8] In the words of Dwayne Huebner (1999), it is "the lure of the transcendent,... a call from the other that we may reach out beyond ourselves and enter into life...." (p. 360). I might recall education via its Latin root in *educere*—to bring forth, to draw out—as the bringing forth of life, newness of life, from within us and in our midst, along with Socrates' notion of the teacher as midwife drawing out, bringing to light—to life, the soul's hidden wisdom. In Italian, the literal translation for to give birth is per dare alla luce—to give (or welcome) to the light. Born of reconceptualist commitments in curriculum studies, the works of Ted Aoki (2005), Max Van Manen (1991), and David Jardine (1992) are oriented thus around the pedagogy of welcoming and nurturing the child.

For Maxine Greene (1973), the teacher herself is the stranger, awakening students to life anew in the work of "making strange the familiar" (1988),[9] as well as visiting upon them the foreign. Huebner (1999) suggests that students too are strangers—and the content of the curriculum, the strange otherness with which both student and teacher are confronted. He adds that love is needed in this uncertain encounter with the unknown stranger, but that schools are dominated by careless structures—inhospitable even to this vulnerable meeting of different minds. Dahlia Beck (1993) claims: "...pedagogy is challenged...opened up by the encounter with the Other...needs the Stranger, in his or her particularities, visage and voice, to recover 'a deep sense of the familial'" (p. viii); "acknowledging Otherness and responding to it affords us the opportunity to shake our sensibilities to 'forms of life, of being, other than our own, yet not disconnected from our own.' It allows us to be/come human.... Encountering the Other empowers the 'Me' to emerge" (p. 90); "a mystery bearer who challenges...the stranger represents the question" (p. 98).

Concerning visitations and curriculum, William Doll (2002) speaks of the ghost of Dewey that hovers, the ghost of control in the curriculum machine that haunts—a strange visitor who often allows no room for other guests. While Doll talks not of hospitality proper, he proposes curriculum as conversation, etymologically related to dwelling, passing one's life, with others, signifying an openness to the other that is mutually transforming—as conversation captures us, we can transcend and transform the self—to borrow from Gadamer—"transposing ourselves into otherness" (p. 49). Here, I am perhaps, however, most interested in attending to the *currere* question—particularly because of this painful experience of a roomless/roam-less "running" where there is no room, a "course" arrested, arresting the "run" of others.

I am thinking of Leah Fowler's (2005) work on, what she calls, a curriculum of difficulty, situated within her interest in the "underside" and "counternarratives" of teaching. Here, she relates the story of Miss Maple, who—in teaching daily encounters a resistant and even disrespectful "host"—begins vomiting every weekday morn, only to gargle, brush, and march back to class for the 10:40 a.m. bell. Fowler describes it as a rage that erupts from lack of control and lack of hope in teaching—which is to say also that there wants "root-room" (Hopkins, 1885), space, for agency and aspiration, to live and grow, to ground and center oneself. In reading Miss Maple's pedagogy, Fowler questions her responsibility for understanding how often her own anger, for which there is no place, is carried into her teaching, seeking room for expression there. She concludes: "Our entire education system is in deep difficulty," and seeks to articulate the "poetics of a teaching life," to "mindfully *dwell in the present moment*... [italics added]" (p. 10) in the call to "work with others at the *center* [italics added] of those difficulties, with a ...compassionate self..." (p. 8). The question of hospitality with respect to self and other bleeds through this labor of and on difficulty, as the need for, and presupposition of, "room," to dwell, to be.

This text has been particularly difficult for me in the reading, as routine vomiting and asthma attacks had become literally my life in academia—no breathing room, no space or way to stomach existence there, sustain nourishment, take in and digest food for thought even—but this dark visitation has also been the strange and welcome call of being—my being—anew, in Martin Heidegger's sense (1927/1962) as *Dasein*, "being-there,"[10] to once again attend, open, to its "there," my there, and the there of academia's being, the now of curriculum studies, too. Let us though turn, more directly, to the question of hospitality—the answer to the call for a room in the inn.

Derrida and Deconstructive Readings on the Question of Hospitality

Derrida (2002) approaches the concept of hospitality—a concept that had particular draw for me, admittedly, as a female raised Christian in the American South[11]—by situating it first within a culture of hospitality, one associated with pleasure and joy. For him, there is no hospitality that does not include the sharing of some sign of joy, "smiling at the other as at the welcoming of a promise" (p. 358). In fact, he describes hospitality as culture itself: "There is no culture that is not a culture of hospitality" (p. 361). Thus, every culture competes to be most hospitable, as a people to regard and present ourselves as such, constructing structures and apparatuses of welcoming. In the call to develop ourselves into a culture of hospitality, we must wait on, extend the self toward, the other; we must be ready to welcome, to host and shelter, and prepare and adorn the self for such, for the coming of the host in all readiness to receive.

Yet, as we turn to Derrida's thought, who returns to the "hôte" (host) in French—the subject of hospitality, we find it is referential of both the one who gives and the one who receives. In typical fashion, through this coupling, he inverts and complicates our conception—hospitality is also, and etymologically, "hostipitality" in his words—hôte, also translated as enemy, is related to the notions of hostage and hostility. Derrida asks: Is there, perhaps, a violence in welcoming the other to, in fact, appropriate for oneself a place? Or perhaps to appropriate (i.e., assimilate, inscribe the place of) the other? He underscores the heart of hospitality as simultaneously poison and remedy (Derrida, 1972/1981), risk and possibility—required, perhaps even redemptive, and potentially reckless.

Albeit, we also are through hospitality called to wait for, and wait upon, the other, as *hostage* of sorts, subject to the visitor who comes—invited *or not*. Generous disposition is not hospitality as there is no welcoming of the other as other. Nor is hospitality mere duty, which is not a genuine welcoming either—"One must…therefore welcome without 'one must'" (p. 361). Via hospitality, we must be willing to *not* be ready, to let ourselves be overtaken, surprised by the unanticipated other we are *not* prepared to receive. As Derrida explicates it, then, within hospitality there is law without or beyond law—the conditional law of hospitality must abide side-by-side albeit also at odds with the unlimited "law" of hospitality beyond law. Here, Derrida (1997/2000) also hearkens back to Kant's ideal of universal hospitality[12] as the world condition for *Perpetual Peace* (1795/1972). Further, we open to the other, facing friend or foe we know not, in the silver "night of non-knowledge" (Derrida, 1990), present in promise to the other, before and beyond law, in the place where no rules apply. In doing so, we also risk ourselves before the other, to transcend ourselves or perhaps to come to know ourselves, to be born anew. In hospitality one is asked to be willing "to let oneself be swept by the coming of the wholly other, the absolutely unforeseeable…stranger, the uninvited visitor, the unexpected visitation beyond welcoming apparatuses" (Derrida, 2002, pp. 361–362). Herein is radical hospitality—not a preference of good-natured souls who simply enjoy entertaining others, nor a principle to be followed in the normative manner of neighborliness or citizenship, but something other, beyond both, even as it conditions such cultural claims upon character and etiquette.

Derrida moves to this call of radical hospitality which "has to consist in receiving without invitation, beyond or before the invitation" (p. 359), unfolding an "unlivable contradiction": "It is to death that hospitality destines oneself—death thus also bearing the figure of visitation without invitation"—a contradiction we unfold whenever we offer hospitality. It is death that may come for good or for ill. He culminates in the "non-dialectizable tension"[13] hidden within the concept of hospitality via the faces of visitation-invitation. Acknowledging that there is no hospitality without danger, without the risk of possible perversion, he affirms an unlivable contradiction that must be lived nonetheless:

> But we know enough to tell ourselves that hospitality, what belabors and concerns hospitality at its core…, what works it like a labor, like a pregnancy, like a promise as much as a threat…is indeed a contradictory conception, a thwarted…conception, or a contraception of awaiting, a contradiction of welcoming itself. (p. 359)

Hospitality must be, owes itself to be, inconceivable, incomprehensible, according to the contradictory and deconstructive law of hospitality. One must open oneself to the other that is not neighbor or brother, not mine, my hôte, as the possibility of impossibility, the experience of the impossible—coextensive with the essential problem at the ground of any aspired-to ethics. "It is always about answering for a dwelling place, for one's identity, one's space, one's limits, for the *ethos* as abode, habitation…home" (1997/2000, pp. 149–151).

Hospitality, then, Derrida (2002) reports, raises questions for us about the concept of concept—sheltering and letting itself be haunted, visited by, another concept. Herein, we see highlighted its integral and umbilical tie to the heart of our academic labors, helping, or haunting, each other and ourselves through the offering of our minds, entertaining together conceptual 'food' for thought.[14] He sees deconstruction as "hospitality to the other, to the other than oneself, the other than 'its other,' to an other beyond any 'its other'" (p. 364), in this way. Drawing upon Levinas, Derrida describes it as "the drama of a relation to the other that ruptures…an experience of the Good that elects me before I welcome it…that proceeds welcoming" (p. 364).

Hospitality in the Post(Partum)-Labors of Curriculum Studies

Room for Joy: Place for Pedagogies of Pleasure, Inclusion, and Care

Principally, perhaps, the call of hospitality in our curriculum labors, is the call to joy, a return to the heart—ever, in truth, at the heart of the life of the mind. Affirming the wisdom of Emily Dickinson (1961), we own the fact that the place we really want to dwell in is possibility, which is also a place of pleasure, promise, and play. In radical openness to the other, we open up a vast terrain fecund with unforeseen and unforeseeable potentialities. In this way, too, we acknowledge, inquire into and indulge in the transformative potential of "play" and authentic "interaction"—through which we also may come together across differences in common moments of goodness and shared pursuits of meaning.

Remembering what we have really "loved 'til now," in the language of Huebner (1999, p. 12) as inspired by Nietzsche—even reconceptualist commitments we unconsciously as yet perhaps continue to carry and can bring to renewed consciousness, we realize that the language of our critical tradition affirms a play engaged to bring into being possibilities that are good and true, just and beautiful. Minding what is a matter of the heart, we remind ourselves that: "Love calls us to the things of this world" (Wilbur, 1988, p. 233). In this way, we are via hospitality returned to laughter—what womanist theologian N. Lynne Westfield (2001) calls serious laughter, a shield through which is spoken the unspeakable, a form of critique. The play and pleasure of laughter is "righteous therapy," in fact, a source of healing[15] that allows us to reconnect with, and to reembody, our being and being-with, our "there." Laughter, putting us into our body, implicitly utters the wisdom of an embodied education, inclusive of mind, body, and spirit.[16] For, "…to describe hospitality is to describe the delightfulness of being human…" (p. 46). Hospitality here highlights the divine delight of being-(in-our-body)-in-the world—heartily laughing and loving our way though it in a full-bodied embrace of (being-with) others. Such, alas, is a delight we too often forget and let slip amid that which distracts, dehumanizes, and deadens, "de-pressing" the expression of joy and laughter. The question of hospitality may help us at least invite ways, and that intentionally, to more fully dwell in this deliciousness, even and especially amid difficulty. What promises, possibilities, pleasures, are we making, taking, partaking of, in curriculum studies—in teacher education, in our academic labors, in our schools? Why do we so little attend the heart, and the body? What of joy and of laughter in our labors? Herein are questions hospitality invites us to wait upon and attend.[17]

Questioning is "the piety of thought"—to borrow from Heidegger (1954/1977, p. 35), but perhaps it is also the play and place of thought. As something of the foundation, fulfillment, and way of academia, it seems uncanny how questioning here can actually lose its way, its play, and thus also its piety and place in and as thought. "The unexamined life is not worth living," the ancient philosophers—lovers of wisdom, discern, and thus initiate study as criticism—a way of inquiring into life toward praxis sublime. However, caught in closed-in, closing-in critique—the kind that seeks the final word and serves to cut off rather than open up further conversation and criticism, the question all too easily collapses, remains unentertained; it is essentially no longer welcome, has no place. Questioning requires the art of hospitality wherein we are not only open to the radical other it may introduce—listening to, learning from, the stranger who comes even as we question or critique her; but also caring for this other, extending and offering our 'there' to him as well. Heidegger (1927/1962) concludes that the meaning of being is, in fact, *care* in the space and place of our temporality. The concept of hospitality invites us, thus, in our curriculum labors to ground them in care, a pedagogy of the personal that acknowledges the relational, contextual, nature of all knowledge and knowing (Palmer, 1993). Nel Noddings (1992) has argued powerfully for the hospitable reconceptualization of the inn of education around centers of care, that is, for self, stranger, community, and consciousness, an invitation that calls us further to its recontextualization so as to be actually lived out together experientially in care.

The classroom, school, field of education—each is also a culture, which means each is also a culture of hospitality, curriculum profoundly about cultures of hospitality too. The present struggles over equity, access and inclusion in education perhaps speak most profoundly to the question of hospitality in our labors—concerning who is defined as "alien," "squatter," or "citizen" (Kliewer, 1998), about who is welcome, where and under what conditions (i.e., Oyler, 1996; Oyler & Preservice Inclusion Study Group, 2006), for whom we care. Practically, we need to critically assess the welcoming apparatuses and structures education engages, and consciously energize and expand inclusive, inviting instruction through them, creating a sense of place where everyone belongs (i.e., Lareau,

2003; Ramsey, 2004; Sapon-Shevin, 1998)—"where no one owns the truth and everyone has a right to be heard" (Kundera, cited in Doll, 1993, p. 151).

Hospitality implies education as a way of being, a way of making and living a life, with others "as best we know how" (Arendt, cited in Greene, 1988). If we teach who we are (i.e., Aoki, 2005; Palmer, 1993), then we must actually be there—present, to welcome and receive the student. Herein, hospitality does indeed call for a vision of home. As theologian-educator Elizabeth Newman (2004) relates it, this sense of place is not so much a building as a people who are called. Arguing that "in the name of welcoming the other, colleges and universities have often come to function more like educational 'hotels'" (p. 91), she claims that they may provide space for others, but do not offer genuine hospitality. Hospitality "calls us to enlarge our hearts by offering our time and personal resources [the gift of ourselves]..." (Conde-Frazier, 2004, p. 172), and invite others also to bring themselves to curriculum labors we undertake together. We must come to know ourselves, and others, though, in order to offer the gifts our humanity brings. As William Pinar (2006), drawing on the work of Wolfgang Klafki, reminds us: to cultivate our humanity, we must begin with our own.

Trading Places, Reordering Spaces: Readin', 'Ritin, and Radical Presence in Education

African-American history—central to understanding contemporary conditions in the United States and its public education system (Pinar, 2004), as rooted in the image of the stranger and a yearning for home, presents us with a profound struggle around the practice of hospitality: the fact that one is never fully free to befriend the other in a racist, sexist world. The reality is that in the experience of oppression, none are loved for their true selves, whereas hospitality requires a place where humanness is not denied but rather embraced. Hospitality, then, in the present moment, must also be heretical, constituted by practices of resilience and resistance—concealed gatherings, hospitable spaces take us even beyond critique. Here is hospitality's link with healing: it invites "soul work for broken bodies, body work for bruised and battered souls" (Westfield, 2001, p. 70). We honor vulnerability and voice, cultivate intimacy and connection, and come together in trust around questions and courses of that which shall ultimately make us all whole. Curriculum work in this way is both transgressive and transformative: it calls for "lunch-counter" curriculum that "talks back" in seeking to create a public space where all are invited to the fellowship of food for thought and talk that nourishes and heals our full humanity.

Hospitality might be elucidated further for us through the image of the banquet feast: no more classes, all sit at the table together (Newman, 2004). In this way, hospitality inverts all "bourgeois" values, calling all to look toward each other, especially the most vulnerable and weakest—"The last shall be first," as Christ claimed, and *I and the other are one.*

> The first step in multicultural living is hospitality.... Hospitality begins a journey toward visibility...defies social arrangements of class, ethnicity, or race...rearranges our relationships.... Through this act of resisting the devaluing of people, we witness to the importance of transcending social differences and breaking sociocultural boundaries that are exclusive. (Conde-Frazier, 2004, pp. 171–172)

Problematizing the pedagogical dichotomy, as teachers we may bring the strangeness of content/curriculum to students and make strange the world through study, but the child also, bringing the new, questions us, visiting upon us that which is other (Huebner,

1999). Hearkening back to the classical ideal of education found in cultivating our humanity, together we entertain the open-minded search for truth, which ever requires openness, each to the other, that transforms, and calls into question the "truths," power relations—the pedagogically privileged and prioritized, that be.

Concerning power, conceptions of curriculum particularly, but more broadly of education and modern life, seem also to be persistently focused on the progressive and the predicated—how to control the course and direct it to desired ends. Dewey critiques this approach to education—which he claims is of the stuff of life rather than of preparation for life—and its adoption of aims in advance of activity. Ends that are educational arise, instead, from within authentic action—from present engagement with life, and others. In classroom discourse, this notion may embrace the importance of "teachable moments," but particularly also those of contradiction, tension, difficulty, and awkwardness as well, and perhaps particularly so. Hospitality acknowledges the mystery and "moreness"[18] of human engagement with the other, including moments of brokenness, stuckness, and vulnerability, as well as progress and possibility.

Hospitality here calls for "an alternative way to think about identity and receiving the 'other'" (Newman, 2004, p. 91). Home actually embodies extensions of ourselves, and it is difficult to receive someone there for long and remain strangers. In this way, a hospitable education is far more self-involving, unpredictable, and risky than that to which we are used: "We do not know what we will discover about the other person or ourselves and how that will impact our lives" (p. 92). In education, this speaks as much to teaching as a vulnerable way of being—the impact of the student upon the teacher—as to its potentially transformative presence in the lives of students.

> "To teach is to create a space"…acknowledges both our sphere of responsibility and our lack of control…a poetics of space…in which teacher and student can practice… radical presence. (O'Reilley, 1998, pp.1–3)[19]

Curriculum, Contradiction, and Communion: The Call to "the Other Beyond its Other"

As such, hospitality in our work is what Newman (2004) describes as a form of:

> …testimony to the brokenness…, while [at] the same time reaching across that brokenness, at once a sign of disunity and hope….welcomed into the life that sustains…, even as our mutual identities…in all their historical particularities, rooted as these are in generations…from different places and times…allowed…to be both guest, receiving the blessing, and host, witnessing to the brokenness…a genuine exchange…. (p. 93)

Awad Ibrahim (2005)—whose "bio-geo/graphy" from Sudan through France to Canadian citizenship toward work in a U.S. university teaching teachers in Ohio, whose reception is predicated upon his name and accent and black immigrant body—engages the question of hospitality through his experience as a foreigner.[20] He finds he must ask the questions of contradiction and beyondness—especially in seeking as the foreigner to become host, in finding his foreignness a resource for hosting, for welcoming his students as teacher. Via what he calls a kind of Freireian praxis, he experiences the giving and gift of hospitality in his teaching as an unconditioned invitation to "a space of deskinning ourselves from ourselves and our comfortable subject positions and hence be able to meet at the rendezvous of true and absolute generosity,…at the rendezvous of humanity" (p 159-160).

Hospitality asks that we embrace Nietzsche's epistemology of the wanderer (Deleuze, 1973), nomadic thought, and life *intermezzo* (Deleuze & Guatarri, 1980/1987), and affirm with Michel Serres (1991/1997) that "learning launches wandering" (p. 8). Yet, it simultaneously calls us to dwell, to connect, to commit, to live in radical openness to the other, risking ourselves, and not as accidental or international tourists. Derrida (1997/2000, 2002), in opening us up here to the question of hospitality, reminds us of the dangers, as well as the delights: the ultimate *indeterminability* of hospitality as lived in radical openness to that which is other. The possibility of transformation is ever present and probable, the encounter with the other beyond its other unknown and inescapable. In encounters with the otherness that is curriculum, one's identity itself is challenged and transformed: in teaching and learning, we are called to die to a part of ourselves such that the new may be born within us—here, too, is the child in our midst we are called to welcome. In the "understanding" of Gadamer (1960/1992), understanding is a happening that only occurs with a "fusion of horizons"—our individual, self-contained horizons thus must be open to giving-way. Can we share understanding, ourselves—move beyond ourselves, each other—without losing ourselves or each other; without dismissing the alterity of otherness, our irreducible and irreplaceable uniqueness; without failing to acknowledge and experience our mutual and exquisite humanness,[21] our common and beautiful humanity?

Post(Partum)-Script to the Question(ing)

...for there is no place at all that isn't looking at you. You must change your life. (Rilke, 1981, p. 147)

But somewhere there is a great mystery that wants to come live in your house and change everything. (O'Reilley, 1998, p. 48)

Indeed, the labors of academia—especially those in curriculum studies—do require and lay claim to the call of hospitality; albeit as we have found, the night has been dark indeed therein as well—little, if any, room having been given to or made for this call. My hope has been that entertaining hospitality here but for a twinkling-star, moonshine-silver moment has reminded us to open ourselves ever to other and deeper, to the "step of stranger," understandings of our way and work. The question of hospitality is, I submit, one we must ever raise and risk—as at the heart of our humanity, as of the essence of education that embraces our exquisite humanness. Ours, perhaps then, in and out of "post"-curriculum studies, is to offer spaces and places of welcome, to invite questioning and conversation, to make, take and remake, room for the strange otherness in our midst that ever calls and questions us. In this way, we must always ask, we must ever live in the question, with the other, at least hospitably, lest the other ever stay other. For herein is the place and space that makes "making room" even possible, by which we come to know who the other is—the other within ourselves too—and truly welcome her or him, giving birth as well to the new within and between us and in our midst.

Before and beyond reconceptualist work in curriculum, the pressing, pregnant power to conceive, to cultivate, our humanity via education calls: From fostering the new life in our midst to fulfilling the democratic vision of peace, we labor to carry on and include the cultural wisdom of all those who have come before, to counter that which dehumanizes and distracts from the dreams we share, and to create the perhaps even undreamed-of-before possibilities that dwell as-yet in the great beyond us. Ironically, though, in our forgetfulness of being (Heidegger, 1927/1962), addiction to doing, and prejudice toward progress, we may lose the understanding and experience of what we have loved until now—the inn of our embodied humanity, the home where is the heart, the question of hospitality itself. Here, what we have loved via the reconceptualist movement may be embraced anew—through the silver night, under starry night—from the manger of the present moment (however strange) in the postpartum labors of love. Perhaps, herein, even labor gives way to laughter, the laughter that heals, in a "peopled" place—of wise men and women, and welcoming—of inexplicable vastness and promise, as well as beauty and joy.

Notes

1. The use of post(partum) here engages a play on the notion of posttimes, engaging post-philosophies—as well as the postulation of a post-reconceptualist moment in curriculum studies. In identifying this moment in the field with the reconceptualist movement—both affiliated with and moving beyond it—this kind of inquiry into the present moment of curriculum studies implicitly raises questions about what has been (re-)conceptualized, (re-)conceived, given birth to anew, in the field, in addition to those concerned with what we do in the present with this legacy, and with where we go from here. I am clearly also playing on the widely known syndrome "postpartum depression" in exploring the want of room, want of hospitality, with respect to our own present postlabors in the field—a kind of night perhaps ever accompanying each new birth.

2. Recent efforts to internationalize curriculum studies, via the founding of the International Association for the Advancement of Curriculum Studies (IAACS), to support conversations within and across national and regional borders, suggests a present openness to sharing with and listening to others, the other, and that, from a variety of intellectual traditions and perspectives (see http://www.iaacs.org; Gough, 2004; Pinar, 2003). The renewed interest in cosmopolitanism in ethics and education (i.e., Appiah, 2006, Hansen, 2007; Snauwaert, 2002, 2006) also reflects this direction.

3. This turn of phrase is rich in its meaning and import, taken from Paulo Freire (1970/1995), in the way of highlighting the dialogic call of an education that humanizes, inviting all to speak their own words and name their own worlds, as it were. In engagement here with it, I also seek to call attention to the interpretive/hermeneutical and experiential nature of education, undertaken through an encounter with an other—whether word- or world-referential, as well as the poststructural orientation to "reading" via Derrida, popularly summarized in the statements: "There is nothing outside of the text; there is nothing but what is outside of the text."

4. Our times are inhospitably similar—for all (Sutherland, 2006), if not particularly for children (i.e., Kliewer, 1998; Kozol, 1991; Polakow, 1993; Quinn, 2003; Steinberg & Kincheloe, 1997), considering the "herods" of classism, racism, sexism, ablism, and corporate consumerism, among others, and the construction and maintenance of "Inns of Exclusion" by them.

5. There is also a growing body of literature lamenting the "ground" academia itself has lost within the academic institution as a result of globalization and corporatization (i.e., Astin & Astin, 1999; Buchbinder & Rajagopal, 1996; Newson, 1992; Shahjahan, 2005; Slaughter & Leslie, 1997).

6. Greene's (1988) work on her struggle "to find (or create) an authentic public space" (p. xi), in which she herself is also included, and Miller's (1990) project to "create those spaces in which all teachers' voices may be acknowledged and valued" (p. xi) speak to and reflect in important ways this issue. Poststructural work in curriculum studies has oft also focused on the gaps and spaces within which we work, perhaps subversively, to realize possibilities within seemingly "roomless" educational realities.

7. For more on this sense of the religious and its relation to education, see Quinn (2001), and Wexler (1996, 2000, 2002).

8. In more recent work, Wang (2004) builds on the work of Aoki's (2005) third space to uncover the potential of an in-between. Here hospitality resides in a liminal space (invitation-visitation) that makes possible the dynamic play of receptivity and self-activity (Pinar, 2006). I am playing with this space in the excessive citations and quotations that follow, and also doing so to evoke the sense of a lively conversation already at play in the field, involving a number of reconceptualist (pre- and post- as well) voices.

9. Through Greene's emphasis here, we see not only the ground for curriculum thought informed by aesthetics and literary theory but also the foreshadowing of important reconceptualist/post-reconceptualist work around "queering" curriculum studies (i.e., Miller, 1998; Pinar, 1994), as well.

10. In *Being and Time* (1927/1962), Heidegger's analysis of human being as *Dasein* emphasizes the assertion that the being that is human is, in fact, constituted by and through its "there."

11. Issues might be raised about the gendered construction of hospitality (McNulty, 2007), although I do not engage them here. Additionally, there are strong histories within the Christian tradition concerning this virtue and practice (see Oden, 2001; Sutherland, 2006), as well as the heritage of "Southern hospitality."

12. For Kant, universal hospitality pertains to the law of world citizenship, and is a condition peace requires. Here, the stranger has the right, which all humans have, upon arrival in the land of another, not to be treated as an enemy, but rather to a temporary sojourn, to associate. Owing to our common possession of the earth's surface, we are called to engage the presence of each other, and once, none had more claim to a particular part of the earth than did any other. In relation to world migrations and immigrant rights issues perhaps, there has been a rise in interest in Kant's work on peace, as well as this concern of hospitality.

13. Derrida emphasizes here the two faces of hospitality—visitation and invitation, at once in competition and incompatible, not dialectical moments in the experience of hospitality; he highlights the contradictory "madness" of the concept of hospitality; that is, to wait without waiting and await the absolutely unexpected.

14. The central metaphor for hospitality across many traditions involves the sharing and breaking of bread. bell hooks and Cornell West (1991) implicitly link the work of academia, as well, with this image, as evidenced in the title of their book: *Breaking Bread: Insurgent Black Intellectual Life.* Huebner (1999), as well, in positing teaching as an art—of giving and sharing, draws upon the poetry of Robert Browning: "God uses us to help each other so, *Lending our minds out* [italics added]…" (p. 24).

15. There is support, in fact, within the scientific community of the efficacy of laughter in healing serious illness like heart disease or cancer (i.e., Siegel, 1986).

16. We possess a growing legacy in the field, particularly through holistic, ecological, feminist, and ecofeminist perspectives, that work to address the obstacles to an embodied education, and imagine its vision in practice (i.e., Jardine, 1998; Riley-Taylor, 2002).

17. Joy here is clearly linked to the aesthetic, the poetic, the beautiful. "Post"-curriculum studies, building on a strong reconceptualist inheritance here, can work further to articulate and actualize hospitable posture and praxis sublime in the way of redressing and expressing our "bliss." Laughter here may be conceived as a counternarrative (Malewski, personal communication, January 2007), or perhaps a counter nonnarrative, and remedy, to the narrative and dis-course of alienation (i.e., notice the connection here with alien and stranger).

18. This term of Dwayne Huebner (1999) is referential of the spiritual, the reality that the human being dwells in the transcendent, that the transcendent dwells within the human being—the understanding that we know more than we can say, say more than we know, and that there is also more than we can ever know; that we are, too, more than we currently are, our not yet—there is an ever-abiding "moreness" to life.

19. What might it mean to theorize and practice presence in these postcurriculum times—*presencing* and *post-ing* critical geographies of teaching (Hargreaves, 2001) in relation to the third space, hybrid face (Asher, 2005), in the in-between time of texts, for example?

20. See also Rosello (2001). *Postcolonial hospitality: The immigrant as guest.*

21. I have adopted this turn of phrase I love from Thomas A. Forsthoefel's work in *Soulsong: Seeking Holiness, Coming Home* (2006).

References

Aoki, T. (2005). *Curriculum in a new key: The collected works of Ted T. Aoki*. Mahwah, NJ: Erlbaum.

Appiah, K. (2006). *Cosmopolitanism: Ethics in a world of strangers*. New York: Norton.

Asher, N. (2005). Engaging postcolonial and feminist perspectives for a multicultural education pedagogy, *Teachers College Record, 107*(5), 1079–1106.

Astin, A., & Astin, T. (1999, November). *Meaning and spirituality in the lives of college faculty: A study of value, authenticity and stress* (Higher Education Research Institute Monograph). Los Angeles: University of California.

Beck, D. (1993). *Visiting generations*. Bragg Creek, Alberta: Makyo Press.

Buchbinder, H., & Rajagopal, P. (1996). Canadian universities: The impact of free trade and globalization, *Higher Education, 31*, 283–299.

Conde-Frazier, E. (2004). From hospitality to shalom. In E. Conde-Frazier, S. S. Kang, & G. A. Parrett (Eds.), *A many colored kingdom: Multicultural dynamics for spiritual formation* (pp. 167–210). Grand Rapids, MI: Baker Academic.

Deleuze, G. (1973). Nomad thought. In D. Allison (Ed.), *The new Nietzsche* (pp. 142–149). Cambridge, MA: MIT Press.

Deleuze, G., & Guattari, F. (1987). *A thousand plateaus: Capitalism and schizophrenia* (B. Massumi, Trans.). Minneapolis: University of Minnesota Press. (Original work published 1980)

Derrida, J. (1981). *Dissemination* (B. Johnson, Trans.). Chicago: University of Chicago Press. (Original work published 1972)

Derrida, J. (1990). Force of law: "The mystical foundation of authority." *Cardozo Law Review, 11*(5–6), 919–1044.

Derrida, J. (2000). Step of hospitality/No hospitality. In A. Dufourmantelle & J. Derrida (Eds., R. Bowlby, Trans.), *Of hospitality* (pp. 75–160). Stanford, CA: Stanford University Press. (Original work published 1997)

Derrida, J. (2002). Hostipitality. In G. Anidjar (Ed.), *Acts of religion* (pp. 356–420). New York: Routledge.

Dickinson, E. (1961). I dwell in possibility. In T. H. Johnson (Ed.), *The complete poems of Emily Dickinson* (p. 657). New York: Little Brown.

Doll, W. (1993). *A post-modern perspective on curriculum*. New York: Teachers College Press.

Doll, W. (2002). Ghosts and the curriculum. In W. E. Doll, Jr. & N. Gough (Eds.), *Curriculum visions* (pp. 23–70). New York: Lang.

Forsthoefel, T. (2006). *Soulsong: Seeking holiness, coming home*. Maryknoll, NY: Orbis Books.

Fowler, L. (2005). A curriculum of difficulty and "the anger in our Miss Maple": The story and the commentary. Retrieved August 25, 2005, from http://www.langandlit.ualberta.ca/archives/vol32papers/fowler.htm

Freire, P. (1995). *Pedagogy of the oppressed*. (M. Ramos, Trans.). New York: Continuum. (Original work published 1970)

Gadamer, H-G. (1992). *Truth and method*. (J. Weinsheimer & D. Marshall, Trans.).New York: Crossroad. (Original work published 1960)

Gough, N. (2004). A vision for transnational curriculum inquiry. *Transnational Curriculum Inquiry, 1*(1). Retrieved October 17, 2007, from http://nitinat.library.ubc.ca/ojs/index.php/tci.

Greene, M. (1973). *Teacher as stranger: Educational philosophy for the modern age*. Belmont, CA: Wadsworth.

Greene, M. (1988). *The dialectic of freedom*. New York: Teachers College Press.

Hansen, D. (2007, February). *The idea of a cosmopolitan education as a response to a changing world*. Special lecture presented at Teachers College, Columbia University, New York.

Hargreaves, A. (2001, December). Emotional geographies of teaching. *Teachers College Record, 103*(6), 1056–1080.

Heidegger, M. (1962). *Being and time* (J. Macquarrie & E. Robinson, Trans.). San Francisco: Harper & Row. (Original work published 1927)

Heidegger, M. (1977). The question concerning technology. In W. Lovitt (Ed. & Trans.), *The question concerning technology and other essays* (pp. 13–35). New York: Harper & Row. (Original work published 1954)

The Holy Bible. (expanded ed.). (1985). New York: Thomas Nelson.

hooks, b. (1994). *Teaching to transgress: Education as the practice of freedom.* New York: Routledge.

hooks, b., & West, C. (1991). *Breaking bread: Insurgent Black intellectual life.* Boston: South End Press.

Hopkins, G. M. (1885). My own heart let me more have pity on. In A. Allison, H. Barrows, C. Blake, A. Carr, A. Eastman, & H. English, Jr. (Eds.), *The Norton anthology of poetry* (p. 859). New York: Norton.

Huebner, D. (1999). *The lure of the transcendent.* Mahwah, NJ: Erlbaum.

Ibrahim, A. (2005). The question of the question is the foreigner: Towards an economy of hospitality. *Journal of Curriculum Theorizing, 4*(21), 149–162.

Jardine, D. (1992). Reflections on education, hermeneutics, and ambiguity: Hermeneutics as a restoring of life to its original difficulty. In W. Pinar & W. Reynolds (Eds.), *Understanding curriculum as phenomenological and deconstructed text* (pp. 116–127). New York: Teachers College Press.

Jardine, D. (1998). *To dwell with a boundless heart: Essays in curriculum theory, hermeneutics, and the ecological imagination.* New York: Lang.

Kant, I. (1972). *Perpetual peace; A philosophical essay.* (M. C. Smith, Trans.). New York: Garland. (Original work published 1795)

Kliewer, C. (1998). *Schooling children with Down syndrome: Toward an understanding of possibility.* New York: Teachers College Press.

Kozol, J. (1991). *Savage inequalities: Children in America's schools.* New York: Crown.

Lareau, A. (2003). *Unequal childhoods: Class, race, and family life.* Berkeley: University of California Press.

McNulty, T. (2007). *The hostess: Hospitality, femininity, and the expropriation of identity.* Minneapolis: University of Minnesota Press.

Miller, J. (1990). *Creating spaces and finding voices: Teachers collaborating for empowerment.* Albany: SUNY Press.

Miller, J. (1998). Autobiography as a queer curriculum practice. In W. F. Pinar (Ed.), *Queer theory in education* (pp. 365–373). Mahwah, NJ: Erlbaum.

Newman, E. (2004). Hotel or home? Hospitality and higher education. In M. Budde & J. Wright (Eds.), *Conflicting allegiances: The church-based university in a liberal democratic society* (pp. 91–105) Grand Rapids, MI: Brazos Press..

Newson, J. (1992). The decline of faculty influence: Confronting the effects of the corporate agenda. In W. Carroll, L. Christiansen-Ruffman, & R. Currie (Eds.), *Fragile truths: 25 years of sociology and anthropology in Canada* (pp. 227–246). Ottawa: Carleton University Press.

Noddings, N. (1992). *The challenge to care in schools: An alternative approach to education.* New York: Teachers College Press.

Oden, A. (2001). *And you welcomed me: A sourcebook on hospitality in early Christianity.* Nashville, TN: Abingdon Press.

O'Reilley, M. R. (1998). *Radical presence: Teaching as contemplative practice.* Portsmouth, NH: Boynton/Cook.

Oyler, C. (1996). *Making room for students: Sharing teacher authority in Room 104.* New York: Teachers College Press.

Oyler, C., & Preservice Inclusion Study Group. (2006). *Learning to teach inclusively: Student teachers' classroom inquiries.* Mahwah, NJ: Erlbaum.

Palmer, P. (1993). *To know as we are known: A spirituality of education.* San Francisco: Harper & Row.

Pinar, W. (1994). *Autobiography, politics, and sexuality: Essays in curriculum theory, 1972–1992.* New York: Lang.

Pinar, W. (Ed.). (2003). *International handbook of curriculum research.* Mahwah, NJ: Erlbaum.

Pinar, W. (2004). *What is curriculum theory?* Mahwah, NJ: Erlbaum.

Pinar, W. (2006, May). *"Bildung" and the internationalization of curriculum studies*. Paper presented at the International Association for the Advancement of Curriculum Studies (IAACS) Third World Conference, Tampere, Finland.

Polakow, V. (1993). *Lives on the edge: Single mothers and their children in the other America*. Chicago: University of Chicago Press.

Quinn, M. (2001). *Going out, not knowing whither: Education, the upward journey and the faith of reason*. New York: Lang.

Quinn, M. (2003). Getting thrown around: Little girls and cheerleading. *Taboo: The Journal of Culture and Education, 7*(2), 7–24.

Ramsey, P. (2004). *Teaching and learning in a diverse world* (3rd ed.). New York: Teachers College Press.

Riley-Taylor, E. (2002). *Ecology, spirituality and education: Curriculum for relational knowing*. New York: Lang.

Rilke, R. M. (1981). An archaic torso of Apollo. In *Selected poems of Rainer Maria Rilke* (R. Bly, Ed. & Trans., p. 147). New York: Harper.

Rosello, M. (2001). *Postcolonial hospitality: The immigrant as guest*. Stanford, CA: Stanford University Press.

Sapon-Shevin, M. (1998). *Because we can change the world*. Boston: Allyn & Bacon.

Serres, M. (1997). *The troubadour of knowledge* (S. F. Glaser & W. Paulson, Trans.). Ann Arbor: University of Michigan Press. (Original work published 1991)

Shahjahan, R. (2005, November–December). Spirituality in the academy: Reclaiming from the margins and evoking a transformative way of knowing the world. *International Journal of Qualitative Studies in Education, 18*(6), 685–711.

Siegel, B. (1986). *Love, medicine and miracles*. New York: Harper & Row.

Slaughter, S., & Leslie, L. (1997). *Academic capitalism: Politics, policies, and the entrepreneurial university*. Baltimore, MD: Johns Hopkins University Press.

Snauwaert, D. (2002). Cosmopolitan democracy and democratic education. *Current Issues in Comparative Education, 4*(2), 5–15.

Snauwaert, D. (2006, October). *Cosmopolitan ethics and being peace: The relationship between spirituality, justice and peace*. Special lecture presented at Teachers College, Columbia University, New York.

Steinberg, S., & Kincheloe, J. (1997). *Kinderculture: The corporate construction of childhood*. Boulder, CO: Westview.

Sutherland, A. (2006). *I was a stranger: A Christian theology of hospitality*. Nashville, TN: Abingdon Press.

Van Manen, M. (1991). *The tact of teaching: The meaning of pedagogical thoughtfulness*. Albany, NY: SUNY Press.

Wang, H. (2002). The call from the stranger: Dwayne Huebner's vision of curriculum as a spiritual journey. In W. E. Doll, Jr. & N. Gough (Eds.), *Curriculum visions* (pp. 287–299). New York: Lang.

Wang, H. (2004). *The call from the stranger on a journey home: Curriculum in a third space*. New York: Lang.

Westfield, N. L. (2001). *Dear sisters: A womanist practice of hospitality*. Cleveland, OH: Pilgrim Press.

Wexler, P. (1996). *Holy sparks: Social theory, education and religion*. New York: St. Martin's Press.

Wexler, P. (2000). *The mystical society: An emerging social vision*. Oxford, England: Westview Press.

Wexler, P. (2002). Chaos and cosmos: educational discourse and social change. *Journal of Curriculum Studies, 34*(4), 469–479.

Whitehead, A. N. (1967). *The aims of education and other essays*. New York: Macmillan. (Original work published 1929)

Wilbur, R. (1988). Love calls us to things of this world. In R. Wilbur (Ed.), *New and collected poems* (pp. 233–234). New York: Harcourt.

Suggested Reading Questions

1. In what ways is education in general and curriculum studies in particular (in)hospitable to the other (the outsider)?

2. The author teaches us that hospitality might require not merely listening to but also caring for the other. How might educators differentiate between caring for the other and crafting a system of dependency?

3. If hospitality requires a vulnerable way of being how might one become vulnerable to the other while still maintaining ontological resistance?

4. How might we as curriculum theorists explore the experience of want and therefore imagine different possibilities for living together—in relation to one another?

5. The author suggests that hospitality might in the present moment allow us to embrace anew loved via the reconceptualization movement. How might we heed this call to openness in such a way as to neither consume together (and therefore remake the other in our own image) or tell the story of the other as an original truth (and therefore remain unaffected and unimplicated in the process)?

Response to Molly Quinn
Why is the Notion of Hospitality
so Radically Other?

Hospitality in Research, Teaching, and Life

JoAnn Phillion

Cup of tea in hand, and eager to delve into something other than my own writing, I picked up Molly Quinn's chapter, "'No Room in the Inn'? The Question of Hospitality in the Post(Partum)-Labors of Curriculum Studies." The title piqued my interest: hospitality, hmm, we never discuss that topic, this should be interesting. As I read I encountered more words (and related ideas) seldom appearing in academic writing—love, laughter, pleasure, joy. I also encountered an invitational style; Molly was asking me, and others in curriculum studies and the field of education, to join in her exploration of the personal meaning she finds in hospitality, how it represents (or does not represent) her labors in the field, and how deconstruction of the term illuminates not merely her personal circumstances, or my own, but also the overall human condition. After more tea, more reading, and more thinking, I felt that Molly had beautifully articulated key educational issues and raised key educational questions with her discussion of the myriad, and often ambiguous, meanings of the concept of hospitality. I also found myself asking why the concept of hospitality is so foreign and other to us, so seldom discussed, and what it might look like in our work. I questioned, as does Molly, Why is the notion of hospitality so radically other in our own work?

Hospitality in Research

As I perused Molly's chapter I reflected on my own research, teaching, and life. Her interpretations of the term *hospitality* resonated with my concerns and my feelings in all areas. Working on issues of immigrant and minority education I thought of how vitriolic (and inhospitable) the national discourse on immigrants is in the United States. A nameless, faceless mass of "illegal aliens" without lived histories, wants, and desires for spaces in which to make a home pervade this discourse. The rhetoric is that walls need to be built, bars need to be put in place, and access needs to be denied. Fear and hysteria abound. This inhospitality pervades not only the U.S. discourse but also the global discourse on immigration. Doing research and teaching in Hong Kong I am struck by the similarities there and elsewhere in Asia, mostly focused on questions of national identity, safety, and economics. In Hong Kong, ethnic minorities, and even within-country migrants, are viewed as other; as those who are dangerous, as those who are a drain on the economy because of overgenerous government programs aimed at the undeserving. Molly points out that this is the time and the space for curriculum studies scholars to enter the discourse: "Now, more than ever, curriculum studies has taken up the call to address the ethical questions central to the work of education—the heart of which is the encounter with an other" (p. 102).

As I read I reflected on the inhospitable conditions Mainland Chinese students can face in Hong Kong schools (Yuen, 2002). Since Hong Kong was removed from British rule and returned to China in 1997, there has been an "influx" of Mainlanders into the city that used to be able to close their doors to them. This influx has caused great social and educational upheaval. Ethnically the same as Hong Kong born students, but linguistically, economically, and experientially different, the government discourse and resulting policies is one of acceptance of Mainland students; after all it is the same country, isn't it? The people are the same, aren't they? One should feel welcome in one room (HK) of the home (China), shouldn't one? Yet, inhospitality pervades public discourse and the media characterizes them as other in every way—much as U.S. public discourse can characterize the growing Hispanic population. Teacher discourse on these students has parallels to public discourse; on the one hand Hong Kong born teachers say Mainland and HK students are all the same to them, they see no differences. On the other hand they say Mainland students do not work hard; their English (which is the criterion for grade placement and indicator of effort placed on schoolwork) is poor; Mainland parents are welfare cheats, lazy, and use the system, and their children will be like that (Phillion, in press).

Familiar ring to all this, isn't there? The secret story of hostility (interestingly, part of the meaning of hospitality), oppression, and rejection; the sacred story of being open and welcoming to others (prevalent in HK and elsewhere); and, the cover story of treating everyone the same (see Crites, 1971 for an illuminating discussion of secret, sacred, and cover stories). Thinking in Molly's terms, a hospitable approach would call for what Charles Taylor (1994), the Canadian philosopher, terms *recognition*; that is, acknowledgment of immigrants as being fully human, as filled with potential, as worthy recipients of care. Recognition, hospitality, would call for appreciation of difference as well as belief in our common humanity. These ideas, central in some strands of reconceptualist thought, are brought forward in a unique and compelling way in Molly's chapter. These ideas, peripheral in most educational writing, do appear in work emphasizing the inclusion of the humanities in our research, writing and thinking (Ayers, 2006). These ideas give me a sense of hope for the future of curriculum studies and education.

Hospitality in Teaching

As I thought about the global human condition, and my own research, I also moved closer to home and thought about my teaching. I wondered: Is there room for a practice-oriented perspective in this topic? (And the related, larger question of whether there is room in curriculum studies itself for a practice-oriented perspective.) Surely there is; the questions Molly poses and the discussion developed in her piece are about the living of curriculum work, the front and center places where relationships with others are enacted and where our theories and ideals play out. Molly states that the question of hospitality is "…a living question, one sought to be lived in practice—professionally, pedagogically, personally (p. 101).

My teaching is never far from my horizon of thought as I read. My teaching means the specific students I work with, most often graduate students. In my university, curriculum studies is a place that is seen as a refuge for minority, immigrant, and international students to discuss and investigate their passions (at least by me, some of my colleagues, and many of our students). It is a "home" in the ways Molly did not seem to be able to find in her university. That is not to say that it is an unquestioned haven of refuge. I do grapple with the kind of environment into which I am bringing students. This became particularly apparent as I worked with four Native American students. Through conversations with them and participation in a university-wide project aimed at recruitment and retention of Native American students, I was made poignantly aware of how inhospitable my university was for them. Courses had few if any texts written by Native American, or other aboriginal scholars; faculty, even those doing multicultural and diversity courses, seldom if ever made reference to Native American issues or people. Undergraduate students sometimes (not always) displayed hostility to them as instructors. I felt I had encouraged them to come to a dark, demeaning place, and also abandoned them as I went on sabbatical to Hong Kong with three of them having just arrived.

To continue the Crites (1971) metaphor, the sacred story was that the university, similar to many in the U.S. and elsewhere in the world, was aiming for a more diverse environment to enrich the experiences of students and faculty. The university was willing to fund a project and related speaker series, and eventually a Native American Education and Cultural Center. Things on the surface looked good. The secret story was that underneath, an inhospitable discourse, although generally unintentional, remained. There was a sense of embracing "them" and acculturating "them" to our ways, but that no corresponding changes needed to be made at the institution. Knowledge flowed one way and one way only, therefore business could go on a usual. It was only in small spaces, places such as in my home at a dining room table with food, in small increments of time, such as a 3-hour "graduate class" that these notions could be challenged, both by the students and by me. It was within these spaces and times that we developed a sense of learning from and with each other. Was there a different sense in being off campus, in my home, that created this climate? This notion of curriculum work is articulated by Molly when she says: "Curriculum work in this way is both transgressive and transformative: it calls for 'lunch-counter' curriculum that 'talks back' in seeking to create a public space where all are invited to the fellowship of food for thought and talk that nourishes and heals our full humanity" (p. 109).

Taking another twist on this perspective, how did my students feel in the milieu I thought of as hospitable, like my own home; were they at home? If not in my home, if not in curriculum studies, then where were they at home? We need to "attempt to imagine different possibilities for living there, new ways to make room and welcome, dwellings of fellowship and freedom in the work of curriculum studies" (p. 102). We need to have "room at the inn" in curriculum studies discourse for work like Molly's, work that opens up spaces for engaging in critical discussions; we also need room for more work with minority perspectives, so that students and others can find a place for themselves. The stranger needs to be welcomed and nurtured, and love is needed in these encounters. Love is not saying too much (or is it? I was told to change that word in an article in a curriculum journal a few years ago as it was too strong, too suggestive); not when students feeling unwelcome at school are driven to suicide (Rishel, 2007), not when faculty are leaving the academy because of no sense of belonging (this chapter), and not when a general malaise permeates much of our work. Why is it that, except for small spaces, the hallways of my building, my dwelling, are so seldom filled with laughter, playfulness, light heartedness, joy, even smiles?

Hospitality in Life

In addition to boosting reflections on my research and teaching, I found the concept of hospitality to be generative in "real" life. At home in the evening, after reading this chapter, a fire crackling in the fireplace, quiet jazz in the background, I told my husband about the chapter. We explored dictionaries, thesauruses, and texts on word origins, and what followed was an interesting journey of our own through the etymology of the word *hospitality*. We wandered through discussions of Charles Taylor's (1994) notions of recognition and acceptance, and explored Martha Nussbaum's (1997) idea of cultivating humanity through a focus on world citizenship rather than nationality. We touched on art, psychology, education, and returned to philosophy. Hospitality, in its different guises, fueled an interesting evening. (I have to admit that we later watched the *Daily Show* and *South Park*.)

Hospitality in Curriculum Studies

Hospitality is not the kind of topic that can be easily dealt with, conversations around the term, I think, at least as evidenced by my evening conversation, would be ongoing, incapable of one finite response or paring down to an agreed upon meaning or necessary response. That is what I love about this essay and curriculum studies in general—the discourse is challenging, puzzling, troubling, yet strangely enriching, fulfilling, and generative. The discourses we engage in shape our experiences and who we become; that is why the notion of hospitality and related notions of care, warmth, kindness, and generosity are so important. Hospitality and its related attributes are missing from much of the discourse I read and from most discourses I engage in such as those at faculty meetings.

If a renaissance in curriculum studies is to continue to develop—called post-reconceptualization or something else—and if it is to gain any influence in the broader academic arenas, then we will have to grapple with these ideas, these themes, these concerns over hospitality. It will necessitate talking across borders, if not also ideological positions and intellectual homes. I have been asked how as a narrativist I can talk to a scholar interested in poststructuralism and critical theory, much less write with one (the editor of this collection). The better question to ask is why not talk across these academic homes and discursive boundaries? Grappling with the multiple meanings and implications of terms such as hospitality is a place to start. This is the risk and possibility that Derrida talks about, which Molly eloquently explores in this work. For that, Molly, I owe you thanks—you are opening up an exciting conversation in the field and with our students in our classrooms. With work like this, I think we can be more hopeful, if not for education in general, at least for curriculum studies in particular.

References

Ayers, W. (2006). Trudge toward freedom: Educational research in the public interest. In G. Ladson-Billings & W. F. Tate (Eds.), *Education research in the public interest: Social justice, action, and policy* (pp. 81–97). New York: Teachers College Press.

Crites, S. (1971). The narrative quality of experience. *Journal of the American Academy of Religion, 39*(3), 291–311.

Nussbaum, M. (1997). *Cultivating humanity: A classical defense of reform in liberal education.* Cambridge, MA: Harvard University Press.

Phillion, J. (in press). Multicultural and cross-cultural narrative inquiry into understanding immigrant students' educational experience in Hong Kong. *Compare: A Journal of Comparative Education.*

Rishel, T. (2007). Suicide, schools, and the young adolescent. In S. Mertens, M. Caskey, & V. Anfara (Eds.), *Handbook of research in middle level education: Vol. 6. The young adolescent and the middle school* (pp. 297–322). Charlotte, NC: Information Age.

Taylor, C. (1994). The politics of recognition. In A. Gutmann (Ed.), *Multiculturalism: Examining the politics of recognition* (pp. 25–75). Princeton, NJ: Princeton University Press.

Yuen, Y. M. (2002). Education for new arrivals and multicultural teacher education in Hong Kong. *New Horizon in Education, 45*, 12–21.

Part II
Reconfiguring the Canon

6 Remembering Carter Goodwin Woodson (1875–1950)

LaVada Brandon

Chapter Overview

In this chapter the author discusses Carter G. Woodson as a reconceptualist, historian, and philosopher. She explores Woodson's lived history and the events and occurrences that functioned as a pretext for his theory of real education. Noting the effects of the inability and unwillingness of public and higher education to account for and prepare African Americans to live and prosper within racist contexts, the author outlines Woodson's belief that counterepistemologies were necessary for social reconstruction. Such alternative knowledge would act as a counterforce for the internalization of an inferiority complex among African Americans and therefore enable the ability to envision and actualize other ways of living. The author then illustrates how Dewey's notions of experience are realized through colonial polarities and that Black curriculum orientations are necessary to resurrect memories of historically silenced groups in any effort toward the promise of social change.

> Real education means to inspire people to live more abundantly, to learn to begin with life as they find it and make it better.
>
> —Woodson, 1933/1998a, p. 29)

Carter G. Woodson was a scholar and an organic intellectual.[1] He lived during a period described by historian Rayford Logan as the Nadir (1865–1965), or the lowest point in African American history (Scally, 1985). Marking the 100-year span that followed the emancipation of enslaved African Americans, the Nadir commemorates the simultaneous celebration of African Americans' freedom from chattel enslavement and the desecration of their hopes and dreams for full citizenship, economic and social mobility, and educational opportunities (Riggs, 1987). During this period, decades of apartheid deliberately subordinated African Americans' rights as U.S. citizens. Subordination was made possible through Jim Crow laws, grandfather clauses, literacy tests, lynching, and institutionalized segregation (Tindall & Shi, 1984/1996). According to John Hope Franklin and Alfred Moss (1994) the Nadir was a time period in U.S. history smeared with blatant racial bigotry as well as economic, social, and political disenfranchisement of African American people, due to an abiding belief in Anglo American superiority.

Within this social context, Carter Goodwin Woodson was a prodigy who theorized self-love and self-determination for African American people. A coal miner, an educator, and the first African American of enslaved parents to receive a PhD in history from Harvard University, Woodson (1933/1998a) believed that through studying African American history, which contained alternative perspectives to the dominant notions of truth, *real education* would elicit a new consciousness to arise in African American people, one which would shatter the dispositions that made the Nadir possible. By informing African American students who they are, what they have done, and what they must do, Woodson held that "real education means to inspire people to live more abundantly, to learn to begin with life as they find it and make it better" (p. 29).

In this chapter, Carter G. Woodson is remembered as a reconceptualist, a historian, and a profound education philosopher. Divided into three sections, the essay opens with, "The Making of an Organic Intellectual" to provide readers with a biographical account of Woodson's life. Particularly, this section recounts Woodson's life experiences that aided him in developing his theory of real education. Section two, entitled "Education Worthwhile," shares Woodson's discontent with modern education's unwillingness or inability to prepare "African Americans" to make a living in the context of institutionalized racism. The last section, section three, "Woodson's Real Education," illuminates Woodson's use of "racial politics in dominant US culture" to reconceptualize educational opportunities for African American learners.

The Making of an Organic Intellectual

Carter G. Woodson was born on December 19, 1875, in New Canton, Virginia, to Anne Eliza and James Henry Woodson. His mother, a literate woman, was Woodson's first teacher. She taught him how to read, write, and do arithmetic (Goggin, 1993/1997). Woodson's father was also very influential in shaping his son's early education. Supplying Woodson with functional education,[2] under James Henry's tutelage, Woodson learned that "to accept insult, to compromise on principle, to mislead your fellow man, or to betray your people, you have lost your soul" (Woodson, 1944, p. 35). Mastering skills education[3] by the age of 17, Woodson left home in 1892 to work in West Virginia's coal mines (Clarke, 1995). While working in the mines, he met an African American miner named Oliver Jones, whose home contained a library of Negro literature and was a gathering place for African American intellectuals living in West Virginia's coal mine community (Woodson, 1944). Often in this space, Woodson engaged in discussions on the history of the race with local ministers. Scally (1985) contends that Woodson was fascinated by these exchanges and wanted to know more about the history of his people.

At age 20, Woodson moved to Huntington, West Virginia with his parents and enrolled in Frederick Douglass High School. Each Sunday morning, Woodson carried his father's breakfast to the roadway shop where his father worked. At the roadway shop, Woodson listened to conversations between his father and other Black and White workers, all of whom were Civil War veterans. Through their exchanges, Woodson (1944) became privy to information omitted from traditional history books, such as the relationship among Black and White soldiers and the battle strategies used by infantry. Additionally, in this space, Woodson developed a passion for oral history. Jacqueline Goggin (1993/1997) holds that these narratives later influenced tenets of Woodson's philosophy of history, which held that an "accurate understanding of the past would enlighten the present generation" (p. 121).[4]

Two years later, Woodson completed his studies at Douglass and received his diploma in 1897. In the fall of 1897, he enrolled in Berea College, an interracial institution, in Berea, Kentucky. In 1898, Woodson left Berea before receiving his degree to teach in Winona, West Virginia, where Black miners had established a school for their children. In 1900, he returned home once more to his alma mater, Frederick Douglass High School, teaching and later serving there as principal.

Returning to Berea in 1902, he resumed his studies and graduated with a bachelor's degree in literature within a year. Woodson then traveled to the Philippines to teach Filipino students[5] (Goggin, 1993/1997, p. 16). Here Woodson met a missionary who warned him against Americanizing Filipino learners. Filipino students were required to use the

Baldwin Primer, which featured red apples, polar bears, and blizzards, all unknown in the Philippines (Scally, 1985). Bothered by the irrelevance and disconnectedness of this material, and forewarned against Americanization, Woodson (1933/1998a) declared that in order for a real educator to teach intelligently, she or he must first study the history, language, manners, and customs of the people being taught. He argued that a real educator did not teach children to sing "Come Shake the Apple Tree," when they had never seen an apple tree, but rather to sing "Come Shake the Lomboy Tree," something they had actually often done. Further, he held that real educators spoke with students of their own native heroes, such as Jose Rizal, instead of Washington and Lincoln (p. 153). Predating current discussions on culturally relevant and culturally responsive pedagogy (King, 1992; Ladson-Billings, 2000; McAllister & Irvine, 2004), Woodson's experience in the Philippines lead him to an understanding of the importance of couching lessons learned in and through the lived experiences of the learner. His time in the Philippines would, however, be cut short. After serving as supervisor of schools and being in charge of teacher training, Woodson became ill in 1907 and resigned his position and returned to the United States.

Once well, Woodson ventured on a 6-month journey to Africa, Asia, and Europe. While traveling, he studied educational methods, visited libraries, and met with scholars, who later assisted him in research on African American history. Inspired by his journey, in the fall of 1907, Woodson enrolled at the University of Chicago to obtain a second bachelor's degree in history and a master of arts in history, Romance languages, and literature. Completing his studies in 1908, Woodson was encouraged by his professors to pursue a doctoral degree in history at Harvard University. To support him while attending Harvard, Woodson taught American history, French, Spanish, and English at Dunbar High School in Washington, DC. In *African Americans Who Were First*, Potter and Claytor (1997) maintain that while teaching in DC Woodson found "that his students knew very little about the contributions made by African Americans to the history and culture of their country" (p. 41).

His students' miseducation at Dunbar High School mirrored Woodson's experience at Harvard. With professors excluding the contributions of African Americans, Woodson found Harvard troubling and bothersome. Woodson's take on U.S. history, which included the presence, influence, and participation of African Americans in America's history, was often contrary to the more colonist[6] sagas professed by his history professor and dissertation chairperson, Edward Channing. Accordingly Woodson challenged Channing's view on history. Asserting that the Negro had no history, Channing challenged Woodson to go and find out otherwise. After much strife, having had his initial dissertation draft denied, and changing doctoral committee chairs from Channing to Albert B. Hart and back to Channing, Woodson received his PhD from Harvard in 1912. His dissertation, entitled *The Disruption of Virginia* argued that class conflicts among Whites and enslavement were the economic causes of the struggle between the eastern aristocracy and the western frontiersmen (1912). Goggin (1993/1997) and Scally (1985) contend that Woodson's trials and tribulations with racism at Harvard haunted him. In addition, Clarke (1995) asserts:

> After serving many years as a teacher in public schools, Woodson became convinced that the role of his people in American history and in the history of other cultures was being either ignored or misrepresented. (p. 167)

Woodson likewise came to believe that a direct relationship existed between the misinformation provided to African American learners in their schooling situations and their possibilities for economic prosperity. Constructed as ignorant and slothful yet obedient and willing to serve (Springs, 2008), African Americans were denied job opportunities because of the presumed dominate belief of their intellectual inferiority (Wynter & Meehan, 1996). Consequently, many African Americans who depended on Whites for employment were left in poverty. Disturbed by these circumstances, Woodson declared that real education must reeducate its learners with alternative claims to truth while giving them skills and training needed to be independent of White owned and controlled enterprises. He referred to this schooling as education worthwhile.

Education Worthwhile

Concerned with the economic impoverishment that consumed most African American communities, Woodson witnessed and researched the cases of hundreds of African Americans who had been reduced to vagabondage and peonage because modern education had not sufficiently trained them for work, and because many White-controlled enterprises would not hire Negroes as laborers (Woodson, 1933/1998). Woodson felt "as long as one race is white and the other black there will always be a race problem. The races must either amalgamate or separate" (Woodson, 1922/1928, p. 554). He believed that as long as there was a race problem, then the Negroes, dependent on a racist system in which Whites were taught to despise them, would always be impoverished. Woodson declared:

> [T]he only education worthwhile is that which prepares a [person] for what he will have to do. [Y]outh, then, should not be educated away from [their] environment. [They] should be trained to lay a foundation for the future in [their] present situation, out of which [they] may grow into something above and beyond [their] beginnings. (p. 290)

Woodson found a remedy for African Americans' economic conditions in real education. He implored African Americans trained in classical education and those with industrial training to become self-sufficient That is, he felt African Americans should pursue the training and skills necessary to maintain life above and beyond the White community. In his book chapter, "The Failure to Learn to Make a Living," Woodson (1933/1998a) maintained:

> What Negroes are now being taught does not bring their minds into harmony with life, as they must face it. When a Negro student works his way through college by polishing shoes he does not think of making a special study of the science underlying the production and distribution of leather and its products so that he may some day figure in this sphere. The Negro boy sent to college by a mechanic seldom dreams of learning mechanical engineering to build upon the foundation his father has laid, that in years to come he may figure as a contractor or a consulting engineer. The Negro girl who goes to college hardly wants to return to her mother if she is a washer-woman, but this girl should come back with sufficient knowledge of physics and chemistry and business administration to use her mother's work as a nucleus for a modern steam laundry. (p.39)

Throughout his work, Woodson (1933/1998a) challenged African Americans to be self-reliant rather than continue to play a subservient role in a White economic and political system. He was convinced that African Americans should do for themselves, independent of White control. For "[t]he Negro will never to able to show all of his originality as long as his efforts are directed from without by those who socially proscribe him. Such 'friends' will unconsciously keep him in the ghetto" (Woodson, 1933/1998a, p. 28). Through real education, Woodson (1928/1958) claimed that "[teachers] must hold up before [students] examples of their own people, who have done things worthwhile" (p. iii). Hence, in real education, Woodson advocated reconfiguration of a Euro-centered tale that would give voice to a silenced African and African American perspective and encouraged the use of counterepistemologies to radically change economic, social, and political conditions for African American people.

Woodson's Real Education

In *The Wretched of the Earth*, Frantz Fanon (1963) held that in order for colonized subjects to be convinced of their subordination they had to believe in their inferiority. Carter G. Woodson (1933/1998a) argued that modern education made this inferiority complex possible. He stated:

> The same educational process which inspires and stimulates the oppressor with the thought that he is everything and has accomplished everything worthwhile, depresses and crushes at the same time the spark of genius in the Negro by making him feel that his race does not amount to much and never will measure up to standards of other peoples. (p. xii)

Speaking on behalf of African American learners, Woodson claimed that inferiority was indoctrinated within the African American community from a young age by way of omitting Black history from students' learning experiences. Through a hidden transcript taught in and through colonized schools advocating the superiority of White skin and Anglo values and the inferiority of subjugated people of color, Woodson asserted that African American students were convinced of their inferiority. Specifically, he (1922/1928; 1928/1958) argued that concealing Negro history was necessary for those who have been subjugated to believe in their inferiority and those who were subjugators to believe in their superiority. Hence, Woodson maintained, counterepistemologies would provide the terms necessary for social reconstruction. Knowledge of the history of the Negro, as creators of civilizations, discoverers of iron, domesticators of goat, sheep, and cattle, and founders of great universities like those found in Timbuktu and Songhay, would challenge racist claims of Negroes' intellectual inferiority and delegitimate racist notions used to school all students, both Black and White. Referring here to African American history as a history of the people, Woodson (1935) wrote in the preface of *The Story of the Negro Retold:*

> In proportion as Americans and Europeans become removed from such nonsense as the Nordic myth and race superiority, they will increase their interest in history of other peoples who have accomplished just as much good as they have. So long handicapped by this heresy, however, they still lack the sense of humor to see the joke in thinking that one race has been divinely selected to do all of the great things on this earth and to enjoy most of its blessings .

Thus, for Woodson, producing and circulating critical counterperspectives on Negro history was the key tool for dismantling racism. Negro history taken up through curricular and pedagogical methods associated with real education laid the foundations for educational practices that aim for economic, social, and political emancipation. Real education would inform later work on Black curriculum orientations for African American learners (see Watkins, 1993).

Real Education as a Culturally Relevant Pedagogy

After their emancipation, millions of African Americans lived in extreme poverty. Woodson (1933/1998a) held that African Americans' predicament was a consequence of their being convinced of their inferiority and therefore unable to envision and actualize other ways of living, both individually and in relation with each other. He argued that colonialist education taught African Americans that "[their] black face was a curse and that [their] struggle to change [their] condition [was] hopeless" (p. 3). Woodson claimed that schooled with these lessons through modern education, African American people internalized negative racial images under terms that inhibited the reformulation of a critical and self-affirming racial identity. Specifically, in the *Mis-Education of the Negro* he wrote:

> [T]he philosophy and ethics resulting from our educational system have justified slavery, peonage, segregation, and lynching. The oppressor has the right to exploit, to handicap, and to kill the oppressed. Negroes daily educated in the tenets of such a religion of the strong have accepted the status of the weak as divinely ordained, and during the last three generations of their nominal freedom have done practically nothing to change it. (p. ix)

Woodson placed at least part of the blame at the feet of African Americans for accepting such conditions. Through schooling governed by colonialist supervision, like most historically marginalized subjects, African Americans were cursed with invisibility and erased from knowledge production. The Negro had been wiped from bodies of academic knowledge, and "was unworthy of consideration" (Woodson, 1933/1998a, p. 3). Yet, Woodson felt that African Americans would need to work first on freeing a repressed self from that which distorted self-conception before social transformation and "worthy consideration" would be possible.

Woodson believed that a means to transgress this mis-education was to center the historical accomplishments of the Negro within mainstream schooling. Specifically, he asserted:

> [I]n our system from the elementary school throughout the university, you would never hear Africa mentioned except in the negative. You would never thereby learn that Africans first domesticated the sheep, goat, and cow, developed the idea of trial by jury, produced the first stringed instruments, and gave the world its greatest boon in the discovery of iron. You would never know that prior to the Mohammedan invasion about 1000 A.D., these natives in the heart of Africa had developed powerful kingdoms which were later organized as the Songhay Empire on the order of that of the Romans and boasting of similar grandeur. (p. 22)

Hence, centering African American history, Woodson sought to reeducate the masses and decolonize minds. Franz Fanon (1963) later asserted that decolonization is "the replacing of a certain species of men with another species of men" (p. 35). But for Woodson, decolonization was the praxis of real education.

As an instructional practice, real education uses epics of an honorable African-American past to "foster social reconstruction by helping students [and others] become creative, critical thinkers and active social participants...capable of refining the nature of their own lives in the society in which they live" (Gordon, 1993, p. 264). Thus, by subverting traditional historical discourses with the knowledge of African and African American history, Woodson professed that real education "would dramatize the life of the race and thus inspire it to develop from within a radicalism of its own" (1998b, p. 54). In other words, by including the memories and significant contributions of members of historically marginalized groups, real education enables children of color to recognize the lies inherent in colonialist claims to truth, to be self-determined, and to become instigators of social change. In *The Wretched of the Earth*, Franz Fanon (1963) declared that self-determination is fundamental in overcoming strongholds of colonization. He wrote:

> [When] the native discovers that his life, his breath, his beating heart are the same as those of the settler, he finds out the settler's skin is not of any more value than a native's skin; and it must be said that this discovery shakes the world in a very necessary manner. All the new, revolutionary assurance of the native stems from it. For, if in fact, my life is worth as much as the settler's, his glance no longer shrivels me up nor freezes me, and his voice no longer turns me into stone. I am no longer on tenterhooks in his presence; in fact, I don't give a damn for him. (p. 45)

Woodson held that self-determination and democratization of one's own psyche were critical components of real education because it encourages cultural competency,[7] and enables "African American people to truly think for themselves and act in their community's own true interest" (Gordon, 1993, p. 274). Fervently believing that "the education of any people should begin with the people themselves" (Woodson, 1933/1998a, p. 32), Woodson asserted "real education means to inspire people to live more abundantly, to learn to begin life as they find and make it better" (Woodson, 1933/1998a, p. 29).

Through real education, Woodson (1933/1998a) stressed the importance of couching lessons learned in the experience of the knower. This educational notion was likewise professed through the works of John Dewey. In the next section, Woodson's philosophy of real education is juxtaposed to Dewey's notion of the role of experience in democratic education.

Woodson and Dewey: Experience and Education

Both Carter G. Woodson (1933/1998a) and John Dewey popularized the role of experience in education. However, because their lived experiences were cloaked by their unique subjectivities, Woodson's and Dewey's theories were not at all similar. Woodson held that the role of experience in education should serve to counter notions of racial superiority professed through modern education. Though arguing that experience in education should be seen as communicable and in constant mutation, one that embraces a group's social aims,[8] Dewey (1916/1966) also held:

> Men live in a community in virtue of things which they have in common; and communication is the way in which they come to possess things in common. What they must have in common in order to form a community of society are aims, beliefs, aspirations, knowledge—a common understanding—"like-mindedness" as the sociologists says. (p. 4)

For Dewey, shared interest was a major tenet in his notion of democracy. He stated, "Since democratic society repudiates the principle of external authority, it must find a substitute in voluntary disposition and interest; these can be created only by education" (p. 87). Dewey believed that constituents had to possess mutual or common interests in order to participate in democratic relations (1916/1966). Additionally, although he saw interests changing over time, and maintained that values were not static,[9] he believed there must be shared values as a pretext for a democracy. For Dewey, the threat of anarchy becomes paramount when experience is not governed by education (Shujaa, 1995). Consequently, Dewey advocates for the necessity of a common strand to maintain control in the possibility of disorder. This common strand is achieved through education used as a means to "give individuals a personal interest in social relationships and control, and the habits of the mind which secure social change without introducing disorder" (p. 99). For Dewey, social change meant educating constituents so that democratic ideals of mutual and common interest as well as interaction and intercourse could be realized. But, "social change without introducing disorder" meant educating an American citizenry by molding them to embrace certain cultural beliefs necessary for maintaining a homogenized American culture, an Anglo perspective realized in schools through cultural domination. Dewey wrote:

> Beings who are born not only unaware of but quite indifferent to the aims and habits of the social group have to be rendered cognizant of them and actively interested. Education, and education alone, spans the gap. (p. 3)

Dewey believed that the purpose of education was to indoctrinate particular cultural dispositions into the young of a given society. He argued that education in its most deliberate form was to make a "conscious effort by some organized group to shape the conduct and the emotional intellectual disposition of its young" (as quoted in Childs, 1989, p. 420). Additionally, Dewey (1916/1966) maintained that education was so important that "unless pains are taken to see that genuine and thorough transmission takes place, the most civilized nations will relapse into barbarism and then into savagery" (p. 304). Dewey's concern for education, in my view, is realized through colonial polarities. *[U]nless pains are taken…the most civilized nations will relapse into barbarism and then into savagery.* His posture posits "civilized" and "savage" as binary opposites. Hence, Dewey also positioned experience in education, in binary opposition, either transmitting the knowledge of the "civilized" or regressing to the knowledge of the "savage." Consequently, in arguing on behalf of civilized knowing, Dewey likewise argues in favor of transmitting cultural dispositions of colonialist peoples who oppressed and enslaved women and people of color around the globe. Expounding this position, Vail and White (1991) state that binary oppositions positioned as either/or were formed during colonization to distinguish "they/imperialist" from "us/subjects." They write:

> It was in this [imperialist] intellectual climate, with its concern for constructing boundaries between "civilized" and "primitives" and with its wide acceptance of Social Darwinism, that the discipline of anthropology, dedicated to describing and explaining "their" cultures to "us" began to be professionalized. At one and the same time, Native Americans, Australian aborigines, Pacific islanders, Asians, and Africans came to be the subjects of racist discourse, the victims of imperial expansion, and the objects of study to anthropology, the very existence of which was based on the assumption that "they" differed in fundamental ways from "us." (p. 4)

Crafted by anthropologists through the use of the theory of evolution, these binaries[10] made fixed a relationship between civilized colonialists and their savage subjects, established the distance between good and evil, as well as worked to justify colonization, enslavement, and oppression.

Dewey held that in order for social and political transformation to take place, the masses had to be educated; otherwise, "influence which educates some into masters, [will] educate others into slaves" (1916/1966, p. 84). In other words, Dewey claimed that those with education would rule those without education and a dichotomous relationship between the oppressed and oppressor would remain deeply entrenched in our democratic society. Dewey's claim was seen as visionary and progressive for the time.[11] However, necessitating that the colonizers' truths and experiences be transmitted through education, Dewey disregarded the effects of colonist education on "the souls of black folks."[12]

In *Democracy and Education,* he wrote:

> There is the necessity that immature members be not merely physically preserved in adequate numbers, but they be initiated into the interests, purposes, information, skills and practices of the mature members otherwise the group will cease its characteristic life.[13] (p. 3)

Dewey's use of experience in education elevates one knowing while subordinating another and, likewise, educated some to be masters and others to be slaves.[14]

Charlene Seigfried (1996) asserts that Dewey's lack of sensitivity is a consequence of the subjective nature of his own experience. Specifically, she argues that Dewey "himself is not a member of any group whose experience has been systematically distorted and therefore has not developed a sensitivity to some specific limitations of his own experiential understandings" (p. 170). Hence, Dewey's *being in the world* shaped his vision of experience and education through the lens of American colonialism. However, Woodson's *being in the world* informed his call to visualize experience and education as a tool for social change. Woodson theorized from what Boisvert calls the "tragic dimension in human reality" (cited in Haskins & Seiple, 1999, p. xiv).[15] Tragic dimensions in human experiences are those experiences of Native American, African American, Asian American, and Latin American peoples who were mutilated, silenced, and exploited as a result of Anglo American colonization, conquest, or enslavement. Consequently, the epistemologies of Native Americans, African Americans, Asian Americans, Native Americans, and Latin Americans are those deemed educable, but not educative, in United States schooling. Woodson (1933/1998) wrote:

> The so-called modern education, with all its defects, however, does others so much more good than it does the Negro, because it has been worked out in conformity to the needs of those who have enslaved and oppressed weaker people. (p. xii)

In real education, Woodson used Black history to resurrect the memories of those historically silenced in an effort to incite social change. However, he was not alone in theorizing a model of education for African Americans. W. E. B. DuBois and Booker T. Washington also professed models of education to meet the needs of African Americans.

Woodson's notion of real education resonated with the theories of Booker T. Washington and W. E. B. DuBois. These two African American philosophers preceded Woodson in generating theoretical claims on behalf of African Americans (Gordon, 1993). Both theorists' postures were formed immediately following the emancipation of formerly enslaved African Americans. Booker T. Washington, an accommodationalist and renowned supporter of industrial education, maintained that African Americans needed to be apolitical and provided with education that enhanced their efficiency in the fields of agriculture and domestic science.[16] On the other hand, W. E. B. DuBois, a supporter of classical liberal education, argued that African Americans' "book learning" needed to be an impetus for racial uplift and provide "the talented tenth" with faculties for political participation (Anderson, 1988). Hence, according to DuBois, education should bestow onto the leaders of our race "analytical and critical faculties to help students become worldly, tolerant, and capable of significant societal participation…and planned transformation" (Watkins, 1993, p, 328). Woodson's notion of real education borrowed from and reshaped both Washington's and DuBois' perspectives. Like Washington, Woodson held that Negroes should learn to be more efficient in those occupations in which they were granted employment; that is, agriculture, domestic science, and later industry during the 1930s (Woodson, 1928/1958, p. 287). And, like DuBois, Woodson believed that an educated class was necessary for promoting novelties of thought that would advance African Americans (Woodson, 1933/1998). However, Woodson (1998) asserted that neither industrial nor classical education prepared African Americans for "what they must do" (p. 44). He argued that industrial education for African Americans was merely the mastering of techniques that had been discarded by industries and that classical education's disciplines served only to indoctrinate self-hate in "educated Negroes," as well as contempt for their African American brothers and sisters. Woodson (1933/1998a) maintained:

> Neither [industrial education] nor the struggling higher institutions of a classical order established about the same time, however, connected the Negroes very closely with life as it was. These institutions were concerned rather with life as they hoped to make it. When the Negro found himself deprived of influence in politics, therefore, and at the same time unprepared to participate in the higher functions in the industrial development that this country began to undergo, it soon became evident to him that he was losing ground in the basic things of life. He was spending his time studying about the things that had been or might be, but he was learning little to help him to do better the tasks at hand. (p. 11)

Woodson's vision for African American education and racial uplift was neither pessimistic nor optimistic. It was pragmatic, "wrought out of the reality and history of the African American experience in America" (Gordon, 1993, p. 273)

When Carter Goodwin Woodson reconceptualized ways of being and knowing for African American learners during the 1930s, he theorized real education. Today, many theories embracing best practices for teaching children of color and other historically marginalized groups are commonly accounted for in theories regarding culturally relevant pedagogy (Bridglall, 2006; Brown, 2007; Cooper, 2003; Hyland & Noffke, 2005; Lovelace & Wheeler, 2006; Rozansky-Lloyd, 2005; Seidi, 2007). However, few reference Woodson or his contributions to the fields of educational philosophy generally or within multicultural education specifically. Centering *real education* as a theoretical notion used to advance educational opportunities for historically marginalized learners, this memoir was written as a call to remember Carter G. Woodson, his works, his theory, and his vision for social change.

Notes

1. In *The American Evasion of Philosophy*, Cornel West (1989) uses this term to refer to DuBois, who he calls the Jamesian organic intellectual. An organic intellectual is a grassroots intellectual/pragmatist. I hold that Woodson is also an organic intellectual.

2. Explaining functional education, William Watkins (1993), in *Black Curriculum Orientations: A Preliminary Inquiry* holds: "[P]reparation of life is at the center of the functionalist curriculum. Consistent with colonial education, functionalism is typically basic, largely oral, and frequently includes folklore as part of its curriculum. Learning occurs through imitation, recitation, memorization, and demonstration. A functionalist curriculum shuns abstractions. It is tied to the practical, the useful, and the demonstrable" (p. 325).
3. In *Going to School: The African American Experience,* Booker Peeks (1990) held that skills education teaches reading, writing, and arithmetic.
4. Although the use of the term *accurate* may seem misleading, what I believe Woodson was positing is that multiple perspectives enable one to better understand an event.
5. In 1898, the Treaty of Paris ended the Spanish-American War. As a consequence of the Treaty of Paris, the Philippine Islands were brought under United States jurisdiction. In addition to U.S. military rule occupying the island, superintendents of schools were appointed to recruit American teachers and were charged with training the Filipinos to govern themselves.
6. My use of the term *colonist* refers to the "teaching of the culture of the power elite" (Springs, 2008, p. 64).
7. Ladson-Billings (2000) holds that cultural competency is "[t]he ability to function effectively in one's culture of origin" (p. 211).
8. For specific citation, please reference Dewey (1916/1966) *Democracy and Education* (pp. 6, 7–8, 208, 217, and 232, as well as Dewey (1938/1997) *Experience and Education.*
9. See Dewey (1939) *Freedom and Culture.*
10. Please note, however, that throughout Dewey's text *Experience and Education,* later written in 1938, Dewey is very astute in disrupting the necessity of either-ors.
11. Starting from the late 1800's, public education was free, but not easily accessible to all. Dewey's position, which advocated the education of the masses, was seen as extremely progressive.
12. Taken from the title of DuBois (1903/1995) *The Souls of Black Folks.*
13. Please note that I present this citation not to suggest that informing younger generations of their history is not vital to the existence of a people or social group, but rather to more vividly express a contradiction in Dewey's posture in *Democracy and Education* and his address at the National Negro Conference.
14. However, by the early 1920s Steven Rockefeller (1991, p. 275) notes: "The war experience and his travels in Japan and China led Dewey in the early nineteen-twenties to study the psychological, social, political, and economic causes of racism, which he described as a 'social disease' and to explore ways of overcoming it."
15. In "Dewey's Reconfigured," Casey Haskins (Haskins & Seiple, 1999) provides a critical analysis of John Dewey's notion of experience presented by Raymond Boisvert. In this article, Haskins shares that Dewey had often been challenged by his critics for "his failure to give due attention to the tragic dimension in human experience." Specifically, she states Boisvert argues that Dewey's basic pragmatic vision of the natural and cultural history of intelligence was shaped by a "Baconian optimism about the perfectibility of mankind which resisted acknowledging the primordial tensions between mind and necessity—between human powers and reaches of nature which are residually resistant to human will" (xiv).
16. After Emancipation, these were the primary areas where African Americans were granted employment.

References

Anderson, J. D. (1988). *The education of Blacks in the south, 1860–1935.* Chapel Hill: University of North Carolina Press.

Bridglall, B.L. (2006). Black American students in an affluent suburb: A study of disengagement. *The Journal of African American History, 91*(4), 495.

Brown, M. R. (2007). Educating all students: Creating culturally responsive teachers, classrooms, and schools. *Intervention in School & Clinic, 43*(1), 57.

Childs, J. L. (1989). The educational philosophy of John Dewey. In P. A. Schilpp & E. H. Lewis (Eds.), *The philosophy of John Dewey* (p. 420). Carbondale: Southern Illinois University Press.

Clarke, J. H. (1995). African-American historians and the reclaiming of African history. In M. Asante & K. Asante (Eds.), *African culture: The rhythms of unity* (pp. 157–171). Westport, CT: Greenwood Press.

Cooper, P. M. (2003). Effective white teachers of black children: Teaching within a community. *Journal of Teacher Education, 54*(5). Retrieved February 2, 2008, from http://www.questia.com/pm

Dewey, J. (1939). *Freedom and culture.* New York: Minton Balch Books.

Dewey, J. (1966). *Democracy and education.* New York: Macmillan. (Original work published 1916)

Dewey, J. (1997). *Experience and education.* New York: Touchstone Books. (Original work published 1938)

Fanon, F. (1963). *The wretched of the earth.* New York: Grove Press.

Franklin, J. H., & Moss, Jr., A. A. (1994). *From slavery to freedom: A history of African Americans.* New York: McGraw-Hill.

Goggin, J. (1997). *A life in Black history: Carter G. Woodson.* Baton Rouge, LA: Louisiana State University Press. (Original work published 1993)

Gordon, B. M. (1993). Toward emancipation in citizenship education: The case of African American cultural knowledge. In L. Castenell, Jr. & W. Pinar (Eds.), *Understanding curriculum as racial text: Representations of identity and difference in education* (pp. 263–284). New York: SUNY Press.

Hyland, N. E., & Noffke, S. E. (2005). Understanding diversity through social and community inquiry: An action research study. *Journal of Teacher Education, 56*(4), 367. Retrieved January 13, 2008, from http://www.questia.com/pm

King, J. E. (1992, Summer) Diaspora literacy and consciousness in the struggle against miseducation in the black community. *Journal of Negro Education, 61*(3).

Ladson-Billings, G. (2000). Fighting for our lives. *Journal of Teacher Education 51*(3). Retrieved December 7, 2008, from http://www.questia.com/pm

Lovelace S., & Wheeler, T. R. (2006). Cultural discontinuity between home and school language socialization patterns: Implications for teachers. *Education, 127*(2). Retrieved October 29, 2007, from http://www.questia.com/pm

McAllister, G., & Irvine, J. J. (2004). Cross cultural competency and multicultural teacher education. *Review of Educational Research, 70*(1), 3–24.

Potter, J., & Claytor, C. (1997). *African Americans who were first.* New York: Cobble Hill Books.

Riggs, M. (Producer/Director). (1987). *Ethnic notions* [Video]. (Available from California Newsreel, 149 9th Street/420, San Francisco, CA 9410)

Rozansky-Lloyd, C. (2005). African Americans in schools: Tiptoeing around racism. *The Western Journal of Black Studies, 29*(3). Retrieved October 29, 2007, from http://www.questia.com/pm

Scally, S. A. (1985). *Carter G. Woodson: A bio-bibliography.* Westport, CT: Greenwood Press.

Seidi, B. (2007). Working with communities to explore and personalize culturally relevant pedagogies: "Push, double images, and raced talk." *Journal of Teacher Education, 58*(2). Retrieved January 7, 2007, from http://www.questia.com/pm

Seigfried, C. (1996). *Pragmatism and feminism.* Chicago: University of Chicago Press.

Shujaa, M. (Ed.). (1995). *Too much schooling, Too little education: A paradox of black life in white societies.* Trenton, NJ: Africa World Press.

Springs, J. H. (2008). *The intersection of cultures: Multicultural schools and culturally relevant pedagogy in the United States and the global economy* (4th ed.). New York: Routledge .

Tindall, G. B., & Shi, D. (1996). *American: A narrative history.* New York: Norton. (Original work published 1984)

Vail, L., & White, L (1991). *Power and the praise poem: Southern African voices in history.* Charlottesville, VA: University Press of Virginia.

Watkins, W. (1993). Black curriculum orientations: A preliminary inquiry. *Harvard Educational Review, 63*(3), 321–336.

West, C. (1989). *The American evasion of philosophy: A genealogy of pragmatism.* Madison: University of Wisconsin Press.

Woodson, C. G. (1912). *The disruption of Virginia*. Unpublished doctoral dissertation, Harvard University, Cambridge, MA.

Woodson, C. G. (1928). *The negro in our history*. Washington, DC: Associated Publishers. (Original work published 1922)

Woodson, C. G. (1935). *The story of the Negro retold*. Washington, DC: Associated Publishers.

Woodson, C. G, (1944). My recollections of veterans of the civil war. *History Bulletin*. Washington, DC: Associated Publishers.

Woodson, C. G. (1958). *Negro makers of history*. Washington, DC: Associated Publishers. (Original work published 1928)

Woodson, C. G. (1998a). *The mis-education of the negro*. Trenton, NJ: Africa World Press. (Original work published 1933)

Woodson, C. G. (1998b). *Papers of Carter G. Woodson and the Association for the Study of Negro Life and History, 1915–1950*. Bethesda, MD: University Publications of America.

Wynter, S. (Speaker), & Meehan, M. (Producer/Director). (1996). *The African culture and philosophy* [Video]. (Available from The Center of American and African American Studies, Southern University of New Orleans, Gentilly, New Orleans, LA 70126)

Suggested Reading Questions

1. Woodson argued that too often public education separated knowledge from life context, and therefore did not prepare African Americans to direct their own lives. What is the role of public education in preparing self-directed individuals and communities in a participatory democracy?

2. Woodson believed that modern education convinced African Americans that they were inferior and concealed their true history. What sort of counterepistemologies might be necessary to reconfigure the social, economic, and political conditions of African American people?

3. Given Woodson's emphasis on the connections between civilization, colonization, and White, Western ways of knowing and thinking, what curricular and pedagogical strategies might be necessary to decolonize public education and consequently meet the needs of African American children and youth?

4. While teaching in the Philippines Woodson learned the importance of contextualizing lessons in the lived experiences of the learner. How might students study the curricular construction of the racial self?

5. What role might life memoirs play in connecting instructional and contemporary misrepresentations of race in the curriculum canon?

Response to LaVada Brandon
Honoring Our Founders, Respecting Our Contemporaries
In the Words of a Critical Race Feminist Curriculum Theorist

Theodorea Regina Berry

Historian Rayford Logan identified the period during which Woodson lived as the Nadir (1865–1965) or the lowest point in African American history (Scally, 1985). This seemingly elevates Woodson's achievements as unprecedented. In the 100 years that followed the emancipation of enslaved peoples of African descent, many African Americans accomplished much more than the majority society would have preferred, given the racial climate of those times. Such accomplishments would not have been possible without the multiple avenues, assets, and perspectives shared within the African American community. If emancipation had not only freed enslaved peoples but also freed the hearts and minds of the White majority, Woodson's work may have been considered minor in this 21st century. Indeed, progress for African Americans was slowed, hindered by what Brandon refers to as "decades of apartheid" and "blatant racial bigotry as well as economic, social, and political disenfranchisement." But, while adulation of such an eminent scholar is not unwarranted, as Brandon notes, Woodson was not the only organic intellectual of that period. Brandon begins to highlight this fact toward the end of her chapter.

As a curriculum theorist who espouses and advocates for critical race feminist perspectives, I support the achievements of Carter G. Woodson and the multiple ways his work has uplifted the African American community. Additionally, I view his work as influenced, supported, and enhanced by the multiple and intersecting people he encountered and experiences he lived. Brandon presents one (well articulated) story of his life. There's more to the story and there are certainly more stories to tell. In this responsive paper, I will discuss what I believe are places where multidimensionality and the intersection of Woodson's identities and experiences may exist. Moreover, I will pose questions for consideration that relate directly to this version of Woodson's life and achievements as one who has contributed greatly to thoughts and ideas regarding curriculum for African Americans.

The Organic Intellectual

Brandon identifies Woodson as an "organic intellectual" and upholds the definition put forth by scholar and theologian Cornel West as one who is a grassroots intellectual/ pragmatist. It could, therefore, be interpreted that this is an individual who believes (and practices) theory into action in purposeful, practical ways. While it is clear that Woodson does fit this description, I yearned to see the connections between his life experiences and his life's work. As I became engrossed of the story of this man's life, I found myself wondering how his parents came to embrace education so deeply. How did his mother, a woman who clearly lived through slavery, learn to read, write, and do arithmetic well enough to teach her son before he entered high school? Considering the racial and social history of those times, it is clear she passed along powerful messages to her son regarding the value of education. This is, I believe, one of many grassroots experiences of this eminent scholar.

Post-emancipation/Reconstruction era work of a coal miner was difficult, to say the least. News broadcasts in this early 21st century have given us a glimpse of this dangerous work for today's coal miners. Yet, Woodson was "engaged in discussions on the history of the race with local ministers." This is meaningful without national historical context. Yet scholars such as Anderson and Moss (1991) and Cooper (1989) tell us about the difficulties experienced by African Americans who sought to receive an education during Reconstruction. In short, resources and curriculums were inadequate while teachers were scarce. In the meanwhile, there were White people who were opposed to our people receiving any education at all. While such conversations were, in fact, part of the grassroots experience, I wonder how the perspectives of these local ministers may have shaped Woodson's work. In what ways did the local and national racial and economic climate for African Americans influence the discussions held by these African American intellectuals living in West Virginia?

Brandon informs us that Woodson's father also held a significant role in his intellectual development. Woodson's father (and other Black and White workers) shared their experiences as soldiers in the Civil War. It was through these stories that "Woodson developed a passion for oral history." While it is clear that the love and respect Woodson held for his father would cause him to value the stories he told, in what ways did Woodson see value in the collective, multidimensional story? Did he, in fact, come to understand the multiplicity and intersectionality of the collective, unifiable experience? If so, how?

Woodson completed high school and started college but, then felt the need to become a teacher in a town where Black miners had established a school for their children. It is clear that Woodson felt inextricably tied to the grassroots community where he was introduced to the history of the race. He even returned home to serve his community as an educator. He was using what he learned and sharing it with his community.

I am left puzzled, however, by his decision to travel to the Philippines to teach Filipino students. After earning his degree, why did he not choose to return to his community to continue his work there? This question is not designed to devalue the experiences he gained through this decision. It is clear that the Filipino students shared similar educational woes to those of African Americans and American Indians. In these cases, education was designed to provide functional skills that would Americanize the students. Resources and curriculums were barely adequate. Teachers had to be (or learn to be) creative and empower their students while teaching them to be humble around the White education officials such as superintendents. It is here where Woodson is transformed into a critical race feminist. Here, Woodson takes all of the experiences he has gained thus far and the multiplicity and intersectionality of his identity as a basis for beginning to understand the students he must teach. He starts with a basic concept: "in order for a real educator to teach intelligently, she or he must first study the history, language, manners, and customs of the people being taught." With this concept, Woodson informs us that it is important, even necessary, to learn and understand the multiple and intersecting identities of the student. However, his curricular praxis is in question. While the changes he made may have been viewed as monumental for its time, they were superficial. How did Woodson truly come to know, understand, and live the Filipino culture in ways that its integration into the curriculum was sincere? In what ways was he connected to the community? And how did the community learn about him and the culture of his community?

Woodson taught at the (now famous) Dunbar High School in Washington, DC. Originally named the Preparatory High School for Colored Youth and later named the M Street High School, it garnered a reputation for excellence. Founded in 1870, it was the first public high school for African Americans in the United States. Woodson was among many notable faculty members including Ann Julia Cooper, Mary Church Terrell, and Robert H. Terrell. Many well-educated African Americans taught at this school as a result of the White supremacy and patriarchy that existed in the nation's professions thus excluding them from positions at predominantly White institutions of higher learning. In what ways did Woodson's encounters with his colleagues at this school influence his educational philosophy?

Education Worthwhile Revisited

Brandon takes special care to clearly articulate the connections between the philosophies of Woodson, DuBois, and Washington. While these men are truly considered founders of African American educational thought, I wonder whose voices are missing. Women such as Mary Church Terrell, Mary McLeod Bethune, Anna Julia Cooper, and Pauli Murray are not connected to Woodson in this work nor identified as contributors of African American educational thought. All of these women made great contributions to educational thought while engaging in their work at the grassroots level; they were all, according to West's definition, organic intellectuals. Yet, when conversations regarding the roots of Black education commence, the names of these men remain front and center. This is not to lessen the impact of their contribution to the African American community. However, these women, and many others of this Nadir period, bear messages in their work that were similar to the ideas and concepts held by these men.

Real Education

As a critical race feminist, I support and advocate for an education connected to the students' lived experience. One of the key tenets of critical race feminism is the centralization of the counterstory. Recognizing that the stories of the master narrative (usually constructed by the White majority) are centered within education, I support the inclusion of Black history as part of the students' learning experiences. This should be asserted in clear, definitive ways throughout the curriculum, as opposed to the marginalized ways it often appears throughout textbooks and school learning resources. Woodson and his contemporaries were establishing a precedent for this kind of culturally relevant pedagogy in the classroom experience. However, activists such as Frederick Douglass and Sojourner Truth engaged in a public curriculum that provided this kind of education to everyone.

A real education is not limited to the classroom or the ivory tower. As an organic intellectual, it should have been important to Woodson and others to engage in such pedagogy that was accessible to everyone. Learning from the grassroots is one thing but, as a critical race feminist, it is significantly important to give back to the community that which you have learned. Notions of inferiority may have been more easily dismantled when scholars were participating in a public curriculum.

Woodson and Dewey may have departed regarding notions of experience and education, especially in relationship to democracy; however, Woodson, DuBois, and Washington depart on the notion of a public curriculum. Both DuBois and Washington engaged in very active, pragmatic work to bring their scholarship to the people. However, nowhere in the version of the story presented by Brandon is it clear that Woodson engaged in such work after earning his doctoral degree. In what ways did Woodson use his multiple and varied experiences to lead the African American community from what he terms as a mis-education?

Conclusion

As I said at the beginning of this response essay, there is more to the story and there are certainly more stories to tell. Trying to unearth all of the stories and counterstories in Woodson's life would have taken Brandon and me many hours of research. There were not only their individual stories of teaching and learning, of living, and growing and being but there were also stories of those whose lives had been influenced by this great scholar. You see, stories do not function, live, exist, in isolation (Harris, 1997). They are intertwined with others' stories and counterstories. This connectedness makes our stories of the African American community stronger. And because there is no master narrative, no one story or version of a story, I do not accept one prevailing story—the story that says that existing norms and modes of behavior and assessment of value, worth, and contribution are natural, inevitable, fair, and neutral—each story/counterstory, bears questions and wonderings I alone cannot completely address.

And just as there is no real Truth, there is no Real Education. The key factor I gained from this chapter is the intersectionality and multiplicity embedded in one scholar's life that had a lasting impact on many scholars who followed him. While it is clear that there were concepts and ideas Lew Woodon established that could have been strengthened, he and his contemporaries laid a foundation for many theories connected to identity and praxis, such as critical race feminism. Scholars such as Cornel West, Angela Davis, Patricia Hill Collins, Darlene Clark Hine, and Vanessa Siddle Walker can all trace their roots as organic intellectuals to this particular period of African Americanscholarship. It is, indeed, worth noting the achievements and accomplishments of these scholars and others like them while honoring the work of those who entered before us.

References

Anderson, E., & Moss, A. A. Jr. (Eds.). (1991). *The facts of reconstruction: Essays in honor of John Hope Franklin*. Baton Rouge: Louisiana State University.

Cooper, A. (1989). *Between struggle and hope: Four Black educators in the South, 1894–1915*. Ames: Iowa State University Press.

Harris, A. P. (1997). Race and essentialism in feminist legal theory. In A. K. Wing (Ed.), *Critical race feminism: A reader* (pp. 343–356). New York: New York University Press.

Scally, M. A. (1985). *Carter G. Woodson: A bio-bibliography*. Westport, CT: Greenwood Press.

7 Eugenic Ideology and Historical Osmosis

Ann G. Winfield

Chapter Overview

Drawing from the work of numerous educators and proponents of the eugenic movement, the author discusses how eugenics transmutated from a more explicit emphasis on racial cleansing toward a vision of social control. And eventually, an even more implicit system by way of education that develops and maintains eugenic ideals. The author outlines the development of a science of society and its implication in promising a raced, classed, and gendered scientism. Pointing out categories such as progressive and conservative as inadequate, she highlights that leftists and socialists were also proponents of a eugenics ideology. Then, the author describes how scholars typically attributed with the origins of the field were implicated in promoting an education system that promoted sorting and classifying students based on their perceived worth. Highlighting the ways in which a eugenic history within the curriculum field has been omitted, the author turns to contemporary examples of eugenic discourse, citing examples from the work of educators such as Ruby Payne.

Much is missing. We are directed toward the substance of our understandings by our collective and individual experience, while our awareness of the influence of history, ideology, and the experience of subjugated groups slips away. What is missing must be examined, for as Madeline Grumet (1988) observed,

> If the world we give our children is different from the one we envisioned for them, then we need to discover the moments when we, weary, distracted, and conflicted, gave in, let the curtain fall back across the window, and settled for a little less light. (p. xv)

Throughout the 20th century, the ability of the purveyors of official culture (Bodnar, 1992) to divert attention from meaningful correctives across a broad spectrum of social policy at the same time as they fortified the ideological, economic, and political context in which inequity thrives, has been underestimated. And so we find ourselves, over half a century after the Brown v. Board of Education decision, in a state of what Kozol (2005) has called apartheid schooling. Eugenic ideology,[1] but a blip on a much longer continuum of cultural and intellectual history, permeates what has variously been described as *historical consciousness*, *collective memory*, and *remembrance*, such that we would be presumptive to assume we are immune.[2] Ideological contexts are egregiously absent from the text of our national dialogue, and we are well advised to examine their content as well as the external and internal mechanisms by which they are transmitted through time. Tapping in to such an understanding, it is my hope, will allow us to counter insidiousness with transformative potential.

If effective analysis of "the nightmare that is the present" (Pinar, 2004, p. 5) requires that we fully incorporate both historical rootedness and our own culpability, then so too must effective resistance. After all, the concerted governmental and societal effort to wipe out entire ethnicities, and to direct the lives of poor, non-Aryan, and the otherwise disenfranchised people in the name of eugenics was pursued not by societally marginal hate groups, but by progressives: the nations most respected universities, esteemed scientists and professors, government agencies and officials, wealthy philanthropists and industrialists, and untold numbers of working people from teachers to social workers. Operating within a power differential defined by class, race, gender, and a narrowly defined conception of "normality," "eugenics was a fundamental aspect of some of the most important cultural and social movements of the twentieth century, intimately linked to ideologies of 'race,' nations, and sex, inextricably meshed with population control, social hygiene, state hospitals, and the welfare state" (Dikotter, 1998 p. 467) and, I would add, education.

The work of examining the influence of history is not merely a linear exercise, nor is it external. History seen through curriculum theory is multifaceted and requires that we engage in personal as well as political, economic, sociologic, and philosophical analyses. Grumet describes curriculum theory as the study of what goes on in schools through the interpretive disciplines and calls upon Sartre's notion of *negation* "the creative refusal of human consciousness that says 'not this, but that'" (p. xii). Negation, Grumet argues, allows our glimpse of the future to be imbued with more light, windows to be unfettered. We are too quick, all of us, to shift our gaze, to focus on the window itself rather than the possibility it provides, and to nudge negation toward prescription. This chapter seeks to supplant our tendency to limit the process of negation through an exploration of what is missing from our knowledge of the past and explore the ways in which an insidious racialized scientism known as eugenics provided the foundation for a system of education that has served to fortify inequity ever since.

I am concerned here not only with navigating the historical terrain that has been so sorely neglected in our national dialogue, but also with understanding the underlying assumptions, motivations, and beliefs that led to the movement and continue to shape thinking in the present. Using archival data, along with the writings of a number of eugenic popularizers and educators, I explore how the eugenics movement shifted its focus from racial cleansing to a vision of social control and ultimately to a system of education "in service to eugenics." Racial and class stratification are implicated in the limitations of political democracy and definitions of success wholly reliant on capitalistic verve. Eugenics and education are inextricably linked, creating an ideological legacy that has morphed and dodged its way into the present on a number of fronts and is embedded in each of us, dictating where we cast our gaze and the foci of our analyses.

Even within the field of curriculum studies, the historical panorama is incomplete with historical accounts of the era focused on social efficiency instead. Throughout, I will argue that we (referring here not only to educators and curriculum theorists but to generations of schoolchildren who have been misled) have been severely constrained by what can only be described as an outstandingly conspicuous vacuum in the historical record where eugenics and the enveloping influence of eugenic ideology is concerned. This absence from the discourse comes from the tautological blindness that is self-reflection for the vast majority of us. Thus, we continue to tinker with the same pile of blocks, unaware, and slightly comfortable that way, of all the other blocks that surround us. We must ask why, given the far reaching, liberatory gaze of reconceptualist and post-reconceptualist curricular work, schools remain as entrenched as ever. Curriculum studies has its historical roots deeply and directly implanted in the soil of eugenic ideology and might be considered to have been developed as the basis for policy directly in service of eugenic principles. The boundary between past and present, interior and exterior, work and life is illusory—to gaze intently at it is difficult, but not impossible.

The Elusive Curriculum: Eugenics Past

> Eugenics has always been an extremely nimble ideology. It cannot be isolated from the movements it bolstered and was conscripted by: nationalism, "reform-oriented" liberalism, out-and-out homophobia, white supremacy, misogyny, and racism. Its longevity relies on these confederacies for the simple reason that even as one falls into relative disrepute, others remain intact. (Ordover, 2003, p. xxvii)

Human beings, hundreds of thousands of them, were victims of the eugenics movement in the United States, either through forcible sterilization, antimiscegenation laws, immigration restriction, or the sorting, testing, and tracking policies implemented in schools across the country during the early decades of the 20th century and since. The programs and policies of the eugenics movement, rooted as they were in streams of intellectual history long preceding the 20th century, were evident across the globe and were ultimately responsible for the Holocaust and other genocidal events. In America, victims fell into roughly three areas: poor, non-Aryan, and socially deviant. Those targeted by eugenicists included both urban and rural residents who were often deemed mentally "unfit" and labeled with the dubious term *feebleminded*. They ranged from unwed mothers and young boys who masturbated, to anyone whose poverty, isolation, language, or habits rendered them unacceptable by "polite" society.

When the American Eugenics Society charged their Committee on Formal Education with the task of advancing eugenic teaching in the schools in 1921 (Paul, 1998), their task was aided considerably by the positivistic substrate created by French thinker Auguste Comte half a century earlier. Comte, to whom is credited both positivism and the field of sociology, introduced the idea that societies evolve through three phases —the theological, the metaphysical (wherein human rights supersede human authority), and the scientific, or positive, which, according to Comte, allowed solutions to human problems to be enforced not by the *will of god* or the moral call of *human rights* but human agency and authority instead. Since, as Comte wrote, "the science of society...supplies the only logical scientific link by which all our varied observations of phenomena can be brought into one consistent whole" (1907, p. 2), subsequent arguments about social phenomena adhered to a form that delegitimized observations and perspectives occurring outside the scientific establishment. Positivism thus understood allows us to see that privileged voice and the ensuing era of boundaried, class, gender, and race-based inquiry provided a perfect confluence for the introduction of eugenic ideology within an otherwise progressive period. We have seen this particular convergence since; the superimposition of new ideas on older, collectively rooted understandings comprise the Ruby Payne phenomenon (see Gorski, 2005), the recycling of myths around gender and intellectual proclivity (or specificity), and in the resurgence of explicit race based explanations of ability embodied in Herrnstein and Murray's 1994 *The Bell Curve,* and, more recently, is the endless Jensenian debacle carried on now by a new generation of educational psychologists promoting racialized scientism.

Comte wanted to address the "great crisis of modern history" and envisioned that a "new moral power will arise spontaneously throughout the West, which, as its influence increases, will lay down a definite basis for the reorganization of society" (1907, p. 1).

Comte's positivist philosophy also considered hopeless the task of "reconstructing political institutions without the previous remodeling of opinion and life" and the "synthesis of all human conceptions [to be] the most urgent of our social wants" (p.1). How perfect a context, then, for the likes of two Englishmen, cousin of Charles Darwin and coiner of the term *eugenics* Francis Galton (1822–1911) and eminent statistician Karl Pearson (1857–1936) who together eased the transition from social Darwinism to eugenics through the provision of language and scientific validity for the hierarchical and racial assumptions that had long been an active strand of intellectual history (Blacker, 1952; Chesterson, 1922/2000; Hasian, 1996; Kevles, 1985; Numbers & Stenhouse, 1999).

Francis Galton, an explorer and anthropologist who traveled for decades among "primitive cultures" and wrote about them for the educated public at home (as did many men of privilege at the time), believed that family preeminence in certain fields was hereditary, a theory no doubt modeled on the success of both sides of his family. Galton's grandfather Erasmus Darwin, physician, natural philosopher, poet, and inventor was a venerated inquirer as was his cousin Charles Darwin, while Galton's mother was descended from a long line of wealthy bankers and gunsmiths and was the youngest of seven children (Blacker, 1952). Galton's (1889) *Natural Inheritance* so influenced Karl Pearson that it changed the course of his career. "It was Galton," Pearson (1914) wrote, "who first freed me from the prejudice that sound mathematics could only be applied to natural phenomena under the category of causation. Here for the first time was a possibility—I will not say a certainty—of reaching knowledge as valid as physical knowledge was thought to be, in the field of living forms and above all in the field of human conduct" (p. xvii).

Pearson went on to write a series of papers between 1893 and 1912 titled *Mathematical Contribution to the Theory of Evolution* (1938). Pearson later became the Galton Professor of Eugenics at University College in London from 1911 to 1933 (Numbers & Stenhouse, 1999), having successfully articulated a form of social Darwinism that appealed to the public's sense of progress by declaring that racial struggle provided the very means of improving civilization. For Pearson (1901), "this dependence of progress on the survival of the fitter race…gives the struggle for existence its redeeming features; it is the fiery crucible out of which comes the finer metal" (p. 21). Clear about the role of science, Pearson called his view "the scientific view of a nation" and argued that society could only be "kept to a high pitch of internal efficiency by insuring that its numbers are substantially recruited from the better stocks" (p. 27).

In order to achieve this level of efficiency Pearson employed elaborate statistical analysis to Galton's law of ancestral heredity and predicted that a population could, within a few generations of selective breeding, "breed true" for selected characteristics (Pearson, 1894). Anticipating the development of the first intelligence test by Binet in 1905, Pearson enthusiastically took on Galton's (1889) contention that mental ability was determined by heredity and began to apply his newly developed statistical tools to the problem of inherited mental ability. This work sparked a great deal of further research, especially in the newly developing field of psychology, and became a primary tool in efforts to limit immigration and create more efficient schools.

Of great consequence to our parsing of the operation of ideologies from the past in the present is an understanding of the extraordinarily porous nature of terms such as *progressive* and *conservative*. Pearson was a socialist, but despite his leftist political leanings he thought "such measures as the minimum wage, the eight-hour day, free medical advice, and reductions in infant mortality encouraged an increase in unemployables, degenerates, and physical and mental weaklings" (Kevles, 1985 p. 33). By obscuring the racial and class basis of poverty and advancement in the U.S. eugenicists were able to embrace a social Darwinist conception of the human condition at the same time as it drew in a broad spectrum of supporters. The role of progressive reformers like Margaret Sanger illustrates the extent to which eugenic ideology cannot be understood within a simple progressive vs. conservative matrix.

Founder of *Birth Control Review* in 1916, Sanger incorporated the American Birth Control League in 1922, an organization that became Planned Parenthood Federation of America in 1942. In 1921, she declared birth control to be the "entering wedge for the eugenic educator" and considered "the unbalance between the birth rate of the 'unfit' and the 'fit' is admittedly the greatest present menace to civilization [indeed,] the most urgent problem today is how to limit and discourage the over fertility of the mentally and physically defective" (Sanger, 1921, p. 5). That eugenic ideology was promoted within a progressive context and offered to the public as a way to make the world a better place, speaks to a complexity which cannot begin to be examined when the majority of the educated public in the U.S. know nothing of it. What would have happened if during the women's movement of the 1960s and 1970s the roots of one of the most empowering tools of the century for women were brought into the light? What if, when thousands of White college students boarded buses for Mississippi to register voters and start Freedom Schools, part of the conversation was the internalized nature of ideological tenets from the past? Would we be further along?

Margaret Quigley (1991) tells us that the "eugenics movement was not monolithic: conservatives, progressives, and sex radicals were all allied within a fundamentally messianic movement of national salvation that was predicated upon scientific notions of innate and ineradicable inequalities between racial, cultural, and economic groups" (p. 3). That policy decisions of all types as well as public opinion was predicated on a hierarchical conception of human worth that long preceded the concerns of the times requires us to accept that the stuff of assumptions is far more insidious than mere ignorance.

The remodeling of opinion was bolstered by a veritable public hysteria born of the pathologization of poverty and demonization of immigrants verified for the public by scientists and professors, lecturers and social workers. Newspapers, lecturers, and public displays warned of a "rising tide of feeblemindedness" while White Americans feared an "infertility crisis" as the birth rate continued to decline. President Theodore Roosevelt warned in 1903 that immigrants and minorities were too fertile, and that Anglo-Saxons risked committing "race suicide" by using birth control and failing to keep up baby-for-baby. Since charities, breadlines, and orphanages were interfering with the natural weeding out of the unfit described by social Darwinist tenets, the pathologization of poverty was not difficult. Prominent eugenicists such as Stanford University president David Starr Jordan (1851–1931) (remembered popularly as an ichthyologist and a peace activist) echoed a view that for many must have been something of a relief:

> No doubt poverty and crime are bad assets in one's early environment. No doubt these elements cause the ruins of thousands who, by heredity, were good material of civilization. But again, poverty, dirt, and crime are the products of those, in general, who are not good material. It is not the strength of the strong, but the weakness of the weak which engenders exploitation and tyranny. The slums are at once symptom, effect, and cause of evil. Every vice stands in this same threefold relation. (1911, p. 35)

According to eugenicists, positive (increasing the birth rate of "high grade" persons) and negative eugenics (preventing reproduction among the "dysgenic" classes) was critical to the improvement of the human race, and the weeding out of "idiots, imbeciles, morons, criminals, inebriates, and paupers" (Southern Historical Collection, n.d.). Although 12 states already had mandatory sterilization laws on the books, Harry Laughlin, leading America eugenicist, authored a "model law" which provided for eugenic sterilization of those persons deemed feebleminded, insane, criminal, epileptic, alcoholic, as well as those who were blind, deaf, deformed, and indigent. This law, eventually passed in 30 states, was less susceptible to arguments of constitutionality (and was subsequently adopted by the Nazis who sterilized between 35,000 and 80,000 people during the first year, a number which had grown to 350,000 by the end of World War II) (Black, 2003). Laughlin was awarded an honorary degree by the University of Heidelberg for his work on the "science of racial cleansing" (Kuhl, 1994).

The eugenics movement put forth coherent, consistent social programs in which sterilization, anti-immigrant and antimiscegenation activism were predominant. Despite these successes, however, research disputing the claims of heritability began to find increasing purchase in the press. One common inaccuracy (or perhaps, something else is at work here) holds that once its self-proclaimed scientific legitimacy in the form of Mendelian genetics was disproved, eugenics was discredited and denounced by society at large. Not only is this characterization wholly inaccurate, it is dangerous for its capacity to blind us to the deep and abiding impact of eugenic ideology on American culture. While it is true that the scientific validity of many of the claims made by eugenicists were called into question as early as the 1910s (Paul, 1998), this did little to dispel the momentum garnered by initial campaign tactics. The movement became, as Quigley characterized, "primarily a political movement concerned with the social control of inferior groups by an economic, sexual, and racial elite" (p.1) and education had a major role to play.

It was within this context that the "Fathers of Curriculum"[3] developed a system of education designed largely to classify and sort students according to their perceived societal worth. Prior to the 1920s, eugenicists focused on breeding and the goal of "weeding out the unfit" from the national stock within three generations. The strategic goal was to be thwarted, however, by the increasingly activist progressive public sentiment as well as new research from geneticists which showed that many of the claims of heritability of various traits (from pauperism to sexual deviance) were patently false. The great compromise for eugenicists was to shift the focus from breeding to sorting and organizing people according to their predetermined standing in the hierarchy of human worth. Scientific validation was no longer necessary, so deeply entrenched into the popular mindset were the concept of eugenics. In any case, the public was in the throes of positivistic ecstasy at the time so that anything with a graph or a percent sign was granted legitimacy.

Education provided just the captive audience that Galton (1883) had originally conceived might benefit from "the science of improving the stock [in which] the more suitable races or strains of blood [had] a better chance of prevailing speedily over the less suitable than they otherwise would have had" (p. 23). Having clearly articulated a hierarchy of human worth which held that Blacks were entirely inferior to White races and that Jews were capable only of "parasitism" upon civilized nations, Galton (1904) refined his earlier definition of eugenics to "the study of agencies under social control that may improve or impair the racial qualities of future generations, either physically or mentally" (quoted in Chase, 1975, p. 14). Some of the ways that eugenic ideology entered into public education and the collective memory of the nation were via testing, tracking, vocational and gifted programs, curricular control over history, biology, civics, health and hygiene, a retooling of the aims of education, and finally, after World War II, life adjustment education.

Education of "Service to Eugenics"

> Eugenical truth is the highest truth men will ever know. The climax of all natural processes is the evolution of man. And if man can, by the use of the intelligence which that evolution has given him, aid in his further evolution, it will certainly be the highest achievement which the powers given him by nature will ever enable him to make. Eugenics will not solve all the problems of society; but it hopes to aid in producing a race that can solve them. (Wiggam, 1927, p. 5)

Eugenicists had in mind a critical role for public education in America. The enactment of compulsory education laws in every state by 1918, along with recent developments in the field of intelligence testing provided the movement with a new vista. Indeed, when the World War I era IQ testing of all soldiers indicated that almost 50% of all White recruits and 89% of Black recruits were morons according to the newly developed Stanford Binet test, the eugenics movement seemed more important and believable. In their enormously influential textbook, *Applied Eugenics,* used for decades in high school and college courses, Popenoe and Johnson (1918) reflect the widespread eugenicist stance on the promise of education with their contention that

> Compulsory education, as such, is not only of service to eugenics through the selection it makes possible, but may serve in a more unsuspected way by cutting down the birth rate of inferior families. (p. 371)

Education of service to eugenics allowed for the "very desirable" condition that "no child escape inspection" (p. 371), a goal that in 1918 had yet to be realized by the public educational system. Further, Lewis Terman (1916) had recently retooled the Stanford-Binet intelligence test and, upon administering it to Spanish-speaking and nonschooled African American children he found that

> High-grade or border-line deficiency…is very, very common among Spanish-Indian and Mexican families of the Southwest and also among negroes. Their dullness seems to be racial, or at least inherent in the family stocks from which they come…. Children of this group should be segregated into separate classes…. They cannot master abstractions but they can often be made into efficient workers…from a eugenic point of view they constitute a grave problem because of their unusually prolific breeding. (p. 91)

This scenario has continued to be replicated virtually unabated for nearly a century now. The characterization of poor and non-Aryan children as unable to master abstraction echoes through the Ruby Payne phenomenon currently sweeping school district professional development programs across the country. Although decades of research has discredited the "deficit approach" to explaining opportunity and access in education, Ruby Payne is indoctrinating a generation of teachers with a series of books which contain "a stream of stereotypes, providing perfect illustrations for how deficit-model scholars frame poverty and its educational impact as problems to be solved by 'fixing' poor people instead of [focusing on] the educational policies and practices that cycle poverty" (Gorski, 2005, p. 8). Even more redolent of eugenic rhetoric, Payne explains that

> the typical pattern in poverty for discipline is to verbally chastise the child, or physically beat the child, then forgive and feed him/her…individuals in poverty are sel-

dom going to call the police, for two reasons: First, the police may be looking for them.... (quoted in Gorski, 2005 p. 37)

It seems likely that the resilience of these themes is due, in part, to the trend during the latter half of the 19th century in which psychology became a popular subject pursued by men of means in top European universities. German psychologist Wilhelm Wundt was particularly influential, having trained a generation of young American psychology students in experimental methodology. These students included G. Stanley Hall and James Cattell, who created the field known as educational psychology, distinguished from child study and pedagogy by its focus on mental testing. By relying on biological assumptions, Wundt's emphasis on the organism's physiology and the experimental method deeply influenced U.S. social science by basing psychological thought on Darwinian premises (Pickens, 1968). By 1914, American psychology was a well- defined discipline with clear-cut fields whose promoters were prolific and popular writers and did much to spread the popularity of instinct psychology and its role in education, the echoes of which are clearly evident today.

They echo through the work of Linda Gottfredson (2005), Professor of Education at the University of Delaware (whose research is funded by the Pioneer Fund, established in 1937 by wealthy eugenicist Wycliff Draper and presided over by Harry Laughlin). Gottfredson argued in her article "What if the Hereditarian Hypothesis is True?" that those with lower intelligence's relative risk for "multiple health and social problems" might be lowered if "education and training were better targeted to their learning needs (instruction is more narrowly focused, non-theoretical, concrete, hands-on, repetitive, personalized, and requiring no inferences)" (p. 318). How redolent this is of the sentiments of Henry Herbert Goddard, a student of G. Stanley Hall, the first American psychologist to recognize the potential of intelligence testing for furthering eugenic ideals. Goddard first entered the public eye with the publication of his book *The Kallikak Family* (1912) wherein he traced the progeny resulting from a dalliance between a misguided revolutionary soldier and a "feebleminded" barmaid. Goddard's book was immensely popular and was used in educational psychology classrooms for decades after its publication (Selden, 1999).

Differences in children required different educational responses, Goddard (1912) wrote, and furthermore, the greatest threat to society, was the "high grade," or "moron" type of feeble mind because although they were unfit (but not unable) to reproduce, they nevertheless were able to function in society and thus were a threat to the gene pool:

> Here we have a group who, when children in school, cannot learn the things that are given them to learn, because through their mental defect, they are incapable of mastering abstractions. They never learn to read sufficiently well to make reading pleasurable or of practical use to them. Under our present compulsory school system and our present course of study, we compel these children...and thus they worry along through a few grades until they are fourteen and then leave school, not having learned anything of value or that can help them to make even a meager living in the world. (Goddard, 1912, p. 16)

Thus was the central dogma of eugenics, that "poverty and its pathologies, like affluence and its comforts, were in the blood—and not in the environment in which human beings were conceived, born, and developed" (Chase, 1975, p. 149). Goddard is also famous for his revision of the Binet test and in particular for his system of classification which gave a mental-age value to "imbeciles," "morons," and "idiots." The tests, according to Goddard's interpretation, proved the inferiority of Jews, Italians, Hungarians,

Poles, Russians, and others with blood "known" to be inferior (Goddard, 1911, 1914, 1915, 1916). Goddard's ideas appealed to the public because for the first time there seemed to be evidence that connected hereditary determinism with mental ability. Past and present, we are compelled by our own ideological roots to seek out a scientific way to establish difference, and to establish divergent paths for students that have different abilities, both of which require, and enjoy, public support.

Although educational historians (Curti, 1935/1959; Kliebard, 1975/1997, 1986/1995; Tyack 1974) have focused much of their attention on the influence of psychologists G. Stanley Hall and Edward Thorndike, somehow they have managed to omit the profound degree to which both were steeped in eugenic ideology. The prolific careers of both men are well documented; Hall published 350 papers and 14 books and Thorndike published an equivalent number of papers and over 30 books (Curti, 1935/1959). A core component of Hall's philosophy was his recapitulation theory (ontogeny recapitulates phylogeny) wherein non-White people were in a stage of evolutionary development the pinnacle of which was European American and, since all groups were evolving, the hierarchical division was permanent. Hall believed that the best stock was likely to come from the middle class who should be provided with adequate educational opportunities to ensure continued success. Society, meanwhile, if protected from the "degenerate and criminal minded" among us, would by default begin to solve its problems (Curti, 1959/1935).

Having spent nearly his entire career at Teachers College, Columbia, American psychologist E. L. Thorndike (1874–1949) was enormously influential through both the provision of the Alpha and Beta tests administered to World War I Army recruits and his specifications for the design and choice of teaching materials, instructional organization, and methods of individualizing instruction and assessment. So great was Thorndike's influence that Cremin (1961) claimed "no aspect of public school teaching during the first quarter of the twentieth century remained unaffected" (p. 114). Using chickens, in boxes, with levers, Thorndike developed a theory of learning based on the premise that outcomes could be produced on scientific production of stimulus and response. What is significant about this Cremin tells us, is that "in one fell swoop it discards the Biblical view that man's nature is essentially sinful and hence untrustworthy; the Rousseauan view that man's nature is essentially good and hence always right; and the Lockean view that man's nature is ultimately plastic and hence completely modifiable" (p. 112). In this way, Thorndike was able to redefine human nature as simply a mass of "original tendencies" ready to be exploited for good or bad depending on what learning takes place.

Selden (1999) tells us that E. L. Thorndike and Leta Hollingworth (of gifted education fame) popularized eugenics to generations of prospective classroom teachers and that by using flawed racial interpretations of the intelligence test data after the First World War, psychometricians Carl Brigham and Robert Yerkes were persuasive in making the connection between educational objectives and eugenic proscriptions. Thorndike, oft quoted in the present as saying "everything that exists in quantity and can be measured" had as his goal a comprehensive science of pedagogy on which all education could be based. Neither did Thorndike limit his vision for the impact of science on education to methods but ultimately believed that the aims of education could be scientifically determined as well (Cremin, 1961).

Despite different ideas on the appropriate scope of individual freedom (particularly in their own lives), many believed in the necessity of strong social controls for some groups of citizens, who were seen as fundamentally different and inferior. Thus, the idea that social problems could be addressed through the social control of children and peoples of less evolved ancestry was widespread in the United States. Among eugenicists, Hall's approach is distinguished by what Curti called his near "sentimentality" for "backward peoples, whom he thought of as in the adolescent and therefore peculiarly sacred stage of racial development" (p. 412). Looked at through this lens, and given that the inheritance of acquired characteristics was generally accepted as well, the concepts of "child-centeredness" and "individualized education" so popular during the Progressive era and used so prolifically today compels us to investigate our use and internalization of these meanings. This language of race, class, and gender based oppression was developed by eugenic ideologues in educational psychology, is used today, often cloaked and lauded as the "progressive" (equated in the popular lexicon as "most likely to awaken appreciation for a social justice issues" approach).

Author of the classic curriculum policy text *The Curriculum* (1918), John Franklin Bobbitt articulated his early ideas on the subjects of race, class, and ability in an article entitled "Practical Eugenics" (1909). Bobbitt shared the view common among eugenicists and social Darwinists before them that social policy should seek to remove the protective characteristics of civilized society and allow the forces of nature to take its course in sorting human worth. Claiming that "our schools and charities supply crutches to the weak in mind and morals," Bobbitt's early writings further asserted that schools and charities "corrupt the streams of heredity which all admit are sufficiently turbid" (Bobbitt, 1909, p. 387). Social turbidity was the topic of the day in 1909 and the confluence of science and racist ideology was well established in the minds of many as the key to racial purity and subsequent societal betterment. In this article, which appeared in the journal *Pedagogical Seminary* (edited by colleague G. Stanley Hall), Bobbitt was confident that the problem of child training would be solved by limiting the right to procreate to individuals of "sound sane parentage" since there was little to be done for the children of "worm-eaten stock" (p. 385). In order to purge society of the unfit, Bobbitt proposed the abolishment of the public school system, all charities, and any other public agency that went out of its way to "preserve the weak and incapable" (p. 393). We will see that Bobbitt later learned to tone down his rhetoric while the essential elements of his early philosophy remained intact.

Curriculum theorists conceded, over the course of the following decade, that eradication and elimination of the unfit was both an unrealistic and increasingly unpalatable goal. Bobbitt and others set about developing a theory of education that exerted social control within these newly realized parameters. Regarded as perhaps one of the most influential curriculum texts in American educational history, Bobbitt's *The Curriculum* (1918) defined curriculum in two ways:

1. It is the entire range of experiences, both undirected and directed, concerned in unfolding the abilities of the individual; or
2. It is the series of consciously directed training experiences that the schools use for completing and perfecting the unfoldment. (p. 43)

In what I contend is a direct reference to his eugenic theoretical stance, Bobbitt (1918) further stated that "education must be concerned with both [directed and undirected training experience], *even though it does not direct both*" [italics added] (p. 43). In other words, "undirected" experiences are those that are imbued by heredity, be they functional ability or economic status.

Schools, according to Bobbitt's curricular philosophy, should act as a societal hub for organizing and sorting children according to their relative worth to society. In what was to be a long relationship between business and industry and the field of education, Bobbitt developed a model of what he called *scientific curriculum* in order to exert control into what he considered an "era of contentment with large, undefined purposes" (p. 41). "The controlling purposes of education," Bobbitt continued, have not been sufficiently particularized. We have aimed at a vague culture, an ill-defined discipline, a nebulous harmonious development of the individual, an indefinite moral character-building, an unparticularized social efficiency, or, often enough nothing more than escape from a life of work. (p. 41)

We see that the sorting, testing, and tracking developed by eugenicists is rooted in the melding of scientific efficiency with educational objectives. Bobbitt went on to extol the great progress being made in the development of scientific method for "every important aspect of education" along with the discovery of "accurate methods of measuring and evaluating different types of educational processes," so that educators might be better equipped for "diagnosing specific situations, and of prescribing remedies" (p. 41).

We might be tempted to just stop here, so familiar is the ring of the proscriptions, so clearly are they linked to the substance of "the nightmare that is the present" (Pinar, 2004, p. 5). To do so, however, would be to gaze at the window rather than seeking to unfetter it. Bobbitt knew that it was within the curriculum that deep control would be wrought. It is, he said, the "primordial factor" (p. 41). "The central theory is simple," Bobbitt explained, "human life, however varied, consists in the performance of specific activities. Education that prepares for life is one that prepares definitely and adequately for these specific activities. However numerous and diverse they may be for any social class, they can be discovered" (p. 42). We know from Bobbitt's 1909 writings, his membership in the America Eugenics Society (Selden, 1999), and the context of the times, just how the inherent hierarchy of capabilities and future professions was determined.

To discover the "appropriate" education for "any special class," Bobbitt believed, required a close inspection of the "total range of habits, skills, abilities, forms of thought, valuations, ambitions, etc., that its members need for the effective performance of their vocational labors" (1918, p. 43). Bobbitt's use of *habits and proclivities* as a tool to discover appropriate education for members of various groups effectively brings together curriculum form and function with dominant racial and class definitions of difference. The possibility that appropriate education could be discovered through measurable individual markers rested on the presupposition that education was "established on the presumption that human activities exist upon different levels of quality or efficiency" (Bobbitt, 1918, p. 48). Education had always functioned as a form of societal promise and progress, only now education did so within the boundaries of an ideology that described learning and ability in terms of race and class limitations. It was Bobbitt's contention within the confines of this definition, that "education should aim at the best" and "scientific investigations as to objectives should seek to discover the characteristics of only the best" (p. 50). Bobbitt was to get his wish in the form of testing.

We have seen that, for eugenicists, the great compromise (having reprioritized the ultimate goal of racial cleansing) when it came to the institution of education was that it direct students, according to their inherited lot, into the workplace. These end products, what have come to be known as curricular objectives, have proved to be one of the most enduring legacies of scientific curriculum as it was originally conceived. Another enduring element of Bobbitt's curriculum theory was his ability to combine specificity and ambiguity into a coherent whole. Perhaps reflecting the cultural perspective from which eugenic ideology was derived, Bobbitt's theory was simultaneously specific and ambiguous. It is interesting to note that Bobbitt's proscription for curriculum provided specificity for practical and clearly desirable skills, but his theory was vague and ambiguous where value issues were concerned (Kliebard, 1975/1997). Although Kliebard never mentions eugenics specifically, he nevertheless felt suspicious enough to refer to Bobbitt's combination of specificity and ambiguity as reflective of a "submerged ideology" (p. 34).

During the 1920s and 1930s, American youth in particular were subject to a saturation of information from every facet of their lives. From the chapter on eugenics in high school biology texts that recommended sterilization of the unfit, immigration restriction, and a justification of racial segregation, to the Saturday night showing of *The Black Stork* at the local movie house, young people were charged with carrying the nation to a more eugenic future. Local newspapers heralded the winners of *Fitter Family Contests* in which entrants submit their genealogical charts vying for a medal proclaiming "Yea, I have a Goodly Heritage" (Selden 1999). How far have we come? To what extent does ideological residue coat our own imaginings and filter the light that might be?

How We Might Proceed … Achieving Escape Velocity

> We are living in a dangerous historical moment when state repression is openly being bartered for supposed security from enemies within and without…. A historical dialectic is beginning to unfold. A nascent social movement is building as the full ideological and material force of the state and the avaricious goals of transnational capital bear down on us. (Lipman, 2004, p. 189)

Confusion, hopelessness, and invective all characterize the current debate over human agency, the role of the past, ideological transmission, and seemingly endless examples of historical repetition. In light of the state of affairs outlined by Lipman above, the implications are grave for our nation's schools. An investigation into these implications might be approached from many angles; this one seeks to elucidate the role of a deeply embedded racialized scientism which has long characterized American society. Tied to the natural theology of secularism and its basic principals of human classification, inheritance, and development, scientific racism, past and present, has been used to endorse progressive pedagogic and disciplinary practices, and has operated to define and enforce access in society.

Over 30 years ago, in *Heightened Consciousness, Cultural Revolution, and Curriculum Theory: The Proceedings of the Rochester Conference*, edited by William Pinar (1974), Maxine Greene contemplated Freire's notion of educational liberation as existing in acts of cognition. Greene (1974) wondered "whether anything can be done in schools and what curriculum ought to signify in a world so dominated by bureaucracies and inhuman technological controls" (p. 69) and found that Freire's phenomenological approach suggested new vantage points. Curriculum ought to be conceived, Greene concluded, "in terms of possibility of individuals, all kinds of individuals" (p. 69). What is interesting is that here, at the birthplace of the reconceptualization, the focus was on the fact that the curriculum was "increasingly structured by the schemata of those who think in terms of behavioral objectives, achievement testing, and management capability" (p. 69).

Pinar argues that curriculum studies experiences a sharp shift during the 1990s to a cultural studies orientation, a shift the abruptness of which may prove to be untimely because a "disciplinary throughline" has yet to be articulated. Perhaps a preliminary step to such an articulation consists in identifying the disciplinary throughline that has irrevocably defined the American public sphere from the very beginning. The foundation consists of a presumption of White supremacy in the decimation of native populations, and the relentless acquisition of land, along with a hierarchical and puritanical paradigm for the formation of a new nation. Built upon this substrate, we might begin the tracing with the contention of English physician and surgeon Charles White in 1799 who claimed that "on the basis of anatomical and physiological evidence…blacks are a completely separate species, intermediate between Whites and apes" (quoted in Tucker, 1994, p. 10), a notion which Thomas Jefferson, lauded for his attempts to pass the "Bill for the More General Diffusion of Knowledge," used to justify both slavery, and the exclusion of non-Whites from his educational aims.

Fast forward though the next century where the disciplinary throughline is refined and strengthened by the Civil War, the publication of Charles Darwin's *On the Origin of Species by Means of Natural Selection, or the Preservation of Favoured Races in the Struggle for Life*, the subsequent application of "survival of the fittest" mandate to social problems in the form of social Darwinism, the coining of the term *eugenics* by Darwin's cousin Sir Francis Galton in 1883, and the development of the Progressive era at the turn of the century. Now we are ready to identify the throughline as it has existed over the past century, providing the primary lines of demarcation for the system of education within which we, our parents, grandparents, and children all have been educated.

Anticipating the rhetoric of "standards and accountability" in the 21st century, Charles Davenport declared in 1911 that "the relation of eugenics to the vast efforts put forth to ameliorate the condition of our people, especially in crowded cities, should not be forgotten" (p. 254). Davenport aptly reflects the deeply embedded ideological throughline that has defined the public debate over education ever since:

> Education is a fine thing and the hundreds of millions annually spent upon it in our country are an excellent investment. But every teacher knows that the part he plays in education is after all a small one...the expert teacher can do much with good material; but his work is closely limited by the protoplasmic makeup—the inherent traits of his pupils. (Davenport, 1911, p. 255)

How shall we debate, argue, and despair over the No Child Left Behind Act as an unfunded mandate, as overreliant on standardized tests, and over the callous disregard for the social inequalities? Perhaps we cannot do so. I suggest that to engage in the details of the manifestation of an ideological throughline to which we are utterly opposed is to have our strength sapped, our vision subsumed, our complicity masked. We already know that the present historical moment is engaged in a systematic devaluing of everything that is not tested, that the authority of official knowledge remains unchallenged in the curriculum, and that broad, liberatory aims for schooling have yet to be realized. What we are less clear about is why. The debate has not identified the core of itself, and as a result, liberals, progressives, conservatives, and traditionalists have too often blurred, blended, and overlapped. Stephen Steinberg (1995) understands this, writing that

> the enemy depends on the so-called liberal to put a kinder and gentler face on racism; to subdue the rage of the oppressed; to raise false hopes that change is imminent; to moderate the demands for complete liberation; to divert protest; and to shift the onus of responsibility...from powerful institutions that could make a difference onto individuals who have been rendered powerless by those very institutions. (Steinberg, 1995, p. 135, quoted in Ordover, 2003, p. 131)

We are most dangerous, then, when we fail to look within. At the beginning of the reconceptualization of curriculum studies, Greene (1974) wrote that a "person brought to self awareness by means of dialogue, [and] made conscious of his own consciousness...is likely to seek higher knowledge in the effort to organize his thinking and constitute with his brothers and sisters a richer, more unified, less unjust world" (p. 82). Pinar (2004), argues that "curriculum theory and the complicated conversation it supports seek the truth of the present state of affairs," and our motive should be "erudition, interdisciplinarity, intellectuality, self-reflexivity [we must envision] curriculum as complicated conversation [which] invites students to encounter themselves and the world they inhabit through academic knowledge, popular culture, grounded in their own lived experience" (p. 208). The disciplinary throughline has been articulated, by many, for a long time. What it has not been is internalized, not intellectually, but really.

Notes

1. I use the term *eugenics*, and refer to *eugenic ideology*, with the understanding that eugenics was but one of many iterations of hierarchical ideological mechanisms applied to human beings. In the United States, examples include Great Chain of Being theory, craniometry, phrenology, and social Darwinism, all of which were predecessors of eugenic ideology and served to pave the way for its acceptance. Terminology for the current form of this race, gender, and class way of thinking has yet to be established firmly in the literature, although I often refer to it as racialized scientism.
2. Some contend that eugenics was supported by most scientists and social scientists up until the 1960s (Lynn, 2001). The pervasiveness of support was clear, ranging as it did from Nobel Prize winning scientists Herman Miller, Linus Pauling, Joshua Lederberg, and William Shockley to leading psychologists Edward Thorndike, Lewis Terman, and William McDougall. Further establishing the legitimacy of eugenics for the public were a number of prominent figures such as Charles Wilson, Irving Fisher, and David Starr Jordan, presidents of Harvard, Yale, and Stanford Universities respectively, and finally, President Theodore Roosevelt and Oliver Wendell Holmes, Associate Justice of the U.S. Supreme Court (Lynn, 2001).
3. This is outlined in my book and especially true of John Franklin Bobbitt, Granville Stanley Hall, W. W. Charters, E. L. Thorndike, and generations of school administrators educated in the science of efficiency by Elwood P. Cubberley.

References

Black, E. (2003). *War against the weak: Eugenics and America's campaign to create a master race.* New York: Four Walls Eight Windows.

Blacker, C. P. (1952). *Eugenics: Galton and after.* London: Duckworth.

Bobbitt, J. F. (1909). Practical eugenics. *Pedagogical Seminary*, 385–394.

Bobbitt, J. F. (1918). *The curriculum.* Boston: Houghton Mifflin.

Bodnar, J. (1992). *Remaking America: Public memory, commemoration, and patriotism in the twentieth century.* Princeton, NJ, Princeton University Press.

Chase, A. (1975). *The legacy of Malthus: The social costs of the new scientific racism.* New York: Knopf.

Chesterton, G. K. (1922/2000). *Eugenics and other evils: An argument against the scientifically organized society.* (Ed. Michael W. Perry). Seattle, WA: Inkling Books.

Comte, A. (1907). *A general view of positivism.* London: Routledge and Sons.

Cremin, L. A. (1961). *The transformation of the school: Progressivism in American education 1876–1957.* New York: Vintage Books.

Curti, M. (1959). *The social ideas of American educators.* Patterson, NJ: Pageant Books. (Original work published 1935)

Davenport, C. B. (1911). *Heredity in relation to eugenics.* New York: H. Holt.

Dikkoter, F. (1998). Race culture: Recent perspectives on the history of education. *American Historical Review. 103*(2), 467–478.

Galton, F. (1883). *Inquiries into human faculty.* London, Macmillan.

Galton, F. (1889). *Natural inheritance.* New York: Macmillan.

Galton, F. (1904). Eugenics: Its definition, scope, and aims. *The American Journal of Sociology,* 10, 1–25.

Goddard, H. H. (1912). *The Kallikak family: A study in the heredity of feeblemindedness.* New York: Macmillan.

Goddard, H. H. (1914). *Feeble-mindedness: Its causes and consequences*. New York: Macmillan.

Goddard, H. H. (1915). *The criminal imbecile*. New York: Macmillan.

Goddard, H. H. (1916). *Mental deficiency from the standpoint of heredity*. Boston: Massachusetts Society for Mental Hygiene.

Gorski, P. C. (2005). Savage unrealities: Uncovering classism in Ruby Payne's framework. Retrieved from http://www.EdChange.org

Gottfredson, L. S. (2005). What if the hereditarian hypothesis is true? *Psychology, Public Policy, and Law, 11*(2), 311–319.

Greene, M. (1974). Cognition, consciousness, and curriculum. In W. F. Pinar (Ed.), *Heightened consciousness, cultural revolution, and curriculum theory: The Proceedings of the Rochester Conference* (pp. 131–138). Berkeley, CA: McCutchan.

Grumet, M. (1988). *Bitter milk: Women and teaching*. Amherst: University of Massachusetts Press.

Hasian, Jr. M. A. (1996). *The rhetoric of eugenics in Anglo-American thought*. Athens: University of Georgia Press.

Herrnstein, R. J. & Charles, A. M. (1994). *The bell curve: Intellegence and class structure in American Life*. New York: The Free Press.

Jordan, D. S. (1911). *The heredity of Richard Roe: A discussion of the principles of eugenics*. Boston: American Unitarian Association.

Kevles, D. J. (1985). *In the name of eugenics: Genetics and the uses of human heredity*. Berkeley: University of California Press.

Kliebard, H. M. (1995). *The struggle for the American curriculum 1893–1958*. New York: Routledge. (Original work published 1986)

Kliebard, H. M. (1997). The rise of scientific curriculum making and its aftermath. In D. J. Flinders & S. J. Thornton (Eds.), *The curriculum studies reader* (pp. 31–44). New York: Routledge. (Original work published 1975)

Kozol, J. (2005). *The shame of the nation: The restoration of apartheid schooling in America*. New York: Crown.

Kuhl, S. (1994). *The Nazi connection: Eugenics, American racism, and German National Socialism*. New York: Oxford University Press.

Lipman, P. (2004). *High stakes education: Inequality, globalization, and urban school reform*. New York, Routledge Falmer.

Numbers, R. L., & Stenhouse, J. (1999). *Disseminating Darwinism: The role of place, race, religion, and gender*. Cambridge, England: Cambridge University Press.

Ordover, N. (2003). *American eugenics: Race, queer anatomy, and the science of nationalism*. Minneapolis: University of Minnesota Press.

Paul, D. B. (1998). *The politics of heredity: Essays on eugenics, biomedicine, and the nature-nurture debate*. Albany, NY: SUNY Press.

Pearson, K. (1901). *National life from the standpoint of science:An address delivered at Newcastle, November 19, 1900*. London: A. & C. Black.

Pearson, K. (1914). *The life, letters and labours of Francis Galton*. Cambridge, England: Cambridge University Press.

Pearson, K. L., Napoleon, L., Filon, G., Lee, A. E., & Bramley-Moore, L. (1984). *Contributions to the mathematical theory of Evolution*. London: K. Paul Trench Trèubner.

Pickens, D. (1968). *Eugenics and the orogressives*. Nashville, TN: Vanderbilt University Press.

Pinar, W. F. (Ed.). (1974). *Heightened consciousness, cultural revolution, and curriculum theory: The proceedings of the Rochester conference*. Berkeley, CA: McCutchan.

Pinar, W. F. (2004). *What is curriculum theory?* Mahwah, NJ: Erlbaum.

Popenoe, P. J., & Johnson, R. H. (1918). *Applied eugenics*. New York: Macmillan.

Quigley, M. (1991). *Our refractory human material: Eugenics and social control*. Somerville, MA: Political Research Associates.

Sanger, M. (1921, October). *Birth Control Review*, 5.

Selden, S. (1999). *Inheriting shame: The story of eugenics and racism in America*. New York: Teachers College Press.

Southern Historical Collection. (n.d.). Human Betterment League, University of North Carolina.

Steinberg, S. (1995). *Turning back: The retreat from racial justice in American thought and policy.* Boston: Beacon Press.

Terman, L. (1916). *The measurement of intelligence: An explanation of and a complete guide for the use of the Stanford revision and extension of the Binet-Simon intelligence scale.* Boston: Houghton Mifflin.

Tucker, W. H. (1994). *The science and politics of racial research.* Urbana: University of Illinois Press.

Tyack, D. B. (1974). *The one best system: A history of American urban education.* Cambridge, MA: Harvard University Press.

Wiggam, A. E. (1927). *The next age of man.* Indianapolis, IN: Bobbs-Merrill.

Suggested Reading Questions

1. The author notes that the eugenics movement was not the work of merely fundamentalists and conservatives but also progressives and socialists. What are the implications of bodies of knowledge being remade to unmask unsettling histories and highlight what Patti Lather terms "lovely knowledge?"

2. In what way is eugenics represented via contemporary practices of sorting, tracking, and assigning work in public education?

3. Throughout history scholars such as Herrnstein and Murray have attempted to explain differences in social circumstances by way of racial categorization. What are the implications of explaining differences between races not in terms of subjugation and domination but natural ability?

4. The author draws a relationship between the historical characterization of poor and non-Aryans as unable to master objectives and the current Ruby Payne cultural deficit approach to poverty. How might educators distinguish between forms of intelligence unique to different social classes and urgent issues of scarcity most often associated with the poor?

5. The author credits Thorndike with popularizing eugenics with teachers. What sort of counterperspectives should be produced and circulated to make teachers aware of the influence eugenics has had and does have on the shape of public education?

Response to Ann G. Winfield
The Visceral and the Intellectual in Curriculum Past and Present

William H. Watkins

Introduction

My response to Dr. Winfield's essay, "Eugenic Ideology and Historical Osmosis," is both visceral and intellectual. Visceral because I abhor eugenics and intellectual because I am a teacher, activist, researcher, author, scholar, curriculum theorist, historian, and seeker of truth. I will thusly address Winfield's essay from different angles. As a respondent, I prefer to be at odds with the author because it makes for spirited polemics; however, I find little to quarrel about in this work. I have learned much from it. I encourage it and offer commentary which I hope contributes to its growth and further politicization.

What My Professors Never Taught Me

Matriculating through a rigorous traditional quantitative oriented doctoral program, we students were exposed to the conventional research literature. Our texts never revealed the ideological, especially racial views of the early behavioral psychologists, psychometricians, and curriculum theorists. Portrayed as the leading researchers and theorists of their time, only later did I find that in the words of the old Bootsy Collins song, they were "fakin da funk."

It was obvious, even to the least sophisticated of us, that education and its subdiscipline, curriculum, sought elevation and recognition in the competitive barrel climb of academia. We learned much about the scientific paradigm and its desirability. Statistical design and measures of central tendency were central to our inquiry. We were always in search of R-square. The "appeal to number" was the order of the day while ethnography and qualitative research was discouraged.

As we students toiled in the vineyards of statistical sludge, the psychometricians, testing and efficiency people were presented as the icons of measurement. We read and studied selected works of Edward Thorndike, G. Stanley Hall, Karl Pearson, Louis Terman, David Sneeden, H. H. Goddard, Robert Yerkes, et al. Our organizational inquiry led us to Frederick Taylor. We curriculum people overdosed on Franklin Bobbitt. We were told that these fellas helped make our field scientific. Eugenics ideology was absent from our inquiry. For critique and counterpoint, we read vintage Giroux (1979) who argued that our field was misguided as it unnecessarily sought chevrons in the hierarchy of "scientific" inquiry.

Setting the Stage: Toward Understanding Eugenics

Annie Winfield's brilliant essay both informs and jolts us. She demonstrates that eugenic ideology undergirds a large, even sweeping, spectrum of thought, left and right. In this brief response, I will highlight several points that thundered through and true. Winfield's book, *Eugenics and Education in America: Institutionalized Racism and the Implications of History, Ideology and Memory* (2007), and this essay, built upon that work, help us stand history on its feet. It is tonic for the intellectually undernourished.

The irreverent Winfield is not bound by convention or ideology. She speaks truth to power and lets the chips fall where they may. I must add that Winfield remains firmly within the curriculum discourses. My response will be both within and outside the literature of our field.

Eugenics remains very much with us. It gets recycled through academia every 20 years or so and rears its ugly head in the mass media. We move from Shockley (1972) and Jensen (1973) to Herrnstein and Murray (1994) to whoever is next. A letter to the editor in the *Chicago Tribune* (ca. 2005) explored why the murder rate in Chicago had not dropped as it had done in New York City. The author concluded that New York's more liberal abortion laws 20 years ago had rid society of miscreants in the womb! The eugenics train keeps on rolling down the track.

Eugenics arose in a particular era. It was the era of the economic frontier where ascendant capitalism shaped social and intellectual life. People of color were the beasts of burden. Race relations were a function of the evolving labor market. That laissez-faire frontier has now given way to a techno-global, militarized, fierce, oligopolistic, and structured environment, yet eugenics theorizing remains with us.

Situating Eugenics: Winfield's Gaze

The post-Renaissance world of European ascendance, exploration, and conquest offered a platform for the eugenics movements. That period witnessed the naked and brutal exploitation of people of color. Colonialism demanded that these people first be explained then transformed. Were they pagans? Why didn't they exploit their own resources? How should they be guided and civilized? Anthropology and the emergent social sciences arose in this context.

Winfield dramatizes the often misunderstood eugenics movement:

> Human beings, hundreds of thousands of them, were victims of the eugenics movement in the United States, either through forcible sterilization, antimiscegenation laws, immigration restriction, or the sorting, testing, and tracking policies implemented in schools across the country during the early decades of the 20th century and since. The programs and policies of the eugenics movement, rooted as they were in streams of intellectual history long preceding the 20th century, were evident across the globe and were ultimately responsible for the Holocaust and other genocidal events. (p. 144)

Next, Winfield connects eugenics to the positivism and scientism of the Western intellectual tradition. She notes that Auguste Comte was a party of interest in the story. Comte believed "the science of society...supplies the only logical scientific link by which all our varied observations of phenomena can be brought into the consistent whole" (p. 144). He was thus the father of positivism, which meant that the only authentic knowledge is based on actual sense experience. Such knowledge can only come from affirmation of theories through strict scientific method. Metaphysical speculation is avoided.

Extremely knowledgeable about the history of eugenics, Winfield tells us that our understanding of this phenomenon is incomplete, to our peril. Politics and the selective tradition are hard at work here. Not only is our knowledge incomplete, she insists, it has been affected by the purveyors of the official culture. She sets forth to inform us about the knowledge that is missing.

Introduced to the field of hereditary determinism, we are acquainted with the father of eugenics, Sir Francis Galton. Galton had a prolific intellect, and produced over 340 papers and books throughout his lifetime. He also created the statistical concept of correlation and widely promoted regression toward the mean. He was the first to apply statistical methods to the study of human differences and inheritance of intelligence, and introduced the use of questionnaires and surveys for collecting data on human communities, which he needed for genealogical and biographical works and for his anthropometric studies. He was a pioneer in eugenics, coining the very term itself and the phrase "nature versus nurture." As an investigator of the human mind, he founded psychometrics and was a respected scholar, anthropologist, explorer, and blood relative of Charles Darwin. Believing in hereditary preeminence, he asserted that heredity determined mental ability.

These views were described in his book, *Hereditary Genius* (1869/1952). There he showed, among other things, that the numbers of eminent relatives dropped off when going from the first degree to the second degree relatives, and from the second degree to the third. He took this as evidence of the inheritance of abilities. He also proposed adoption studies, including transracial adoption studies, to separate out the effects of heredity and environment.

He tabulated characteristics of their families, such as birth order and the occupation and race of their parents. He attempted to discover whether their interest in science was "innate" or due to the encouragement of others. Ongoing studies were published in another work, *English Men of Science: Their Nature and Nurture* (1874), which illuminated, but did not settle, the nature versus nurture question. His work provided interesting and provocative data on the sociology of scientists of the time.

Galton recognized the limitations of his methods in these two works, and believed the question could be better studied by comparison of twins. His method was to see if twins who were similar at birth diverged in dissimilar environments, and whether twins dissimilar at birth converged when reared in similar environments. He again used the method of questionnaires to gather various sorts of data, which were tabulated and described in a paper "The History of Twins" (1875). In so doing he anticipated the modern field of behavior genetics, which relies heavily on twin studies. He concluded that the evidence favored nature rather than nurture.

Galton invented the term *eugenics* in 1883 as he set forth many of his observations and conclusions in a book, *Inquiries in Human Faculty and Its Development*. He believed that a scheme of "marks" for family merit should be defined, and early marriage between families of high rank be encouraged by provision of monetary incentives. He pointed out some of the tendencies in British society that he considered dysgenic, such as the late marriages of eminent people, and the paucity of their children. He advocated encouraging eugenic marriages by supplying incentives for those able to have children. Winfield informs us that eugenics was not simply a splinter movement inhabited by lunatics, emergent fascists, and ne'er-do-wells. Rather, it was accepted in respected quarters. Its theorems became a thread, even building block, running through the foundations of accepted ideological and institutional life.

We are informed that "socialist" Karl Pearson, preeminent and influential mathematician and progressive reformer Margaret Sanger were drawn to eugenics. A casual student of social movements, I was unaware and intrigued by this apparent ideological oxymoron. Winfield's discussion here unintentionally ties to a larger body of inquiry critiquing America's early 20th century left wing, especially socialist, practice. Scholars of American radicalism, for example, those collaborating with William Z. Foster (1952), suggest American socialists were oddly and uniquely anticommunist and far removed from the Bolshevism of Europe. Eugenic racism apparently found space to operate here.

Winfield further informs us that early 20th century America witnessed a pathologization of people of color, those who lived in poverty, and a demonization of foreign people. Those discourses quickly extended to criminals, the insane, drunks, and those with birth defects. Classification schemes soon followed where labeling people as "idiots," "imbeciles," and "morons" identified the unacceptable. Such schemes helped distinguish the worthwhile from the worthless.

Winfield tells us that we haven't known enough about the broad appeal of eugenics, which ranges across both sides of the political terrain. Political science 101, we remember, teaches about the political spectrum. As charted, we learned that, in degrees, the right favors laissez faire while the left welcomes the safety net. We are "consoled" that a major negotiation between the two occurs. Public policy is presumably forged somewhere in the middle. Winfield asserts eugenic sentiment has influence throughout the spectrum.

Eugenics, she argues has been one of the building blocks of our culture. As civil society was forged in America, eugenics was woven into apartheid and progressivism alike. Most damaging, eugenics has been a part of both the conservative and liberal reform community. In other words, eugenics transcends the nation's social life. Beyond its sociopolitical and cultural manifestations, eugenics has been an important feature in the shaping of our academic disciplines, especially the social sciences. Winfield posits that it is entrenched in our intellectual tradition.

Defining Eugenics

Winfield proceeds to cull definitions of eugenics. Those definitions tell us that scientific eugenics was multifaceted addressing both individual and societal issues. Beyond views on individualism and fit, eugenicists and social Darwinists took up political objectives, such as social control. Eugenicists were consumed with social engineering and spoke of perfecting humanity. They found certain aspects of modern society threatening.
For all scientific racists, diversity and heterogeneity spelled trouble on two accounts. First, they believed nature made the races antagonistic and a diverse society would inevitably witness conflict. Second, they were obsessed with miscegenation. Examining the views of Gobineau (1854/1967), the "Father of Racism," I wrote (2001):

> Gobineau's theoretical racism was articulated in his magnum opus, entitled *Essai sur l'inégalité des races humaines*, completed in 1854. In it, he wrote that the racial question overshadowed all other issues in history. The inequality of races explained all destinies. Of most significance to Gobineau was social decay, or social decline. He rejected social decline as the product of excesses of misgovernment. Rather, he insisted that it was the product of miscegenation between the races. He argued that tribes were unable to remain pure and virile when the mixture of blood has been introduced. (p. 26)

Winfield points to scientism as the justification, rationale, and shield of the movement. The scientific revolution underlay intellectual life at the turn of the 20th century. Social scientists spoke of the magic of number demanding that we quantify everything.

Patriots defined the scientific society as planned and gradual social change because many feared America might experience the turmoil caused by unequal wealth in Europe. Industrialists and efficiency people looked to Taylorism/Fordism to organize production. The brokers of culture hoped for a cohesive functioning society. Eugenics spoke to their collective needs.

Public Education, Testing, and Eugenics

As Winfield deepened her inquiry, we might want to reflect on the context and state of education in the early 20th century. Extensive change and growth occurred. Schools were expanding rapidly. Increases in enrollment was evident. Even the now recovering Southern states were committing increased funds to the endeavor. The concepts of mass and compulsory schooling gained in popularity. A professional school bureaucracy was taking shape (Tyack, 1974). Most importantly, the changing corporate–industrial labor market demanded better educated workers and a clerical class to manage production. The testing and measurement movement, initiated by Alfred Binet quickly became institutionalized in the U.S.

Intelligence came to be a defining rationale for the social order in the early 20th century (Gonzalez, 1982). Tests of "intelligence" piloted on incoming soldiers found favor and support from behavioral psychologists in the measurement-hungry environment of public schools. Those in possession of knowledge were seen as more fit to manage the social order. Intelligence replaced work as the essence of human capital. The organization and leadership of society was to be placed in the hands of the intelligent. Intelligence came to be associated with leadership, property ownership, and worth, and IQ testing emerged as the "scientific" way of discerning intelligence. More importantly, IQ tests provided the "proof" of human difference. Difference emerged as the central organizing rationale of capitalism and its system of public education in the United States for all modernity. All could not, nor would not, achieve in the differentiated society.

Intelligence: Establishing the Concept of Difference

Democracy suggests universalism, more specifically, universal access where all can partake and participate. Presumably, schools will help us get there. Popular mythology holds mass public education is designed to level society and create opportunity for all. Notions of equalitarianism underlie the democratic agenda. Eugenicists, upholding democracy, held that not all people were capable of achievement. Individual differences relegated people to their "place" in the accessible society.

No discussion of eugenics and intelligence would be complete without including the research and theorizing of Edward Thorndike, who with his students used "objective" measurements of intelligence on human subjects as early as 1903. By the time the U.S. entered World War I, Thorndike had developed methods for measuring a wide variety of abilities and achievements. During the 1920s he developed a test of intelligence that consisted of completion, arithmetic, vocabulary, and a directions test, known as the CAVD. This instrument was intended to measure intellectual level on an absolute scale. The logic underlying the test predicted elements of test design that eventually became the foundation of modern intelligence tests.

Winfield quotes the celebrated work of Lawrence Cremin (1961) writing about Thorndike's influence, stating that "no aspect of public school teaching during the first quarter of the twentieth century remained unaffected" (p. 150). She explores Thorndike's role in the Alpha and Beta tests administered to soldiers in World War I. Embraced by school people, those tests forever defined assessment for students. Thorndike and colleague Leta Hollingworth racialized intelligence. Their findings suggested people of color were limited in intellectual performance.

Thorndike's book *Individuality* (1911) signaled the concretization of "differential psychology" which was built upon hereditarian inheritance. This body of thought served as justification for why some children achieved, others did not. Thorndike wrote:

> The mental capacities of human beings at birth, or at conception, vary widely, probably as widely as their capacities to become tall or strong. Their original propensities or proclivities, or emotional and temperamental tendencies vary, and perhaps as widely as their facial contours or finger-prints. (cited in Clifford, 1968, pp. 314–315)

Thorndike became an adamant supporter of testing and measuring intelligence. His views were widely supported by American eugenicists, racists, and Aryan theorists. Harvard psychologist Hugo Musterberg (1909) effectively articulated the hereditarian/difference implication for education:

> We have brought the work of education under one formula. This is not meant to indicate that education should be uniform. Everybody ought to be made willing and able to realize ideal values, but everybody is called to do it in his own way. The child who comes from the slums, the child who never saw a green meadow, and the child who never saw a paved street, cannot be educated after a uniform pattern. The education of the boy cannot be the education of the girl, the education of the intelligent child must differ from that of the slow-minded child…. Yet still more important are the differences between the individual tasks which the life after school will put before the individuals. To make the child willing and able to realize ideal values, means also to secure the subtlest adjustment to these later differences. The laborer and the farmer, the banker and the doctor all must help in building up the realm of values. But they are equally prepared for it only if they are prepared for it in very different ways. (cited in Gonzalez, 1982, p. 142)

Winfield correctly ascertains that the now "scientific" notion of difference would be exploited. H. H. Goddard, through his popular book *The Kallikak Family* (1912), relied on difference theory and he further joined intelligence to the eugenics idea. We learn that it was Goddard who revised Binet's initial test and advanced mental-age classifications such as moron and idiot. He also wrote of the inferiority of southern and eastern Europeans. His ideas foreshadow a century of eugenicist thinking on intelligence and race.

Re-W(r)ighting the Story

Getting to the heart of the matter, Winfield not only explores the perpetrators of eugenics, she also calls attention to the gratuitous omissions they have been granted in the literature. Winfield spotlights previous historiographies of the unfolding of public education. She inserts the missing eugenicist component. She writes:

> Although educational historians (Curti 1935/1959; Kliebard, 1975/1997, 1986/1995; Tyack, 1974) have focused much of their attention on the influence of psychologists G. Stanley Hall and Edward Thorndike, somehow they have managed to omit the profound degree to which both were steeped in eugenic ideology. The prolific careers of both men are well documented; Hall published 350 papers and 14 books and Thorndike published an equivalent number of papers and over 30 books. (Curti, 1935/1959, p. 16)

Turning from the psychologists, Winfield narrows her gaze to the educational, and especially, curriculum theorists who built on the eugenicist idea. Franklin Bobbitt is central to her inquiry. Winfield's central objective in this work is to illustrate the role of eugenics in curriculum theory and public education. By virtue of his position, Franklin Bobbitt is the quintessential and obvious study. Bobbitt's views were evident prior to the publishing of his opus, *The Curriculum* (1918). Winfield reviews his article "Practical Eugenics" (1909). She writes:

> Bobbitt shared the view common among eugenicists and social Darwinists before them that social policy should seek to remove the protective characteristics of civilized society and allow the forces of nature to take its course in sorting human worth. Claiming that "our schools and charities supply crutches to the weak in mind and morals…." (p. 151)

Summarizing another article from the journal *Pedagogical Seminary* (1909), Winfield notes that Bobbitt addressed child rearing. He advocated that only selected people be allowed to parent otherwise little could be done for the children of the unfit. Concerned that the evolving societal safety net was shielding the weak and incapable, he called for the abolishment of public schooling and charities.

Later reconciled to public schooling, Bobbitt offered direction and theorizing about curriculum and instruction in an environment where achievement was viewed as a function of race and social class. Winfield notes that his definition of curriculum includes notions of perfecting. Moreover, she argues, Bobbitt's scientific curriculum is an amalgam of testing, measurement dogma, Taylorism, and hereditarianism. She concludes Bobbitt envisioned schools as instruments for sorting, testing, and tracking. Bobbitt is illustrative of an important shift of emphasis in eugenics theorizing from breeding to sorting. Bobbitt's historical reputation as a respected curriculum theorist is irrefutable.

Eugenics, Neoliberalism, Crisis, and the Future

In the end, Winfield is overwhelmed yet clear. She writes:

> Confusion, hopelessness, and invective all characterize the current debate over human agency, the role of the past, ideological transmission and seemingly endless examples of historical repetition. (p. 153)

Mass education is a noble, and perhaps, sacred endeavor, yet even efforts at school reform are guided and co-opted by the forces of the past. Today's liberals hope schools can create and guarantee access. Schools should give voice and hope to the voiceless and hopeless. Winfield is pained to note that although the larger sociopolitical culture embraces democratic views of schooling that culture remains tainted with hereditarianism and intellectual racism. Nowhere does escape seem possible. Even liberal and progressive reformers are trapped by the scourge of the past.

If egalitarian ideas and learned people cannot redress inequity, who or what can? We seem hopelessly mired in a history that foreshadows and governs the present to repeat the past. The totalizing presence of No Child Left Behind evidences the repetition and resilience of our inherited views.

Daunted but not defeated, Winfield looks for avenues of hope and change. She finds encouragement among conscious educators and curricularists not imprisoned by the past. She notes the presence of Maxine Greene, the influence of Paulo Freire, and William Pinar's reconceptualization movement as examples of "vantage points" for enlightened thinking.

Venturing beyond Winfield's work, I would like to raise questions that politicize White supremacy and eugenics in the new era. What is the new era? For me, the new era is the techno-global revolution which is replacing the industrial era that replaced agrarian society. The "chip" has led to digitization which has transformed, even re-created the labor market, commodity production, information management, education, communications, the arts and governance. Our cities, our jobs, our laws, our pensions, our educational structures, and fundamental aspects of our lives and culture are unrecognizable from a few years ago.

Following a period of unprecedented prosperity in the late 20th century, all is not well in the new order. Capitalism is in free fall. At this writing, recessionary trends are joined by seemingly endless war. Deindustrialization and the destruction of the safety net thrusts millions into uncertainty and unspeakable poverty. The erosion of the middle class is euphemistic for the pauperization of large numbers of White people. Hence, race relations are recast. The new economics and politics demand new examinations. We are in uncharted waters. The workings of the new economy are uncertain. Driven by capitalist accumulation, perhaps the biggest changes have occurred in economics and politics. Neoliberalism and neoconservatism (Harvey, 2005; Hoogvelt, 1997) have taken effect. The call to market economics is eliminating the "public." No more public aid, public housing, public medicine—even public schooling is in jeopardy.

Like the economy, the politics of the nation are blurry. Old ideologies and alliances have morphed. Former protectors of the safety net now support the call to the market. Civil politics has given way to stolen elections, authoritarianism, and the resurgence of an imperial mentality. Militarism, private armies, illegal and brutal conquest of foreign lands is now the order of the day.

Always complex, race issues must be totally reexamined. Race and the economy are, and have always been, wedded. In times of plenty, prosperity, and civility race do not seem to attract the same attention and acrimony. In times of recession and austerity, race somehow finds its way back into public discourse.

The racial base of the ruling order is White. Like any hegemonic group, they hope to protect their base if possible. We might question if the new concentrations of wealth and changing labor market allows the White working class to retain its privileges. The inevitable question is what to do with the new pariahs, mostly Black and Brown; however, they are now joined by others who while Whites are losing their privileges.

The race issue has once again expeditiously found its way back into the headlines. From the Jena 6 to the presidential election to everyday practices in local communities, race is on the agenda. The mass media is giving urban racial violence extensive coverage. All disputes are now identified as gang related. People of color, especially youth, are being demonized and depicted as unfit for civilized society. Their very presence is now presented as a problem. The rapid expansion of White poverty hardly attracts a bleep in the news. It might be argued that the ruling order would rather "raise" race than the more threatening and volatile issues of the inequities of capitalism.

The continued racialization of public schooling and school reform are raised by Winfield, then, comes at the right time. School restructuring is wedded to gentrification and greatly impacts those living at the margins of society. Already experiencing drop-out rates hovering around 40%, proposed privatization and restructuring will likely leave inner city schools dangling in uncertainty and inferiority. Many cities will undoubtedly experience large populations of deschooled people. Winfield tells us we must look to the past to know our future.

Eugenicists have and will continue to address and assess the new social and economic order. As equal opportunity *haters*, they will find people of color genetically inferior as well as Whites, "morons," and "imbeciles." Avoiding the realities of political economy, they will likely defend the social order while renouncing those who do not succeed in it.

We can only speculate how repressive and authoritarian the new order might become. In the worst case scenario, the genocides and cases of ethnic cleansing practiced on other people might be a dress rehearsal for what is to come in the U.S. All of the prerequisites are already in place. The country's history of slavery, cruelty, legal executions, and present-day torture has both prepared and desensitized people to state violence.

The current interest in genetic engineering is of equal concern. The leap from genetically constructed fruits and meats to human beings is already underway. The quest for perfect people is juxtaposed to the savagery of demonized people in our midst.

In America we don't talk about removal and partition practices; however, they enjoy increasing popularity while demonstrating a eugenic twist. Most egregious is the prison industrial complex where now over 2,000,000 people languish. Little to no effort is invested in rehabilitation. Immigration alarmists tell us there are 12 million undocumented people residing in the U.S. alone. The call for deportation and elimination has become strident. Finally, as a student of history and world traveler, I have read about and seen the great walls of China and Turkey; however, I thought "walls" were a relic of the past. Here we are in the 21st century and walls are being erected at the Rio Grande and the Gaza Strip. Enough said!

Appearing as lunacy to some, eugenics endures. Proponents hold they are part of nature's master plan where the weak and unfit are weeded out. Their claim is to the purity of science. They embrace "remedy." Eugenicists argue the racial struggle makes society stronger. Civilization is improved by being rid of its dead weight. They want the country to breed true.

We are left with sweeping issues and questions to ponder. The ultimate question eugenics raises is about human life. How much is a human life worth? Is human life losing value in the new order? Finally, will the repetition of history allow eugenic remedies to find favor in the new social order? Winfield helps us know what questions we need to ask.

References

Bobbitt, J. F. (1909). Practical eugenics. *Pedagogical Seminary*, 385–394.

Bobbitt, J. F. (1918). *The curriculum*. Boston: Houghton Mifflin.

Clifford, G. J. (1968). *Edward L. Thorndike: The sane positivist*. Middletown, CT: Wesleyan University Press.

Cremin, L. (1961). *Transformation of the school: Progressivism in American education 1876–1957*. New York: Knopf.

Curti, M. (1959). *The social ideas of American educators*. Patterson, NJ: Pageant Books. (Original work published 1935)

Foster, W. Z. (1952). *History of the communist party of the United States*. New York: International.

Galton, F. (1874). *English men of science: Their nature and nurture*. London: MacMillan.

Galton, F (1875, November 18). The history of twins. *Nature, 13*, 59.

Galton, F. (1883). *Inquiries in human faculty and its development*. New York: Macmillan.

Galton, F. (1952). *Hereditary genius: An inquiry into its law and consequences*. New York: Horizon Press. (Original work published 1869)

Giroux, H. (1979, December). Toward a new sociology of curriculum. *Educational Leadership, 37*, 248–253.

Gobineau, A. de (1967). *Essai sur l'inégalité des races humaines* [Essay on the inequality of the human races]. New York: Fertig. (Original work published 1854)

Goddard, H. H. (1912). *The Kallikak family: A study in the heredity of feeblemindedness.* New York: Macmillan.

Gonzalez, G. G. (1982). *Progressive education: A Marxist interpretation.* Minneapolis: Marxist Educational Press.

Hall, G. S. (1904). *Adolescence: Its psychology and its relations to, psychology, anthropology, sex, crime, religion and education.* New York: D. Appleton.

Harvey, D. (2005). *A brief history of neoliberalism.* New York: Oxford University Press.

Herrnstein, R., & Murray, C. (1994). *The bell curve: Intelligence and class structure in American life.* New York: Free Press.

Hoogvelt, A. M. M. (1997). *Globalization and the post colonial world: The new political economy of development.* Baltimore: Johns Hopkins University Press.

Jensen, A.R. (1973). *Educability and group differences.* New York: Harper & Row.

Jensen, A. R. (1995, January). Psychological research on race differences. *American Psychologist, 50*(1), 41–42.

Kliebard, H. M. (1996). *The struggle for the American curriculum 1893–1958.* New York: Routledge. (Original work published 1986)

Kliebard, H. M. (1997). The rise of scientific curriculum making and its aftermath. In S. J. Flinders (Ed.), *The curriculum studies reader* (pp. 31–44). New York: Routledge. (Original work published 1975)

Schockley, W. (1972). Genetics, dysgenics, geneticity, raceology: A challenge to the intellectual responsibility of education. *Phi Delta Kappan,* 297–307.

Taylor, F. W. (1911). *Principles of scientific management.* New York: Harper.

Thorndike, E. (1911). *Individuality.* Boston: Houghton Mifflin.

Tyack, D. (1974). *The one best system: A history of American urban education.* Cambridge, MA: Harvard University Press.

Watkins, W. H. (2001). *The white architects of black education: Ideology and power in America, 1865–1954.* New York: Teachers College Press.

Winfield, A. (2007). *Eugenics and education in America: Institutionalized racism and the implications of history, ideology and memory.* New York: Lang.

Part III

Technology, Nature, and the Body

8 Understanding Curriculum Studies in the Space of Technological Flow

Karen Ferneding

Chapter Overview

This chapter addresses the next moment in curriculum studies with a focus on the flow of knowledge production or the need for curriculum scholars specifically and educators in general to address the nature of humanity's relationship to its technological inventions. She explains that via technics that are manifested today as complex networks of techno-science, postmodern humanity becomes more seduced by technology's force. This is like the role of a magician's apprentice, the author explains, who becomes consumed by the power of cybermatic alchemy and endeavors to transform the raw materials of nature into simulacrum. This author suggests technology has become humanity's quest for salvation and accordingly humanity that once created technological inventions becomes its servant. To counter this phenomenon, the author turns toward two concepts—transepochal state and historical rupture—to describe a pivotal historical moment in knowledge production that involves issues like global warming and environmental degradation. The author emphasizes that educators must turn from their focus upon the instrumental and the givenness of that which exists toward the creative potential of the inner self, studies of the dialectic between self and society, and a spiritual–ethical foundation for stewardship and compassion.

Being Within and of the Flow

Change is a fundamental principle of human reality. Confucius, standing on the edge of a river is said to have stated: "Everything flows on and on like a river, without pause, day and night." His observation expresses how the nature of reality is characterized by the flow of change. Change, as noted by the ancient Chinese text, *I Ching*, signifies the mystery, the essence of all that exists. Within Taoism, the yin and yang forces dance a continuum of dialectic flow.

While coming into being within the flow in what is known as the 20th century, I awoke to the image of the atomic bomb. I peered at its unfathomable power crouched beneath a desk in a classroom with small windows reflecting the absolute grayness of a winter sky. Today, the image still haunts me, and its reality marked the beginning of a lifelong quest to understand the nature of humanity's relationship to its technological inventions. To me, its essence symbolizes the implosion of change, control, ir/rationality, and transcendence. It is my humble observation that humanity's relationship to the flow, via the ir/rationality of technoscience, is not so much to experience or understand, but rather to control.

Even so, our experience of change within the flow of time is related to our ontology, the nature of our beingness in time. We are Heidegger's *Dasein*, thrown into a specific historical matrix of time and space manifested as a unique consciousness. However, for human beings, the flow is demarcated by the immanent. The fact remains that we are beings of consciousness—a consciousness of our own mortality. Indeed, it could be said that culture exists as an expression of imagination and language to mask our profound fear—a grand design of our "denial of death" (Becker, 1973). Also, in his book *Escape from Evil*, Ernest Becker (1975) explains that the social need for the King to act as hero, the quest of heroism—the wars, plundering, and conquest—is akin to demonstrating the favor of the gods, the destiny of the right of the ruler to wield the greatest and absolute power over fate and men—and, ultimately, nature. To wage war, a quest of an inevitable bloodbath, is to engage death, and thus embody the power of the gods.

At the base of the human psyche regarding all this drama is the *causi sui* project— being a god unto oneself—and its ensuing guilt for existence/beingness itself. How does one live this game of beingness, of conscious existence, but not knowing why, especially if one has to die? What is the point? And so, meaninglessness hides in the shadows of the psyche as the true enemy that stirs our deepest fears.

Sophocles' Oedipus indicates the depth of our mysterious beginnings—nature (no time) and humanity (temporality), prophesy, fate, destiny, and human freedom. The symbolic power of the Oedipus narrative arises from nonrationality; its origin unknown as the origin of nature herself. Indeed, Freud's psychological theory related to the phallus is central to Western societies' conceptualization of the human psyche and illustrates the mysterious symbolic power of possibility and inevitability, of hope and fear, wrapped up in one upright symbol of human power and powerlessness. But, ultimately, the phallus seems no match against the depth of our guilt and fear. Thus, our "will to control" (will to power) exists as a salve for the psyche; culture being one manifestation, technics another. And one might consider the meaning of the collapse of their distinction as in the case of the present condition of "technoculture."

Technics as Salve/ation

A particular image from Fritz Lang's 1936 film *Metropolis* depicts the main character, dressed in workman's clothing, desperate to stop a huge clock that automates an immense and cavernous industrial machine. The image illustrates the nature of being within mechanized time. Within industrialization one can no longer live time as an eternal flow, but rather service it as artifice, a cybernetic system of control. The image shows the character literally struggling with machinic power manifested as reified time and thus signifies how humanity, striving to capture and conquer time, is in fact attempting to transcend it. For example, in his book, *The Religion of Technology*, David Noble (1997) explains how, historically, Western societies' relationship with technology arises from humanity's quest for transcendence and salvation. Technology obviously gives expression to production, invention, and science. However, it also operates at the level of mythos, a religion in his words, that in fact is *the* expression of the *causi sui* project. The aim of the *causi sui* project is to undo humanity's fall from grace and restore Eden on earth. This calculated destiny to create a prelapsarian state of perfection, achieved via the acquisition of scientific and technological knowledge, shall cleanse the past sin of disobedience—which means that anything that expresses the feminine shall not inspire the New Eden.

Indeed, Noble's thesis indicates that since woman signifies the essence of nature herself, and woman has been alleged to be the cause of the downfall, nature is also not to be trusted. Rather, like women in general, she is to be used. This rather utilitarian approach, whose origins are found in ancient agrarian-based systems of social organization (Becker, 1973; Eisler, 1995), generated a "dominator model" of culture (Eisler, 1995, 2000). Such a condition manifested at the dawn of the Middle Ages and by the period of early industrialization indicates a state of separation from nature, a position of objectification that is also the basis of scientific thinking and what we have come to understand as the historical condition of modernity. Its particular rationality, what Herbert Marcuse (1964) describes as "instrumental rationalism," exists within Western/ized societies as an unconscious commonsense way of knowing regarding technology and nature. Instrumental rationality, as practiced via science, expresses the ideology of progress as truth (Lyotard, 1984). Therefore, to question the tenets of the "religion of technology" is to engage in blasphemy.

But I learned that there are those who dare to engage in such questioning. For example, in her 1962 book, *The Silent Spring*, Rachel Carson, a marine biologist, reported on the negative environmental effects of DDT and other pesticides. Her book was a harbinger of the present crisis in global environmental degradation. During a 1963 interview she stated:

> We still talk in terms of conquest. We still haven't become mature enough to think of ourselves as only a tiny part of a vast and incredible universe. Man's attitude toward nature is today critically important simply because we have now acquired a fateful power to alter and destroy nature. But man is a part of nature, and his war against nature is inevitably a war against himself.

And it was significant to me that such a controversial book was written by a woman; the very reason why it was dismissed by some. In a rather cautious manner, the author described how thoughtless industrialization was destroying the natural habitat upon which life exists.

However difficult it was to imagine that humanity was engaged in the practice of un/conscious self-destruction, as with the image of the Bomb—the quintessential weapon of mass destruction—the notion of pollution became naturalized as the state of affairs within 20th century living. It seemed ironic to me that while satellite technology gave us a dramatic and awe-inspiring view of our beautiful planet, Ohio's Cuyahoga River, so filled with industrial pollutants, was literally on fire. One can only wonder if Confucius had stood before this river, what manner of inspiration it may have elicited from the wise old sage.

Ways of Knowing Technological Flow

To say that change can be manifested by technological innovation is to state the obvious. And, in this case, it is significant to remind ourselves that the obvious is often overlooked. *Technoculture*, a term used to describe the melding of the technological and social spheres, indicates the state of postmodern reality. However, even though we live within and of technological systems, rarely do we consider them as shaping forces. Rather, we understand all technologies and technological systems, no matter their complexity, as mere tools that are completely under our control and which are the means to the end of greater efficiency. This is the story of Western progress and capital.

As theorized by Heidegger (1977), this rather instrumental position regarding technics is correct but is not true, for it tells only half of the story. Technology and technological systems indeed exist as tools but such tools are not neutral or without bias. Technological innovations operationalize human intention and are related to the production of knowledge and thus power (Foucault, 1980). For example, like its predecessor the railroad, information and computer technologies (ICT) exist as a physical infrastructure but transport digital electronic data streams instantaneously, making terrestrial space superfluous. In fact, the acceleration of time via ICT is directly related to the deterriorializing of space.

Therefore, within our postmodern moment the characteristic of instantaneity demonstrated by ICT processing indicates that the delay inherent in the experience of cause and effect has collapsed, and what in effect exists is the realm of premonition. And so it seems that the flowing river that inspired Confucius has become a virtual stream of electronic digital pulses. We no longer witness the flow of time and beingness via the reality of nature that inspires metaphoric wisdom. Rather, via technics, we have actualized the metaphor and imagine that we are also the keepers of the virtual river's flow.

But things are in fact even more complex. In the essay, *The Question Concerning Technology*, Martin Heidegger (1977) explains that technology, "is no mere means, it is a way of revealing." In fact, technology's essence or beingness is not only a way of revealing (*episteme*), but also a process that is essentially poetic *(poiesis)* (p. 12). Moreover, technology manifests within a realm where "revealing and unconcealment take place, where aletheia, truth happens" (p. 13).

Heidegger is inviting us to understand technology as part of the sacred, the mystery. However, our relationship to technology is quite the contrary. We do not have the language or paradigmatic framework to conceive technology as possessing an essence. In contrast, the scientific paradigm and loss of a sense of the sacred with regards to nature has created a relationship that Heidegger describes as *gestell* or "enframement," a condition that is similar to Herbert Marcuse's "instrumental rationalism." According to Heidegger, because of the condition of enframement, all that we create via technique becomes "Standing Reserve," an essentially utilitarian position.

Enframement is not just a condition, it is a destiny, and thus indicates technology's reflexive nature. While other possibilities exist, the particular destiny of enframement is essentially one of hubris. As nature becomes transmogrified into standing reserve, so is humanity. Ironically, humanity cannot encounter itself, its own essence, while living this destiny. This is so because, while engaged in the condition of enframement, humanity's existence is not connected to *poiesis*, but rather to the maintenance of the condition of enframement itself. Thus, the destiny of enframement is one of maintenance, a keeper of what can be described as "the ordering of the machine." The destiny of enframement is not so much a condition of autonomous technology run amuck as much as it indicates a condition of profound separation from nature. Indeed, Marshall McLuhan (1964) has described such a fate for humanity in that, via our inventions, we act as "servo-mechanisms" for our own narcissism.

Philosopher Don Ihde (1979) asks, in the tradition of Heidegger, what are the conditions of possibility that make technology possible? As a phenomenologist, Ihde perceives our relationship to technology as one that is grounded in our embodiment. He characterizes this relationship by means of various degrees of technology's opacity. For example, when we drive a car, we are experiencing technology *through* a machine. One can also have an experience *with* a machine as a hermeneutic text. An example is Big Science's instrumentation such that, via output/data, a unique system of code or language is generated. Therefore, technology operating as a hermeneutic via instrumentation creates a specific symbolic system. Indeed, the "world" created by instrumentation can be taken as "real" and as such enables reification. A particular realism is constructed, "instrumental realism," as instrumental reductivity is systematically ignored and with reification engaged. This new realism becomes convincing as a form of metaphysics because "what was invisible becomes present" (p. 47), and simultaneously the mundane world becomes downgraded and forgotten. In fact, our experiences with direct senses in the flesh become secondary to those generated by our instrumentation.

The construction of our abstraction of the world moves us further away from nature and Mystery and deeper into our "technological cocoon" (Ihde, 1979). And this in fact is Ihde's third category of the technological–human relation—the "atmospheric" (p. 13). The machinic condition as a "technosphere" is ubiquitous and humans in effect exist *inside* the machine that is manifested as a "technological cocoon." The human–machine relation therefore:

> …pervades the entirety of the correlational possibilities of possibilities. Machines become, in our technological culture, part of our self-experience and self-expression…. They become a technological texture to the World and with it carry a presumption toward totality. In this sense, at every turn, we encounter machines existentially. (p. 15)

Televisual and Internet "spaces" are expressions of a technosphere. We have undeniably entered the space of virtual flow. In addition, Gray Kochhar-Lindgren's (2005) vision of postmodern technoscience reveals a disturbing posthuman sensibility. It seems as if the destiny of enframement has reached its second phase predicted by Heidegger—the self-enslavement of humanity via its own practice of turning nature into standing reserve. Humanity, in effect, gets its just desserts.

He elaborates on Karl Marx's vision of industrial capitalism as a condition where humans are mere appendages of a mechanical machine animated by an autonomous force, which is in fact the transference of human labor (energy) into the machine. It is a condition that expresses the immortality of technological capitalism—a machinic vampirism, bloodthirsty after human ingenuity/imagination/power. Humanity, once the creator of its technological inventions, has become its servant. We serve what Ernst Junger describes as the "technological mind" and the "artifice of technique" (1960, p. 41). Kochhar-Lindgren explains: "With the emergence of the social brain and the automaton of capitalism, however, the artifice is exteriorized as a more encompassing exoskeleton and is literalized as electronic intelligence" (2005, p. 86). Kochhar-Lindgren's vision seems to parallel Ihde's perception regarding humanity's embodiment within a technosphere.

The individual, asserts Kochhar-Lindgren, has little power within the autonomous technological system, but rather it is the collective as a social body, which "forms a database—a base for the circulation of information for the sake of moneymaking—[that] has such powers" (2005, p. 87). He concludes:

> We are freed up by our machinery to either become unemployed or work longer hours [intensification]. Capitalism always ups the ante in the casino of the global economy and what is always at stake is time—time is money…. And for Marx, both the system and the subject within the system have a destiny—their own vanishing. (p. 89)

Marx's vision of human destiny indicates a dialectical–historical mechanism that implodes in a self-destructive morass of automated excess. However, beyond this point of inevitable cataclysm, as the story goes, the relationship between humanity and its machines is transformed, alienation is ultimately overcome. Kochhar-Lindgren states that cybernetics offers the means to create a "new foundation"—the end of human history, and the beginning of the posthuman. This condition, however, would necessarily entail an ironic turn—"*a humanization of the machine and the mechanization of the human*"[italics added] (2005, p. 90).

Indeed, Kochhar-Lindgren describes the present *transepochal state*, as being characterized by humanity's sense that "something is changing, something different is emerging. We can all feel it; we are trying to articulate it" (p. 194). Kochhar-Lindgren (2005, p. 196) refers to the posthuman vision of Jean Baudrillard (2001), who in the book, *The Vital Illusion*, reflects on the domination of technology with its "rage to overcome death, will enact 'the perfect crime'"—the creation of a cybernetic controlled world that will empty itself of the human as well as the evidence that such a crime of destruction has occurred. The technological system, therefore, becomes a tautology that initiates the end of mystery. Or, in contrast, Baudrillard envisions that technology could be "an immense detour toward the radical illusion of the world…an absolutely unpredictable movement that would finally bring us to the other side of metaphysics"—a metaphysics that gives expression to the mystery through love.

As one can see, technology manifested as a (false) god drives a hard bargain. Having chosen what appears to be the destiny of enframement, humanity can create a system of transcendence via technics, but in the process courts its own enslavement. However, if posthumanism means the demise of the metanarrative anthropocentrism and a turn toward a consciousness of stewardship and mutuality regarding nature, then the posthuman harkens the possibility of an "evolutionary moment" akin to a "spiritual awakening." But will it be an awakening of "electronic spirituality?"

Globalization as the Technologizing of the World

It is perhaps easy to dismiss visions of posthuman destiny as "scorched earth" alarmism or sci-fi nonsense. However, social scientists who attempt to articulate the concept of "globalization" and its sociocultural effects also make reference to something akin to Kochhar-Lindgren's *transepochal state*. Many indicate that the infrastructure of ICT is foundational to the condition of globalization, thus underscoring the relationship between technology and social and economic systems. Therefore, although the present condition of postmodern globalization can be conceived as a continuum of modernity, it nevertheless is distinctive as a specific historical "moment" (Appadurai, 1998; Bauman, 1998; Castells, 2000).

It is essential to realize that, as transportation systems, electronic technologies act to shape our relationship to time and space, which are the basic coordinates of the lifeworld. In this sense, such technologies act to *constitute* human social reality (Carey, 1989; Castells, 2000; Innis, 1951, 1952; McLuhan, 1964). For example, in his book *The Rise of the Network Society*, Manuel Castells (2000) describes how the present condition of an electronic global network, "does fundamentally change the character of communication" and that "communication decisively shapes culture" (p. 356).

Quoting the work of Neil Postman, Castells (2000) states,

> … "we do not see…reality…as 'it' is, but as our languages are. And our languages are our media. Our media are our metaphors. Our metaphors create the content of our culture." Because culture is mediated and enacted through communication, cultures themselves—that is our historically produced systems of beliefs and codes— become fundamentally transformed and we will be more so over time, by the new technological system. (p. 356)

Traditionally, according to Castells (2000), space exists as *crystallized time* engendering sociospatial structures that provided the material support for time-sharing social practices. In contrast, technoculture or the "network society" is constructed around a deterritorialized *space of flows* consisting of images and sounds, information, capital, and organizational transactions. The *space of flows* is not just one element of social organization. Rather, it functions as the expression of processes dominating economic, political and symbolic life. In addition, network society via ITC and electronic media experiences time as *timeless time* (timelessness), a condition indicated by instantaneity, simultaneity, and an ahistorical ephemerality. This is a unique experience to human reality.

The hyperreality of the televisual creates a seductive sensorial simulation of reality characterized by a consumerist-based social imagination that configures self-identity and cultural norms. It acts to "frame the language" of society's communication (e.g., politics, business, art, sports), for as Castells (2000, p. 364) explains, media as the "symbolic fabric of our life," affect consciousness and behavior "just as real experience works on dreams." Moreover, the shaping nature of media is characterized by rootlessness, alienation and psychological distancing. The televisual flow, configured as commodity culture, acts in a reciprocal or reflexive manner—it essentially operates as a cybernetic feedback system.

In fact, in the following quotation, Castells (2000) explains how network society operates as a "cultural system" characterized by *real virtuality,* a condition similar to Ihde's technological cocoon.

> What is then a communication system that, in contrast to earlier historical experience, generates *real virtuality? It is a system in which reality itself (people's material/symbolic existence) is entirely captured, fully immersed in a virtual image setting, in the world of make believe, in which appearances are not just on the screen through which experience is communicated but they become the experience.* All messages of all kinds become enclosed in the medium have become so comprehensive so diversified so malleable that it absorbs in the same multimedia text the whole of human experience, past, present and future. (p. 404)

This condition weakens the symbolic power of traditional sources of socialization (religion, values, political ideology) and creates a "secularization of society" related to the dominance of commodity culture. "Societies are finally and truly disenchanted because all wonders are online and can be combined into self-constructed image worlds." The televisual system of *space of flows* and *timeless time* are "material foundations of a new culture…where make-believe is belief in the making" (Castells, 2000, p. 406). Indeed, humans have superseded nature, "because of the convergence of historical evolution and technological change we have entered *a purely cultural pattern* [italics added] of social interaction and social organization" (Castells, 2000, p. 508).

The cultural system of *real virtuality* has generated a new type of self that "is obsessed with the binary reference to instantaneity and eternity: me and the universe, the self and the Net" (Castells, 2000, p. 493). Castells (2000) in fact believes that the reconciliation of the biological individual with the cosmological whole "can only be achieved under the condition of the merger of all times, from the creation of ourselves to the end of the universe. Timelessness is the recurrent theme of our age's cultural expressions, be it in the sudden flashes of video clips or in the eternal echoes of electronic spiritualism" (p. 494).

In addition, Wertheim (1999) explains that the social construction of space is historically associated with spiritual transcendence. Reification and mechanization of space by means of certain technologies—perspective drawing, cartography, and instrumentation such as the telescope—transformed space from a "place" of transcendent realism of God and the soul to the physicality of the human and matter (p. 87). She believes that the omission of spiritual space from the Western worldview is the reason why cyberspace (the realm of the Internet and televisual) as an immaterial realm has become "a spiritual space" (p. 39).

Similarly, Appadurai's (1998) conceptualization of globalization involves the generation of various types of "global cultural flows" or "scapes" by means of ICT and electronic media that act as "the building blocks of...multiple imagined worlds that are constituted by the historically-situated imaginations of persons and groups spread around the globe" (p. 33).

Appadurai (1998) focuses on the cultural consequences of globalization and associates the flow of media and ideas with social imagination. The *ideoscape,* which emphasizes democratic ideals, and the *mediascape* configure the social imagination such that, "ordinary lives today are more often powered not by the givenness of things but by the possibilities that the media (either directly or indirectly) suggest are available" (Appadurai, 1998, p. 55).

The deterritorialized space of social imagination exists as a staging ground for action via the power of the local or the "vernacular" to generate "subversive micro-narratives" that challenge globalizing forces (p. 10). However, despite the possibility of resistance, *imagination as social practice* also functions as escape. The fetishism of the commodity and hyperconsumerism indicates that the consumer is not an actor, but rather a chooser. This condition is illustrated by how the AK-47, symbolic of the commodification of war and violence via the global arms trade, secures its symbolic presence in B-grade violent films, and thus exists as a globalized iconic cultural code for Third World poor men and youth. The AK-47 signifies a complex interaction of economic factors, gender politics, and the fantasy of macho self-assertion (Appadurai, 1998, p. 31). For Third World poor men, the AK-47 signifies transcendence of their lack of real agency. In effect, imagination has broken out from the space of art to that of ordinary life (Appadurai, 1998, p. 5).

It is clear that the power of the mediascape to generate social imagination is concomitant with a breakdown of traditional socializing forces (e.g., the family, church, school, and state). For Appadurai, (1998, p. 9), this condition has generated a severe "rupture" in the historical evolution of traditional and industrialized societies. Culturally, the implications for the condition of globalization are not only extreme economic and social stratification—only 1.4% of global wealth is owned by the poorest countries (Davis, 2006)—but also the absorption of traditional cultures into the mediascape; integration of all messages into a common cognitive pattern characterized by commercialization (e.g., interactive educational programs look like videogames); diverse cultural expressions are captured within a televisual domain as a commodity; and widespread social and cultural differences descend into ethno-religious based wars and technologically induced "instant wars" that characterize a new form of military–corporate domination (Castells, 2000).

Indeed, Mike Davis (2006, p. 205) explains that the U.S. State Department, World Bank, and United Nations perceive that a "permanently redundant mass" of millions of poor people, who inhabit Third World megaslums, and their acts of resistance, constitute an unprecedented threat to geopolitical security. This "urbanization of insurgency" shall be met with a "low-intensity world war of unlimited duration" that utilizes high-tech surveillance technologies including "robo-soldiers" designed specifically for such urban warfare. U.S. urban areas, such as Los Angeles, are to be test sites for these high-tech systems of containment. Resistance to the "perfect logic" of surveillance society, no matter its impetus, is perceived as the "Achilles heel" in the cybernetic equation. Davis concludes that, "If the empire can deploy Orwellian technologies of repression, its outcasts have the gods of chaos on their side" (p. 206).

The "Transepochal State" and Curriculum Studies' "Next Moment"

By examining the social visions of other writers, I have offered a position from which one may understand the human condition regarding the complexity of humanity's relationship to its technological inventions. The sketch that I have drawn via the palette of others' imaginings configures an image of a fateful transcendence via the destiny of enframement. Indeed, such a story conjures the silent ghost of responsibility and the haunting sirens' call of our lost freedom. If we are to be gods unto ourselves, what is, essentially, the purpose of such an endeavor? Efficiency? The efficiency of our disappearance? What does the "mechanization of the human" mean? How are we to live this fate crafted by our own hands and imagination? An individual or a society cannot actively engage praxis or resistance against a condition that remains invisible through willful denial or a self-deceit maintained by the seduction of consumption and the ecstasy of technological utopianism.

Gray Kochhar-Lindgren's (2005) *transepochal state* and Appadurai's (1998) condition of *historical rupture*, I believe, attempt to describe a decisive "moment" in the flow—a turning point. And their composite sketch of our era must necessarily be viewed within the context of accelerated environmental degradation and the condition of global warming/ climate change. Each one of us is being asked to stop and consider the apparent "inevitability" of our collective destiny. Thus, I invite those who engage in the practice of curriculum studies' "post-reconceptualization" to consider the "next moment" in curriculum studies within the context of the present technologically inspired *transepochal state*.

As humanity quietly disappears into its self-generated emptying, perhaps the discordance and suffering such a condition naturally creates will foster an awakening and an active resistance. However, as noted by curriculum theorist James B. Macdonald (1971/1995), humanity is sleepwalking on a tightrope. In an essay entitled, "A Vision of a Humane School," he references the poet and visionary William Blake, "Do what you will, this life is a fiction and is made up of contradiction" (p. 51).

Macdonald (1995) elaborates on this idea of contradiction and the human condition and explains in the following quotation the nature of our current "serious contradiction."

> The contradiction lies within the tension of humanness and technology. The question is whether men will dehumanize themselves through the creation of a technological environment and its consequent social arrangements.
>
> What will awaken men from the idiocy of their technological compulsions? Will we be saved by superior intelligence from the unknown universe? Will there be a second coming of Christ? Perhaps, but then, perhaps not. Will California quake and crumble in the Pacific as a warning to men? Or shall we simply risk the possibility of beginning again after we have purged ourselves in the fire of nuclear redemption? (p. 49)

He recognizes the despair such sobering reflection generates and explains that as educators, we cannot but hold on to hope—specifically, as it is defined by Eric Fromm: "To hope means to be ready at every moment for that which is not yet born, and yet not to become desperate if there is no birth in our lifetime" (1968, p. 50). Thus, we are called not only to have hope, but also to trust and have faith. The moral center upon which education stands calls us to have the courage to face the reality of our self-constructed contradictions. And I believe that Macdonald, writing in 1971, was a visionary having stated so clearly that the central contradiction defining our post/modern era is the tension between our humanness and our technological inventions.

If we sense the nature of the current *transepochal state*, the question naturally arises, what ought we to do? In terms of educational policy, it is clear that current reforms, as exemplified by No Child Left Behind and its antecedents that emphasized technology-based reform (Goals 2000, A Nation at Risk), are based on standards and accountability schemes that reflect the instrumental values of efficiency and control (Ferneding, 2003). Indeed, as Macdonald (1971/1995) observes, schools are "too relevant to our society," meaning they reflect the "shoddiness that pervades our general social experience" (p. 51). Moreover, the ideology of achievement reflects the fetish of competition that drives society at large. As a socializing environment, education's purpose has shifted from a context that can explore our humanness via a curriculum based on the humanities to an environment of containment that inculcates the givenness of that which exists. This condition is antithetical to the moral basis of education and has dire consequences to the health of a democratic society, especially as the surveillant eye of the neural net penetrates deeper into the life-world.

Pinar, Reynolds, Slattery, and Taubman (1995) explain how the reconceptualists, inspired by philosophy, aesthetics, and theology, challenged the dominance of the Tyler rationale, whereby emphasis is placed on the rationalization of curriculum development (e.g., objectives, evaluation, selection, organization), as a way of envisioning education and curriculum studies. The purpose of the reconceptualist movement is not so much the development of curriculum per se, but rather the quest to understand education in relation to self and the human condition. For example, Duane Huebner (1999), who emphasizes the centrality of love and transcendence regarding the aim of education, perceived modernity as a specific human condition characterized by immersion within a technological order. This technological order is subject to the reification of knowledge and the instrumentality of relational knowing and thus carries the seed of dehumanization. He explains that the technicist position that influences education today uses knowledge "as a manifestation of power, not as a manifestation of reverence and duty" (p. 368). The technicist position also risks the formation of idols, "and participation in the structure of idolatry" (p. 366). Huebner invites educators to embrace the "lure of the transcendent" as a means toward debilitating those mechanizing forces that threaten to dehumanize.

Macdonald (1971/1995) also makes reference to the intersection of transcendence and the technological order. He describes the nuclear and electronic age as "an operating pattern" and a "cultural milieu that has never existed before" (p. 74). He indicates a generalized condition of technological ubiquity that seems to suggest a posthuman condition with which individuals must struggle to transcend: "Humanity will eventually transcend technology by turning inward, the only viable alternate that allows a human being to experience oneself in the world as a creative and vital element" (1971/1995, p. 75). He further explains that freedom is central to understanding the purpose of education and proposes a "transcendental development ideology" model of curriculum development. This model emphasizes metaphysics and individuation and ultimately counters the dominance of technological rationality by emphasizing "aesthetic rationality" (p.79).

While an emphasis on transcendence offers an avenue towards hope, it leaves me uneasy. I wonder if Macdonald or Huebner underestimated not so much technology's ability to constitute social reality, but rather how much humans would willingly celebrate this outcome. And, it is not so much the practicality of actualizing a curriculum model based on metaphysics and individuation in schools, although this is a mighty issue. Other concerns arise. What is the meaning of transcendence within postmodern technoculture? Has the meaning and condition or need for transcendence changed in relation to the emergence of an information or network society and "electronic spiritualism"?

Ralph Waldo Emerson, writing in the tradition of American transcendentalism (1830s–1860s), taught us about civil disobedience and the relationship between an individual and a system. And today we can still ask, how does one live within a controlling or, as conceived by Foucault, disciplining system that configures the self and the care of the soul? But perhaps most important at present is the question: How has the *nature* of this controlling system changed? And thus, how has the manner in which one might re/act changed? What is the nature of self within the context of an environment in which our relation to time and space has fundamentally shifted? How does one negotiate the splintering of the self within a/spatial a/synchronous environment of the televisual and "real virtuality"? In other words, how might one seek transcendence if the cultural sphere has become escape itself—an unreality that nevertheless possesses, indeed constitutes, the nature of our lived experiences? Is this what Castells meant by stating that, at this (transepochal) time, culture has finally superseded nature? Consider Ihde's technosphere or Castell's real virtuality. Stated in another manner: What is it that we transcend if, via ICT, the nature of our lives is such that technology actualizes the ephemerality of transcendence itself? I believe we sense such profound transformations in our world even while we are in denial that our inventions can elicit such changes. This is the nature of how we live the present *transepochal state* that harkens posthumanism.

Macdonald (1971/1995) warns us that because we are immersed within visual culture we have lost our ability to gain access to our inner self and creative potential. The dialectic between the inner and outer self has become diminished because much of our power is given over to the latter dimension. He emphasizes that having visions is not the same as creating them. What is necessary, via education one hopes, is to develop more explicit means by which to give conscious power to creative visualization. Therefore, imagination and imaginative contemplation signal a return to the source of creative humanism and a "reawakening of the human potential."

Maxine Greene (1988, 1995), who also believes that an aesthetic turn within education can awaken self-reflection, imaginative thinking, and a desire for possibility, describes human freedom as the "leitmotiv of our time" (1988, p. 25), a point also raised by Macdonald (1971/1995). She refers to a conditioned environment of our own un/making, dominated by bureaucratic and technological forces that, according to Hannah Arendt, create an administered world based on scientific positivism expressed as "Rule by Nobody." When people acquiesce to such determining forces, a state described by Greene as "submergence" into the commonsense logic of the given, neoliberal radical individualism acts to normalize an ethos of "negative freedom" or "freedom from" such that it is nearly impossible to associate freedom as a goal with universal concern for what is good or right (Greene, 1988). Also, ironically, Dewey's progressivism, which associates democratic freedom with critical thinking (and thus education), is problematic because it arose from a historical context of technological progress. Consequently, according to Greene (1988, p. 44), Dewey and his generation were naïve about the power science and technology would have to literally constitute social and economic systems. Given this, Greene (1988) asks:

> What is left for us in this positivist, media-dominated and self-centered time? How, with so much acquiescence and so much thoughtlessness around us, are we to open people to the power of possibility? How, given the emphasis on preparing the young for a society of high technology, are we to move them to perceive alternatives, to look at things as if they could be otherwise? And why? And to what ends? (p. 55)

Greene invites educators to consider how a return to a careful study of the dialectic between self and society can awaken one from the seduction of the given. Self-knowledge anchored within the ethics of freedom and democratic values can elicit action or praxis to actualize "transformative education" towards the end of social justice (Greene, 1988). She imagines that self-reflective teaching and a curriculum based on the arts can help to revitalize the imagination (Greene, 1995).

However, within the context of a cultural realm dominated by electronic media, what is the meaning and nature of the imagination? How has it been transformed by the shaping forces of systems that have altered our relationship to time and space? Indeed, a subtle but critical change has occurred. Televisual's *timeless time* lived as the seduction of consumption was once considered an escape from the painful and mundane realities of everyday living. It was understood to be "mere entertainment." But today, the televisual nature of media and ICT's cyberspace not only function as sources of ritualized pleasure. Rather, they exist as a virtual "place" where we work, shop, flirt, and essentially live life as a game. Consider the meaning of Macdonald's "inner dialectic of the self" in relation to the creation of cool avatars and "My Space" nodes of perpetual virtual self-reconstruction.

As noted above, the reconfiguration of the social imagination is also central to Appadurai's (1998) conceptualization of globalization. He explains that imagination, once operating within the confines of art, "has broken out into ordinary life" (p. 5). Appadurai's conception of "imagination as social practice" is complex; while social imagination operates as a means of resistance, it can also be co-opted by the aesthetic and seductive nature of the televisual. In fact, Heidegger (1977) conceptualizes the nature of technology as being grounded in *poiesis*. Ihde (1979) states that, according to Heidegger, "technology and art belong to the danger and possible salvation of the same epoch of Being" (p. 115). Indeed, what if not only technology but also the realm of art has succumbed to the condition of enframement and thus not only reflects, but, according to art critic Donald Kuspit (2005), celebrates the condition of commodification? And as a social condition, we must come to understand how commodification actualizes the anaesthetizing of the social imagination and as such is a form of dehumanization. It may be that dehumanization is both the cause and effect of the "disenchantment of the world," and in this sense is truly an unfortunate destiny.

Conclusion

In conclusion, the meaning of the present *transepochal state* is not definitive. However, if our inventions hold the potential to act as virtual pacifiers that lull us into deeper states of electronic spiritualism, our quest is to awaken from the seduction of such transcendence. Until we do so, the question, "What ought we to do?" cannot be raised. In addition, education as an institution, and as an imaginative potentiality, can participate in the rediscovery of the human potential only if the technical rationalist structuration that defines its purpose and nature is dismantled. This act of dismantling, ironically, must necessarily arise from the realm of possibility—the realm of human imagination, which is undergoing immense transformations within the present *transepochal state*.

If concern for freedom is the "leitmotiv of our times" (Greene, 1988), one must necessarily ask what we have done thus far with our freedom, with our imagination. According to the wise teacher in Daniel Quinn's (1992) novel, *Ishmael* (who just happens to be a gorilla) humanity has managed to imprison itself within a narrative "that casts mankind as the enemy of the world" (p. 75), a condition that, I propose, essentially describes Heidegger's state of enframement. I understand the state of enframement as an acute state of separation from nature, from others and from the self. When we feel separated from others or within ourselves, it is impossible to feel love. Given this, it is imperative that we understand the relationship between technology and transcendence regarding the immanence of power. Such reflection is not simply a counterdiscourse of "technological pessimism" (Segal, 1994), but rather, as Huebner suggests, an opportunity to "probe deeper into the educational landscape to reveal how the spiritual and moral is being denied in everything" (Pinar et al., 1995, p. 862).

And while I propose this with *great* caution, it is possible that science, via the findings of quantum physics, specifically in tandem with growing ecological disaster, may inspire a desperate humanity. If we are fortunate it will not be in a manner that fosters a deeper submergence into electronic spiritualism. Rather, inspired by its own findings, such as the theory of relativity and quantum physics (e.g., uncertainty principle), those who practice science may truly perceive the principle of reflexivity regarding the nature of mind and epistemology and in turn act in a manner that acknowledges how humans bear significant responsibility as cocreators of their world.

It is certain that if Big Science continues to operate within the paradigm of scientific materialism, a reductionistic philosophical position that courts nihilism and naturalizes dehumanization, human imagination shall be limited by a destructive paradigm that makes it an "enemy of the world." If, as educators, we seriously consider Huebner's assessment that "the spiritual and moral is being denied in everything" (cited by Pinar et al., 1995, p. 862), how is it that we unwittingly acquiesce to the operation of a technoscience that is without a consciousness of ethics, much less a spiritual–ethical foundation of compassion and stewardship? For me, *the* question that characterizes the current postreconceptualist moment has already been posed but obviously remains unanswered: "What will awaken men from the idiocy of their technological compulsions?" (Macdonald, 1995, p. 49).

References

Appadurai, A. (1998). *Modernity at large: Cultural dimensions of globalization.* Minneapolis: University of Minnesota Press.

Baudrillard, J. (2001). *The vital illusion.* New York: Columbia University Press.

Bauman, Z. (1998). *Globalization: The human consequences.* New York: Columbia University Press.

Becker, E. (1973). *The denial of death.* New York: Free Press.

Becker, E. (1975). *Escape from evil.* New York: Free Press.

Carey, J. (1989). *Communication as culture.* New York: Routledge.

Carson, R. (1962) *The silent spring.* New York: Houghton Mifflin.

Carson, R. (1963, April 3). *The silent spring of Rachel Carson.* CBS Reports television program transcripts Retrieved February 20, 2007, from http://www.rachelcarson.org/

Castells, M. (2000). *The rise of the network society* (Vol. 1, 2nd ed.). Malden, MA: Blackwell

Davis, M. (2006). *Planet of slums.* New York: Verso.

Eisler, R. (1995). *The chalice and the blade.* San Francisco: HarperCollins. (Original work published 1987)

Eisler, R. (2000). *Tomorrow's children.* Boulder, CO: Westview Press.

Ferneding, K. (2003). *Questioning technology: Electronic technologies and educational reform policy.* New York: Lang.

Foucault, M. (1980). *Power/knowledge: Selected interviews & other writings 1972–1977.* New York: Pantheon Books.

Fromm, E. (1968). *The revolution of hope.* New York: Harper & Row.

Greene, M. (1988). *The dialectic of freedom.* New York: Teachers College Press.

Greene, M. (1995). *Releasing the imagination.* New York: Teachers College Press.

Heidegger, M. (1977). The question concerning technology. In D. Kreell (Ed.), *Martin Heidegger: Basic writings.* (pp. 3–35). New York: Harper & Row.

Huebner, D. (1999). *Lure of the transcendent.* Mahwah, NJ: Erlbaum.

Ihde, D. (1979). *Technics and praxis.* Boston: Reidel.

Innis, H. (1951). *The bias of communication.* Toronto: University of Toronto Press.

Innis, H. (1952). *Changing concepts of time.* Toronto: University of Toronto Press.

Junger, E. (1960). *The glass bees.* (Trans. Louise Bogan & Elizabeth Mayer). New York: Straus & Giroux.

Kochhar-Lindgren, G. (2005). *Technologics: Ghosts, the incalculable, and the suspension of animation.* Albany, NY: SUNY Press.

Kuspit, D. (2005). *The end of art.* Cambridge, England: Cambridge University Press.

Lyotard, J. (1984). *The postmodern condition.* Minneapolis: University of Minnesota Press.

Macdonald, J. (1995*). Theory as a prayerful act* (B. J. Macdonald, Ed.). New York: Lang. (Original work published 1971)

Marcuse, H. (1964). *One-dimensional man: Studies in the ideology of advanced industrial society.* Boston, MA: Beacon Press.

McLuhan, M. (1964). *Understanding media: The extensions of man.* New York: McGraw-Hill.

Noble, D. (1997). *The religion of technology: The divinity of man and the spirit of invention.* New York: Knopf.

Pinar, W., Reynolds, W., Slattery, P., & Taubman, P. (1995). *Understanding curriculum.* New York: Lang.

Porte, J. (1988). *Representative man: Ralph Waldo Emerson in his time.* New York: Columbia University Press.

Quinn, D. (1992). *Ishmael.* New York: Bantam Books.

Segal, H. P. (1994). The cultural contradictions of high tech: Or the many ironies of contemporary technological optimism. In Y. Ezhari, E. Mendelsohn, & H. P. Segal (Eds.), *Technology, pessimism and postmodernism* (pp. 175–216). Amherst: University of Massachusetts Press.

Tyler, R. (1976, October). Two new emphases in curriculum development. *Educational Leadership,* 61–71.

Wertheim, M. (1999). *The pearly gates of cyberspace: The history of space from Dante to the internet.* New York: Norton.

Suggested Reading Questions

1. In what ways might educators help students investigate their relationships with technology?
2. What forms of curricular understanding might move technological concepts from their "givenness" of instrumental rationality toward the poetic, artistic, and spiritual?
3. The author suggests that without deterritorialization of media we risk the configuration of our social imaginations to the given. What forms of aesthetic inquiry and media analysis might create sites for imagining alternate realities?
4. Posthuman suggests lines among human, machine, and nature have become less distinct (for example, prosthetic limbs and pacemakers). What sorts of ethical commitments might frame humanity's relationship with technology in ways that help actualize more just and equitable societies?
5. Technology has refigured society's notion of time and space and challenged educator's notions of childhood. What sort of curriculum lenses might assist students in exceeding utilitarianism to focus on digital art and what the author terms "electronic spirituality"?

Response to Karen Ferneding
Smashing the Feet of Idols
Curriculum Phronesis as a Way through the Wall

Nancy J. Brooks

> I think, then, that the chief task of philosophy is to justify…and to defend practical and political reason against the domination of technology based on science. That is the point of philosophical hermeneutics. It corrects the peculiar falsehood of modern consciousness: the idolatry of scientific method and of the anonymous authority of the sciences…. (Gadamer, 1975, p. 316)

To interpret the moment of post-reconceptualization, Ferneding looks back to the first moments of the reconceptualization and three of the scholars who served as midwives at its birth: James Macdonald, Dwayne Huebner, and Maxine Greene. I take great comfort in the works of these scholars. I came to academe much later in life than most and well after the reconceptualization. As someone with nearly 20 years of school-based experience, the work of these intellectuals helped me make sense of the field of curriculum studies, of academe, and of the world in general. Having survived the first massive federal intrusion upon our field, these scholars stand as examples of intellectuals who persevered, finding "lines of flight" (Deleuze, 1995, p. 19) in difficult times.

To this list of exemplars I would add Paul Klohr, whose oeuvre is perhaps written more in the hearts and minds of his students than in print, but who has been nevertheless every bit as influential in the field. With Macdonald, Huebner, and Greene, Klohr has demonstrated for us that, "It is not a question of worrying or of hoping for the best, but of finding new weapons" (Deleuze, 1995, p. 178). Although the weapons this band of scholars created in the form of new curriculum discourses were rejected by the mainstream educational establishment, they were able to hew out a space that provided for "the passage to the Reconceptualization" (Pinar, 2007, p. 10).

We now stand in an era in which it appears that the power of our society's "technological compulsions" is stronger than ever, in both methodological and ideological terms. Not only has the discourse of putative national economic in/security subsumed that of education in general, but in many states the province of state educational oversight has now been expanded from K-12 to P-16. In some places, professors of education are summoned to state workshops for instruction on how to teach their classes. The common sense of many of these "reforms" seems generally accepted—it is either seldom questioned or the questions are seldom aired. Technology as both general and educational method and discourse is inextricably entwined with the global economic order. In the words of David G. Smith (2003):

> The most important challenge for curriculum work in the new millennium may be to develop the ability to deconstruct precisely as theory the unquestioned assumptions underwriting regnant forms of global economic procedure. Without this, curriculum work, even in the name of justice and equity, will hit its head against a wall.

> *The key is to find a way through the wall to change the thinking that constructs it* [italics added]. (p. 36)

Illuminating and transforming this wall of theoretical assumptions was exactly the concern of H. G. Gadamer, as stated succinctly in a piece that was published nearly 35 years ago. Gadamer, a former student of Martin Heidegger, explained his perspective on the problem of science/technology—summarized in the words of the quote above—while in dialogue with critical theorists.

In the mid- to late 20th century critical theory gained much more of a following, especially in the U.S., than Gadamer's philosophical hermeneutics. In spite of the reams of scholarship produced on it, it appears from our standpoint now, however, that critical theory has failed on its own to awaken our society from our electronic slumbers. However, I am wondering if conditions might now be more hospitable to Gadamer's approach—or at least a reinvigoration of it—especially in regard to his key use of the intellectual virtue of *phronesis*, translated variously as "practical reason," "practical wisdom," "moral knowledge," or "prudence."

Drawing from Aristotle, Gadamer (1997/1960) distinguished this kind of knowing from *theoria*, or "knowing on the basis of universal principles" (p. 21). *Phronesis* is "directed towards the concrete situation" and "must grasp the 'circumstances' in their infinite variety" (p. 21). *Phronesis* also differs from technical knowledge (*technē*) in several important ways: (1) It is not a technique to be learned, but is better described as the ability to choose the right thing in the midst of a difficult situation; (2) it includes an important element of self-knowledge, emphasizing the importance of historical consciousness, and (3) it involves an element of sympathetic understanding.

In the brief article "Hermeneutics and Social Science" Gadamer (1975) recounted major philosophical trends that have brought us to a place where "our cultural self-understanding is dominated by the one-sided concept of scientific procedure resulting in unlimited technology" (p. 310), a one-sidedness that is "obvious to the extent that one senses the richness and breadth of the humanities" (p. 311). He attributed Western society's infatuation with science to people's longing for the type of normative patterns that evaporated following two world wars. The central problem of Western society, according to Gadamer, is that this longing leads the citizenry to invest science with exaggerated authority. Through this process the concept of practice has become understood as the application of science to technical tasks, resulting in the degradation of practical reason to technical control.[1] In the resulting highly technologized and controlled society, "The crucial change is that practical wisdom [*phronesis*] can no longer be promoted by personal contact and the mutual exchange of views [conversation] among the citizens… many forms of our daily life no longer require personal decision" (p. 313). As educators, we can clearly identify with this in the way the need to select curricula and even instructional methods is being removed from our plate of responsibilities.

Gadamer (1975) rejected critical theorists' claim that emancipatory reflection could unmask the impact of "capitalistic, bureaucratic" interests on public opinion (or "common sense"). He objected on the basis that the critique of ideology "implies its own freedom from any ideology" and "enthrones its own norms and ideals as self-evident and absolute" (p. 315). He proposed the dialogical process of his philosophical hermeneutics—with *phronesis* as its goal and guide—as a better approach to communication and a continuing exchange of views. He gave a nod to the power of rhetoric, especially as it was beginning to manifest itself in the mass media, and to its role in the transmission of monological scientific culture. But he concluded that "Both rhetoric and the transmission of scientific knowledge…need the counterbalance of hermeneutical appropriation, which works in the form of dialogue. And precisely and especially practical and political reason can only be realized and transmitted dialogically" (p. 316).

Of course, Gadamer's work is not new to curriculum studies. Many curriculum scholars have drawn from it, and indeed, the reconceptualization itself—*understanding* curriculum—has been a hermeneutic endeavor. Atkins (1988) and Stanley (1992) have even written specifically on *phronesis*. The obvious question, then, is why I am hopeful that the time may now be ripe for *phronesis* to function as "the key through the wall" of our society's technological compulsions.

I might begin by surmising why, if it has such potential, *phronesis* has not engendered the same enthusiasm as critical theory in the post-Sputnik years, whether within or without the walls of the academy. That will undoubtedly become clearer as we gain more historical distance. Obviously, the notion of practical judgment is not as "sexy" as that of false consciousness. For curriculum scholars, perhaps the association of *phronesis* with the word *practical* was too threatening at a time in which they were trying to break free from "the intellectually restricting consequences" (Pinar, 2006, p. 158) of having to address all of their scholarship to teachers and administrators. Or it could be that the status of "practical wisdom" did not compare favorably to *theoria* as an intellectual project due to the early intensity of the "theory/practice" controversy.

But times have changed in regard to all of these possible conditions. Some of the shine is off of the intrigue of critical theory. As to the second condition, curriculum studies has built up a wealth of scholarship unburdened by the old ties to curriculum development, some of which has even broken ground for us to understand the greater possibilities for *phronesis*. In addition to the work of Atkins (1988) and Stanley (1992), Henderson and Kesson (2004) have more recently developed their "curriculum wisdom" paradigm for problem solving around the notion of a "robust *phronesis* that is deepened and extended through its interactions" (p. 56) with six other inquiry modes they have identified. Outside of our own field, interest in *phronesis* has also been growing, perhaps most noticeably demonstrated by Danish scholar Bent Flyvbjerg's (2001) attempt to use it as a basis upon which to "restore social science to its classical position as a practical, intellectual activity aimed at clarifying the problems, risks, and possibilities we face as humans and society, and at contributing to social and political praxis" (p. 4)

In the case of the third condition, that of the comparable status of *phronesis* as an intellectual activity, the status of *theoria* has itself changed. The notion of any type of knowledge having the status of being enduring and foundational is now much more suspect. As Eisner (2002) has written,

> Our confidence in episteme is less secure that [sic] it once was. The reasons are several. Pluralism has become more salient in our approach to knowledge. We are, in general, less confident about finding the one best way, even though in some circles this ambition still lingers. (p. 376)

Contributing to this may be the impact of discoveries in the physical sciences that demonstrate our inability to know, predict, and control as we once anticipated. In addition, over the past several decades materialist perspectives have gained significant ground, emphasizing that science which arises from specific historical conditions is not value free. The result of these changes in our understanding of knowledge is perhaps a little less reverence for *theoria* and a greater appreciation for *phronesis* as an intellectual activity.

It is possible, though, that the condition most responsible for the failure of *phronesis* to take hold earlier was its lack of attention to the nature of power. A number of scholars have noted this weakness and attempted to rectify it through some melding of the work of Gadamer and Foucault. Indeed, this is Flyvbjerg's (2001) approach. In some regard, then, the years of attention to critical theory may have actually been laying the groundwork for a more effective development and employment of the concept of *phronesis*. Certainly, with its appreciation for the humanities, its emphasis on self-knowledge, historical consciousness, and conversation, *phronesis* scholarship has found a home in curriculum studies. Indeed, as an intellectual activity focused on practical judgment, it would seem to provide an umbrella and a language broad enough for any kind of curriculum work. Perhaps more importantly, it may be able to make the leap beyond the academy to "correct the peculiar falsehood of modern consciousness" (Gadamer, 1975, p. 316).

Whether the key of *phronesis* will lead us through the wall of our technological assumptions, I cannot say. However, Ferneding has clearly laid out for us the implications of our changing reality. As we exist more and more in a technology-mediated environment, the contradictions that lie within the "tension of humanness and technology" grow ever stronger. Perhaps it is not by coincidence, but from necessity, that Western scholars are returning to *phronesis*. According to Flyvbjerg (2001), *phronesis* is most important among the intellectual virtues because "it is the activity by which instrumental rationality is balanced by value-rationality…" (p. 4). He elaborates:

> Since Weber…the domain of instrumental rationality has continued to grow and has tended to marginalize value-rationality. Today the problems involved in this development relate not only to Weber's concerns with social and cultural affairs, but to the biosphere as well and to humankind's existence as a species. (pp. 61–62)

If Flybjerg is correct and humankind does not re/learn the function and importance of *phronesis*, it is possible that a grim future awaits, if any future at all.

Note

1. We should note that the concept of *phronesis* has been disappearing from Western scholarship for hundreds of years—to the extent that we have no analogous term for it as in the cases of "theory" from *theoria* and "technique" or "technical" from *technē* (Flyvbjerg, 2001, p. 57).

References

Atkins, E. (1988). Reframing curriculum theory in terms of interpretation and practice: A hermeneutical approach. *Journal of Curriculum Studies, 20*(5), 437–448.

Deleuze, G. (1995). *Negotiations* (M. Joughlin, Trans.). New York: Columbia University. (Original work published 1990)

Eisner, E. W. (2002). From episteme to *phronesis* to artistry in the study and improvement of teaching. *Teaching and Teacher Education, 18*, 375–385.

Flyvbjerg, B. (2001). *Making social science matter: Why social inquiry fails and how it can succeed again* (S. Sampson, Trans.). Cambridge, England: Cambridge University Press.

Gadamer, H.-G. (1975). Hermeneutics and social science. *Cultural Hermeneutics, 2*, 307–316.

Gadamer, H.-G. (1997). *Truth and method* (2nd rev. ed., J. Weinsheimer & D. G. Marshall, Trans.). New York: Continuum. (Original work published 1960)

Henderson, J. G., & Kesson, K. R. (2004). *Curriculum wisdom: Educational decisions in democratic societies*. Upper Saddle River, NJ: Pearson.

Pinar, W. F. (2006). *The synoptic text today: Curriculum development after the reconceptualization*. New York: Lang.

Pinar, W. F. (2007, April). *Disciplinarity and the intellectual advancement of U.S. curriculum studies: The Canon Project*. Paper presented to the annual meeting of the American Association for the Advancement of Curriculum Studies, Chicago.

Smith, D. G. (2003). Curriculum and teaching face globalization. In W. F. Pinar (Ed.), *International handbook of curriculum research* (pp. 35–52). Mahwah, NJ: Erlbaum.

Stanley, W. (1992). *Curriculum for utopia: Social reconstructionism and critical pedagogy in the postmodern era*. Albany, NY: SUNY Press.

9 The Posthuman Condition
A Complicated Conversation

John A. Weaver

Chapter Overview

The author discusses the Greek understanding of technology as both skill and art and notes that it can be a creative and destructive force depending on how it is put to use by humans. The author then describes the difference between technology that enhances humanity's unconcealment and modern technology which has been framed simply as a neutral tool, one that makes possible increased efficiency. Noting Heidegger's insights on modern technology, the author discusses the posthuman condition which has reclaimed the poiesis of technology at the same time it has opened the door for unprecedented abuse of the human body. Turning to the curriculum field, the author notes that curriculum scholars are largely silent on the topic of biomedicine, which the author attributes to a rigidity and lack of digital art. Next, the author describes a posthuman condition where humans return to nature and technology enters the body. The author provides three vignettes which demonstrate how new biomedical technology raises conceptual and ethical concerns. Lastly, the author calls on curriculum theorists to claim their voice in the biomedical field.[1]

But Where Danger is, Grows

—The Saving Power also (Hölderlin cited in Heidegger, 1977, p. 28)

Martin Heidegger cited this epigraph from the 18th century German romantic poet, Heinrich Hölderlin in his famous essay "The Question Concerning Technology" to describe the Janus face of technology, which could be poetically creative or destructively dehumanizing; it all depended on what humans let technology do. Like humans, animals, and other things, technology had an essence, and that essence was not technological. The struggle and destiny of technology was to unconceal this essence. The process of unconcealing its essence was a process of bringing forth. This bringing forth of technology's essence was captured in the Greek understanding of technology as *technē* or *poesis*. *Technē* was simultaneously technique or instrumentalism and skill or art. When humans permitted technology's *poesis* to burst forth, the useful and creative force of technology shone and acted as a device to enhance humanity's own unconcealment. This unconcealment of the *poiesis* of technology helped unleash the creative passions and desires of humanity in every aspect of human existence. With the help of *technē* the peasant became a nurturer of the land, the bridge became a peaceful causeway across a river, and the artist emerged as a truth teller.

When technology was unable to unconceal itself, the danger Hölderlin warned about appeared. It is when Heidegger begins to discuss the lost power of technology to bring forth its essence and the essence of humans at a pivotal point in his essay, he stops talking about technology in general and specifically uses the word *modern* technology to raise his concerns about the destructive force of technology. It is modern technology that has lost its way from technology's Greek roots and enframed the potential of technology and humans to unconceal themselves. Enframement prevents technology from revealing its essence and limits technology to a crass instrumentalism in which technology is viewed as a neutral tool, constructed simply to assist a more efficient society. Such a one-sided and impoverished visioning of technology as a tool dangerously reduces things and humans to objects or standing reserves. With the creation of dams, a mighty river is no longer permitted to fulfill its destiny as a majestic symbol of the power and beauty of nature; instead it is now a source of electricity to be used whenever the people need it. In a very prophetic statement, Heidegger, who personally knew something about treating humans as standing reserves but could not unconceal the courage to speak about his own experiences, warned against the use of humans as standing reserves when he wrote: "The current talk about human resources, about the supply of patients for a clinic, gives evidence of this [idea of humans as standing reserves]" (Heidegger, 1977, p. 18).

Heidegger's insights about modern technology and the creation of standing reserves out of humans is prophetic because we have entered the biomedical[2] age in which numerous cases can be discussed to demonstrate how technology has simultaneously reclaimed the poetic roots of Greek *technē* and opened the door for an unprecedented and unrelenting abuse of the human body as a site of standing reserves. In this chapter, I want to discuss the posthuman condition that has reclaimed the *poiesis* of technology and taken us to the abyss of human abuses. Modern technology has ushered in an era of biomedical innovations from the Human Genome Project, the Visible Human Project, pharmaceutical wonder drugs, organ transplants, stem cell research, and human regeneration. More specifically, it is the rise of computer technology and the digital age that makes all of these scientific creations possible. These technologies have ushered in not only a biomedical age but also an explosion in the realm of art. Animation, graphic novels, films, and television are experiencing a renaissance because of the digital image. It is no coincidence that artists are experiencing a renaissance at the same time scientists are. Artist and scientist have once again become intertwined, the Greeks have been rediscovered, Heidegger can rest more securely in his grave. A scientist cannot perform his craft of reading DNA strands, cell lines, blood stains, brain scans, or organ matches without summoning their interpretive skills to read digital images and computer print outs. Without a will to interpret, scientists cannot function. At the same time, artists cannot create their cutting edge art without computer images, video montages, and computer programs.

Yet, no one, including Heidegger, should rest too easily or exalt in an overabundant jubilation too soon. Just as a renaissance of art and science is occurring, people around the world are perhaps no more vulnerable to abuse and terror than they are today and in the near future. The posthuman condition has not only rewritten the code of humanity, it has rewritten the rules of insurance, organ donation, body ownership, human subjectivity, medical care, patent laws, entrepreneurial investment habits, and property rights. All of these disparate fields of economics, politics, and culture now emerge with the body as the center of dispute and struggle. In the remainder of this chapter I want to explain why curriculum theorists have to enter into this complicated conversation, define what the posthuman condition is, and demonstrate how the posthuman condition reshapes human subjectivity, social justice, and human dignity. I will end this chapter with some ideas on what curriculum theory can do to become more active in defining the posthuman condition.

A Complicated Conversation and Our Voices of Silence?

> The problem in our culture is not illiteracy, but the literalisms that make us ill....
> When people say they are frustrated I think they lack art. (Doll, 2000, xiii)

I begin this section with some thoughts from our most thoughtful and poetic curriculum theorist, Mary Aswell Doll, because her words also capture my concerns with curriculum theory and its lack of a relationship with the biomedical revolution. William Pinar has described curriculum theory as a complicated conversation. It certainly is. Curriculum theorists have extended the field of education to include popular culture, youth cultures, psychoanalysis, women's studies, gay and lesbian studies, ethnic studies, and the list goes on. We have entered these discussions with an enthusiasm that has been lacking in many fields for decades, and in the case of education, perhaps centuries. Yet when it comes to the biomedical field, the technology that brings the world biomedicine, and the posthuman condition, curriculum theorists are almost united in silence. There are certainly some voices in the wilderness such as Peter Appelbaum, Karen Ferneding, Annette Gough, and Noel Gough urging curriculum theory to pay attention to how their bodies and subjectivity are being reshaped and reconstituted economically, politically, and culturally. But these voices are too few and have not led to theorists entering into the complicated conversation of the posthuman condition. There are plenty of voices in curriculum theory such as Dennis Sumara, Brent Davis, Rebecca Luce-Kapler, Bill Pinar, David Jardine, and countless others who have theorized the body but rarely in connection with technology and still less rare with biotechnology.

This silence stems from two phenomena within curriculum theory and both are captured in Doll's epigraph. First, when it comes to technology curriculum theorists are too rigid, too paranoid, too literal. Most curriculum theorists are fearful that technology has and will attack their subjectivity. Such a view interprets technology as a tool, something that is not a part of our humanity but an intruder that threatens our creativity and autonomy. The problem with this literal demarcation line drawn in the sand between technology and humans is that the winds have already blown the line away. It is easy to anecdotally and empirically demonstrate how humanity has merged with, or emerged from, technology to not only violate human subjectivity but to make it better. Second, curriculum theorists are frustrated because they lack art, digitally enhanced art. Certainly, curriculum theorists do not lack art in the traditional sense of poetry, literature, painting, and essays. There is no other field within education that is more artistic than curriculum theory. The art curriculum theorists lack is digitally enhanced art. A new will to art has emerged that is impossible to understand without grasping the impact of technology on art. As I mentioned in an essay in *The Journal of Curriculum Theorizing*,

> the will to art is a building block to other dimensions of life. The Cliché art imitates life is just an overused statement, but reversed to read life imitates art in the digital age marks an important shift.... Literally, new media artists are creating new worlds, new environments in which the users/viewers create experiences, feelings, and actions as they interact within the art installation. (2005, p. 85)

These new worlds are missed when frustration and fear dictate how curriculum theorists approach technology.

Lacking digital art, however, is the least of our worries as curriculum theorists. By not engaging the biomedical world and the posthuman condition, curriculum theorists risk their own sense of social justice and self. As I will demonstrate below, there are no aspects of our sense of justice and self left untouched by the posthuman condition. To ignore the posthuman condition is to abandon all sense of justice, equality, hope, and identity. If we leave biomedical science to the scientists then nostalgic literalism and frustration is all we will have left. We can no longer, in spite of the frustrated voices of scientists, leave science to the scientists. They cannot be trusted. Curriculum theorists, and all citizens of a democracy must raise their voices or, without any attempt at hyperbole or hyperbull, there will be no democracy to talk about.

The Posthuman Condition: What Is in a Name?

 I use the name *posthuman* because it is the best term to capture the diversity and complexity of the intersection between humans and technology since the 1980s. Often when I use the term *posthuman* in conference papers or classroom lectures, audience members object to the name because they assume it literally means after human. If the term *posthuman* has any connotations of "after" in its meaning, it is only referring to the end of the humanist definition of modern Western man. I specifically use the gender and regionally specific "Western man" here because the Enlightened, humanist term used *man* as a universal catch-all phrase that functioned as a synecdoche for all of humanity. The assumption was that "Western man" represented reason and could therefore speak for all other people. Through "Western man" no other(ed) peoples needed to speak. The humanist term *Western man* also implies a separation and superiority between "man," nature, and technology. Separated from nature and technology, the most commonly held belief was that since man was separate and superior from nature, it was within man's purview to exploit nature as "Western man" deemed necessary. Since "Western man" was separate from technology, then technology was a mere tool used by humans to better their lives. While the first relationship created environmental crises, the second has created an instrumental logic that has exploited segments of the world's population through slavery, industrialization, and wars.

The posthuman condition challenges these assumptions. The lines between "Western man," or now any type of man, no longer exist with nature or technology. In the posthuman condition humans return to nature and technology now enhances or enters into the human body. As a result of these major changes in the realities of the worlds we inhabit, the posthuman condition marks a radical transformation, both discursively and materially of human beings. This transformation is best captured in two terms *cyborg* and *fyborg*. A cyborg constitutes a body that is physically altered to enhance an individual's capabilities. For instance, a pacemaker, artificial hearing implant, a surgically implanted microcomputer chip, or a prosthetic limb makes an individual a "cyborg." A technological device has become a part of the human body and because of that "addition" the body is able to perform what nature was unable to do. Let me provide you with an anecdote. Recently, I was walking from my office to our student computer laboratory. While I was walking there, a student with a prosthetic limb darted across the room. What was amazing about this momentary experience was that the young woman's gait was just as natural with the prosthetic limb as with a natural leg. There was no limp, no signs of displacement. It serves as evidence of how far humans have become cyborgs and connected to technology. A *fyborg*, a term coined by Gregory Stock (2003), refers to any bodily enhancement/transformation through any temporary technological intrusion into the body. For instance, the use of stem cell lines to create an organ, gene therapy, PET or CAT scans, cosmetic surgeries, or kidney dialysis are examples in which technology is used to insert, as uninvasively as possible, a new DNA strand, treated blood, healthier neuron pathways, or a new organ. In all of these cases, technology enters into the body or connects to the body but does not remain there. In all of these cases, when successful, the individual is healthier and life is prolonged.

While each of these examples physically alters the human body, posthuman scholars suggest there are subtle, and potentially dangerous, metaphorical shifts in thinking about the human body as well. As a result, humans not only begin to look and feel differently they also think differently. As Eugene Thacker notes the posthuman body is "approached on the level of information…that, as information, can be technically manipulated, controlled, and monitored" but also seen as containing a material essence (2003, p. 89). Katherine Hayles in her work *How We Became Posthuman* (1999) suggests the posthuman body is also discursively viewed as "the original prosthesis we all learn to manipulate" in which "there are no essential differences or absolute demarcations between bodily existence and computer simulation, cybernetic mechanism and biological organism, robot teleology and human goals" (p. 3). If the posthuman body is interpreted as a seamless and permeable organism that shares a common ontological and physiological space with machines then there is nothing from stopping individuals from whimsically replacing their "natural" human parts with more efficient, pleasing, and effective replacements. The danger lies in the loss of materiality of the human body and more specifically, if the body is seen only as information, then, given current power dynamics throughout the world, certain bodies will matter more than others. We can already witness this phenomenon through stories of people from poorer nations selling their organs to wealthier people who need a transplant but refuse to place their names on a donor waiting list in their home country. The fear of reducing the body to information code is also expressed in the reproduction research in which women throughout the world risk injury and perhaps death in order to donate eggs for "harvesting.

Neither Hayles nor Thacker believe the answer to these power plays and ethical dilemmas is to stop the posthuman condition from developing. Even a cautious and careful critic of the posthuman condition like Hayles admits within the title of her book that it is impossible to stop something that already has happened. Many people throughout the world have already become posthuman. The way to challenge any reduction of the posthuman condition is to reintroduce the materiality of the human body within biomedical, political, economic, and cultural discourses. Thacker introduces a way in which the biomedical field simultaneously views the body as an informational code and as fundamentally material. When a biomedical expert enters a human body with their computer based technology they do so with two assumptions in mind. First, the unhealthy body is viewed as information with a deficient code that can be removed and improved much as a bad computer code can be removed and improved. Second, they assume the removal of this deficient code will mark an improvement in the human's lifespan. After the biomedical expert alters the code of the body, however, the assumption is the individual will return to a "recuperated, healthy, homeostatic body" or a material state in which the individual is able to sustain life on their own. Such an assumption implies the need for a materiality that distinguishes the individual from other individuals and organisms (Thacker, 2003, p.89).

Given these concerns and states, the posthuman condition then can be defined as the rise of a new human condition in which the individual is seen as the embodiment of information code that is consistently interacting with the environment around it in a unique manner that no other individual can experience. Such a definition of an individual implies that each individual is constantly reshaping and remaking themselves, sometimes into healthy and other times unhealthy states. In either state, individuals can choose to enhance their chances for healthier lives through temporarily invasive medical treatment. However, these health "choices" imply that individuals are constantly

negotiating with their environment not only biomedically but also politically, economically, and culturally. As a result, the posthuman condition implies that individuals are
constantly at risk for political and economic exploitation, requiring a rigorous defense
of what human dignity means and what it means to live in a democratic world. Any loss
of human dignity and the favoring of one body over another or the improvement of one
body at the expense of someone else strikes a blow against the creation of a democratic
world based on respect for individual rights. Anything less than respect for individual
rights risks placing individuals as standing reserves readily at hand to serve the health
needs of other individuals.

The Art of Biomedical Fields and Humans as Standing Reserves in the Posthuman World

In this section, I will provide vignettes to highlight the various ways the posthuman condition is constructed and defined. Not one of these vignettes is a thought experiment in
science fiction writing. Each case demonstrates how this new biomedical technology can
be used and, unfortunately, abused.

Redefining a Preexisting Condition

Before the posthuman age a preexisting condition merely meant if a client changed
insurance companies while receiving treatment for an illness or a previous illness such as
cancer reappeared, the insurance company could deny coverage. In the posthuman age,
insurance companies are requesting blood samples from prospective clients to look into
a future that may never emerge. Insurance companies use the blood to study an individual's DNA to determine if they have any strands that are known to cause certain diseases.
For instance, there is a DNA strand that, if found in an individual's genetic makeup,
could cause breast cancer. If disease causing strands are found in an individual's genetic
makeup it does not mean you will contract that disease, with a few exceptions such as
Huntington chorea, it merely means you are predisposed to that disease. In other words,
if you have the DNA strand that causes breast cancer, you smoke, and live next to a chemical plant you will most likely contract breast cancer because of environmental issues than
genetic predisposition. However, insurance companies are using blood samples to deny
coverage to clients who show any predisposition towards any potential disease. Insurance
companies are only willing to insure healthy clients and only willing to insure clients
for those illnesses and diseases that they are less likely to contract. While scientists have
developed a way to help individuals understand their future life history and help them
live longer, healthier lives, insurance companies are using this information to limit their
liability and maximize their profits. To date no state legislature has made it illegal for
insurance companies to deny coverage based on genetic potentialities that might never
emerge. However, the U.S. House of Representatives by an overwhelming majority has
passed antidiscriminatory legislation, but the Senate has yet to act. Insurance companies, like most other big conglomerates, have shifted the burden of responsibility onto
the individual while constructing market conditions that insure a lucrative and stable
flow of profits.

Victor Frankenstein Was Right Only His Method Was Wrong

In Mary Shelley's classic gothic novel *Frankenstein*, the ambitious Dr. Frankenstein tries
to bring back to life a poorly reconstructed human. He succeeds through the use of

electricity, some nighttime digging in cemeteries, and some handy stitching. Of course, the whole technique is far fetched and until most recent times the whole idea was considered to be outrageous. Times have changed, however, and Mary Shelley has proven to be prophetic. One of the purposes for stem cell research is to create a way to regenerate tissue structures and to reverse the aging process. The key to all stem cell research is to "harvest" pluripotent stem cells at the birth of a child before the stem cells are either discarded as *waste*, a term that does not imply lack of profit potential, or able to age and grow into a specific type of cell. If the pluripotent cells are "harvested" and stored, the stem cells can be used at a later date to create a badly needed kidney, liver, lung, or heart transplant or they can be used to inject into an aging man or woman who wishes to look 30, 40, or 50 years younger. As Eugene Thacker notes, "once a patient's cells can be prompted to regenerate into particularized tissue structures, they can then be transplanted back into the body of the patient, in a strange kind of biological "othering" of the self" (2003, p. 91).

The fight against aging or the desire to look young again is a strong impulse within humans, but it is an impulse that raises some important ethical and humane questions. The whole process of "harvesting" stem cells and then storing them is referred to as "banking." The terminology used to describe the regenerative process reduces the child and mother of the cord blood cells to the status of host thereby placing in doubt their status as humans with inalienable rights. Perhaps more important, is the question of who should receive the cord blood cells. There are the autologous donors who bank the cells for their own potential usage in case they need an organ transplant in the future. What about the nonautologous stem cells and the patient who wishes to receive stem cells merely to look or feel young again? If the market is permitted to be the sole determiner of who the recipient of stem cells will be, then the rich and well insured will be permitted to never grow old while the majority of people will live a disadvantaged, normal life cycle. The same logic used by drivers of Hummers and other tanklike vehicles—I can afford the gas so I should be able to drive whatever I want—will be used to justify inequalities in biomedical practices—I can afford the medical treatment to regenerate my tissue structure so why should I not do it?

Who Owns Me?

In 1976 Dr. David Golde advised John Moore to have his spleen removed to avoid the spread of hairy-cell leukemia. Later Moore discovered that Golde used Moore's spleen to create an immortal cell line of the protein lymphokines. According to Catherine Waldby and Robert Mitchell (2006), lymphokines are difficult to produce and Golde literally stumbled on a goldmine of the proteins. Moore eventually discovered what Golde did with his spleen and sued the California university system and Golde. Initially, Moore lost, then won in the California Appellate court, then lost in the California State Supreme court, and finally lost in the U.S. Supreme Court. Minus the Appellate court, the three judicial bodies ruled that Moore could not own a part of his body, and since Golde and his team of scientists eventually altered the cells found in Moore's body they could claim ownership on the stem lines and Moore was not due any compensation. For Moore to claim ownership over his body the courts reasoned would impede scientific innovation and society would not benefit from the many medical innovations reaped from Moore's spleen.

The Moore case raises important ontological issues. If one cannot own oneself, then who does? Taken at face value such a decision to deny ownership over one's body reaffirms long-standing traditions to view the human body as beyond economic value, and such a stance prevents anyone from selling body parts for money. In the biomedical age, however, questions of ownership are complicated. When a child is born the doctor cuts the umbilical cord, severing physical ties to the mother. Housed in the cord is pluripotent stem cell, cord blood. Technically this cord blood has been labeled as hospital waste which enables hospitals to sell the blood to cosmetic companies to use in their products or to simply discard it. With the rise of stem cell research, the cord blood has become more valuable and its disposition more contentious. Technically, cord blood was never "waste" but a part of a human being. So who owns the cord blood and if it is the hospitals and the patient does not choose to "bank" the cord blood, then can the hospital do whatever they wish with the cord blood, including create cell lines for research? An even more troubling question is that while it is reasonable to prevent humans from owning their own body, why is it corporations or universities can own parts of humans after they have been slightly modified, and why is it after modification corporations or universities do not owe the donor any compensation for developing a cell line from their blood? One can see an inequity in power relations when it comes to human bodies. When it comes to individual rights the human body transcends value but when it comes to corporate or university patent rights humans can be, literally, a source of income.[3]

Do You Suffer from Restless Leg Syndrome?

In the history of human pathology the tradition was to discover a disease and find a cure. In today's environment a drug, usually not new or innovative, is introduced into the market and a new disease is invented to fit the effects of the drug. Human pathology has been placed on its head in order to fit the needs of pharmaceuticals while the health of patients has become secondary. Pharmaceutical corporations are by far the most corrupt conglomerate to ever control the United States. Even the tobacco industry looks at Big Pharma with envy. Whenever the pharmaceutical industry is threatened with taxation or regulation, their standard reply is that such a tax will reduce the creation of innovative drugs from ever reaching the market. Never has a more profitable lie been uttered. Most of the innovative drugs that have been developed since the 1990s have come from either the National Institutes of Health or publicly funded university research. From 2000 to 2004, 32 new drugs were approved by the FDA to enter the U.S. market, of those only seven came directly from pharmaceutical funded research (Angell, 2005). If ailing people were dependent on drug companies to help them, their life expectancy would be much less than the 79 to 80 years average most Americans live today. As it turns out, pharmaceuticals have deceived the American public into believing they are providing a public service when in reality they are using the health of Americans to reap unprecedented profits.

Armed with the largest lobbyist organization in the business world, Big Pharma has controlled legislation to insure maximum profits and entered into agreements with the FDA that gives away publicly funded research for virtually nothing. Most of the drugs that are introduced onto the market are not geared toward life-threatening diseases because the pharmaceutical companies believe there is not a big enough market to maintain a strong profit margin. Drugs that are created to help small populations of patients with life-threatening diseases are referred to as orphan drugs because the patients die off too fast to replenish the market demand. Most of the drugs introduced into the American market are more non-life-threatening diseases and are often me-too drugs. Me-too drugs are those drugs that are molecularly slightly different from drugs already on the market. So while many diseases, including most forms of cancer have no treatment alternative to radical chemotherapy, many health problems including depression and acid reflux have multipharmaceutical options.

The Big Pharma fleecing of America is even more controversial when one considers how research on the effectiveness of a drug is conducted. When a new drug is tested most of the time it is not tested against any rival drug. For instance, when Paxil, an antidepressant drug, was tested it was not tested against Prozac but against a placebo. Even when most drugs are tested against placebos, the placebo is sometimes just as effective. When the *New England Journal of Medicine* published a study on hypertension, the authors reported that when compared with drugs from Pfizer, Merck, and AstraZeneca, an old time diuretic was most effective (Angell, 2005, p. 96).

The controversies surrounding pharmaceutical drugs raise many disturbing questions. For a nation that has openly declared a war on drugs, how has it become such a drug dependent society? Given that most drugs are not rigorously tested, how can we trust the effectiveness and long term safety of these drugs? How many drugs like Vioxx are out there? And why is it illegal for Americans to import drugs from Canada because they are supposedly unsafe, but FDA regulations have been compromised and weakened seriously compromising patient safety? What does Big Pharma's ownership of America's government say about the state of democracy in the United States? How much does a democracy cost on Wall Street these days?

The Posthuman Condition and Curriculum Theory

In the section above I could have discussed the impact of cosmetic surgery or the impact of legal drugs on youth cultures but these are important topics for later discussions. The point of mentioning cosmetic surgery and prescription drugs is to demonstrate how pervasive and unavoidable the posthuman condition is. Curriculum theorists have to intervene in this discussion over the posthuman condition for numerous reasons. First, as I tried to point out in the discussion of biomedical issues, the very meaning of what a democracy means is as stake. Curriculum theorists have a proud lineage traversing the past as far back as John Dewey, George Counts, and Jane Addams. What these three educationalists have in common is a strong commitment to social justice and a radical notion of democracy. Today, democracy is being reduced to the right to vote while corporations fleece our nation of every last penny to line their pockets with unprecedented profits as schools remain underfunded from preschool to higher education levels. While the majority of individuals witness a dwindling impact on decisions made about public funds, more and more taxpayer dollars are going to corporations in the form of tax breaks, tax abatements, and the transfer of taxpayer funded research. Second, no matter what we do as a vocation, the posthuman condition influences how one defines one's subjectivity. Again, corporations are colonizing our bodies to reap the profits of cutting edge biomedical innovation while most individuals are blocked from obtaining basic health care. How deeply corporations colonize bodies and how much access individuals have to biomedicine depends on one's race, gender, social class, ethnicity, and geographical location. Upper class, White, Western, European males are more likely to have access to biomedicine than all the other categories. Inequity is being defined in new ways: access to health care and biotechnology. Third, in the name of democracy and democratic science, curriculum theorists have to become what Donna Haraway refers to as a "bumptious technoscientific actors" (1997, p. 94). A bumptious technoscientific actor demands a voice in the biomedical conversations. They demonstrate the audacity to ask their doctor what studies have been conducted for the new drug they are prescribing and who funded the studies. More importantly, they ask doctors and policy makers why we need to drug young people—so they can become better test takers? Doctors and policy makers will not be pleased with their new inquisitive patients but we are not on this earth to please doctors and policy makers. In a democracy, they are present to serve our health and educational needs. A bumptious technoscientific actor demands to know what happens to the cord blood after their child is born and what the hospital will do to share in the benefits of life the mother and newborn have created through their cord blood. Hospitals will claim waste is not part of the mother or newborn any longer and is therefore the hospital's property, but humans are not here to serve hospitals. Human life is too valuable to let hospitals classify part of a human being as waste and then profit from it. Curriculum theorists have to become these bumptious technoscientific actors and claim their voice in the biomedical world because our voices are more important than any profit margin or younger looking wealthy octogenarian. Vanity should not guide biomedicine but the health needs of organ recipients should and the market should not dictate who is entitled to an organ. In a democracy, people should decide who is entitled and then all life should be valued and no one denied because of the lack of money or access. Adding our voices to the biomedical conversation will complicate it indeed but insurance companies, biotech corporations, Big Pharma, and the medical profession should never have an easy life. Their functions in our posthuman world are too vital for them to take any one life too lightly and place profits over individuals.

Let me end where I began with Heidegger and merge his thought with Haraway's bumptious technoscientific actor. Haraway is the posthuman progeny of Heidegger's thought. Like Heidegger she is interested in our essence, our being, but for Haraway it is an essence and being that is partial, contingent, and dependent on technology. In a Heideggerian sense the bumptious technoscientific actor becomes a voice for promoting the unconcealing of our potential as posthumans as well as the conscientious advocate against the temptation to treat some humans as standing reserves. Perhaps more important it is the bumptious technoscientific actor who finds art in the posthuman condition and restores *poiesis* into our cultures. This actor is not a theater performer but sees the importance and value of the arts and the sciences together. It's a role perfectly suited for curriculum theorists, the only scholars capable and willing to restore *poiesis* in education.

Acknowledgment

I wish to thank Erik Malewski and two anonymous reviewers. Your comments and insights were insightful and very helpful in the development of my ideas.

Notes

1. I use the term *biomedical* to cover the many different names to describe the merging of science, medicine, and technology. Other terms are often used to describe biomedical changes in our society including *bioinformatics*, the reading of genetic code, *biotechnology*, the convergence of computer information systems with genetics, or *bioengineering*, the use of the human genome and technology to reconstruct the human body. Adele Clark and her coauthors describe biomedicalization as a "shift from enhanced control over external nature... to the harnessing and transformation of internal nature...often transforming 'life itself'" (Clarke, Shim, Mamo, Fosket, & Fishman, 2003, p. 164).
2. For more insights into the debates and concerns over stem cells see Waldy and Mitchell (2006), Paul Rabinow (1999), *French DNA: Trouble in Purgatory,* and Sarah Franklin and Ceilia Roberts (2006), *Born and Made: An Ethnography of Preimplantation Genetic Diagnosis.*
3. For anyone interested in pharmaceutical corporations and their products see Angell's book *The Truth about Drug Companies.* If you are interested in the global impact on pharmaceuticals and the theoretical issues surrounding drug development see Eugene Thacker (2006) *Global Genome,* Kaushik Rajan (2006) *Biocapital,* or Andrew Lakoff (2005) *Pharmaceutical Reason.*

References

Angell, M. (2005). *The truth about drug companies: How they deceive us and what to do about it*. New York: Random House.

Clark, A., Shim, J., Mamo, L., Fosket, J., & Fishman, J. (2003). Biomedicalization: Technoscientific transformations of health, illness, and U.S. biomedicine. *American Sociological Review, 68*(4), 161–194.

Doll, M. A. (2000). *Like letters in running water: A mythopoetics of curriculum*. Mahwah, NJ: Erlbaum.

Franklin, S., & Roberts, C. (2006). *Born and made: An ethnography of preimplantation genetic diagnosis*. Princeton, NJ: Princeton University Press.

Haraway, D. (1997). *Modest_witness@second_millennium.femaleMan©_meets_oncomouse™*. New York: Routledge.

Hayles, K. (1999). *How we became posthuman: Virtual bodies, in cybernetics, literature, and informatics*. Chicago: University of Chicago Press.

Heidegger, M. (1977). *The question concerning technology and other essays* (W. Lovit, Trans.). New York: Harper Torchbooks.

Lakoff, A. (2005). *Pharmaceutical reason: Knowledge and value in global psychiatry*. New York: Cambridge University Press.

Rabinow, P. (1999). *French DNA: Trouble in purgatory*. Chicago: University of Chicago Press.

Rajan, K. (2006). *Biocapital: The constitution of postgenomic life*. Durham, NC: Duke University Press.

Stock, G. (2003). *Redesigning humans: Choosing our genes, changing our future*. New York: Mariner Books.

Thacker, E. (2003). Data made flesh: Biotechnology and the discourse of the posthuman. *Cultural Critique, 53*(2), 72–97.

Thacker, E. (2006). *Global genome: Biotechnology, politics, and culture*. Cambridge, MA: MIT Press.

Waldby, C., & Mitchell, R. (2006). *Tissue economies: Blood, organs, and cell lines in late capitalism*. Durham, NC: Duke University Press.

Weaver, J. (2005). Digital aesthetics. *Journal of Curriculum Theorizing, 21*(1), 77–94.

Suggested Reading Questions

1. The author suggests that the role of education is to guide technology toward the unconcealment of its own capacities as a poetic and creative force. How might curriculum scholars craft alternate onto-epistemological lenses with which to challenge the notion that humans are standing reserves?

2. If, as the author suggests, curriculum theorists are too rigid and literal when it comes to technology—and fear it will attack their subjectivity—what ideas and concepts might assist with envisioning technology in figurative ways as well as in ways that enhance and expand subjectivity?

3. The posthuman condition indicates that technology as an inorganic form has entered the organic human body and rendered such distinctions suspect. What sort of ethical commitments might be necessary to help ensure that technology is used to enhance rather than abuse the human body?

4. The author, following the work of Donna Haraway, asserts that curriculum theorists must become technocratic actors. In what ways might the capacity to insert one's voice into biomedical conversations be shaped by race, class, and gender privilege?

5. Given the author's use of vignettes to highlight the construction and definition of the posthuman condition, how might teachers and educators incorporate this condition in their teaching and learning?

Response to John A. Weaver
Questioning Technology
Heidegger, Haraway, and Democratic Education

Dennis Carlson

I think John Weaver raises some very important questions about technology and education that need to become a part of the "complicated conversation" in curriculum studies, and in pedagogical practice. His essay helps reframe the conversation on technology by reconceptualizing the very idea of technology. In the commonsense world of educational practice in most public schools and classrooms, teachers think of technology as all that stuff related to computers—entering data on student achievement into computer programs, using computers to "drill" students on test-preparation skills and knowledge content, and perhaps more recently, in more affluent schools, using computer technology to link their computers to an overhead screen and to students' laptop computers, all linked to the Internet. This is the "new" technology in public education, although as Weaver suggests, it has some very "old" roots in Western culture. The point here is that technology is not just something teachers pick up because it is lying around. Rather, it incorporates a way of "thinking" about curriculum, pedagogy, and the educational process that needs to be unpacked rather than uncritically taken for granted. We must proceed, as Heidegger did, by questioning technology, and rethinking technology as *technē*, a way of bringing something into presence, of producing something according to one worldview or another, one way of "being in the world" or another.

The questioning of technology, I would agree, has only really begun in education, although this questioning also has a history and comes out of a heritage. Michael Apple (1990), for example, and others (including myself) have been influenced by a neo-Marxist theory of the technical control of labor in industry and the deskilling of work (Braverman, 1974), as well as the application of this theory to a theory of schooling in capitalist America (Bowles & Gintis, 1976). The argument here—and I think it is still a compelling one, even if it was presented in too reductionistic a form—is that technical control is ideological in the sense of being a manifestation of a broader interested worldview associated with modern, industrial capitalism, a worldview actively engaged in constituting human subjectivity and disciplining and training the body to make it more "productive." Foucault (1979) has added much to this analysis in recent years, in his suggestion that modern public schools are organized by three "normalizing" technologies of disciplinary power: the examination, the rank ordering and classification of students, and the hierarchical observation of student bodies through a "panoptic" gaze. For Foucault these are not technologies that are mere reflections of economic technologies, since schools seem to share as much with prisons and mental institutes as they do with the organization of the workplace. But he clearly recognized that capitalism was an expression of a particular *technē*, one more about disciplinary power than "freedom," "equality," or "social justice."

More recently, I think the psychoanalytic work of Marxist Felix Guattari (1996) provides a useful poststructural theory of technology. He defines capitalism as the "semiotization of a certain mode of production" (p. 233). Symbolization "machines" or microtechnologies provide the "codes" used to produce certain informational or knowledge outputs. From this perspective, schooling is less a structure than a process, in which the curriculum is a "machine" that gets the wheels turning, to produce some "product" with a use or exchange value—the student body, and more narrowly achievement test scores. The student body is itself produced through these machines as a machine, a certain kind of "desiring machine" whose desires have been wired and disciplined to make it more productive, and to make it more responsive to having its desires for meaningful, nonalienated, "authentic" work sublimated through extrinsic rewards and consumerism. What gives transnational capitalism its special power is that it has been able to reorder various heterogeneous activities and domains of cultural production—such as public education—under a single semiotization *technē*, consisting of various "machines," such as the standardized test.

We will need other technologies, other "machines," to fundamentally address class and race-based achievement gaps in public education, and in the process reconstruct public education so that it more consistently and effectively lives up to its democratic promise (Carlson, 2007). I agree with Weaver that Heidegger can be useful in formulating a "saving" *technē*, along with Haraway. In *Leaving Safe Harbors* (2002) I offered my own views on Heidegger's (1977) "Question Concerning Technology" essay, and also Haraway's (1991) notion of a posthuman, "free" cyborg, as they relate to the articulation of a new, democratic progressivism in American education and public life. Here I want to briefly develop a few themes I mapped out in somewhat different terms in that book. As Weaver indicates, Heidegger hoped to recuperate some of the "original" meaning of the word *technē* in ancient, pre-Platonic culture to "think" the ground of a "saving power." Such an effort to build a counter-*technē* by returning to an originary, "authentic" *technē* that was somehow there in "pure" form at the beginning, is, of course, a questionable project and can be articulated with a rightist cultural politics. At the same time, it may be useful to return to a particular premodern heritage of "thinking" *technē* that may now seem quite foreign, to help us imagine a more "authentic" and less alienating *technē*. This *technē* he associates with the Aristotelian tradition of "thinking" technology in terms of causation—that which causes something to come into presence. Heidegger turns to the trope of the "chalice" in a religious ceremony to provide an example of the coming together of four causes, in Aristotelian terms the material, formal, final, and efficient causes. If we think of the chalice as the curriculum, we can see how each of these causes has to be adequately accounted for, how they play a part in the coming to presence of a high-stakes testing curriculum, and also, potentially at least, a more emancipatory and liberatory curriculum.

The "material" cause refers back to the material (metal) that is shaped and reshaped to make the chalice, and also the material culture within which the chalice is made present—on a table, within a cathedral, within a community, and so on. This leads us to ask questions about how curriculum texts get produced, and the economic marketing of texts. It also leads us to question the material structuring of the economy and the workplace, and of public life, for which the curriculum prepares young people. Marxism, of course, was a materialistic movement to the extent that it viewed the material economic "base" as deterministically shaping the "superstructure" or consciousness of people. While the Marxist tradition gave too much determining power to the material cause, it is clear that material culture, and particularly the material structuring of the workplace and the economy, play a powerful role in shaping the curriculum in public schools—both the formal curriculum and the "hidden curriculum." The restructuring of the new global labor market is having a powerful effect on the curriculum in schools serving the new working class and underclass; and we cannot pretend that achievement gaps and chronic underachievement among inner-city youth can be "fixed" apart from some rather dramatic changes in economic policy, in the way work is organized in the economy, and in equality of opportunity in the labor market. It will do little good to try to "reason" our way to democratic progress in education without fundamentally addressing these very real, material concerns.

The "formal" cause of the chalice coming into presence is the pragmatic cause, the need for a technology that will hold wine. In the age of NCLB and high-stakes testing, formal causation in curriculum development takes the form of a narrow instrumentalism that mobilizes curriculum "machines" to produce achievement-level outputs (test scores), at the expense of genuine efforts to raise achievement and expectations in schools serving youth marginalized by class and race. This is what the critical theorists of the Frankfurt school called "instrumental rationality," or "purposive rationality," a technology that is interested only in immediate ends, even if these immediate ends (higher test scores) are attained through the use of a reductionistic skill-based curriculum that is ultimately inconsistent with the development of "higher order" or "critical" thinking skills, to say nothing of the development of critical citizens in a democratic society. A democratic curriculum, as Dewey maintained, must emerge out of, and serve to advance, pragmatic aims as well—but clearly he envisioned a far different kind of pragmatic causation. First, a democratic curriculum needs to be pragmatic in the sense of being "student-centered" (Dewey, 1916), "culturally relevant" (Ladson-Billings, 2001), and "culturally responsive" (Gay, 2000). It must refer back to the interests and motivations of young people in their pragmatic life-worlds, the "habitus" they inhabit. Second, a democratic curriculum is a pragmatic technology in the sense of being guided by experimentalism and the motivation to address "real life" problems in the life-world. Democratic pragmatism suggests an openness to the process of learning, or of developing curriculum, an openness grounded in continuous reflection on practice and reconstruction of practice in light of reflection. The focus is on the pragmatic field of action in unique sites, in which unpredictability, unknowability, and unintelligibility are the norm and in which teachers and students must negotiate what counts for knowledge as they go. What makes this Deweyan form of pragmatism democratic is the concern that it be guided by a "fuzzy vision" of a "good society" (Carlson, 1997). This visionary component is what turns "vulgar pragmatism" into "critical pragmatism" (Cherryholmes, 1988).

The "efficient" cause of the chalice is the active will and intention of the crafts person and artist who brought it into concrete presence. Heidegger generally argued that the "efficient" cause was overvalued and overemphasized in modern, Western culture, as if it were the only cause. Nietzsche, the prophet of the "will to power," certainly seemed to elevate its status. But the "efficient" cause should also not be down-played. In the Hegelian–Marxian tradition, and in Freire's critical pedagogy, part of what it means to become fully self-conscious is to recognize that we play an active role in producing culture and self, and that oppressed and silenced peoples need not accept their fate passively and fatalistically. Democratic forms of curriculum and pedagogy make students "producers" of texts rather than merely "consumers" of texts; and they shift responsibility to students to interpret texts within communities of interpreters. As Derrida (2004) observed (and in this he followed Heidegger) that the most important questions that drive the educational encounter—whether in an elementary school classroom or a university campus—have to do with responsibility: "For what and to whom are we responsible?" (p. 83). Certainly for teachers, and for education faculty, these are the essential questions we must raise today, in the age of NCLB and the National Council for Accreditation of Teacher Education (NCATE).

The "final" causation that brings the chalice into presence is the ceremony in which it is used, within a church, within a certain religious heritage. This cause leads us to recognize that we all speak and write within heritages which produce us as much as we produce them. Academic disciplines and fields are heritages, although traditionally not very democratic heritages. So too are liberal, critical, and radical heritages of social theory linked to democratic *praxis*. It is the responsibility of the educators and public intellectuals to keep this collective memory alive; and we play a compliment to a heritage when we question it and critically reread it. It is, at the same time, possible to understand the "final" cause as consistent with a certain brand of poststructural thinking, that language or discourse is the constitutive force in culture, rather than human agency, that in fact discourse is involved in producing the "knowing" subject and "productive" body. In this case, the "efficient" cause seems to be erased almost entirely. A concern with human will and agency is replaced by a concern with an analysis of discourse as a technology that produces human subjects. What is important about Heidegger's formulation of the *technē* that brought the chalice into presence is that it does not force us to choose one cause over another, but rather encourages us to see how they all intersect in an "authentic" work or educational experience.

Does Haraway's "cyborg" represents the coming-together of these causes in a new *technē* that—as Weaver argues—"marks a radical transformation, both discursively and materially, of human beings?" Certainly, the idea of the cyborg posthuman body is consistent with developments in popular culture and material culture, and consequently in youth identity formation. Young people already are, to a large extent, cyborg subjects, plugged into globalizing communities of users and a vast array of information which they are using to educate and reeducate themselves, although certainly the experiences of urban youth are different from suburban, White youth in this regard. In most urban schools I visit, the computer is still being used to program students, lead them down predictable paths, and produce standardized learning outcomes. And among middle class cyborg youth, the possibilities opened up by the new technologies are largely "wasted" on idle chatter and mind-numbing games. Heidegger might say that what the new cyborg subject too often lacks is a "final" cause, a grounding in a progressive heritage of becoming which it upholds, criticizes, and assumes responsibility for advancing. While it certainly is true that people are, now quite explicitly, assembling and reassembling themselves out of parts available on the global grid, this process does not necessarily "go" anywhere unless it is grounded in critical, democratic heritages, and a language of "social justice" and (yes) even "human rights." It is the responsibility of teachers, and teacher educators, I believe, to ground the new cyborg subjects in democratic heritages and interpretive traditions, and to situate them as well with a real material world that has been prestructured in ways that limit our capacity to reassemble ourselves along whatever lines we choose.

References

Apple, M. (1990). *Ideology and curriculum* (2nd ed.). New York: Routledge.

Bowles, S., & Gintis, H. (1976). *Schooling in capitalist America: Educational reform and the contradictions of economic life*. New York: Basic Books.

Braverman, H. (1974). *Labor and monopoly capital: The degradation of work in the twentieth century*. New York: Monthly Review Press.

Carlson, D. (1997). *Making progress: Education and culture in new times*. New York: Teachers College Press.

Carlson, D. (2002). *Leaving safe harbors: Toward a new progressivism in American education and public life*. New York: Routledge.

Carlson, D. (2007). Are we making progress? The discursive construction of progress in the age of "no child left behind." In D. Carlson & C. P. Gause (Eds.), *Keeping the promise: Essays on leadership, democracy, and* education (pp. 3–26). New York: Lang.

Cherryholmes, C. (1988). *Power and criticism: Poststructural investigations in education.* New York: Teachers College Press.

Derrida, J. (2004). *Eyes of the university.* Stanford, CA: Stanford University Press.

Dewey, J. (1916). *Education and democracy.* New York: Macmillan.

Foucault, M. (1979). *Discipline and punish: The birth of the prison* (A. Sheridan Trans.). New York: Vintage Books.

Gay, G. (2000). *Culturally responsive teaching: Theory, research, and practice.* New York: Teachers College Press.

Guattari, F. (1996). Capitalist systems, structures and processes. In G. Genosko (Ed.), *The Guattari reader* (pp. 223–227). Oxford, England: Blackwell.

Haraway, D. (1991). *Simians, cyborgs, and women: The reinvention of nature.* New York: Routledge.

Heidegger, M. (1977). *The question concerning technology and other essays* (W. Lovit, Trans.). New York: Harper Torchbooks.

Ladson-Billings, G. (2001). *Crossing over to Canaan: The journey of new teachers in diverse classrooms.* San Francisco: Jossey-Bass.

Part IV

Embodiment, Relationality, and Public Pedagogy

10 (A) Troubling Curriculum
Public Pedagogies of Black Women Rappers

Nichole A. Guillory

Chapter Overview

This chapter focuses on rap as a principal language form and an integral part of the in school and out of school curriculum. The author suggests that rappers are public pedagogues and explores the notion that Black female rappers talk back to dominant discourses and construct alternative representations for their publics, ones that are simultaneously stereotypical and disruptive. The author analyzes lyrics to reveal how Black female rappers school or educate their audiences on sexual desire, heterosexual politics, and Black lesbian sexuality. More specifically, she discusses how Black female rappers frame desire and pleasure within heterosexual relationships; how power, money, language, and culture are connected within expressions of Black women's sexual identities; and how Black lesbians' sexual contexts and desires queer the space of hip-hop by way of explorations of same gender attraction. The author suggests the scripts Black female rappers offer are necessarily in dialogue with a long history of representations of Black women. In this sense, Black women rappers are explored as public pedagogues who raise important epistemological questions, and both trouble and enable dominant discourses.

Crack Music:[1] An Introduction

Rap is a musical form, a phenomenon, a culture, a commodity too important for teachers to ignore. Rap's hyper(Black)masculine hard edge, propensity for constant change, tendency toward contradiction, over-the-top braggadocio, privileging of the individual, spirit of rebelliousness, and takeover of mainstream U.S. popular culture all speak to hip-hop generation youth. Constantly changing, rap influences how many students express all of who they are—their style of dress, language, class, race, sexuality, and gender. Our students belong to the hip-hop generation, and many of them consume rap's troubling[2] representations. These representations inevitably seep into the cracks of schooling spaces.

As a supervisor of teacher interns, I have experienced countless moments in which high school students bring representations of rap culture with them into English class to enliven the study of dead texts, that is texts chosen for them by teachers who are under pressure to follow a district-mandated lockstep curriculum and to make sure students pass standardized tests. I have witnessed students' appropriation of familiar rap images, characters, and tropes to make meaning(s) of less familiar canonical texts. For instance, students have represented Victor Frankenstein's monster with a gold tooth and what they describe as a "pimp gangsta hat" cocked to one side during their study of Mary Shelley's novel, and they have drawn a platinum grille on their illustration of the Pardoner during their study of Chaucer's *Canterbury Tales*. When asked about their representational choices, students connected their drawings to themes of excess and greed in Shelley's and Chaucer's texts, respectively. Instead of lauding students' obvious critical and creative engagement with these texts, teachers in both instances told me that their students had "gotten out of hand" and had "strayed too far" from the authors' actual descriptions. I have left these meetings wishing that more students would "get out of hand" and "stray too far" so as to interrupt the monotony of standardization in public schooling.

The secondary English teachers and the teacher education faculty with whom I work have been mostly unwilling to acknowledge the pedagogical function of rap. While some have been willing to admit the pedagogical "usefulness" of raps as supplementary resources or as an effective scaffolding technique to motivate "unmotivated" students to participate in academic literacy activities, very few recognize the necessity of understanding rap as an art form that has transformed the way hip-hop generation students speak, write, dress, resist, and frame the world. Very few educators recognize the necessity of understanding rap's contradictory representations, the context in which it was born and now lives, its co-optation and commodification by corporate America, and its impact on mainstream U.S. popular culture.

I maintain that the pedagogical worth of raps does not lie in how well they are able to fit inside an existing traditional curriculum; for example, as objects of study alongside thematically similar canonical texts. This kind of thinking promotes school study of only those texts that offer "positive" messages to young students, and as we know, raps that receive the most airplay and attention are not those that offer uplifting messages and unproblematic representations. Con(s)t(r)aining rap so that it can be studied with texts on a district-mandated reading list does not make it valuable pedagogically. Rap is a powerful language on its own and a necessary part of the at-large public curriculum, and when rap is conceived in this way, rappers become public pedagogues.

Ida B., Angela D., and M.i.s.s. E: Generations of Black Women Talking Back

Situated in the current cultural movement of hip-hop, Black women rappers' writing and performance of lyrics are examples of educational phenomena that Pinar (2001) says happen outside the school, "those pedagogical elements of political and social movements (such as the anti-lynching campaign), and individuals (such as Ida B. Wells) whose political or racial or feminist labor was in a profound sense performed as pedagogical" (p. 26). Two women rappers in particular, Missy Elliott and Eve, conceptualize their roles as performers in pedagogical terms. Missy expresses her intent to help children through "modeling" and by "extending" understanding:

> Women in hip hop are more positive. You're almost giving that mother instinct, and you think about the children. Not to say anything bad about the males, but from their standpoint, it's more, "Yo, it's cool right now to talk about this." I have to extend further cause kids respect entertainers. Whether you want it or not, you are a role model. I'm going to be talking to kids about abuse, cause I went through watching my father abuse my mother, and I was sexually abused at eight. There's so many people being abused or watching their parents fight, and they need to know how you got over it and what they can do. We should touch more positive stuff these days, cause the world is getting crazier and crazier. (Missy quoted in Oumano, 1999, para. 26)

Though Missy constructs the role of teacher as "ideologically congruent with women's supposed innate nurturing capacities" (Munro, 1998b, p. 3), she still understands that her work has pedagogical potential. Pinar's description (2004) of Ida B. Wells as teacher, whom he says "imagine[d] her classroom more expansively to include the American public" (p. 44), is also fitting for Missy because she breaks the silence that often surrounds violence and sexual abuse of women and children in Black families.

Eve is also reflective about her role as teacher and her power to speak back to the stereotypical images of Black women:

> I'm conscious of me being an entertainer and having a voice. I feel I do have to teach along the way. I'm only 22 and got a lot more to learn, but I feel I know enough about respecting myself that I can pass that on. I have to say something to know that I kind of made a difference, or at least made people know that I stand for something other than just wanting to make somebody shake their ass or sing my songs. (Eve quoted in Edwards, 2001, p. 126)

In using her voice to "make a difference," Eve fashions a pedagogical identity around talking back to stereotypical images of Black women.

Though the production of images of Blackness in the White imagination remains mostly the domain of privileged White men, Black women have resisted (and still do resist) the stereotypical constructions of Black womanhood. Black women across generations have built a language to defend our name in public, challenging the underlying power structures of naming by talking back to and against the dominant discourses that have tried to define who we are. It is that act of speech, of "talking back," that hooks (1989) says is "no mere gesture of empty words, that is the expression of our movement from object to subject—the liberated voice" (p. 9). What happens when a Black woman talks back to negative images of herself? In these moments, Black women engage in an act that has been mostly forbidden us in public discourses. hooks (1989) describes the act of back talk:

> In the world of the southern black community, "back talk" and "talking back" meant speaking as an equal to an authority figure. It meant daring to disagree and sometimes it just meant having an opinion…. To make yourself heard if you were a girl child was to invite punishment, the back-hand lick, the slap across the face that would catch you unaware, or the feel of switches stinging your arms and legs. To speak then when one was not spoken to was a courageous act—an act of risk and daring. (p. 5)

So when we speak against the stereotypical images of Black women as mammies, matriarchs, welfare mothers, whores, bitches, gold diggers, and babymamas, we are also speaking back to the underlying power structures, and by extension the people in control of those power structures, responsible for the production and circulation of demeaning representations of Black women.

Contemporary participants in a continuing history of Black women involved in the struggle of resistance to defend our name in public discourses, Black women rappers are important voices in/writers of the public conversation about the collective struggles of Black women: our struggle to define ourselves rather than be mis(represented) by others; our struggle for respect and treatment as peers in male-dominated work spaces; our struggle to express our lesbian, bisexual, heterosexual, transgender, and questioning selves; our struggle against violence by male partners in heterosexual relationships; and our struggle to build community and mobilize ourselves. Familiar to Black women across generations and across the Diaspora, these struggles are most often the discursive strands that Black women rappers write into their complicated representations of young Black women's identities.

As Black women rappers construct representations for their publics, they "inscribe whose knowledge and what knowledge counts" (Munro, 1998b, p. 3). They participate in curricular acts of representation (Castenell & Pinar, 1993; Munro, 1998b) that are simultaneously stereotypical and disruptive, discomforting and liberating. Complex and contradictory, Black women rappers' representations reflect the complicated context of the hip-hop generation, which Morgan (1999) so aptly describes:

> We have little faith in inherited illusions and idealism. We are the first generation to grow up with all the benefits of Civil Rights (i.e., Affirmative Action, government-subsidized educational and social programs) and the first to lose them. The first to have the devastation of AIDS, crack, and black-on-black violence makes it feel like a blessing to reach twenty-five. Love no longer presents itself wrapped in the romance of basement blue lights, lifetime commitments, or the sweet harmonies of The Stylistics and The Chi-Lites. Love for us is raw like sushi, served up on sex platters from R. Kelly and Jodeci. Even our existences can't be defined in the past's simple terms: house nigga vs. field nigga, ghetto vs. bourgie, BAP vs. boho because our lives are usually some complicated combination of all of the above. (pp. 61–62)

Lessons about the contradictory spaces many Black women often occupy are far from standardized in Black women's raps. In their songs, Black women rappers often call themselves bitches, glorify marijuana smoking, express an insatiable desire for sexual intercourse with men, idolize material possessions, reveal a distrust of sisterhood among Black women, celebrate Black ghetto culture, and tote the ultimate phallic symbol, the gun. But they also seize the term *bitch* from misogynist rap discourse and recode it with woman-friendly connotations; encourage Black women to defend themselves against male violence; stress the necessity of sexual and financial independence for Black women; and resist objectification of the Black woman's body.

In the following sections of this chapter, I focus on how some Black women rappers perform a complicated public pedagogy in which they talk back to or "trouble" the essentializing discourses that have defined Black women as whores, gold diggers, welfare queens, and babymamas. I understand Black women rappers to be public pedagogues, and I consider how they enact "talking back" pedagogies[3] around representations of power and Black women's sexualities. I locate moments in the lyrics of Black women rappers that demonstrate how they "school" their audiences about the representation of Black heterosexual and lesbian relationships. Specifically, in my reading of lyrics by Missy Elliott, Mia X, Queen Pen, Foxy Brown, and Lil Kim, I identify representations that speak to three themes: sexual desire, heterosexual politics, and Black lesbian sexuality.

I discuss how these women rappers communicate Black women's sexual desire and pleasure in the heterosexual sex act; how they link power, money, and sexuality in expressions of Black women's sexual identities; and how they queer the space of hip-hop by offering representations of Black lesbian sexuality. As I consider the complexity of these women rappers' sexual expressions, I ask: What do these women have to say about sex, sexuality, and control over Black women's bodies? How do these rappers articulate Black women's sexual desire? How do they communicate in their lyrics, if at all, Black women's resistance to sexual objectification, sexual oppression, and even sexual violence in relationships with Black men? To what extent do these women rappers affirm patriarchal notions of sexual roles of male and female lovers? Do some lyrics ever move out of heterosexist discourse and make room for queer readings or offer representations of Black lesbian sexuality?

Keep Movin': Sexual Desire and Pleasure

Black women rappers focus on women's pleasure and (hetero)sexual satisfaction in their raps by representing women who boldly communicate their sexual desires, make the first move in sexual encounters with men, and insist on oral sexual gratification from men before engaging in sexual intercourse with them. A few songs even have women declaring that men are totally unnecessary for women's sexual pleasure. I do not mean to suggest that women rappers' expressions are always unproblematic, sexually autonomous narratives. In fact, mainstream Black women's raps often feature women who focus on pleasing men, rather than themselves, and I maintain that these representations reflect the tendency in rap discourse not to portray woman-centered sexual desire and pleasure. They seem unable to escape traditional patriarchal male-female roles in heterosexual relationships that define women in terms of their capacity to serve the will and sexual desires of men.

I agree with Goodall's (1994) finding that there is a "growing sexual freedom in [women's] rap, an increasing willingness on the part of [women] rappers to display and address issues of their own bodies and sexuality" (p. 85). I realize that these women work in an industry where sexually explicit lyrics are most often big money-makers. So what seems like uninhibited, independent sexual expression may actually be a marketing strategy to sell more records. After all, as Burford and Farley (1999) conclude about the rap industry, "it pays to be nasty" and "there's money to be made in the profane" (p. 72). Even so, these women's lyrics, though sometimes conflicted, raise important questions about control over Black women's bodies and expressions of Black women's sexuality.

The woman in Missy Elliott's rap "Sock It To Me"[4] (1997) takes charge of her sexuality and actively seeks out a male sexual partner. She raps: "I was looking for affection/So I decided to go/Swing that dick in my direction." Inverting the traditional male–female roles in heterosexual courtship patterns, she resists waiting for a man to pursue her and chooses instead to make the first move toward a sexual liaison. The woman in the song is not a passive player in the heterosexual courtship game. Rather, she is in control of the timing of the heterosexual encounter. Missy chooses to have the woman in this song claim her desire and act on it. In doing so, she speaks through the historical silence surrounding Black women's sexualities,[5] and her audience is reminded that women are sexual beings who desire sexual pleasure. Even though Missy says she will be "out of control," she represents a woman who seems very much in control of defining the terms of a sexual encounter. She tells the man what to do with his penis, specifically to swing it in her direction. Missy's representation of Black female sexual pleasure begins with a woman who takes charge and then decides to let herself go (out of control) to experience the sexual pleasure she desires.

Missy's choice to have this woman seek out a man's penis is not without contradiction. Perhaps she is talking back to Black male rappers' constructions of women as commodities, our bodies available for men's sexual consumption. In severing the Black man's penis from the rest of his body, she is able to possess him, and by extension, his power. The woman demands that the man, now the object of desire, fulfill her sexual fantasies. Or perhaps Missy's move can be read as a playful gesture, one with serious intention, to remind us of the more familiar pattern in men's rap that exhibits Black women's bodies as a collection of sexual parts. Though resistant on some levels, the lyrics do not escape phallocentric ideology or heterosexism which privilege the phallus as the ultimate source of power, and the lyrics only redirect objectification toward the male body, not do away with objectification altogether. Though the song is not totally successful at subverting racist and sexist imaging of the Black woman as "out of control," read "hypersexual and wild," the song still is a valuable representation by a Black woman about heterosexual matters. The woman in "Sock It to Me" makes a conscious choice to seek sexual fulfillment, and she defines the terms of the sexual encounter demanding that the man "do it long and slow with a back stroke."

Perhaps unintended but still significant is the connection between movement and sexuality when the woman in Missy's song declares that her "hormones are jumping like a disco." Not a new theme in Black music in general and in Black women's music in particular, mobility, whether real or imagined, is especially meaningful to Black folks whose movement has historically been limited or denied altogether. In her work on early 20th century women blues singers, Davis (1998) locates a thematic coupling between a woman's ability to move and her ability to exercise autonomy in her sexual life:

> For people of African descent who were emerging from a long history of enslavement and oppression during the late nineteenth and early twentieth centuries, sexuality and travel provided the most tangible evidence of freedom.... For women especially, the ability to travel implied a measure of autonomy, an ability to shun passivity and acquiescence in the face of mistreatment and injustice and to exercise some control over the circumstances of their lives, especially over their sexual lives. (pp. 67, 74)

The woman in Missy's rap is similar to Black women blues singers who, in their efforts to "redefine black womanhood as active, assertive, independent, and sexual, urged women to 'keep movin,' movement which did not necessarily mean a territorial change" (Davis, 1998, p. 75). Davis suggests that to keep moving also meant action or a woman's ability to go forward and act in the world, to resist and survive mistreatment in a sexual relationship. Refusing to be confined by conventional notions of sexuality and desirability, the woman in Missy's rap is also active. Movement is emphasized as she describes the sex act and her role in it.

In similar fashion, movement figures prominently in Mia X's rap entitled "Sex Education" (1998). Mia X creates a teacher persona through which she performs a Black female sexuality that works against silence, passivity, and shame in the open expression of heterosexual desires. Through a fictional persona, Mia X, the "southern diva who keeps you hotter than grandma's heater," boasts about her sexual prowess. She highlights motion in the sexual performance. In fact, she calls herself "a rodeo girl" in control of moving the sexual act toward its climax. She claims that her "up and down" and "round and round" movements have the man "sweating like a Jane Fonda workout."

Mia X's performance of a Black female sexuality does seem bold in its sexual explicitness, but it is not without its contradictions. Mia X's sexual expression seems in keeping with racist and sexist representations of Black women. First, she describes a sexual encounter in which she is not an equal partner (her legs are "spread like 9:15"), and in keeping with heterosexism, Mia X places emphasis on pleasing the man, never even mentioning her own desires. Male desire, not women's, is the impetus for the sexual encounter. At the beginning of the song, she declares herself "The best teacher/Certified in opening wide, guaranteed to please ya," and she ends with similar phrasing, "I aim to please/And all my students come back." The language here suggests commodification of the woman's role in the sex act; she performs a service with a (money back?) guarantee. The language also draws attention to the Black woman's body as easily accessible, available, and thus sexually deviant (hooks, 1992). Significant to this representation is Mia X's pedagogical persona. That she "aims to please" is, interestingly enough, in the context of her image as teacher. A "dutiful daughter" (Munro, 1998a, p. 272), she is patriarchy's exemplary teacher placing the (sexual) desires of the Father before her own. Her male sexual lover, whom she calls "Daddy"[6] at one point in the song, matters more in the pedagogical (and sexual) space.

Foxy Brown also places more importance on fulfilling men's sexual fantasies in her rap "Candy" (2001). Like Mia X, Foxy performs a Black female sexuality that does not always resist racist and sexist representations of Black women. In her rap, Foxy, playing the role of "stewardess," directs men's attention to her body—and by extension the Black woman's body—which she says tastes "just like candy." Her efforts to "catch his eye" by "showing a little cleavage, licking her lips, adjusting her tits, and switching her hips" create a sexualized scene in which the body parts of the Black woman become the objects of the male gaze.

Foxy creates a lyrical sexual fantasy that invites the male gaze by placing emphasis on the visual appeal of specific body parts. Calling attention to her dark complexion and her breasts, mentioning her expertise in lying on her stomach and throwing her legs back, and accepting the lesser role in the pilot–stewardess dichotomy, Foxy performs a Black female sexuality that is centered in the objectification of the Black woman's body and in the satisfaction of male desire. The woman becomes the Dark Continent upon which men can stake their (erect) claim (White, 2001). Foxy's invitation to the nameless man in the rap—suggestive of an invitation to male listeners in general—to "imagine [her] nude, stretched out…nipples all out, bent over the sink" does not evoke the beauty and sensuality of Black women's bodies but reinforces the stereotypical representation of Black women's bodies as territories to be penetrated, occupied, and ravaged by men. Foxy's representation reminds me of the images of Black women in male rappers' videos, those that Rose (1994) describes as a "virtual meat market" (p. 169) of Black women's bodies.

Not until the last few lines of the rap does Foxy's performance of a Black female sexuality position women differently. Even though she directs men's attention to her naked body once again, she proclaims her "priceless-ness" and boasts of her skill when in the "top" position. This shift is the only time in the rap "Candy" that the Black woman is constructed with a measure of sexual agency. "When I'm on top, the whole show stop" suggests a Black woman who is more of an equal player in the sexual liaison, perhaps one who is more in control of her own sexual pleasure. Perhaps this moment in Foxy's rap is too little, too late to overcome the repeated objectification of the Black female body as "eye candy" for men, but it should not be overlooked as an important reminder of the ongoing struggle between Black women and men for control of Black women's bodies.

Missy Elliott's rap "One Minute Man" (2001) represents a more woman-centered narrative of sexual pleasure. Focusing attention on her own sexual satisfaction, the woman in Missy's rap says she wants nothing to do with men who are quick to orgasm. She wants a man with staying power, one whom she insists must "come prepared" to handle whatever she "throws" to him. Intent on "keeping him up all night," the woman invites the man "to show [her] what [he's] got" and "give [her] some more." In other words, the man must impress her with his sexual prowess and prove himself worthy to be considered her sexual partner. In this interesting inversion, Missy places the woman's desires ahead of the man's, and she empowers the woman to claim sexual pleasure on her own terms.

Missy wrote the song to include a male rapper's performance, and in the original version, Ludacris raps a verse taking on the persona of a mechanic. He is a full-service sex technician. Calling himself "an all-nighter" capable of "shooting all fire," he brags about the effects of his virility and stamina on women. He claims to be able to make women "so wet that they body start to leak" and to make them "see stripes" after sexual encounters with him. Posing as the ultimate fuck-all-night-big-dick Black man, a familiar construction in male hip-hop discourse, he distances himself from the men for whom the woman in Missy's song has no sexual desire. Ludacris calls these men "one minute fools" who are unable to understand why women do not want to have sex with them.

Missy's rap forces Ludacris to engage in familiar boasts about a Black man's extraordinary sexual prowess. But Missy places Ludacris' performance in the rap after her two verses and just before the ending chorus in which she declares over and over that she does not want a one minute man, placement which could be read to suggest that Missy is prompting Ludacris to defend his persona against charges of sexual inadequacy. If read in this way, Missy, a Black woman, calls into question Black male rappers' representations of Black male sexuality and forces Ludacris to reconstruct Black masculinity. Exposing one woman's dissatisfaction with "one minute men," Missy creates a rupture in male rap discourse by privileging a woman's sexual satisfaction.

Missy creates an even more significant rupture with her song "Toyz" (2003). The woman in Missy's rap declares that she does not need her man anymore for sexual fulfillment because her sexual toys please her much better, and she repeats over and over again in the chorus of the song that "every girl must have a toy" for their own sexual enjoyment. Taking on a sexually autonomous role, Missy says she will remain unaffected even if her lover decides to "hit every chick on the block" because "she gon be alright once [she] turn this power on." On cue after this line, a small motor sounds, suggestive of a vibrator. In the first and second verses, Missy criticizes her man's sexual performance ("You don't get the job done when I need a little loving") and refuses to engage in sexual intercourse with him ("Don't come waking me up, cause I ain't giving you nada"). Missy's representation here is of an independent woman who chooses not to depend on a man to fulfill her sexual needs. Confident in herself and her toy, she says, "It works for me and lasts longer than the battery."

Missy's performance is of a woman who no longer romanticizes her heterosexual relationship and instead recognizes the realities and limitations of it. Unhappy with the terms of her current relationship, she chooses to abandon the ideals of love with her male partner, but she is unwilling to sacrifice her own sexual pleasure. A desiring subject, she is content to love and please herself. In the outro to the song, Missy dismisses her male lover from her bedroom and her life cautioning him against slamming the door when he leaves because it might "fuck up her concentration" with her toy.

Missy's image of a strong, sexually independent woman in this song complicates how Black women are typically represented in rap discourse. The image talks back to constructions of Black women that objectify, degrade, and confine rather than humanize, respect, and liberate. Missy's representation resists the familiar stereotype in rap discourse that casts Black women as passive players in matters of sexual desire, in other words, the tendency in rap discourse to represent Black women as important only to the extent they act in the (sexual) service of men. An important rupture in patriarchal discourse, Missy's song calls into question how Black women are most often represented in rap discourse and teaches us how to represent Black women who are in control of and define the terms of their own sexual pleasure.

"Precariously Perched": Heterosexual Politics

When Black women rappers represent a negotiation of sexual power relations between Black women and men, their lyrics are angrier, more resistant, less passive than their lyrics about women's sexual desire and pleasure. Black women rappers seem to have less difficulty expressing the frustrations, fears, and struggles of heterosexual Black women than they do articulating woman-centered desire. Rose (1994) quotes from Cornel

West's interview with Stephanson (1988) in which he describes the complicated intimacy between Black women and men:

> The pressure on [African] Americans as a people has forced the black man closer to the black woman: they are in the same boat. But they are also at each other's throat. The relation is internally hierarchical and often mediated by violence: black men over black women. (West in Stephanson, 1988, quoted in Rose, p. 149)

Black women are "precariously perched" (Hammonds, 1997a, p. 145) in heterosexual relationships. In a space of intersectionality, "the dual positioning of women of color as women and as members of a subordinated racial group renders [us] vulnerable to the structural, political, and representational dynamics of both race and gender subordination" (Crenshaw, 1993, p. 112). With financial freedom that many Black women do not enjoy, Black female rappers are able to voice some of the vulnerabilities Black women face at one time or another in heterosexual relationships. Enlightening pedagogy, the raps offer advice to women and warnings to men, which converge around questions of power and sexuality. Rose (1994) further describes these songs:

> These raps are not mournful ballads about the trials and tribulations of being a heterosexual woman. Similar to women's blues, they are caustic, witty, and aggressive warnings directed at men and at other women who might be seduced by them in the future. By offering a woman's interpretation of the terms of heterosexual courtship, these women's raps cast a new light on male–female sexual power relations and depict women as resistant, aggressive participants. (p. 155)

Blending themes of women's pleasure with sexual politics, Lil Kim's rap "Not Tonight" (1996) is a complicated performance of a Black woman defining the terms of sexual pleasure and negotiating her positioning in a heterosexual relationship. Lil Kim tells the story of sexual encounters with two fictional male partners, Jimmy and Rondu, both of whom Kim concludes are less than satisfactory lovers even though they provide her with expensive jewelry, clothes, and cars. Characterizing Jimmy as a "trick," Kim begins the rap by placing herself in the position of prostitute who performs sexual services that please him, specifically fellatio and anal sex, in exchange for drugs, credit cards, and access to his car. All the while, however, Kim admits to using the material possessions given to her by Jimmy to seek out attention from other men. In the narrative, Kim has Jimmy pay her with the things she values, but he is not what she wants in a sexual partner. She describes how Jimmy's sexual performance was satisfying to her only twice out of 10 times.

Up to this point in the rap, Kim constructs an all too familiar image of the Black woman in rap discourse: the gold-digging ho, a woman who is involved with a man only to the extent that she can gain access to his money. Kim's representation is indeed problematic, but she flips the script at the end of her story about Jimmy when she makes known her desire for oral sex, questions Jimmy's manhood, and dismisses him because he does not (perhaps cannot) satisfy her. Kim assesses Jimmy's manhood by privileging her own desires. What she wants is of more value than the material possessions Jimmy can afford to give her. Following Kim's declaration is a chorus of women singing: "I don't want dick tonight/Eat my pussy right." An important shift in rap discourse, a Black woman chooses to define pleasure by refusing the Big Black Dick, so often constructed by male rappers as irresistible to all women. She defines a Black woman's sexual identity based on what the woman desires, not in reaction to what men want.

Kim constructs a similar story about Rondu, whom Kim also dismisses because of his inadequate sexual performances. Even Rondu's mention of his new car is not enough for Kim to agree to a sexual hook-up with him. He is a joke as a lover. Kim not only ridicules the sexual interactions she has had with Rondu, but she criticizes his penis specifically. Calling it "trash," Kim attacks the image on which Black male rappers often hang their manhood in their songs, a move by Kim that calls into question the supposed power and potency represented by the Black penis. Kim ridicules and rejects it in favor of the fulfillment of her own sexual desires. In an interesting script reversal, Kim proposes to pay Rondu $10,000 if he leaves her alone, a sum that totals more than the worth of Rondu's jewelry, which he used to try to seduce Kim. In these lines, Kim constructs a more powerful position for the Black woman; she defines the terms of the relationship. Nothing Rondu has to offer, including his flashy shows of jewelry, entices her. Her body is not for sale.

In the last verse of the rap, Kim is explicitly pedagogical calling attention to the "moral" of her story. Connecting issues of women's sexuality and capital, Kim teaches us the significance of money in relationships between Black women and men. Kim connects her ability to define the terms of a sexual relationship ("You ain't licking this, you ain't sticking this") with her ownership of material wealth ("I got my own Benz, I got my own ends"). Using her position of power in a heterosexual relationship, she refuses to compromise her sexual desires, and she prioritizes her pleasure over her man's in her performance of a Black woman's sexuality. The Black woman represented in this way can choose not to have sex in exchange for money, cars, and jewelry.

Kim chooses to end the rap with representations similar to the ones she constructed in the story about Jimmy in the first verse: "Me and my girls…. Fuck for car keys and double digit figures." Perhaps Kim is unwilling or unable to dismiss the familiar gold-digging image of the Black woman and the hypersexual braggadocio common in male rappers' constructions of Black female sexuality. Perhaps Kim uses these images to gain her audience's attention long enough so that she can include representations that rupture the patriarchal discourse of male rappers. In any case, Kim's representational choices are pedagogically significant. They expose the fragility of the images male rappers most often use to represent Black manhood in their raps; they sometimes reify and sometimes resist the demeaning sexual stereotypes often used to represent Black women in rap discourse; and they call for an intersectional framework to understand representations of race, gender, and class tensions in heterosexual relationships between Black women and men.

Lil Kim is not the only Black woman rapper to construct representations of Black women's sexuality that are complicated by issues of money and class. Foxy Brown performs raps that represent Black women willing to engage in sexual intercourse with men only if they are paid in some way. I select Foxy's rap "I Can't" (1999) in particular because she is explicit about her intention to "school" or teach women audiences what to do to make heterosexual relationships work to their benefit.[7] Foxy insists that women negotiate—perhaps dictate—the terms of a sexual encounter so that it becomes a means to a woman's financial gain. In her rap "I Can't," Foxy cautions women against falling for men too quickly and giving in to their sexual advances because she says women risk losing power in the relationship. She warns women about the games men play to gain control over them, specifically promising marriage to trick women into sleeping with them. Maintaining that men "game a lot," Foxy offers a game plan of her own for sexual relations with men, which includes a long list of luxuries that she expects them to provide, such as Christian Dior handbags, Prada shoes, diamonds, and license plates that read "Property of Mahogany Brown," a name Foxy gives to a persona she sometimes assumes on wax.

Foxy insists on ownership of the car she is given and wants that ownership labeled on the license plates, a public notice that the car belongs to a Black woman.

Foxy's plan for sexual encounters with men is largely based on a Black woman's ownership of property. Foxy's use of the phrase "Property of" can be read as a moment in which the construction of Black women as commodities, as objects to be bought and sold, is called into question. Positioning the Black woman in her rap as an owner of expensive items, Foxy links a Black woman's sexual freedom to her financial stability. Foxy's lesson is clear: a woman who has her own money is more powerful in heterosexual relationships than a woman struggling to make ends meet. Not having to depend on just any man for monetary support, she has a greater degree of autonomy in choosing a sexual partner. Assuming the role of teacher, Foxy stresses that she uses "pussy" to keep men "chasing her," and she warns women not to "get up off it" too quickly.

Foxy's "Pussy is Power" message can be read in more than one way. Foxy's use of representations that connect a woman's site of sexual pleasure with power can be thought of as a counterreading that ruptures the phallocentric discourse of male rappers; however, her construction of the Black woman's "pussy" as a mode of currency for access to a man's expensive things reifies male rappers' representations of Black women as scheming gold diggers. My attempts at reading Foxy's text has resulted in multiple questions: How are poor and working-class Black women supposed to negotiate Foxy's brand of "pussy politics" that depends so much on a woman's access to material wealth? Is Foxy's brand of "pussy politics" yet another construction of the Black woman as jezebel, whose body is an object for sale? Can Foxy's "pussy politics" ever really "change the plot" of patriarchal hip-hop discourse that privileges a male-over-female hierarchy in the representation of heterosexual partnerships?

Women Loving Women: Black Lesbian Sexuality

Even though the women rappers' lyrics I have read thus far are valuable expressions that show negotiations of and struggles for power by Black women in heterosexual relationships, none of them reject heterosexual arrangements altogether. Instead, they reinforce heterosexuality. In the homophobic and misogynistic discourse of rap, representations of lesbian and gay sexualities are rare. Yet I am sure such raps are performed more than I am aware, songs which allow for queer readings but are not overt in their representation of lesbian and gay sexual partnerships.

Queen Pen queers the hip-hop space, firmly entrenched in heterosexist representations, with images of women seeking sexual pleasure from other women in her rap "Girlfriend" (1997). Queen Pen takes on the playa persona, typically a male figure who can "pull" or seduce many women, often without them knowing he is not monogamous. She recodes the playa persona,[8] which is often used in male rap discourse, and carves out a space from which she constructs representations of urban lesbian identity. She becomes a woman playa whose sexual prowess and cunning result in "mad bitches wanting [her]" and "mad niggas checking for [her]." Taunting the boyfriend of the woman with whom she has had sex the previous night, Queen Pen boasts that she's "had" his girlfriend and ridicules his sexual ineptitude, a representation that can be read as a challenge to the traditional power roles associated with masculinity. Queen Pen, a Black woman, brags about "having" the Black man's girlfriend, a power play that places Queen Pen in a more dominant position than the Black man. That Queen Pen as the playa (typically a male role) has "had" his girlfriend suggests "possession" of the Black woman, an all too familiar (hetero)sexist representation. Though she inverts the typical hierarchical relationship between Black women and men by taking over the male position, she does not create a representation that subverts the traditional roles linked to the heterosexual relationship. Taking on the playa persona locks Queen Pen into representations of Black sexuality that are more about ownership and occupation, rather than partnership and reciprocality.

Queen Pen creates a liberating representation when she pays particular attention to the Black woman's body in her narration of a flirting scene between women outside a bar. She takes notice of the "rhythm of [the woman's] thighs" as the woman moves toward her several times; her description highlights the sensuousness of the Black woman's body. Allowing the Black woman's body freedom to move to its own rhythm, Queen Pen resists the usual objectifying representations of containment in rap discourse that construct the Black woman's body as something to be occupied and taken over by men.

Queen Pen's narrative pokes fun at women who try to keep their desire for other women hidden. In exposing their attempts at initiating a sexual encounter with women (on the down low) even though they are already involved in a heterosexual relationship, Queen Pen deconstructs the rigid categories we assign to sexual identity and exposes the instability of heterosexuality. Blurring the line between gay and straight, Queen Pen raps, "It's my business what I do/Him or her, he or she, inside you/If I choose to juggle both, then it's all on me." Her vagueness in these two lines could be read as a representation of Black female bisexuality or hesitancy in representing a narrowly defined lesbian sexual identity. Whatever the reading, Queen Pen creates a space in which representations of Black women's sexualities move out of a heterosexist framework to complicate the already complicated discourse of rap.

(A) Troubling Curriculum?

All of the women rappers I have chosen to include in this chapter have crafted expressions that talk back in multiple ways to the racialized sexual imaging of Black women. Sometimes complicit in perpetuating the production of demeaning representations and sometimes resistant to their continuance, the texts that I have read have not always included positive, woman-centered representations of Black women's sexualities. Even though my readings show some women rappers' texts to be contradictory and problematic, the representations they offer are pedagogically important, not merely in a classroom usage kind of way, but also to the at-large public curriculum. Black women rappers' representations reveal as much about their individual experiences as they help to make more complex our shared understanding of the underlying intersections of, and sometimes tensions among race, gender, class, generation, and sexuality.

A kind of "curriculum as complicated conversation" (Pinar, Reynolds, Slattery, & Taubman, 1995, p. 848), the many scripts Black women rappers offer to the U.S. public are in dialogue with a long history of representations of Black women. Rather than close down conversation, Black women rappers are public pedagogues who raise important epistemological questions: What does it mean when Black women construct knowledge about sexuality in public discourses? What does it mean when *hip-hop generation* Black women construct this knowledge? What critiques are Black women rappers offering to their audiences about the experiences of Black women from the hip hop generation? How do these critiques connect to the historical and contemporary essentializing discourses that have represented Black women in static and demeaning ways? Why do audiences displace their discomfort with hypersexualized images onto women rappers and not onto the male executives who are largely responsible for the production of these images?

While I may not make the same representational choices that Black women rappers make in their imaging of Black women's sexual identities, I understand the need for them as performers (teachers) to reach their audiences (students) where they are, for as Eve comments:

> You got to talk like your people to get through to your people (Eve quoted in Tate, 2001, p. 161). Some of [my] songs may be vulgar as hell, but I make them like that on purpose so certain people can listen. (Eve quoted in Solomon, 2000, p. 206)

I hope that we are listening to what Black women rappers have to say because we have much to learn from their boldness in resisting objectification and pushing boundaries. Imagine the excitement we could conjure in our classrooms if we were so bold.

Notes

1. See Kanye West (2005).
2. *Troubling* seems a fitting term to describe rap texts. To disturb the mental calm and contentment of; to cause discomfort to; to annoy, vex, or bother; to agitate or stir up; civil disorder, disturbance, or conflict—all of these meanings are suggestive of the complexity of rap, its problematic or objectionable content as well as its potential for unsettling our taken-for-granted assumptions and shaking up the status quo.
3. I intentionally use the plural term *pedagogies* to note that its "use is important to signify the multiple approaches and practices that fall under the pedagogy umbrella whereas rely[ing] on the singular form is to imply greater unity and coherence than is warranted" (Gore, 1993, cited in Daspit, 2000, p. 165).
4. I am reminded of Aretha Franklin's refrain "Sock It to Me" in her classic song "Respect."
5. See Hammonds (1997a), Higginbotham (1992), Hine (1989), hooks (1998), Lorde (1984), and Spillers (1989) for discussions of history of silence surrounding representations of Black women's sexualities.
6. I am reminded here of early 20th century blues women singers (e.g., Bessie Smith, Ma Rainey) who also often referred to male lovers as "Daddy" in their songs.
7. Other women rappers express intent to teach women that a sexual encounter can be a means to their financial gain. See also Queen Pen's "Pussy Ain't For Free" (2001) and Trina's "Da Baddest Bitch" (2000).
8. The playa is a hip-hop reversioning of the "Mack" made popular in 1970s blaxploitation films.

References

Burford, M., & Farley, C. J. (1999, August). Dignity or dollars. *Essence*, 72–76, 132–138.

Castenell, L. A., & Pinar, W. F. (Eds.). (1993). *Understanding curriculum as racial text: Representations of identity and difference in education*. Albany: SUNY Press.

Crenshaw, K. W. (1993). Beyond racism and misogyny: Black feminism and 2 live crew. In M. J. Matsuda, C. R. Lawrence III, R. Delgado, & K. W. Crenshaw (Eds.), *Words that wound: Critical race theory, assaultive speech, and the first amendment* (pp. 111–132). Boulder, CO: Westview Press.

Daspit, T. (2000). Rap pedagogies: "Bring(ing) the noise" of "knowledge born on the microphone" to radical education. In T. Daspit & J. A. Weaver (Eds.), *Popular culture and critical pedagogy: Reading, constructing, connecting* (pp. 163–182). New York: Garland.

Davis, A. (1998). *Blues legacies and black feminism*. New York: Vintage Books.

Edwards, A. (2001, March). Independent woman. *Vibe*, 121–126.

Goodall, N. (1994). Depend on myself: T.L.C. and the evolution of Black female rap. *Journal of Negro History*, (79), 1. Retrieved March 31, 2000, from http://www.web2.infotrac.galegroup.com database.

Gore, J. (1993). *The struggle for pedagogies: Critical and feminist discourses as regimes of truth*. New York: Routledge.

Hammonds, E. M. (1997a). Black (w)holes and the geometry of black female sexuality. In E. Weed & N. Schor (Eds.), *Feminism meets queer theory* (pp. 136–156). Bloomington: Indiana University Press.

Hammonds, E. M. (1997b). Toward a genealogy of black female sexuality: The problematic of silence. In M. J. Alexander & C. T. Mohanty (Eds.), *Feminist genealogies, colonial legacies, democratic futures* (pp. 170–182). New York: Routledge.

Higginbotham, E. B. (1992). African-American women's history and the metalanguage of race. *Signs: Journal of Women in Culture and Society, 17*(2), 251–274.

Hine, D. C. (1989). Rape and the inner lives of black women in the middle west: Preliminary thoughts on the culture of dissemblance. *Signs: Journal of Women in Culture and Society, 14*(4), 912–920.

hooks, b. (1989). *Talking back*. Boston: South End Press.

hooks, b. (1992). *Black looks: Race and representation*. Boston: South End Press.

hooks, b. (1998). Naked without shame: A counter-hegemonic body politic. In E. Shohat (Ed.), *Talking visions: Multicultural feminism in a transnational age* (pp. 65–73). Cambridge, MA: MIT Press.

Lorde. A. (1984). *Sister outsider*. New York: Crossing Press.

Morgan, J. (1999). *When chickenheads come home to roost: A hip-hop feminist breaks it down*. New York: Simon & Schuster.

Munro, P. (1998a). Engendering curriculum history. In W. F. Pinar (Ed.), *Curriculum: Toward new identities* (pp. 263–294). New York: Garland.

Munro. P. (1998b). *Subject to fiction: Women teachers' life history narratives and thecultural politics of resistance*. Buckingham, England: Open University Press.

Oumano, E. (1999, June 5). Girl power. *Billboard*. Retrieved October 21, 1999, from http://www.findarticles.com

Pinar, W. F. (2001). *The gender of racial politics in America: Lynching, prison rape, andthe crisis of masculinity*. New York: Lang.

Pinar, W. F. (2004). *What is curriculum theory?* Mahwah, NJ: Erlbaum.

Pinar, W. F., Reynolds, W. M., Slattery, P., & Taubman, P. M. (1995). *Understanding curriculum: An introduction to the study of historical and contemporary curriculum discourses*. New York: Lang.

Rose, T. (1994). *Black noise: Rap music and black culture in contemporary America*. Hanover, NH: Wesleyan University Press.

Solomon, A. (2000, December). The natural. *The Source*, 205–210.

Spillers, H. (1989). Interstices: A small drama of words. In C. S. Vance (Ed.), *Pleasure and danger: Exploring female sexuality* (pp. 73–100). London: Pandora Press.

Tate, G. (2001). All about Eve. In *Vibe hip-hop divas* (pp.158–163). New York: Three Rivers Press.

White, E. F. (2001). *Dark continent of our bodies: Black feminism and the politics of respectability*. Philadelphia: Temple University Press.

Selected Discography

Foxy Brown. (1999).*Chyna doll*. Violator Records.

Foxy Brown. (2000). *Broken silence*. Def Jam Recordings.

Kanye West. (2005). *Late registration*. Roc-a-Fella Records.

Lil Kim. (1996).*Hardcore*. Big Beat Records.

Mia X. (1998). *Mama drama*. Priority/No Limit Records.

Missy Elliott. (1997). *Elliott, Supa dupa fly*. Elektra Entertainment Group.

Missy Elliott. (2001). *Miss E…so addictive* Elektra Entertainment Group.

Missy Elliott. (2003). *This is not a test*. Elektra Entertainment Group.

Queen Pen. (1997). *My melody*. Lil Man/Interscope Records.

Queen Pen. (2001). *Conversations with queen*. Motown Records.

Trina. X. (2000). *Da baddest bitch*. Slip-n-Slide Records.

Response to Nichole A. Guillory
The Politics of Patriarchal Discourse
A Feminist Rap

Nathalia Jaramillo

Multiple feminist and feminized theories and pedagogies advocate an understanding of women's oppression *and* agency in social life across various domains. Biofeminists dispute genetic arguments and reclaim the cultured self; ecofeminists examine the relation between the degradation of nature and the exploitation of women; postmodern feminists focus on the interplay between language—discourse and performative registers—and women's identity formation; materialist feminists ground their analyses of women's oppression in the historical and concrete dimensions of capitalist society; critical race feminists apply the lens of "race" to differentiate oppression among women; queer-feminists contest hetero-normativity and the construction of gender; and various other feminists examine the intersection of identity, power, and social relations on the subjective formation of "woman." There is no one way to apply a feminist analysis to women's oppression or to advocate a pedagogy, or praxis, to help establish the conditions for women to free themselves from mental (and manual and sexual) slavery (to borrow Bob Marley's timeless lyric). Missing from the list above are postcolonial feminists, indigenous feminists, Chicana feminists, Islamic feminists, transnational feminists, socialist feminists, psychoanalytic feminists, and so the list continues. My intent on naming the various "feminisms" is not to simplify or dilute the importance of each strand of feminist theorizing. On the contrary, these "feminisms" indicate an obvious and permanent shift in global politics. For one, the oppression of women can no longer go unnoticed or unattended (even while their exploitation persists), and second, feminist theorizing has much to say about domination in general, and the coexistence of militarism, speciesism, imperialism, capitalism, colonialism, and the exploitation of women (and men) and their bodies worldwide. To the extent that feminist theory and practice can avoid liberalization and incorporation into the neoliberal project of human and earthly exploitation and to the extent that it continues to offer an oppositional and counterhegemonic praxis in our pursuit for a more socially just and humane world we are better positioned to create a world of our own making. The varied analyses and social practices that stem from feminist praxis aid our understanding of the changing roles and experiences that people encounter as the information society becomes more perverse, poverty more deep-rooted, militarism more brute, capitalism more expansive, and in some isolated cases, socialism more possible.

I raise this feminist rap (rap defined here as chat, chatter, conversation) because upon reading Nichole Guillory's essay, "(A) Troubling Curriculum," I was *troubled* by my initial reaction to place her analysis of women's discourse on sex and sexuality in rap music in sharp contradistinction to my understanding of women's agency in these spheres. I wanted to engage Guillory's work in a way that enables a self-described materialist feminist like me to think about the pedagogical potential of hip-hop as a counterhegemonic space that youth and women access to "talk back" to dominant society and to develop their critical capacities for being in the world. I considered the importance of social location from where people speak; a need to understand, in Adrienne Rich's words, "how a place on the map is also a place in history" (1985). I begin this essay by locating my place on the map.

My brush with popular culture began as a latch-key suburban first-generation Colombian-American teen of the 1980s, when the Material Girl (or the person devout fundamentalists refer to as the Great Whore of Babylon) taught me that Jesus wasn't necessarily a White man, that papa shouldn't preach, and that eventually I'd learn what makes a virgin feel so good inside. Hours spent in front of a TV watching music videos and listening to the radio had an undeniable impact on my thinking in and of the world. I did not have the language or the critical capacities to reinterpret popular media and its role in my personal formation or its function as an evolving multitrillion dollar globalized industry that reproduces sex, drugs, and rock and roll for a profit. I consumed "pop" blindly and uncritically and spent my weekly allowance at the Wherehouse Music Store, devouring music that would speak directly to my need to rebel from a strict orthodox Catholic upbringing. The Material Girl became a permanent shadow in my mind, a shape shifter from debutante to devilish-eyed vixen, a reference point for enacting womanhood in popular society. At various levels, she "talked back" to the pious, religiously sanctified, and patriarchal relations of mainstream society. As a young, sensuous, and Catholic child of immigrants, she disrupted the flow of the American Dream (i.e., family of four in a new home with a minted blue Cadillac Seville parked in the driveway) and established benchmarks of rebellion for many young women in the early stages of their identity development. And yet, to isolate her performances and lyrics from the class structure from where she spoke and from where she was listened to, is to miss the complexity of the basis and outcome of mass produced discourse. That she impacted a middle-class, repressed teen in the throes of forming her identity (and in many ways purging the identity allotted to her through family and institutionalized religion) speaks to the interconnectedness between one's personal context, history, and experience and the meaning of language in everyday life. Language is an important site for human agency, but when we only consider subjectivity in language and by language, we fail to enter into a space of critical self-reflexivity.

In consideration of the historical precincts of material production and consumer-oriented "popular" markets that connect "discourse" and "being," I thought about the "pedagogical" elements that Guillory discusses in her essay. I share her sentiment that popular culture and hip-hop specifically, can offer a powerful means for connecting students to texts and ideas that may appear archaic and far removed from the concrete realities (and influences) of their lives. In this spirit, I will focus on Guillory's assertion that Black women rappers (and *raperas*) or "public pedagogues" act as,

> important voices in/writers of the public conversation about the collective struggles of Black women: our struggle to define ourselves rather than be mis(represented) by others; our struggle for respect and treatment as peers in male-dominated work spaces; our struggle to express our lesbian, bisexual, heterosexual, transgender, and questioning selves; our struggle against violence by male partners in heterosexual relationships; and our struggle to build community and mobilize ourselves. (p. 211)

In thinking about the objectification and sexual repression of the female body, and the systematic patriarchal violence inflicted on the sexes, I was taken by the Guillory's focus on the female body (as sexual and desirous) in rap music as a disruption of patriarchal discourse.

The Body

Guillory's detailed analysis of women's rap lyrics brought to mind the contradictory forces inscribed on the body in a postmodern, late capitalist society. Her writing on Black women rappers' focus on sex and asserting their pleasure in the sexual encounter (whether with a man, woman, or battery-operated hand-held device) compelled me to think about the politics of sex in popular culture. The mapping of phallic desire on the female body and the unequal relation between a woman's sexual fulfillment and a man's sexual power is the focus of many lyrics "deconstructed" in Guillory's essay. Recalling, for example, Missy Elliot's lyric "swing that dick in my direction," Guillory writes of shifting power between the sexes where, in the case of Elliot, Guillory asserts, "in severing the Black man's penis from the rest of his body, she is able to possess him, and by extension, his power. The woman demands that the man, now the object of desire, fulfill her sexual fantasies." While at some level we can appreciate the "inversion" of patriarchal discourse in these lyrics (the woman possesses the penis, rather than being possessed by it), it is difficult so situate this analysis outside of the context from which these unequal sexual relations emerge (i.e., history of slavery and colonization). This "inverted" discourse brought to mind the question: does the female version of male objectification make it any less patriarchal? If we adopt the worldview that only men can advance (and speak) patriarchy, then we sublimate women to the status of biological citizens: ovaries = nonpatriarchal. In doing so, we lose sight of the very conditions and relations that give rise to human exploitation, to the fragmentation of the body into its (economically) "productive" parts, and to the commodification of the bodies and images of youth as a form of "sex work" (Hill-Collins, 2006). Men and women can tease out their sexual prowess in the public sphere under the veil of enacting "agency," but ultimately, many fall prey to the sex work industry "not primarily as commercial workers as is popularly imagined, but rather, as representations of commodified Black sexuality as well as potential new consumer markets eager to consume their own images" (Hill-Collins, 2006, p. 305). In the hip-hop industry, sex work pays big; it gives the illusion that the historically marginalized are in fact incorporated (literally, into INCs), that the historically voiceless are heard, and that there is no greater human equalizer than the dollar sign. Patriarchy establishes hierarchical and often violent relations between the sexes, but it is also an intricate part of an overarching system of capitalist exploitation that maximizes on the perceived differences between the sexes.

My argument here is not a moral or ethical one; it is an argument predicated on an understanding of the body, as laboring, sensuous, and historical (see McNally, 2000). Discourse cannot disinter the body from where it is concretely located. To read the body discursively, and to claim that the opposition between the language of the body and the social location of the body is "given" (i.e., acknowledge women's objectification of men's bodies but appreciate the power of their "oppositional" discourse) reinforces the duality of mind and body. In this framework, an understanding of the body as seemingly liberated from domination vis-à-vis discourse separates the body from its place within the broader politic of colonialist-capitalist social relations. When we sever words from the living, sensuous, consuming, and producing body we separate language from the meaning derived in everyday life.

In thinking of women rappers' texts as "at-large public curriculum" with the potential of complicating our "shared understanding of the underlying intersections of and sometimes tensions among race, gender, class, generation and sexuality" (Guillory, p. 220), I thought about whether female subjectivity could be asserted in nonsexualized terms, or if female identities have been so exploited and objectified as sexed entities that a central (and necessary) means to assert agency is through sexuality. I do not claim to have a response to these issues. The need for public spaces to emerge where women can assert their sexuality is a necessary counterpart to the overwhelming logic of patriarchal–capitalist exploitation. But whether or not women do so in a way that does not reinscribe the same form of exploitation remains an issue to contend with when we consider the social struggles faced by our communities.

Guillory's essay brought many issues, contradictions, and tensions to bear. She compelled me to think beyond a U.S. setting and to explore how rappers/*raperas* contest the unified and objectified "woman" subject, as a racial, ethnic, laboring, heterosexual, and lesbian body in a transnational context. Here, again, the politics of location becomes central to an analysis of discourse and social struggle. Hip-hop (rap), conceived as a discourse of marginality with its roots in the African diaspora, has taken significance transnationally, shaping what Marc Perry describes as "contemporary forms of Black diasporic consciousness and subjectivity" (2008). Perry discusses the performative contours of hip-hop as mobilizing notions of racial selves in ways that are "at one time both contestive and transcendent of nationally bound, hegemonically prescriptive racial framings" (p. 2). In his discussion of *raperas* like the Cuban group *Las Krudas*, Perry notes "women often assert black, female-centered critiques of gendered forms of power as they intersect with those of race and sexuality. In doing so, they make important interventions within the male-dominant space of Cuban hip-hop as well as broader spheres of racialized patriarchy as they currently take shape within a transformative Post-soviet era Cuba." Las Krudas, call for resistance, a "rejection of such self-objectifying gendered conformity in which black women move towards a self-actualization for and in the image of themselves. Indeed, las Krudas with their dreadlocks, full-figured bodies, in-your-face feminist discourse, and unorthodox performance style clearly represent radical departures from both conventional Cuban images of feminine as well as the standard masculinist hip-hop fare" (Perry, 2007, p. 7).

Eres Bella—Las Krudas

> You are beautiful being you,
> ebony in flower, black light
> You are beautiful being you,
> the body isn't the only virtue.
> You are beautiful being you,
> ebony in flower, black light
> You are beautiful being you,
> intelligence is your virtue

A Note on Pedagogy

We have reached a point in history where hip-hop and pop culture in general have become deeply embedded in larger capitalist and transnational–state social formations. This can offer an important space for young people to both contest and reproduce these relations. I agree with Guillory that women rappers/*raperas* offer an important perspective on the locality of their experiences and that young and old alike interpret rappers' messages in equally context-specific ways. How women make their mark in the hip-hop industry that both conforms and offers a site of resistance to the dominant patriarchal–capitalist social order will be largely informed by where they stand and how they choose to speak. There is no one or right way for women to make their voices heard just as there is no one feminist theory or practice that will liberate women from oppression. Liberation takes place in praxis; in the daily struggles of developing a critical consciousness and agency to transform (and transcend) the oppressive social structures and relations that have historically tempered our free development. We inhabit sensuous bodies that struggle to make meaning in this often complex and contradictory world. Pedagogically, our hope resides in creating the conditions for students to critically interrogate their subjective identity formations and the messages and images conveyed to them through popular media; that we encourage embodied understandings of the social world and how we are implicated in it; and that we aim towards living in a world of our own making. This includes questioning the politics of discourse and looking toward an engaged public pedagogy that enables thought and action to be consistent with each other.

References

Hill-Collins, P. (2006). New commodities, new consumers: Selling blackness in a global marketplace. *Ethnicities*, 6, 297–317.

McNally, D. (2000). *Bodies of meaning: Studies on language, labor, and liberation*. Alban, NY: SUNY Press.

Perry, M. (2007). *Black feminist arisings: Contestive [re-]articulations of race and gender in Cuban hip-hop*. Paper presented at the Caribbean Studies Association, Salvador de Bahia, Brazil.

Perry, M. (2008, October). Global black self fashionings: Hip-hop as diasporic space. *Identities: Global Studies in Power and Culture, 15*(6), 141–152.

Rich, A. (1985). Notes toward a politics of location. In M. Díaz-Diocaretz & I. M. Zavala (Eds.), *Women, feminist identity, and society in the 1980's: Selected papers* (pp. 7–22). Philadelphia: John Benjamins Publishing Company.

11 Sleeping with Cake and Other Touchable Encounters
Performing a Bodied Curriculum

Stephanie Springgay and Debra Freedman

Chapter Overview

The chapter explores the call to create hybrid interdisciplinary montages within curriculum studies by naming performance art as a material manifestation of a bodied curriculum. The authors discuss the ethical, political, social, as well as the raced, classed, and gendered implication of being in relation with other bodies in different and hereto unknown ways and explore what these unsettling encounters produce in terms of different ways of thinking and being in the world. The authors focus upon the work of Canadian performance artist Diane Borsato in order to develop frameworks for thinking about human touch and relationality. Next, they turn to a discussion of learning as a form of becoming that takes place through and with others not in isolation as conventionally conceived. More specifically, they attend to the implications difference has for ethical constructs of teaching and learning. They suggest that ethics understood through relationality requires approaches to knowledge that are not absolute but specific to the complexities of bodied encounters. Lastly, they propose that the present and next moments of curriculum theorizing will require openness to as yet unknown ways of thinking and processes of becoming.

Introduction

In her book *Places of Learning* Elizabeth Ellsworth (2005) explores the potential for thinking about education as something "in the making," as an embodied, experiential, and relational process. Her research examines multimedia projections, public events, and performance art to present emergent pedagogical qualities, or rather, places in the making. Ellsworth positions these places as anomalies—as irregular, peculiar, or difficult to classify when viewed from the "center" of dominant educational discourses. We believe that the intimate performances and interventions enacted by contemporary Canadian artist Diane Borsato, need to be considered from this perspective—not as "things" already made into concrete facts, projects to be taught, nor metaphors for teaching and learning, but in the making—"harboring and expressing forces and processes of pedagogies as yet unmade, that provoke us to think or imagine new pedagogies in new ways" (Ellsworth, 2005, p. 6). Barbara Kennedy (2004), in writing about film from a feminist Deleuzian perspective, contends that film (or in our case performance art) needs to be understood not as a text with a meaning, but "as a body which performs, as a machine, as an assemblage, as an abstract machine" (p. 5), where "perception" is explored as experience and sensation.

Responding to curriculum scholars, Lisa Cary (2006) and Bill Pinar (2004), who suggest that curriculum theory is at a pivotal point to be re-reconceptualized by exploring "hybrid and interdisciplinary constructions, utilizing fragments from philosophy, history, literary theory, the arts…to create conceptual montages" (Cary, 2006, p. 33), we examine the performance art of Diane Borsato to guide us in performing and materializing a bodied curriculum. While embodiment has been addressed as integral to education (see Bresler, 2004) a bodied curriculum attends to the relational, social, and ethical implications of "being-with" other bodies differently and to the different knowledges such bodily encounters produce (Springgay & Freedman, 2007). It is a practice of being oriented to others, to touch, to reflect, and to dwell with others in relation. A bodied curriculum opens up subjectivity to the in-between of corporeality, materiality, and difference shifting the perception of embodiment as universal, toward an understanding of bodies and knowledges as difference. In an effort to "make present" this relational knowing we explore Diane Borsato's intimate performances and bodily encounters. Borsato's work explores everyday activities and materials through the body—of paying attention to the absurdities, ambivalence, and unthought encounters that exist between bodies.

In the first section of our chapter we focus on two of Borsato's intimate performances "Touching 1000 People" and "Sleeping with Cake" in order to develop the theoretical constructs of "touch" and "being-with." From here, we extend such understandings of relationality to a bodied curriculum and in particular attend to the ethical implications of teaching and learning "with" others as difference. We conclude the chapter proposing that a (post)reconceptualization of curriculum theory requires an openness to the unthought and a process of becoming that is always incomplete.

Touching One Thousand People and Sleeping with Cake

Imagine walking down the street of a large urban city. How do you encounter and face the stranger? How do you hold your body? How do you materialize and mark your space? For most of us, the authors included, we are inclined to embark on the dance of avoidance—the refusal of contact, touch, or conscious encounter. We side step and we walk around—marking our territory as an uncomplicated space. But imagine walking down a busy street and suddenly a hand reaches out to caress your shoulder. Or envision yourself reaching for a plump juicy red apple and finding your fingers slightly intertwined with those of another. Picture yourself accepting change at the checkout counter and being gently fondled by a thumb and forefinger; or sitting on a crowded public bus and feeling your shins being softly nuzzled by the sole of an athletic shoe. Having come across research that suggested that touching people in a seemingly unconscious manner could possibly affect their well-being, artist Diane Borsato subtly came in contact with 1,000 perfect strangers. Whether it was simply grazing someone's hand or lightly caressing an arm, Borsato sought to change the well-being of the city, improving its mood (and her own) through touch (Borsato, 2001). As an exercise in "diligently counting—463, 464, 465"—her performative piece became an exercise in "paying attention" (Borsato, 2001, p. 65). Moreover, her absurd task renders meaningful the nonvisible sense—touch—as a way of knowing and encountering self and other.

Western thought has always privileged vision as the dominant sense equating it with light, consciousness, and rationalization (Vasseleu, 1998). The other senses, marked by the body's effluence, were understood as interior sensibilities and thus of lesser value (Classen, 1993). In fact the nonvisible senses such as touch, taste, and smell were characterized as emotive senses and therefore gendered female or culturally dark, vulgar, and deviant. For instance the differences between the following two turns of phrase signify the ways in which Western thought has constructed knowledge as separate from and in opposition to the body. "I see" has commonly meant I know or understand, while "I feel" is often associated with intuitive knowing, which has historically been condemned as ridiculous and dismissed as trivial.

While vision is premised on the separation of the subject and object, creating a rational autonomous subject, as a contact sense touch offers contiguous access to an object. Touch alters the ways in which we perceive objects, providing access to depth and surface, inside and outside. Touch as a way of knowing can be understood through two modalities. First, touch is the physical contact of skin on matter. The second modality is a sense of being in a proximinal relation with something. In visual culture this has often been addressed as synaesthesia, a term which refers to the blurring of boundaries between the senses so that in certain circumstances one might be able to say that one can taste a painted image. A further understanding of proximity has been taken up by corporeal phenomenologists (e.g., Merleau-Ponty, 1968) and feminist scholars (e.g., Ahmed & Stacey, 2001; Grosz, 1994) who argue that knowledge is produced through bodied encounters, which can be interchangeable with the terms *interembodiment* or *intercorporeality* (Weiss, 1999).

More specific, interembodiment, an approach explored by feminist scholar Gail Weiss (1999) emphasizes "that the experience of being embodied is never a private affair, but is always already mediated by our continual interactions with other human and non-human bodies" (p. 5). Interembodiment poses that the construction of the body and the production of body knowledge is not created within a single, autonomous subject (body), but rather that body knowledge and bodies are created in the intermingling and encounters between bodies. Accordingly, Madeline Grumet (1988) writes that:

> Trapped in the dualisms of individualism and idealism, we become convinced that whatever we see in our "mind's eye" is a private vision, split off from what others know and feel, split off from the synesthesia that integrates all our perceptions, split off from the body, the other, the world. (p. 129)

Rather, intersubjectivity, she argues is characterized as a sharing between self and others. Elizabeth Ellsworth (2005) concurs, arguing that a relational learning experience "acknowledges that to be alive and to inhabit a body is to be continuously and radically in relation with the world, with others, and with what we make of them" (p. 4). How we come to know ourselves and the world around us, our subjectivity, is performed, constructed, and mediated in relation with other beings. It is this relationality that is crucial. Rather than knowledge formed through the rational autonomous I, knowledge is the body's immersion, its intertwining and interaction in the world and between others (Merleau-Ponty, 1968). However, as feminist scholars have noted, embodiment (from a Merleau-Pontian perspective) ignores the specificity of gender or sexuality (Stawarska, 2006). Embodiment universalizes the body on the basis of the standard male norm. Likewise, as Beata Stawarska (2006) claims, Merleau-Ponty's theories of intersubjectivity erase the particularities of difference lived and encountered with, in, and through different bodies. To that extent, our interest in touch and relationality resides in the notion that we are always "with" others, not to consume or assimilate one another's experience and subjectivity, but that in the event of the "with," difference and thus, thought is produced. This understanding of with as difference, we argue, involves a reconceptualization of the body—embodiment—in terms of the concepts touch and spac(e)ing.

When we touch something we connect with it, we encounter it in an intimate way. While intimacy can be understood as "knowing someone in depth, knowing many different aspects of a person or knowing how they would respond in different situations,"[1] we want to think about intimacy through Jean Luc Nancy's (2000) notion of being-with. To be a body is to be "with" other bodies, to touch, to encounter, and to be exposed.

As such, intimacy is not simply about the possibility or impossibility of ever knowing the other fully or deeply, but rather names the meetings and encounters between bodies (Ahmed, 2000). Bodied encounters, we argue, in and through touch, produce intercorporeal understandings and in doing so imagine an intimate curriculum premised on difference.

For Borsato, the intimacy of "Touching 1,000 People" altered the way she moved through the city. She writes,

> I started to feel much closer to familiar cashiers, and I think I felt compelled to smile more at strangers around me, and at service people in general. I found myself feeling responsible to "touch," in even a small emotional way, grumpy taxi drivers, indifferent waiters, and anyone else who seemed to need such touches…. As I moved through the city throughout the month—counting, negotiating the streets with my palms as eyes—I even started noticing all the dogs that needed comforting as they waited anxiously outside of shops. (2001, p. 65)

As a result of touching, Borsato and the strangers she encountered began to unravel an unthought experience. Through the act of touching (both literally and in terms of proximinal relationships) the subject is able to make sense of something and simultaneously make sense of themselves. To make sense of something, to know it, to create it, is to come into contact with it, to touch it, and thereby produce a body (Perpich, 2005). In other words, in the moment of encounter—touch—self and other emerge, not as already predetermined subjects/objects but as subjects in the making.

While Borsato, and the research she drew upon, suggested that physical touching would alter people's moods in a positive way, Borsato also observed that different individuals reacted differently to acts of being touched. She writes;

> I also began to recognize the differences in people's feelings of entitlements to space and how it related to what I perceived to be their age, cultural background, gender, and class. For example, it seemed much harder to touch teens than older adults, much harder to touch finely dressed women than men, much easier to touch very old people, etc. Site also mattered. For example, it was much easier to touch people in the supermarket than in a fancy department store or a museum. (p. 65)

Feminist scholar Sara Ahmed (2000) makes sense of these individualized reactions by suggesting that the concept of who is a stranger needs to be challenged. It is commonly believed that a stranger is "any-body" we do not know. Rather, Ahmed (2000) contends, a "stranger is *some-body* whom we have *already recognized* in the very moment in which they are 'seen' or 'faced' as a stranger…we recognize somebody *as a stranger*, rather than simply failing to recognize them" (p. 21). A stranger is some-body we recognize as "strange," or as Ahmed (2000) implies, "it is a figure that is painfully familiar in that very strange(r) ness" (p. 21). Strangers are recognized as not belonging, as being out of place. In order to recognize some-body as strange(r) there needs to be closeness, proximity—a touching encounter. Likewise, in order to recognize some-body (or for that matter some-thing) as out of place there needs to be a demarcation and enforcement of boundaries and of space. It is the "coming to close"—the bodied encounters which produce a body (the stranger) in the moment of exchange and thereby bring into being knowledge of self and other, and the other's otherness. The subject, writes Ahmed (2000), "is not, then, simply differentiated from (its) other, but comes into being by learning how to differentiate between others" (p. 24). Put another way, the Westernized autonomous individual is no longer the central axis upon which all else is judged, rather selves and others simultaneously become differentiated. Thus, bodied encounters *as* difference dislocate fixed boundaries and involve *spatial* negotiations between bodies.

Spac(e)-ing

Like vision and touch, our dominant understanding of space is Cartesian. Space is an empty place marker into which things are placed and encountered. For instance, most individuals would think of the body (which is an object) as being in space (a void), rather than constituting space itself. Post-Cartesian views about the ontological status of space include substantivalism and relationalism. Substantivalism claims that the world consists of material objects and a further entity called space. Space is no longer empty but a separate object in and of itself. Thus, space can be observed as a discrete unit in the same way that one might be able to observe objects. Relationalism denies this objective existence of space and argues that objects are related to each other by spatial relations. Accordingly, space does not exist as such, but rather in terms of spatial relations and patterns (James, 2006). Nancy's "being-with" emerges both as an affirmation of relationalism but also as a radical critique in terms of the relation between the experience of space and of embodiment. In a similar way, Gilles Deleuze's thinking on space exists as a passage, a network of movements (to), and force. While Nancy develops the concept of the body (or what he calls *sense*) as an element of spacing, Deleuze theorizes the interval or the in-between. Both, for the sake of our arguments, assist us in thinking of bodied encounters *as* difference, a position that enables us to examine a (post)reconceptualization of curriculum as bodied. In what follows we develop a relational understanding of space in order to establish a conceptual framework for thinking of interembodiment outside of universalizing structures.

In binary thought we think of opposing terms; for instance mind and body, self and other, or light and dark. Likewise, as Irigaray (1993) claims, the use of one term as the neutral or universal term to define both is the basis of Western language and culture. For instance there is not simply the term *mind* and another independent term *body*, but rather there is only one term, "the other being defined as what it is not, its other or opposite (Grosz, 2001, p. 94). Irigaray's claim is that the one term, and in this example—the body—is erased and that the body emerges only as supplement or complement to the privileged other term—the mind. The supplementary term is the one that must be overcome, transcended, or refused. Similarly, the Other does not exist separate from or independent of the self, but is always defined in relation to the sovereign subject.

However, when we speak of the in-between, in a Deleuzian sense, it is not a physical place bounded by fixed entities (i.e., mind and body) rather, it is a space of movement, of development, and of becoming. The in-between, according to Grosz (2001), "is that which is not a space, a space without boundaries of its own" (p. 91). The in-between does not negate either term (i.e., mind and body) but resists the privileging of one to the other. In our example of mind and body then, the body comes into being not as a supplement to, or reliant on the mind, but under its own terms, its own force, movement, and assemblage. The in-between claims Grosz (2001) "is what fosters and enables the other's transition from being the other of the one to its own becoming, to reconstituting another relation, in different terms" (p. 94).

The in-between pervades the writings of many contemporary philosophers under various terms including: différence, repetition, iteration, liminality, the interval etc. The in-between is a "space in which things are undone, the space to the side and around, which is the space of subversion and fraying, the edges of any identity's limits. In short, it is the space of the bounding and undoing of the identities which constitute it" (Grosz, 2001, p. 93). It is a space of juxtaposition and realignment that opens bodies and thought to new arrangements and possibilities.

This may be why the middle, according to Deleuze, is the best point from which to begin, where thought unravels itself.

> The middle is by no means an average; on the contrary, it is where things pick up speed. Between things does not designate a localizable relation going from one thing to the other and back again, but a perpendicular direction, a transversal movement that sweeps one and the other away, a stream without beginning or end that undermines its banks and picks up speed in the middle. (Deleuze & Guattari, 1987, p. 25)

Contrary to dichotomous relations, in the middle something passes between two terms such that they are both modified putting them to strange new uses. To be in-between is to become; and "becoming is bodily thought" (Grosz, 2001, p. 70). The in-between is where "thought, force, or change, invests and invents new series, metamorphosizing new bodies from the old through their encounter" (Grosz, 2001, p. 70). Thus, the in-between becomes an unhinging of expectation and sequence, not to replace them with their opposites but with reordering of something new altogether. Thus, the in-between is entirely spatial and temporal. Grosz (2001) suggests that space be reconfigured as indeterminate, unfolding, serial, multiplying, complex, heterogeneous, and as an opening up to other spaces. This, she argues requires a thinking of the materiality of space—shifting our understanding of it in terms of proximity and entwinement.

While Deleuzian theories position space as the in-between, Nancy's use of the term *being-with* seeks to think of embodiment in terms of the concepts of touch and spacing. The term *space*, for Nancy, should be understood as being constituted in meaning. Being (for instance the self) does not exist prior to knowledge and meaning, but being comes into existence through the act of creating meaning and knowledge. Nancy's reconceptualization of space leads him to formulate a materialist, or a bodily ontology (James, 2006). In this sense, space cannot be thought of as a separate entity; rather, the experience of space unfolds as a spatial–temporal event between bodies, which is understood as open and ecstatic. Bodies/things, Nancy argues, exist through a spacing—a spacing of space. In doing so, Nancy contends that space be thought of as "an opening or exteriority which never closes or folds onto itself" (James, 2006, p. 104). This spacing or the in-between is intangible and ungraspable in the sense that it is not an "object" or something that we can "see" with our eyes and thus point to and say "hey I found the in-between sitting over here." Spacing exists in the relationships between bodies/things.

Spacing is crucial to thinking about embodiment in terms of touching. For instance, we often think of touch as a physical contact of skin on matter, but spacing allows us to conceive of touch as intangible, as something in a proximinal relationship with something else. Spacing does not imply a measure of distance (i.e., 1 meter or 500 miles) rather spacing constitutes the very place where things happen between bodies. Thus, touching as a way of knowing implies that I can know the other without fixing her or reducing her to an object.

> It captures the tension between the need to intangibly touch the other, while maintaining a respectful distance from her. The intangible touch is not one that does violence to the other by violating her corporeal boundaries; rather, it is a reciprocal touch that gives me access to the other's limit, the borders of her body. To touch the other is to interrupt a logic that attempts to know the other by subsuming her into

categories of the same, a logic that attempts to fix the other, confer an identity on her, an identity that renders her body either meaningful or worthless. To touch the other, in both a tangible and intangible sense, is to gain access to her specificity, to be exposed to it, to be affected by it and to respond to it, but not to subsume it or annihilate it. (Sorial, 2004, pp. 220–221)

In this way, touch creates a space where difference emerges not as "something different from" but as difference itself. This understanding of difference, we argue, is enacted in Borsato's visceral experiment titled "Sleeping with Cake." In this private performance she filled up her bed with "about 10 cakes—a few chocolate cakes, cherry cakes, vanilla cakes, lemon cakes and a flan—and slept surrounded by them for an entire night" (2001, p. 63). Seeking comfort from presence and touch it was not the taste of each different cake that made itself present, but the materiality of the cake—how it felt next to her in bed.

> Even while I was sleeping I was tremendously aware of the cakes all around me. I was shocked to appreciate how dense a cake really is (especially my homemade cakes, it seems). All these points of pressure on the bed around me made it feel like I was sleeping with 10 cats. I could smell the intense sugar of them all night long, and being surrounded by such lusciousness was even somewhat erotic, something I had predicted I wouldn't experience on account of the sticky crumbs and frosting. (2001, p. 63)

It wasn't that Borsato came to know the objects in her bed as "chocolate cake" or "strawberry frosting" but as events that presented themselves in-between, or in the spacing between her body and the bodies of the sweet cakes. For Borsato, what became known was the intimacy of the encounter, and with/in this intimacy she was propelled to recognize the relationality between bodies. This relationality, we argue, is where knowledge is created, mediated, and ruptured, presenting itself for future relational events. Moreover, in-between or through spac(e)ing a bodied curriculum emerges. A bodied curriculum is important if we are to conceive of a curriculum that leaves open the possibilities of ethical interactions between self and other.

A Bodied Curriculum

The body has always been of importance to the theories and practices of curriculum. Understanding curriculum as *bodied* offers an exploration of the production of subjectivities not premised on self/other dichotomies. Engaging with all of the senses and in particular the experience of touch, a bodied curriculum materializes as encounters between bodies. Writing about complexity and education, Brent Davis and Dennis Sumara (2006) insist that complexity thinking orients educators to question "How should we act?" (p. 25). Rather than seeking facts (what is) or interpretation (what might be) complexity thinking compels educators to consider "more useful interpretive possibilities" (p. 26) foregrounding the role of the knower in the known. Moreover, complexity thinking, like Deleuzian spac(e)ing and the in-between, maintains that systems are composed of necessarily different parts which are mutually dependent. The constituent parts are diverse, self-organizing, self-regulating, and constantly shifting in unpredictable ways. For example, bodies are composed of interconnected sets of complex systems such as cells, tissues, and organs. Each of these complex systems exist individually and in relation to each other, to form and transform embodied responses and experiences. However, "because complex systems defy preconceived hypotheses mapping these responses, they remain inherently and productively elusive of predictions" (Stevens, 2005, p. 278). Moreover, complexity thinking causes us to expect difference, "to see it as a crucial and inalienable aspect to being human" (Stevens, 2005, p. 278).

Many of Borsato's performances exemplify this understanding of a bodied curriculum. Enacted on busy urban streets, in the privacy of her own bedroom, or in the homes and restaurants inhabited by others, Borsato engages with others in unusual and purposeful ways. Assigning herself the task to cook alongside each of her Aunts, Borsato's performance, "Cooking with Zias" shifts the attention from "learning to cook" a prescriptive curriculum based on recipes, organized procedures, and particular ingredients, toward a bodied curriculum situated in the everyday, where bodied encounters become the performance. Although a passion for food brought the women together, it was the relationality of bonding, of conversation, and of the incompleteness of the event that constitutes it as a bodied curriculum. Borsato explains this: "I spent seven different afternoons talking about food, culture, the generation gap, women's roles, sex, love, art, and family gossip" (Borsato, 2001, p. 62). Sometimes, Borsato notes, the encounters with her aunts, many of whom she had never spent time with before, were awkward, and filled with the weighty presence of uncertainty and partiality. Meaning, write Davis and Sumara (2006) "emerges more from what is absent, tacit, literalized, and forgotten than from what is present, explicit, figurative, and conscious" (p. 38).

This attention to the unspoken calls to mind the work of Maxine Greene (1973) who encourages educators to conceptualize curriculum through a "stranger's vantage point on everyday reality" (p. 267) , to search for the unknown and the unfamiliar not to reveal or expose such details but rather to see what "other possibilities" being in unfamiliar spaces evoke. Maxine Greene, Madeleine Grumet, and Janet Miller are among the many curriculum scholars who work to understand how encounters with the arts could open curriculum spaces. While our efforts to reconceptualize a bodied curriculum are indebted to their work, and to those scholars who have theorized curriculum as an "aesthetic text," our aim is not to (only) think about how works of art destabilize our assumptions providing us with transformative, creative, and unfamiliar possibilities of teaching and learning, rather, our interest lies in examining the encounters that exist between bodies and thereby produces particular body-subjects. Thus, it isn't so much that Borsato's work is an unusual form of art, or that witnessing her work, which we might add is almost an impossibility because of their intimate and private nature, might provoke unfamiliar or taken for granted responses; rather, the moment of unfamiliarity that is generated through her work is the impossibility of ever completely knowing self and other. In much the same way, a bodied curriculum is framed in terms of "evolving relations among interacting agents" (Davis, Sumara, & Luce-Kapler, 2007, p. 57). In a bodied curriculum "events of learning are about constant co-adaptations of interacting parts—an ongoing structural dance" (p. 58). A bodied curriculum can be explained by a Deleuzian understanding of thought. For Deleuze, thought is a process, which participates, colludes, or collides with other processes. Through an array of intermingling processes an individual is capable of being affected by sensations that have no specific link to an object of origin.

Take for instance another of Borsato's touching experiments, in which she assembled sentimental objects such as her steel-toed boots and a worn copy of her favorite book *A Natural History of the Senses* and boiled each of them for many hours to see if she could distill their sentimental essence. However, after hours of boiling the objects, much like one would make broth, Borsato discovered that she was unable to "boil out sentiment like a flavour for a soup" (Borsato, 2001, p. 63). Each object's meaning was not something that could be abstracted or removed; rather, its meaning was lived and embodied within its materiality. Meaning "was in the presence of the objects themselves, in their existence as whole, unique, touchable, heavy things" Borsato, 2001, p. 63). Boiling and making broth of her objects Borsato was unable to know her objects more—she may have discovered their particular odors or how long each object took to distill, but she was unable to know the other fully or completely. However, while Borsato was unable to extract the sentiment from each object, her performative gestures propelled her to experience a mode of being together with her objects that exceeded the boundaries of the experiment. By staging these bodied encounters unthought of possibilities will break through the conventions of daily interactions and involve self and other in transformative experiences. This, suggests Zygmunt Bauman (1993), is a mode of relationality not governed by rules and expectations but an encounter that demands an attentiveness to alterity, to the uniqueness of the Other. Building on Bauman's work, educational philosopher Sharon Todd (2003) writes that such encounters are "a togetherness born out of the immediacy of interaction, a communicative gesture that does not have as its end anything except its own communicativeness, its own response" (p. 48). As such, Borsato's intimate and touching gestures "offer insight into how the surprising and unpredictable forms of relationality that arise in the immediacy of an encounter with difference carry profound relevance for ethical interaction" (Todd, 2003, p. 4).

Left with smelly broth, much like the sticky remainders of "Sleeping with Cake," we are confronted with an "ethics of embodiment" (see La Jevic & Springgay, 2007; Springgay, 2007; Watt, 2007). An ethics of embodiment, we contend shifts how "we as teachers, students, and teacher-educators perceive our 'selves' and others' 'selves' so that we do not simply incorporate or appropriate 'others' and their stories into the ones we already and always have been telling about ourselves or 'them'" (Miller, 2005, p. 229). "Being-with" compels us to examine and take responsibility for the meanings we make, "understanding all the while that the meanings and categories by which we typically comprehend and live our daily existence can be altered" (Miller, 2005, p. 229). Embodiment as difference underscores the importance of learning to live "with" others, touching not to consume or inhale, but opening up to particularities and possibilities of what each may become.

An Ethics of Embodiment: "Tangles of Implication"

In understanding the term *ethics* we draw on feminist cultural theorist Sara Ahmed (2000) who argues that ethics is distinct from morality, where morality is a set of codes and behaviors. "Ethics," she offers "is instead a question of how one encounters others *as* other (than being) and, in this specific sense, how one can live with what cannot be measured by the regulative force of morality" (2000, p. 138). When education takes up the project of ethics as morality, it is interested in particular principles that govern bodies such as regulations, laws, or guidelines (Todd, 2003). In this instance ethics as a moral curriculum is designed to assist students in learning how to live and act. It is made into concrete practices, duties, and systems of oppression. Ethics becomes a particular acquisition of knowledge that is rationalist in its features.

In contrast, Sharon Todd (2003) suggests that an ethics understood through social interaction, and where knowledge is not seen as absolute gives importance to the complexities of the ethical and bodied encounter. This, Todd and Ahmed both claim, insists on transitioning from understanding ethics as epistemological (what do I need to know about the other) and rather problematizes ethics through a relational understanding of being. Embedded in feminist/social ethics relationality (touch) rests on a complex view of everyday experience "in terms of human relations and social structures" (Christians,

2003, p. 223). Such an understanding discloses the impossibility of putting oneself in the place of others.

A feminist/social approach to ethics asks questions about power—that is, about domination and subordination—instead of questions about good and evil. Such an approach to ethics is centered on action aimed at subverting rather than reinforcing hegemonic relationships (Jagger, 1994). Butler (2006) in her revisitation of Irigaray's work contends that the ethical relation is premised on the "*never yet known,* the open future, the one that cannot be assimilated to a knowledge that is always and already presupposed" (p. 115). Ethics does not claim to know in advance, "but seeks to know who that addressee is for the first time in the articulation of the question itself" (p. 115). This argument, Butler (2006) suggests poses a more difficult question: "How to treat the Other well when the Other is never fully other, when one's own separateness is a function of one's dependency on the Other, when the difference between the Other and myself is, from the start equivocal" (p. 116). It is the *never yet known* that Todd (2003) argues is at the heart of educational relationships, stating that "our commitment to our students involves our capacity to be altered, to become someone different than we were before; and, likewise, our students' commitment to social causes through their interactions with actual people equally consists in their capacity to be receptive to the Other to the point of transformation" (p. 89).

Thus, ethics shifts from "getting to know the other" to an understanding grounded in bodied encounters—being-with—that are themselves ethical in nature. It is an ethics conceived of through touch and spacing. This Todd (2003) contends moves education from being "focused on acquiring knowledge about ethics, or about the Other, but would instead have to consider its practices themselves as relation to otherness and thus as always already potentially ethical—that is, participating in a network of relations that lend themselves to moments of nonviolence" (p. 9). The intimacy of touching places us in relation to openness and risk, and to what we cannot know beforehand, enabling us "to be vulnerable to the consequences and effects that our response has on the Other" (p. 88).

It is this understanding of ethics as being-with that is at the heart of a bodied curriculum. Embracing the unknown, bodies transform curriculum requiring us to consider "tangles of implication." Bodies imbricated in ethical and intimate touching encounters challenge us to examine "our desires for and enactments of, as well as our fears and revulsions toward, those identities and practices that exceed the 'norm'" (Miller, 2005, p. 223). Moreover, a bodied curriculum as difference points to possibilities for agency and transformation by examining the ways,

> in which students and teachers might negotiate the official discursive terrains of schooling that bound the "design and development" of curriculum as well as "identities." By investigating our "tangles of implication" in what we might come to see as contradictory and conflicting discursive constructions, we also might glimpse spaces through which to maneuver, spaces through which to resist, spaces for change. (p. 223)

These "tangles of implication" are what Borsato engages with through her performance works. Touching strangers, sleeping with cake, cooking with her aunts, and even licking and distilling objects, Borsato's intimate explorations through touch invites "one another to risk living at the edge of our skin, where we find the greatest hope of revisioning ourselves" (Boler, 1999, p. 200). A bodied curriculum asserts that knowledge is corporeal; it is produced in and through touch—fostering our own becoming.

In performing a bodied curriculum, the possibilities for dynamic interaction become exposed, recontextualizing, complicating, and purposefully rendering teaching and learning unknowable.

Note

1. Retrieved March 16, 2006, from http://en.wikipedia.org/wiki/Intimacy, 2006.

References

Ahmed, S. (2000). *Strange encounters: Embodied others in post-coloniality.* London: Routledge.
Ahmed, S., & Stacey, J. (2001). *Thinking through skin.* London, UK: Routledge.
Bauman, Z. (1993). *Postmodern ethics.* London: Blackwell.
Boler, M. (1999). *Feeling power: Emotions and education.* New York: Routledge.
Borsato, D. (2001). Sleeping with cake and other affairs of the heart. *The Drama Review, 45*(1), 59–67.
Bresler, L. (Ed.). (2004). *Knowing bodies, moving minds: Towards embodied teaching and learning.* Boston, MA: Kluwer Academic.
Butler, J. (2006). Sexual difference as a question of ethics: Alterities of the flesh in Irigaray and Merleau-Ponty. In D. Olkowski & G. Weiss (Eds.), *Feminist interpretations of Maurice Merleau-Ponty* (pp. 107–125). University Park, PA: Pennsylvania State University Press.
Cary, L. (2006). *Curriculum spaces: Discourse, postmodern theory, and educational research.* New York: Lang.
Christians, C. (2003). Ethics and politics in qualitative research. In N. Denzin & Y. Lincoln (Eds.), *The landscape of qualitative research* (pp. 208–243). New York: Sage.
Classen, C. (1993). *Worlds of sense: Exploring the senses in history and across cultures.* New York: Routledge.
Davis, B., & Sumara, D. (2006). *Complexity and education: Inquiries into learning,teaching and research.* Mahwah, NJ: Erlbaum.
Davis, B., Sumara, D., & Luce-Kapler, R. (2007). *Engaging minds: Changing teaching in complex times* (2nd ed.). New York: Routledge.
Deleuze, G., & Guattari, F. (1987). *A thousand plateaus: Capitalism and schizophrenia.* Minneapolis: University of Minnesota Press.
Ellsworth, E. (2005). *Places of learning: Media, architecture, pedagogy.* New York: Routledge.
Greene, M. (1973). *Teacher as stranger: Educational philosophy for the modern age.* Belmont, CA: Wadsworth.
Grosz, E. (1994). *Volatile bodies.* Bloomington: Indiana University Press.
Grosz, E. (2001). *Architecture from the outside: Essays on virtual and real space.*Cambridge, MA: MIT Press.
Grumet, M. (1988). *Bitter milk: Women and teaching.* Amherst: University of Massachusetts Press.
Irigaray, Luce. (1993). *An ethics of sexual difference.* Ithaca, NY: Cornell University Press.
Jaggar, A. (1994). *Living with contradictions: Controversies in feminist social ethics.* San Francisco: Westview Press.
James, I. (2006). *An introduction to the philosophy of Jean-Luc Nancy.* Stanford, CA: Stanford University Press.
Kennedy, B. (2004). *Deleuze and cinema: The aesthetics of sensation.* Edinburgh, Scotland: Edinburgh University Press.
La Jevic, L., & Springgay, S. (2007). A/r/tography as an ethics of embodiment: Visual journals in pre-service education. *Qualitative Inquiry. 14*(1), 67–89.
Merleau-Ponty, M. (1968). *The visible and the invisible.* Evanston, IL: Northwestern University Press.
Miller, J. (2005). *Sounds of silence breaking: Women, autobiography, curriculum.* New York: Lang.
Nancy, J. L. (2000). *Of being singular plural.* Stanford, CA: Stanford University Press.

Perpich, D. (2005). Corpus meum: Disintegrating bodies and the ideal of integrity. *Hypatia, 20*(30), 75–91.

Pinar, W. (2004). *What is curriculum theory?* Mahwah, NJ: Erlbaum.

Sorial, S. (2004). Heidegger, Jean-Luc Nancy, and the question of Dasein's embodiment. *Philosophy Today, 48*(2), 216–218.

Springgay, S. (2007). An ethics of embodiment. In S. Springgay, R. Irwin, C. Leggo, & P. Gouzouasis (Eds.), *Being with a/r/tography* (pp. 153–165). Rotterdam, The Netherlands: Sense.

Springgay, S., & Freedman, D. (Eds.). (2007). *Curriculum and the cultural body.* New York: Lang.

Stawarska, B. (2006). From the body proper to flesh: Merleau-Ponty on intersubjectivity. In D. Olkowski & G. Weiss (Eds.), *Feminist interpretations of Maurice Merleau-Ponty* (pp. 91–106). University Park, PA: Pennsylvania State University Press.

Stevens, P. L. (2005). ReNaming "Adolescence": Subjectivities in complex settings. In J. Vadeboncoeur & L. P. Stevens (Eds.), *Re/Constructing "the adolescent": Sign, symbol and body* (pp. 271–282). New York: Lang.

Todd, S. (2003). *Levinas, psychoanalysis, and ethical possibilities in education.* New York: SUNY Press.

Vasseleu, C. (1998). *Textures of light: Vision and touch in Irigaray, Levinas and Merleau-Ponty.* New York: Routledge.

Watt, D. (2007). Disrupting mass media as curriculum: Opening to stories of veiling. In S. Springgay & D. Freedman (Eds.), *Curriculum and the cultural body* (pp. 147–162). New York: Lang.

Weiss, G. (1999). *Body image: Embodiment as intercorporeality.* New York: Routledge.

Suggested Reading Questions

1. The authors suggests that under patriarchy and Western notions of intellect, knowledge has been thought of as separate from body. What are the implications of the authors' suggestion that the world might be changed in a positive direction through touch?

2. Following the work of feminist philosophers, the authors take up the term *interembodiment* to highlight the experience of embodiment as never private, but taken up in the relationships between nonhuman and human bodies. If knowing is a public affair, what are the implications for how teachers theorize teaching, learning, and studying?

3. Given the emphasis on intimacy as encounters between bodies (rather than knowing another fully), what is the significance of touch as a pedagogical act that allows subjects to make meaning of the world and simultaneously make sense of themselves?

4. Drawing on the work of Maxine Greene, the authors encourage educators to explore curriculum through the stranger's perspective on everyday life. How might unfamiliarity and the impossibility of knowing the self and an-other becoming sites of most valuable for conceptualizing "knowing in the making?"

5. The authors note when the Canadian performance artist Diane Borsato began to rely on touch, it radically altered her perceptions of her surroundings. How might an embodied curriculum attune us to diverse ways of encountering the world?

Response to Stephanie Springgay and Debra Freedman Making Sense of Touch

Phenomenology and the Place of Language in a Bodied Curriculum

Stuart J. Murray

In *The Visible and the Invisible*, Maurice Merleau-Ponty writes:

> If my left hand is touching my right hand, and if I should suddenly wish to appre-hend with my right hand the work of my left hand as it touches, this reflection of the body upon itself always miscarries at the last moment: the moment I feel my left hand with my right hand, I correspondingly cease touching my right hand with my left hand. But this last-minute failure does not drain all truth from the presentiment I had of being able to touch myself touching: my body does not perceive, but it is as if it were built around the perception that dawns through it. (1968, p. 9)

In describing our sense of touch, Merleau-Ponty speaks to our fundamental orienta-tion in the world, the prereflexive or precritical manner in which the human body sets the scene for intersubjective relations in and through touch. Being-with others is not, then, originally a matter of information exchange, as if we were seamlessly communicat-ing data, the content of some abstract proposition or other. In this regard, educational curricula are often out of touch, and increasingly so as we adopt corporatized "account-ability practices" that include quantifiable "learning outcomes," "key performance indi-cators," and the like.

Touching and being-touched for Merleau-Ponty stand in a phenomenological relation of ambiguity. It is impossible to say precisely when touching crosses over into being-touched, when activity become passivity, when the subject who touches becomes the object of the touch, and vice versa. We never possess the object in touch; we are equally possessed by it. Thus, there is a "miscarriage" in this relation, a kind of wild "reversibil-ity" (p. 147), and a radical unknowing that becomes immaterial, as it were, through the material wisdom of the body itself. The body is neither cause nor effect; rather, we might say that the body occasions "the perception that dawns through it." Thus, intersubjectiv-ity is not a sharing between a preestablished self and other, but it is first in and through that relation that self and other are meaningfully constituted, and without which a lan-guage of "self and other" would be incomprehensible.

Diane Borsato's art project *Touching 1,000 People* is likewise an occasion to make sense of touch and to explore the ways the touching–touched body might enter "the next moment" of curriculum studies. I wonder, then, how what I have called the "material wisdom" of the body might translate into something that could affect the curriculum in material ways. I am wary of the embrace of terms like *becoming, the in-between*, or of unre-constructed notions of "*proximity*," "*difference*," and "*performativity*." Certainly, I do not deny the important ludic permutations that these concepts enable, and there is something to be said for unstructured play: it fosters creativity and curiosity (at a time when these are in short supply in the academy). But our theoretical tools must also be put to work, materialized, made practicable. Gilles Deleuze and Foucault once remarked: "Practice is a set of relays from one theoretical point to another, and theory is a relay from one practice to another" (1977, p. 206). How, then, do we best ensure that our theories are not out of touch? How do we set them into motion? Deleuze continues, "No theory can develop without eventually encountering a wall, and practice is necessary for piercing this wall" (p. 206). In this spirit, I would like to dwell for a moment on what Merleau-Ponty calls the "miscarriage" of the touching-touched, to prise open the space of "the in-between" to expose the troubled face of this relation, and to amplify this inherent phenomenological ambiguity towards a practice—an ethic—of discomfort. I will suggest that in the "miscarriage" or "last-minute failure" of the touching–touched relation we might light upon a failure that is pedagogically productive, a site of critical resistance.

In a review essay discussing Borsato's work, the artist–curator Kathleen Ritter writes:

> Borsato's minor physical contact—a gentle nudge, discreet grazing, or brush of the hand—turns the act of touching into transgression. The work is performative and temporal. It exists in the moment of its enactment…. Borsato's touching, the action performed outside of socially expected behaviour which I first imagined to be a careful and gentle brush on the shoulder proved to be, upon discovery, a somewhat uncontrolled and erratic flinging movement of arms that at times *hit* rather than *touched*. The act was not performed in a desire to be touched back. Instead it imposed a distance between Borsato and the subject of her movements; people invariably moved away from her as she touched them. (2005, n.p.)

Ritter adds a significant critical dimension to Borsato's work, helping to contextualize how and why difference is important in the intersubjective relation of touch. The resistance, or failure, "imposes a distance" and is telling; these are not just bodies, but gendered bodies, racialized bodies, bodies marked by their socioeconomic status, by their own histories, and so on. As Borsato herself writes, "I also began to recognize the differences in people's feelings of entitlement to space and how it related to what I perceived to be their age, cultural background, gender, and class" (2001, p. 65). The resistance is a wall, in Deleuze's sense, bringing into relief the myriad conditions under which bodies can appear as touchable or untouchable in the first place. In her recent work, Judith Butler describes these conditions as the "scene of address" (Butler, 2005; Murray, 2007). Here we might begin to distinguish the caress from the grope, for example, prising open the space between touching and touched, problematizing our interpretations, and calling out for a critical reading. It is hard to name the point when touching crosses over into being-touched, when a playful reversibility is performed and the performative uptake is "felicitous," in J. L. Austin's (1975) sense; but here, reversibility is interrupted, and we become painfully aware that an incommensurable being-in-the-world separates us, the touching from the touched, and that the space in-between is sometimes an unbridgeable gap.

Not so much a "space," now, we are confronted with a site that bristles with meaning, that "exists in the moment of its enactment," as Ritter says. I am suggesting that this site become a worksite, the occasion to bring the prior and enabling conditions of touch to language, to expression. This is what Borsato does with these rather private performances when she reflects on them publicly. She brings them to language, affectively. "I started to feel…," she writes, "I felt compelled…," "I found myself feeling responsible…" (Borsato, 2001, p. 65). In this vein, Ritter writes:

> language is the vehicle in which the works travel back to the art community after the performance. The work comes to be known through language, myth, anecdote,

description, rather than through traditional exhibition methods…. In this way, the work is only available to its *other* intended audience—the art community—by its telling, at the artist's talk, published documents, rumors that circulate about the work, etc. (2005, n.p.)

Language is therefore crucial, and especially when communication "miscarries," when it interrupts, discomfits, or transgresses—and this holds true not just for us when we touch and are touched, but for public art, for educational practices, and so on. The failure ought to prompt us to ask why, to bring-to-language, to struggle to express not just feelings, but the myriad prepersonal and precritical conditions that set the limits of my personal experience, my engagement, my encounter with the other. This is the critical work that emerges from out of a material, bodily resistance, a failure to know, to possess, or to master the world. It is through language that we ask questions; and it is through language that we learn the significance of our bodies, that we do not coincide perfectly with ourselves, that our right hand, when it reaches to touch our left hand touching, "always miscarries at the last moment," a moment of unknowing, an existential gap, a lack, that teaches me how to be-with others, for this touch, too, this being-with, miscarries.

For Merleau-Ponty, this material dimension of human existence opens us onto language and the kind of conversation that Springgay and Freedman seem to yearn for in their chapter:

> A genuine conversation gives me access to thoughts that I did not know myself capable of, that I was not capable of, and sometimes I feel myself *followed* in a route unknown to myself which my words, cast back by the other, are in the process of tracing out for me. (1968, p. 13)

My words exceed me, they circulate, between me and the other, crossing that unbridgeable gap where I dare not go; my words trace out for me a route unknown, and yet even though they trace out and light the way, I feel myself *followed*, by words that go on before but also tarry behind—or perhaps it is the other who follows, but if Merleau-Ponty is unclear in this, his language only underscores the verbal aspect of the other's being-with-me. In these relations, the body does not enjoy a self-immediacy; my relation to my body, just as my relation to the other, is mediated, uncertain, the occasion for reflection, for conversation, and for asking questions. My response to a "bodied curriculum," then, would be a linguistic turn, of sorts. While the implicit dimensions of the body are necessary, bodies are not in themselves sufficient, and to the body I would add the need for an explicit language to think through the ways that that body is able to be present to itself and to others. It is in language that the self becomes a question to itself. Here once again I turn to Merleau-Ponty:

> If we are ourselves in question [Si nous sommes nous-mêmes en question] in the very unfolding of our life, it is not because a central non-being threatens to revoke its consent to being [*son consentement à l'être*] at each instant; it is because we ourselves are one sole continuous question, a perpetual enterprise of rebuilding ourselves [*de relèvement de nous-mêmes*] on the constellations of the world, and of rebuilding things on our dimensions. (1968, p. 103, translation modified)

Here, Merleau-Ponty poses the question of our being a question to ourselves. His language opens a kind of unbridgeable gap, I believe, because if we ourselves are the *sole* question, there can be no other orienting question, no other, no Archimedean point from which to pose the question that "we ourselves" somehow *are*. His is somehow an ironic assertion, too, because it is spoken by he who is, in these terms, unknown to himself, who speaks from within a continuous self-questioning, rather than from a position of knowledge or truth. And yet, the question is pressing because this question speaks directly to the "perpetual enterprise of rebuilding ourselves...and of rebuilding things."

To *be* the kind of question that we ourselves *are* suggests the eternal enterprise of self-fashioning, learning and relearning who and what we are, and how we relate to the world and to others in it. The language of the subject's self-questioning thus strikes me as crucial because it bears upon the rhetorical conditions, the speech conditions, the scene of address within which I find myself, and in and through which I will be able to *say* who I am—a being who speaks, and whose speech never fully coincides with his being, never completely fills that being with propositional or logical "contents." The language itself performs a kind of opening, a doubling of the subject through grammatical reflexivity—*nous sommes nous-mêmes en question*: we are those beings who stand *in* relation to ourselves questioningly. And so part of the question lies hidden in the unremarked and unremarkable reflexivity of the grammar, in the relation between the self and itself as the self takes up the terms in and by which its relation to itself will unfold, hesitate, miscarry, and continuously seek new relations of being.

"There are two circles," Merleau-Ponty writes, "or two vortexes, or two spheres, concentric when I live naïvely, and as soon as I question myself, the one slightly decentered with respect to the other" (1968, p. 138). At the risk of uttering a prescriptive statement, I will close by suggesting that education is nothing without the slight decentering of educational subjects, without at least a momentary suspension of naïveté, the inaugural moment of self-questioning and, indeed, self-doubt. If we are to make sense of the ways that the world touches us, and if we are to sustain discomfort in the face of the other, in the face of difference, then we must learn—and teach—the language of ethical critique. Bodies arrive on the scene with many dissonant conversations already underway. Dissonant as they may be, some will speak to and bolster my prejudices, others will include me, some may exclude, while still others will set forth in advance the terms by which my body will be experienced by me, how it will appear in the world, and how—if I am so entitled—I may touch or be touched. The ongoing task of our "bodied curriculum" is perhaps to find the language to enter these conversations, without necessarily reproducing them.

References

Austin, J. L. (1975). *How to do things with words* (2nd ed.). Cambridge, MA: Harvard University Press.

Borsato, D. (2001). Sleeping with cake and other affairs of the heart. *The Drama Review, 45*(1), 59–67.

Butler, J. (2005). *Giving an account of oneself.* New York: Fordham University Press.

Deleuze, G., & Foucault, M. (1977). Intellectuals and power: A conversation between Michel Foucault & Gilles Deleuze. In M. Foucault, *Language, counter-memory, practice* (D. F. Bouchard, Trans., pp. 205–217). Ithaca, NY: Cornell University Press.

Merleau-Ponty, M. (1968). *The visible and the invisible* (A. Lingis, Trans.). Evanston, IL: Northwestern University Press.

Murray, S. J. (2007). Ethics at the scene of address: A conversation with Judith Butler. *Symposium: Review of the Canadian Journal for Continental Philosophy, 11*(2), 415–445.

Ritter, K. (2005). How to recognize a furtive practice. A user's guide. *Lieux et non-lieux de l'art actuel.* Montréal: Les Éditions Esse. Retrieved February 21, 2008, from http://www.dianeborsato.com/rittertext.html

12 Art Education Beyond Reconceptualization

Enacting Curriculum Through/With/By/For/Of/In/Beyond/As Visual Culture, Community, and Public Pedagogy

B. Stephen Carpenter II and Kevin Tavin

Chapter Overview

The authors of this chapter explore the notions of reconceptualization and post-reconceptualization at the crossroads of art education and curriculum studies. They discuss ongoing efforts to shift from traditional modes of art making and art thinking toward ones that are critical, political, and contextual, ones with the capacity to account for visual culture and ethical obligations to the broader public. They explore the creative self-expression movement of the 1920s and the discipline oriented movement that has its origins in the 1960s and transformed into the discipline based art education movement of the 1980s and 90s. These movements are explained as the pretext to the reconceptualization as visual culture, which is explained as a response to new images and technologies, relationships between humans and lived experienced in a networked world, and ways of theorizing visuality, and new spaces for visual culture. Exploring art-based research community based pedagogy, and eco-art education, the authors suggest art education is in the midst of a reconceptualization or new ways of assembling within a postmodern world. Having mapped out the present moment, the authors conclude by envisioning the next moment through a series of questions and statements about what the post-reconceptualization of art education might look like.

Introduction: Prepost

A post-reconceptualization of art education relies on a presupposition that there has already been—or some scholars have at least pushed the limits of—a reconceptualization of art education in the first place. Unlike curriculum studies in general, we believe the field of art education, and more specifically the area that deals directly with and appeals to K-12 art teachers, did not experience a reconceptualization movement in the past that, for example, challenged and changed profoundly and directly the primary concepts and functions of curricula, to move from curriculum development in art education to understanding curriculum as symbolic text (Pinar, Reynolds, Slattery, & Taubman, 1996).

While remarkable similarities exist between the history of art education and the history of curriculum studies in general, such as the battle between social efficiency and progressive movements and their various social wings; the rise and tyranny of behavioral objectives and "basic principles"; the prominence of the classical curriculum; the focus on disciplinary structures; and the emphasis on humanistic curricula, we believe that there is one fundamental difference: the reconceptualization of art education is in a *current* state of struggle and reform and not something to write about or reflect upon as a marker of the recent or distant past. We set out to make our case by distinguishing between considerations of a reconceptualization of curriculum in art education from the work of curriculum theorists and scholars such as Barone (1991), Heubner (1975),

Padgham (1988) and others who have engaged in reconceptualization of curriculum as ~~aesthetic~~[1] and symbolic text (Pinar, Reynolds, Slattery, & Taubman, 2004). Curriculum from this perspective is characterized as a project in which "the curriculum comes to form as art does, as a complex mediation and reconstruction of experience. In this regard, curriculum can be linked to any art form..." (Pinar et al., 2004, pp. 567–568). While we acknowledge this perspective on curriculum theorizing with respect to art as important, we want to make clear that in this chapter we are concerned with curriculum reconceptualization—perhaps narrowly so—within the field of visual art education rather than other arts, such has been the case in the work of scholars like Blumenfeld-Jones (2004, 2006), Grumet, and Figgins (see Pinar et al., 2004, pp. 567–605). Moreover, we are cautious of some of these approaches to considering curriculum as ~~aesthetic~~ text as, according to Pinar et al. (2004), they are based on the work of modernist artists and "twentieth century 'modernist painters'" (p. 573) rather than works and artists characterized by and engaged within postmodernism and discourses of pluralism.

In this chapter, we approach the question of reconceptualization and post-reconceptualization of curriculum in art education primarily from a perspective as art educators interested in curriculum work rather than as curriculum theorists who are engaging the arts as symbolic or metaphorical discourses to theorize curriculum. That said, we acknowledge that some scholars have contributed to curriculum research from both the curriculum in art education and curriculum theorizing as ~~aesthetic~~ texts perspectives, such as Barone (1983), Eisner and Vallance (1974), Greene (1988), and others, with the work of Elliot Eisner perhaps being the most significant (see Pinar et al., 2004, pp. 567–605).

We believe that the reconceptualization of art education, while broad and oversimplified in our depiction of it here, is engaged in an ongoing attempt to shift from traditional modes of artmaking and "art thinking" toward a profoundly critical, historical, political, and self-reflexive understanding of visual culture and social responsibility, coupled with meaningful and transformative student production in a variety of forms and actions. If this struggle within art education is indeed taking place in the current historical juncture, how then can we move beyond something that is just now beginning to take shape?

Perhaps a good place for us to begin to respond to this question with respect to the reconceptualization of art education is to address questions that were vitally important to the reconceptualization of curriculum studies three decades ago. For example, what is the current state of "the field" of art education? What discourses and movements have emerged that may constitute a reconceptualization? After addressing these important questions, we might then be better positioned to offer a reflection on what a post-reconceptualization in art education might look like.

The Current State of "the Field" of Art Education

Throughout the last century, the field of art education in the United States underwent a number of paradigm shifts. The two most prominent shifts being the creative self-expression movement, which began in the 1920s and achieved a dominant position in art education after World War II, and the discipline-oriented movement that emerged in the early 1960s and gained prominence during the 1980s and 1990s in the form of Discipline-based Art Education (DBAE). These two movements, either in tandem or individually, have functioned as the foundation of most current art education curricula in public K-12 schools as well as preservice preparation programs in U.S. colleges and universities. In both cases, the creation and study of works of art is a common denominator.

Under the auspices of The Getty Education Institute for the Arts, DBAE[2] was promoted in the early 1980s as an alternative theory to previous movements in art education, including the creative self-expression movement. A precursor to the DBAE movement and other attempts to reconceptualize art education curricula came as a result of the 1965 Penn State seminar (Clark, 1984). The seminar encouraged the group of interested art educators, which included artists, aestheticians, art critics, sociologists, psychologists, administrators, historian, and others, to focus on problems of form, content, and pragmatics (Clark, 1984) inspired by papers presented by Jerome Bruner, Elliot Eisner, June King McFee, Vincent Lanier, and Manual Barkan, among others. Clark (1984) noted that the seminar participants "were already grappling with various redefinitions for art education curricula" (p. 226) and the need for "large scale curriculum development in art education" (p. 230). Clark (1984) identifies a number of curriculum projects that were influenced by the Penn State seminar but concludes that none were "fully accepted as serving this need" (p. 230).

Building upon declarations made at the Penn State seminar, proponents of DBAE in the early 1980s assertively argued that art educational theories and practices lacked "substance and content to place it on par with other academic subjects" (Asmus, Lee, Lindsey, Patchen, & Wheetley, 1997, p. 116). Advocates claimed that by advancing the study of artworks typically considered "masterworks," through disciplined inquiry and promoting the creation of student artwork based upon these so-called masterworks, DBAE offered a more comprehensive education for all students. This initiative was also seen as having the potential to improve the academic status and economic competitiveness of American students (Delacruz & Dunn, 1995). Art education under the purview of the creative self-expressive movement and DBAE focused primarily, if not exclusively, on K-12 instruction rather than higher education or nontraditional sites of education. This point not withstanding, many higher education teacher preparation programs modified their curricula as a means to endoctrinate novice art teachers into a creative self-expression or DBAE ideology that promoted the study and creation of works of art.

As a new construct, DBAE immediately attracted scrutiny and criticism from within and outside the field of art education. Opponents of DBAE argued that it was too restrictive in content, too prescriptive in theory, too academic in practice, and too Eurocentric in nature (Clark, 1997). Other critiques have been based on feminist (Collins & Sandell, 1988), multicultural (Chalmers, 1992), and child-centered critiques (London, 1988). Still other criticisms focused upon the role of general education in the curriculum (Hamblen, 1987) and the cognitive nature of learning (Parsons, 1998). Unlike the cataclysmic change of the curriculum field where vociferous criticism and competing paradigm wars helped propel the reconceptualist movement, the critics of DBAE were unable to initiate major change beyond DBAE in art education. After more than a decade of attempts, continuous critiques, and reinvention of various kinds, their arguments, while effective on some level, were merely perceived as snapping "at the heels of a sluggish though still powerful beast" (Berleant, 2004, p. 14).

In what is essentially his comprehensive report on the DBAE curriculum reform initiative, Brent Wilson (1996), lead evaluator of the Getty supported regional institutes noted, DBAE "will have to respond to changing societal, artistic, and educational conditions and to the interests of new individuals who decide to join the continuing task of forming and reforming DBAE" (p. 227). Into the 1990s, curriculum theorists, scholars, politicians, administrators and others within and outside art education, enacted many challenges to, and calls for, paradigms shifts in art education prior to the current reconceptualization. Struggles over the aims, goals, and direction of art education were, and are, ongoing. Only after the Getty cut off funding in the late 1990s, however, did art education in the U.S., like the curriculum field in the 1970s, find itself "up for grabs," with enough space created for the current reconceptualization.

In the late 1990s, a growing number of U.S. art educators took advantage of this theoretical space and called for a paradigm shift toward the inclusion of and emphasis on visual culture. Their arguments challenged the canonicity of the art curriculum as it was generally understood; advocated for the study of an expansive range of objects and images including popular culture examples; and raised issues about visuality and everyday life (Duncum, 1999, 2001; Freedman, 2000, 2001; Tavin, 2000, 2003; Wilson, 2000). Related to such considerations for extending the mapped curriculum territory and content of art education, scholars have also been concerned with other areas of inquiry among which include arts-based pedagogy/research/studies (Barone, 1995; Barone & Eisner, 1997; Eisner, 1995; Fordon, 2000; Springgay, Irwin, & Kind, 2005; Springgay, Irwin, Leggo, & Gouzouasis, 2008; Sullivan, 2004), authentic instruction (Anderson & Milbrandt, 2005), community-based art education (London, 1994; Owens & Wang, 1996; Stephens, 2006; Ulbricht, 2005), service learning (Jeffers, 2005; Taylor, 2002, 2004a; Taylor & Ballengee-Morris, 2004); public pedagogy (Tavin & Robbins, 2006); culture jamming (Darts, 2004); computer technology (Carpenter & Taylor, 2003, 2006; Keifer-Boyd, 2005); and eco-theory and environmental pedagogy (Blandy & Hoffman, 1993).

These related areas function as separate discourses within and outside art education. In many ways their proponents embrace the challenges supported by scholars who advocate visual culture or other related perspectives as viable responses to the traditions of creative self-expression and discipline-centered approaches. While not exhaustive or mutually supportive, these simultaneous areas of curriculum discourse support our premise that art education is in a current state of struggle; a state that we interpret here as a reconceptualization of art education. Below, we examine more closely a few of these approaches—visual culture, arts-based research, community-based pedagogy, environmental and eco-art education—as a sample of the more extensive list of related areas we acknowledged above. We offer these examples as a means to consolidate our exploration in this chapter, as we believe an exhaustive examination of these and the other areas is beyond the scope of our current project. Further, we consider the roles of these areas in the current reconceptualization of curriculum in art education for the sake of moving our discussion forward and not to exclude other areas.

Visual Culture

The call for the reconceptualization of art education in/as visual culture is in part a response to the current inventory of images and technologies associated with global virtual culture, new relationships between humans and their experience as networked subjects, new levels of theorizing about visuality, and the growing number of sites/sights/cites[3] of visual culture within the field of art education (Freedman & Stuhr, 2004). Although the meaning of *visual culture* in art education discourse falls within contested spaces and its character, function, scope, methods, and legitimacy are all marked by debate, the term is generally used as a referent for three interrelated concepts: the ontological, substantial, and pedagogical dimensions of visual culture. These three concepts form a rubric that helps to name, position, and problematize the current cultural condition in which visual representations saturate public and private spaces and play a central role in the construction of consciousness, identity, and the creation of knowledge.

The project of visual culture as art education ranges from investigations of visual images and technologies that profoundly affect understanding, to the hermeneutics of visualizing and visuality (Cooley, 2004; Duncum, 2005; Elkins, 2003; Tavin, 2003; Taylor,

2007; Taylor & Carpenter, 2007). This practice includes an inclusive register of images, artifacts, objects, instruments, and apparatuses as well as the experience of networked and mediated subjects in a globalized 21st century. Thus visual culture as art education today allows for a different type of analysis than in past paradigms, one that can draw from new and newly emerging images, technologies, and cultural experiences that involve cybernetics, digital imaging, monitoring, optical enhancement, satellite mapping, simulation, surveillance, and virtual reality, for example (Darley, 2000). This analysis is informed by and we hope informs disciplines, fields of study, and academic projects such as African American/Black studies, critical sociology, cultural studies, film and media studies, new art history, postcolonial studies, visual anthropology, and women's studies, and theories such as critical semiotics, critical theory, critical race theory, deconstruction, feminism, hyperreality, literary criticism, phenomenology, poststructuralism, psychoanalytic theory, and queer theory (Tavin, 2003).

Arts-Based Research

The influence and emergence of arts-based research (Springgay, Irwin, & Kind, 2005; Springgay, Irwin, Leggo, & Gouzouasis, 2008; Sullivan, 2004) and arts-based educational research (Barone, 1995; Barone & Eisner, 1997; Eisner, 1995) have also played an important role in the curriculum development and curriculum theory discourse in art education in the past decade. While primarily limited to postsecondary learners and educators, arts-based research calls into question the paradigms of traditional research methods and methodologies while at the same time continues to gain acceptance within traditional circles of research and scholarship. Some critics of such efforts take issue with the hyphenated label, a signifier that would mark such a project as an excuse or an exception to—read less than—the more established grand narratives of quantitative, scientific, and qualitative research. Supporters counter with arguments that, hyphenated or not, arts-based research offers critical space for the construction and presentation of new knowledge that would be otherwise marginalized with respect to more traditional and accepted modes of research.

Community-Based Pedagogy

Like most pedagogical labels, community-based pedagogy—sometimes referred to as community-based learning or community-based education—eludes clear definition (Ulbricht, 2005). Community-based pedagogy "is not discriminatory and extends beyond classroom walls" (London, 1994; Stephens, 2006) and includes strategies for learners "to learn what they want to learn from any segment of the community" (Owens & Wang, 1996). London (1994) favors the role of the child and their lived experiences in their community rather than prescribed learning activities directed by the teacher. McFee (1961/1970) and McFee and Degge (1977) contributed much to the early considerations about the purposes and goals of art education with respect to a community-based pedagogy in art education. More recently, art educators such as Neperud and Krug (1989) have supported culturally responsive art education.

   Green (1999) following the lead of Gablik (1991), Giroux (1992), Lacy (1995), and Neperud and Krug (1989), calls for a reconceptualization of art education "as cultural criticism." Green (1999) borrows Lacy's (1995) term *new genre public art* as inspiration for students to "conceptualize new art forms, engage the community in projects that are socially constructive, and recognize art making as an intellectual, scholarly endeavor" (p. 80). At its best, this endeavor resists being reified as a mere intellectual project fitting within the existing canon of art. It strives to embody collaborative practices among artists and their audiences, and the engagement of multiple audiences through empathy and appreciation. This sense of "new genre public art" builds on exposure, deconstruction, and rejection of modernism's constructs and myths of "art" and "audience." In fact, making the very notion of art problematic may allow the ambiguity of the meaning, content, and intention of community-based projects to avoid the trappings of the past. However, while Green (1999) acknowledges this movement as part of a reconceptualization in art education, she limits the possibilities of such a movement to their implications for classroom practice and artmaking rather than also extending these ideas to more theoretical and conceptual curriculum considerations.

Environmental and Eco-Art Education

Broadly demarcated, scholarship in environmental education and eco-theory is generally concerned with resisting the dichotomies of human/culture verses environment/nature, repositioning humans as the center of power in such relationships, and underscoring the interrelationships among all things living and nonliving. Recently, eco-theory in art education has manifested specifically in terms of writing on eco-responsibility (Hicks & King, 2007; Stout, 2007), eco-political pedagogy (jagodzinski, 2007), eco-lore and eco-education (Bequette, 2007), and critical place-based pedagogy (Graham, 2007). Writing around the time of the attenuation of DBAE, art educators Blandy and Hoffman (1993), drawing on the work of other scholars (Gablik, 1991; Ornstein, 1990), framed eco-theory within art education in response to

> those who have pursued environmental problems in the pursuit of emphasizing a sense of place within daily actions, developing a consciousness of self, local, and larger communities, promoting language that affirms life-sustaining relationships, and analyzing critically analysis taken-for-granted concepts within existing arts institutions that affect the environment. (p. 23)

Perhaps an ultimate goal of eco-theorists, then and now, is to "ask us to radically revise the way in which we perceive the world" (Blandy & Hoffman, 1993, p. 25).

Blandy and Hoffman (1993) note various aspects of and perspectives on "a community-based orientation to art education" (p. 26). Such perspectives, however, tend to be anthropocentric and omit considerations of a "bioregional perspective" (p. 28). Art education scholars who have been interested in advancing art education curriculum through eco-theory acknowledge that such practice "will require art educators to ask for a high degree of self-investment and reflection from students. Changing lifestyle patterns, developing a pro-active stance, and challenging existing non-environmentally sound practices by family, friends, and colleagues will be required" (Blandy & Hoffman, 1991, p. 28). For example, in the field of art education Taylor (1997) describes an eco-based art experience informed by the work of Gablik (1991) that is focused on social responsibility. Recommendations for applying such theories to art education have gravitated toward those who espouse the selection of "art to study in art education contexts [that] can work to reinforce an art education of place" (Taylor, 1997, p. 28).

In other words, the applications of such theories remain bound to the studio-based, artmaking preferences of the dominant art educational practices and do not necessarily extend to conceptual pursuits such as curriculum theorizing in art education. To move beyond such dominant practices suggests that reconceptualization of an art education of place is ongoing. For example, place-based education is a reconceptualization of environmental education and becomes a curriculum in which students might see "their two-year project lead to the town's installation of a new water system" (Sobel, 2004, p. 19) and result in improved community health. Place-based education is an interdisciplinary and community situated reconceptualization of environmental education that emphasizes lived engagement with the environment and social action but is not bound to dominant practices of environmental education. A reconceptualized art education of place might also disconnect from traditional dominant artmaking and studio practices and establish itself as a site of lived engagement and social action through expanded possibilities for considerations of visual interpretation, performance, and events.

The (Current) Reconceptualization of Art Education

The range of areas we first identified at the beginning of the chapter and the smaller set of perspectives we have just elaborated on above are all interested in the role of art objects in the process of advancing positive personal and social change. Gude (2004), Taylor (2004b), and others have advanced proposals for reconceptualized perspectives of the very core of art education curriculum. In the past few years these scholars have put forth separate but critically compatible frameworks that challenge traditional approaches to art education, which have been based on modernist conceptions of aesthetics, in favor of postmodern, pluralistic, and reconceptualized considerations of digital, hypermediated, and visual culture informed approaches to art education. Such radical revisions of perception include the reconsideration of the various means, purposes, goals, outcomes, and sites of art education, a practice in keeping with our premise that art education is deeply embedded in a contemporary of reconceptualization. Such considerations, we believe, carry the markers of a current state of reconceptualization in art education that has not yet taken hold per se but rather is in the process of defining and clarifying itself.

Similar to the reconceptualist movement in curriculum studies over three decades ago, the current reconceptualization of art education is in part a reaction to the changing conceptions of self, world, and artworlds brought on by the postmodern condition and postmodern theorizing. This current position is in opposition to the disciplinary hegemony, decontexualized curricula, and knowledge standardization inherent in the prevailing forms of art education of the past (Reid, 1978). Propelled by postmodernism, the current reconceptualization in art education is struggling through its charge for and challenge to traditional, official, and operational curricula in art classrooms. Further, these considerations actively make space for content within unquestioned null curricula, those areas of cultural production and content omitted from previous curricular texts. In this sense, the current reconceptualization of art education embodies the need to both understand art education curricula as *symbolic representation* as well as embrace different symbolic representations as *legitimate content* for the field. Following the lead in curriculum studies, the reconceptualization of art education asks "what can be created of what we have been conditioned to be?"—by routine and by omission (Pinar et al., 1996, p. 51).

Seeing curricula as symbolic representation, Taylor, Carpenter, Ballengee-Morris, and Sessions (2006) suggest that "rather than basing curriculum on learning a medium or technique, we recommend that art teachers base their units of instruction on a problem, issue, or question gleaned from works of art and visual culture" (p. 39). Similarly, Stewart and Walker (2006), Ballengee-Morris and Stuhr (2001) and others have called for the reconceptualization of art curricula from traditional modes of media and methods to big ideas, enduring ideas, and key concepts that help guide art instruction and visual culture pedagogy. For example, *Visual Culture in the Art Class: Case Studies* (Duncum, 2006) offers explicit cases of pre-school, elementary, and middle school curricula that move beyond modernist elements of art and principles of design, and other archaic concepts of art, toward a thematic, issues-based, reconceptualized study of visual culture.

Turning toward symbolic representations as content for a reconceptualized art education, scholars such as Carpenter and Taylor (2003), Darts (2004), Freedman (1997), Tavin (2002) and Taylor (2000 2004b), advocate for students to critically investigate popular culture through digital and hypermediated means. For example, Darts (2004, 2006) argues that visual culture is an effective vehicle for teachers and students to examine social justice issues and engage democratic principles toward social change. Although cultural production is one part of such an approach, learners in this model make explicit their critical investigations of cultural practices and interpretations of daily visual experiences.

We acknowledge that the examples above indicate a radical departure from art education curricula of the past; however, we must underscore that a reconceptualized art education need not focus on or have as its ultimate goal the exacting prescription of what teachers can and should do with students in educational contexts. In understanding *curricula* as symbolic representation, we believe a reconceptualized art education curriculum should resist the notion of "best practices." Just as the reconceptualization of the curriculum field three decades ago called into question the degree to which curriculum theorists and theory must inform or be beholden to practical application and curriculum development, similar questions shadow the discourse surrounding visual culture and related movements in art education such as arts-based pedagogy/research/studies, community-based art education, public pedagogy, computer technology, eco-theory and environmental pedagogy, and other agendas. As Pinar (1999) acknowledges, "Schools are no longer under the jurisdiction (it was probably always more professional than legal) of curriculum theorists" (p. 14). Similarly, we believe that the current state of curriculum reconceptualization in art education revolves around tensions based on various assumptions, such as the assumed responsibility of theorists to inform the practices of art education practitioners and the misguided impossibility of practitioners to engage in meaningful curriculum theorizing about art education.

Playing on the premise of reconceptualizing theory as a practice, of stepping curriculum theory away from obligations to curriculum development, what and where might intellectual, interpretive practices in response to symbolic representations in the social and cultural environment lead art educators? How might an interdisciplinary reconceptualized art education help teachers think more comprehensively about their subject matter as embodied in visual lived experiences? Without limitations on always returning to classroom practice, where might such reconceptualization explorations take art education theorists? These points are central to determining the status and indeed troubling the waters of the current reconceptualization in art education and any musings on what a post-reconceptualization might look like.

In sum, through a prereconceptualized approach in art education, the making of products—whether works of art, critical writing, performances, or forms of activism—seem to be an assumed, ultimate goal. In our current evolving reconceptualized condition of art education, the making of such products seems to have taken the form of socially conscious commentary in ways that struggle to resemble traditionally accepted products. In both cases, the focus on a limited concept and range of classroom production perpetuates a belief in the intrinsic value of an art work, regardless of the socially conscious content, allowing critics such as Fry (1996) to argue, "actual life requires moral responsibility, yet in art we have no such moral responsibility—it presents a life freed from the binding necessities of our actual existence" (p. 79). In a post-reconceptualized approach, the making might become more than the mere process of establishing change and taking action.

To this point, we have posited that art education is at least still within the meaningful and necessary process of working through its own reconceptualization of at least the past decade, thanks to the attention of scholars who are concerned with visual culture and related areas such as arts-based pedagogy/research/studies, community-based art education, public pedagogy, culture jamming, computer technology, and eco-theory and environmental pedagogy. A post-reconceptualization of the field of art education, we believe, must therefore call for a move beyond, as well as with the reconceptualization efforts already established within, the broader scope of education and toward a next logical step.

(Imagining) The Post-Reconceptualization of Art Education

In order for us to consider a post-reconceptualization in art education, we acknowledge that we have only begun to scratch the surface of a comprehensive project of working through much of what we see as the current reconceptualization in the field. Imagining a post-reconceptualization in art education requires us to envision approaches to art education where the practical, technical, creative self-expression centered and discipline-based approaches to instruction and learning have been moved aside—except where they are means to/of inquiry and not ends in and of themselves—in favor of those approaches that demand and embody knowledge construction toward the always incomplete work of positive change, action, political (re)positioning, social reconstruction, cultural inquiry, and democratic living. In this final section, we put forward more questions than answers as we imagine a post-reconceptualization in/of art education with the understanding that, from our perspective, an actual or comprehensive reconceptualization of art education has not yet been, or may ever be, realized.

First, we wish to make explicit that we recognize a continuum of curriculum in art education from prereconceptualization to post-reconceptualization. Included in such a continuum resides the idea of the process of curriculum as a change from "exclusively school materials to curriculum as symbolic representation" (Pinar et al., 1996, p. 16) and from a mostly ahistorical perspective to a profoundly historical understanding (Pinar et al., 1996). Discipline-centered discourse in the 1960s, DBAE, and multicultural perspectives have greatly influenced the role and attention of history and culture within art education. This point not withstanding, we believe in order for art education to move through reconceptualization and into a post-reconceptualized existence it must confront and reconcile its lack of "a profoundly historical understanding."

The current reconceptualization of the field of art education, we believe, has yet to reconcile how theories and issues of visuality reside within curricula of the past or even how they might function as curricula in the present. The politics of visuality, primarily informed by and through visual culture, offer a meaningful site for consideration of a reconceptualized art education. For instance, art educators might consider how a particular hegemony of sight (and particular sites) has existed through different scopic regimes throughout modernity. For example, one particular scopic regime—Cartesian perspectivism—was and still is used to help name, order, and control humans, nature, and the world, legitimated through the "official" school curriculum:

> The profane faith in visual representation was particularly crucial to the modern interpretation…as mechanistic order. To bring what is present before the mind's eye

is to assay "ideas" for their evidential truth, to make them secure and available for calculative, instrumental projects, to tie them to the mechanical legality of natural causation. (Sandywell, 1999, p. 41)

In a reconceptualized art education, the politics of visuality can also be helpful to problematize a more general binary model of history. Through theories of visuality, for example, modernism's dominant linguistic discourse of structuralism, in which every element of meaning is locked into signification in relation to "the other," begins to unravel and proves inadequate as a means to understand history as an ongoing set of temporal modes. With these modes in mind, "visual culture might venture to ask how bodies of thought produced a notion of vision in the service of particular politics or ideology and populated it with a select set of images, viewed through specific apparatuses and serving the needs of distinct subjectivities" (Rogoff, 1998, p. 21). Taking seriously the politics of visuality, a reconceptualized art education might attempt to interpret how visual experience and the visualized subject is constructed within social systems, practices, and structures. The politics of visual culture can question how social and political oppression was developed in the past through spectacle and surveillance and how it is maintained in the present through the practices of display and spectatorship.

We wonder to what degree social justice, cultural democracy, and cultural freedom are currently at play, or at work, in a reconceptualized art education and what such roles might look like in a post-reconceptualized art education. Gaztembide-Fernández (2006) suggests, "The current turn in curriculum study needs to be less about definitions and more about work, about action, about dedicating our efforts and our labor to projects that touch the lives of real people, ourselves, our kin, our students, our colleagues, our audiences" (pp. 134–135). Perhaps this might be understood as the difficult work of "interstanding" theory rather than defining theory. In other words, such work might consist of operating on and through theory in order to set ourselves and the world in question in order to reconstruct meanings and develop agency for promoting democratic public spheres, ethical imperatives, and social justice.

Might "interstanding the politics of visuality" support a democratic project that addresses real life issues regarding real life struggles? Might this project position art education curricula as both performing in culture and being performed on through active interpretation? A pedagogy of/as performance art (Garoian, 1999) encourages and enacts interstandings among visuality and politics through embodied forms of knowing and learning. Garoian (2001) argues that this type of performativity may "reposition viewers as critical participants and enables their creative and political agency... relevant to their personal identities" (p. 235). In our view, such goals have not been fully explored in the field of art education. Attention to these areas within an interdisciplinary, reconceptualized art education might lead to consideration of the curriculum as existing beyond the structures of formalized and traditional education. That is, rather than considering the implications of interdisciplinary art curricula in terms of learning *in*, *with*, or *through* art and visual culture, a post-reconceptualized interdisciplinary art education curriculum might promote learning *as* and *because* of the politics of visuality.

Finally, what about considerations of curriculum beyond symbolic representation? One consideration might be the importance of Lacanian psychoanalytic theory to the field, which may include a move from symbolic *cites* and *sights* toward a focus on the psychic register of the Real. jan jagodzinski's work has been invaluable in bringing attention to issues beyond representation and discursivity—the seeable and sayable—to the unconscious realm (jagodzinski, 2001, 2003, 2004a, 2004b). If the current reconceptualization in art education focuses on the dramatic aspects of visual culture, where identity politics and ideological critique offer up possibilities for naming, perhaps a different form of art education, informed by Lacan, for example, might move us closer toward a traumatic (not dramatic) presence, where the unnamable signifier is the Real of the decentered subject (jagodzinski, 2004a).

Lacan's early theories of the "mirror stage" locate the construction of decentered self in relation to visual images. According to Eagleton (1996):

> The child who is still physically uncoordinated, finds reflected back to itself in the mirror a gratifyingly unified image of itself; and although its relation to this image is still an "imaginary kind"—the image in the mirror both is and is not itself, a blurring of subject and object still obtains—it has begun the process of constructing the centre of self. This self, as the mirror situation suggests, is essentially narcissistic: we arrive at a sense of "I" by finding that "I" reflected back to ourselves by some object or person in the world. (p. 143)

Lacan saw this process as one of "desiring." He argued that desire comes from a lack, which we continuously strive to fill. Therefore, we are constantly searching for images to fill that gap (Eagleton, 1996). This desiring is connected to both gazing and being the recipient of the gaze. This unconscious activity is constantly sliding back and forth between the "object" (being gazed at) and the "subject" (doing the gazing) while escaping the possibility of signification, alluding language, and being ultimately impossible to represent. Unconscious desire of the Real is beyond symbolic representation (Tavin, in press; Walker, Daiello, Hathaway, & Rhoades, 2006).

Exploring the area of unconscious desire may help promote a different type of art education *as* and *because* of the politics and power of visuality in everyday life. This speculation is of course a fantasy about a fantasy of the future of art education; a reconceptualization where art education as a field is more reflexive about its own history and politics, anxieties and fears, practices and preferences, and "interstands" its own unconscious attractions to phantasmagoric imaginations.

Notes

1. We intentionally strike through (graphically cross out) this term. We believe it is already under a form of erasure which undermines its conceptual adequacy and raises questions about its politics and relevance (Tavin, 2007).
2. For a more complete discussion on the theory and development of DBAE and the role of the Getty Education Institute in the history of art education in the United States, see Wilson (1996).
3. According to jagodzinski (2004b), *cite* is "that which is sayable," *sight* is "that is which seeable," and *site* is "that which is feelable" (p. 40).

References

Anderson, T., & Milbrandt, M. (2005). *Art for life: Authentic instruction in art*. Boston: McGraw-Hill.

Asmus, E., Lee, K., Lindsey, A., Patchen, J., & Wheetley, K. (1997). Discipline-based arts education: A conceptual framework for learning and teaching the arts. *Visual Arts Research, 23*(2), 114–123.

Ballengee-Morris, C., & Stuhr, P. (2001). Multicultural art and visual culture education in a changing world. *Art Education, 54*(4), 6–13.

Barone, T. (1983). Education as aesthetic experience: "Art in germ." *Educational Leadership, 40*(4), 21–27.

Barone, T. (1991). Assessment as theater: Staging an exposition. *Educational Leadership, 48*(5), 57–59.

Barone, T. (1995). The purposes of arts-based educational research. *International Journal of Educational Research, 23*(2), 169–180.

Barone, T., & Eisner, E. (1997). Arts-based educational research. In R. M. Jaeger (Ed.), *Complementary methods for research in* education (pp. 73–103). Washington, DC: American Educational Research Association,.

Bequette, J. (2007). Traditional arts knowledge, traditional ecological lore: The intersection of art education and environmental education. *Studies in Art Education, 48*(4), 360–374.

Berleant, A. (2004). *Re-thinking aesthetics: Rogue essays on aesthetics and the arts.* Burlington, VT: Ashgate.

Blandy, D., & Hoffman, E. (1993). Toward an art education of place. *Studies in Art Education, 35*(1), 22–33.

Blumenfeld-Jones, D. S. (2004). Dance curriculum then and now: A critical hermeneutic analysis. In W. Reynolds & J. Webber (Eds.), *Expanding curriculum theory: Dis/positions and lines of flight* (pp. 125–153). Mahwah, NJ: Erlbaum.

Blumenfeld-Jones, D. (2006). Aesthetic consciousness and dance curriculum: Liberation possibilities for inner city schools. In K. Rose & J. Kinchloe (Eds.), *Encyclopedia of urban education* (pp. 508–518). Westport, CT: Greenwood.

Carpenter, B. S., & Taylor, P. G. (2003). Racing thoughts: Altering our ways of knowing and being in art through computer hypertext. *Studies in Art Education, 45*(1), 40–55.

Carpenter, B. S., & Taylor, P. G. (2006). Making meaningful connections: Interactive computer hypertext in art education. In C. D. Maddux & D. Johnson (Eds.), *Type II Uses of technology in education: Projects, case study, and software applications* (pp. 149–161). Binghamton, NY: Haworth Press.

Chalmers, F. G. (1992). DBAE as multicultural education. *Art Education, 45*(3), 16–24.

Clark, G. (1984). Beyond the Penn State seminar: A critique of curricula. *Studies in Art Education, 25*(4), 226–231.

Clark, G. (1997). Critics, criticism, and the evolution of discipline-based art education. *Visual Arts Research, 23*(2), 13–17.

Collins, G., & Sandell, R. (1988). Informing the promise of DBAE: Remember the women, children, and other folks. *Journal of Multicultural and Cross-cultural Research in Art Education, 6*(1), 55–63.

Cooley, H. R. (2004). It's all about the fit: The hand, the mobile screenic device and tactile vision. *Journal of Visual Culture, 3*(2), 133–155.

Darley, A. (2000). *Visual digital culture: Surface play and the spectacle in new media genres.* New York: Routledge.

Darts, D. (2004). Visual culture jam: Art, pedagogy, and creative resistance. *Studies in Art Education, 45*(4), 313–327.

Darts, D. (2006). Art education for a change: Contemporary issues and the visual arts. *Art Education, 59*(5), 6–12.

Delacruz, E., & Dunn, P. (1995). DBAE: The next generation. *Art Education, 48*(6), 46–53.

Duncum, P. (1999). A case for an art education of everyday aesthetic experiences. *Studies in Art Education, 40*(4), 295–311.

Duncum, P. (2001). Visual culture: Developments, definitions, and directions for art education. *Studies in Art Education, 42*(2), 101–112.

Duncum, P. (2005). Critical thinking in, about and through visual culture. *Journal of Research in Art and Education, 6*(1), 21–35.

Duncum, P. (Ed.). (2006). *Visual culture in the art class: Case studies.* Reston, VA: NAEA.

Eagleton, T. (1996). *Literary theory: An introduction.* Minneapolis: University of Minnesota Press.

Eisner, E. (1995). What artistically crafted research can help us understand about schools. *Educational Theory, 45*(1), 1–6.

Eisner, E., & Vallance, E. (1974). *Conflicting conceptions of curriculum.* Berkeley, CA: McCutcheon.

Elkins, J. (2003). *Visual studies: A skeptical introduction.* New York: Routledge.

Fordon, A. E. (2000). Arts-based educational studies: An "adventurous" option to arts-based educational research. *Educational Foundations, 14*(3), 51–62.

Freedman, K. (1997). Visual art/virtual art: Teaching technology for meaning. *Art Education, 50*(4), 6–12.

Freedman, K. (2000). Social perspectives on art education in the U.S.: Teaching visual culture in a democracy. *Studies in Art Education, 41*(4), 314–329.

Freedman, K. (2001). How do we understand art? Aesthetics and the problem of meaning in the curriculum. In P. Duncum & T. Bracey (Eds.), *On knowing: Art and visual culture* (pp. 34–46). Christchurch, New Zealand: Canterbury University Press.

Freedman, K., & Stuhr, P. (2004). Curriculum changes for the 21st century: Visual culture in art education. In E. Eisner & M. Day (Eds.), *Handbook of research and policy in art education* (pp. 815–828). Reston, VA: The National Art Education Association.

Fry, R. (1996). An essay in aesthetics. In C. Harrison & P. Wood, P. (Eds), *Art in theory 1900–1990: An anthology of changing ideas* (pp. 78–83). Oxford, England: Blackwell.

Gablik, S. (1991). *The reenchantment of art.* New York: Thames & Hudson.

Garoian, C. (1999). *Performing pedagogy: Toward an art of politics.* Albany, NY: SUNY Press.

Garoian, C. (2001). Performing the museum. *Studies in Art Education, 42*(3), 234–248.

Gaztembide-Fernández, R. A. (2006). Is curriculum work? (with Sloan, K., Franck, K., McDermott, M., & Gershon, W.) In J. Milam, K. Sloan, S. Springgay, & B. S. Carpenter, II (Eds.), *Curriculum for a progressive, provocative, poetic, + public pedagogy* (pp. 131–162). Troy, NY: Educator's International Press.

Giroux, H. (1992). *Border crossings: Cultural workers and the politics of education.* Routledge.

Graham, M. (2007). Art, ecology, and art education: Locating art education in a critical based-placed pedagogy. *Studies in Art Education, 48*(4), 375–391.

Green, G. (1999). New genre public art education. *Art Journal, 58*(1), 80–83.

Greene, M. (1988). The artistic-aesthetic and curriculum. *Curriculum Inquiry, 6*(4), 283–296.

Gude, O. (2004). Postmodern principles: In search of a 21st century art education. *Art Education, 57*(1), 6–14.

Hamblen, K. (1997). Second generation DBAE. *Visual Arts Research, 23*(2), 98–103.

Hicks, L., & King, R. (2007). Confronting environmental collapse: Visual culture, art education, and environmental responsibility. *Studies in Art Education, 48*(4), 332–335.

Huebner, D. (1975). Poetry and power: The politics of curriculum development. In W. Pinar (Ed.), *Curriculum theorizing: The reconceptualists* (pp. 271–280). Berkeley, CA: McCutchan.

jagodzinski, j. (2001). Revisiting social theory in art education: Where have we been? Where are we today? Where *are* we going? Where could we go? *Journal of Social Theory in Art Education, 21,* 1–24.

jagodzinski, j. (2003). Unromancing the stone of "resistance": In defense of a continued radical politics in visual cultural studies. *Journal of Social Theory in Art Education, 23,* 104–139.

jagodzinski, j. (2004a). Questioning fantasies of popular "resistance": Democratic populism and radical politics in visual cultural studies. *Journal of Social Theory in Art Education, 24,* 257–299.

jagodzinski, j. (2004b). *Youth fantasies: The perverse landscape of the media.* New York: Palgrave Macmillan.

jagodzinski, j. (2007). The e(thi)co-political aesthetics of designer water: The need for a strategic visual pedagogy. *Studies in Art Education, 48*(4), 341–359.

Jeffers, C. (2005). *Spheres of possibility: Linking service-learning and the visual arts.* Reston, VA: National Art Education Association.

Keifer-Boyd, K. (2005). Technology interfaces with art education. *Visual Arts Research, 31*(1), 1–3.

Lacy, S. (1995). *Mapping the terrain: New genre public art.* Seattle, WA: Bay Press.

London, P. (1988). *Beyond DBAE: The case for multiple visions of art education.* North Dartmouth, MA: University Council on Art Education.

London, P. (1994). *Step outside: Community-based art education.* Portsmouth, NH: Heinemann.

McFee, J. K. (1970). *Preparation for art.* Belmont, CA: Wadsworth. (Original work published 1961)

McFee, J. K., & Degge, R. M. (1977). *Art, culture, and environment: A catalyst for teaching.* Belmont, CA: Wadsworth.

Neperud, R., & Krug, D. (1989). People who make things: From the ground up. In In R. Neperud, (Ed.), *Context, content, and community in arteducation: Beyond postmodernism* (pp. 141-168). New York: Teachers College Press.

Ornstein, G. F. (1990). Artists as healers: Envisioning life-giving culture. In I. Diamond & G. F. Ornstein (Eds.), *Reweaving the world: The emergence of ecofeminism* (pp. 279–287). San Francisco: Sierra Club.

Owens, T., & Wang, C. (1996). Community-based learning: A foundation for meaningful educational reform. Retrieved January 29, 2007, from http://nwrel.org/scpd/sirs/10/t008.html.

Padgham, R. (1988). Correspondences: Contemporary curriculum theory and twentieth-century art. In W. Pinar (Ed.), *Contemporary curriculum discourses* (pp. 359–379). Scottsdale, AZ: Gorsuch Scarisbrick.

Parsons, M. (1998). Integrated curriculum and our paradigm of cognition in the arts. *Studies in Art Education, 39*(2), 103–116.

Pinar, W. (1999). Response: Gracious submission. *Educational Researcher, 28*(1), 14–15.

Pinar, W. (2006). *The synoptic text today and other essays: Curriculum development after the reconceptualization.* New York: Lang.

Pinar, W., Reynolds, W., Slattery, P., & Taubman, P. (1996). *Understanding curriculum.* New York: Lang.

Pinar, W., Reynolds, W., Slattery, P., & Taubman, P. (2004). *Understanding curriculum* (2nd ed.). New York: Lang.

Reid, W. (1978). *Thinking about the curriculum.* London: Routledge.

Rogoff, I. (1998). Studying visual culture. In N. Mirzoeff (Ed.), *The visual culture reader* (pp. 14–26). London: Routledge.

Sandywell, B. (1999). Specular grammar: The visual rhetoric of modernity. In I. Heywood & B. Sandywell (Eds.), *Interpreting visual culture: Explorations in the hermeneutics of the visual* (pp. 30–56). New York: Routledge.

Sobel, D. (2004). *Place-based education: Connecting classrooms & communities.* Great Barrington, MA: Orion Society.

Springgay, S., Irwin, R. L., & Kind, S. W. (2005). A/r/tography as living inquiry through art and text. *Qualitative Inquiry, 11*(6), 897–912.

Springgay, S., Irwin, R. L., Leggo, C., & Gouzouasis, P. (2008). *Being with a/r/tography.* Rotterdam, The Netherlands: Sense.

Stephens, P. G. (2006). A real community bridge: Informing community-based learning through a model of participatory public art. *Art Education, 59*(2), 40–46.

Stewart, M. & Walker, S. (2005). *Rethinking curriculum in art.* Worcester, MA: Davis.

Stout, C. (2007). Eco-responsibility and art education. *Studies in Art Education, 48*(4), 331.

Sullivan, G. (2004). *Art practice as research: Inquiry in the visual arts.* Thousand Oaks, CA: Sage.

Tavin, K. (2000). Teaching in and through visual culture. *The Journal of Multicultural and Cross-Cultural Research in Art Education, 18(1)* 37–40.

Tavin, K. (2002). Engaging advertisements: Looking for meaning in and through art education. *Visual Arts Research, 28*(2), 38–47.

Tavin, K. (2003). Wrestling with angels, searching for ghosts: Toward a critical pedagogy of visual culture. *Studies in Art Education, 44*(3), 197–213.

Tavin, K. (2007). Eyes wide shut: The use and uselessness of the discourse of aesthetics in art education. *Art Education, 60*(2), 40–45.

Tavin, K. (in press). The magical quality of aesthetics: Art education's *objet a* (and the new math). *Studies in Art Education.*

Tavin, K., & Robbins, C. (2006). If you see something, say something: Visual culture, public pedagogy, and the war of terror. In J. Milam, K. Sloan, S. Springgay, & B. S. Carpenter, II (Eds.), *Curriculum for a progressive, provocative, poetic, + public pedagogy* (pp. 97–112). Troy, NY: Educator's International Press.

Taylor, P. G. (1997). It all started with the trash: Taking steps toward sustainable art education. *Art Education, 50*(2), 13–19.

Taylor, P. G. (2000). Madonna and hypertext: Liberatory learning in art education. *Studies in Art Education, 41*(4), 376–389.

Taylor, P. G. (2002). Singing for someone else's supper: Service-learning and Empty Bowls. *Art Education, 55*(4) 6–12.

Taylor, P. G. (2004a). Service-learning and a sense of place. *The Journal of Cultural Research in Art Education, 22,* 33–44.

Taylor, P. G. (2004b). Hyperaesthetics: Making sense of our technomediated world. *Studies in Art Education, 45*(4) 328–342.

Taylor, P. G. (2007). Press pause: Critically contextualizing music video in visual culture and art education. *Studies in Art Education, 48*(3), 230–246.

Taylor, P. G., & Ballengee-Morris, C. (2004). Service-learning; A language of "we." *Art Education, 57*(5), 6–12.

Taylor, P. G., & Carpenter, B. S. (2007). Hypermediated art criticism. *The Journal of Aesthetic Education, 41*(3), 1–24.

Taylor, P. G. Carpenter, B. S., Ballengee-Morris, C., & Sessions, B. (2006). *Interdisciplinary approaches to teaching art in high school.* Reston, VA: NAEA.

Ulbricht, J. (2005). What is community-based art education? *Art Education, 58*(2), 6–12.

Walker, S., Daiello, V., Hathaway, K., & Rhoades, M. (2006). Complicating visual culture. *Studies in Art Education, 47*(4), 308–325.

Wilson, B. (1996). *The quiet evolution: Changing the face of arts education.* Los Angeles: J. Paul Getty Museum.

Wilson, B. (2000). The parable of the para-site that ate art education. *Journal of Multicultural and Cross-cultural Research in Art Education, 18,* 24–30.

Suggested Reading Questions

1. The authors note that cuts in funding for art education opens up spaces for the reconceptualization of the field. How might we characterize the relationship between power, resources and knowledge production in academic fields?

2. In the reconceptualization in art education the division between art and audience in the meaning making process has been rendered suspect. What is the significance of shifting meaning from the intention of the artist to the readings of audience members?

3. In a parallel move to curriculum studies, art education shifted from a focus on the basic principles of design to understanding visual culture. Given what the authors describe in the final section entitled "Imagining the Post-Reconceptualization of Art Education," what elements might characterize the next moment in the field?

4. How might an emphasis on lived experiences in relation to visual culture bring new perspectives to the field of art education?

5. How might an analysis of the ways the visual subject is constructed within present social conditions lead to new forms of media literacy?

Response to B. Stephen Carpenter II and Kevin Tavin
Sustaining Artistry and Leadership in Democratic Curriculum Work

James Henderson

It is a pleasure to respond to Stephen Carpenter and Kevin Tavin's curriculum essay, and my response will be based on a line of inquiry I initiated 22 years ago. In 1986 I began collaborative work on a *reflective teaching* text that would be situated within curriculum reconceptualization; and this project, which was informed by Gadamer's (1975) examination of the dialogical "play" at the heart of disciplined human understanding, eventually resulted in three distinctive editions. During this period, I realized that the reflective teaching I was advocating was positioned within a more comprehensive *transformative curriculum leadership* which I needed to clarify; so I eventually coauthored three editions of a curriculum leadership text. Kathleen Kesson and I (1999) also coedited a book on democratic curriculum leadership. Our work on this text led to the realization that democratic curriculum leadership was informed by a particular application of the "Socratic" interplay between dialogue, self-examination, and disciplined inquiry (Hadot, 1995). Based on this insight, Kathleen and I (2004) published a book on curriculum "wisdom." In this text, we present an *arts of inquiry* map that is informed by Schwab's (1978) argument that the "arts of the practical" and the "arts of the eclectic" are central to good curriculum work. Kathleen and I quickly realized that educational practitioners could not make use of the *arts of inquiry* map without additional curriculum studies background, and we began to think about the creation of a supportive professional development text. We are currently working on this book; and as we proceed, we have been exploring the distinction between inquiry method and *inquiry montage*.

I will shortly discuss the notion of *inquiry montage* in more detail; however, I first want to provide an overview of how I will respond to Stephen Carpenter and Kevin Tavin's essay based on my brief autobiographical introduction. I will begin by affirming the importance of their argument in light of my collaborative work on *reflective teaching*. I will then challenge Stephen and Kevin to consider the *transformative curriculum leadership* implications of their advocacy. Finally, I will invite them to further clarify their curriculum studies position from an *arts of inquiry* frame of reference, and my invitation will be based on a further explanation of the *inquiry montage* that Kathleen Kesson and I are creating.

Reflective Teaching

As Dewey (1910) notes in his classic text, *How We Think*, reflection is embedded in recurring cycles of framing problems, enacting solutions, and examining action premises and consequences. When this problem solving is grounded in an understanding of how to remake democratic educational "experience and its discursive representations so that we see the past and present more clearly and where our seeing might lead us" (Pinar, Reynolds, Slattery, & Taubman, 1995, p. 866), an interesting teaching–learning dynamic is established. By acquiring a complicated understanding of curriculum, the thoughtful educator is positioned to teach for complicated understanding. In concise terms, the educator is developing his or her capacities to facilitate a balanced "3S" understanding— to teach for a Subject matter understanding that is embedded in a democratic Self and Social understanding (Henderson & Gornik, 2007). This is precisely the curriculum problem solving perspective advanced by Stephen and Kevin. They argue that art educators must not only function as subject matter experts, they must address the democratic good life. I applaud Stephen and Kevin's holistic commitment and advocacy (the 3S: subject matter, self, and social understanding).

Transformative Curriculum Leadership (TCL)

By rethinking "subject matter" as the facilitation of 3S understanding, educators are positioned to enact a TCL problem solving process. This is a challenging collaborative undertaking incorporating a complex set of practices: reconceptualizing educational standards; cultivating reflective inquiry; enacting systemic deliberations grounded in integrated designing, planning, teaching, and evaluating decision making; building learning communities; and engaging in public intellectual activities (Henderson & Gornik, 2007). This systemic reform work deconstructs the curriculum understanding/curriculum development binary that pervades much of the early curriculum reconceptualization literature. In the spirit of Pinar's (2006) point that, "Curriculum development after the reconceptualization supports passionate intellectual classroom practice that engages our worldliness…" (p.xii), Stephen and Kevin write as "art educators interested in curriculum work," and they call for "operating on and through theory…in order to reconstruct meanings and develop agency for promoting democratic public spaces, ethical imperatives, and social justice" (p. 245). I applaud this professional agenda, and I invite Stephen and Kevin to further think about ways they can foster this agency both within art education and between art educators, as well as among other subject matter specialists.

Supported by a grant from the Martha Holden Jennings Foundation, Rosemary Gornik and I are currently working on the establishment of an online Curriculum Leadership Institute (CLI) that advances such professional collaboration and networking. Given the current lack of understanding of curriculum leadership, we are finding this to be difficult work. In general, current educators are positioned to address the "what's" and "how's" of their work but not the "why's." As art educators who think deeply about the "why's" of their work, I invite Stephen and Kevin, as well as all readers of this chapter, to consider becoming active participants in this CLI effort.

Rosie Gornik and I are in the process of creating a flexible and fluid curriculum leadership *certification process* that can be locally adapted. The process is anchored in a particular "canonical" (Pinar, 2008) interpretation:

- The fundamentals of curriculum problem solving as informed by the tradition of American pragmatism (Cherryholmes, 1999);
- The historical distinction between instructional and curriculum leadership;
- The complicated relationship between standardized management, constructivist best practice, and curriculum wisdom problem solving (Henderson & Gornik, 2007);
- The importance of "ethical fidelity" (Badiou, 2001) in TCL problem solving and the implications for long-term experiential learning and collegial support

After studying this subject matter, educators create and enact TCL plans. Academically based educators advance the certification process in institutional or professional organizational settings,[1] while pre-K-12 educational practitioners initiate TCL problem solving in school settings. Accordingly, I invite Stephen and Kevin to acquire the necessary background and then consider establishing a curriculum leadership *certification process* at their respective institutions or at annual meetings of their arts education professional associations. Furthermore, I invite them to consider how art educators who are interested in curriculum leadership might reach out to teacher educators in other subject matter fields. By doing so, they would be engaged in interprofessional collaboration that is an essential feature of school-based TCL problem solving.

Arts of Inquiry/Inquiry Montage

While attempting to introduce TCL problem solving as outlined above, Rosie Gornik and I have noted a significant problem that is directly parallel to the inaccessibility of the arts of inquiry map in *Curriculum Wisdom* (2004). Most progressive educators appreciate the importance of integrating curriculum studies into their reflective practices, and they agree that reflective teaching should be interpreted as "reflective inquiry." However, they generally have not developed their capacities to ground their reflections in complicated curriculum understanding; consequently, their ability to practice two key components of TCL problem solving—reconceptualizing subject matter and enacting systemic deliberation—is constrained.

The Socratic gestalt as outlined above provides further insight into this capacity-building problem. Pinar (2004) presents an elegant argument for enacting curriculum as complicated conversation in a context of currere examination and notes that this work is based on "faith in the possibility of self-realization and democratization, twin projects of social and subjective reconstruction." (p. 8) Kathleen Kesson and I have decided to extend Pinar's argument. Inspired by Dewey's (1938/1998) *Experience and Education*, we think it is vital to inquire into the democratization of educational experience. Pinar et al. (1995) reflect this professional commitment when they write:

> What John Dewey said in reference to philosophy might be said in reference to the contemporary curriculum field:
> A [curriculum theory] which was conscious of its own business and province would then perceive that it is an intellectualized wish, an aspiration subject to rational discriminations and tests, a social hope reduced to a working program of action, a prophecy of the future, but one disciplined by serious thought and knowledge. (Dewey, quoted in Westbrook, 1991, p. 147, 866)

Kathleen and I have decided that curriculum dialogue and self-examination should be informed by multimodal inquiry into democratic educational experience.[2] In effect, we are adapting the Socratic gestalt for a particular curriculum leadership purpose.

In our quest to advance a *reflective inquiry* grounded in contemporary curriculum studies and focused on democratic educational experiences, we have embraced the notion of "montage" as both method and form. Montage in film is an alternative to cinematic continuity, a mode of editing in which scenes are juxtaposed in such a way as to create meaning through collision, conflict, or contradiction. In photography, it is a process in which multiple photographic images are cut, rejoined to create new images, and sometimes rephotographed to create a seamless image. In audio production, montage collages are produced through the integration of portions of existing scores or recordings from either one or multiple sources. New technologies in digital film editing, photography, and recording are opening up all kinds of possibilities for synergistic effects in the context of multiple art forms. In sum, montage is a mode of artistic/intellectual production that advances the creative fusion of elements. Since *reflective inquiry* in TCL problem solving requires the creative fusion of a diverse set of curriculum study projects, we are in the process of creating a supportive *inquiry montage*.[3]

I find it interesting that Stephen and Kevin's paper is written in a montage spirit, but I don't find it surprising. After all, much of "avant-garde" art of the 20th century takes this approach (Badiou, 2007). However, I do invite Stephen and Kevin to consider how their art education argument might be informed by an *arts of inquiry montage*. Space does not allow me to pursue this invitation in more detail; instead, I will conclude this essay with a question directed to Stephen and Kevin and to all the readers of this chapter: Given our collective passion for social justice and other important values associated with democratic living, how do we build and sustain our capacities to engage in the necessary, day-to-day curriculum problem solving and leadership?

Notes

1. This work is being piloted at Kent State University, Monmouth University, and Mount Union College.
2. This decision is informed by Jay's (2005) argument for the "heterodox" study of human experience.
3. Our work is informed by Irwin and Cosson's (2004) presentations of "a/r/tography" projects.

References

Badiou, A. (2001). *Ethics: An essay on the understanding of evil* (P. Hallward, Trans.). London: Verso.
Badiou, A. (2007). *The century* (A. Toscano, Trans.). Cambridge, England: Polity Press.
Cherryholmes, C. (1999). *Reading pragmatism.* New York: Teachers College Press.
Dewey, J. (1910). *How we think.* New York: D. C. Heath
Dewey, J. (1998). *Experience and education.* West Lafayette, IN: Kappa Delta Pi. (Original work published 1938)
Gadamer, H. G. (1975). *Truth and method* (G. Barden & J. Cumming, Eds. & Trans.). New York: Seabury.
Hadot, P. (1995). *Philosophy as a way of life: Spiritual exercises from Socrates to Foucault* (M. Chase, Trans.). Malden, MA: Blackwell.
Henderson, J. G., & Gornik, R. (2007). *Transformative curriculum leadership* (3rd edition). Upper Saddle River, NJ: Merrill/Prentice-Hall.
Henderson, J. G., & Kesson, K. R. (Eds.). (1999). *Understanding democratic curriculum leadership.* New York: Teachers College Press.
Henderson, J. G., & Kesson, K. R. (2004). *Curriculum wisdom: Educational decisions in democratic societies.* Upper Saddle River, NJ: Merrill/Prentice-Hall.
Irwin, R. L., & de Cosson, A. (2004). (Eds.). *A/r/tography: Rendering self through arts-based living inquiry.* Vancouver: Pacific Educational Press.
Jay, M. (2005). *Songs of experience: Modern American and European variations on a universal theme.* Berkeley, CA: University of California Press.
Pinar, W. F. (2004). *What is curriculum theory?* Mahwah, NJ: Erlbaum.
Pinar, W. F. (2006). *The synoptic text today and other essays: Curriculum development after the reconceptualization.* New York: Lang.
Pinar, W. F. (2008). *Intellectual advancement through disciplinarity: Verticality and horizontality in curriculum studies.* Rotterdam: Sense.
Pinar, W. F., Reynolds, W. M., Slattery, P., & Taubman, P. M. (1995). *Understanding curriculum: An introduction to the study of historical and contemporary curriculum discourses.* New York: Lang.
Schwab, J. J. (1978). *Science, curriculum, and liberal education: Selected essays* (I. Westbury & N. J. Wilkof, Eds.). Chicago: University of Chicago Press.
Westbrook, R. B. (1991). *John Dewey and American democracy.* Ithaca, NY: Cornell University Press.

Part V

Place, Place-Making, and Schooling

13 Jesus Died for NASCAR Fans

The Significance of Rural Formations of Queerness to Curriculum Studies

Ugena Whitlock

Chapter Overview

This chapter explores constructions of sexual identity and gender roles within the working class rural settings. Using an autobiographical lens as a White, blue collar, rural Southern lesbian raised as a fundamentalist Christian, the author theorizes place-making by way of the particularities of race, social class, gender, sexuality, and religion. Recognizing that queer images tend to be associated with urban culture, through her own life, she discusses what it means to think and live queerly within rural Southern cultures. Next the author describes place as social, cultural, and geographical constructs before turning to the specificities of North Alabama where she grew up. Next, she describes rural queerness as multiple, varied, and complex and in excess of (while not losing account of) prevailing images of oppressive and graphic violence against people in rural settings: Offering a description of what it was like to learn about lesbians in a small country town, the author explores queer memory and the formation of her own identity with particular focus on her relationship to the church. She concludes with a discussion of the ways queer fundamentalist Christian conversations complicate the field of curriculum studies.

Gay identity and community were dialectically shaped in the cities—spaces of anonymity and economic independence, seemingly free of so-called small-town values. Clearly, gayness and place have been linked in particular ways. But how might we frame queer identities and ancestries in other ways? That is, in other places? In a regionalist critique of an urban-focused American lesbian and gay history, I would like to assess queerness in the towns and small cities of the still agrarian South. Specific socioeconomic conditions there suggest specific place-based experiences of sexuality and memories thereof. (Howard, 2003, p. 149–150)

Jesus take the wheel… (Carrie Underwood, 2005)

They say there is no real change of seasons in the South, but that is not true. There is deer season, dove season, squirrel season; or, for the racing fan, there are the spring and fall races at Talladega, the Aaron's 312 and 499 and UAW-Ford 500, respectively. And, just like the myriad-colored foliage of a fall weekend in Vermont, the spectacle at the Motor Speedway on race weekends in April and October is a sight to see! Traveling along Interstate 20 last October on my way from Atlanta to Birmingham, I was struck by the number of recreational vehicles (RVs) I kept passing. Admittedly, I myself had been in the market for an RV, so I was more likely to take note of the bus-sized half-million-dollar motor homes that tooled along the highway with diesel horns gleaming on their roofs. When I reached Talladega, I soon realized why.

The Talladega Motor Speedway in Talladega, Alabama, has a 40-year-old history as a major NASCAR racetrack. In addition, the races bring in millions of dollars in revenue to Talladega and surrounding areas. Local restaurants have 2-hour waits, and there are no hotel rooms to be had. But the enormity of the event—the most profound evidence of the season's change—is the transformation of the Speedway property.

I have passed the Speedway at different times of the year, and on any given day, it is impressive, if only for its size and its isolated positioning in an abandoned air strip in middle Alabama. From I-20, I see the arena looming in the distance, and as I drive directly in front of the grandstand, I can see that crisscrossing over the road that approaches it are sets of racing-flag-shaped arches that remind me of swords crossed over the bridal couple at a military wedding. It impresses me every time.

On this day in October, after having passed scores of RVs, I approached the Speedway unprepared for what I was about to behold. All along the slope of the landscape surrounding the arena, for as far as the eye could see were motor homes, recreation vehicles of all kinds. Vintage Airstream campers were parked alongside junky slide-on pickup campers, which shared space with the aforementioned Allegro buses. Every few feet, grounds staff had placed porta-potties, just in case, I suppose, RVers did not wish to fill up their waste tanks. And the color! Many traveling race fans had hoisted their banners of preference atop their homes on wheels, or tents, as the case may be. NASCAR flags abounded and football flags, and, of course, confederate battle flags. From the highway I could see tailgaters cooking and grilling and otherwise fellowshipping. They had come not only to see a race, but to commune.

In Talladega, racing is life, and folks take it seriously. Incidentally, in the motion picture, *Talladega Nights: The Ballad of Ricky Bobby,* Will Ferrell portrays the title character, who must defeat a dreaded opponent—who is French (!)—to retain his NASCAR title. The film created a stir among local residents, not so much for portraying the hero as a raving Southern lunatic who runs around the track in his underwear, but because it was filmed at the track in Daytona, Florida. The very idea that a movie called *Talladega Nights* could be filmed anywhere other than the Talladega Motor Speedway was incredible to local fans. This is a town that sells T-shirts and rear window static cling decals of the late Dale Ernhardt's number 3 with angel wings attached to memorialize the driver's ascent into NASCAR heaven.

The title of this paper is taken from a church sign I spotted in Talladega that weekend. While there may have been 150,000 fans camped out surrounding the Speedway, churches most likely had to be cleverly creative to draw some of them over to services on Sunday morning. "Jesus died for NASCAR fans" seemed to me to fittingly capture not only the particularities of religion in a Southern country place, but it also lends itself to a queer reading of this particular Southern place. Not to read too much into one church sign, it did seem to succinctly capture raced (no pun intended), classed, gendered, and religious positioning of the everyday lives of people who live for race weekends, for example. The assurance of redemption is given to a section of the population that is predominately—but surely not exclusively—White, low- to lower middle class, male, and straight. While the South may not be essentialized as religious—we have neither a monopoly on religious thought and practice, nor does every Southerner claim to be religious—the presence and influence of organized religion in the South cannot be overstated. Queer narratives that emerge from Southern place attest to this presence, even as they trouble it.

Reconceptualist scholars contend that the educational reconstruction of the South is vital to the fate of the United States itself; they recognize that, while the South does not have exclusive rights to a sense of place, what it does have is heightened sentiment towards the *past.* And, although the layers of racial, class, gendered, and sexual oppression are complex, one hardly has to scratch the surface to see them in the South. White

Southerners feed this sentiment—*nostalgia*—without acknowledging, much less troubling, underlying histories. Educational reconstruction of the South begins with reconstructing White Southern understanding of those histories while *constructing* sensibilities of reparation. Yes, I am suggesting that in one capacity or the other, White Southerners should demonstrate the willingness to pay. I do not know as yet what form *payment* might take, but until we are willing to engage in progressive conversation with one another, we will never find out. One way in which I seek to destabilize the pillars of historical place that bolster White Southern solidarity is to question conventions of personal and institutional Southern identity. Rending the Southern veil of nostalgia is queerly fundamental.

This chapter explores rural formations of queer subjects in nonmetropolitan spaces and then examines how those formations might inform curriculum conversations by adding threads of complexity. From an autobiographical narrative within an interdisciplinary theoretical framework, I offer a storying of constructions of sexual identity and gender roles within the specificity of working class rural settings. Drawing from particularities of the local, my perspective is that of a White, blue collar, rural Southern lesbian, raised a fundamentalist Christian, yet mine is not a story of queer migration to an academic, urban utopia. Rather, I narrate and theorize my own story as it is contextualized by race, social class, gender, sexuality, and religion—and by place. As Halberstam (2003) suggests, it is important to recognize that there are gay, lesbian, bisexual, and transgender (GLBT) people who choose to live their lives in rural settings. I contemplate one of those lives—mine—in a critical examination of queer images in rural Southern cultures. According to Halberstam, "…it is not always easy to fathom the contours of queer life in rural settings because…queers from rural settings are not well represented in the literature that has been so much a hallmark of twentieth-century gay identity" (p. 164). In discussions of queer images in global contexts, those lives lived, sometimes invisibly, within the contexts and contours of rural place have powerful stories to tell, stories that have a place in a reconceptualized curriculum.

The Dixification of Queerness

Before I move on to a discussion of rural place and queerness, it seems expedient to sort out some terms and concepts. *Queer* and *place*, for example, will probably have very, very different connotations here than elsewhere, given the particular contexts. First, *place* is a constructed idea, like race or gender, and may thus be considered through a variety of lenses. Place for me is ultimately *Southern* place, with the corresponding images and constructions I associate with it. Some of these images I describe below, others include music, food, local people, and attractions. It is important for me to offer the disclaimer that Southern place, the South, and Southerner mean different things to different people. M. J. Cash (1940) explained that there are at the same time one and many Souths; that his work *The Mind of the South* is still cited over half a century later is significant. People still wonder about "the mind" of the South and are no closer to understanding it than they were then. I contend that there is a collective impression of Southern place based on history, social structures, and cultural markers, with which individual people may or may not identify. Therefore, it is important not only to "tell the South," but also to tell the self: the self within place helps us make meaning of the one South and the many Souths.

So, place is a social, cultural, geopolitical construction, as well as a geographic location. History contributes to its identity makeup, as do the creation, perpetuation, and claiming of stereotypes steeped in that history. Economic factors and social class are mutual referents with place, as are race, sexuality, and religion. We can think about place in terms of these concepts, and we can think about these concepts in terms of place. The contexts are overlapping and complicated; my study of place—like queerness—is inter-disciplinary. Southern place is a character in my story; it is the both the subject of con-templation and the means through which I contemplate my autobiographical narrative in order to consider larger social contexts. Social, cultural, and political motifs are writ large upon Southern landscapes; their implications are, therefore, far reaching—into the curriculum field, for instance.

I do specifically refer to the region in North Alabama where I grew up; Colbert County was carved out of Franklin County after the Civil War to give North Alabama another—White, male, Confederate-sympathizing—representative in the state legislature. Its char-ter was abolished by the "Radical" Reconstruction Constitutional Convention of 1867, reinstated 3 years later. Colbert County (the "t" is pronounced—no French-sounding pretense for the folks who live here) is named after Chief George Colbert, half-Chicka-saw, half-Scot ferry operator on the Natchez Trace. Colbert County is situated along the rocky, once-unnavigable Tennessee River at the base of the foothills of the Appalachians. The river was dammed up and tamed as part of the Tennessee Valley Authority (TVA) project, which, in conjunction with Roosevelt's Rural Electrification Administration, brought electricity to rural homes. Before 1935, only one in 10 farms had electricity, a condition that in itself puts this particular place in marked contrast to urban centers at that time. The area began producing steel in the late 1880s and at once became industri-alized. My daddy worked for Reynolds Metal Company, which had produced aluminum for World War II, and later, Reynolds Wrap for a generation of postwar wives. Reynolds Metal was the last of the major industrial plants to shut down in the 1990s. Now, the area is neither predominantly farm country nor industrial center. As its own identity has been thrown into question, it seems a fitting place to base a study of the mutuality of place and identity constructedness.

Littleville, Alabama, recently put up signs at both ends of the town limits along Highway 43 proclaiming itself "Gateway to the Shoals"—an identity claim that basically acknowledges its status as a place on the way to another place. Littleville is 9 miles from Ivy Green, Helen Keller's 1880 birthplace in Tuscumbia. My granddaddy swore on his deathbed that her father, Captain Keller, had owned a summer camp along a creek not a mile from our home; for me, a young girl growing up in the country, was a means of connecting with another Alabama girl who did not on appearances fit in easily with the surrounding countryside. According to official reports, the population of Littleville is 978; it ranks below or significantly below the state average in median household income ($32,583), median house value ($60,800), percentages of Black (0.0%) or Hispanic (0.08%) populations, and percentage of the population holding a bachelor's degree (7.7%). The only category in which it ranks above the state average is median age (37.9). It is poor, White, uneducated, and aging. It is the place I consider home.[1]

Littleville was a dry county until the mid-1970s (for the uninitiated, there are actually some counties that do not sell alcohol—those that do are, naturally, wet), one of the last times conservative Christians took for granted that enough *other* "decent folks" would get out and vote. They did not, but drinkers and businessmen did—along with those who had been foolish enough to believe that alcohol taxes would be used to improve local roads. As Littleville borders a dry county, it has effectively put the Franklin County boot-leggers out of business, relegating them instead to local lore. I actually swapped bootleg-ger run stories with a professor at a major university—in the South, of course. That folks made their way over back roads and through the woods to walk up to a sliding window of the bootlegger's house on Saturday night and then went to church on Sunday morn-ing is but one dichotomous circumstance that makes it easier to conceive of Southern queerness. As long as appearances remained a certain way, nobody was very interested in digging too far back in the closet. In my South, people went to great lengths to keep up appearances.

As complicated as place is for me to theorize, it is easier for me to grapple with than queerness. Like place, queer is unstable and nonunitary. It can, in the words of St. Paul, be all things to all people (I Corinthians 9:22), or so it seems to me, which also seems to me to work in my favor. I will, however, attempt to state certain parameters within which I discuss queer and queerness. *Queer* often names or describes identities and practices that "foreground the instability inherent in the supposedly stable relationship between anatomical sex, gender, and sexual desire" (Corber & Valocchi, 2003, p. 1); so to begin with, queer disrupts assumptions concerning causal relationships among sex, gender, and sexuality that serve to normalize heterosexuality. I suggest that the constituent images and attributes of place, to which I will refer simply as *place*, are complicit in reinforcing normative, compulsory heterosexuality, which, in turn, becomes important to the construction of place. Thus, if place is considered a significant identity construction, so too must be heterosexuality and its normativity.

It is important, then, to find language by which to discuss queer and place in the same narrative. To this end, I find John Howard's *Men Like That: A Southern Queer History* (1999) very helpful. His history of queer life in Mississippi traces queer desire throughout rural landscapes. Howard writes,

> …throughout the twentieth century, queer sexuality continued to be understood as both acts and identities, behaviors *and* beings. It was variously comprehended—depending in part on race and place—along multiple axes and continuums as yet unexamined by historians…. Along with the traditional concerns with identity, community, and politics…my primary emphasis is on desire as an organizing category. (p. xviii)

Howard's comments acknowledge the comprehensiveness of thinking about queerness to include thinking, doing, and being. And yet, by assigning desire as an organizing category, he proposes queerness as a means of contextualization—not the basis of *who* we are or *how* we think or act, but as part of the interrelated conditions through which we are and think and act.

Throughout my narrative about place, desire, and sexuality, I find myself wanting to write *lesbian* instead of *queer*. I therefore sometimes write *lesbian* instead of *queer*. I do not conflate the two, but turn again to Howard to help explain my differentiation. The quote, while rather lengthy, articulates difference in usage among *same-sex* (homosex, as per Howard), *queer*, and *gay*. He writes,

> [The emphasis on desire as an organizing category], rare in queer history, requires an elaboration of terminology. I use the amalgam homosex to indicate sexual activities of various sorts between two males. Queer holds multiple meanings, in both the historical and theoretical contexts of this study. When writing of particular moments in history, I use the widespread, contemporaneous understanding of things queer, as noted above. However, generally in referring to "queer Mississippians"—those who engage in queer sex or harbor queer notions—I am employing an expansive definition that goes well beyond homosex to encompass all thoughts and expressions of sexuality and gender that are nonnormative or oppositional. Though gay is always employed as an identity-based descriptor, queer may or may not be, depending on the individual. (Howard, 1999, p. xix)

For the remainder of this chapter, my use of *queer* and its derivatives imply similar multiple meanings to those Howard notes: "contemporaneous understanding of things queer" and nonnormative, oppositional thoughts and acts, for example. Likewise, *lesbian* is an identity-based descriptor; it is what I would fill in the blank "I am a _____" with. It gives a nod to my feminist thought and my woman–woman desire.

"Lovin' Done Country Style…": Rural Formations of Queerness

With a nod to Loretta Lynn's anthem to heterosexual country womanhood, "You're Lookin' at Country" (1971), sexual cultures "done country style" are particular to the places where they are constructed and nurtured, the "country," for example, or, in my case, the rural ("country") South. Further, rural queerness is as multiple and varied as there are rural queers. Are images of queerness predominantly metropolitan because queered metropolitan spaces are privileged over queered rural spaces (as they are, ultimately, in nonqueered spaces), or is it the other way around? The question is deceptive; both its parts are too interrelated to be reducible to cause and effect. So phrased, the question displays the bifurcating tendency to discuss one in terms of the other, rather than considering and interrogating particularities of place in relation to specificities of rural queer lives. As Judith "Jack" Halberstam notes (2003),

> Indeed, most queer work on community, sexual identity, and gender roles has been based on and in urban populations and exhibits an active disinterest in the productive potential of non-metropolitan sexualities and genders and identities. Most theories of homosexuality within the twentieth century assume that gay culture is rooted in cities, that it has a special relationship to urban life…. In practice, we might find that rural environments nurture elaborate sexual cultures even while sustaining surface social and political conformity. (p. 162)

In terms of queer curriculum studies, the assumption is often one of unitary queerness understood to be metroqueer. Yet an examination of queerness nurtured by rural environments that concurrently sustains social and political structures of conformity and conservatism not only disrupts unitary constructions of queerness, it also queerly disturbs those very structures. Not incidentally, it helps us understand rural place better by disrupting notions of unitary rural subjectivity, queer or otherwise.

What images do we have of rural queer lives? I am reminded again of Shreve McCannon's entreaty to Quentin Compton: *Tell about the South. What's it like there. What do they do there. Why do they live there. Why do they live at all…*(Faulkner, 1936/1990, p. 142).[2] Because, of course, my own rural space is Southern, my telling will be in Southern voice. When McCannon's charge is considered from a queered perspective, it transforms the telling of the South and the telling of queerness, unsettling conventional narratives of Southern place and metronormative assumptions of queer folks. Prevailing images distort and discount lived experiences by focusing almost exclusively on oppressive, graphic violence perpetuated against rural queers: Brandon Teena and Matthew Shepard, for example. Such objectification is no more an accurate portrayal of queer lives than defining "The Black Experience" solely in terms of slavery or "The Jewish Experience" solely in terms of the Holocaust, yet these presumptuous objectifications are often reinforced by popular culture, public attitudes, and behaviors—notably in public schools and curriculum. In "The Brandon Teena Archive" (2003) Halberstam notes

…the rural context allows for a very different array of acts, practices, performances and identifications…. And so in relation to the complicated matrix of rural queer lives, we tend to rely on the story of a Brandon Teena or Matthew Shepard rather than finding out about the queer people who live quietly if not comfortably in isolated areas or small towns all across North America. (p. 164)

Tell about living a queer life in the South. What is it like there? What do we do there? Why do we live there? The stories of those of us, who live, sometimes quietly—sometimes not, sometimes comfortably—sometimes not, are situated in place. Thus, from the stories that *tell* the lives, we gain better understanding *of* the lives. In addition, we may gain better understanding of the place: a place that both nurtures these lives as it nurtures those who would seek to end them with violence. The same Jesus who died for NASCAR fans died for Southern queers, those who follow racing and those who do not.

This, then, is the crux—pardon the pun—for Southern queer fundamentalists. Christ's followers who congregate here on earth generally do not welcome both groups with open arms. It is highly unlikely that an openly gay, lesbian, or transgendered person would be able to enter a Southern rural church—like the one in which I grew up—and receive the blessed assurance of salvation. For many of us to enjoy communion with the saints would require a confession of our "sins" and renunciation of our sexuality. Or, we might practice salvation of the closet and hope that redemption supersedes the guilt and shamefulness of passing. Or, we might do as Paul suggests (Philippians 2:12) and "work out our own salvation" in countless other ways, but almost always, for me, with "fear and trembling." The choices seem bleak, even as the proclamation that Jesus died for us might appear hollow. And yet, I find my theorizing, and direction for this study, in the apostle's next words, "For it is God which worketh in you both to will and to do of His good pleasure" (v. 13). Religious and sexual ecstasy, embodied spirituality—God in us—all are formations of queerness to be explored within the contexts of Southern place. In NASCAR country.

Not surprisingly, queer studies have been slow in theorizing place in the construction of queer identity, instead normalizing metropolitan queers as "authentic" and metropolitan centers as the exclusive places where one can "fully participate in the various cultural, social, and political networks inhabited by other queers" (Spurlin, 2000, p. 183). In "Remapping Same-Sex Desire: Queer Writing and Culture in the American Heartland," William Spurlin contends,

> …queer inquiry has shown little interest in cross-cultural variations of the expression and representations of same-sex desire…with its narrow Eurocentric, and therefore imperialistic gaze, queer studies has not seriously engaged how queer identities and cultural formations have taken shape and operate outside of large metropolitan locations. (p. 183)

When rural narratives are considered at all, it is usually in relation to rural queer migration. *Southern* rural narratives of queerness—like this one—are almost never considered. In *Men Like That: A Southern Queer History* (1999), John Howard notes that the rural countryside is considered a "hinterland, a geopolitical closet from which sexual migrants flee" (p. xix), which reminds me of Stella Kowalski's reply to Sister Blanche: "You take it for granted that I'm in anything I want to get out of!" (Williams, 1947)[3] Granted, there are rural escapees living in urban spaces, many of whom disparage and denounce their growing-up places in no uncertain terms. They have their stories, and the telling of them fuels what Spurlin refers to as the "myth of the queer child," who "saves money and gets on a train bound for New York or some other coastal city in search of a new life more compatible with his or her emerging sexual identity" (p. 182). This is in keeping with a larger privileging of urban places over rural ones. Despite rats and other general sleaze, it is figured cities remain sophisticated spaces where bright young, middle-class White men can make their fortunes. After all, it is figured, what kind of life can be had in the crude, uncultured, slow backwoods? *Why do they live there? Why do they live at all…?*

The myth of the queer child, according to Spurlin, presumes another myth prevalent in queer studies,

—that of the metropolitan centre as a mecca for queer community, self-servingly constructed by urban queers, where lesbians, gay men, bisexual, transsexuals, and transgendered people from the non-metropolitan peripheries, such as the rural South and the Midwest in the United States, can gather to escape oppressive familial and social relations back home. (pp. 182–183)

It is precisely these familial and social relations, particular to Southern (in my case) rural place, that I recount in an attempt to understand rural formations of queerness. I suspect more Southern queers than might be imagined experience oppressive relations to differing degrees, if we experience them at all. And many of us have no desire to escape, preferring to navigate those relations in order to find those that nurture and sustain us. Some of us may even attempt to escape and then return; familial and social relations constructed and embedded in place end up being what we escape to, not from, which is also problematic.

It should be noted that I am not suggesting a Southern rural idyll, where the cotton is high and sweet tea flows like water. Queer narratives, like any others, can neglect to trouble the intricacies of place and thereby lack critical dimension. We must be willing to rend the veil of nostalgia, else we fall prey to the temptation that vexes every Bubba and (you waited for it, and here it is: *Gone with the Wind* reference) Scarlett and Ashley: looking to the South for succor. We must examine the degree to which we are of-the-place, and question what that might mean—for us and for the place. We are not, after all, relieved of complicity or responsibility within the place narrative just because our narratives might also be queer. Little attention has been paid in queer curriculum studies to the lived experiences of Southern rural queers, to the particular place-based formations and "experiences of sexuality and the memories thereof" (Howard, 2003, p. 150). I suggest such narratives might throw into question what we think we know about queerness and place—thus adding important layers of complexity and disturbance to complicated curriculum conversations.

Rural place as a closet metaphor erases the life stories of those of us whose queer identities are constructed in and by place. Halberstam surmises,

The rural queer, within this standardized [escapee] narrative, emerges from the dark night of a traditional and closeted world and blooms in the sunshine of modern gay urban life. In reality, many rural queers yearn to leave the city and return to their small towns and many recount complicated stories of love, sex, and community in their small town lives which belie the closet model. (p. 163)

When you're lookin' at me, you're lookin' at country—woman, White, Southern, lesbian, Christian, queer curriculum scholar, mother, sister, daughter, partner. Not one of these descriptors would have fit in exactly the same way had I been born and raised anywhere else. What do I find when I look at me? What does country look like? And what can we learn about place and queerness and curriculum from the looking?

"Them Ol' Nasty Lesbians": Place and Queer Memory

Queer studies—curriculum or otherwise—neglect responsibility to queer history and memory when they fail to include the stories of those of us who were not raised nor identify as big city queers. To be fair, I understand the promotion of gay culture in cities because they are, as Howard suggests, spaces of anonymity. Yet they are also places where the nonanonymous congregate and form communities of socialization and support. True, the entertainment industry paints distinct pictures of urban queers—consider the set of *Queer Eye for the Straight Guy*, for example. When the Fab 5 watch the culmination of their efforts at the end of the show, they watch from the vantage point of a luxury apartment, martinis in hand. *Queer Eye* is a reality show; in reality, the closing credits reveal that the "luxury" apartment was provided by such-and-so company. This picture of fun-loving, care-taking, yet sophisticated queerness is so carefully constructed as to be both safe and appealing to straight viewers. These guys don't have a hidden agenda. They exist only to remake your wardrobe, kitchen, décor, hygiene, and culture—then, poof, they retreat to the queer Manhattan bat cave. And—they leave you *straight*.

Fictional shows like *The "L" Word* and *Queer as Folk* have a much broader canvas upon which to construct urban queer life. While the characters must undergo some sort of dramatic conflict—drug addiction, discrimination, relationship perils, family drama—in the end, the warm group of a half-dozen bosom friends are there for each other. Moreover, they are there for each other in a quaint neighborhood (complete with a trendy, hedonistic nightspot and a sort of queer-den-mother's restaurant, in the case of *Queer as Folk*) or in the trendy LA neighborhoods of West Hollywood. These shows seem like different sides of the same queer coin, so I did some checking (The "L" Word, Wikipedia, 2007). Both are actually shot in Vancouver, BC, and are produced by sister companies. Both portray gay men and lesbians as affluent professionals unhampered by financial or material concerns—fabulous characters with plenty of disposable income and plenty of playtime who romp around creating their own drama. Both are prime time soap operas that often offer complex plot twists, yes, but reveal about as much complexity of gay and lesbian characters as *Gray's Anatomy* reveals about doctors, which, by the way, is set in the metropolis of Seattle.

After a season I stopped watching *The "L" Word*—lost interest in it, really—because I didn't know those girls. I don't mean to suggest that I only watch television shows that have characters with whom I identify, but *The "L" Word* had made such a grand entrance onto the popular culture landscape to an audience starved for images of ourselves (Walters, 2003). *The "L" Word* message, it seems, is clear: lesbians live in cities, are predominantly White, are more secular than religious, and are securely ensconced in the upper class. Not a country girl in the bunch. It follows then, or so it seems to me, that by framing queer identities within rural settings—by finding us in small towns and out in the country—we may not only trouble assumptions about how place-based experiences constitute queerness, but we might also gain understanding about class, race, region, and religion. To that end, I turn to my own queer memory.[4]

For a town of fewer than a thousand residents, Littleville has a disproportionate number of churches—five at my last count: one Methodist, two Baptist, one Christ Vineyard, and mine, the Church of Christ. I never presume nor wish to represent the views of all White Southerners, Littlevillians, or "Members of the Church," as folks in my particular denomination refer to themselves, but a look backward through queer memory falls within these bounds. I try to (re)collect these memories and examine them, and of course I examine them within these contexts, among others.

Littleville has not changed much over the past half-century, all things considered. In fact, I often tell friends that when I "go home" to Littleville, I also feel as though I am going back in time. My daddy tells me that when he was a kid of 14, he could listen from his window and hear the jukebox at the old café playing *Tenderly*, by Rosemary Clooney, or the desolate, bellowed moans of a train whistle, slowing for a crossing at which it would not stop. When I was born, we lived in a little gray house by those tracks, at that same crossing. The deafening call of the trains was one of the earliest sounds I ever heard, and I cannot hear it today without thinking about home.

Like most locations in the world, I suppose, Littleville, Alabama, is "known" for something. Down the road in Franklin County, for example, was where it had been rumored for years that anybody could find a hired gun, where one could put a hit on somebody— if one had need of such a service. Everybody in Littleville knew that everybody in the country knew this. Publicly, Littleville itself is nationally known as being a speed trap.[5] Although it is one of those small towns about which folks can joke, "Be careful when you're driving through or you'll miss it," its several backstreets and one thoroughfare are well-patrolled and represent a significant flow of revenue for the municipality. Privately, though, there had been rumors for years about the "Littleville Lesbians," a provocative group that had existed long before Desperate Housewives.

Now, I realize here that I need to clarify what I mean by *lesbian*, since there are at least three ways to classify them in Littleville alone. First, there are the women who seem to be performing the stereotypes: they drive trucks, work construction, and hang out at the softball field. Then there are the women who are out and social but do not dress and perform masculinity. They are also to be found at the softball field; the difference is these gals attract fewer glares and stares at the Catfish Haven restaurant (more about Catfish Haven later). At this point I want to assert that I am resistant to reinforcing a butch/femme binary in my description. I must offer description, but with the understanding that these women are as individual and un-fitting as metropolis queers. I am also attempting to capture something of the local perspective of a population that does not itself "fit" into small town life. And *that* is one aim of this chapter: to turn the small-town gaze back upon itself, to queer the gaze, as it were, and show ruptures within this collective subjectivity.

I am unwilling to label the third group "lesbian" at all; they are the married women who identify as straight and entertain female lovers—usually those from the aforementioned groups—in their homes while their husbands are at work. Although the visible group creates quite a stir, these not-so-desperate housewives represent a much greater threat to the inhabitants of this Christian-identified, rural, working class community. Whether they are gay-curious, secret lovers, or in some other way practicing same-sex, they make up an underground network as veiled in secrecy as the Priory of Sion. They are risk taking, pleasure seeking sexual outlaws who seek to connect with other women and who are virtually indistinguishable from one's mother, sister, or wife. Heck, they could even *be* one's mother, sister, or wife. As it turns out, that is *exactly* who they are.

The title of this section, "Them Ol' Nasty Lesbians," refers to my first awareness of women-centered women. Years before, this particular couple had bought an old stucco house not a half mile from my parents' house in Littleville. Whenever I passed by, I saw them working on renovating their place—patching up chipped stucco, painting the house (a dark green), putting up a fence around the yard. We never spoke; I'm not even sure they ever saw me—a 12-year-old kid just walking down the road. Gradually the old place came to life again. They put two yellow Labrador retrievers in the yard, and every holiday they decorated house and yard with the appropriate tacky lights and plastics.

Let me tell you of my known encounter with a lesbian. No, this is no kind of coming out story; instead, it occurred while I was still firmly ensconced in matrimony. I was 30 years old when my uncle's wife of 19 years left him for a woman. The contexts surrounding this incident provide an interesting glimpse into rural formations of queerness, and more particularly, into that of lesbians, a segment of women underrepresented in literature. From what I can make of it, my uncle's wife started out as a heterosexual-identified housewife looking for social outlets and then transitioned into a woman-identified woman, but that is her story. Mine is to observe and study the gaze. It is important to me that I look back and pay attention to memory, to attend now to scenes dismissed as interesting yet inconsequential. For one of the most unusual, puzzling aspects of my own queerness is the feeling that this part of my self has no past, no background. Queer memory, however, is not to be conflated with queer origins (Probyn, 1996) or the myth of the queer child.

One day, I saw my uncle, my daddy's brother, talking to Daddy in our back yard. I could see that Uncle Joe was crying but couldn't tell what they were talking about. After several days of Mother and Daddy whispering around the house and stopping midconversation whenever my brother or I came into the room, Mother decided to tell me what was going on. (Although by this time I was 30 years old, my parents had only referred to sex two times in my presence—both times without actually saying the word.) Joe's wife was leaving him for another woman, one who worked at the same factory that he did. They had met at the ballpark, and the woman, Belinda, had begun picking up Mandy, Joe's wife, and taking her to town during the day while he was at work. Looking back, I realize that the circumstances surrounding this small-town—and family—scandal had many complexities and facets. At the time, it was all very simple; there were good guys—my family—and bad gals—the illicit couple. I remember asking my mother if the woman was anybody we knew. She replied, yes, I had probably seen her. "She lives with them women down the road...them ol' nasty lesbians."

Not long afterward, I saw Belinda at the Catfish Haven. Catfish Haven is the most lucrative restaurant in Littleville. Actually built into the side of a hill with a flowing spring, there is a walkway over an indoor pond where patrons can watch the fish swim, without, probably, pondering too carefully the intended fate of the fish. The place is a nondescript structure in need of a paint job that goes mostly unnoticed during the week, but on Saturday night and Sunday after church, cars are parked all the way to the road. You can order a one- two- or three-piece catfish dinner with all the appropriate trimmings—including a huge slice of dill pickle in case you swallow a bone. This Sunday, as we went there for lunch along with the rest of the church crowd, my mother noticed a woman—short, with a key ring on her belt and wearing construction boots—getting out of a long, white car. "I wish you'd look," she said, "there's ol' Belinda ____." I craned my neck from the back seat of Mother's Caprice Classic to see what Belinda looked like—to see what a lesbian looked like up close.

I had seen her before—not at the little green house with the Christmas tacky, but at the restaurant. I realized that she was the sister of one of my classmates, Denise, at Littleville Elementary School, who was by this time a waitress at Catfish Haven. Belinda had her regular booth from which she had lunch, coffee, and the day's newspaper. Today I watched her go inside from her car, and even then, before the theory, before knowing about postcolonial gazes and the like, I felt myself watching her—me, freshly sanctified from a good Sunday churching and her, an animal-freak to be ostracized, condemned, and, at all costs, avoided.

My first queer images were in direct opposition to the image invoked by my mother, yet hers was stronger. Lesbians were "them," the unclean, those whose very existence must be spat out if mentioned at all. I've considered that conversation, particularly the phrase, many times since I've lived as a lesbian. I've spent years working through the implications of my mother's words, including earning a PhD, writing a book, and presenting at conferences all over the world. What I haven't done is come out to my parents. Oh, I know they know: I moved to Louisiana to be with my partner; then she moved to Georgia to be with me. We've bought a house together—we even have a couple of dogs in the yard and put out Christmas tacky. But I don't say my words so she doesn't have to say hers. My greatest fear is that all I can ever be in my mother's eyes is one of "them ol' nasty lesbians."

Just As I Am

I look back and try to consider how my own experiences in that small country church helped shape my sexuality, my queer memory itself. Try as I might, I cannot remember any overt teachings at church against homosexuality in the modern world. Now, I have lived away from Littleville for many years, and I feel certain that it has probably come up in some form or another in sermons or adult Sunday School lessons since then. I do not remember it being mentioned very often from the pulpit, though, and mainly heard it referenced—in cryptic, King James Version terms, I might add—in exegetical study of the Bible. There are approximately 10 verses that might remotely refer to same-sex acts—and some are a real stretch—so we only talked about them as we came across them (unless, of course, the [male] teacher wanted to make analogies between the wickedness of the modern world and the fall of the Roman Empire). I do remember that. The point is, I believe that there is a misconception among nonfundamentalist Christian populations that conservative Christians are hate-mongerers, and worship services are radical diatribes against gays and lesbians. And, judging from various position statements, televangelist rants, and 700 Club episodes, one's suspicions are not wholly unjustified. Condemnation by the tenets of organized religion fuel the guilt and self-loathing so many of us Christian queers experience.

To be responsible to queer memory, however, means that I must survey the relationship between the site of my earliest spiritual encounters and my queer lesbian identity. So, as does Angelia Wilson (2000), I "hold up a mirror to my Southern homeland" (p. 157), and, also like her, I study the reflection without even the pretense of objectivity. Wilson writes, "Every child of the South has, consciously or unconsciously, constructed their identity in relation to rather strict gender/sexual rules" (p. 160), and further, "One cannot fully grasp American politics without understanding the extent to which normative Christianity dictates the political, social, and sexual agenda" (p. 165). The Southern construction of gender and sexual rules and the dictates of normative Christianity are powerful influences upon rural formations of queerness in the South, formations that are both personal and political. For me, these overarching, culturally and socially significant issues are sometimes best theorized from the remembering of one small scene, one such as I describe below.

I titled this section "Just As I Am" with multiple layers of meanings in mind. Besides the obvious reference to identity, it is, as anyone who has seen a Billy Graham Crusade over the past 40 years knows, the title of the altar call, or invitation song (as it is called in the Church of Christ: altar call sounds too Catholic). Invitation songs immediately follow the preacher's sermon, which may last anywhere from half an hour upwards—depending on the congregation (on the way to Catfish Haven on Sundays, Church of Christ members pass Baptist churches still in session, happy to beat the crowd, glad that

"Baptists keep 'em all day." Baptist funerals usually run long, too.) When the preacher utters something to the effect of, "If there is anyone here who needs to make his life right with God, or who has not accepted Christ and is in danger of being forever lost in eternity, please come, as we stand and sing." (Notice how I quote this so effortlessly.) These songs are often mournful, depicting both the threat of impending damnation and the opportunity for salvation. One has only to accept the Savior, the Lamb of God:

> Just as I am without one plea,
> But that thy blood was shed for me,
> And that thou bidst me come to thee,
> O Lamb of God, I come; I come.

> Just as I am, thy love unknown
> Has broken every barrier down.
> Now, to be thine, yea, thine alone
> O Lamb of God, I come; I come.

Between the second and third lines of each stanza, there is a crescendo in a minor key, giving an extra emotional tug. I have heard preachers ask the song leader to "give 'er one more round," expecting that one more repentant sinner will come forward.

This song has seven stanzas, and by the time we got to the last one, I felt what I can only describe as controlled ecstasy. The Church of Christ is not one of the charismatic or Pentecostal denominations; all things, including actually having any ecstasy in church, must be done decently and in order (I Corinthians 14:40). We do not shout or witness, do not have choirs or Christmas pageants. Within this setting, ecstasy is subdued. The equating, comparing, or correlating of queer sexual ecstasy with religious impassioned emotions—of religious and sexual desire—must, for the time being, be left for another discussion although Kate Chedgzoy makes provocative forays into the conversation in her "Region, Religion, and Sexuality: Pilgrim Through This Barren Land" (2000). My brief glimpse here leads me to note that in my own lived experiences, the coming unto Christ and the coming to sexual climax are both, under the right conditions, spiritual ecstatic experiences in which desire is central. Both involve spiritual, mutual surrender to a lover.[6]

From my queer fundamentalist memory, ecstasy has a dark side—the highly motivational and influential fear of being lost. Wilson states, "For those of us who grew up in the church, there is nothing more personally frightening than rejection and damnation to hell" (2000, p. 127). Looking back, it is difficult to tell whether, as my heart swelled and voice rang out between that second and third line of "Just As I Am," whether I was motivated more by ecstatic desire for Christ or my fear of going to Hell. Regardless, the spiritual manifestations were physical, emotional, and psychological. I knew the joy of a sated lover. My church experience helps me name my queer desire, as my queer desire helps me name my religious ecstasy. It is my particular rural formation of queerness, and it is not unrelated to curriculum studies.

Conclusion

In *Below the Belt: Sexuality, Religion and the American South*, Angelia Wilson (2000) relates a story about visiting an Operation Rescue office in Dallas, Texas, and interviewing Flip Behnam, the antiabortion activist who converted Norma "Jane Roe" McCorvey to Christianity. Wilson is a lesbian, the Texas-born daughter of a Methodist minister; she is a professor of social policy at the University of Manchester, England, yet read her comments, particularly the last lines:

> He escorted me to a counseling room where I flicked through some brochures while waiting for him to return. There is a reason you never see pictures of aborted fetus. Flip joined me and after explaining the project, I asked the first question. For the next 90 minutes I sat captured by his voice, by his logic, by his exuberant belief.... I wanted to be back in my car, back in my ivory tower, back to a place where I could forget. Even now editing the tapes of him, hearing his voice again, a part of me can't help thinking he makes sense. A small part of me. (p. 104)

A most significant, long-lasting formation of queerness, one shaped by a Southern brand of Christian fundamentalist thought is that parts of this thinking still makes sense to part of me. Conservative positioning still makes sense to me because fundamentalist thinking is often polarized into right or wrong, sin or righteousness, redemption or loss, salvation or damnation. There are gray areas and contradictions to be sure—antiabortion vs. procapital punishment stances, for example. But the old arguments are well-crafted and well-rehearsed, peppered with scripture, and that part of me which holds those scriptures to be the inerrant Word of God finds it hard to discount the persuasions. Moreover— and this is one of the most baffling secrets I keep—part of me wants the positions to be "right," and I give a quiet, private *Yes-s-s-s!* when a well-placed point is made (even when it is made on Fox News, a reprehensible place where I sometimes find myself). There is another stanza to "Just As I Am," one in which the sinner entreats that she is impatient to *cleanse my soul of one dark blot*. No matter how far I may be from Littleville, Alabama, I am never far removed from the one dark blot. It is a blot about which I have been singing since I was 5 years old, it is so deeply engrained. It is a very queer blot.

However, queer fundamentalist conversations are as complicated as the queer gaze of memory. I am most interested in exploring sources, constructed in the rural Southern particularity of fundamentalist Christianity, that simultaneously nurture the formation of spirituality and queer sexuality in individual rural lives. This is not to suggest a rural idyll of queer sexuality, which would be no more existent than the imagined South for which so many Southerners are nostalgic (McPherson, 2003). Nor, of course, does the state of being queer privilege one to critique the South or Southern-style religion, any more than being a Southern fundamentalist Christian privileges one to critique queerness. The rural South is a contested site, where race, class, gender, religion, and sexuality play out continually and comprehensively. Voices of gay, lesbian, transgendered, and bisexual people who were raised and perhaps choose to remain on these landscapes add layers of complication, complexity, and understanding that are significant to both queer studies and curriculum studies.

A final note about Talladega: Following race weekend, I headed back to Georgia. Just after I passed the church with the provocative sign, I came upon the Speedway property. This time, it was a desolate wasteland of some trash, yes—the remnant of a moderate-sized city occupying the landscape for 4 days. But the most striking image was that of the hundreds of porta-potties that were left to follow the slope of the land in a kind of postmodern pastoral.

Notes

1. The demographic information may be found at the following Web site. Retrieved spring 2007, from http://www.city-data.com/city/Littleville-Alabama.html

2. Interestingly, Faulkner uses Shreve to further the individual story of the Sutpen family and the broader story of the South. As Quentin Compson "tells the South," that is, the Sutpen saga, McCannon conceives of it in epic proportions—"It's better than the theatre...better than Ben Hur..." (p. 176).

3. Mainly, the line itself is such a treasure that it begs (me, at least) to be used. Also, the notion of the changing South as represented by Blanche and Stella—and Stanley, the brute who brings with him the infusion of new blood to the fading, emaciated place—is captured in Stella's rejoinder.

4. In fact, I had trouble finding any network shows that did not follow a similar formula. (LOGO, the gay-themed network owned by MTV, does try with its "Real Momentum" series.) The only one I could find in which urban-place did not itself figure was *Normal, Ohio*, which premiered on Fox in 2000 and starred John Goodman, the likeable actor just off his successful stint on *Roseanne* as Dan Connor. Here is the Fox press release for Normal, Ohio:

   > Goodman stars as William "Butch" Gamble, a beer-drinking, sports-loving Midwesterner who happens to be gay. Butch has decided to leave the liberal city of Los Angeles and return to his Ohio hometown—filled with less tolerant family members. His top priority is making amends with his son, Charlie. In the meantime, he's shacking up with his kid sister, Pamela. There are definitely no comforts of home—unless you count the warmhearted bickering!" Retrieved March 5, 2007, from http://www.tv.com/normal-ohio/show/35/summary.html

   Little wonder that Fox aired only six episodes.

5. Speedtrap.org is one of those fun sites about which I wonder, "Are there really people whose life's mission is to maintain a speed trap site?" Nevertheless, it exists at the following address. Retrieved February 27, 2008, from http://www.speedtrap.org/speedtraps/ste.asp?state=AL&city=Littleville

6. I believe that exploring this notion of "coming unto Christ and the coming to sexual climax" is central to queer studies of religion and Southern place. I turn to Lacan's *feminine juissance* (1998) as I continue my work on queer memory, place, and formations of queerness.

References

Cash, M. J. (1940). *The mind of the south.* New York: Alfred Knopf.

Chedgzoy, K. (2000). Region, religion and sexuality: Pilgrim through this barren land. In R. Phillips, D. Watt, & D. Shuttleton (Eds.), *De-centering sexualities: Politics and representations beyond the metropolis* (pp. 110–122). New York: Routledge.

Corber, R. J., & Valocchi, S. (Eds.) (2003). *Queer studies: An interdisciplinary reader.* Malden, MA: Blackwell.

Faulkner, W. (1990). *Absalom, Absalom!* New York: Vintage International. (Original work published 1936)

Halberstam, J. (2003). The Brandon Teena archive. In R. J. Corber & S. Valocchi (Eds.), *Queer studies: An interdisciplinary reader* (pp. 159–169). Malden, MA: Blackwell.

Howard, J. (1999). *Men like that: A Southern queer history.* Chicago: University of Chicago Press.

Howard, J. (2003). The talk of the county: Revisiting accusation, murder, and Mississippi, 1895. In R. J. Corber & S. Valocchi (Eds.), *Queer studies: An interdisciplinary reader* (pp. 142–158). Malden, MA: Blackwell.

Lacan, J. (1998). On feminine sexuality: The limits of love and knowledge. In J-A. Miller (Ed.), *Book XX: Encore, 1972–1973* (pp. 48–51). New York: Norton.

Lynn, L. (1971). You're lookin' at country. On *You're lookin' at country* [CD]. Los Angeles: Decca Records.

McKay, A. (2006). *Talladega nights: The ballad of Ricky Bobby* [Motion picture]. Los Angeles: Sony Pictures.

McPherson, T. (2003). *Reconstructing Dixie: Race, gender and nostalgia in the imagined South.* Chapel Hill, NC: Duke University Press.

Probyn, E. (1996). *Outside belongings*. New York: Routledge.

Spurlin, W. J. (2000). Remapping same-sex desire: Queer writing and culture in the American heartland. In R. Phillips, D. Watt, & D. Shuttleton (Eds.), *De-centering sexualities: Politics and representations beyond the metropolis* (pp. 182–198). New York: Routledge.

Underwood, C. (2005). Jesus take the wheel. *On Some hearts* [CD]. New York: Arista.

Walters, S. D. (2003). *All the rage: The story of gay visibility in America*. Chicago: University of Chicago Press.

Williams, T. (1947). *A Streetcar Named Desire*. New York: Signet Books.

Wilson, A. R. (2000). *Below the belt: Sexuality, religion and the American South*. London: Cassell.

Suggested Reading Questions

1. Given the author's explanation focused on subjugated place-based experiences of queer sexuality, what other subjugated groups might be explained through place-based inquiry?

2. In what ways might autobiography be used to unveil assumptions regarding the ways race, class, gender, and society shape self-understanding and the cultural scripts made available to different individuals?

3. The author distinguishes between identity-based terminology, such as gay and lesbian, and queer, which signifies nonnormative and oppositional thoughts and acts. How might identity based politics be characterized in contrast to queer politics?

4. What are the implications queer place-based curriculum studies for the reconceptualization of school based curricula?

5. How might educators use place-based studies to engage in their own curriculum inquiries?

Response to Ugena Whitlock
Curriculum as a Queer Southern Place

Reflections on Ugena Whitlock's
"Jesus Died for NASCAR Fans"

Patrick Slattery

My iPod, note pad, and reading materials were stuffed into the seatback pocket in front of me in preparation for takeoff. I was on a nonstop flight from Texas to Florida. As the Boeing 737 pulled away from the gate, I settled comfortably into my fourth row window seat. The middle seat remained empty, providing a little extra room to stretch. I planned to read Ugena Whitlock's article "Jesus Died for NASCAR Fans: The Significance of Rural Formations of Queerness to Curriculum Studies" while on this flight. How interesting, I thought, that I was quite literally flying across the *Heart of the Dixie* as I prepared to read her narrative on sexuality and religion in rural Southern U.S. culture.

The flight path over Louisiana bisected my family roots in Shreveport and my hometown of New Orleans. As I started reading Ugena's manuscript, I caught myself glancing out my window scouring the distant landscape for familiar landmarks: the LSU campus where I was an undergraduate computer science major in 1971 and where Ugena and I both completed our doctoral degrees in curriculum theory; the bluffs of the Mississippi River at Vicksburg where my ancestors on my mother's side are buried near the Civil War battlefield; or the beginning of the Natchez Trace leading to Whitehall, my cousin's north Mississippi Plantation home in Columbus.

Between each compelling page of Ugena's gothic southern narrative of rural formation of queerness, I strained my neck across the aisle to look out of the windows on the right side of the plane in an attempt to catch a glimpse of Cat Island off the coast at Biloxi, Dauphin Island and Orange Beach south of Mobile, Santa Rosa Island at the border of Alabama and Florida, or any of the other Gulf Coast haunts of my youth. I wanted to visibly touch the soul of my southern roots as I pondered my own coming of age and coming out in the South. "How queer it is!" I chuckled under my breath.

"Perhaps I can spot Escambia Bay and my kid brother's neighborhood in Pensacola where he lives with his middle-class family of six?" I thought. Kevin has lived in the same house since 1976 when his home was our launching pad to the beaches beyond Gulf Breeze. Years later I heard that Santa Rosa Island is sometimes called "The Gay Riviera" of the Gulf Coast. I have partied, played, prayed, and puked all over these Gulf Coast beaches since the late 1950s. Not even the litany of Andrew, Betsy, Camille, Ivan, Juan, Katrina, and all of the other massive hurricanes of my lifetime could destroy the complex memories of those pristine Southern beaches on the Gulf of Mexico.

I was deep in thought somewhere over rural Alabama—perhaps north of Pensacola and south of Ugena's inspired Talladega Motor Speedway—when a flight attendant caught my attention. "Would you like something to drink, sir?" she called with notepad ready and elbow resting on the aisle seat headrest. I hesitated. I almost spoke the words, "Water, please." I did not want an alcoholic beverage to numb my nostalgic reflections just as I was about to start writing some initial reactions to Ugena's paper. I always bring along several free cocktail coupons on Southwest flights, but on this flight I resisted the alcohol for a split second. One thing swayed my fateful decision. There was a boisterous and obnoxious young man in the aisle seat at the end of my row. His handsome physique caught my attention when he boarded the plane, but I avoided eye contact to forestall conversation. As the 3-hour flight progressed, I also noticed that his oversized boots matched his inflated ego. For the first half of the flight he had been downing vodka tonics at an alarming rate and hitting on the women flight attendants with heterosexual zest—much to the consternation of the women but much to the delight of his equally handsome traveling buddy seated across the aisle.

I placed Ugena's manuscript on the empty seat between us, slowly inhaled a reflective breath, and called back to the very patient flight attendant: "I will have a double vodka with cranberry juice and a lime." I handed her two cocktail coupons; she smiled and wrote down my order. This gave Mr. Macho a critical moment to invade my space, glance at the title of Ugena's paper, and initiate a conversation. "Jesus! Derek and I are going to the Daytona 500, too!" he exclaimed with a clear assumption of instant male bonding. Apparently, he only had time to glance at the first part of the title: "Jesus Died for NASCAR Fans." I was horrified that he assumed that I must be flying into Orlando—with him and Derek—to rent a car and drive out to Daytona Beach for one of the most important NASCAR races of the season.

In the haste of the moment, I decided not to tell him that I was actually meeting my boyfriend in Orlando and driving down to Miami to hang out with gay and lesbian friends on South Beach. However, I did mention that I had never been to a NASCAR race, and neither had I ever been a NASCAR aficionado. Big mistake—on both fronts! The "boyfriend on South Beach" comment would have shut him up for the rest of the flight (or perhaps longer). But the "never been to NASCAR" comment gave him a perfect opening to talk (for the rest of the flight). "Then why the heck are you reading about Jesus and NASCAR?" he said with a degree of quizzical frustration in a slow southern drawl. I wondered to myself, "Should I tell breeder and his mate Derek why I am reading this queer paper?"

By now Derek was straining his neck across the aisle and ready to jump into the center seat between us. I quickly pondered, "What should I say? Do I invite Derek over for a three-way conversation? Do I talk to the boys about Christology, eschatology, and NASCAR? Do I dare talk about rural formations of queerness?" None of these seemed like good possibilities. I wanted to start writing about Ugena's paper and not talk to two straight boys about queer theory. Maybe. Suddenly I had another mischievous thought, "Might these good old boys possibly be family—or even weekend sports buddies with benefits?" No way. My gaydar registered zero. But many devious possibilities raced through my head at NASCAR speed.

Perhaps I was reading the situation through the internalized homophobia of my younger days on the Gulf Coast beaches when I was very much like these two Southern boys. These guys might be different. The double vodka and cranberry juice arrived just in time. I was now trapped (curiously engaged?) in a complicated conversation of testosterone-bonding across the Southwest aisles and Southern miles with my very drunk Confederate brothers.

For the rest of the flight we engaged in a delicate dance of mutual desire that actually became quite intriguing. We each stripped bare several layers of normative-shattering autobiography, including my knowledge and excitement about SEC football and Derek's tolerance of his step-sister's gay brother-in-law at Thanksgiving dinner. Their desire to introduce me to NASCAR culture at Daytona Beach was only matched by my desire to introduce them to queer culture at South Beach. But desire, as Ugena writes, has multiple layers of social and psychological complexity. In fact, the complexity of desire permeates the curriculum theorization of many scholars of the post-reconceptualization generation.

Ugena Whitlock cites John Howard's (1999) *Men Like That: A Southern Queer History* in order to point the way toward such desire and cultural negotiation as an organizing category. The "multiple axes and continuums" of identities, behaviors, and beings in Ugena's paper—and in John Howard's text as well—were being played out at 35,000 feet above Dixie at hyper NASCAR speed. I will get back to Bo and Derek in a moment. (Yes, their names were really Bo and Derek.) Considering my Aunt Billie Claire, Uncle Juicy, Aunt Put, Uncle Lilly, and all the myriad peculiar names in Southern families, Ugena and I both know that our formations of queerness in the South are rooted by birth and by name in the chthonian soil of Louisiana bayous and the red clay hills of Alabama. William Faulkner, as Ugena points out, taught us as much through his characters Ike McCaslin and Quinten Compton.

Bo and Derek reminded me of Ike and Quinton. Ugena writes, "Because my own rural space is Southern, my telling will be in a Southern voice." Ugena concludes—and I strongly agree—that the telling deconstructs metanormative assumptions of queer folks and also transforms the telling of the South. As we have learned from Foucault, my (re) telling of Ugena's narrative of her memory of the church sign at Talladega to Bo and Derek on a flight over Dixie to a north Florida NASCAR race and a culturally diverse south Florida beach was a queering of many spaces beyond the literal Southwest Airlines jet cabin. The intersections of Dayton Beach and South Beach, NASCAR and Jesus, rural queerness and Curriculum Studies, Patrick and Ugena and Bo and Derek, all inform and queer each other. This is a central argument in Ugena's paper, and it is a central tenet of both postmodern theory and post-reconceptualization curriculum theory as well. Perhaps, as William Pinar (1988, 1991, 1998, 2001, 2004) has suggested in many of his books and papers, the South provides a rich metaphor of place that can inform a renewal in curriculum studies in the spirit of Faulkner and psychoanalysis (Pinar, 1991). A "Southern strategy" for social psychoanalysis necessarily demands a complicated and integrated conversation about religion and sexuality (along with race and homosexuality and gender and queer identities). Ugena masterfully guides us on this intellectual journey.

A significant theme in Ugena's paper is a little gem buried in note 6 about Jacques Lacan's feminine juissance. She writes, "I believe that exploring this notion of 'coming unto Christ and the coming of sexual climax' is central to queer studies of religion and Southern place [and to] queer memory, place, and formations of queerness." I agree. I have also explored this important connection in my artwork and in my writing (Slattery, 1994, 2001, 2006).

In the 2005 Egon Guba lecture at the American Educational Research Association (AERA), I discussed the following about one of my art installations:

> This installation is a construction and reconstruction of memories of my body in junior high classrooms. I collected artifacts from scrapbooks, yearbooks, and family closets. I also imagined furniture and icons which I searched for in antique stores and junk yards. I worked within to reconstruct images from my unconscious, while remembering Jackson Pollock's admonition that the creative process also involves consciousness of the overall effect of the piece. While the symbols are particular to my Catholic school experience, I believe that the issues I raise in this art installation are universally applicable. Repression of the body, sexual fantasies, uncontrollable sexual responses, and guilt and anxiety about sexuality are all part of the educational experience of students who sit in school desks. Since there is no student seated in the desk in this installation—only a class photo, first grade hand prints, and a cast

of my hand—the viewer is reminded of the absence of the body and the attempt to repress sexuality in the school curriculum. Such curricular governmentality creates an environment where rape and abuse can flourish. This is a lesson lost on religious leaders, Catholic bishops, and other institutional leaders who prefer to shame children, perpetuate victimization, silence discourse, and cover up abuse. (Slattery, 2005, p. 10)

The abuse of children that results from the decoupling of sexual and spiritual climax in Southern Baptist churches and Roman Catholic schools must be uncovered. One of my favorite Louisiana authors is Walker Percy. In his last novel before his death, *The Thanatos Syndrome*, Percy (1987) tackled this problem directly. In the novel, the central character is a psychiatrist and recovering drug addict who went to prison for selling prescription narcotics at the Interstate 10 rest stop. His name is Tom More. With the ingenious help of his attractive cousin, Dr. Lucy Lipscomb, More uncovers a criminal experiment to "improve" behavior patterns in south Louisiana through the secret use of drugs in the water supply. Later in the novel Tom More stumbles on a ring of child molesters and pedophiles at the local school, Belle Ame Academy, who are leading this drug experiment. The most striking example of strangeness of which Tom More takes note is the inability of some of the infected children and adults to have self-reflection and context. These individuals can respond to questions with the accuracy and precision of a savant, and yet display no sense of self-reflection nor a sense of the context in which the language is being used. Sexual abuse of children and educational manipulation of students flourishes in this Southern novel for many reasons, not the least of which is the bifurcation of sexuality and human spirituality in the school curriculum. This novel not only supports Ugena's thesis in her paper, it tells an important narrative in the Southern literary tradition.

What we see in Southern literature, in contemporary curriculum literature, and in Ugena Whitlock's narrative of rural formations of queerness is a yearning for practices of freedom and justice. There is a commitment to queering the educational spaces so that there will be inclusion, agency, self-reflection, sustainability, understanding, and democracy. Postmodern authors and post-reconceptualization curriculum theorists do not advocate for schools and societies void of ethics and values. Rather, we work for profound commitments to democracy and freedom. We are not nihilists and relativists detached from society. I believe that the present moment in curriculum studies is certainly contested and fragmented, but this does not diminish the tremendous commitment to justice inherent in our work. Ugena concludes, "The rural South is a contested site, where race, class, religion, and sexuality play out continually and comprehensively. Voices of gay, lesbian, transgendered, and bisexual people who are raised and perhaps choose to remain on these landscapes add layers of complication, complexity, and understanding that are significant to both queer studies and curriculum studies." The shifting space of the postmodern in curriculum literature offers the possibility of creating a productive disequilibrium that will bring understanding—and perhaps even mutual acceptance and compassionate engagement—to the bifurcated forces in schools and society.

So, what does NASCAR have to do with this queer shifting space in curriculum studies? Well, by the end of the flight and after several more vodka tonics and vodka cranberry juices, Bo and Derek convinced me to travel with them from Orlando to Daytona Beach for my first NASCAR experience, and I convinced Bo and Derek to join us after the Daytona 500 on a trip to South Beach to learn about queer culture. Not! But it sure would make a great ending to a Southern narrative about the significance of rural formations of queerness to curriculum studies.

References

Percy, W. (1987). *The thanatos syndrome.* New York: Farrar, Straus, & Giroux.

Pinar, W. F. (1988). Time, place, and voice: Curriculum theory and the historical moment. In W. F. Pinar (Ed.), *Contemporary curriculum discourses* (pp. 264–278). Scottsdale, AZ: Gorsuch, Scarisbrick.

Pinar, W. (1991). *Curriculum as social psychoanalysis: The significance of place.* Albany, NY: SUNY Press.

Pinar, W. (1994). *Autobiography, politics, and sexuality: Essays in curriculum theory, 1972–1992.* New York: Lang.

Pinar, W. (Ed.). (1998). *Queer theory in education.* Mahwah, NJ: Erlbaum.

Pinar, W. (2001). *The gender of racial politics and violence in America: Lynching, prison rape & the crisis of masculinity.* New York: Lang.

Pinar, W. (2004). *What is curriculum theory?* Mahwah, NJ: Erlbaum.

Slattery, P. (1994, Fall). Curriculum development and postmodernism. *Louisiana Philosophy of Education Journal: Official Proceedings of the Louisiana Philosophy of Education Society, XIX,* 5–26.

Slattery, P. (2001). The educational researcher as artist working within. *Qualitative Inquiry, 7*(3), 370–398.

Slattery, P. (2005). *Artist, activist and professor: The role of autobiography in my qualitative research.* Invited Egon G. Guba address, American Educational Research Association, Qualitative Research SIG, Montreal, Canada.

Slattery, P. (2006). *Curriculum development in the postmodern era* (2nd ed.). New York: Routledge.

14 Reconceiving Ecology
Diversity, Language, and Horizons of the Possible

Elaine Riley-Taylor

Chapter Overview

This chapter explores the ways non-Westerners and Westerners understand their relationship with other humans and the natural world. The author explores the intersection of autobiographical story telling and postmodern forms of ecological theory. Noting the historical work that makes her scholarship possible, the author turns toward a description of prior work, such as the writing of Huebner that made discussions of the spirit in education possible. The author turns to an autobiographical exploration of coming to understand spirituality and ecology as relational and therefore something larger than a human project. Next she explores the language of spirituality and language of place within curriculum studies. She suggests language is a key site for sharing knowledge across generations and therefore constitutes a "commons" or public space. Providing a description of her own commons, the author points to relational and process epistemologies for offering a view of knowledge that makes significant place and time, ones within which thought and understanding are made available for living. Lastly, she outlines an ecological perspective that accounts for provisional truths relative to the scale of circumstance and context, the way language shapes available thought, and how self is made in relationship with place.

The Western Apache people commonly end a prayer with the words: *may it soon be usefully so* (Basso, 1996, p. xvii). The simple statement nods to a larger intention: that what has been spoken will begin taking root as does the single seed, dampened and swelling, moving through the rich black earth toward the warmth of day; life borne out of the sweetness of mystery and depth, gives rise to that which may be experienced, that which may be heard or seen or felt or signified in some way, so that the meaning made will somehow nourish and give direction to the living that will follow.

Moving within the Relations of Place

Summer mornings are chilly in this part of Northern Arizona. I move out of the house, across the yard, and down to the pass that runs beneath the highway, making my way to a hillside of National Forest land, a "commons" area covered in old growth Ponderosa Pine. The "commons" are those "aspects of human and natural communities that are mutually supportive and freely available to all" (Bowers, n.d). A public space, the Forest Service woodlands encircling Flagstaff are home to herds of elk and deer, to bobcat, cougar, rabbit, squirrel, and a variety of birds indigenous to the area. I stoop down to study the animal tracks verging east from the path along what looks to be a small animal run. The narrow run disappears beneath the trunk of a fallen pine grown over in a swirl of prickly brush. The tracks deepen sharply at the spot before the log, where they, also, end abruptly. The small deer most likely took the log in a single jump and, yes, the tracks pick up on the log's other side—initially deep, then growing more shallow once the animal returns to a normal gait. As I walk, I think about a paper that I am writing for a curriculum studies conference to be presented in the spring at Purdue University. The 2006 conference will mark what many theorists consider to be a watershed period in curriculum history—a "Reconceptualization" of the field that began in the late 1950s and coalesced over the decades that followed. (Note: The period has come to be called a reconceptualization, but was not called that by those involved during the time, nor was it ever considered any sort of "unified" movement.)

There's a shrill cry, high above me. The sound comes again, "aahheeow." Looking up, I see a circling pair of Red Tail hawks far above the path I'm walking. I think about this place and the diversity of life existing on the Colorado Plateau where Flagstaff sits. I realize that the talk that I prepare for the conference will have to begin here, on this ground and in this place that feeds the spirit and renews the senses. Animal and plant diversity in these forests makes for a rich environment that not only enhances the aesthetic experience of living in the area, but also contributes to the ecological balance that sustains and keeps the land vital. Even so, there is a prevalent tendency among many people, here—as there is across the United States—to view the natural world as merely a "resource" for purposes of human consumption. An early initiator of the reconceptualization, Dwayne Huebner (1999), shows how many Westerners' view relationships with the natural world or even with people. He says that the "prevailing mode of thought would seem to be the subject-object mode, whereby man's [sic] basic attitude toward the world of nature and the world of people is that it is something to be known, to be used" (1999, p. 89).

The period of reconceptualizing curriculum opened possibilities toward self-reflexive and critical forms of scholarship, and increased curricular languages for examining the "self" and the modes of authority institutionalized within the social order. This "Post-reconceptualization" conference would bring new curriculum scholars whose work was representative of emerging trends in the field into dialogue with people and ideas integral to the field's historical foundations. The intergenerational and dialogical intention of the conference, itself, could be said to have been made possible by the flowering of ideas that the "Reconceptualization" evoked (1969–1980; Pinar, 2007).

Overview

The following chapter moves between ecological forms of postmodern theory (Spretnak, 1997) and personal voice—autobiography and story—to ground theory more firmly into "lived" worlds (Butterfield, 1994; Grumet, 1980; Miller, 1997; Pinar & Grumet, 1976). In some ways, these conceptual tools are mine for this framing due to a generation of scholars before me, whose work came to "redefine" the meaning of curriculum theory and what it is to do curriculum work.

Curriculum Stories: Beginnings from the Ground of Change

The decades of the late 1950s, up through the 1970s, brought a "coming of age" that could be seen more clearly, later, with the benefit of hindsight. In many ways reflective of the liberating changes loosening political and social constraints across Western culture at the time, the field began to break free of the historically limited interpretation of "curriculum," beyond that of a syllabus or static document, to a way of "understanding" (Pinar, 2007; Pinar, Reynolds, Slattery, & Taubman, 1995) educational issues based within the combined historical and social wisdom gathered over an expanse of time (Huebner, 1999). The first half of the 1900s had mired the curriculum field within a pattern of reformist movements, akin to a revolving door that opened upon whatever "next best thing" was deemed appropriate, typically justified in the name of "social control" (Kliebard, 1987). The "ahistorical nature" of the field, according to Herbert Kliebard (1975), was representative of a "lack of dialogue...between present day practitioners... and their professional forebears" (p. 41). He wrote that "issues arise...usually in the form of a bandwagon and then quickly disappear in a cloud of dust.... Sometimes these issues have their counterparts in an earlier period, but this is rarely recognized" (p. 41).

Kliebard and other reconceptualist-era thinkers (Huebner, 1999) pointed to the need for an accurate and intentional sedimentation of the field's history that would counter its "uncritical propensity for novelty and change" (Kliebard, 1975), providing a "funded knowledge or a dialogue across generations" (p. 41). The limited language of Frederick Taylor's (1911) scientific management and Franklin Bobbitt's factory model (1918), "bound the field of the 1900s within a mode of thinking and...limited framework" that narrowed curriculum to a "production model...with efficiency as the criterion for success" (Kliebard, 1970, cited in Pinar, 1975, p. 49). A field that was "clearly more managerial than curricular" in terms of "educational innovation" embedded school life in the language of regimentation (Kliebard, 1987, pp. 94–98).

The call for "alternatives came from reconceptualists, fed up with a strictly 'utilitarian justification' for education policy and curriculum decisions" (Kliebard, 1970, as cited in Pinar, 1975, p. 48). Over time, a case was made for a different sort of curricular language (Huebner, 1999) that would challenge the instrumentalist notions of schooling held in the metaphors of the "platoon" or "industrial efficiency" (Kliebard, 1987), and later, in metaphors of "business" (Wexler, 1996) and of "technology" (Aoki, 1999; Bowers, 1997). Precedents were established for a stable and measured approach to curriculum as a field of study (Huebner, 1966, cited in Pinar et al., 1995), and the meaning of "curriculum" moved from a developmental "how to" model toward an expanded notion of curriculum as "understanding." In their synopsis of the field entitled, simply, *Understanding Curriculum*, Pinar et al. (1995) captured the momentum of the shift when they wrote:

> [t]he field no longer sees the problems of curriculum and teaching as "technical" problems, that is, problems of "how to." The contemporary field regards the problems...as "why" problems.... [T]he view, today, is that solutions to problems do not just require knee-jerk, commonsensical responses, but careful, thoughtful, disciplined understanding. (p. 8)

With this new language of "understanding" came a broadened view of "knowledge," beyond a static immovable repository of facts and truth, to a more actively, pliable and provisional "knowing" based upon contingent factors within a given context. The change has allowed for more embodied forms of knowledge and for a variety of methodological tools open to scholars working to "understand" curriculum, according to what makes sense within their given context and based upon their personal ways of knowing.

As a curriculum theorist, my work attempts to rethink instrumental, Westernized notions of curriculum and challenges a traditional educational emphasis on the "mental/rational domain" to the exclusion of other ways of knowing and making meaning of experience. Reflecting on changes within a reconceptualized field, Bill Schubert recalls (in Marshall, Sears, & Schubert, 2000) that he was first drawn into curriculum by a desire to "share with others the powers of ideas in making sense of one's life" (p. 174). Curriculum theorists work to *make sense* of a wide range of ideas, understandings, and methodologies, including critical, hermeneutic, phenomenological, gender, and postmodern theory toward "understanding" human experience (Pinar et al., 1995). I like the word *sense* for its layered understandings, which include mental/rational ways of knowing as well as incorporating the knowing of the body, the heart, and even the spirit. Such "embodied" ways of knowing are often found within cultural myths or individual stories, situated within a particular place that signifies a larger meaning within that culture or to an individual storyteller. These sorts of stories frequently depict a turning point or an experience that brings some form of understanding that makes it worth passing on to others in the mind of the teller. An experience of this nature could be described as an "opening" onto vistas that were previously closed from view. I know for myself, such "knowing" often comes as a result of some effect in my environment; that is, I see an image or hear a musical strain, or a phrase that turns, just so; it is as if someone had left a window open and a fresh wind blowing through had left me, changed.

I resonate with strands of postmodern thought that have moved the individual "I" out of the center (Smith, 1996) and replaced it with a "relational self" (Gergen, 1999). For me, the latter construct suggests an expansion of human knowing, outward, including— and moving beyond—an "individual I" and recognizing the shifting, composite nature of identity which stands, always, in relation to a given context. Speaking from multiple positions and incorporating personal voice with theory, I find, allows me to problema-tize the taken-for-granted overreliance on mental/rational forms of understanding and "get at" more embodied (Hocking, Haskell, & Linds, 2001; Lakoff & Johnson, 1999) and relational forms of knowing (Riley-Taylor, 2002) wherein my strongest hopes for educa-tion lie.

Spirituality as a Relational and Therefore Ecological Way of Knowing

Relationship is the medium of our lives as human beings. At a cellular level, our bodies take direction from the minutest strands of genetic material, while our lives are struc-tured by the cycles of a distant moon and stars. Every interlocking level of life is imbued with a vitality that connects each pulsing, sensate form (Abrams, 1996). "Ecology" is defined as the network of relations that exists between "organisms and their environ-ment" and also refers to the "relationships between human groups and their physical and social environments" (*American Heritage Dictionary,* 1996). "Spirit" is, from my perspec-tive, the vital force by which all things are connected. When I attempt to speak of spirit, however, I do so carefully—if not reluctantly—so as not to presume that I may know how others conceive of spirit (or if they think of it at all)—for an understanding of spirit is different across geographic zones; it is different across cultures; it is certainly different from one human being to another. I can only speak of spirit, then, in personal terms as a daughter of the 1960s, growing up within an Anglo, middle-income family amidst the traditions and strong bonds of kinship, and also the pretensions and double standards, that characterize "Old South" Mississippi. As with so many other aspects of people's lives, my own perceptions of spirituality may be different from the African-American women with whom I grew up; different, still, from those practiced by the White, bible-belt Chris-tian women who schooled me on Sunday mornings; different, again, from the Navajo, and also, from the Hopi women (Qoyawayma, 1964/1992) whom I have taught, and with whom I've worked, over the last 6 years in a teacher education program at Northern Arizona University. My spiritual views may overlap with some of these perspectives, but, I also understand that human beings' embeddedness within culture, language, and place significantly affects their spiritual understandings.

My own view of "spirit" is not that of a distant spectator, not a being that subsumes par-ticularities into an all-knowing, all-controlling static form. Nor is my own emergent view of spirit that of a "metaphysics of presence" which has dominated Western thinking since the early Greeks (Garrison, 2000), no Platonic "recollection" of what once existed, nor a circling back to retrieve some lost past as an escape into a land of ideal forms that life may only imitate (Wachterhauser, 1986, p. 418). Rather than trying to ground all knowing (or Spirit) into a preexisting structure, my understanding of spirit comes in waves—through some ineffable language of the body, the emotions, the mind. Spirit breathes a fresh wind of renewal and in-spires my own perceptions with a sharpened awareness or an unexpected insight. At these times, I become aware of my own connection within a larger mystery that cannot be contained. I could define spirit as a shifting system of dynamic relations—even while it remains, nonetheless, a *constant* underlying my experience of living. By calling it a "constant," I do not mean to say that it is static for I see spirit, rather, as a space encompassing the both/and; that is, openness *and* closure, fluidity *and* boundedness, mutability *and* structured form (Doll, 1993). I see it as akin to the breathing-out-and-breathing-in of life itself; spirit's "cycles" pull and release, widen and narrow, as an emergence of the present moment. Yet, an understanding of spirit is also embodied within a history of geography and time, the experience of human and land which moves in dialogical interaction increasingly characterized within the current context. As Wexler (2000) characterizes such spirituality by a sense of fluidity, perhaps likened to a "flow… in between place and person…[such that n]either the self nor the environment is inert, reified, or empty of meaning, power, or the history of experience" (p. 136).

Spirit's connection with the land is integral, for me. The word *ecology* embodies my own framework for viewing life as a relational process from which all things arise, and I ground that process within the notion of "Spirit," an unknowable source from which all life emanates and all life is fed. From this perspective, then, life can be seen as an ongoing experience of the sacred and human beings as an integral part of something much larger than the strictly human project. In this way, the relationship that humans share within the earth's ecology is one that is spiritual in nature.

An ecological understanding of curriculum as "embodied," foregrounds how the stories of our lives reveal layers of meaning that can be analyzed and explored. An embodied theory of curriculum draws life from an historical foundation laid down before, to then nourish and inform what will become within a reflexive and dynamic process toward "understanding" (Pinar et al., 1995). Such a theory of curriculum is brought to life—indeed, "lives and breathes"—in and through the discourse, recognizing that any field of study lives in language as a "particular discursive practice, or a form of articulation that follows certain rules and which constructs the very objects [that] it studies" (Pinar et al., 1995, p. 7). An ecological theory of curriculum would construct a more fully aesthetic understanding that expands the limits of language and opens to all of the varied aspects of human capacities to know: the visual, auditory, and olfactory senses, the touching, the tasting, the myriad abilities that can vitalize the knower toward a deeply held *sense of understanding*.

Spirituality and the Language of Curriculum

I am filled with these thoughts as I wander a muddy lip of the drying bed of Mormon Lake, some 25 miles south of Flagstaff. Just ahead about 50 feet, a Great Blue Heron artfully steps the same undulating line where the lakebed center's muddy core gives way to soft, then solid, ground. *The bird freezes.* A single thrusting motion, forward, brings Heron beak to break the water—a quick immersion, beak-into-shallows, then upright, again, guzzling the slick and wiggling prey. Mormon lake is in constant flux. At times, the largest lake in Arizona—while at others, Mormon is virtually no lake at all, just a lowland mudflat, encircled by a field of yellow wildflowers. My lightweight boots grow heavier, now, with a patina of clinging silt, one thin layer upon the next. Feet turn uphill, combing through tangles of feathery amber-green stems, each encased in the tiniest cloak of fuzzy protection, sinewy lengths terminating in the brightest "pop" of yellow petal. My eyes move back toward the lake, distance-painting-land in solid color. I "breathe in" the veritable profusion, so much more than I can say.

If there has been a prevailing condition of *the Spiritual* predating human existence on the planet (and therefore human language), then reducing spirit into words is a difficult task—and, I might add, not always necessary. Still, in justifying the relevance of spiritual language within curriculum discourse and for the benefit of personal exploration arising from spiritual sense-making, there are times one feels compelled to speak. In spite of Spirit's "unspeakability," there are curriculum workers who have drawn spiritual language into the "complicated conversation" that is curriculum (Doll, 2002; Hendry, 1998; Huebner, 1999; Kesson, 2002; MacDonald, 1995; Noddings, 1992; Purpel, 2002; Quinn, 2001; Riley-Taylor, 2002). Notably, from the 1950s on, Dwayne Huebner's (1999) work has increasingly drawn the language of "spirit" in and through his scholarship as embodied in such terms as: *wonder, calling, care, vocation, values, ethics, transcendence, wholeness, meaning, depth,* and the *vital principle.* Huebner notes that the primary association for the word *spirit* is its use within an array of Eastern and Western religious traditions, such as

> Buddhism, Hinduism, Islam, Judaism, Christianity…Native Americans, and the peoples of Africa—[which] all acknowledge the spiritual as an integral aspect of human life. For all of these religious traditions, human beings participate in a spiritual dimension of existence, something more than the material, the sensory, and the quantitative. To speak of the "spirit" and the "spiritual" is not to speak of something "other" than humankind, [but] merely "more" than humankind as it is lived and known. (pp. 342–343)

I resonate with the sense of "spirit" as the "moreness" to which Huebner refers, because it is of *this* world, not another. Within education circles, he says, talk can be "about lived reality, about experience and the possibility of experiencing" (p. 344). Thus, his sense of *moreness* avoids religious traps, while making room for the "unimagined…[and] the possibility of new ways, new knowledge, new relationships, new awareness…indicat[ing] that life is more, or can be more, than the forms in which it is currently lived" (pp. 343–344). The Navajo use of the holistic term *beauty,* or *hozho,* is representative of such spiritual "sense-making" from a framework of lived experience in that it

> refers…to the world when it is flourishing; … to the community, flourishing in the world; … to things we make, which flourish and play a role in the flourishing of other things; and…to ourselves, flourishing as makers, as people inhabiting a community that inhabits a world. It is a word for the oneness of all things when they are joined together… Hozho has many things to teach, but it teaches first that beauty is one thing: everything. (Sartwell, 2004, pp. 135–136)

Beauty as an all-encompassing "relationality" that subsumes all things within its reach, is not, however, an idea that is all sweetness and light. The Navajo way includes, also, the discord, contradictions, and difficulties bound up in the figure of "coyote," the "trickster/demon" and master of chaos and disequilibrium (p. 140). These things, too, are part of *hozho.*

Mapping Geographical Place-Names: Languaging Life

There are human behaviors and political structures and institutions that can lead to dangerous imbalances affecting diverse cultures and forms of life at risk for their survival.

Diversity plays a critical role toward maintaining the health and ecological balance of the planet—not only diversity of plant and animal species, but also diversity of cultures (Shiva, 2000a). Language is one of the "commons" at risk of disappearing with the Western globalizing practices around the world that flatten the world's cultural contours and homogenize human differences.

Languaging is viscerally tied to place, culture, and history. Anthropologist Keith Basso (1996) says that "all views articulated by Apache people are informed by their experience in a culturally constituted world of objects and events with which most of us are unfamiliar" (p. 40). For the Western Apache, "place-making" is a narrative art that combines historical reflection, oral narrative, and mentoring within a process of re-creating the past within the present in order to teach and to share the wisdom of cultural understanding. A place-making event is a form of drama, although it is not a theatrical production. Rather, such an event typically occurs through an artistic form of story-telling. Basso describes his 3-month journey by horseback to create a map of the place names within Western Apache tribal lands at the request of the Tribal chairman. The methods of Apache historians are different from those used by Anglo historians in "documenting" records of the past. Basso says the words of Western scholars lie "silent and inert on the printed English page; it is history without voices to thrust it into the present. Removed from the contexts of daily social life…geographically adrift" (p. 33).

Conversely, the form of Apache place-making is a sort of spoken history, told as if the historical action were taking place in the moment. *The women are gathering their baskets and coming slowly toward the water as the serpent moves away.* Apache people situate the story-telling event in the places where the stories are said to have occurred, but the story is told as if it were happening in the present time. The place-names "hold" the stories as a record of the "community of memory" (Bowers, 1995, p. 149).

Apache place-names are poetic combinations evoking images that directly depict "how a place appears" and "why an event that occurred at a particular time and location is significant." Examples from among the many place-names that the map-makers recorded were:

> They Are Grateful For Water
> She Carries Her Brother on Her Back
> Lizards Dart Away In Front
> Green Rocks Side By Side Jut Down Into Water
> Circular Clearing with Slender Cottonwood Trees

As the group came to each place to be mapped, it's history was "unfolded" from the composites of words, holding sediments of stories, embedded meanings teased open with the "telling" by the native elder. Joseph Campbell (2004) has said that the sociological function of such cultural stories is to suggest to the people how they may live in ways that will sustain the capacity of the tribe to survive. As an anthropologist, Basso (1996) explains that the trends heard in each of the stories are of "disruptive social acts, with everyday life gone out of control…conclud[ing]…with a stark reminder that trouble would not have occurred if people had behaved in ways they knew they should" (p. 28).

Elder Wisdom: A "Commons" across Generations

Languages carry "intergenerational knowledge" that is the basis of a community's traditions of self-sufficiency and systems of mutual support, according to Bowers (2003a, 2003b). Thus, as language is lost, so is a significant portion of the culture itself. It is the end, Bowers (1995) warns, of the "community of memory" of past generations (p. 149). The loss of the "cultural and environmental commons" he describes as the world's cultures and bioregions…[that] have not yet been monetized and brought into the industrial approach to markets…. [The commons represent] sites of resistance to the spread of a world monoculture and to the further spread of poverty to those who lack the means to participate in a money economy. (Bowers, 2005a, pp. 3–4)

The "enclosure of the commons" (Bowers, 2005a, 2005b) is a trend occurring around the world as industrial capitalism expands its reach to "progressively" incorporate into private property, more and more of what was never "owned" before: whether speaking in terms of the appropriation of land that had been the common ground for a village to share, or the ownership of water where water was previously an uncontrolled substance "belonging" to an entire village; or in terms of genetically altered and patented seeds that had previously been grown and saved by farmers over generations of crops and people (Shiva, 2000a, 2000b). Rather than allowing "traditions of knowledge and patterns of mutual support that have enabled communities to be relatively self-sufficient" over time to be eroded by an unquestioning view of "progress," Bowers (1995, 1997, 2001) says we should critically evaluate which traditions contribute to the long-term sustainability of the planet and its life forms, and which do not—so as to conserve those "cultural and environmental commons" that will support the earth's longevity (pp. 3–4). The aim is not to suggest that all traditional knowledge is inherently useful in contributing toward sustainability, nor is it to fetishize or appropriate lifestyles from people who've lived in a different time or place. The point is to save the unique characteristics contained within endangered, cultural ways of knowing for the richness that these forms of diversity offer, certainly, to the cultures in question, and, to the well-being of the planet as a whole. The fallacy that all change and growth is a positive thing is a "traditional belief" that people within industrialized cultures might do well to reconsider.

Habitats in "Common"

My home sits on a ridge a few hundred yards above a municipal golf course running north/south through a section of the small city of Flagstaff. The sky is still dark when I come up the stairs to find Jim in the kitchen making coffee. I stop with a distant sound that comes from outside—a pounding—that is audible, though very faint. Running toward the back sliding glass door I peer out through through the glass into darkness. As my eyes begin to adjust, the moving shapes, below, come into sharp relief. "It's a herd of elk running on the golf course," I call out to Jim who's still in the kitchen, "maybe 10 or 12 of them, mostly females." Reaching for binoculars, I watch the headlights from a few early-dawn commuters as they fly along the highway, not 10 feet from where the herd has now stopped to graze. The cars begin to slow—then stop—edging up to the curb, I guess, to get a better view. Meanwhile, the elk are cautiously grazing on one of the golf course putting greens. In recent years, severe drought conditions have brought record numbers of animal species down out of the forests in search of food and water. In other cases, the development of green space has eliminated habitat for animals that are then left with nowhere to go. Focusing binoculars on the herd, I can see from their stirring that they appear to be alarmed by the attention and proximity of people and cars. With tossing heads and flaring nostrils, the elk quickly break into a run along the highway's edge, a pounding sound of galloping hooves, once more, clearly audible in the morning air. They reach the rise of highway and the pedestrian passage, crossing underneath. As if in one motion, they turn sharply, eastward, through the underpass, and beyond, to the steep incline taking them to the Ponderosa forest ridge, above.

The idea that growth moves forward in a linear direction that is, by its nature, for the "good" is a common fallacy underlying mainstream Western thought and embodied in the metaphor of *Progress*. Metaphors are the conceptual building blocks (Lakoff & Johnson, 1980, 1999) that structure human thinking into narrow frameworks limited within a "network of cultural presuppositions" (Lakoff & Johnson, 1980, p. 57). You might say that these concepts "think us," rather than the other way around because they limit what we think within preordered constraints, so that some things come into focus, while others fade from view. So, these "assumptions, values, and attitudes" (p. 57) are laid down over our experiences as we live them. Lakoff and Johnson (1980) say that metaphorical meaning-making is not "a conceptual overlay which we may or may not place upon experience as we choose" (p. 57), but that meanings are made within the conceptual constraints that are imposed by the metaphorical constructions in which we think and move and act. In this way, experience is shaped by the language in which we live. For example, take the *Life as a Relational Process* metaphor:

I view the land as a relational system—one with which I feel a visceral connection. It is the land from which we arise, and the land upon which we grow into relationships, both at an intrapersonal level and at the level of social relations. The land sustains humans' most basic needs of food and water, air and shelter; the land offers us life. As with all living things upon it, the land lives within cycles at every level and dimension: cycles of the sun, the moon, the stars; cycles of wind and drying heat; cycles of moisture, summer monsoon and winter snow filling up aquifers and deep water wells, drawing the elk, the coyote, the humans, all drawn by the life-giving substance of water. Humans, too, move through their lives from start to finish within relational cycles. From the beginning of life, born of the mystery that begets all living forms, human lives are lived in process; they unfold in "cascades" (Wilson, 1984, p. 115) that emanate from "early childhood… into cultural and social patterns" (Orr, 2004, p. 138) of giving and receiving, a reciprocity of relations imbuing networks with meaning. Across all sentient forms upon the Earth, "Life," itself, is the common bond: life as an energy animating all things; life as relationality connecting within a shifting, dynamic network that signifies at every confluence of factors; life as circulating forces entangled within a giving and receiving, a gaining and a losing, light and shadow's symbiotic play of reciprocal relations.

A metaphor such as *life as a relational process* foregrounds some things as important while diminishing others. My metaphors shape the ways I am able to think and categorize experience into understandings that are meaningful to me. For example, what of all of the categories of phenomenon that relational metaphors block from sight? I hold that there is beauty in the relationality of life; does not this notion embody, also, a darkly abiding despair? Relational metaphors such as those above have been used to suggest a planetary vision of a "relational system" (e.g., *earth as an organic body*) within which those living upon it may contribute to its long-term well-being and be nourished, in return. However, the *earth as an organic body* metaphor also provides a conceptual framework to, then, imagine that it is "reasonable" for the overall "body" of the system to eliminate those aspects considered harmful or which are not in its "best interests." Relational frameworks have been used to "rationalize" the concept of a "unified master race" that fueled the horror of the Holocaust in 20th century Nazi Germany or the "human cleansing" practiced within certain totalitarian regimes up through history to contemporary times.

Relational and process epistemologies are relevant for this discussion because they are my own first principles. But regardless of the metaphors I use, I have come to know that it is critical to unpack the assumptions that underlie one's language (Kohli, 1995; Munro, 1998), and especially those ideas that one holds, dear. When "knowing" becomes hardened into categories and institutionalized into systems of control, it becomes dangerous. In the case of spiritual beliefs, the danger of such assumptions is when they're institutionalized into concrete forms and "rationalized" so to impose control by those with power over those without. The 17th century Enlightenment-inspired migration of people from Europe to the "new Americas" was to escape precisely such oppression. If institutionalized by systems of power, certain contemporary forms of right-wing Christian politics that today threaten the freedoms of democracy, could be another example. That which we take for granted becomes like "law," entrenched and seldom questioned—and, therefore, dangerous.

Instances of Opening: An Ecology of Living and Other Stories

Curriculum studies has come to embody a wide range of possibilities for understanding curriculum as a multilayered, indeed, many-storied field that is rife with diversity. I don't mean to suggest that those of us working in curriculum are now living the "happy story"; but, I *am* suggesting that we are in a better position to deal with the many complex issues that we face *because* of the changes that a "reconceptualized" field has brought. A widened view of knowledge as contingent and contextual has embodied curriculum within the power of "story"—stories of significance, stories that embody the knowledge that a generation has held as "worthy to pass on" to those who come next. A reconceptualized curriculum field has become increasingly aware of the critical nature of its own intergenerational knowledge in widening, deepening, and complexifying the "complicated conversation" that has redefined the domain (Pinar, 2007). Within cycles of human cultures, the knowledge of the culture's lifeways is passed on, embodied and shared through language. Such understanding is rethought and interpreted, anew, as a past within the context of present time and lived worlds. In this way, knowledge is made significant in the place and time within which it is "present-ed" (as a *verb*, i.e., it is made "present") for the living. With each new iteration, what is passed on is changed somehow, imbued with the tenor of the times. There is always those understandings which seem to "hold," withstanding time's passage to remain relevant and vital. These are elements which come to be understood for ways that they nourish and sustain a healthy, living world.

I conceive of an ecology of living in at least two layers: (1) at a personal level, that is, as a pursuit of self-awareness; and (2) how the "self" stands in relationship to "place," that is, to the environmental world that makes up the physical context and the social web that immerses each person. Relationship to place can be seen differently by different people. David Orr (2004) says that "we learn to love [what is] familiar...to bond with what we know well" (p. 137). He points out that sometimes "prisoners...prefer their jail cells to freedom; city dwellers...shun rural landscapes or wilderness; and rural folk...will not set foot in the city" (p. 137).

Thus, an ecological perspective is not synonymous with environmental advocacy. Instead, such a framework would aim to recognize the relationality of all life, which includes not only unity but also diversity. It would resist an attitude that one size could ever be appropriate for all. An ecological framework (Berry, 2000) would take into account that thinking and decision making must occur in the local places, with particular people in particular circumstances—and that struggles may always occur, yet again. Critical postmodern thought has foregrounded the "messiness" that necessarily exists within a diverse and complex world. An ecology of living would acknowledge that there are times when all cannot be controlled and when that which can be known is only that uncertainty exists; that there are times when truth must be recognized in terms of its pluralities, provisional truths that are relative to one context, the scale of a particular circumstance, time, or place. These are times when I am called to widen, that is, to be willing to open so to understand from a different angle or to step into another pair of shoes. I might describe such a "turn" as an "instance of opening" to widen, to include, to broaden my own capacities for understanding, and to incorporate ways of knowing that I might not typically access. I am reminded of Jim Garrison's (2000) statement when he says that "the moment we approach any philosophical notion no longer by thinking to refute it but by asking how it can be said, the ground shifts beneath the traditional arguments" (p. 2). Such shifting ground may unexpected offer an emergence of an "instance of opening" across contradictory positions; that is, a widening to try and understand both sides, perhaps agree to disagree, thus allowing for the contradiction—a both/and equilibration.

An ecology of living would resist a set pattern, method, or means of control—but is, rather, a partial vision of contours, elements that would be critical to include from my own view. Certainly, it would require recognition of the complex ways that linguistic structures "have us" rather than the other way around (Bowers, 1995; Foucault, 1979; Lakoff & Johnson, 1999), and so it would call for a willingness to listen and for the critical abilities to unpack the hidden assumptions structuring any encounter of communication (Bloom & Munro, 1996; Kohli, 1995). It could require the skillful mediation of a person with a critical understanding of ways to establish forums wherein effective dialogical exchanges may more genuinely occur. Meanwhile, the social inequities of power relations and differential ways of knowing and communicating must be considered and accounted for (Foucault, 1979). Moreover, it requires a broader perspective than one centered solely on the "individual," but a way of knowing that accounts for the reality that people-are-nested-within-cultures-are-nested-within-environments (Jardine, 2000); thus, it necessitates an ecologically informed way of knowing that will "meet the test of not destroying the habitat[s]" around the world that all living things need to survive (Bowers, 1995, p. 131). An ecology of living could be a metaphor for making sense of our lives. Huebner's (1999) notion of *moreness* comes to mind. A far cry from the Western metaphor of Progress—not more material goods, more prestige, more power, but the life-affirming framework of Huebner's "moreness" suggests that as long as there is life, there are possibilities for change, for renewal, for bringing a world into balance. There is no end to *horizons of the possible*, recognizing that each path is unique and brings with it differing material and social conditions. There is an element of choice, perhaps, but choice is always mediated by internal and external worlds. The "happy story" is, in reality, a "complicated conversation" (Pinar, 2007)—even an arduous journey—that we must try and be willing to make, once more, yet again, in the spirit of "understanding" and of "openings" onto new and possible worlds—may it soon be usefully so.

References

Abrams, D. (1996). *The spell of the sensuous: Perception and language in a more-than-human world.* New York: Vintage.

Aoki, T. (1999). Toward understanding "computer application." In W. F. Pinar (Ed.), *Contemporary curriculum discourses: Twenty years of JCT* (pp. 168–176). New York: Lang.

Basso, K. H. (1996). *Wisdom sits in places: Landscape and language among the Western Apache.* Albuquerque: University of New Mexico Press.

Berry, W. (2000). *Life is a miracle: An essay against modern superstition.* Washington, DC: Counterpoint.

Bloom, L. A., & P. Munro (1996). Conflicts of selves: Nonunitary subjectivity in women administrators; life history narratives. In J. A. Hatch & R. Wisniewski (Eds.), *Life history and narrative* (pp. 99–112). London: Falmer.

Bobbitt, F. (1918). *The curriculum.* Boston: Houghton Mifflin.

Bowers, C. A. (1995). *Educating for an ecologically sustainable culture: Re-thinking moral education, creativity, intelligence, and other modern orthodoxies.* Albany, NY: SUNY Press.

Bowers, C. A. (1997a). *The culture of denial: Why the environmental movement needs a strategy for reform-ing universities and public schools*. Albany, NY: SUNY Press.

Bowers, C. A. (1997b). *Let them eat data: How computers affect education, cultural diversity, and the pros-pects of ecological sustainability*. Athens: University of Georgia Press.

Bowers, C. A. (2001). *Educating for eco-justice and community*. Athens: University of Georgia Press.

Bowers, C. A. (2003a). Revitalizing the commons or an individualized approach to planetary citi-zenship: The choice before us. Retrieved March 23, 2007, from http://www.c-a-bowers.com/

Bowers, C. A. (2003b). *Mindful conservatism: Rethinking the ideological and educational basis of an eco-logically sustainable future*. Lanham, MD: Rowman & Littlefield.

Bowers, C. A. (2005a). Educating for a sustainable future: Mediating between the commons and economic globalization. Retrieved March 23, 2007, from http://www.c-a-bowers.com/

Bowers, C. A. (2005b). Educational reforms that contribute to ecojustice and the revitalization of the commons. Retrieved March 23, 2007 from http://www.c-a-bowers.com/

Bowers, C. A. (n.d.). Some thoughts on the misuse of our political language. Retrieved December 31, 2007, from http://www.c-a-bowers.com/

Butterfield, S. (1994). *Black autobiography in America*. Amherst: University of Massachusetts.

Campbell, J. (2004). *Pathways to bliss: Mythology and personal transformation*. Novato, CA: New World.

Doll, W. (1993). *A post-modern perspective on curriculum*. New York: Teachers College Press.

Doll, W. (2002). Struggles with spirituality. In T. Oldenski & D. Carlson (Eds.), *Educational yearn-ing: The journey of the spirit and democratic education* (pp. 10–21). New York: Lang.

Foucault, M. (1979). *Discipline and punish: The birth of the prison*. New York: Random House.

Garrison, J. (2000). Dewey after Derrida. In V. Richardson (Ed.), *Handbook of research on teaching* (4th ed., pp. 69–81). New York: Macmillan.

Gergen, K. J. (1999). *An invitation to social construction*. London: Sage.

Grumet, M. R. (1980). Autobiography and reconceptualization. In W. F. Pinar (Ed.), *Contemporary curriculum discourses: Twenty years of JCT Counterpoints* (No. 70). New York: Lang.

Hendry, P. M. (1998). *Subject to fiction: Women teachers: Life history narratives and the cultural politics of resistance*. Buckingham, England: Open University Press.

Hendry, P. M. (2005, Spring). Disrupting the subject: Julian of Norwich and embodied knowing. *Journal of Curriculum Theorizing, 21*(1), 95–108.

Hocking, B., Haskell, J., & Linds, W. (Eds.). (2001). *Unfolding bodymind: Exploring possibility through education*. Brandon, VT: Foundation for Educational Renewal.

Huebner, D. (1966). Curriculum as a field of study. In H. Robison (Ed.), *Precedents and promise in the curriculum field* (pp. 94–112). New York: Teachers College Press.

Huebner, D. (1999). *The lure of the transcendent*. Mahwah, NJ: Erlbaum.

Jardine, D. W. (2000). *Under the tough old stars: Ecopedagogical essays*. Brandon, VT: Foundation for Educational Renewal.

Kesson, K. (2002). Tantra: The quest for the ecstatic mind. In Jack Miller (Ed.), *Nurturing our wholeness* (pp. 30-47). Brandon, VT: Foundation for Educational Renewal.

Kliebard, H. M. (1975). Persistent curriculum issues in historical perspective. In W. F. Pinar (Ed.), *Curriculum theorizing* (pp. 39–50). Berkeley, CA: McCutchan.

Kliebard, H. M. (1987). *The struggle for the American curriculum, 1893–1958*. New York: Routledge.

Kohli, W. (1995). Educating for emancipatory rationality. In W. Kohli (Ed.), *Critical conversations in philosophy of education* (pp. 103–115). New York: Routledge.

Lakoff, G., & Johnson, M. (1980). *Metaphors we live by*. Chicago: University of Chicago Press.

Lakoff, G., & Johnson, M. (1999). *Philosophy in the flesh: The embodied mind and its challenge to Western thought*. New York: Basic Books.

Macdonald, B.J. (Ed.). (1995). *Theory as a prayerful act: The collected essays of James B. Macdonald*. New York: Lang.

Marshall, J. D., Sears, J. T., & W. H. Schubert. (2000). *Turning points in curriculum: A contemporary American memoir*. Upper Saddle River, NJ: Merrill.

Miller, J. (1997, March). *Un-telling teachers' stories as curriculum history*. Paper presented at the Amer-ican Educational Research Association Conference, New York.

Noddings, N. (1992). *The challenge to care in schools: An alternative approach to education.* New York: Teachers College Press.

Orr, D. W. (2004). *Earth in mind: On education, environment, and the human prospect.* Washington, DC: Island Press.

Pinar, W. F. (1975). *Curriculum theorizing.* Berkeley, CA: McCutchan.

Pinar, W. F. (2007, May). *Crisis, reconceptualization, internationalization: U.S. curriculum theory since 1950.* Paper presented at East China Normal University, Shanghai.

Pinar, W. F., & Grumet, M. R. (1976). *Toward a poor curriculum.* Dubuque, IA: Kendall/Hunt.

Pinar, W. F., Reynolds, W. M., Slattery, P., & Taubman, P. M. (1995). *Understanding curriculum: An introduction to the study of historical and contemporary curriculum discourses.* New York: Lang.

Purpel, D. (2002). Social justice, curriculum, and spirituality. In T. Oldenski & D. Carlson (Eds.), *Educational yearning: The journey of the spirit and democratic education* (pp. 86–102). New York: Lang.

Qoyawayma, P. (1992). *No turning back: A Hopi woman's struggle to live in two worlds.* Albuquerque: University of New Mexico Press. (Original work published 1964)

Quinn, M. (2001). *Going out, not knowing whither.* New York: Lang.

Riley-Taylor, E. (2002). *Ecology, spirituality, and education: Curriculum for relational knowing.* New York: Lang.

Sartwell, C. (2004). *Six names of beauty.* New York: Routledge.

Shiva, V. (2000a). *Tomorrow's biodiversity.* New York: Thames & Hudson.

Shiva, V. (2000b). *Stolen harvest: The hijacking of the global food supply.* Cambridge, MA: South End Press.

Smith, D. G. (1996). Identity, self, and other in the conduct of pedagogical action: An East/West inquiry. In W. F. Pinar (Ed.), *Contemporary curriculum discourses: Twenty years of JCT* (pp. 458–473). *Counterpoints* (No. 70). New York: Lang.

Soukhanov, A.H. (Ed.). (1996). *American heritage dictionary of the English language* (3rd ed.). Boston: Houghton Mifflin.

Spretnak, C. (1997). *Resurgence of the real: Body, nature, and place in a hypermodern world.* New York: Addison-Wesley.

Taylor, F.W. (1934/1911). *The principles of scientific management.* New York: Harper.

Wachterhauser, B.R. (1986). *Hermeneutics and modern philosophy.* Albany, NY: SUNY Press.

Wexler, P. (1996). *Holy sparks.* New York: St. Martin's Press.

Wexler, P. (2000). *Mystical society: An emerging social vision.* Boulder, CO: Westview.

Wilson, E.O. (1984). *Biophilia.* Cambridge: Harvard University Press.

Suggested Reading Questions

1. How has the language of reconceptualization marked a decisive shift from utilitarian and business efficiency to understanding curriculum as personal and embodied forms of knowing?

2. According to the author, relational forms of knowing and an embodied curriculum connect knowledge of self to spiritual sense-making. How might such an autobiographical exploration open up curriculum to the language of spirituality and of place?

3. The notion of place-making is described by the author as a combination of historical reflection, oral narrative, and mentoring. In what way might these contribute to our understanding of teaching and learning as a shared, intergenerational flow of ideas?

4. What might be some of the forms of knowing that the author considers hardened oppressive categories and institutionalized systems of control that have been formed and shaped by the discourse on unity and rationality?

5. The author states that curriculum can be understood as a multilayered, many-storied, diverse field. What implications might this have for a curriculum that is sensitive, contextual and multicultural?

Response to Elaine Riley-Taylor
A Poetics of Place
In Praise of Random Beauty

Celeste Snowber

> The same stream of life that runs through my
> veins night and day runs through the world
> and dances in rhythmic measures.
>
> —Tagore, 1997, p. 87

Blue gray waves ebb and flow in a rhythm, which underlies each moment at the Peruvian coast where I stay on sabbatical for a few weeks. Pounding waves tussle rocks of all sizes into a symphony of crashing and clapping—stone to stone. I am startled; my senses alive as I return to creation's lullaby. The ocean may change the location of rocks, stones, seaweed, shells, wood, but it is a life-giving force, steady and sure that all is encompassed within. In this ecology of wonder I am once again drawn into humus and humility, connected to what gives life. Elaine Riley-Taylor gives us life at every turn, where we are arrested once again to know that it is from the landscape of creation where our words flow. Language is rooted in the senses, the senses and lifeblood of the body (Abram, 1996; Snowber, 2002) Not only though our words, but in our actions and our lives she beckons the reader to hear, see, smell, and touch the place where ecology and curriculum meet, but also more than anything, we are beckoned to beauty. In this beauty we are asked to be connected to all things, creation and ourselves. And in this place there are layers of meaning waiting to be unfolded.

I can only respond with a language, which has an intimate connection to the land and sea, where a poetics of place inhabits the life world. I respond in language which roots back to the earth, where poetics is a way of theorizing (Leggo, 2001, 2006; Snowber, 2005). Riley-Taylor has given us a solid background of theorists who have opened up ways of thinking that honor relations of place. My response is to continue that conversation by an invitation to the idea of random beauty as an ecological place to listen; to reconnect to the voice within and the landscape without. Elaine reminds us that the Navajo use of the term *beauty* or *hozho* as representative of a spiritual "sense-making," and one of the first things that *hozho* has to teach us is beauty is everything. I am caught by this concept, because Riley-Taylor's work is imbued with beauty and provocation, inviting us into a deep connection with self, other, and the natural world. Beauty, of course, can be dissonant. Beauty has a transforming presence as writer, John O'Donohue says, "True beauty can emerge at the most vigorous threshold where the oppositions in life confront and engage each other" (2005, p. 19). Beauty has the capacity to stop us at the shore of our own lives and is caught in the swell of the wave.

Random Beauty

Breath stops
in the rush of wind
I stroll creation's canvas
rugged coast in aching light

I release
in the weight
of a lover's arms
I lilt in the face of sea
you sweep bits and
pieces of beach life

Black stones, smoothened shapes
darkened ovals, misshapen hearts,
circles half broken, feathers cut,
wood split, pebbles scattered,
shells: blue, beige and brown,
sculpted nature's icons into
sand art, a visual feast.
As if placed by a gentle hand,
a skilled artist
you perch each object
in the elbow of sand.

Subtle designs
abound on the edge of air's
force, ferocious velocity
carves an intricate pattern,
of random beauty

Collage of Our Own Lives

There is a complete randomness in the sea objects or sea jewels on the beach, as I would call them. There is no particular pattern to their placement, as there is no particular pattern to the sky, which shifts from one moment to another. It is a random beauty and yet there is an order of the spectacular to this particular place. There is science here, reasons why each piece of sea life has transformed into something else, there is a rational to the weather and shifting wave patterns. I am awed by the physics of waves, but tangibly awed by physical beauty. There is both order and chaos in this beauty. I must ask the questions in the lived curriculum, where is the call to beauty, where is the order, where is the chaos? How do they interconnect, play and be/long together and ultimately transform us?

In the midst of the throws of my own life, both my teaching/academic life and personal life, I find it difficult to notice the beauty of it all, or the patterns and shapes, which I might really cherish. I am too close. We all live too close to our lives, and it is often only in retrospect, sometimes years later when we begin to live in gratitude for what has been, and ultimately to what is. Increasingly, as I age, I think I have less and less perspective on what is really reality. I don't see the whole collage. I only see the fragments, threads, notes, and this is where I often become overwhelmed. How can I stand back from my own life and see the collage of fragrances and textures, hues and colors that permeate the whole? How can I find ways to not get seduced by the parts? When I walk the beach laced with pebbles, seaweed, pieces of the sea I gaze at the wonder of both the whole and the parts. I pick a stone or worn sea glass and roll them in my hand and delight in the sounds. The clumps of beach debris are living art formed in random ways, which echoes the work of an artist. And each singular stone cries out its extravagance. Stones deep to bone.

Sky Deep to Bone

sky deep to bone
thick with light
earth poised to feet
parse my heart

stone close to sea
amber bleeding tree
sun on fraying wood
conjugate my torso

My desire is to see all those pieces of the lifeworld as part of the complex, wonderful, outrageous random beauty of a life well lived. This to me is a "living in gratitude" for what is. To *be* with what is. I am not always here; I live in the longing for gratitude, the longing to be with what is. Loving what is, as a lover, with both the quirks and things that annoy me, and the things that make me wildly over the edge. They are all true. And this too is an ecology of place.

Teachers of Random Beauty

I sit on the edge of stone, soaked and molded by the force of waves. Here I break into the moment. Fresh beige laces the heart, the smell of seaweed and salt sit on skin, and all moments are held in this one, just looking—just seeing, smelling, hearing the ocean's notes. They be/hold me in an embrace, one where time stops, the tyranny of details to be accomplished and flesh once again drinks in wonder. The ocean's pedagogy is to turn to w(one)der, the one of creation, which halts one into an aesthetic arrest, but an arrest of motion. To be arrested into motion, the motion of waves, the motion of the heart, the motion of the blood.

Ocean's edge teaches me the beauty of randomness. Like no other landscapes, the borders of the sea with all its natural jewels—clam and oyster shells, pieces of seaweed, weathered sea glass, stones of all shapes and textures, wood caressed by time, of salt. They hearken me to drop into a timelessness where I could collect and pick beauty for hours and be deeply happy. The patterns are exquisite and here the artist is the ocean, the form: tussling of objects to a new arrangement. The ocean's edge has become my teacher. I listen for her beauty. I have come to need it as nutrients for my soul, vitamins for my body. At the ocean, I go on foot with the body, and words emerge from this bodily connection. I am reminded of the philosopher Hélène Cixous saying, "writing is not arriving; most of the time it's not arriving. One must go on foot with the body" (1993, p. 65). In the simple act of walking its torso, picking and releasing its sea jewels, I am restored, recentered to remember what matters. For all the plans I have, and many of us have, they often go awry, and yet the profound beauty of a life is what happens when the plans don't work, when we are once again jolted by surprise. The sea edge teaches me once again to accept, make peace with the experiences and events happening in my life and in others, even if I don't understand with my visible eye. She unfolds the invisible to me through the visible. Is this not what art does? Is this not what living a creative life is? Is this not curricular practice and ultimately an ecology of living?

To Let Light Be

> unending hours
> silence falls
> in the heart
> and one smells
> the scent of home
>
> lavender is the treasure
> admist greens:
>   kelly and olive
> beneath browns:
>   amber & chocolate
> white, clear & beige
>
> jeweled fragments
> shards of weathered
> glass off/on
> shores, high/low
> inter/intra tidal
> waters, ferry swept—
> they gather on edges
> of pebbles and mud
> cobbles and sand
>
> cobalt blue cries
> out boldly in morning
> light, a new
> crop of glass has
> been thrown by
> transitions from
> the sea to
> beach
>
> one wonders the
> story behind each
> piece: the age, the
> hand that carried
> or drank from its lip
> A word is
> behind/beyond
> each fragment
> ruins of luminescence
> to let light be.

When I smell seaweed it has the scent of home, familiarity, somewhat like comfort food, permeating my cells—I feel alive. I grew up with seaweed, salt water, and jagged rocks on the New England coast in a small peninsula town, where one was never far from the Atlantic. The back rocks near my house were my playground, and my sanctuary where I learned the first lessons in dropping down and listening to the sea. It was the school for reflective practitioners. No book or curriculum could have beaten the daily lessons, which included withstanding storms, hurricanes, and moods of tides. One never knew what to expect, the weather was a canvas onto which each day would unfold its beauty and purpose. Life was abundant in each fragment and shift of temperature and color. One could wear the appropriate clothing, but there were so many changes, one really never knew.

I feel just as at home in the university classroom. I enter and know I am home, not knowing what I will find day to day, or what climate or temperature will emerge, but it is a place of home, a place of salt, where I am keenly alive, and become more alive to myself, to others, and to the curiosities and wonder we will fish for together. My task is not different than at the edge of the sea: listen, look, and be. And from here, I will know how to continue to open up the space, which nourishes all of us, the place where magic lies. The classroom is as much as a sacred place as the ocean, another fierce landscape that has its own story, waiting to be read, told, and retold.

The ecology that Riley-Taylor presents to us is far more than an ecology of the land, but one of the spirit, body and he/art. It is an ecology of relationality to all living. She beautifully lays this out as she draws on relational and process epistemologies, but more so she calls us to attention through beauty. And in this, both this chapter and her work on ecological education (2002), models what O'Donohue says: "Beauty is not just a call to growth, it is a transforming presence wherein we unfold towards growth almost before we realize it" (p. 8).

I keep dwelling in an interplay of invisible and visible. Another life is at work continually, the undercurrent of a voice which cries out in a gentle whisper, "listen to the wind," "smell the moist rain," "praise the laughter," "have your tears—for they are your prayers." The small wonders are the gourmet meal of the curriculum of life, waiting and wooing us to its table. A table which calls forth playing in the food of random beauty. May we dine, eat, and drink from the juice of delights.

References

Abram, D. (1996). *The spell of the sensuous: Perception and language in a more-than-human world*. New York: Vintage.

Cixous, H. (1993). *Three steps on the ladder of writing*. New York: Columbia University Press.

Leggo, C. (2001). Research as poetic rumination: Twenty-six ways of listening to light. In L. Neilsen, A. Cole, & J. G. Knowles (Eds.), *The art of writing inquiry* (pp. 173–195). Halifax: Backalong Books.

Leggo, C. (2006). Attending to winter: A poetics of research. In W. Ashton & D. Denton (Eds.), *Spirituality, ethnography, and teaching: Stories from within* (pp. 140–155). New York: Lang.

O'Donohue J. (2005). *Beauty: The invisible embrace*. San Francisco: HarperCollins/Perennial.

Riley-Taylor, E. (2002). *Ecology, spirituality, and education: Curriculum for relational knowing*. New York: Lang.

Snowber, C. (2002). Bodydance: Fleshing soulful inquiry through improvisation. In C. Bagley & M. B. Cancienne (Eds.), *Dancing the data* (pp. 20–33). New York: Lang.

Snowber, C. (2005, December). The mentor as artist: a poetic exploration of listening, creating, and mentoring. *Mentoring and tutoring: Partnership in learning, 13*(3), 345–353.

Tagore, R. (1997). *A collection of Indian poems by the Nobel Laureate Rabindranath Tagore Gitanjali*. New York: Scribner. (Original work published 1913)

15 Thinking Through Scale
Critical Geography and Curriculum Spaces

Robert J. Helfenbein

Chapter Overview

This chapter is focused on the relationship between critical geography and curriculum studies. The author discusses the ways in which three lenses—spaces that speak, spaces that leak, and spaces of possibility—might extend curriculum theory by way of new language and additional conceptual tools. The author then explores the historical development of critical geography as a subset of the field of geography. Critical geographers are interested in space, place, power, and identity, the author notes. Working with spatial analyses the author explores what these concepts might mean for the study of the lived experiences of children, parents, and teachers. He concludes with a description of how the relationship between subjectivity and space and the fluid character of social and spatial products as illuminated by critical geography might inform the field of curriculum studies.

> I have become convinced both that the implicit assumptions we make about space are important and that, maybe, it could be productive to think about space differently. (Massey, 2005, p. 1)

This chapter explores the conjuncture between new scholarship in geography—known as critical geography—and curriculum theorizing. The hope here resides in extending the always already "complicated conversation" that is curriculum theory and by exploring the themes, theories, and analysis of another field new insights might come to light. As feminist geographer Doreen Massey offers in the epigraph, thinking about space differently and interrogating our spatial assumptions could be productive. The question at the root of this chapter revolves around not just acknowledging the importance of the spatial in schooling but attempting to think about those school spaces differently. A critical geography insists on multiple scales of analysis, a sliding scale, and this capability of theorizing on scales from the body to global capital and back again offers curriculum theory a new analytic lens. This is a theoretical journey, so the bulk of the piece is in connecting ideas and not in the specifics of research methods. However, another study done in the urban school district of Indianapolis, Indiana is offered in part as an exemplar of the application of this theorizing to research (see Helfenbein & Gonzalez-Velez, 2005).

> I have come a long way to tell you a story—
> it is a story of a finger and an eye.

John Pickles begins his book *A History of Spaces: Cartographic Reason, Mapping and the Geo-Coded World* (2004, p. 3) with this quote from renowned geographer Gunnar Olsson. Olsson's point is that the work of geography is to draw attention to, to draw a line. But of equal importance in this dramatic reduction is the way in which both finger and eye indicate subjective positions—*my* finger points; your eye perceives. Bodies, positions, perception, lenses all come into play in this geography, this way of mapping and of making meaning of maps. This type of *critical geography* concerns itself then with identities and difference, borders and borderlands, reproduction and resistance, the global and the local; but, to be considered critical, it does all this at once—it is the geography of the "yes, and" opposed to the "either, or." It is a geography of the lived experience of subjects, or, as appropriate here, in looking toward new possibilities in the study of curriculum, the lived experience of schools.

To introduce this chapter, I suggest that the lens of critical geography provides for three things in these extensions of the curriculum theory map: (1) spaces that speak; (2) spaces that leak; and (3) spaces of possibility. It may be that the only maps I can draw are maps of possibility (Helfenbein, 2004) but it is with sincerity that I suggest that students and teachers continue to finds ways to negotiate the structures of high school, perhaps "work around reproduction" and not only come to resistance, but resilience. Curriculum theorizing, as in a broader social theory, has indeed taken up a series of spatial metaphors to assist in thinking through subjectivity, identity, and transgression (see Cary, 2006; Kincheloe & Pinar, 1991; Whitlock, 2007). The significance of a geographic term like *place* and its import epistemologically resonates through the work of the reconceptualists. A critical geography offers this already productive tradition some new language, some new tools; the finger points.

For the sake of clarity, however, definitions and intersections offer a starting point and, in the spirit of praxis, provide an exemplar of an analysis informed by critical geography. The methodology employed in the example study (Helfenbein & Gonzalez-Velez, 2005) takes its lead from the subset of critical geography known as multiscalar analysis (or often, simply scalar geography). Briefly, as the review of critical geography theory affirms this approach, scalar geography rejects the notion of single scale representations of the social in favor of overlapping analyses of forces at multiple scales, all simultaneously "at work." Returning to geographer John Pickles (2004), the importance of a scalar geography is in "comparing maps of a region or country and recognizing the remarkable diversity among them [that] illustrates the importance of understanding that 'these spaces are produced'" (p. 96) and, if you will, the impossibility of representation. How many maps would it take to be true? The wrong question to be sure as in recognizing this impossibility points us to seek the multiplicity and rethink the set of maps we rely on. This too, is a geography of "yes, and" as maps themselves and the choices of mapmakers limit one's sense of the complexities of moments and spaces.

Critical Geography

One might begin an exploration like this one with the question of what makes a geography *critical*. Geography work, like every contemporary field, holds centers and margins and as theoretical directions emerge and expand, scholars take up those directions and apply them to the work of thinking through space and scale. The margins of geography began with a critique of positivism using existentialism and phenomenology and started to infuse questions of identity, difference, and the self into spatial analysis (Tuan, 1977). Feminist and Marxist geographies also emerged, highlighting the production of gendered and capitalist spaces respectively. Place became a concept for theorizing and the sense of a close, lived, bounded nature was challenged by pointed to how places are situated within and impacted by complex arrays of forces. For feminist geographers— most notably Doreen Massey—"place is a locus of complex intersections and outcomes of power geometries that operate across many spatial scales, from the body to the global" (see Hubbard, Kitchen, & Valentine, 2004). As these and other epistemologies moved through the "posts" a small group of geographers influenced by the work of cultural studies via Birmingham began to coalesce. This coalescence is often (and incidentally often not) referred to as critical geography and critical geography refuses to think of the "either, or" of traditional geographies (and theorizing) but rather insists on the "yes, and" of what is being called both the "next moment" and the "poststate."

So, then, to take up critical geography as a theoretical framework means to be concerned with the interrelationships of space, place, power, and identity (Allen, 2003; Harvey, 2001; Massey & Jess, 1995; Soja, 1989, 1996). Geographers have long been interested in the concepts of space and place—in fact, geography curricula often begin (and sadly end) with these as two of the Five Themes of Geography (Segal & Helfenbein, 2008)—but the critical distinction comes in the analyses of the relationships, intersections, and conjunctures between the two and in coming to postmodern analyses of how both operate with/in fields of power and work on/in identity formation. For geographers, place is the localized community—filled with meaning for those that spend time there. Quite simply, it has significance; however temporally and however interrelatedly with time itself, it has significance. This is not to say, however, that places are in any way prepolitical, utopian, or transcendent of social forces for indeed places are particularities wrapped up a myriad of relations. Forces of economic, social, and cultural practices work on both the inhabitants of the place and work to form the place itself. Space constructed through discursive, interpretive, lived, and imagined practices becomes place (de Certeau, 1984; Soja, 1996). Place, in this conceptual form, must be seen as only possible in the interactions that constitute it.

Much of critical geography has been a response to and a call for analysis of the changing relationships between space and place in late capitalism and the globalized condition (Allen, 2003; Breitbart, 1998; Harvey, 2001; Massey & Jess, 1995; Soja, 1989, 1996). Globalization itself is a spatial term wrapped up in all the complexities of economy, sovereignty, and hybridity. How *place* relates to an increasingly globalized *space* forms a point of departure for analysis of economic relations, democracy, and identity. These larger cultural forces all involve manifestations of power in the social realm and work on both people and places in multiple and fluid ways. Mapping those relations of power remains a central axis to the work of critical geographers and holds the affinitive connection between the field and the complementary work of critical theory and cultural studies (in fact, these fields share and exchange foundational writers such as Marx, Lefebvre, and Foucault). Some writers argue that coming to articulate the conditions of power and its effects on lived society are not only academic trajectories but a central part of the moral obligation of all social scientists and specifically, the geographer (Harvey, 2001; Soja, 1989).

An important object of analysis in critical geography and indeed broader social theory is the border and its changing nature in a globalized space. In traditional geographic study borders play a major role in coming to understand place and politic. In geography education, for example, outline maps and continents or states made of felt come to mind. However, in this new theoretical trajectory—spatial metaphor itself—of critical geography, borders and boundaries are troubled, crossed, and complicated. Boundaries come to be understood as part of the process of place-*making*, part of how meaning is made in places in response to larger structural/spatial forces not of our own making. This social construction of borders implies that the meanings of both the border and the place defined within are neither guaranteed nor essential (Massey, 1995; see also Hall, 1996). Yet, as real and imagined borders exist in embedded networks of history, politics, and power they do indeed have a materiality—real effects on lived experience. In fact, social structures can no more be understood without some conception of the spatial than can the spatial be analyzed without inclusion of the social (Soja, 1989). This is not to say that borders and boundaries create a sense of place in any pure or guaranteed way (again, see Hall, 1996), but rather of note is the notion that multiple possibilities exist within the bounded space and in the possibility of border crossing. It is precisely in this interaction that spaces speak, spaces leak, and spaces themselves are possibilities.

Critical geographers suggest that typically in social science research the concepts of space, place, identity—and its oft conflated term, *culture*—all get characterized in isomorphic fashion problematically assuming the neutrality of space. Four distinct but overlapping problems arise: (1) what of those who inhabit the borderlands? (Anzaldua, 1999); (2) how do we account for differences within particular places; (3) what of the hybrid cultures of postcoloniality?[1] (Bhabha, 1994); and (4) how do we come to understand social and cultural change within spatial context? (Gupta & Ferguson, 1992). All four issues come out of a sensitivity to that location often referred to as "the margin." To be "on the margin" or, more politically, "marginalized" implies a position, a location, in relation to power and structures of power. What then can we say of those locations, or indeed, more importantly, what do those who inhabit those places say of how they mean? Hybridity too—along with change, both forced, chosen, and some combination of the two—proves complexly tied to a sense of self, perception, and perhaps even economy and subjects may take up forms in particular times and spaces to gain some use value (see Helfenbein 2006b). Here is where, in my view, this work rests in relation to the underlying basis of Birmingham cultural studies and critical qualitative research. Through the lens of critical geography we must not only turn to those on the margin but turn to them so that we may hear them speak.

Understanding space, place, power, and identity as a set of interactions provides for critical geography a frame within which to rethink all three. But again, as issues of the globalized context arise, new reconceptions (postreconceptions?) become necessary. It is my contention that globalization represents fundamental restructurings of fundamental forces and, at the same time, privileges aspects of society in new and unseen ways. Contrary to the brief theoretical moment when global capital, high-speed travel, and information technology seemed poised to "kill" place, these important changes bring about places that mean differently. As Gupta and Ferguson (1992) state,

> In the pulverized space of postmodernity, space has not become irrelevant: it has become reterritorialized in a way that does not conform to experience of space that characterized the era of high modernity. It is this that forces us to reconceptualize fundamentally the politics of community, solidarity, identity, and cultural difference. (p. 9)

*Re*territorialization then becomes the object of analysis. Indeed, *de*territorialization holds a predominant part of the process of the globalized condition but this is no end, no death, as inevitably spaces become reterritorialized by forces both structural and (yes, and!) agentic.

Critical Geography and Education

To turn now to how the lens of critical geography relates to educational (and specifically curricular) theory, certain themes should be obvious. Agency, structure, meaning, power, identity, difference: all reside squarely in the purview of contemporary theorizing about school and schooling. Think here about the connection of larger social forces, social constructions of knowledge, and educational public policy. What might it mean for those interested in the "lived experience of schools" that Tom Friedman (2005) says (and state superintendents hold aloft) "the world is flat" and that education is our only hope? What does it mean for citizens and those who teach citizenship when U.S. Senator John McCain says "the war on terror knows no borders" following air strikes on Pakistan killing civilians instead of their intended targets? What might it mean when a midsized Midwestern city simultaneously calls itself the "heartland" and marketers for a local radio station advertise "world class rock for a world class city"? This brief sampling of questions points to global economic shifts, rearticulations of political sovereignty, and even, in the case of economic development, political affiliation, and what counts as "rock," collective identity in an urban setting. Thinking about schools and schooling can certainly not be limited to thinking about processes in pedagogy or curriculum as all of these forces are at work—space is everywhere.

Often in educational research there remains a tendency to think of schools as bounded systems—systems that begin and end with four walls and the sounding of school bells. Schools, in fact, are very complex social systems that are all bound up in a "tangled web of practices" that include connections to government (local, state, and federal), community, historical context, economic structure and shift, and fluid notions of community, culture, and identity (Ellis, 2004; Nespor, 1997; Tyack & Cuban, 1995). Attempting to understand practices in educative spaces requires the embrace of multiple levels of analysis and inquiry, multiple scales. This complexity of forces—all working on the actors involved—comes clear with the addition of the lens of critical geography.

To date, spatial analysis seems to be enjoying an increased presence in contemporary critical research and theorizing but the work is sporadic and no one has drawn the line through the work of these varied scholars. A productive connection from this work to the new questions of curriculum offers both a sense of growing trajectory as well as a sense of the possibilities of continuing this work. While not explicitly claiming the discipline of geography, some prominent scholars have applied a spatial analysis to educative practice: classroom geographies (Johnson, 1982; McKinney, 2000); and the recent work of cultural studies approaches to education (Dimitriadis & Carlson, 2003; Giroux, 2000; Hytten 1999). There are the various ethnographies about specific schools and the lives of students such as Eckert (1989), Kozol (1991), Pope (2001), Valenzuela (1999), and Yon (2000), to name only a few. Of course, there are the books that address geography as a subject, as in elementary education (i.e., Sobel, 1998), or secondary social studies education (i.e., Kincheloe, 2001; Segal & Helfenbein, 2008). Certainly there are other books that have taken on the notion of place such as Pinar and Kincheloe's *Curriculum as Social Psychoanalysis: The Significance of Place* (1991) and its inheritor Whitlock's *This Corner of Canaan: Curriculum Studies of Place and the Reconstruction of the South* (2006), and McLaren's *Life in Schools* (1994). *A Natural History of Place in Education* (Hutchison, 2004) begins to investigate place as a theoretical concept applied to schools but jumps quickly to the spatial analyses of architecture and classroom configuration. While critical geographers are generally not used in their sources, and no mention of the formal concept per se exists in their work, many of the concerns inherent to critical geography are taken up by these various scholars; for example, the ways in which identity and power are implicated in relations with place.

In curriculum theory, however, the language and, to some extent, the authors of critical geography—notably Bhabha (1994) and Tuan (1977)—are evoked in Hongyu Wang's (2004) *The Call from the Stranger on a Journey Home: Curriculum in a Third Space* and, rather interestingly employed in Clifford Mayes (2004) *Seven Landscapes: A Holistic Theory of Curriculum.* Cary's *Curriculum Spaces: Discourse, Postmodern Theory and Educational Research* (2006) offers a compelling combination of postmodern theorizing and critical discourse analysis marking innovative notions of "curriculum spaces" as the landscape of discursive formation/s. Furthermore, in recent publications and conference presentations other movements have arisen using space and place as both metaphorical constructs and as ways in which to place an analysis of embodied selves. Pinar (2004) writes:

> public education is, by definition, a political, psycho-social, fundamentally intellectual reconstruction of self and society, a process in which educators occupy public and private spaces in-between the academic disciplines and the state (and problems) of mass culture, between intellectual development and social engagement, between erudition and everyday life. (p. 15)

Discussions of democracy and the public sphere (including Pinar's) similarly represent renewed attention to the spatial but also the implications of virtuality on spatial formations and meaning making. Such recent inclusions of place and space, while not explicitly naming critical geography as a source, represent an important movement in contemporary educational discourse to which critical geography can contribute and furthermore, offer curriculum theorizing as a particular site of such work.

Two recent texts do merit brief discussion here. Elizabeth Ellsworth's (2005) *Places of Learning: Media, Architecture, Pedagogy* offers conceptions of pedagogy and place that, in my view, closely parallel the contemporary work of curriculum theory. Her compelling phrase "the experience of the learning self in the making" (p. 5, and throughout) calls attention to not only the lived experience of schools but also how these selves are located in places, in relation. She further pushes us to think of bodies and experiences in both temporal and spatial ways. She states that,

> pedagogy involves us in experiences of the corporeality of the body's time and space. Bodies have affective somatic responses as they inhabit a pedagogy's "time and space"—all within the "midst of learning." (p. 4)

It is the undetermined nature of these responses, wrapped up in the multiplicity of forces that work on subjects that seems to blur the line between what Ellsworth calls pedagogy and what curriculum theorists call curriculum. While this contention might (and probably should) be debated, the connection with critical geography's call for a more rhizomatic analysis of subjects, spaces, and places seems clear.

It would also be insufficient to not explicitly mention Bill Pinar's (2004) *What Is Curriculum Theory?* and its call for both a rethinking of public and private spheres and, in relation to the American South, "a curriculum of 'place'" (p. 241). Pinar suggests that curriculum in the South holds particular regional characteristics not easily dismissed or transcended. Calling characteristically for a reflective, autobiographical Southern study, Pinar suggests that in this model "curriculum...becomes a place of origin as well as destination, a 'ground' from which intelligence can develop, and a 'figure' for presenting new perceptions and reviewing old ones" (p. 246). One might think of this project as asking *how where we are makes us who we are* but we would be remiss to not also ask the inverse—*how who we are makes where we are* (see Helfenbein, 2005); none of these answers is guaranteed. Adding critical geography to this configuration would suggest that curriculum could be seen as not only origin and destination, figure and ground, but, in the pursuit of recognizing subjects in process and in multiplicity, curriculum is also the space-in-between. That space-in-between can also be thought of as those spaces that speak, those spaces that leak, and those spaces of possibility.

The complexity of a critical geography analysis deepens our understandings of the rhizomatic interactions that make up the places where educative moments occur. Student and educator perceptions of place indeed play an important role within the varied interactions of educative practice (Helfenbein, 2005). A notion of place and an understanding of the complex geographies of power and community are essential for coming to know how institutions like schools work (or don't) and how identities are formed. The layers of analysis suggested by this spatial turn represent a critical approach to understanding schools and students—and hopefully allow students to understand themselves—as participants in a "tangled web of practices."

The complexities of these tangled webs are formidable in all places but particularly so in those places where students find themselves labeled, limited, or forgotten. Coming to understand the tensions in these complicated webs, the contradictions, competitions, and congregations within, is both necessary to recognize the various forces influencing the students' lived experience as it is vital to our attempts to how students respond to them.

What does Critical Geography offer Curriculum Theory?

The question is a good one. What does a new theoretical lens add to the already rich and flexible field of curriculum theorizing? What would that work look like? A look through that lens at a study entitled *Urban Middle School Faculty and Perceptions of Place* (Helfenbein & Gonzalez-Velez, 2005) might provide the beginnings of an answer. A qualitative, quasi-ethnographic method was used in exploring faculty perceptions of place in a dramatically shifting urban landscape. I begin with my field notes from an initial interview at the school,

> Walking into the counselor's conference room this spring, waiting for my study participant to send an email and gather herself before our interview, I noticed the loud and jarring sound of a highly revved car engine. It's a familiar sound but one in which most folks stop and turn toward as if someone is driving too fast, or it might be stylish car worth noticing, or, perhaps most likely, in anticipation of an impending accident. The sound was not unusual but the fact that I heard it so distinctly in a middle school conference room—wait…there it is again—was. As I pieced things together and confirmed with my, now joining me, participant I realized that it was in fact the Speedway, some type of time trials. This was, after all, [a city known for racing]. "Yes," she said with the shrug of someone surprised that the obvious had been mentioned, "we'll hear that all spring."

What might it mean to the educators in this troubled middle school that the sound of racecars travels across the empty parking field and permeates their classroom walls as they teach these children? To adopt the phrase that first attracted me to curriculum theory, how does this affect the "lived experience" of children, parents, and educators? More work needs to be done to answer this question to be sure but certainly we can theorize as to the spatial relationships that mark this school as unique, as to ways in which this space speaks.

To share another piece of the story of this middle school, it is important to note that this school is a part of Indianapolis Public Schools (IPS), an urban district noted for low- performance on the state's accountability system and seemingly always mentioned in opposition to the "township schools." A student of mine was observing a physical education class in his field placement and struck up a conversation with an assistant principal that I will take a liberty and relate.[2]

P: Where ya from?
S: XXXX township.
P: Oh, yeah. Good schools. Say, what do you think is the biggest difference between XXXX and IPS schools?
S: [the student told me he paused, nervous on how to answer, sensing a test] Well… maybe the teachers teach differently, maybe their expectations….
P: [interrupting] Nope. It's the kids.
S: Well…maybe…but it seems like the teachers…
P: [interrupting] Nope. It's the kids. It's the kids.

I acknowledge that this story doesn't follow the conventions of qualitative research but it does point to a striking educational reality—place matters. Place matters to the degree that this IPS principal describes her own school—to a preservice teacher I might add— in oppositional terms to the amorphous "township schools" with not so lightly veiled connotations of race, class, and culture. She does so in a way that removes any culpability from her or her faculty. Any failing or negative seen by this future educator is a result of the kids, kids that come from a particular place. What does this add to Pinar's (2004) "complicated conversation" and how does it help to acknowledge the "nightmare of the present?" *Where* these kids come from—even though these borders often split alleys, share trashcans, or cross stoplights in this city—speaks to the construction of difference, of subjectivity, and the ways in which it is deployed. These spaces speak and in some cases curse.

The most striking and complicated feature in the drive out of the urban core of India-napolis to the school studied in "Urban Middle School Faculty and Perceptions of Place" is Speedway (Helfenbein & Gonzalez-Velez, 2005). Speedway is a loosely defined spatial marker within the larger and locally significant township. The name is a reference to the locally iconic racetrack and a brand identified with everything from but not coinciden-tally to, strip clubs, pawn shops, and liquor stores. Westington[3] is not technically in the incorporated town or the larger township although the racetrack itself is visible from the front of the rather bleak school grounds (and events like time trials are heard through-out the spring). Westington lies in the borderlands, a borderland imbued with multiple and shifting meanings. This space both speaks and leaks.

A meeting with the director of a local community center proved useful in understand-ing the history of Westington and the surrounding neighborhood. This project involved both the wide scale of contextual work to the tightened focus on individuals and their perceptions. As we began our inquiry into this particular place with a tight scale on the neighborhood level, the school community was initially marked by a geography of absence—we couldn't find it! Even in a nationally marketed GIS database whose signa-ture work was a detailed topography of neighborhoods and social networks, the commu-nity where Westington resides was not included. Again, what was so different about this place that it was left off the map? Through the course of my interview with the commu-nity center director, a story unfolded of a once pleasant, middle-class neighborhood that slipped over the years into deep decline. In response to a question about his efforts in the area, although they extend past his technical jurisdiction, he responded with his fear that it might turn into the "worst urban slum in [this city]." Speedway, in contrast and just across that large empty parking lot in front of the school, flourishes with projects of gen-trification and renewal. But, notable here is the speaker. The language of "might turn" should be interrogated, but the fact remains that this community worker had crossed the borders of his jurisdiction and set up the after-school program in which the relationships that sparked this project were formed—the spaces leak.

In Indianapolis, the geography of the public schools returns us to the question of scale and its inherently political nature. Indianapolis Public Schools (IPS) is the urban school district (read: Black schools historically) and the townships have developed into suburban nodes—although they are remarkably and increasingly urban—surrounding the traditional urban core, even though most other public services were consolidated under local governance in 1968 (Reynolds, 1998, p. 186). White flight was rampant with the threat of desegregation as it was across the nation, but the difference is that they did not have to go far. Desegregation and White flight can be seen as exemplars of the political characteristics of scale (I remind the reader of the earlier discussion of deterritorialization to reterritorialization) playing out in particular ways in this particular place. Efforts at gentrification follow the historical model of protecting spaces as racial and socioeconomic diversity encroach. All of those characteristics point to the particularities of curriculum, or more consistently, curriculum spaces—the context within which the lived experiences of school take place.

In tightening the scale—the sliding scale of a critical geography—to focus on our school a quick analysis reveals a sliver of cachment area for IPS between two township districts known for a very different racial makeup. Closest to WMS resides Speedway, the unique community revolving around the historic auto racetrack and its seasonal, profitable, if unsavory temporary industry. The landscape is flat and barren largely to accommodate large fields for parking for the 250,000 seat event. The town of Speedway, although benefiting from its proximity, needed a buffer zone from the expansive needs of bringing in such numbers on a seasonal basis, but also a buffer from the particular types of enterprise that go along with it, and finally a buffer from the threat of desegregation. The geography here is one of borders that serve both social and political purposes. What is different about this place is becoming clear.

Other aspects of this study include: (1) a tightening yet again of the scale to get a sense of the teachers' perceptions of this particular place and how they fit with, don't fit with, or inform the theorization briefly sketched out here; and (2) sliding the scale to its extreme—the global—to add to the list of forces at work in these communities and WMS. Anecdotally, the sense that the glory days of Speedway's educational system along with the larger townships are over due to new demographic shifts seems pervasive. Did Indianapolis follow the now famous "onion model" of urbanization for a time but now such a model no longer holds? Perhaps, but it seems more likely that with the spatial variable of the racetrack and the social variable of the politics of race, Indianapolis developed in somewhat unique ways. But what of the spaces of possibility?

This study "Urban Middle School Faculty and Perceptions of Place" reinforced some heartfelt beliefs about the role of research and teacher development. The act of interviewing—or preferably, talking with—educators so central to this exemplar brought up issues that all involved felt needed attention. When teachers are given the chance to critically look at their practice and the lived experiences of their students, they see things they might miss in the clamor of the school day; they see blind spots. Collaborative inquiry into the complicated conversation of curriculum *itself* can help transform practice. The lack of these critical conversations with educators helps to create these blind spots and an active part of the work of theorizing should be to uncover those fields.

But furthermore, a brief turn to theory might prove useful in coming to make sense of the context and conversation presented in the study of Westington Middle School and the dilemma of how one makes theory of use to the participants in the field. Henri Lefebvre (1970/2003) writes about what he calls "blind fields" in a recently translated book *The Urban Revolution*. He points out that what is interesting about a blind field—or for our purposes, a blind spot—is not what is missing from view but rather, the process by which something is obscured. To put it more simply, "How is it that we've been blinded?" is a much more important question than, "What are we missing?" Lefebvre states, "the blinding is the luminous source…that projects a beam of light, that illuminates *elsewhere*. The blinded is our dazed stare, as well as the region left in shadow. On the one hand a path is opened to exploration; on the other there is an enclosure to break out of, a consecration to transgress" (p. 31).

This conception of the blind spot serves to get a handle on how the participants at WMS in this study can all reference the poverty and changing demographics of the neighborhood, but the support needed for the kinds of services and community connection at the school remains lacking. The teachers in this study are conscientious, caring, and thoughtful about their practice and the kids they teach. Yet, this blind spot remains. How can this be? We contend that all the pressure on schools—and particularly urban schools in this age of accountability—to be able to document student achievement in a climate of very real, high stakes testing (a very tangible curriculum issue), does exactly what Lefebvre describes. It is a beam of light that is the blinding—it illuminates elsewhere, it turns our attention. This turning creates a blind spot, the region left in shadow. Sadly, in this case, this region is positive connection with a rapidly changing school community. Yet, as Lefebvre points out, this beam of light does point to a new path. It cannot be argued that student achievement doesn't need to improve or that accountability has not pointed those schools that have historically failed our children and at what cost? And when and where do we turn our attention to those regions in shadow? The pointing to them, both for and with teachers in the field, provides that cognitive break, that border crossing, that space of possibility.

Spaces of Possibility: Conclusions

To again "think through scale" I offer two levels which focus our attention on the potential for critical geography for curriculum theorizing. Taylor (2005), in talking about the possibilities of critical geography for curriculum in composition studies, defines the role of critical educators as "ultimately about disorientation, reorientation, [and] a more useful psychogeographical mapping" (p. 4; see also Kitchens & Helfenbein, 2005). I might suggest this describes what we as teachers do every time we try to get students to think. But perhaps more interestingly (widening the lens), this descriptor of critical education follows precisely the nature of capital in the post-Cold War socioeconomic present. Globalization, or compellingly in my view, Empire as described by Hardt and Negri (2000, 2004), moves through the process of disorientation (or deterritorialization), reorientation (reterritorialization), and mapping (or, dare I say it, hegemonic inscription). For example, I offer that forces of globalization work on educative spaces and those that inhabit them in new and consequential ways. Globalization, as it is seen, is the pulsing extension of the contradictory processes of capital throughout the spatial realm. By offering the descriptor *pulsing* I suggest that these forces extend and retract—what Lefebvre calls the "incessant to-and-fro"—in the hopes of new markets, the reinscription of old ones, and the extraction of markets where there once were none, which becomes a point important to the connection to public education. Lefebvre (1970/2003) argues that fundamentally these processes follow the broadly conceived characteristics of urbanization. As these processes extend through the spatial, we see—sometimes slowly, sometimes quickly—the urbanization of everything (Helfenbein, 2004).

The notion that critical education efforts might resemble the changing nature of global capital could be troubling or could lead to old slippage that affirms resistance as reproductive; or, one could take the lead again from Hardt and Negri to characterize these odd bedfellows as merely two sides to the same coin—in this case Empire and Multitude. This coin and the way it flips, resides in and is primarily involved in the spatial relations that are both produced and producing in human relations and in that uncertainty, hope is not lost. Reynolds (2003) seems to agree when he says,

> The ability of theory to enable agency is a basis in curriculum studies, critical pedagogy, and cultural studies as well. Finally, the exploration of spaces or, as Deleuze would have it, lines of flight, that would provide however temporary popular cultural resistances as political resistances is another shared concern. Multidisciplinarity would provide a place for workers both in curriculum and culture to study together in these areas. (p. 103)

Critical geographies of education then seek out these lines of flight and attempt to broaden the lens of our analysis in ways that differ from but are built upon the inclusion of place in curriculum studies. Kincheloe and Pinar (1991) offer that if place is taken seriously it enables a historicized epistemology for curriculum inquiry. Looking to place as a way to see inward, this approach becomes what they call social psychoanalysis. Whitlock (2006) and Casemore (2008) take that charge into their own explorations of place and self, race, sexuality, power, and identity. What a critical geography offers, in addition to those powerful contributions, is a way to look outward, a way to include the contemporary dynamics of global capital into the curriculum set of questions. Taking these multiple scales into account—from self, the local, and place to power, the global, and space—offers an explicit privileging of agency in a changing world and an ability to include the speed and impact of late capitalism in the analysis. In effect, after our return to place, we must now again return to space: the geography of the "yes, and," the geography of relations, a Critical Geography.

To conclude (or perhaps, begin?), I return to the finger and the eye, a phrase intended to remind the reader of the subjectivity of the map-maker and the subjectivity of those who make meaning of the maps. Agency, as Reynolds marks it as the goal of theory, is what this finger ultimately hopes to point to, to draw your eye to. This finger points to both the social grid in which those schooling and those schooling find themselves in but also the ways in which, spaces in which, they wriggle free. This notion is rooted in coming to understand new relations (and old inscriptions) between selves and world. As Rob Shields (1999) states,

> Space is a medium—and the changing way in which we understand, practice and live in terms of our space provides clues to how our capitalist world of nation-states is giving way to an unanticipated geopolitics—a new sense of our relation to our bodies, world and planets as a changing space of distance and difference. (p. 147)

Shields's point here reinforces the newest (30 years or so) directions in geographic theory—the recognition that space is productive, the conduit for, and the product of social relations. Necessarily all three, this multifaceted characterization serves more than simply pointing out the complexity of any spatial analysis but also points to two important distinctions: (1) the subjectivity of our relationship to spaces or for the sake of this chapter, *how spaces speak*; and (2) the lack of guarantee, or determinism, in the nature of both social and spatial production, or, *how spaces leak*. Many taking up these two distinctions and their subsequent objects of analysis (e.g., power, identity, positionality, the border, and, perhaps most importantly, a rethinking of the global and the local) have come to call their work critical geography and also point to agency, *the spaces of possibility*.

Note

1. This story was related to a Middle School Methods class that meets in an IPS school. I have told the story as I remember it and make no claim to its literal representation.

References

Allen, J. (2003). *Lost geographies of power.* Malden, MA: Blackwell.

Anzaldua, G. (1999). *Borderlands: La frontera* (2nd ed.). San Francisco: Aunt Lute Books.

Bhabha, H. (1994). *Location of culture.* New York: Routledge.

Breitbart, M. M. (1998). "Dana's mystical tunnel": Young people's designs for survival and change in the city. In T. Skelton & G. Valentine (Eds.), *Cool places: Geographies of youth cultures* (pp. 306–328). New York, Routledge.

Cary, L. J. (2006). *Curriculum spaces: Discourse, postmodern theory. and educational research.* New York: Lang.

Casemore, B. (2008). *The autobiographical demand of place: Curriculum inquiry in the American South.* New York: Lang.

de Certeau, M. (1984). *The practice of everyday life.* Berkeley: University of California Press.

Dimitriadis, G., & Carlson, D. (Eds.). (2003). *Promises to keep: Cultural studies, democratic education, and public life.* New York: Routledge Falmer.

Eckert, P. (1989). *Jocks and burnouts: Social categories and identity in the high school.* New York: Teachers College Press.

Ellis, J. (2004). The significance of place in the curriculum of children's everyday lives. *Taboo: The Journal of Culture and Education, 8*(1), 23–42.

Ellsworth, E. (2005). *Places of learning: Media, architecture, pedagogy.* New York: Routledge.

Friedman, T. (2005). *The world is flat: A brief history of the twenty-first century.* New York: Farrar, Straus, & Giroux.

Giroux, H. A. (2000). *Impure acts: The practical politics of cultural studies.* New York: Routledge.

Gupta, A., & Ferguson, J. (1992). Beyond "culture": Space, identity and the politics of difference. *Cultural Anthropology, 7*(1),6–23.

Hall, S. (1996). The problem of ideology: Marxism without guarantees. In D. Morley & K. Chen (Eds.), *Stuart Hall: Critical dialogues in cultural studies* (pp. 25–46). New York: Routledge.

Hardt, M., & Negri, A. (2000). *Empire.* Cambridge, MA: Harvard University Press.

Hardt, M., & Negri, A. (2004). *Multitude: War and democracy in the age of Empire.* New York: Penguin Press.

Harvey, D. (1989). *The condition of postmodernity: An enquiry into the origins of cultural change.* Cambridge, MA: Basil Blackwell.

Harvey, D. (2001). *Spaces of capital: Towards a critical geography.* New York: Routledge.

Helfenbein, R. (2004). A radical geography: Curriculum theory, performance, and landscape. *Journal of Curriculum Theorizing, 20*(3), 67–76.

Helfenbein, R. (in press). The urbanization of everything: Thoughts on globalization and Education. In S. Tozer, B. Gallegos, & A. Henry (Eds.). *Handbook of research in social foundations of education.* Mahwah, NJ: Erlbaum.

Helfenbein, R. (2006a). Space, place, and identity in the teaching of history: Using critical geography to teach teachers in the American South. In A. Segall, E. Heilman, & C. Cherryholmes, (Eds.), *Social studies—The next generation: Re-searching in the postmodern* (pp.111–124). New York: Lang.

Helfenbein, R. (2006b). Economies of identity: Cultural studies and a curriculum of making place. *Journal of Curriculum Theorizing, 22*(2), 87–100.

Helfenbein, R., & Gonzalez-Velez, Y. (2005). Urban middle school faculty and perceptions of place. In J. A. Anderson, M. J. Dare, & K. M. Powell (Eds.), *The urban education inquiry project.* Monograph no. 1. (Available from the Center for Urban and Multicultural Education, 902 W. New York St, ES 3116, Inner City, IN 46202)

Hutchison, D. (2004). *A natural history of place in education.* New York: Teachers College Press.

Hytten, K. (1999). The promise of cultural studies in education. *Educational Theory, 49*(4), 527–543.

Johnson, N. B. (1982). School spaces and architecture: The social and cultural landscape of educational environments. *Journal of American Culture, 5*(4), 79–88.

Kincheloe, J. (2001). *Getting beyond the facts: Teaching social studies/social sciences in the twenty-first century.* New York: Lang.

Kincheloe, J., & Pinar, W. (Eds.). (1991). *Curriculum as social psychoanalysis: The significance of place.* Albany, NY: SUNY Press.

Kitchens, J., & Helfenbein, R. (2005). *Curriculum as critical geography: Space, place, and education.* Paper presented at the Annual Meeting of the American Association for the Advancement of Curriculum Studies, Montreal, Canada.

Kozol, J. (1991). *Savage inequalities: Children in American schools.* New York: Crown.

Lefebvre, R. (2003). *The urban revolution* (R. Bonnono, Trans.). Minneapolis, MI: University of Minnesota Press. (Original work published 1970)

Massey, D. (1994). *Space, place, and gender.* Minneapolis: University of Minnesota Press.

Massey, D. (1995). The conceptualization of place. In D. Massey & P. Jess (Eds.), *A place in the world? Places, cultures, and globalization* (pp. 117–128). New York: Oxford University Press.

Massey, D. (2005). *For space.* Thousand Oaks, CA: SAGE.

Massey, D., & Jess, P. (Eds.). (1995). *A place in the world? Places, cultures, and globalization.* New York: Oxford University Press.

Mayes, C. (2004). *Seven landscapes: A holistic theory of curriculum.* Lanham, MD: University Press of America.

McKinney, M. (2000). *A place to learn: Teachers, students, and classroom spaces.* Unpublished Dissertation, University of North Carolina, Chapel Hill.

McLaren, P. (1994). *Life in schools: An introduction to critical pedagogy in the foundations of education* (2nd ed.). White Plains, NY: Longman.

Nespor, J. (1997). *Tangled up in school: Politics, space, bodies, and signs in educational process.* Mahwah, NJ: Erlbaum.

Pickles, J. (2004). *A history of spaces: Cartographic reason, mapping and the geo-coded world.* New York: Routledge.

Pinar, W. (2004). *What is curriculum theory?* Mahwah, NJ: Erlbaum.

Pope, D. C. (2001). *Doing school: How we are creating a generation of stressed-out, materialistic, and miseducated students.* Yale University Press.

Reynolds, M. A. (1998). The challenge of racial equality. In W. J. Reese (Ed.), *Hoosier schools: Past and present,* (pp. 173–193) Indianapolis: Indiana University Press.

Reynolds, W. M. (2003). *Curriculum: A river runs through it.* New York: Lang.

Segal, A., & Helfenbein, R. (2008). Geography education. In L. Levstik & C. Tyson (Eds.), *Handbook of research in social education* (pp. 259–283). New York: Erlbaum.

Shields, R. (1999). *Lefebvre, love, & struggle: Spatial dialectics.* New York: Routledge.

Sobel, D. (1998). *Mapmaking with children: Sense of place education for the elementary years.* New York: Heinemann.

Soja, E. W. (1989). *Postmodern geographies: The reassertion of space in critical social* theory. New York: Verso.

Soja, E. W. (1996). *Thirdspace: Journeys to Los Angeles and other real-and-imagined places.* Oxford: Blackwell.

Taylor, H. (2005). *Gimme some space: How composition can benefit from critical geography.* Paper presented at the Annual Meeting of the American Association for the Advancement of Curriculum Studies, Montreal, Canada.

Tuan, Y. (1977). *Space and place: The perspective of experience.* Minneapolis: University of Minnesota Press.

Tyack, D., & Cuban, L. (1995). *Tinkering toward utopia: A century of public school reform.* Cambridge, MA: Harvard University Press.

Valenzuela, A. (1999). *Subtractive Schooling: U.S.-Mexican Youth and the Politics of Caring.* SUNY Press.

Wang, H. (2004). *The call from the stranger on a journey home: Curriculum in third space.* New York: Lang.

Whitlock, R. U. (2007). *This corner of Canaan: Curriculum studies of place and the reconstruction of the South.* New York: Lang.

Yon, D. A. (2000). *Elusive culture: Schooling, race, and identity in global times.* New York: SUNY Press.

Suggested Reading Questions

1. The author speaks of interrogating our spatial assumptions about school space and attempts to remap the way we understand space by providing three things—spaces that speak, leak, and possibility. How does this new lens of critical geography reimagine the sociospatial construction of women in curriculum theory and practice?

2. How does a critical geography of space in education that calls for an intellectual shift from modern ways of categorizing space, place, and scale to a postmodern engagement with the ways in which we understand identity, difference, and power give educators a new language and tool to challenge the differential spaces of schooling and educational reforms?

3. In traditional geography, the mapping of borders defines our understanding of both place and social relations. How might the spatial metaphor complicate our understanding of "border politics" and impact the ways in which we think and speak of different forms of oppression in our everyday lives within schooling, social formations and globalized networks?

4. The author suggests that space is everywhere—being created and re-created in economic development, political affiliations, and collective identity in different settings. In the context of schools and schooling, the construction and dissemination of knowledge and educational policy, how might it become possible to create spaces of action in the midst of such complexities?

5. How might critical geography be used to link individual lived experiences to global, economic, political, and social changes in the world?

Response to Robert J. Helfenbein
The Agency of Theory

William F. Pinar

What might it mean, Robert Helfenbein (this volume) asks, that the sound of racecars lacerates the classrooms in the school where he works? He asks how that screeching sound might affect the "lived experience" of children, parents, and educators?

The sound of racecars in classrooms: the distraction of the sound, its violence, the evocation of danger, of speed, of traveling too fast, in competition with each other, to see who reaches the finish line first. Is it a car race the Republicans had in mind with No Child Left Behind (NCLB)? The title of the legislation contradicts its content, given that competition guarantees someone will be left behind. In this life-risking rush to nowhere, what can be the meaning of the race?

The sound of race cars in schools positions us on the sidelines, teachers and students confined to empty parking lots construed as classrooms: Everywhere the sound of elsewhere. More than a few students see no exit, only the dead-end that a curriculum severed from lived experience so often seems. What can be the meaning of a race when one's car is left at the starting line, without gas, mechanics, or promoters? The Republicans' pillorying of the poor ensures many a child is left behind, not only without a head start, no start at all. In NCLB, teachers are directed to rescue them by raising test scores.

In this critical geography of curriculum spaces,[1] every child is left behind, littered along the sidelines listening as others go somewhere fast. Where are they headed anyway? Baghdad? Where can they go in the U.S., a place threatened not only by global capital and information technology, but by the Republicans' Orwellian assault on our national calling to life, liberty, and the pursuit of happiness. Who can even hear these phrases in the screeching sound of cars racing to nowhere? And if these phrases are still audible to us, what can they mean given that speed, competition, and violence characterize the race run in this nonplace of Empire?

The screeching sound of standardized tests deafens the voting public to the cries and whispers of those left behind. As Helfenbein points out, our attention is turned elsewhere, on those tests, not on the savage inequality of our schools, not on the scapegoating of teachers and, now, of education professors. In his chapter, Helfenbein employs visual, as well as auditory, images; he raises his finger to direct our attention to the map of the present, to its arbitrariness, its routes to nowhere, endangering life and limb, distracting us from the emptiness of the parking lot in which we stand stranded, waiting for the next moment.

In the next moment, will the younger generation find wriggle room, seat-belted tight as we all are in classrooms racing to nowhere, on an overheated planet plagued by pandemics? In pointing to the map critically—underscoring the subjectivity of the map-maker and the subjectivity of those who study it—can we find routes yet unmarked, not yet blocked by homeland (in)security? Robert Helfenbein thinks so. He invokes conversation, more precisely, the communicative action that collaborative inquiry promises, in order to recall the agency of theory.[2] Theory is the agency of the finger, pointing else-where, even while we keep our eye on the road, attuned not to the screeching sound all round us, but to that audible inner space wherein we can create "wriggle" room.

Helfenbein points out that this "notion is rooted in coming to understand new rela-tions (and old inscriptions) between selves and world" (this volume, p. 314). In my terms, the phrase implies the regressive, progressive, analytic, synthetic reconstruction of the subjective and the social through the academic. The *Cambridge Dictionary* tells us wriggle means "to twist your body, or move part of your body, with small, quick movements."

While not so quick anymore, I have been twisting for some time, or so it feels. By Nixon's election in 1968 and first wave of Republican-led school deform—it was, then, back-to-the-basics—it was clear to many of us that the official curriculum was no lon-ger negotiable. Curriculum development, as our predecessors knew it, was no longer an option. And we—in the early 1970s, *we* constituted the next moment—turned to the unof-ficial curriculum, to the subjective sphere. Employing the concepts of phenomenology and autobiography, we worked to enable teachers to create, as Helfenbein nicely phrases it, curriculum-in-between, that space, as Ted Aoki so memorably theorized it, between curriculum-as-plan and curriculum-as-lived (Pinar & Irwin 2005). In that intersubjec-tive space of conversation, teachers could, we thought, reclaim their agency; animate the curriculum in its immediacy and meaning. We twisted the idea of curriculum to mean autobiography; in-between text, teacher, and student, curriculum became that articula-tion of what we experienced as we studied (Miller 2005; Pinar & Grumet, 1976/2006).

We developed curriculum, not through protocols disguised as principles, but through understanding the subjective experience of study.[3] Later, we understood that understand-ing as also historical, racialized, gendered—well, many of you know those discursive domains by means of which we labored to understand curriculum after the reconceptu-alization (Pinar, Reynolds, Slattery, & Taubman, 1995).

In recent years I have twisted the notion of the synoptic text, now textbooks for teach-ers that summarize and juxtapose research in the subjects they teach, interdisciplinary research complicating the topics they and their students live. The synoptic text today, I suggest, is a form of curriculum development, connecting the subjective to the social through academic knowledge. The lived experience of curriculum has always been for me one interrelated phrase, even if during the first 20 years of my career I focused on the first three words. They remain interrelated as I now focus on the last two.

On the map of our present difficulties we find more than Republicans and those Democrats complicit in the conservatives' 35-year assault on the schools. We see regions now faint with age, areas, for instance, where we once enjoyed jurisdiction—curriculum development in the schools most prominently—but at which today we can only point. Understanding curriculum is no consolation prize—its absence in the founding para-digmatic moment helped seal our predecessors' fate—but without opportunities to write the curriculum some of us cannot help but feel stranded on the sidelines.

Also on the map of the present, there, to the right, we see our own institutional homes, increasingly inhospitable places of confinement where we are overworked, under suspicion by "scientific" colleagues now propped up by NCLB, insulted by right-wing politicians who, if they could, would erase us from the map. Administrators are paid not to represent us. We are sidelined with busywork: National Council for Accreditation of Teacher Education (NCATE) most prominently. Rendered ill-tempered by our victimiza-tion, sometimes we fight among ourselves. We have no time to think, no time to read any-thing but student papers, memos, and e-mails. How can a field advance intellectually if its participants are disabled, by their employers, from study? Whatever rooms are available to us in our places of confinement are not rooms of our own. Within this undermining infrastructure, the field itself feels threatened, and we have established a Commission on the Status of Curriculum Studies in the U.S. to document our dilemma and to chart a course of action.

Apart and together, we still enjoy occasions to act. For us, action is, above all, intellectual action: acting on ourselves, for our students, with our colleagues. At this, the first state-of-the-field conference since May 3–5, 1973 in Rochester, New York (Pinar, 1974), let us begin to map the moment that comes next. After listening to each other for 3 days, we will, on Sunday morning, speak to each other again. Through such communicative action, we might, as Robert Helfenbein reminds, not only strengthen our resolve, but embody resilience.

Resilience, *Webster's Dictionary* reminds, is "the capability of a strained body to recover its size and shape after deformation caused especially by compressive stress." Once, curriculum constituted the majority field in schools and colleges of education. Once, we developed the curriculum, including the means by which teachers assessed student study of it. While I am hardly nostalgic for that past, I affirm our field's right to the opportunity our predecessors lost.[4]

On this February morning at Purdue University in Indiana, for the moment safe from the screeching sound of cars careening to nowhere, let us follow Robert Helfenbein's finger, and the fingers of the other keynoters, as they point to a map on which we might locate the next moment. Animated by the agency of theory, let us wriggle free from the confinement of the present. In the resilience intergenerational solidarity creates, let us walk together through the present into the future. Let us begin this weekend.

Notes

1. Lisa Carey, too, employs this phrase, if differently (Carey, 2006).
2. Helfenbein refers to Reynolds's (2003) depiction of agency as the goal of theory.
3. Study—not learning, not teaching—complements curriculum (Block, 2001, 2004; McClintock, 1971).
4. I intend that verb to underscore both the field's victimhood and its culpability: see Pinar (2006, chapter 7).

References

Block, A. A. (2001). Ethics and curriculum. *Journal of Curriculum Teaching, 17*(3), 23–38.

Block, A. A. (2004). *Talmud, curriculum, and the practical: Joseph Schwab and the rabbis.* New York: Lang.

Carey, L. (2006). *Curriculum spaces: Discourse, educational research and postmodern theory.* New York: Lang.

Helfenbein, R. (2006, February 16–19). *Thinking through scale: Critical geography and curriculum spaces.* Paper presented to The Next Moment, a State-of-the-Field Conference held at Purdue University.

McClintock, R. (1971). Toward a place for study in a world of instruction. *Teachers College Record, 73*(2), 161–205.

Miller, J. L. (2005). *The sound of silence breaking and other essays.* New York: .Lang.

Pinar, W. F. (Ed.). (1974). *Heightened consciousness, cultural revolution and curriculum theory: The proceedings of the Rochester conference.* Berkeley, CA: McCutchan.

Pinar, W. F. (2006). *The synoptic text today and other essays: Curriculum development after the reconceptualization.* New York: Lang.

Pinar, W. F., & Grumet, M. R. (2006). *Toward a poor curriculum.* Troy, NY: Educator's International Press. (Original work published 1976)

Pinar, W. F., & Irwin, R. L. (Eds.). (2005). *Curriculum in a new key: The collected works of Ted T. Aoki.* Mahwah, NJ: Erlbaum.

Pinar, W. F., Reynolds, W. M., Slattery, P., & Taubman, P. (1995). *Understanding curriculum.* New York: Lang.

Reynolds, W. M. (2003). *Curriculum.* New York: Lang.

16 Complicating the Social and Cultural Aspects of Social Class

Toward a Conception of Social Class as Identity

Adam Howard and Mark Tappan

Chapter Overview

This chapter explains Americans' continued commitment to the American Dream in spite of evidence of increased stratifications over the last 40 years. Given what the authors term the *egalitarian myth*, they suggest that the general American public needs to be better prepared to talk about social class issues. They note that there is a clear correlation between social class status and educational success but disagreement over how to explain this relationship. Rather than rely upon economic analysis on cultural deficit theories, the authors rely upon social, cultural, and personal aspects to explain the complex ways social class shapes educational experiences and outcomes. They explore social class as an identity that invokes ideologically mediated action, a moral relational constitution, and available ideologies. As such, they describe social class identity as performed. They close by emphasizing that social class is as much a lived experience as it is the result of economic factors and therefore requires the study of cultural forces that reproduce unequal relations.

Illusions and Dreams

The United States is not only the most highly stratified society in the industrialized world but does less to limit the extent of inequality than any other industrialized democracy. Class distinctions operate in virtually all aspects of American life. Over 30 million people in the United States live in poverty; school success remains linked tightly with a student's social class status; most Americans live in class-segregated communities; and even with all the advances in medicine in recent years, the differences in health and lifespan are widening between the poor and affluent (Scott & Leonhardt, 2005). Moreover, since the 1970s, the top 1% of households has doubled their share of the national wealth to 40% while the total net worth of the median American household has fallen. The top 1% now has more wealth than the entire bottom 95% (Sklar, Collins, & Leondar-Wright, 2003). According to the U.S. Census Bureau (2004), the share of income of the poorest one fifth of households dropped from 4.2% to 3.5%.

Yet even with these considerable class distinctions, most Americans remarkably hold on to illusions about living in an egalitarian society. In fact, most Americans believe that the contours of social class have become blurred, and some argue that they have even disappeared in recent years (Scott & Leonhardt, 2005). Today, most Americans hold tightly to the "rags to riches" faith; that is, they believe it is possible to start out poor, work hard, and become rich. According to a *New York Times* poll (Leonhardt, 2005), 75% of Americans believe that chances of moving up from one class to another have risen over the past 3 decades, a period in which social class has played a greater, not lesser, role in shaping the everyday realities of Americans. Class awareness and class language are receding in the United States at a time when the gap between rich and poor in the country has widened (hooks, 2000).

It is against American principles for people to belong to a social class group. Although the general public recognizes that people occupy different class positions, the prevailing belief is that these arrangements are not fixed. Anyone who works hard enough can realize the "American Dream," and mobility—that is, the movement of families up and down the economic ladder—is the promise that lies at the heart of this dream. Poverty, therefore, is an aberration of this promise and of the American way of life. Surveys indicate that over half of the American public believes "that lack of effort by the poor was the principal reason for poverty, or a reason at least equal to any that was beyond a person's control.... Popular majorities did not consider any other factor to be a very important cause of poverty—not low wages, or a scarcity of jobs, or discrimination, or even sickness" (Schwarz & Volgy, 1992, p. 11). For most Americans, poverty is seen as unfortunate but temporary and as an end product of the poor themselves (Mantsios, 2003). The prominent belief held in the United States is that the poor have brought their "predicament" upon themselves and their conditions will change only when they change. Unlike the despised poor, most celebrate the wealthy for living the American promise. The wealthy as a class do not exist but instead are understood as the most talented, the most ambitious, and the most successful. The lines between most Americans and the wealthy are blurred by the illusion that affluence is attainable and achieved mostly on the basis of individual merit and through hard work. For most, American society is divided between the inferior poor and everyone else.

The egalitarian myth, and the rhetoric Americans hear from public leaders and in the media and other everyday venues that support this myth, comforts American middle classes while offering hope to the poor (Boudon, 1990/1994) and "allows the dominant class to appear not as a class but as representative of the whole society" (Larrain, 1992, p. 52). These fantasies of egalitarianism, moreover, steer people away from talking about social class and from revealing the taken-for-granted realities of different class positions. Social class has been and remains a taboo subject in American culture. As Ortner (1991) points out, "American natives almost never speak of themselves or their society in class terms. In other words, class is not a central category of cultural discourse in America" (p. 169). Rosenblum and Travis (2003) add, "[b]ecause social class is so seldom discussed, the vocabulary for talking about it is not well developed" (p. 22). Without this vocabulary, the general American public is ill-equipped to engage in the type of complicated conversation that is needed to understand the evasive nature of social class in American society. This inability to understand the impact of social class in America extends to the relationship between social class and schooling.

Social Class and Schooling

With relatively few exceptions (e.g., Ripple & Luthar, 2000; Seyfried, 1998), educational researchers generally agree that there is a high correlation between students' class status and school achievement and attainment (e.g., Brantlinger, 2003; Coleman, 1988; McLoyd, 1998; Metz, 1998; Nieto, 2005). Consistently, research studies document the differences in school circumstances and outcomes between poor and affluent students (e.g., Burton, 1999; Oakes, 1985; Orfield, 2000; Persell, 1997). A variety of issues and questions relating to social class have been explored in educational literature, such as achievement patterns (Brooks-Gunn & Duncan, 1997; De Civita, Pagani, Vitaro, & Tremblay, 2004; Hauser, Simmons, & Pager, 2000; Kao, Tienda, & Schneider, 1996); funding and resources (Education Trust, 2001; Ingersoll, 1999; Kozol, 1991); tracking (Ansalone, 2001; Oakes, 1985; Varenne & McDermott, 1998); disadvantages of poor children as they enter formal schooling (Phillips, Brooks-Gunn, Duncan, Klevanov, & Crane, 1998; Stipic

& Ryan, 1997); the overrepresentation of poor students in special education (Artiles & Trent, 1994; Barton & Oliver, 1997; Connor & Boskin, 2001); and the leveling of students' aspirations (MacLeod, 1987; Willis, 1977). This extensive body of research has documented the various ways that schools reflect the social class divisions of the larger society fairly consistently through their structures, practices, and policies and the lived experiences of, and the interactions among, those within schools.

Agreement that there is a correlation between social class status and educational success has not extended, however, to an agreement about how to explain the relationship. Several different approaches to this problem have been offered—none of these, we would argue, ultimately provide useful explanatory frameworks, nor help us to engage in a complex and nuanced conversation about social class in the U.S.

Traditional approaches to understanding the relationship between social class and schooling (e.g., Anyon, 1980, 1981; Arnowitz, 1980; Bowles & Gintis, 1976) rely heavily on economic analysis that has a tendency to disregard the social and cultural elements of social class. Within this analysis social class is primarily connected to just how much capital, in its various forms, one has or does not have. Several scholars have also argued that traditional reliance on Marxist analyses and functionalist justifications no longer to work in understanding the complexities of social class in shaping educational experiences (e.g., Van Galen, 2007). More recent efforts to address these complexities by exploring the social and cultural elements of social class have been steeped in deficit-laden perspectives. The most popular among these current approaches is the framework for understanding the "culture of poverty" offered by Ruby Payne (2005).

Payne's well-known book, *A Framework for Understanding Poverty* (2005), has come to dominate the literature on social class issues in schooling. Since 1996, Payne and her assistants have conducted hundreds of workshops per year to as many as 25,000 participants in school districts across the U.S. as well as in Australia and New Zealand. They claim to help teachers and administrators understand and learn how to work with students from poverty (Bohn, 2006). Her for-profit organization, aha! Process, Inc. publishes her books to accompany these workshops; *A Framework for Understanding Poverty* has sold over 1 million copies. All of Payne's books have appealed to a large audience of educators looking for simple answers to urgent problems in their work with children from poverty.

Payne's principal message is that poverty is not only a monetary condition. She describes it as a culture with particular rules, values, and knowledge transmitted from one generation to the next that inform people how to live their lives. Payne goes on to argue that children growing up in a culture of poverty are unsuccessful in school because they have been taught the "hidden rules of poverty" instead of the "hidden rules of being middle class." Even though her argument recognizes what researchers have previously substantiated on how the middle class culture of schools disadvantages poor, working class students (e.g., Anyon, 1981; Apple, 1996), Payne frames the culture of poverty, and its hidden rules, as inferior to middle class culture. She claims that public school teachers who are predominantly from the middle class do not understand and are not able to relate to their students from poverty. She argues that teachers do not appreciate the hidden and essential rules for survival in poverty. Payne, therefore, sees her primary goal as bridging this gap between middle class teachers and their poor students by helping teachers understand the culture that their students from poverty going with them to school, and by teaching educators the significance of and the techniques for teaching students in poverty the hidden rules of the middle class.

Payne's work has been increasingly criticized by antipoverty and antiracist educators and activists in recent years for failing to recognize the role that social and economic structures, including schools, play in perpetuating poverty, and for reifying stereotypes of the poor (Gorski, 2006a, 2006b; Ng & Rury, 2006). Gorski (2006a, 2006b) argues that her framework promotes the culture of classist assumptions that infiltrates U.S. schooling. Although Payne's framework acknowledges the social and cultural elements of social class that are largely ignored by traditional approaches, she reinforces classist assumptions through her simple and comfortable solutions to complex, difficult problems. She casts the poor as culturally deficit while excusing the affluent from the responsibility of challenging conditions that reinforce social class divisions. The popularity of her work demonstrates just how enduring these deficit sentiments are in the U.S.

Some scholars, like Osei-Kofi (2005), have argued that Payne's work does not have sufficient merit to warrant scholarly critique. Bohn (2006), for example, points out that since Payne's work is self-published it does not have to be verifiable, reproducible, valid, or reliable. Bohn argues that there is nothing more substantive about Payne's work than a few random anecdotes about poor children and their families. Most critics argue, however, that Payne's work has flown under the radar far too long and has become too influential to ignore. The popularity of the vast array of products and services available through Payne's business has made her one of the most influential voices in today's education milieu. As Keller (2006) points out, "The dispute over the value of Ruby Payne's ideas seems to be taking place far from the trenches of public education. There, the opinion is largely pro-Payne" (p. 2). The reality is that Payne's framework remains popular among teachers even with the increased criticism from scholars. Our suupposition is that teachers are mostly supportive of Payne's solutions because they are provided with a framework for placing blame on poor students for their lack of academic success in schooling.

Many scholars (e.g., Brantlinger, 2003; Howard, 2008; Nieto, 2005) have argued that cultural deficit theories, like Payne's, and the frameworks that these theories support were debunked in the 1970s when theorists began to argue that schools reproduce the economic and social relations in society and therefore tend to serve the interests of the dominant classes (e.g., Bourdieu & Passeron, 1977; Bowles & Gintis, 1976; Jencks, 1972; Spring, 1972). These theoretical projects placed schools within a political framework and explained the principals role of schooling as reproducing the class divisions in our society. These theorists argued that schools therefore not only reflected structural inequalities of the larger society but also maintained them. Katz (1975), for example, demonstrated that from the beginning, public schooling was "universal, tax-supported, free, compulsory, bureaucratically arranged, class-biased, and racist" (p. 106). These conflicting features, according to Katz, derived from the primary purpose of public schooling, which was to prepare and train different groups of people for different roles in society. Bowles and Gintis's (1976) *correspondence principle*—that is, "the close correspondence between the social relationships which govern personal interaction in the work place and the social relationships of the educational system" (p. 12)—explains that this function of the school is apparent from their physical and organizational structures to their curriculum and instruction. Schools with mostly poor students, for example, are generally factory-like fortresses that operate with controlling mechanisms, whereas schools with mostly affluent students provide the space for students to be more autonomous. Moreover, relations between poor students and their teachers reflect more dominant–dominated relationships than between affluent students and their teachers (McDermott, 1977).

Although the arguments of social reproduction theorists such as Bowles and Gintis (1976) have been criticized for being too simplistic and overdetermined (e.g., Apple & Weis, 1983; Giroux, 1992; Morrow & Torres, 1994), their theories have had a tremendous impact on educational thinking since the 1970s. The stated purpose of schooling to serve as an "equalizer" was questioned critically in these works and established a solid argument that "schools had historically been engaged in the service of a dominant class to control not only the lives but even the ideas of dominated groups" and "school failure became a perfectly understandable byproduct of this control" (Nieto, 1996, p. 234). Other theorists expanded on the tenets of social reproduction to explore the inherent political nature of schooling and to offer a wide range of explanations of the ways that schools tend to reproduce rather consistently the inequalities that exist in society (e.g., Apple, 1982; Arnowitz, 1980; Fay, 1987; Giroux, 1981, 1992). These theories also laid the groundwork to challenge the explanations that attributed cultural and intelligence deficits of the poor to lesser educational outcomes that gained great momentum in the 1960s (Bereiter & Engelmann, 1966; Jensen, 1969; Reissman, 1962), and had tremendous impact on social and educational policy made in the following years (Nieto, 2005).

Yet, as we have suggested above, while the strong links between social class and schooling are widely acknowledged, social class is not widely used as an analytical category for understanding the social, cultural, and political landscapes of schooling in the United States. Influenced by the lack of class language and class awareness in the larger society, it is not surprising that the academy has been relatively silent about social class and the concept has been and remains a troubling concept for many scholars. In fact, as Robertson (2000) observes, "It has become unfashionable in academic circles to talk about class, as if class no longer mattered and the historic concerns of class theorists—such as inequality—have disappeared" (p. 19). Class, in other words, is not a central category of thought for many scholars during a time when the gap between the quality of education for poor and minority students and that for affluent White students is widening and class divisions in schooling and in the larger society are growing deeper.

The time is obviously ripe to look for new explanatory frameworks, and new ways to generate conversations about social class and schooling. We agree, in other words, with those who argue that past and present approaches to understanding social class in schooling need to be reconceived within newer theoretical perspectives in order to revive conversations about class in educational scholarship (e.g., Van Galen, 2007). We propose that one way to move toward a new theoretical terrain is to rely more on social, cultural, and personal aspects than on economic factors for understanding the complex ways in which social class shapes educational experiences and outcomes. When it is discussed in academic circles social class is typically understood as something we *have*, rather than being intimately connected to who we *are* (i.e., as a dimension or aspect of personal *identity*; Howard & Tappan, 2007). To think about social class as identity, however, is not to deny or diminish the importance of various economic factors that create unequal relations; rather, it is to underline the relationship between these economic factors and identity formation, and to acknowledge that, heretofore, not only has social class largely been missing from our conversations about identity (Bettie, 2003), but also that identity has, heretofore, not been a common analytic category used to understand the dynamics of social class.

Social Class Identity as Ideologically Mediated Action

Social class as identity is a lived, developing process (Anyon, 1980) that is constructed by a particular form of socialized knowledge conditioned in a specific habitus (Bourdieu, 1984); that is, a system of dispositions that develops from social training and past experience (Reed-Danahay, 2005). The habitus "could be considered as a subjective but not individual system of internalized structures, schemes of perception, conception, and action common to all members of the same group or class" (Bourdieu, 1977, p. 86). Bourdieu (1984) argues, in fact, that class encompasses individuals who share homogeneous conditions of existence, sets of dispositions and preferences, and are capable of generating similar practices in social settings. Every aspect of an individual's social condition contributes to the development of the habitus and class membership. An individual's class position is homologous to others whose lives are similarly affected by social conditions. Therefore, social class is defined by the social conditions of lived experience and the intrinsic rules of an individual's social world. Individuals form particular ways of knowing and doing, values, beliefs, assumptions, and relations with others and the world around them that reflect their social class positionality.

To better understand this conception of social class as identity we turn to a *sociocultural* approach to identity formation (Howard & Tappan, 2007; Tappan, 2000, 2005, 2006). Our perspective is also informed by recent scholarship on the role that position-centered ideology plays in reinforcing and reproducing dominance and power (Thompson, 1990). As such, we would argue that identities are fundamentally forms of *self-understanding*: "people tell others who they are, but even more important, they tell themselves and then try to act as though they are who they say they are" (Holland, Lachicotte, Skinner, & Cain, 1998, p. 3). These self-understandings are not, however, simply individual, internal, psychological qualities or subjective understandings that emerge solely from self-reflection (Damon & Hart, 1988), or as a result of the resolution of deep-seated intrapsychic conflicts or struggles (Freud, 1923/1960). Rather, identities link the personal and the social—they are constituted relationally (Apple & Weis, 1983; Wexler, 1992); they entail action and interaction in a sociocultural context (Penuel & Wertsch, 1995); they are social products that live in and through activity and practice (Holland et al., 1998); and they are always performed and enacted (Butler, 1990, 1991; Willie, 2003).

Recent research on the construction of racial identity, moreover, points to the importance of understanding *how* identity is culturally produced and reproduced, rather than focusing, simply, on *what* identity is. As such, this scholarship challenges the conventional understanding of identity as embodied through naturalized categories (Dolby, 2000) to one in which identity is produced, as Stuart Hall (1996) argues, "in specific historical and institutional sites within specific discursive formations and practices, by specific enunciative strategies" (p. 4).

Following Penuel and Wertsch (1995), we have thus found it most helpful to view identity as a form of "mediated action." Informed by the work of both Vygotsky (1978) and Bakhtin (1981), the concept of mediated action entails two central elements: an "agent," the person who is doing the acting, on the one hand, and "cultural tools" or "mediational means," the tools, means, or resources appropriated from the social world, and used by the agent to accomplish a given action, on the other (Wertsch, 1995, 1998; see also Tappan, 2000, 2005).

Methodologically, adopting a mediated action approach to identity formation ultimately means focusing less on what persons say about their own "inner" psychological states or conflicts, and more on what they *do* with particular cultural tools or resources that shape and mediate their sense of self-understanding in specific situations and circumstances (see also Holland et al., 1998). As such, "when identity is seen in this framework as shaped by mediational means or cultural tools, questions arise as to the nature of cultural tools and why one, as opposed to another, is employed in carrying out a particular form of action" (Penuel & Wertsch, 1995, p. 91)

The cultural and historical tools, resources, or mediational means that are most critical for identity formation are the *ideologies* that are available in a particular social-cultural-historical context. This insight, of course, comes first from the psychologist Erik Erikson (1968), who argues that, particularly during adolescence, ideologies give young lives meaning and purpose, ideologies give youth something to which to be loyal and true, and ideologies connect the past, present, and future:

> [C]ultural tools in the form of ideologies provide individuals with a coherent world view, something that, in [Erikson's] view, youth desperately need to fashion an identity. In that way, these ideologies are empowering, providing youth with a compass in a contradictory and complex world. At the same time, [however], these resources are, according to Erikson, constraining, in that individuals are limited in who they can become by the array of choices of ideology, career, and self-expression. (Penuel & Wertsch, 1995, p. 90)

Thus, for example, *moral* identity (to consider one important dimension of identity) consists, using this viewpoint, of an understanding of oneself as a moral person that comes not from oneself alone, gaining access to, or reflecting on, one's "true" or "essential" moral self (see Blasi, 1984). Rather, it comes from ongoing dialogue with others in one's social world—dialogue that is necessarily shaped and mediated by specific cultural tools and ideological resources. Chief among these tools and resources are what can be called *moral ideologies*—voices or orientations, religious or secular, that are carried and transmitted via others' words, language, and forms of discourse (Tappan, 1992, 1997; see also Gilligan, 1982). One finds one's moral identity, therefore, primarily in the ideologically mediated moral action in which one engages, not simply via a process of self-reflection. Moral identity is, as Tappan (2005) points out, "at its core, a function of the ongoing dialogical interchange between self and others" (p. 49). As such, identity development necessarily entails a process of "ideological becoming" (see Bakhtin, 1981), whereby one appropriates the words and language of others, and in so doing struggles to strike a balance between "authoritative" and "internally persuasive" forms of discourse (see Tappan, 2000, 2005).

Given the critical relationship between ideology and identity, it is important to acknowledge the critical role that ideology also plays in maintaining, reinforcing, and reproducing the dynamics of power, privilege, and oppression (Apple, 1995). To study and understand ideology, argues John Thompson (1990), "is to study the ways in which meaning serves to establish and sustain relations of domination" (p. 56). Thompson expands Marx's analysis of relations of class domination and subordination as the principal axes of inequality and exploitation in human societies, to offer a more inclusive perspective on the ways in which ideology establishes and maintains various forms of dominant-subordinate power relations. In so doing, he identifies five general modes through which ideology can operate to establish and sustain relations of domination: "legitimation, dissimulation, unification, fragmentation, and reification" (p. 60).

As such, Thompson's analysis echoes Gramsci's (1971) theory of hegemony, which claims that dominant groups use ideologies much more effectively than physical force or violence to keep subordinate group members in their place, and to rebuff any attempts at resisting the status quo. Ideologies serve this purpose by convincing subordinate group members of the legitimacy of their position in the social hierarchy, as Ellen Brantlinger (2003) clearly illustrates in her research on the ways in which middle class parents negotiate and rationalize the advantages their children enjoy in school. In particular, when she analyzed the narratives of middle class mothers about their children's school experience for patterns of domination and subordination, Brantlinger found clear evidence of all five of Thompson's (1990) ideological operations, as well as many of the associated "strategies of symbolic construction": "[middle-class mothers'] depictions of their own and Other people's children provide the rationale and justification for the case they make for their children's need for distinctive and separated school circumstances....[for example,] mothers readily relegate Other people's children to segregated settings and lesser conditions while claiming that such arrangements are in the Other's best interest" (Brantlinger, 2003, p. 36).

Finally, our argument is supported by Butler's (1990, 1991) claim that identity is fundamentally *performed* or *enacted* (see also Goffman, 1959; Willie, 2003). Butler (1991) suggests, in particular, that identity is fragile, that the roles one plays are unstable, and hence actors must continually repeat their performances of identity, in different contexts, and for different audiences, in order to provide some measure of stability and certainty:

> [I]f heterosexuality [for example] is compelled to repeat itself in order to establish the illusion of its own uniformity and identity, then this is an identity permanently at risk.... If there is, as it were, always a compulsion to repeat, repetition never fully accomplishes identity. That there is a need for repetition at all is a sign that identity... requires to be instituted again and again, which is to say that it runs the risk of being de-instituted at every interval. (p. 24)

So, if identity is a form of mediated action, and if it is performed or enacted (repeatedly, perhaps, in different contexts, for different audiences), then one's performance of one's identity must entail the use of specific cultural tools/mediational means—particularly ideologies and ideological operations. Thus a fundamental question for researchers studying the manifestations and implications of ideologically mediated identity is to identify the ideological resources that are appropriated in a given social-cultural-historical context, and to understand how these resources are used to mediate the performance of identity in that context—in both positive and negative ways (Tappan, 2006).

We must note, however, that in our view identity as an ideologically mediated form of action/performance does not imply that persons are simply automatons, blindly following cultural and ideological dictates and scripts. Douglas Foley's (1990) ethnography of a small Mexican American town in south Texas is quite instructive in this regard. In his study, Foley shows how a school in this small town serves to construct a cultural ideology grounded in traditional American values. Members of this school community resist and challenge, as well as enact and maintain, expected roles. By performing different roles in various contexts, members constitute cultural meanings and practices that in turn shape their ways of being and behaving. As such, Foley argues,

> Cultural traditions are constantly being homogenized and invented in modern capitalist cultures. This culture concept makes problematic the anthropological notion of an "authentic," stable cultural tradition that produces stable social identities. The idea of shifting "lifestyles" tends to replace the idea of distinct, unchanging social identities. (p. 193)

Foley further explains that students, in particular, are not simply socialized through an "imposed cultural hegemony of ideas" (p. 193) but instead, they enact and practice their identities in a variety of ways, in a variety of contexts.

Cultural meanings, or ideologies, therefore, are neither imposed hegemonic structures nor stable. Individuals do not perform prescribed parts in enacting and practicing their identities. They are constantly shaped and reshaped by the complex interactions of individuals' everyday realities and lived experiences. As many have argued (e.g., Apple, 1995), hegemonic ideologies are imposed on people in schooling and in larger society, but these meanings take on different values and forms as individuals mediate these cultural meanings in constructing their identities.

Our own empirical work on social class as identity focuses primarily on the ways affluent students use the array of available cultural meanings for understanding the world around them and stabilizing themselves in that world (Howard, 2008; Howard & Tappan, 2007). We find that affluent students use various ideological modes to rationalize their schooling and life advantages, construct between-class divisions, establish within-class solidarity, and discredit others. These ideological operations, however, are not simply methods or competencies that affluent students know how to use; they are also formative elements of their identities. Ideology and identity thus meet at the boundary between individuals' inner and outer worlds. Their identity is produced in relation to and coordination with their ways of knowing and thinking. Through this coordination and relationship, an individual's identity is not given, but an activity, a performance, a form of mediated action. This activity/performance is one of coordinating the values and views that form the foundation of individuals' immediate social context with those that underline their ideologically-mediated social class identities. By examining how social class as a component of identity is actively produced and reproduced, we draw new attention to the salience of social class for understanding the workings of everyday life and for fashioning particular ways of knowing and doing.

Conclusion

Conceptualizing social class as an aspect or dimension of identity allows us to see more clearly some of the limitations of other approaches to understanding the role that social class plays in the U.S. educational system. In addition, this approach opens up the theoretical terrain for a comprehensive analysis of the social and cultural elements of social class, and encourages a new and different conversation about these complex and complicated issues. It enables, therefore, a critical exploration of the ways in which social class interacts and intersects with other aspects of one's identity, including race, gender, sexuality, nationality, and religion. In so doing, this approach does not isolate social class into a category as through it exists separate from the other dimensions of who we are. Rather, it attempts to understand identity in terms of the full interplay of these multiple personal, social, and cultural dimensions.

Turning our scholarly efforts toward the lived experiences of social class rather than only the economic factors can elaborate and extend our understandings of the various social and cultural forces that are at play in reinforcing and reproducing unequal relations. By critically examining the social and cultural aspects of social class we can work toward developing the necessary cultural script to extend beyond commodified notions that divert attention from, and protect, the concealed and sophisticated processes involved in the cultural production of these unequal power relations. By mapping out and exposing the contours of the social and cultural elements of social class, we can engage in the type of complicated conversation that is needed to understand more fully how the success of some relates to the failure of many and for entering new theoretical terrains that revive our explorations of social class. It is only through engaging in complicated conversations about social class that we can develop a theoretical framework that has yet to be imagined. We can then perhaps begin to stretch our imagination to think of schooling in ways that allow us to analyze class stratification, not simply to reproduce it.

References

Ansalone, G. (2001). Schooling, tracking, and inequality. *Journal of Children & Poverty, 7*(1), 33–47.

Anyon, J. (1980). Social class and the hidden curriculum of work. *Journal of Education, 162*, 67–92.

Anyon, J. (1981). Elementary schooling and distinctions of social class. *Interchange, 12*, 118–132.

Apple, M. (Ed.). (1982). *Cultural and economic reproduction in education: Essays on class, ideology and the state.* London: Routledge & Kegan Paul.

Apple, M. (1995). *Education and power.* New York: Routledge.

Apple, M. (1996). *Cultural politics and education.* New York: Teachers College Press.

Apple, M., & Weis, L. (1983). Ideology and practice in schooling: A political and conceptual introduction. In M. Apple & L. Weis (Eds.), *Ideology and practice in schooling* (pp. 3–25). Philadelphia: Temple University Press.

Arnowitz, S. (1980). Science and ideology. *Current Perspectives in Social Theory, 1,* 75–101.

Artiles, A. J., & Trent, S. (1994). Overrepresentation of minority students in special education: A continuing debate. *Journal of Special Education, 27,* 410–437.

Bakhtin, M. (1981). *The dialogic imagination* (M. Holquist, Ed.; C. Emerson & M. Holquist, Trans.). Austin: University of Texas Press.

Barton, L., & Oliver, M. (1997). Special needs: Personal trouble or public issue? In B. Cosin & M. Hales (Eds.), *Families, education and social differences* (pp. 89–101). New York: Routledge/The Open University.

Bereiter, C., & Engelmann, S. (1966). *Teaching disadvantaged children in the preschool.* Englewood Cliffs, NJ: Prentice-Hall.

Bettie, J. (2003). *Women without work: Girls, race, and identity.* Berkeley: University of California Press.

Blasi, A. (1984). Moral identity: Its role in moral functioning. In W. Kurtines & J. Gewirtz (Eds.), *Morality, moral behavior, and moral development* (pp. 128–139). New York: Routledge Falmer.

Bohn, A. (2006). A framework for understanding Ruby Payne. *Rethinking Schools, 21*(2). Retrieved January 11, 2008, from http://www.rethinkingschools.org

Boudon, R. (1990/1994). *The art of self persuasion: The social explanation of false beliefs* (M. Slater, Trans.). Cambridge, England: Polity Press. (Original work published 1990)

Bourdieu, P. (1977). *Outline of a theory of practice.* Cambridge, England: Cambridge University Press.

Bourdieu, P. (1984). *Distinction: A social critique of the judgment of taste.* Cambridge, MA: Harvard University Press.

Bourdieu, P., & Passeron, J. C. (1977). *Reproduction in education, society and culture.* Beverly Hills, CA: Sage.

Bowles, S., & Gintis, H. (1976). *Schooling in capitalist America.* New York: Basic Books.

Brantlinger, E. (2003). *Dividing classes: How the middle class negotiates and rationalizes school advantage.* New York: Routledge Falmer.

Brooks-Gunn, J., & Duncan, G. J. (1997). The effects of poverty on children. *Future of Children, 7,* 55–71.

Burton, R. L. (1999). A study of disparities among school facilities in North Carolina: Effects of race and economic status. *Educational Policy, 13*(2), 280–295.

Butler, J. (1990). *Gender trouble: Feminism and the subversion of identity.* New York: Routledge.

Butler, J. (1991). Decking out: Performing identities. In D. Fuss (Ed.), *Inside/out: Lesbian theories, gay theories* (pp. 13–29). New York: Routledge.

Coleman, J. (1988). Social capital, human capital, and schools. *Independent School, 48*(1), 9–16.

Connor, M. H., & Boskin, J. (2001). Overrepresentation of bilingual and poor children in special education classes: A continuing problem. *Journal of Children & Poverty, 7,* 23–32.

Damon, W., & Hart, D. (1988). *Self-understanding in childhood and adolescence.* New York: Cambridge University Press.

De Civita, M., Pagani, L., Vitaro, F., & Tremblay, R. E. (2004). The role of maternal educational aspirations in mediating the risk of income source on academic failure in children from persistently poor families. *Children and Youth Services Review, 26,* 749–769.

Dolby, N. (2000). Changing selves: Multicultural education and the challenge of new identities. *Teachers College Record, 102*(5), 898–912.

Education Trust. (2001). *The funding gap: Low-income and minority students receive fewer dollars.* Washington, DC: Author.

Erikson, E. (1968). *Identity: Youth and crisis.* New York: Norton.

Fay, B. (1987). *Critical social science.* Ithaca, NY: Cornell University Press.

Foley, D. (1990). *Learning capitalist culture: Deep in the heart of Tejas.* Philadelphia: University of Pennsylvania Press.

Freud, S. (1923/1960). *The ego and the id.* New York: Norton. (Original work published 1923)

Gilligan, C. (1982). *In a different voice.* Cambridge, MA: Harvard University Press.

Giroux, H. (1981). *Ideology, culture, and the process of schooling.* Philadelphia: Temple University Press.

Giroux, H. (1992). *Border crossings: Cultural workers and the politics of education.* New York: Routledge, Chapman & Hall.

Goffman, I. (1959). *The presentation of self in everyday life.* Garden City, NY: Doubleday Anchor.

Gorski, P. (2006a). Classist underpinnings of Ruby Payne's Framework. *Teachers College Record Online.* Retrieved January 11, 2008, from http://www.tcrecord.org

Gorski, P. (2006b). Savage unrealities: Classism and racism abound in Ruby Payne's Framework. *Rethinking Schools, 21*(2). Retrieved from January 11, 2008, http://www.rethinkingschools.org

Gramsci, A. (1971). *Selections from the prison notebook* (Q. Hoare & G. N. Smith, Eds.). New York: International.

Hall, S. (1996). Who needs "identity"? In S. Hall & P. du Gay (Eds.), *Questions of cultural identity* (pp. 1–17). London: Sage.

Hauser, R. N., Simmons, S. J., & Pager, D. I. (2000). *High school dropout, race/ethnicity, and social background from the 1970s and the 1990s* (Working paper no. 2000–12). Madison, WI: University of Wisconsin-Madison, Center for Demography and Ecology.

Holland, D., Lachicotte, W., Skinner, D., & Cain, C. (1998). *Identity and agency in cultural worlds.* Cambridge, MA: Harvard University Press.

hooks, b. (2000). *Where we stand: Class matters.* New York: Routledge.

Howard, A. (2008). *Learning privilege: Lessons of power and identity in affluent schooling.* New York: Routledge.

Howard, A., & Tappan, M. (2007, April). *Privilege as identity.* Paper presented at Annual Meeting of American Educational Research Association, Chicago, Illinois.

Ingersoll, R. (1999). The problem of underqualified teachers in American secondary schools. *Educational Research, 28*(2), 26–37.

Jencks, C. (1972). *Inequality: A reassessment of the effect of family and schooling in America.* New York: Harper & Row.

Jensen, A. R. (1969). How much can we boost IQ and scholastic achievement? *Harvard Educational Review, 39,* 1–123.

Kao, G, Tienda, N., & Schneider, B. (1996). Racial and ethnic variation in academic performance. *Research in Sociology of Education and Socialization, 11,* 263–297.

Katz, M. B. (1975). *Class, bureaucracy, and the schools: The illusion of educational change in America.* New York: Praeger.

Keller, B. (2006, May 3). Payne's pursuit. *Education Week,* 1–3.

Kozol, J. (1991). *Savage inequalities: Children in America's schools.* New York: Crown.

Larrain, J. A. (1992). *The concept of ideology.* Aldershot, England: Gregg Revivals (Routledge).

Leonhardt, D. (2005, May 14). A closer look at income mobility. *New York Times.* Retrieved July 20, 2007, from http://www.nytimes.com/pages/national/class/index.html

MacLeod, J. (1987). *Ain't no makin' it: Leveled aspirations in low-income neighborhoods.* Boulder, CO: Westview Press.

Mantsios, G. (2003). Media magic: Making class invisible. In T. E. Ore (Ed.), *The social construction of difference and inequality* (2nd ed., pp. 81–89). New York: McGraw-Hill.

McDermott, R. P. (1977). Social relations as contexts for learning in school. *Harvard Educational Review, 47*(2), 198–213.

McLoyd, V. (1998). Socioeconomic disadvantage and child development. *American Psychologist, 53,* 185–204.

Metz, M. H. (1998, April). *Veiled inequalities: The hidden effects of community social class on high school teachers' perspectives and practices.* Paper presented at the annual meeting of the American Educational Research Association, San Diego, CA.

Morrow, R. A., & Torres, C. A. (1994). Education and the reproduction of class, gender, and race: Responding to the postmodern challenge. *Educational Theory, 44*(1), 43–61.

Ng, J., & Rury, J. (2006). Poverty and education: A critical analysis of the Ruby Payne phenomenon. *Teachers College Record Online.* Retrieved January 11, 2008, from http://www.tcrecord.org.

Nieto, S. (1996). *Affirming diversity: The sociopolitical context of multicultural education* (2nd ed.). White Plains, NY: Longman.

Nieto, S. (2005). Public education in the twentieth century and beyond: High hopes, broken promises, and an uncertain future. *Harvard Educational Review, 75*(1), 43–64.

Oakes, J. (1985). *Keeping track: How schools structure inequality.* New Haven, CT: Yale University Press.

Orfield, G. (2000, April). *What have we learned from school reconstitution?* Paper presented at the Annual Meeting of the American Educational Research Association, New Orleans, LA.

Ortner, S. (1991). Reading America: Preliminary notes on class and culture. In R. G. Fox (Ed.), *Recapturing anthropology: Working in the present* (pp. 163–189). Santa Fe, NM: School of America Research Press.

Osei-Kofi, N. (2005). Pathologizing the poor: A framework for understanding Ruby Payne's work. *Equity & Excellence in Education, 38*(4), 367–375.

Payne, R. (2005). *A framework for understanding poverty.* Highland, TX: aha! Process, Inc.

Penuel, W., & Wertsch, J. (1995). Vygotsky and identity formation: A sociocultural approach. *Educational Psychologist, 30,* 83–92.

Persell, C. H. (1997). Social class and educational equality. In J. A. Banks & C. A. M. Banks (Eds.), *Multicultural education: Issues and perspectives* (3rd ed., pp. 87–107). Boston: Allyn & Bacon.

Phillips, M., Brooks-Gunn, J., Duncan, G., Klevanov, P., & Crane, J. (1998). Family background, parenting practices, and the Black/White test score gap. In C. Jencks & M. Phillips (Eds.), *The Black/White test score gap* (pp. 229–272). Washington, DC: Brookings Institution Press.

Reed-Danahay, D. (2005). *Locating Bourdieu.* Bloomington: Indiana University Press.

Reissman, F. (1962). *The culturally deprived child.* New York: Harper & Row.

Ripple, C. H., & Luthar, S. S. (2000). Academic risk among inner-city adolescents: The role of personal attributes. *Journal of School Psychology, 38*(3), 277–298.

Robertson, S. L. (2000). *A class act.* New York: Falmer Press.

Rosenblum, K. E., & Travis, T.-C. M. (2003). *The meaning of difference: American constructions of race, sex and gender, social class, and sexual orientation* (3rd ed.). New York: McGraw-Hill.

Schwarz, J. E., & Volgy, T. J. (1992). *The forgotten Americans.* New York: Norton.

Scott, J., & Leonhardt, D. (2005, May 15). Shadowy lines that still divide. *New York Times.* Retrieved July 20, 2007, from http://www.nytimes.com/pages/national/class/index.html.

Seyfried, S. F. (1998). Academic achievement of African American preadolescents: The influence of teacher perceptions. *American Journal of Community Psychology, 26*(3), 381–402.

Sklar, H., Collins, C., & Leondar-Wright, B. (2003). The growing wealth gap: The median household net worth matches the sticker price of the new Ford Excursion. In T. E. Ore (Ed.), *The social construction of difference and inequality* (2nd ed., pp. 90–95). New York: McGraw-Hill.

Spring, J. (1972). *The rise and fall of the corporate state.* Boston: Beacon Press.

Stipic, D., & Ryan, R. (1997). Economically disadvantaged preschoolers: Ready to learn but further to go. *Developmental Psychology, 33,* 711–723.

Tappan, M. (1992). Texts and contexts: Language, culture, and the development of moral functioning. In L. T. Winegar & J. Valsiner (Eds.), *Children's development within social contexts: Metatheoretical, theoretical, and methodological issues* (pp. 93–117). Hillsdale, NJ: Erlbaum.

Tappan, M. (1997). Language, culture, and moral development: A Vygotskian perspective. *Developmental Review, 17,* 78–100.

Tappan, M. (2000). Autobiography, mediated action, and the development of moral identity. *Narrative Inquiry, 10,* 81–109.

Tappan, M. (2005). Domination, subordination, and the dialogical self: Identity development and the politics of "ideological becoming." *Culture and Psychology, 11*(1), 47–75.

Tappan, M. (2006). Reframing internalized oppression and internalized domination: From the psychological to the sociocultural. *Teachers College Record, 108*(10), 2115–2144.

Thompson, J. (1990). *Ideology and modern culture.* Stanford, CA: Stanford University Press.

U.S. Census Bureau. (2004). Historical income tables: Households. Retrieved July 20, 2007, from http://www.census.gov/hhes/income/histinc/h0201.html

Van Galen, J. A. (2007). Introduction. In J. A. Van Galen, & G. W. Noblit (Eds.), *Late to class: Social class and schooling in the new economy* (pp. 1–15). Albany: State University of New York Press.

Varenne, H., & McDermott, R. (1998). *Successful failure: The school America builds.* Boulder, CO: Westview Press.

Vygotsky, L. (1978). *Mind in society: The development of higher psychological processes* (M. Cole, V. John-Steiner, S. Scribner, & E. Souberman, Eds.). Cambridge, MA: Harvard University Press.

Wertsch, J. (1995). The need for action in sociocultural research. In J. Wertsch, P. del Rio, & A. Alvarez (Eds.), *Sociocultural studies of mind* (pp. 56–74). New York: Cambridge University Press.

Wertsch, J. (1998). *Mind as action.* New York: Oxford University Press.

Wexler, P. (1992). *Becoming somebody: Toward a social psychology of school.* London: Falmer Press.

Willie, S. (2003). *Acting Black: College, identity, and the performance of race.* New York: Routledge.

Willis, P. (1977). *Learning to labor: How working class kids get working class jobs.* New York: Columbia University Press.

Suggested Reading Questions

1. The authors state that U.S. society suffers from an inability to speak of the relationship between social class and schooling. How might this view be supported by the argument that this is due to the reductive nature of economic analysis at the cost of cultural factors that shape the experience of poverty?

2. According to the authors, Ruby Payne frames the culture of poverty as inferior to middle class culture. How might such an understanding of poverty, based on cultural deficit arguments, explain poverty, reinforce unequal relations, and differences in schooling and society?

3. In what ways does conceptualizing social class as identity become a counterforce of the role economic factors play in the identity formation of social groups and class stratification?

4. The authors suggest that the performative nature of identity is situated and produced in specific sites. What is the relationship between situated identity and identity as a form of mediated action?

5. How might curriculum studies scholars begin to envision future schooling as a process that makes space for interrogating social inequities rather than reproducing it?

Response to Adam Howard and Mark Tappan Toward Emancipated Identities and Improved World Circumstances

Ellen Brantlinger

Howard and Tappan have written a thoughtful and engaging essay in which they assert that rather than seeing identity solely as economic status it is beneficial to use the concept of identity to create an explanatory framework for understanding social class. To provide the rationale for class analysis, they preface their chapter with a compelling review of the growing inequities in schools and society. They make a broad theoretical sweep to explain the relevance of correspondence theory, habitus, performance theory, and ideology to understanding class relations. I was delighted that the authors' mentioned "moral ideologies" because I am convinced that the moral prerogatives that undergird scholarly work must be articulated. I personally am explicit in insisting on the necessity of basing one's scholarly contributions on a social reciprocity morality that acknowledges human commonalities and interdependence, and considers human's impact on the environment (Brantlinger, 2007, 2008, in press). I choose to base my practice on a socially inclusive, communitarian ethic that contrasts to the reigning competitive, individualistic moralities that validate social hierarchies in meritocratic schools and other arenas of capitalist social life.

Citing numerous classical and current sociologists, linguists, and feminist scholars, Howard and Tappan argue that identity can be used as a conceptual tool for understanding class relations. Although they take the first step in recognizing identity phenomena in class realities, they do not show how this level of scholarly focus might contribute to class equity. To counter the impact of ubiquitous and lethal deficit hypotheses, scholars should always be critically oriented in their aim to alter inequitable and unjust conditions related to class, race, gender, sexual orientation, and ethnicity. Howard and Tappan fail to clarify how identity is a meaningful construct in understanding class or a valuable tool for enabling a social class equity agenda. Their next project might be to demonstrate how the microlevel study of social identity is better—or at least as good as macrolevel analyses of economic relations—in bringing about peace, prosperity, and constructive interdependence among American and world citizens.

Countering Ruby Payne

In their chapter, Howard and Tappan debunk the ideas of the populist writer and profiteer, Ruby Payne. They also critique Payne's audiences' lack of insight into her distorted versions of social class distinctions. Eliciting Gramsci's essential question, "who benefits," they note that practitioners appreciate Payne's victim blaming because it negates the negative impact of class structure (hierarchical class system, class privilege) and lets powerful players off the hook regarding personal responsibility to others. Additionally, cultural deprivation versions of poverty's origins serve to deflect blame from the moral flaws of higher-income people's advantaging their own class to the deficiencies in impoverished children and families. Howard and Tappan rightly attribute the persistence of class deficit theory to the fact that it serves the middle class's interests.

I concur with the authors' condemnation of the Payne enterprise. As a Court Appointed Special Advocate (CASA) volunteer, I must attend certain inservice programs and in the past was a participant in a day-long "Bridges Out of Poverty" workshop (Payne, 2005). Priced at $40 per head, with at least 150 participants, despite claims to nonprofit status, someone in Payne's burgeoning organization made money. The session was led by a woman who claimed low-income family background. She presented herself as an example of how someone living in poverty would think and act. She referred to the mostly professional audience as people who held middle class perceptions of themselves and their life options. Witty and self-deprecating—the Rodney Dangerfield of class theory—the presenter was guided by a highly scripted PowerPoint presentation (replicated in handouts). She charged through various situations designed to illustrate the way class works and fired off questions. Correct answers were aligned with deficit viewpoint and there was no opportunity to ask independent questions. When I challenged the victim-blaming implications of her examples, the presenter promptly shifted her gaze and praise to participants with conforming responses. She never looked at me or called on me again. Presumably to divert common criticism of the Payne materials, the presenter promised to address "exploitation" and "social structure." These focal levels were never covered. I heard from the conference sponsor that my evaluation was the only negative one in the batch.

I report on my own experience with Payne's work to illustrate that focusing on a broadly defined concept of identity does not ensure a critical perspective. Payne's theories are not out-of-sync with Howard and Tappan's claim that identity aspects of social class are valuable as an analytic tool. In fact, Payne emphasizes that social class is a sociocultural phenomenon that links to, and shapes, the class-distinctive personal identities and behaviors of people. Like Howard and Tappan, Payne foregrounds class identity and social milieu as more important than societal economic structures and family finances in creating class distinctive actions and unequal life outcomes. The fact that identity can be used to shore up deficit theory should provide the impetus for critical scholars such as Howard and Tappan to fine-tune their definition of the identity concept in order to exclude approaches not consistent with the desired outcome of diminishing the damaging impact of social class distinctions. Howard and Tappan do not identify themselves as critical theorists; however, because they scrutinize privilege and repeatedly reference critical scholars, I place them in this camp. As critical scholars, their goal should be to go beyond explanation about social life to a commitment to work toward social class transformation. Although I agree that identity is an important conceptual tool for progressive scholars, cultural deprivationists such as Payne strategically use the concept to further entrench deficit theories. A generalized identity construct does not avoid the deficit-oriented pitfalls found at other focal levels (institutional structure, discourse, ideology) of social research that the authors reference. That said, my advice is that Howard and Tappan expand their discussion of identity so it is clear and tight enough to ensure the elimination of appropriation by deficit theorists. As it currently stands, the generalized notion of identity straddles multiple philosophical/theoretical ways of understanding social class.

Identity's Role in Social Life

Stuart Hall (2005) sees identity as strategic, positional, and dynamically constructed within particular historical, cultural, and language contexts. Identity operates subjectively through a *representational system* replete with *signifying practices* that have the power to mark, assign, and classify (p. 295). For Hall, human *difference* is meaningful for identity production because it creates a binary between self and Other. Hall argues: *"culture depends on giving things meaning by assigning them to different positions within a classifactory system"*[italics in original] (p. 303). Although "typing" (classifying) is necessary for humans to understand and navigate the world, stereotyping uses a few simple, vivid, memorable, and easily grasped traits to reduce, essentialize, naturalize, and fix individual difference. Wexler (1992) calls such relatively unrefined images as caricatures of social identities (p. 9). Stereotypes provide the rationale for *"symbolically fixing boundaries"* and *"ritualizing exclusion"* (Hall, 2005, p. 306, 307). Stereotyping is most evident when there are huge power inequities among people. Social class stereotypes exist as a means to justify societal inequalities and the oppression of Others (Brantlinger, 2003). Clearly, according to Hall's definitions, Payne's theories of social class differences use stereotypes to provide the justification for class privilege. Unfortunately, Payne is not alone. Practitioners often base their work on the scientific creation of stereotypes (use of classifications, standardized tests that compare outsiders to insiders' norms). Stereotypes define the nature of individuals' specialized needs and script roles for those labeled to play in school and society. Identity therefore is not only composed of subjective understandings, it is imposed externally by role prescriptions combined with societal messages about what it means to be from certain groups. Typically, privileged individuals have the power to construct and advertise their own positions and character as superior (Howard, 2008). Construction of self as superior is socially relational because it depends on finding Others to be socially inferior.

Constraining Identity

Social class stereotypes and symbolic boundaries limit the subjective resources available to individuals to construct their own identities in ways that are satisfactory to them and that further their unique life goals. The fact that stereotypes do not always benefit the already advantaged often goes unrecognized. For example, privileged students may feel compelled to develop their cultural, social, educational, and economic capital in order to retain their class position. Such efforts can sideline more authentic desires and rachet up within-group competition in stressful ways. Disadvantaged students are obviously restricted by such institutional practices as tracking and special education classification and placement. Low-income people internalize the negative images of their class and, consequently, may not try options that are actually potentially available to them. After visiting a low-income school that involved violin lessons for all primary grade students, a teacher related that a "Harley-looking dad thanked the violin instructor, remarking: 'I thought playing the violin was only for fucking rich kids.'" This statement illustrates the father's own sense of class identity, class boundaries, and his perceptions of his son's restricted possibilities. It also shows that when schools break out of typical social class modes of curriculum then children, parents, teachers, and community members may begin to think differently about class distinctions and individual possibilities: "Emancipating" Identity

Because I fault Howard and Tappan for not sufficiently refining their concept of identity to exclude its use by deficit theorists, I make use of Freire's (1973) term *emancipation* to delimit the construct. Freire used education as a tool to raise individuals' consciousness about the reality of their worlds and, particularly, the constraints certain societal structures as well as representational and signifying phenomena place on their lives and their thinking. Whether the target student is from a privileged or disadvantaged back-

338   *Ellen Brantlinger*

ground, the ideal of a universal subject who has an *emancipated identity* should be the goal of critical understanding. Such individuals would eschew social bias and hierarchy as they endorse a social reciprocity moral code. Recognizing their own and others' innate human worth and interdependence, difference would not be equated with inferiority. Individuals with an emancipated identity would use their transformed (democratically and equity-focused) agency to fight oppression and improve world circumstances. According to this specific definition of (emancipated) identity, Payne's work would be dismissed because it wrongly reads the world and does not end with social equity. In meritocratic schools and unregulated capitalist societies, institutional structure and cultural messages reinforce ideas about human difference as problematic. In contrast, socialist societies ideally do not stratify citizens into social hierarchies. This does not mean that homogeneity or assimilation are advocated. Various desired identities and social roles (i.e., social and cultural variation) would be voluntarily assumed by subjects. Hence, differences would be horizontally, rather than vertically, distinctive.

Conclusion

Howard and Tappan took readers on an interesting, well-informed, and relevant tour of ideas about social class relations; however, they did not go far enough in detailing what they want for social class relations. Hence, I encourage them to hone in on their identity focus to alter its nebulous and inactive status so that they can provide guidelines for practice that benefits the larger social good.

References

Brantlinger, E. A. (2003). *Dividing classes: How the middle class negotiates and rationalizes school advantage.* New York: Falmer Routledge.

Brantlinger, E. A. (2007). (Re)turning to Marx to understand the unexpected anger among "winners in schooling: A critical social psychology perspective. In J. Van Galen & G. W. Noblit (Eds.), *Late to class: Social class and schooling in the new economy* (pp. 235–268) Buffalo, NY: SUNY Press.

Brantlinger, E. (2008). Playing to middle class self-interest in pursuit of school equity. In L. Weis (Ed.), *The way class works: Readings on school, family, and the economy* (pp. 243–259). New York: Routledge

Brantlinger, E. (in press). Impediments to social justice: Hierarchy, imposed identity (disability classification), science, and faith. In W. Ayers, T. Quinn, & D. Stoval (Eds.), *Handbook for social justice in education.*

Hall, S. (2005). From representation: Cultural representations and signifying practices. In E. R. Brown & K. J. Saltman (Eds.), *The critical middle school reader* (pp. 295–310). New York: Routledge.

Howard, A. (2008). *Learning privilege: Lessons of power and identity in affluent schooling.* New York & London: Routledge.

Payne, R. (2005). *A framework for understanding poverty.* Highland, TX: aha! Process, Inc.

Wexler, P. (1992). *Becoming somebody: Toward a social psychology of school.* London: Falmer.

Part VI

Cross-Cultural International Perspectives

17 The Unconscious of History?
Mesmerism and the Production of Scientific Objects for Curriculum Historical Research

Bernadette M. Baker

Chapter Overview

This chapter discusses key historical events related to the conception of mesmerism, animal magnetism, and hypnosis and how such events influenced the field of education in general and curriculum studies in particular. The author notes that such studies cannot be limited to particular notions or formal disciplines given these concepts originated during the 19th century, a time when neither nation nor field was differently developed. The author discusses the ways in which distinguishing between various states of consciousness—far from settling debates over the truth of human nature—incited a new series of debates and investigations focused on hypnotic states. After providing two vignettes, she illustrates four ways mesmeric phenomena influenced what is now the field of education and its assumed objects or foci. Noting the important but largely underexamined work of Alfred Binet and unconscious studies, the author describes their influence on concepts of Being in and out of schools. While previously there were questions as to whether the hypnotized subject was in or out of the body or interpenetrated with a planetary fluid, by the late 1800s the mind was presumed to exist in the body and the unconscious became associated with primitiveness and exoticism. The author notes that the altered states associated with mesmerism impacted the inscription of children in multiple ways, including suggestibility studies. Lastly, she reveals the ways in which mesmerism is related to the making of the psychoanalytic field, the assumption in scientific study that the heart stands in the way of reason, and the very contours of the field of curriculum studies.

> the critique of scientific reason to which the failure of psychoanalysis leads us…has as its correlate the problem of hypnosis.
> —Chertok & Stengers, 1989/1992, p. ix

A precise understanding of the nature of self, mind, ego, or consciousness is not the key to an understanding of existence, essence, or identity, or vice versa; truths are not simply those things that exist the way they appear; perception is not dependent upon induction into discursive regularities that make appearance possible—such provocations, so seemingly counterintuitive, bespeak the limits of Western philosophy. Shaping, troubling, and exceeding those limits across the 19th century were a series of events that Henri Ellenberger (1960/1970) has called "the discovery of the unconscious." This chapter is an examination of the understudied impact that key events related to such an apparent discovery—animal magnetism, mesmerism, and hypnosis—held for the formation of an educational field more broadly and for the production of scientific objects that have become the repetitive focus specifically of a curriculum history subdiscipline.

It is impossible to delimit such a study to the territory of a discrete nation. Geopolitical entities do not speak for themselves. Nation-formation was an uncertain and fledgling activity across the 19th century. Scholars, events, and translations traveled and the boundaries they crossed were not construed so simply nor so directly in terms of homogeneous, stable geographical territories or idealized projections of state cultures and languages. Thus, while one can make reference to sites of practice, such as in France and in the U.S. when "unconsciousness studies" are the topic, these sites have to be understood in the Derridean sense as conceptual and discursive before geographical, not as forms of representation, nor efforts toward essentialization. Even when documentary sources seem to emanate so repetitively from places now considered parts of Europe and the U.S. their beginnings appear far more messy and numberless, especially when colonization and proto-anthropology are taken seriously as conditions of possibility for the formation of Western sciences (Abraham, 2006; Anderson, 2002; McLeod, 2000), especially when the deep histories of irreconcilable cosmo-theological traditions circulating within "the West" are acknowledged, and especially when "elementary units of habitation" (J. Richardson, in press) (such as reservations, slave "plantations," cities, towns, farmhouses, etc.) mottle the landscape.

It is similarly difficult to delimit such a study to the trajectories of a specific science, largely because the sciences for most of the 19th century were not as formalized as one might presuppose—the biophysical sciences, the humanities, and the social sciences could not be named as such. Rather, borders in multiple forms were being worked out, transgressed, and forged anew. Often forgotten in this vein is the further difficulty of separating what today would be called popular and high culture, especially where claims about mind, medicine, education, and healing were being made (A. Richardson, 2001).

Animal magnetism, mesmerism, and hypnosis,[1] reemerging in Anglophone literature of the mid-19th century decades and formalizing at the turn of the 20th century, are challenging to unpack given the complexity, profundity, and breadth of issues to which they were and still are in many instances tied. They reerupted across a century in which many pointed debates revolved especially around post-Kantian theories of reason and the formation—and troubling—of what would today be called ocularcentrism—whether we only see objects in terms of the categories for seeing that we have been taught or whether we see objects and then categorize them. Such debates, from the early 1800s on, included: equivocation around the physiology of the eye, such as whether seeing was reducible to eye and whether mental images were explainable as an organic event; the emergence of perception as important to processes of comprehension; whether concepts such as perspective and perspectivalism were ways of controlling more radical proliferation of observations (i.e., separating observer from observed, making the angle exterior and knowable, and fixing it in advance); debate over what was admissible as sensory, such as whether perception involved something beyond sensory portals; disagreement over sensory portals as objective, whether sensory portals always carried the same content for each receiver, whether that content was reliable, and whether it traveled along organic routes (e.g., the trouble that performance of magic tricks and visual illusion experiments generated at midcentury, as well as early 19th century studies of the effects of alcohol, drugs, and head injury). In the broth of theories put forward from no single locus of authority, such argument over what constituted the material, the spiritual, the mental, and the bodily indexed a broader disagreement over truth-production and the attendant status anxiety.

Truth-production had come to matter, then. Determinations of sociomoral standing hung in the balance and this status anxiety infused a vast array of sites of expression, from the "religious" to the "artistic." Drawing lines between states, such as waking, sleeping, somnambulic, dreaming, unconsciousness, and so forth was not just wound into preexisting debates over the truth of human nature but interrupted them—an apparently new series of phenomena, potentials, and capacities were brought spectacularly and more regularly into view. A compelling vignette drawn from an official 19th century investigation into *le magnétisme animal* is illustrative of the fascination that such interruption, issues, and debates held.

In Paris in 1831 a *Report of the Experiments on Animal Magnetism* was presented by a Committee of the medical section of the French Royal Academy of Sciences. Described in that report were tests conducted on one Pierre Cazot, a 20-year-old hat maker described as a family man with character of high repute, a reliable worker, born of an epileptic mother and subjected for 10 years to fits which occurred five or six times a week. Cazot was admitted into a Parisian hospital at the beginning of August 1827. While there he was subjected to what was called synonymously animal magnetism or mesmerism. It appeared to induce a particular state ("magnetic slumber" or "somnambulic state") now associated with hypnosis. Cazot's reported ability to enunciate the exact date, time, and severity of his next fit whilst in a somnambulic state was under question and observation. After being put into the proper condition Cazot was asked to forecast his next fit. On August 24 the Committee recorded Cazot's portrayal of his next two attacks.

Nothing could awaken him [out of a somnambulic state]. We pressed him with questions. How long will your fits continue? For a year—Do you know whether they will follow close upon each other? No—Will you have any this month? I shall have one on Monday the 27th at twenty minutes from three o'clock—Will they be severe? Not half so severe as the one I had last.—Upon what other day will you have another attack? After exhibiting some symptoms of impatience, he answered: Fifteen days hence, i.e. on the 7th of September.—At what hour? At ten minutes before six in the morning (Colquhoun, 1831–1833, p. 171).

After being told by Cazot's doctor that the first fit occurred as scheduled, the Committee dutifully gathered just before 6 in the morning on September 7, 1827, to see if he would have the second, reporting:

In order to witness the second fit, your committee met, at a quarter before six of the morning of the 7th of September, in the Salle St Michel of the hospital de la Charité. There we learnt that, upon the previous evening at eight o'clock, Cazot has been seized with a pain in his head which had tormented him all night; that this pain had caused the sensation of ringing of bells, and that he had experienced shooting pains in the ears. At ten minutes to six, we witnessed the epileptic fit, characterized by rigidity and contraction of the limbs, the repeated projection and jerking back of the head, the arched curvature of the body backwards, the convulsive closing of the eyelids, the retraction of the ball of the eye towards the upper part of the orbit...etc. (Colquhoun, 1831–1833, p. 173).

Cazot was called upon repeatedly for nearly a year to project and fulfill such prophecies, even after describing what could be done to prevent his next attack. The Committee concluded that upon coming out of somnambulism Cazot had no memory of the dates he named or his actual fits either. As proof, they tried to trick him by telling his doctor a wrong date. They wanted to see whether anyone was cheating by informing Cazot in advance when to turn on such massive convulsions for all and sundry to gather around and describe. Whether theorized today as suggestibility, imagination, intuition, precognition, or self-fulfilling prophesy the Committee reported that Cazot always had his fits right on time—except for one.

After being kicked by a horse the following May, Cazot fell, hitting his head on the wheel of the wagon and dying from the blow. His prediction of his largest fit ever in the upcoming August could subsequently not be verified. In the final report the Committee theorized how he could miss foreseeing his death but not his fits.

On the basis of this and other experiments, the *Report* subtly contested two earlier investigations from 1784, submitted in Paris, which had dismissed animal magnetism as a charlatan practice. Animal magnetism was a theory of a universal fluid that linked all planetary, solar, animate, and inanimate things. Popularized via the physician Frantz Anton Mesmer in the 1780s it provided a monistic depiction and correction of health problems: one fluid, one disease, one cure. Under this etiology of the universe, the healer, rather than a mineral magnet, mobilized and concentrated existing fluid (conceptualized roughly as energy rather than as wet) to diffuse whatever was blocking the fluid's travel through an object, thereby restoring harmony. In treating people (as opposed to plants, animals, planets, water, objects of glass or wood, as well as the sun), blockages were to be removed through making passes, movements of the hands over or on the body of a reclining patient. The reports of the 1780s put the controversial matter to rest or so it seemed, stating outright that a universal fluid did not exist. These early official investigations, headed in one case by Benjamin Franklin, did note that inexplicable effects were being produced in patients undergoing the mesmeric passes.

In embarrassed and incredulous tones the new report printed in Paris in 1831 documents more diverse phenomena than simply Cazot's performance, which the Committee states they cannot and choose not to explain and which they recommend for further investigation to the Royal Academy. They overtly refuse to enter in upon the question of whether there really is a universal fluid and repeatedly remind the Academy of their initial mistrust and skepticism around such practices, reminding them also of their high moral standing, their experience with clinical procedures, and their very genuine concern for integrity at every stage.

In the early 1830s the report was translated into English and relaunched animal magnetism onto a field of popular debate, 60 years after it had first fascinated continental Europeans and Scandinavians. In Anglophone publications of the 1830s, 1840s, and 1850s in Canada, the U.K., and the U.S., for instance, mesmeric practices would come to notice, being wound into and out of existing belief systems in ways that held enormous implications for the formation of scientific fields and conditions of truth-production.

I have argued elsewhere (Baker, 2007) that broader perceptions of chaotic fluidity and the lustering and planishing of mesmeric phenomena directly bore on activities now associated with education in at least four ways: shaping principles of behavior management, contouring the boundaries of expertise and authority in educational research, elevating the role of Will in intelligence testing and child development theories, and redefining what constituted public and private realms. This chapter elaborates how century-long debates over the validity of animal magnetism, mesmerism, and hypnosis infused the production of scientific objects, including belief in mind as a legitimate site of engineering; the classification of children; the formation of scientific strategies of sympathy and criticism; and the production of the rational, broad-spirited social scientist who must work upon him- or herself, as well as others, to be in a condition to both extract and receive truth.

Such objectifications were important for establishing parameters of an educational field, as well as linking it more broadly to those sciences today considered social. It also suggests how such mesmeric-inspired objectifications and delimitations interpenetrated what curriculum history has, until recently, taken as its mainstream domain—educational policy, classroom practices, curriculum reforms, and textbooks focused on compulsory public schooling and on what Rosemarie Garland Thompson (1997) calls "the figure of the normate."

The chapter examines contours of such objectifications especially through the work of Alfred Binet (who coined with Théodore Simon the term *intelligence testing*, which mutated later into the IQ) and William James (who popularized the terms *stream of consciousness* and *pragmatism*). Much curriculum historical research has examined the connection between discourses that traveled between Germany and the U.S. in the late 19th century, particularly in the figure of John Dewey's version of pragmatism. There has also been quite an extensive examination of the role of a largely Protestant psychology in mental measurement movements. There has been little to no attention paid to the eruption of "unconsciousness studies" in France, their traveling and mutation, the implications of Binet's primary area of training and expertise—hypnosis—or to James's contributions to educational discourse on mind via his involvement in mental healing and parapsychological movements that furnished much of the substance of his public lecturing to teachers and to others. Binet was a source that James overtly referenced when seeking experimental evidence for some of his most rigorous analyses. As the examples below from their work indicate, debates over mind, consciousness, and the unconscious were absorbed into certain practices to the point that a phantasmic retrieval becomes necessary to understand how the "common sense" of Anglophone educational research over much of the 20th century became restricted to examining formal institutions, particularly public schools, and curriculum history to policy or classroom practice implicitly devoted to certain "kinds" of children and teachers in those schools. Such research, in turn, repeatedly circles around particular theoretical assumptions, such as the belief that the "minds" of the young are "influenced" by the experiences of schooling and that this process is somehow key to understanding the existence, essence, or identity of a society.

The pivotal role of mesmeric debates in science-formation and inciting crises of authority have been attended to in histories of anthropology (Stocking, 1986; Wallace, 1983), law (Laurence & Perry, 1988); literary criticism (Mills, 2006; A. Richardson, 2001); medicine (Pattie, 1994; Thornton, 1976); parapsychology (Berloff, 1987; Dingwall, 1967); philosophy (Darnton, 1968); psychiatry (Ellenberger, 1970); psychology and psychotherapy (Chertok & Stengers, 1989/1992; Gauld, 1992; Hale, 1971; Tinterow, 1970); science (Waterfield, 2003; Winter, 1998); sociology (Gilman, 1993); and theology (Fuller, 1982). But significantly, they have not been attended to in Anglophone histories of education or in curriculum history. An engagement with such debates has the potential to indicate what educational research has marshaled under its umbrella and at what cost it has ignored some key aspects of its "own" domain-formation. This chapter thus elaborates the parameters and intertwining of apparently disparate events in ways that re-member the effects of such discourses for curriculum history; that is, in ways that link the very possibility of a wider field called education, in part, to the many attempts to write monistic explanatory scripts over and against perceptions of unruly multiplicity, excess, or fluidity.

Mesmerism and the Parameters of an Educational Field

It is helpful to understand the formalization of an academic educational field emerging across the middle to late 19th century as dependent on the intersection of at least two constructs: childhood-as-rescue and the public school (Baker, 2001). The relations that simultaneously constituted such constructs and undermined any claims to unity in fledgling nations such as France and the United States were interpenetrated and reshaped by mesmerism's catalytic eruption. The incitement to discourse that emanated from description of mesmerized subjects and the reported phenomena cut so directly and so deeply to the core of conceptualizations of Being, existence, presence, life, death, and governance that reactions often swung between vehement incredulity and jubilant support.

In the 1830s, William L. Stone, Superintendent of New York Public Schools and editor of a well-respected New York-based newspaper, published a pamphlet about his observation of animal magnetic trials, defending the fine line he trod between such polarization in trying to theorize the events. After some criticism of his pamphlet, Stone responded by collecting case studies from around the country, including instances of how children in the classroom were "magnetizing" each other. In his Letter to Dr. Brigham, Stone (1837) argued,

> The inference from your letter is, that I have suddenly become a convert to Animal Magnetism, to the whole extent claimed and practiced by Frederick Anthony Mesmer, the founder of the art, and contended for by Wolfart and Kluge, and the other German and French enthusiasts, who have written in explanation and support of the system. This is an error. I am not a positive believer in the system, because I know not what to believe; and yet, I am free to confess, that I have recently beheld phenomena, under circumstances where collusion, deception, fraud, and imposture, were alike out of the question, if not impossible, which have brought me from the position of a positive skeptic to a dead pause. From the evidence of my own senses, I have been compelled if not to relinquish, at least very essentially to modify, my disbelief; and I can no longer deny, although I cannot explain, the extraordinary phenomena produced by the exertion of the mental energy of one person upon the mind of another, while in a state of what is termed magnetic slumber. (p. 5)

When animal magnetism was reignited in the U.S. in the 1830s through characters such as Charles Poyen, the self-proclaimed "Professor of Animal Magnetism" who traveled from France to spread the word on the East Coast, through William Stone, and phrenologist Robert Collyer, self-proclaimed "Professor of Mesmerism and Pyschography," who traveled from England to deliver a series of popular lectures in the South, Midwest, and North, the subjects used in itinerant lectures, demonstrations, and stage shows were often female household servants or enslaved, medical patients, a traveling "clairvoyant" used for staging demonstrations, or the magnetizers themselves. In the midcentury decades, mesmeric-based theories of human nature interpenetrated abolitionist and feminist movements as well as underpinned the religious devotions of Phineas Quimby, Andrew Jackson Davis, and Mary Baker Eddy.[2]

Midcentury the site of fascination was not just the skull phrenologists loved to squeeze, but also the epigastric region and the extremities, fingers and toes. Debates emerged over whether the hypnotized subject's self was "inside" or "out," discrete from the magnetizer or not, and interpenetrated by a universal fluid that was extraplanetary or not. Lectures, experiments, and trials in North America, continental Europe, Scandinavia, the British Isles, India, Haiti, and Brazil were reported, conducted in the home, sometimes at a university or hospital, and sometimes in a public hall. Such reports and trials became so controversial that the city of Boston held an investigation into the plausibility of the practice in the 1830s, with representatives deciding that while they could not confirm or deny the existence of a universal fluid, they could say something unique was happening to magnetized subjects.[3]

The possibility of permanently confined populations in asylums changed the location and theorization of mesmeric-based studies, however. Without prior confined populations and the stabilized observational grid thought necessary for comparison, experimental studies of children described as backward, vicious, or degenerate and women described as hysterical—the two main targets of psychotherapeutic research—were less likely. The restricted location and repetition in "clinical" and "laboratory" settings, which continuously claimed experimental status, distinguished these activities from stage show hypnotism, Christian Science, and nontraditional spiritualism and mediumship. Experimental studies in late-19th century Europe, such as in Jean Martin Charcot and Pierre Janet's Salpêtriére school which Binet and Freud attended, and its opponent, Hippolyte Bernheim's Nancy school, and in the United States, such as at the Vineland Institute in New Jersey, foregrounded altered states as a key research tool. Mind was fundamentally presumed to exist, as was body. Once this assumption was in place, the point was to ascertain how mind worked, particularly in relation to mechanisms now described as unconscious.

Mind as Scientific Object

The methods developed through laboratory mesmerism assumed mind's location as on the inside of a physical shell. The early 1800s debates over materialism, that is, whether mind was reducible to an organ such as brain, had fallen away, with mind now being restricted to the head, in most theories, the brain only, and as operating via procedures which were only able to be ascertained under controlled conditions of studying of hysterical or insane patients. The term *unconscious*, coming into Anglophone novels and brain-based research at the turn of the 1800s, took on new meaning by 1900 on the basis of such studies. Under the influence of Janet, Charcot, and Freud especially, unconscious meant not just a lack of awareness, but a repository site—in some accounts a hot, steamy, if not tropical, repressed, sex-laden, and chaotic zone and in others a ruthlessly efficient, automated, cold machine that took care of business so that the conscious mind would not have to. The unconscious as depicted in the first dynamic psychiatry especially, started to resemble colonial and anthropological descriptions of "cannibals," "natives," "barbarians," and also "noble savages" whose darkness, distance, exoticism, and mysteriousness began to occupy recesses of the "White" mind through theories such as recapitulation (ontology recapitulates phylogeny) and cultural-epochs (Baker, 2001).

Three levels of altered states were often depicted on the basis of studies of confined hysterical women and degenerate children. Similar phenomena were repeatedly reported and debated, although caveats were often placed around the dangers of templating: there may be more than three states; the three states may be mixed in form and displayed suddenly, originally, and separately; they may or may not be produced in succession within a subject; and the order may differ.

1. The cataleptic state—motionless unless otherwise instructed; eyes open; fixed gaze as if fascinated; complete insensibility to pain; limbs light when raised by someone else and stay there; retains muscular and sensory activity; tendon reflex disappears; does respond to suggestion and hallucinations.
2. The lethargic state—achieved by closing eyelids or putting subject in dark place after (1) above, followed often by emission of a peculiar sound from larynx; complete insensibility to pain; limbs relaxed, flaccid, and drop when raised; sometimes sensory organs retain activity; efforts to influence patient by means of suggestion or intimidation are fruitless; tendon reflex is exaggerated; image of death.
3. The state of artificial somnambulism—also called magnetic sleep; eyes closed or half-closed; no tendon reflex; different kind of rigidity of limbs—not as relaxed as lethargic state; skin insensible to pain; reacts to mesmeric passes; easy to induce very complex automatic actions via commands and suggestions; retention of sight, smell, and sound activities. (Binet & Fére, 1888, p. 160)

No single soul-mind-body connection could dominate the debates—the connections remained both nebulous and highly contentious in many accounts that discussed mesmerism and the unconscious. For some observers, the altered states attributed to mesmerism indicated natural laws of "bodily" and "mental" operation that proved a materialist physiology which held across people, for others mesmeric phenomena were proof of God's existence, evidence of a vitalist origin that was deliberately beyond human grasp, and that signaled purposeful creation. In some instances, then, mind operated implicitly as the new legitimate expression for soul—it becomes more "scientific" to name the everlasting, mystical, and dynamic property that was thought to leave the body upon death as mind rather than as soul. In other instances, mind and body were treated as being less than the divinity attributed to soul—they were related but ultimately of a lower status in a tripartite configuration that saw soul's immateriality as unable to be subjected to mechanical laws, unlike mind and body. Different again were the debates when taken farther in a scholar such as William James, where mind was hypothesized to continue after death and to have potentially new laws of operation in the afterlife. In his *Principles of Psychology* James argued that psychology had to admit of soul precisely because the question of origin of design was not answered by physiologists. This indicates how, by the turn of the 20th century, the impact of mesmeric debates-practices ranged across far broader domains than those linked with hypnosis today. Such debates preceded publication of Darwin's *Origin of the Species*, however, bringing into pointed relief more than just a "science versus religion" discourse—such debates actually helped to shape the lines that came post-Darwin to be refigured around science and religion, human and nonhuman, natural and supernatural, and life and death. To that end, the making of mind into a scientific object across the 19th century entailed a messy secularization of interests in what might now be called the divine, the theological, and the religious, with the unconscious becoming the new zone whose rules of operation proved elusive and mystical—exactly what a pursuit in service to Christian theology or mechanical naturalism required in order to appear elevated above "common sense."

Fabricating Types of Children

Across the 19th century, debates over animal magnetism, mesmerism, and hypnosis eventually helped reorient the inscription of children labeled special and delinquent from a moral structuralism framed by appeals to pauperism and poverty to a neurophysiological functionalism framed by appeals to genetico-national morbidity and problems of consciousness, volition, and suggestibility. Practices of phrenomesmerism constituted a crossover point in such shifting inscriptions of human kinds, human nature, and human mind, a midcentury moment in which faith-based initiatives, scientific methods, and antireligious spiritualisms were not distinct and where demarcations between this worldly and otherworldly and spirit and flesh were up for grabs. By the end of the 1800s, the child genius is launched out of the tree of insanity and into an oppositional position in the field. Amid the shift, compulsory public school attendance is enforced for some youth, while academic fields work out their respective and messy domains of obligation, roughly psychology to habit and belief; medicine to diagnosis and correction; education to imitation and emulation; and parapsychology to "extra"ordinary phenomena and psychic energy.

Within this wider shift and crystallization of disciplines, the altered states and phenomena that came to be associated with mesmerism and with mind impacted the inscription of children in several distinct ways. First, mesmeric therapy was recommended and tried as a form of disability treatment and intervention for children labeled vicious and degenerate. The methods circulated in modified forms through institutions especially in Europe and the United States. "Suggestive therapeutics" while perhaps most associated with Edgar Bérillon in the 1880s and 1890s was discussed in a flurry of literature at international conferences, in educational, scientific, and medical journals, and in textbooks and pamphlets. In Anglophone literature, J. Milne Bramwell and Osgood Mason were staunch proponents. The "hypnopedagogic method" was applied to children for whom "ordinary" education proved insufficient to repress "impulsive tendencies" including, for instance, kleptomania, onanism, laziness, restlessness, deceitfulness, incontinence, disobedience, chronic temper-tantrums, and nail biting. It was believed to constitute a "moral orthapaedics" and by 1898 Bérillon in particular claimed to have had a great deal of success with it. Five principles were enumerated :

1. Assess the suggestibility of the child through specific tests. Ready responsiveness means that the child is intelligent and docile, easy to instruct and educate.
2. Induce a state of hypnosis, or a passive state of some kind, preferably before suggestions are undertaken.
3. Once hypnotized, impose moral direction by imperative suggestions, expressed with authority and clarity.
4. With imperative verbal suggestion one should associate a psychomechanical discipline in order to create a center of psychic arrest; this will render the child incapable of performing the forbidden act. For example, for the chronic masturbator the arms are raised in the air and it is suggested that the arms are paralyzed. The child is then assured that the next time an impulse to onanism arises the paralysis he/she now feels will return immediately. Where the habit is laziness, then it is movement rather than inertia that is imposed.
5. The child should be woken quickly and the same phenomena obtained with conscious participation. (Gauld, 1995, pp. 492–493)

Debates raged over whether such practices ought to be used in "regular" classrooms and if so, whether they would "weaken the Will" of children who were not seen as ill, thereby ruining their educability. For the "degenerate" child, then, presumption of a weak "will" made them fit for hypnotic therapy. Paradoxically, their suggestibility would indicate their "intelligence," their potential to be persuaded, transformed, and redeemed.

Second, mesmeric debates contributed to advice for citizen-production through behavior management of "the normals." Alfred Binet, whose primary area of training and study was hypnosis, wrote with Féré one of the most comprehensive treatises on animal magnetism in the late 1800s, as well as publishing his clinical studies on "alterations of personality" and "double consciousness" upon which both William James and Lewis Terman were to rely. In *Animal Magnetism*, Binet and Féré argued that differing results will be obtained "if the patients are subjected to a different *modus operandi*; if, in other words, they do not receive the same hypnotic education [induction procedure]" (Binet & Féré, 1888, p. 172). Either way a compelling consideration remained, construed within a shift from overt sovereign power to the dispersed, disciplinary, and institutionalized authority of nation-building and welfare states: "The question arises how it should be possible for one person to exert over another the power of making him speak, act, think, and feel as it pleases the experimenter to dictate?" (Binet & Féré, 1888, p. 172). Binet overtly theorized through several of his texts whether it was ethical to subject "normal" children to hypnosis and gave examples of possible appropriate uses. For instance, in their chapter titled "The Application of Hypnosis to Therapeutics and Education," Binet and Féré discuss the modification of instincts in children through the example of a hen, which disinclined to sit, was made to do so with seemingly no memory of how it was persuaded:

> The efficacy of suggestion by teachers may, as we believe, be shown by the possibility of modifying certain instincts *by suggestion* in the case of animals. One of the present writers repeatedly witnessed a curious practice employed by a farmer's wife in the district of Caux. When a hen has laid a certain number of eggs in a nest of her own selection, and has begun to sit, if there is any reason for transferring her to some other nest, the hen's head is put under her wing, and she is swung to and fro until she is put to sleep. This is soon done, and she is placed in the nest designed for her; when she awakes, she has no recollection of her own nest, and readily adopts the strange eggs. By means of this process, *hens may sometimes be made to sit which had shown a previous disinclination to do so* [italics added]. This modification of instinct by suggestions seems to show that the educational use of suggestion is not so absurd as some authors assert it to be. (Binet & Féré, 1888, p. 360)

In certain circumstances, then, mesmeric experiments had a significant impact on how claims about the nature of influence and the nature of children were formulated. With the implications for the formation of a shared national imaginary hanging in the balance, scholars concerned with the physiology of influence asked by what processes people came to think the same things. Studies of "the unconscious" had moved by the 20th century from the mid-19th century period fascination with catalepsy and lethargy to a more focused concern with hysteria and "sexual deviation." New models of mind, dipsychism and polypsychism, for instance, were proposed and new models of education developed to take advantage of the physiology of influence and the study of suggestion (Ellenberger, 1960). The redefinition of hypnosis by Bernheim's Nancy School in France as *suggestion induced to enable further suggestion* blurred the difference between somnambulic and waking states. Suggestion became used with such frequency and in such a wide variety of ways that it began to lose any shared reference points (Ellenberger, 1960, p. 151). It is here that the absorption into teaching practices for "normal" citizen-children becomes most evident; Corporal punishment was barred in child-centered movements (harking back to Rousseau), so in its absence how was a teacher to get "the normals" to do what she wanted?

The models developed were, as Winter has already noted, not only reactions to, but assimilations of mesmerism. They relied on a particular understanding of unconscious mental action, of influencing the Will through the power of looking and verbal commands, and of trances and psychic manipulation. Only in retrospect would it be possible to portray the new mental physiologies developed as unambiguously different from and opposed to mesmerism (Winter, 1988, p. 8).

This is borne out, for instance, in how novel and controversial the idea was of suggesting to a child what you wanted them to really do. In 1888 Binet and Féré argued:

> Strictly speaking, suggestion is an operation producing a given effect on a subject by acting on his intelligence. Every suggestion essentially consists in action on a person by means of an idea; every effect suggested is the result of a phenomenon of ideation, but it must be added that the idea is an epi-phenomenon; taken by itself it is only the indicative sign of a certain physiological process, solely capable of producing a material effect. (p. 171)

They argued further:

It is possible not only to make suggestions to subjects in the waking state [after coming out of hypnosis], but also to persons who have not been hypnotized at all. Learned men have been agitated by these latter experiments, which have aroused in them doubt and dissatisfaction. They have no difficulty in admitting that suggestions may be made to hypnotized subjects, since they are not in normal health, but they cannot understand how they should be made to individuals who are awake, not under hypnotism, and that this should be done by modes of action in daily use in our relations to one another. (Binet & Féré, 1888, p. 178)

In terms of teaching, then, "If it is the characteristic of suggestion to address itself to the subject's intelligence, it follows that there are as many forms of suggestions as there are modes of entering into relations with another person" (Binet & Féré, 1888, p. 178). In his 1900 book *La Suggestibilité* Binet presented a historical overview of experimental work done in the field of suggestion, including his own contributions, and laid out educational applications of suggestibility for schoolchildren and soldiers. He argued that group experiments produce:

1. a division of functions, with some children becoming leaders and others followers;
2. an increase in suggestibility; and
3. a strong tendency toward imitation, which is the advantage of collective education—imitation and emulation are "powerful stimulants for progress."[4]

Thus, the ties that bound nation-building to collective compulsory education, compulsory education to imitation and emulation, and emulation to evolution and progress of "humanity" become clearer and the stakes high. Whenever mesmeric experiments took place, a national imaginary could be transformed, for the discourses within which it was nested were so often oriented toward citizen-production, racialized purification, ability-reproduction, and sexuality-straightening, via mastery of a "zone" previously considered private or out of reach. Mesmeric practices had raised uncomfortably stark issues spoken of in terms of class and gender and also became the occasion for reflections about the basis of racial distinctions and the "natural laws" that had helped one people to "bend" another to its "Will" (Winter, 1998, p. 7). It thus brought to the surface issues of equality, endowment, and national security that linked hens to children, classrooms to armies, and Africa to the Americas and Caribbean.

Scientization of Sympathy and Critique

Mesmeric debates helped produce mind as a scientific object and "kinds" of children as (Il)legitimate ontologies, grouped around refigured racializing, sexualizing, and able-izing discourses that drew relations between external phenotype and internal structure as markers of morality and control of Will. They also became absorbed into the *critique* of such productions, objectifications, and causal links—notions of sympathy, critical reversals, and uncertainty over origin, cause, and effect were, in a sense, other kinds of "less visible" scientific objects made manifest out of the criticism of previous calcifications. William James's ruminations are a compelling instance of this, of how mesmeric debates helped inform what could and could not fall within the domain of human control, what counted as epistemological, and what could arise as a welfare spirit of sympathy and critique.

As an eminent Harvard philosopher and psychologist, James was also an ardent supporter of mental healing movements, studied "psychic phenomena" such as mediumship, telepathy, and automatic writing for over 20 years, gave a famous series of lectures to teachers across the 1890s on how mind works, and a more public series of lectures regarding exceptional mental states based on his seminars at Harvard, in which he argued we all have a bit of insanity within us. The lectures on abnormal mental states rely heavily on mesmeric debates for their sources and their insights. They begin with a reframing of what the problem is in regard to current beliefs about mental states. The difficulty lies more in attitudes toward such states than in the absolutely fixed character of the phenomena themselves:

> We make a common distinction between healthy and morbid but the true fact is that we cannot make it sharp. No one symptom by itself is a morbid one—it depends rather on the part that it plays. We speak of melancholoy and moral tendencies, but he would be a bold man who should say that melancholy was not an essential part of every character. Saint Paul, Lombroso, Kant, each is in some way an example of how melancholy in a life gives a truer sense of values.
>
> The flux between mental states means not only are they related to each other but that morbid and healthy do not cancel each other out. This does not imply an equality between states, however, so much as underscores how the morbid is in service to the healthy, both simply in order to recognize it and more substantively to give it "material" with which to work: "A life healthy on the whole must have some morbid elements." (James, 1960, Lect. 1, p. 15)

James argued further that "If dreams don't interfere with our waking life they only enlarge our knowledge" of it, that even our experience of everyday waking reality may be only a fragment of the whole: "Who shall say that the ordinary experience is the only possible one?" (p. 16). What makes dreams characteristic of some states of consciousness is that in dreams all "associations are complete" whereas in the waking state, where ideas are allowed expression, it is usually controlled associations that give logical continuity to the progression of thoughts. Thus, waking reality has by its very nature a tendency to exclude apparently random associations, while at the same time it admits only those ideas most pertinent to the object of attention (pp. 16–17). Narrowing only occurs in certain states, of which dreaming is one, while vividness occurs in almost all, including dream states. What objects remain before the mind's eye become more intense, vivid and lively, as if they were borrowing energy from the other mental objects that are excluded. In this economy of explanation, the implications for teaching and instruction are forged: as attention becomes more and more restricted, *"all other ideas are forced out of the picture"* [italics added] (p. 17).

There is one "fundamental fact" that James stresses as such: "The sound mind is a system of ideas in gear, integrated with every other idea, and having a field, a focus, and a margin; the margin [however] *controls*" (p. 18; original emphasis). The widest possible association of meanings in the interpretation of an idea is what constitutes a sound mind and in a healthy life there are no single ideas. So *the process of association in waking and dream state differs* (and arguably in death also for James)—in dreams single ideas can stand alone, in waking reality this is never the case. Ordinary sleep, trance, and death form a continuum, from many lights, to one single light burning brightly, to no light (death). In addition, daydreaming, thinking under conditions of intense concentration, alcoholic intoxication, and sleep-drunkenness are all experiences in normal waking life that are similar to mental processes while dreaming (p. 21).

Significantly, James argues here that individualization presupposes and proposes—each mind responds differently to such episodes and "Why this is so, why minds differ, is one of the great questions in theoretic psychology. As yet, there is very little contribution to its solution" (p. 21). Drawing heavily from Janet's ideas of dissociation and the synthesizing capacity of consciousness, James proffers a theory for this difference. Janet's postulation was that altered mental states follow from incapacity to fix the attention, due to mental or moral weakness. Such weakness may be due to hereditary depletion or the nerve force, but shows itself only after a series of traumatic or exhausting experiences, which then exert a negative influence on the synthesizing function of the brain. When this capacity for sustained attention is dispersed, dissociation of certain parts of consciousness from waking life occurs, thus casting psychic fragments into the unconscious secondary existence to displace waking awareness, at which time one becomes more susceptible to suggestion and to hypnosis (p. 22). Janet called this altered state somnambulism, meaning a second psychological existence clearly distinct from the first and alternating with it, a state in which intellectual phenomena are sufficiently developed for someone to perceive sensations and even to understand the signs and language of normal experience, but a state nonetheless totally forgotten when "the subject" returns to normal condition (also called *déboulement de la conscience*). Under Janet, hypnosis helps redefine the child who is not paying attention to the teacher as a problem, as morally and mentally weak. Moreover, anyone who can be hypnotized becomes suspected of such weakness of will. James does not follow fully this line of reasoning, however.

Hypnotism is introduced in his first lecture as one of the most important experimental methods known for artificially inducing subliminal states of consciousness, allowing apparently controlled observation of states strikingly similar to natural somnambulism, in that it also appeared to break up the mind into two or more parts. James argued that the prevailing theory of the time was that in the normal condition of mind the waking state and the subliminal consciousness work in perfect harmony, blended into a unity now considered one conscious personality. In hypnosis the two systems were thought dissociated. Waking consciousness is split off from the rest of the nervous system while subliminal consciousness is laid bare and comes into direct contact with the external world. Characteristics of normally subdued states of consciousness can then be observed; and in this condition the hypnotized subject will more easily receive instructions and perform actions suggested by the hypnotist (p. 24).

James asserted that hypnotism had been rediscovered since Mesmer and denied by scientists:[5] "It was the theory of suggestion, however, that finally robbed hypnotism of its former marvel. Mesmer's theory of a universal fluid through all of nature, later theories that it was the will of the strong over the weak—all these explanations are now exploded" (p. 25). He defined hypnosis as possibly only partial sleep, as not requiring a strong "will" of the hypnotizer because you need only to suggest an idea of which the mind takes hold. The subject's mind is hypnotized only in the passage from waking to sleeping state, hence we all go through this passage at least twice a day—the hypnagogic state. In a comment that educators were to find handy in years to come, James argued that the idea was to prevent the subject from reaching deep sleep and to catch them on the way, for then they will immediately act upon an idea. In the process, then, animal magnetism was redefined: "everything depends on the subject allowing himself to be entranced and hardly anything on the operator, except that he must engender the subject's trust and be able to fix attention on the relaxed condition" (p. 25). Crucially, hypnosis was placed in the control and decision-making capacity of the recipient, not of the mesmerizer.

The key point of this elaboration of and fascination with hypnosis was, as for Binet, the characteristic that presents itself in this state—suggestibility. James asserted that it was the main symptom of hypnosis and by suggestibility he meant the intrusion into the mind of an idea that is at first met with opposition by the person, then accepted uncritically, and realized unreflectively, almost automatically. In turn, this means vividness and motor efficacy, the former producing intense emotional excitement that banishes all other ideas and creates a state of monoideism and the latter referring to the ease with which the idea can then be translated into muscular activity—an increase in the reflex excitability: "This is unquestionably the true explanation" concludes James. This countered Bernheim's Nancy school theory where it was argued that there was no such thing as a hypnoid state; rather, hypnosis was due to suggestibility alone. James argues, however, that it was a genuinely peculiar state, carrying increased suggestibility in its train. The fall of the threshold of consciousness enabled a single idea to be implanted and motor activity to follow but only when this opening of doors to the subliminal had taken place (pp. 25–26). Even in states that are similar, such as crowd-induced excitement or when remarkable feats considered impossible before are performed, the result he explains is caused by the narrowing of the field of consciousness that permits the suggestibility to take hold (p. 27).

The opening lecture ends with a summary of six phenomena that are common to both hypnosis and dream states: (1) both wake you when you say wake (i.e., you can program in either state to awaken); (2) both are anesthetic to most impressions; (3) in both there is a possible rapport; (4) suggestions are obeyed in both; (5) memory is often gone in both, although memories can be recalled from within such states upon revisiting (e.g., Bernheim had demonstrated that the memory for events occurring under hypnosis could be transferred to the subject's dreams during natural sleep); and (6) in both the aftereffects of a suggestion that is implanted in one state can appear in another (e.g., posthypnotic suggestions). James concludes by arguing that "In all this we notice *dissociation*, polyzoism [Frederick Myers' notion of 'the property in a complex organism of being composed of minor quasi-independent organisms'], and polypsychism"—a plurality of states or consciousness (pp. 33–34).

James's introduction of Myers's version of "the subliminal consciousness" was his reference to the unconscious and a crucial turn in the objectification of mind—he proffered it as the most likely explanation for this multiplicity—an explanation that had to rely on apparently mystical themes that loosely resonated both with reincarnation theses or with spiritism. As Eugene Taylor (1983, p. 5) notes, James in the end could not avoid frequent allusions to what he called "the occult" as part of the "scientific" explanation for exceptional mental states.

Moreover, the largesse offered to insanity, to the possibility of insanity in all of us, had a limit-point that still operates today. The malleability of exceptional mental states, their touchability, and the optimism that might reorient the prior negative view, their treatability and the attendant sympathy, had a bottom line. The bottom-line lunatic could not be helped at all. There were for James, as for his contemporaries, beings so beyond the usual organization of sensibility that seemingly nothing could be done. The largesse emerges, then, in two directions that exceed James's work but that swirl through its concerns: first, around those Lewis Terman would later describe as "high grade defectives"—something had to be done with "them" because they were not quite fit for any single thing; second, around the nuances, reversals, ephemerality, diffusion, and dispersal of insanity "in us all"—this version of insanity is only that which might appear in watered down form and is actually in service to the intensification of abilities. The old ways of seeing insanity and the new forms of sympathy promoted thus have as a silent point of reference geniuslike or psychic capacities to which such morbidity is in service. Such morbidity can appear only as temporary hysterias, dissociations, depressions, and so on, that lend material to both health and the creative act. The generosity of the dispersal, the sympathy and the criticism of harshness that it enables, is secured on the basis of a deeply rooted, immobile, fundamentally unshakable other kinds of otherness—a being positioned as so beyond reform, restitution, or recovery of the five senses in working order that they become the bottom-line lunatic—that which an associationist system of psychology of mind relies upon in order to make other "reforms" or accommodations appear inclusive, charitable, and sensitive.

Subject Matters: Mesmerism and the Spirituality of the Educational Social Scientist

> The greatness of psychoanalysis resides, we believe, in the fact that its failure forces us to pose the problem of "reason" itself, and more precisely, the problem of the model of rationality guiding modern sciences. (Chertok & Stengers, 1989/1992, p. viii)

There is a final scientific object worth discussing here, beyond the objectification of mind and classification of children that emanated from and was shaped in part by mesmeric debate—that of the broad-spirited (adult) social scientist. This was a special kind of scientific object, to which strategies of sympathy and critique were indebted, which relied first on the purification efforts of theoretico-experimental sciences as a point of contrast, and second on working the apparent schism between "heart" and "reason."

> Theoretico-experimental sciences are distinguished by the practice of making their version of "reason" depend on the power to "give reasons" for or to explain phenomena. This version of reason thus presumes the power of predicting outcomes, of controlling in order to replicate, of purifying to insure the implication of a theory—the power, in sum, to make a phenomenon "admit" its truth. (Chertok & Stengers, 1989/1992, p. xvi)

Proto-social sciences such as psychoanalysis, experimental psychology, and education could not fully approach their emergent domains in the same way. This is in part due to the problem that suggestibility posed, because "the infant's relation with its caretakers are already characterized by what we should recognize as a form of suggestion." The muddiness of suggestibility is what enables the separation between biophysical and social sciences; because suggestion puts "truth" in question, that is, it problematizes the possibility of constructing a theory on the basis of experiment or experience. "Suggestion is impure; it is the uncontrollable par excellence...the question of suggestion always arises when 'heart' and 'reason' are no longer conceived as being in opposition, when 'heart' is no longer considered an obstacle to the legitimate power of (theoretico-experimental) reason" (Chertok & Stengers, 1989/1992, p. xvi–xvii).

It is especially around the problems posed by the unconscious and suggestibility studies that education's domain-formation has encountered some of the dilemmas apparent in the field of psychoanalysis, in which the history of hypnosis and earlier mesmeric debates have been more overtly acknowledged as playing a vital role. Such dilemmas give over more broadly onto the formation of the ethical social scientist—for instance, the therapist, the lowly teacher, and the elevated university-based researcher who attempt to make social phenomena admit truths that are difficult to purify and to replicate.

A comparison and the interplay between the field of psychoanalytics—that with which the unconscious is perhaps most strongly associated today—and education is thus instructive. Psychoanalytic theory and practice at the turn of the 20th century "does not simply reproduce the model of other rational practices. The 'heart' to which psychoanalysis addresses itself is not conceived in such a way as to guarantee a science resembling other sciences (by contrast to the role 'behavior' plays in experimental psychology, for example)" (Chertok & Stengers, 1989/1992, p. viii). Rather, two differences mark the uniqueness, differences that circulate profoundly through both Binet's research into animal magnetism and suggestibility and through James's turns to hypnosis and exceptional mental states—through, that is, their idiosyncratic struggles to disarticulate explanations of mind and of altered states from charges of dabbling with the occult.

First, like education, in making psychoanalysis into a field one objective was to create a practice that would render intelligible the obstacle "heart" poses to the efforts of "reason." A second objective was to create a practice that would *not* be limited to making "heart" an object of science, like any other, only more complex. Consideration of certain states as mental and as exceptional, as sites for elaborating "epistemologies" of special education, therapy, self-healing or New Thought moved back and forward between these objectives. The difference that this difference of navigating "heart" and "reason" made is crucial and the pivotal role of mesmerism in bringing them into sharp relief is indicated in several different sites. For instance, James's reference to the mystics and the scientifics, in which he recounts this travel from disreputable obscurity ("animal magnetism") to scientific status ("hypnotic suggestion") captures well the sentiment of many mental healing movements in the United States at the time and the tensed relation they held to chemical medicine—a relation that became even more strained after the refinement of several chemical anesthetics which displaced the use of hypnosis to achieve anesthesia for surgery and dentistry. Binet's concern over whether suggestion was an appropriate strategy to use with healthy children is another instance, while Freud, too, struggled with the implications of hypnosis for thinking through the problem that heart posed to reason. While defining psychoanalysis as that field which emerges from the moment it rejects hypnosis as a therapy, Freud repeatedly required hypnosis as much as dreams to argue that there was an unconscious beyond the ego's control: "Even before the time of psychoanalysis, hypnotic experiments, and especially posthypnotic suggestion, had tangibly demonstrated the existence and mode of operation of the mental unconscious" (Freud, quoted in Borch-Jacobsen, 1989, p. 93).

Such field-formations in their departures from theoretico-experimental sciences did not by default homogenously inscribe what it meant to reason or to be ethical in the social sciences, however. In comparing the formation of fields in France and the U.S., Chertok and Stengers note that in a long tradition marked by philosophers such as Bachelard, "scientific reason" in France has not at all been understood as empirical but instead understood on the basis of the power of the "concepts" it creates, where the use of the term *concept* excludes ideology, professional interests, and individual psychology. French epistemology thus came to identify the creation of psychoanalysis with a rupture: "the epistemological value of the Freudian *concept* of the unconscious is based on this difference from the aggregate of knowledge preceding it" (Chertok & Stengers, 1989/1992, p. xii). The difference that Freud's American heirs invoked creates a new representation of the relations between "heart" and "reason." Through all its mutations in the United States, the psychoanalytic unconscious is marked by one constant:

> it is always linked with the theme of "truth," and more precisely "resistance to truth," taking "truth" here to refer to the painful but uniquely effective pathway toward a "cure." "Heart," in the sense of an obstacle refusing to submit to the reasons of reason, is therefore central to the Freudian conception of the human psyche. But the relation in the US heirs between "heart" and "reason" is no longer this traditional relation. (pp. xiii–xiv)

The latter inflections required a kind of *subject who could be produced in a new relationship to truth*. It is here, in this new relationship to truth, that an emergent educational field blurs local national markers in ways that an emergent field of psychoanalysis does not. It is in this relationship to truth that the ethics of the teacher and university-based expert who were to be the bearers of the new educational science were formed. The new relation makes an emergent educational field take on the shape and feel that renders it so recognizable in transnational locations that have been dominated by Christianity—that apparent blend which attempts to meld "spirituality" with "theoretico-experimental" status in settings that refuse purified experimental design, in part on the basis of suggestibility's muddying role.

The new relationship between subject and truth had at least two levels: it involved working between an apparent conscious and unconscious, with strategies of suggestibility that imitated the hypnotic relation, persuading a child to confess an interior, to form new chains of association, and to "internalize" in the unconscious after some minor resistance what an adult wanted them to do. It also involved work of the teacher or researcher—an early and continuous division—upon themselves, in preparation for the truth-telling and truth-production that the now-public access to the formerly private unconscious had provided.

This new relation had several further characteristics. These characteristics are still discernible in contemporary reform efforts, in the tenor of academic reviews, and in the moral high grounds presupposed around what "good" teaching and "relevant" educational research would look like. First is the exclusion of the principle of care of the self amid the elevation of the principle of "know thyself." In *Hermeneutics of the Subject* (1981/2005) Foucault argued that the Cartesian approach had referred to knowledge of the self as a form of consciousness and,

> What's more, by putting the self-evidence of the subject's own existence at the very source of access to being, this knowledge of oneself (no longer in the form of the test of self-evidence, but in the form of the impossibility of doubting my existence as a subject) made the "know yourself" into a fundamental means of access to truth…. But if the Cartesian approach thus requalified the *gnothi seauton*, for reasons that are fairly easy to isolate, at the same time—and I want to stress this—it played a major part in discrediting the principle of care of the self and in excluding it from the field of modern philosophical thought. (p. 14)

This separation underwrites the distinctions between what Foucault calls philosophy, science, and spirituality. Philosophy was

> the form of thought that asks, not of course what is true and what is false, but what determines that there is and can be truth and falsehood and whether or not we can separate the true and the false. We will call "philosophy" the form of thought that asks what it is that enables the subject to have access to the truth which attempts to determine the conditions and limits of the subject's access to the truth. (p. 15)

What he next lays out are the dimensions of spirituality in its split from philosophy and science, a shearing that I suggest found its place in the formation of social sciences. A second characteristic helping shape the educational social scientist, then, was how "spirituality's" pathways to truth were construed via the necessity attributed to the conversion of the subject, whether in the form of "suggestive therapeutics" and "moral orthapedics" for children, teacher training primarily for teenage girls, or the objectification of exceptional mental states in Harvard University seminars:

> If we call this "philosophy," then I think we could call "spirituality" the search, prac-
> tice, and experience through which the subject carries out the necessary transforma-
> tions on himself in order to have access to the truth. We will call "spirituality" then
> the set of these researches, practices, and experiences, which may be purifications,
> ascetic exercises, renunciations, conversions of looking, modifications of existence,
> etc., which are, not for knowledge but for the subject, for the subject's very being, the
> price to be paid for access to the truth. (p. 15)

Third, this version of spirituality as it appeared in the West at least had itself three
main qualities. First,

> Spirituality postulates that truth is never given to the subject by right. Spirituality
> postulates that the subject as such does not have right of access to the truth and is
> not capable of having access to the truth. It postulates that the truth is not given to
> the subject by a simple act of knowledge (*connaisance*), which would be founded and
> justified simply by the fact that he is the subject and because he possesses this or that
> structure of subjectivity. It postulates that for the subject to have right of access to the
> truth he must be changed, transformed, shifted, and become, to some extent and
> up to a certain point, other than himself. The truth is only given to the subject at a
> price that brings the subject's being into play. For as he is, the subject is not capable
> of truth. I think that this is the simplest but most fundamental formula by which
> spirituality can be defined. (Foucault, 1981/2005, p. 15)

This establishes the grounds for doing the work on the subject that is deemed necessary for the subject to be a knowing one and establishes the structures of exclusion
around the bottomline lunatic who can never prove that she or he knows themselves
under such conditions of proof. This work of and on the subject involves two kinds—*eros*
and *askesis*.

> It follows from this point of view there can be no truth without a conversion or a
> transformation of the subject. This conversion, this transformation of the subject—
> and this will be the second major aspect of spirituality—may take place in differ-
> ent forms. Very roughly we can say (and this is again a very schematic survey) that
> this conversion may take place in the form of a movement that removes the subject
> from his current status and condition (either an ascending movement of the subject
> himself, or else a movement by which the truth comes to him and enlightens him).
> Again, quite conventionally, let us call this movement, in either of its directions, the
> movement of eros (love). Another major form through which the subject can and
> must transform himself in order to have access to the truth is a kind of work. This
> is a work of the self on the self, an elaboration of the self by the self, a progressive
> transformation of the self by the self for which one takes responsibility in a long
> labor of ascesis (*askesis*). Erōs and askēsis are, I think, the two major forms in Western
> spirituality for conceptualizing the modalities by which the subject must be trans-
> formed in order finally to become capable of truth. This is the second characteristic
> of spirituality. (p. 15)

Last, the truth-effects have to become visible in the subject and understood as caused
by the work the subject did on themselves to prepare for the transformation or conversion that gave access to truth. James's proposition that those hypnotized actually decide
and permit themselves to be put in this condition illustrates this theme:

Finally, spirituality postulates that once access to the truth has really been opened up, it produces effects that are of course, the consequence of the spiritual approach taken in order to achieve this, but which at the same time are something quite differ- ent and much more: effects which I will call "rebound" ("de retour"), effects of the truth on the subject. For spirituality, the truth is not just what is given to the subject, as reward for the act of knowledge as it were, and to fulfill the act of knowledge. The truth enlightens the subject; the truth gives beatitude to the subject; the truth gives the subject tranquility of the soul. In short, in the truth and in access to the truth, there is something that fulfills the subject himself, which fulfills or transfigures his very being. In short, I think we can say that in and of itself as an act of knowledge could never give access to the truth unless it was prepared, accompanied, doubled, and completed by a certain transformation of the subject; not of the individual, but of the subject himself in his being as subject. (p. 16)

The mesmerized subject performs a service to self and others that blurs the discrete- ness of these very locations. Transformed into an altered state via his or her own per- mission, the truths of the mind, of behavior, and most of all, of how "relations" can be formed, are thoughts revealed, their secret hiding place exposed and now made govern- able. The teacher and the university researcher who gain (uneven) status and revel in this new order are to be the bearers of truth effects for themselves, for the children in their care, and for education as an important spiritualizing system, upholding a point of view that lends space to the social scientist as a necessary invention—a view that assumes that studying and engineering minds will unlock the key to a society's mechanism, trans- forming a nation into a collective unity and securing a homogeneous morality simultane- ously expressed and encoded as secularized and competing forms of Christianity.

Conclusion

Beneath what science knows about itself is something that it doesn't know; and its history, its becoming, its periods and accidents obey a certain number of laws and determinations. These laws and determinations are what I have tried to bring to light. I have tried to unearth an autonomous domain that would be the unconscious of knowledge, which would have its own rules, just as the individual human uncon- scious has its own rules and determinations. (Foucault, 1968/1996, p. 54)

Foucault argues that in a Renaissance episteme the principle of knowledge-produc- tion was resemblance, in the classical age following it was the separation of words from things and their arrangement in orderly tables, and in a modern episteme it was the search for historical origins that formed the basis of the organization of knowledge. If understood within this framing it is easy to see how mesmeric debates operated as an instance of and incitement to discourse in the formation of modern subjectivities. However, mesmeric debates troubled this very kind of analytical or big-picture framing, because they so overtly problematized the question of origins or beginnings, of pro- cesses of attribution, of linkage and sequence, of linear time and cause-effect analysis between discrete points, of who is speaking—what is memory and what is volition—and significantly, of the distinctiveness of a unique, individualized possession of mind. That is, they questioned the purifiability or isolation of any "thing" as a discrete, singular, and coherent entity. They could thus been seen as falling within as well as transforming a broader moment in which conditions of truth, object- and subject-closure, and systems of bonding and ethics became triangulated as issues, and were directly discussed as in need of resolution and action. In a broader shift from monarchical and Papal systems of governance into new inventions called nations and welfare states, such debates helped to forge "mind" as an obscure and challenging site of engineering at which ego-formation, citizen-shaping, and relationship-building should be targeted. In particular, they most pointedly placed the nature of rationality and influence at stake, occupying both an ambiguous and central position in the working out of distinctions between human/non-human, matter/spirit, life/death, and normal and extraordinary.

In pushing to the fore such issues of govern-ability and the (non)closure of subjects-objects, mesmeric debates became an important fulcrum upon which the separation of sciences, the fabrication of scientific objects, and the formulation of what could constitute an investigative approach turned. As Alison Winter (1998, pp. 6–8) has already noted in regard to mesmerism, the existence of a scientific or medical orthodoxy must not be presupposed; the very constitution of this orthodoxy was at issue. Definitions of science across the mid- to late 19th century were malleable and there was no agreement on what could be said about natural law, nor was it obvious when, where, and how one could say it. Chertok and Stengers (1989/1992) concur in regard to the pivotal role animal magnetism played in the very formation of sciences as sciences:

> Animal magnetism is inseparable from the project of constituting a science. Similarly, hypnosis, which succeeded magnetism, activated a relation *purified* of any belief in a supernatural causality; it had as its goal to explain what previously had appeared supernatural in terms of scientific knowledge, to discover the scientific truth beyond trances, ecstasies, possession, thaumaturgical prodigies, and so on. Nevertheless, both hypnosis and magnetism have had troubled relation with scientific reason. The practical invention of the hypnotic relation, which endeavors to submit "heart" to a rational reading, has had the effect of providing a privileged terrain where "heart" and scientific reason confront each other, a terrain where proclamations of rational conquest alternate with admissions of defeat. (p. x, italics in original)

It is not surprising, then, that debates over such phenomena appear across a range of "theological," "national," and "welfare" debates that infused the emergent biophysical, humanities, and social science fields in the late 19th century. What is more surprising perhaps is the relative absence of attention to them in education more broadly and curriculum history specifically. In raising the question of human/nonhuman distinctions, and of cause, effect, proximity, and distance, and significantly, of subject- or object-closure, mesmerism brought into relief how the "giving of reasons," of asserting origins or causality for events had shifted, narrowed, cleaved, and in some senses, reversed. Rather than explaining madness, for instance, through demonology and treatment to exorcism or shamanism, such experiments in the "discovery of the unconscious" in the West shifted the locus of explanation from air–sky arrangements between Pagan spirits or a monotheistic Creator much closer to the ground—into the "body," into an immediate environment, or into family history. The work of Binet and James, among others, "where proclamations of rational conquest alternate with admissions of defeat" indexes how the "rationalities" of many social sciences including education and beyond psychoanalytics were an instance of this shift in the locus of cause, becoming dedicated to and honed in on a heart–reason problematization and mired in the difficulty that "suggestion's" muddying aspects seemed to present.

This muddying effect was, however, only possible if backgrounded on a faith in the a priori discreteness of entities—suggestibility is raised as problematic, then, only in regard to such presumptions regarding how causes should be identified, isolated, and purified, reduced to a single, manipulatable origin or site. This inclination gave a "feel" that is still recognizable today in such social sciences, navigating new pathways of truth-production in desperate attempts to find causality for objects that did not seem to remain stable or retain the same features in the process of studying them. The apparent problem of interpenetration, intersubjectivity, or nonclosure between researcher and researched, would not go away.

The subfield of curriculum history took shape within this broader series of problematizations. It has for the last three decades been concerned with the sociopolitics of epistemology, including the formation of school subjects and what is and is not presented for learning. A journey through the impact of mesmerism, both transnational in terms of discursive flows and particular in terms of temporary coagulations, thus points to an additional kind of subject matter—not the compartments now known as mathematics, science, literacy, and social studies, for instance, but the simultaneous *reduction* and *porousness* of what Foucault (1966/1973) calls "the questions of the human being, consciousness, origin, and the subject" (p. 16). The so-called subject of education to whom such compartments of knowledge are meant to matter, be delivered, and stored in the unconscious as memory reveals its narrow parameters, one privileged enough to attain or occupy the status of the human in terms of the figure of the normate and thereby to become the implicit focus of curriculum historical research.

The division between ontology and epistemology, so often taken-for-granted as the very basis of an educational field—knowledge as ejected from body and able to be passed on through strategies of instruction and body as located in the classroom and housing mind—becomes exposed for its cultural specificity even from "within" the West, for its historicity and fragility, for its dependence on coherent and bounded entifications that nonetheless seemed to leak. Animal magnetism, mesmerism, and hypnosis operate as unresolved dilemmas that have posed questions to Being, to place-force style (Newtonian) analysis, to the elevation of death as the unspeakable boundary that focuses social scientific work on everything that happens before "it," and to the adequacy of analyzing that apparently discrete realm called Life repetitively and naively under the terms *society* and *relations of power*.

This inspires a series of questions that bring the traditional proclivities of mainstream curriculum historical work into view: Why does it at first blush, appear ridiculous to reconsider education and curriculum history in light of animal magnetism, mesmerism, and hypnosis? Why do they seem initially so far apart? Why do teachers not hypnotize children on their first day at school? Why would the very thought of such a thing seem to cross a big line, and enter into a shady and dubious realm that brings the term *brainwashing* to the fore? Why are other forms of suggestion, reward, punishment, behavior management, contouring of desires, not considered brainwashing, and now permissible in a classroom? Why is it legitimate for Olympic athletes of varied ages to be regularly hypnotized as part of their training, a sign of how seriously they are taking their representation of the nation?

I am not here proposing such strategies in terms of for or against. Rather, as one of the many considerations that engaging with mesmeric debates through characters such as Binet and James draws one into, and that what such questions above indicate pertains to how the boundaries of the ethical form as a given field forms. It is important to excavate where the lines are laid not just around sciences and normalcy (subjects/unsubjects), but also around what constitutes the colonizing and the brainwashing. That is, not because letting such lines just sit there might hide something sinister in "the unconscious" of "our" present that automatically controls and limits options, but because if democracy is to be raised to the level of question-formation and not just invoked to organize the answers in "multiple forms," then such questions seem to cut stingingly to the core of systems for viewing, judging, and treating that the social sciences claim as their specialty and their preserve. What formats of relation-formation, influence, and suggestibility become acceptable? What uses of authority are validated and debarred? To what extent might the emergent (and contemporary) social sciences such as education be suggestive of "softer, gentler" forms of colonizing or imperial processes that have escaped the attention of studies directed at the biophysical sciences and technology and their relation to accumulation? (McLeod, 2000).

As the quote above from Foucault indicates, even in scholarship that so overtly contests the notion of *consciousness* as a guide to writing history as his does, the *un*conscious has become such a widespread and appealing concept, taking up slack in explanations for explanations. I have traded here on that double position, that there are ways of rethinking history that not only attend to "conditions of possibility" for the production of scientific objects of which we may be less aware, but that awareness can help point to the levels that limit the very orders of knowledge being so historicized—in short, one encounters the threshold of the conditions being considered, rethinking curriculum history as both vehicle and effect of 19th century mesmeric debates.

This "suggests," finally, that such a history of education and of curriculum is not necessarily a history of a particular institution—it is a history of the practice of education and curriculum of which the institution forms one element. In taking this approach, I submit here that such an effort works because it fails—the aporia, paradoxes, and practicalities of the enterprise are not intended to be resolved or made less ambiguous. Lacanian psychoanalytics operate on the basis that it is valuable because it fails: "It is precisely insofar as psychoanalysis disappoints the (false) hope of a cure that it has an indisputable value. Like hypnosis, the hope of a cure is considered to be a deceptive lure" (p. xii). Traditionally, education and curriculum history as a subfield have implicitly taken up as scientific objects formations such as mind, types of children, sympathy and critique, and the virtues of the broad-spirited social scientist, especially of teaching-as-a-form-of-influence, without much investigation of the discursive thresholds that had to be crossed for such objects to come into view. Once they do, a new series of questions present themselves that are difficult to face, that are less about saving the child, the society, and the world through the engineering of mind and more about the extent to which such transformative–redemptive pursuits might operate as, at best, inadequate if not disingenuous forms of therapy, and at worst, imperialistic.

Notes

1. *Animal magnetism* was Franz Anton Mesmer's appellation for the application of Newtonian physics to healing. It stood in contrast to mineral magnetism, which was a well-known healing method at the time and now to terrestrial magnetism (Mesmer, 1958). *Mesmerism* was at first a pejorative term applied to the therapy when Mesmer moved to Paris and began his famous sélon treatments. In 1842 James Braid coined the term *hypnosis* and subsequently reflected it was not appropriate because what was observed was not a form of sleep. Somnambulism and the somnambulic state were sometimes used synonymously for animal magnetic slumber as well, not referring strictly to sleep-walking but to a state that appeared after a hypnotic induction. I am arguing here that these three terms are linked historically into an important event, the apparent "discovery of the unconscious" as Henri Ellenberger calls it. I am not arguing that the theories that undergirded each deployment were continuous or that hypnosis as practiced in the late 19th century is at every level equivalent with animal magnetism as practiced in the late 18th century.

2. For period accounts see Charles Poyen St. Saveur (1837); William L. Stone (1843).

3. See Robert Fuller (1982) for a discussion of the Boston city council report.
4. See Stephen Jay Gould's discussion of the appropriation of Binet's work in the United States in his 1981 *The Mismeasure of Man.*
5. In psychology, physiology, and medicine, wherever a debate between the mystics and the scientifics has been once and for all decided, it is the mystics who have usually proved to be right about the *facts*, while the scientifics had the better of it in respect to the *theories*. The most recent and flagrant example of this is "animal magnetism," whose facts were stoutly dismissed as a pack of lies by academic medical science the world over, until the non-mystical theory of "hypnotic suggestion" was found for them—when they were admitted to be so excessively and dangerously common that special penal laws, forsooth, must be passed to keep all persons unequipped with medical diplomas from taking part in their production. (James, 1897/1960, p. 28).

References

Abraham, I. (2006, September). The contradictory spaces of postcolonial techno-science. *Economic and Political Weekly, 210*–217.

Anderson, W. (2002). Postcolonial technoscience. *Social Studies of Science, 32,* 643–658.

Baker, B. M. (2001). *In perpetual motion: Theories of power, educational history, and the child* (Vol. 14). New York: Lang.

Baker, B. (2007). Animal magnetism and curriculum history. *Curriculum Inquiry, 37*(2), 123–158.

Beloff, J. (1997). *Parapsychology: A concise history.* New York: Palgrave Macmillan.

Binet, A. (1900). *La Suggestibilité.* Paris: Schleicher.

Binet, A., & Féré, C. (1888). *Animal magnetism.* New York: Appleton.

Borch-Jacobsen, M. (1989, Summer). Hypnosis in psychoanalysis. *Representations, 27,* 92–110.

Chertok, L., & Stengers, I. (1992). *A critique of psychoanalytic reason: Hypnosis as a scientific problem from Lavoisier to Lacan.* Stanford, CA: Stanford University Press. (Original published 1989)

Collyer, R. (1843). *Lights and shadows of American life.* Boston: Brainard.

Colquhoun, J. C. (1831–1833). *Report of the experiments on animal magnetism, translated with an historical and explanatory introduction, and an appendix, by Esq. Edinburgh. Made by the committee of the medical section of the French Royal Academy of Sciences.* London: Cadell & Whittaker.

Darnton, R. (1968). *Mesmerism and the end of the enlightenment in France.* Cambridge, MA: Harvard University Press.

Dingwall, E. J. (1967). *Abnormal hypnotic phenomena: A survey of nineteenth-century cases* (Vols. 1–4). London: Churchill.

Ellenberger, H. (1970). *The discovery of the unconscious: The history and evolution of dynamic psychiatry.* New York: Basic Books. (Original work published 1960)

Foucault, M. (1973). *The order of things: An archaeology of the human sciences.* New York: Vintage Books. (Original work published 1966)

Foucault, M. (1996). Foucault responds to Sartre. In M. Foucault (Ed.), *Foucault Live* (pp. 51–56). New York: Semiotext(s). (Original work published 1968)

Foucault, M. (2005). 6 January 1982: First hour (G. Burchell, Trans.). In F. Gros (Ed.), *Michel Foucault: The hermeneutics of the subject: Lectures at the Collége de France. 1981–1982* (pp. 1–24). New York: Palgrave Macmillan. (Original work published 1981)

Fuller, R. C. (1982). *Mesmerism and the American cure of souls.* Philadelphia: University of Pennsylvania Press.

Gauld, A. (1992). *A history of hypnotism.* Cambridge, England: Cambridge University Press.

Gilman, S. L. (1993). *Freud, race, and gender.* Princeton, NJ: Princeton University Press.

Gould, S. (1981). *The mismeasure of man.* New York: Norton.

Hale, N. G. (1971). *Freud and the Americans: The beginnings of psychoanalysis in the United States, 1876–1917.* New York: Oxford University Press.

James, W. (1960). William James on psychical research. In G. Murphy & R. O. Ballou (Eds.), *Proceedings of the Society for Psychial Research.* New York: The Viking Press. (Original work published 1897)

Laurence, J.-R., & Perry, C. (1988). *Hypnosis, will, and memory: A psycho-legal history*: Guilford Press.

McLeod, J. (2000). Metaphors of the self: Searching for young people's identity through interviews. In J. McLeod & K. Malone (Eds.), *Researching youth* (pp. 45–58). Hobart, Tasmania: Australian Clearinghouse for Youth.

Mesmer, F. A. (1958). *Maxims on animal magnetism* (J. Eden, Trans.). Mt. Vernon, NY: Eden Press.

Mills, B. P. (2006). *Fuller and the mesmeric arts: Transition states in the American renaissance*. Columbia: University of Missouri Press.

Pattie, F. (1994). *Mesmer and animal magnetism: A chapter in the history of medicine*. Hamilton, NY: Edmonston.

Richardson, A. (2001). *British romanticism and the science of the mind*. New York: Cambridge University Press.

Richardson, J. G. (in press). Institutional sequences and curriculum history: Classical vs. scientific knowledge and the formation of a new nation. In B. Baker (Ed.), *New curriculum history*. Rotterdam, The Netherlands: Sense.

St. Saveur, C. P. (1837). *Progress of animal magnetism in New England. Being a collection of experiments, reports, and certificates from the most respectable sources. Preceded by a dissertation on the proofs of animal magnetism.* Boston: Weeks, Jordan.

Stocking, G. W. J. (1986). *Malinowski, Rivers, Benedict, and others: Essays on culture and personality*. Madison: University of Wisconsin Press.

Stone, W. L. (1837). *Letter to Doctor A. Brigham on animal magnetism, being an account of a remarkable interview between the author and Miss Loraina Brackett while in a state of somnambulism*. New York: George Dearborn.

Taylor, E. (1983). *William James on exceptional mental states: The 1896 Lowell Lecture*. Amherst: University of Massachusetts Press.

Thompson, R. G. (1996). *Extraordinary bodies*. New York: Columbia University Press.

Thornton, E. M. (1976). *Hypnotism, hysteria, and epilepsy: A historical synthesis*. London: Heinemann Medical.

Tinterow, M. (1970). *Foundations of hypnosis*. Springfield, IL: Charles C. Thomas.

Wallace, E. (1983). *Freud and anthropology: A history and reappraisal*. New York: International Universities Press.

Waterfield, R. (2003). *Hidden depths: The story of hypnosis*. New York: Brunner-Routledge.

Winter, A. (1998). *Mesmerized: Powers of mind in Victorian Britain*. Chicago: University of Chicago Press.

Suggested Reading Questions

1. Baker uses two vignettes to illustrate the influence of mesmerism in the field of education. How have the conceptual and discursive practices around mesmerism shaped the classification of children and theories of behavior management in classroom practices?

2. According to Baker, what is the influence of Binet's use of hypnosis and William James's involvement in mental healing on debates over mind, consciousness, and the unconscious on the way we conceive of schooling and schools?

3. The author argues that debates over animal magnetism, mesmerism, and hypnosis have led to fabricating different types of children. How might such an inscription of children directly relate to the formation of various academic disciplines?

4. Baker suggests that the field and power of suggestibility links education to progress. How might this argument illustrate the ways in which race, class, and gender issues become part of the national imaginary and the project of nation building?

5. The author notes that psychoanalysis has played a major role in reinforcing the Cartesian binary of mind and body, heart and head. How might the construction of such binaries establish structures of exclusion and frame a universal morality?

Response to Bernadette M. Baker
The Unstudied and Understudied in Curriculum Studies

Toward Historical Readings of the "Conditions of Possibility" and the Production of Concepts in the Field

Erik Malewski and Suniti Sharma

It vibrates like an arrow in the course of an irreversible and asymmetrical address, the one that goes most often from father to son, master to disciple, or master to slave ("I'm going to teach you how to live"). Such an address hesitates, therefore: between address as *experience* (is not learning to live experience itself?), address as *education*, and address as *taming* or *training* [dressage]. (Derrida, 2006, pp. xvi–xvii)

In its function, the power to punish is not essentially different from that of curing or educating. (Foucault, 1995, pp. 302–303)

It might be said that since Foucault one of the most enduring and accommodating technologies of education has been the question, under what conditions has such knowing been made possible? This question can unsettle our bodies of knowledge, inciting as-yet unknown ways of thinking, creating new languages, and beseeching the reexamination of disciplinary truths. This question can also safeguard questioners from the risky practice of examining the implications of her or his actions, quell the thirst for knowledge, and foster fundamentalist outlooks upon the world. The question of the relationship connecting particular conditions and the possibility of knowledge seems to reside between such deconstructive and dialectical tactics—and no matter recent tendencies toward one or the other—curriculum studies is made up of both. As Edgerton (1996) teaches us, the work of such a question fluctuates somewhere between readings and the conditions that elicit such readings (p. 47). Edgerton began to outline these indeterminable qualities when she explored the possibilities for curricular translations at the crossroads of cultural studies and multiculturalism, guided in her work by the question, "What knowledge might lessen violence to ourselves and the world?" She then positioned this question within education's desire for nonhierarchical love and, in ways that are common to the reconceptualized curriculum field, as the very terms required for educational reform.

For Edgerton, the difference a question that addresses the conditions for knowing makes is to be found in the discourse available to the questioner. She sensed that the sorts of questions engaged through reading practices should propagate breakdowns and ruptures in understanding that exceed both the reader and author. We relay this particular ethic within concerns over the current state of the field and infer that the "next moment" in curriculum studies resides in the questions the field will ask itself about the conditions that make its thought possible. Susan Edgerton's question about curricular translations can be turned toward present and future moments in the field itself: "how might curriculum studies lessen violence against ourselves and the world?" As something other than insisting upon an answer and therefore risking that we move through it, we attempt to dwell upon the question itself and the ways it might induce us to think. As a way to proceed, we follow along the pathway of what Michael Apple (2004) describes as being attentive to the shape of the questions asked and the manner in which they are answered. To begin to make our point, we offer what has become a less controversial point of view: a question that incites charges of failure, neglect, and carelessness.

One question curbs unsettling debates and difficult thoughts over curriculum and pedagogy: How are curriculum scholars helping to prepare educators to respond to the volatile situations of the real world? A review of educational topics suggests that calls to answer this question—or ones similar to it—proliferate. Accordingly, beliefs about the ability of the field to offer requisite responses are linked to how curriculum scholars address the following: economic struggles, ecological devastation, test scores, sexual relations, technological innovations, classroom pedagogy, curriculum planning, suicide ideations, symptoms of depression, racist attitudes, gay and lesbian issues, communicable diseases, and science and math competitiveness. Without question, each case offered here has its own specificity that requires study of its historical conditions and contemporary processes, not merely in regards to the changing terms under which different individuals and social groups sense they are affected—and therefore experience anxiety or distortions of self—but also for those who feel safe or outside of the demands such anxiety provoking knowledge makes. After decades of crisis after crisis, curriculum studies, like other educational disciplines, has been called on as a professional field to find ways to deliver information that will prevent catastrophes or provide the warning signs of impeding disasters or, at the very least, typographies of risk factors, all so that educated decisions can be made. With the call to "do something quickly," the procession of dangerous situations that require immediate remedial action can lead to ahistorical and atheoretical terms for reform, ones where government and business leaders, and increasingly teachers and faculty, feel as if they must attempt to solve problem after problem without time to study the conditions out of which such problematics arise. Britzman and Dippo (2000) aptly remind us that faced with the responsibility for fixing the horrors of the world but lacking the insights necessary to do so can have a splitting effect: the reconceptualization of the educator's world into multitudes of insiders and outsiders.

In its most common form, the images of crises have embedded in them a crescendo effect whereby they seem to appear out of contemporary circumstances, build to a point of uncontrollability, and unleash themselves on society. The historical economic, political, and social conditions that led incrementally or cyclically to these issues, or the interrelationship of seemingly disparate elements of modern life, and therefore the discursive nature of the plethora of crises we now face, are lost. Pinar (2004) notes that these crises have historically been spurred on by business and government leaders who find teachers are an easy group to blame for social ills. Here educators and, more recently, education faculty, become scapegoats. Portrayed as out of touch, self-interested, and underprepared for dealing with contemporary problems, the terms for accountability measures are set as the general public requires assurances that there is a stable body of knowledge and that such knowledge will set us on the road to not just intellectual but economic, political, and national advancement. From the outside looking in, it seems that curriculum studies is not responsive to the needs of real world people.

These expectations have not come exclusively from the outside, however; many educators have welcomed them as organizing axes for developing what is characterized as applicable, practical scholarship (see Dimitriadis in this volume). Too often the answer to the call for relevance involves expanding the knowledge base in targeted areas or developing frameworks to guide decision-making processes. In the midst of all the insta-bility that makes a crisis a crisis, comes what Lather (2003) terms lovely knowledge—readiness claims and "fail-proof" ideas underwritten by philosophies of control. Quite ironic, it is the attempt to safeguard the promise of public education from falling into continuous crisis that has lead to what Pinar (1993) termed "the fragmented self" that shields against the possibilities of thought: traumatic knowledge is read as a disruption to the normalcy of common sense; ordering knowledge eclipses investigations into the origins of ideas; clarity is elevated above play and imagination; and parts become more central to the curriculum than interrelationships and connecting patterns. The prob-lem is this: there is no agreement over what epistemologies might engender harmonious relations, educational experiences are of most valuable in a society marked by strife and catastrophe, and pedagogical practices are capable of producing in students' transfor-mative moments of learning.

Embedded in all these situations marked by urgency and necessity there are more compelling and challenging questions. Bernadette Baker has put forth a series of them, and elaborates on how historical debates over the validity of animal magnetism, mes-merism, and hypnosis shaped the discourse on the objects of curriculum research. She argues that educational scholarship has largely ignored key aspects of its own domain formation: Why does it at first blush appear ridiculous to reconsider education and cur-riculum history in light of animal magnetism, mesmerism, and hypnosis? And, there are other questions too: Why does hypnotizing children bring the term *brainwashing* to mind while other forms of suggestion such as behavior management and contouring of desires are permissible in the classroom? What can it mean that it is legitimate for Olympic athletes of various ages to be regularly hypnotized as part of their training but not the subjects of education? How is it that certain forms of authority are deemed legitimate while other forms are banned?

These questions, as Baker indicates, are important not because such categories mask something evil lurking in the unconscious but because the ways the unknown is treated and viewed has implications for the very conditions out of which both democracy and education become possible. Such questions raise more uncertainties about how to think about what has been and what might be in curriculum studies. To envision the future of curriculum studies without falling into safeguarding our axiomatic truths—what Ben-jamin (1977) might describe as the truth that stands in the way of truth (see Hartman, 1999; Lather, 2000)—or the ways in which knowledge befits our idealizations and fulfills our expectations—we have a responsibility to think within contemporary conflicts and paradoxes. This necessitates that we grapple with a sense of the past and future that attends to the question, What knowledge might lessen violence against ourselves and the world? Questions such as this, and more general questions about the state of the field allow us to consider curriculum studies' desire for relevance and its aptitude not only for transformation but its openness to work that ushers in a different state. It also allows curriculum theorists to consider how the field might be reimagined by studying the con-ditions under which our terms and categories have become possible and our practices acceptable. As Baker's work attests, thinking thoughts of the present necessitates that we consider the work of curriculum studies as positioned at the intersection of institu-tional frameworks and embodied relations: the space between innovation and tradition, between innocence and complicity.

As Dewey (1938/1997) teaches us, curriculum studies must craft its work at the cross-roads of what could be—to make a difference in the educational experiences of those who live them—and the realities of the present—how the field is shaped by institutions, governments, policies, and the expectations they place upon higher education. There is the optimistic impulse that we have already rethought history to attend to the conditions that made the present possible and yet there remains an ever-present uneasiness that such awareness can limit the very orders of knowledge being historicized. Using an array of lenses, a number of curriculum scholars have raised key questions about the nature of our work: "Must we observe the golden rule of pedagogy and withhold from others what has been withheld from us?" (Grumet, 1988, p. 128); "How might reconceptualized versions of curriculum enable students and teachers to work together in learning environments where knowledges are viewed as their joint constructions of meanings?" (Miller, 1992, p. 248); "Can the claims for higher academic achievement be demonstrated?" (Watkins, 1993, p. 336); "What would be the parameters of a praxis under erasure?" (Lather, 2003, p. 263); and "What do we make of the world we have been given, and how shall we remake ourselves to give birth to a new social order?" (Pinar, Reynolds, Slattery, & Taubman, 1995, p. 866). Across these questions are themes of suppressed knowledge, divisive curricula, deconstructive problematics, unstudied histories, and practices that are oppressive despite emancipatory intentions. We believe them to be markers that set the stage for next moments in the field.

Next, might questions such as these disarticulate the axiomatic truths of curriculum studies? Nearly 35 years ago, Pinar (1975) raised the issue of experience in education, surfacing a key tension in the field between the technical, ahistorical, and atheoretical character of curriculum studies and its perpetual crisis. He teaches us that its technical character was spurred by commitments to the authority of developmental discourse both in education and the broader world, but his approach highlights the need to investigate the discursive thresholds of history that had to be crossed in order for our concepts of a reconceptualized field to come into view. In 1978 he wrote:

> what must constantly be attended to in a curriculum field that is reconceptualized from the technical, pseudo-practical tradition that is its past, reconceptualized from the narrowly scientific present that myopically continues its tradition, to the emancipatory discipline it must become, is the historical–biographical function of any given issue. (1994, p. 71)

The notion that developmentalism has been conferred upon the field as if its style has the capacity to transcend the particularities of being human—living and learning by way of a life in context—has, as Pinar notes, a long history. Baker's 1999 *American Educational Research Journal* article on developmentalism, progress, and schooling offers such an indicator. Baker was concerned over the enthusiasm educational practitioners and scholars alike have for developmentalism and what it produces as its larger effect in pushing aside more indeterminate discourses, ones that attempt to account for how or why developmental discourses have come to matter so much. In an effort to illustrate the effect developmentalism had on conceptions of learning during the early 1900s, she states,

> Generally speaking, the move toward *centering* developmental conceptions of the child and curriculum suggested a new relationship between the child, teacher, and knowledge. The child, instead of being perceived as a subject that would fit around the order of knowledge in the school, was newly positioned as the central subject around whom knowledge should be ordered. The teacher, rather than looking for true knowledge in the classics, was now to look into the child, via science, for true knowledge of development. (Baker, 1999, p. 201)

Baker provides an alternate way to think about knowledge that lessens violence by looking toward the past to think differently about the future: the truths held as self-evident are not only historically and culturally specific, they can be studied for how they shape notions of the "good" or "dangerous" curriculum and the conditions under which teacher–student relationships become possible at different historical junctures. For Baker, the aim is not to destabilize developmentalism with the same types of reasoning that allowed developmentalism to take root. Rather, the more appropriate question focuses upon how and why technocratic and developmental viewpoints have come to matter so much. Here the focus is on what learning becomes possible when we begin to work out of the bizarre, idiosyncratic, and unstudied histories that mark our efforts to establish criteria, "an opening out onto the complexities that inhere in judging the dangerous and the good" (Baker, 1999, p. 829).

To raise questions in regard to themes such as developmentalism, the unconscious, trauma, hypnosis, and mesmerism as key to understanding the thinking that gets thought in curriculum studies is no small matter. Rather, it is one where the understandings we have and implications of our work are troubled through the study of our epistemological unconscious, the fundamental assumptions that underwrite knowledge at different historical moments: the constitutive limits of discourse and the rules that enable its productivity. As Baker illustrates in this chapter and her scholarship elsewhere (1998, 2002), it is much easier to dismiss inquiries into origins and withdraw into despair, euphoria, careerism, and distortions of history to avoid questions of difficult, unsettling knowledge and the curious beginnings of our taken-for-granted beliefs. In a field driven by crises from both the inside and outside—with all the pressures for advancement from the former and answers from the latter—there is less room for aporias and working at the crossroads of what we have termed "difficult, unsettling knowledge" and what Baker and Heyning (2004) have called "denaturalization projects" (p. 31).

Unsettling knowledge are those ideas that disturb the convenient truths through which we organize our thoughts and make meaning of our experiences in the world. These are the theories that creep up on educators and disturb them with difficult thoughts: that education is not synonymous with rationality and control, but also that one might become unreasonable, irrational, and intractable, that the persistent crises in the field—whether forced upon the field from the outside or the result of internal eruptions—will exceed all reason and discompose all prior efforts at advancement. Unsettling knowledge invokes skepticism. As Baker (1999) teaches us, we have dismantled developmentalism but paradoxically in an effort to move and progress forward have left developmentalism intact (p. 830), shedding doubt on our capacity to use deconstruction as more than a mere tool in our own efforts toward transcendence. Teachable moments, such as the ones that Baker provides, give us awareness of our inability to think beyond the conditions that make our knowledge possible, tendencies to transfer our insecurities onto our thoughts of others, and vulnerabilities that become evident in the face of truths that discompose other truths. They might even have unwanted effects and increase our enthusiasm for institutional perspectives and technical considerations. Regardless, unsettling knowledge is required. It can pry us away from our pillars of certainty and force us to confront what Derrida has termed "the certainty of the undecidable" (1990, p. 1035): the need for a certain letting go of the truths that matter most in hopes that they might turn on themselves to question the very conditions that made them possible and provoke inquiry into the relationship between the history of the field and the very creation of its objects. In our next moments—post-reconceptualization—we might open spaces to indulge what ultimately cannot be decided, to move toward producing and learning out of the failures and breakdowns in any efforts toward further understanding, to embrace what Lather

(2004) describes in reference to the work of de Man as, "blindness and insight, where the necessary exclusion is the very organizer of whatever insight might be made and critical texts always turn back on the very things they denounce/renounce" (p. 1).

Unsettling knowledge can break the desire to engage in affirmative actions, develop best practices, or establish a central body of scholarship in the field. These deranged knowledges act as a counterforce to certainty because knowledge with the capacity to agitate functions as a reminder of the inadequacy of our categories—that the best we have to offer might not be good or worthy enough to pass on. Indeed, if curriculum studies must waver between a vision of tomorrow and the realities of today, then questions over unsettling knowledge cannot be settled by frameworks, best practices, or learning competencies. There are no fundamental principles that will help here only questions over how the building blocks we cannot do without have come to matter so much, to become unquestioned truths of the field. Instead, one must risk a position in ways that Derrida teaches us is adequate to the status of a position. That is, we must engage in the risk of continuous rereading practices that recognize that any position will always be something less than what it professes. In this chapter, Baker reminds us of the importance of this risk taking, "I have traded here on that doubled position, that there are ways of rethinking history that not only attend to the 'conditions of possibility' for the production of scientific objects of which we may be less aware, but that such awareness can help point to the levels that limit the very orders of knowledge being historicized" (p. 362). Yet, to gain insight into concepts with the authority to tak[e] "up the slack in explanations for explanations" (p. 362), to consider how ongoing historical debates over the validity of developmentalism and unconscious infused the very production of the concepts curriculum studies holds most dear, requires opening spaces for scholars and practitioners alike to explore the character of our responses to these dilemmas.

Even after 30 years have passed since the first efforts to reconceptualize the field, too much of what both graduate and undergraduate students read on curriculum is inadequate to the task of encountering and working through unsettling knowledge. Unsettling knowledge cannot raise awareness by learning the steps toward developing effective curricula, attending trainings that teach the best curriculum content to meet learning objectives, or parading through the facts and figures that make up a chronology of the field. Neither can distortions that purport competencies as the grounds for learning or a series of successor regimes as the basis for the field be of much assistance if we are to follow Baker's assertion that "truths are not simply those things that exist the way they appear" (p. 341). Such distortions dissociate curriculum from the very real dilemmas surrounding the fundamental assumptions that make possible the appearance of our most sacred and prized objects. To think through distortion in curriculum studies and create the terms for the sorts of conversations Baker implores us to have, we need to forego crisis rhetoric that privileges developmentalism and technical modes of thought, and as an alternative encounter questions over ethical commitments that illuminate some of the difficulties associated with unsettling thoughts. Out of the questions curriculum scholars have asked, we have found some themes that cut across the numerous theoretical clusters that comprise curriculum studies and might become a resource for meeting the call for ongoing complicated (to which we add difficult) conversations: unconsciousness studies, conditions of possibility, ocularcentrism, anxieties of truth production, validity studies, legitimate discourse, acceptable mechanisms for persuasion, deceptive lures, and so on. We think it might be these themes that provide the capacity to reconfigure "What truths do we hold as self-evident?" into "How did these truths come to matter so much that they became self-evident?" And possibly, to further extend the conversation, to question, "What does it mean to be a curriculum scholar when more frequently our work is questioned for its relevance from the outside while from the inside our work has taken on a new sense of urgency and importance?"

In order to trace the movement toward unsettling knowledge, we make a turn from curriculum studies proper toward an example from anthropology, Scheper-Hughes's (1992) ethnography focused on the lived experiences of the poor in northeastern Brazil, *Death Without Weeping: The Violence of Everyday Life in Brazil*. The shift toward anthropology and what it makes possible for envisioning different possibilities and as-yet unknown intellectual orientations gives us one mode of thought that can implicate us in our readings and meaning making strategies. The participants in Scheper-Hughes's study waver someplace between determination and despair, and the tension between the relentless search for laughter and pleasure and living conditions characterized by distress, hunger, and suffering sustains the very terms under which community is made and unmade. In particular the study focuses on mother love and child death in the Alto do Cruzeiro region and the City of Bom Jesus da Mata, places where material and psychological scarcity and devastation shape the conditions out of which moral thought and ethical practice arise. The researcher takes the reader on a journey through innumerable crises: chronic hunger, sickness, death, underemployment, alcoholism, murder, child abduction, global capitalism, malnutrition, medicalization of hunger, routinization of human suffering, and colonialism and its effects on the ability to have trust, love, keep faith, and find moments of pleasure among communities members who suffer material and symbolic violence on an everyday basis. Events involving thirst, hunger, and neglect, however, do not provide the full picture of their lives. Furthermore, the urgent and horrific nature of life for the Brazilian poor is not presented as something the researcher used to advance a body of knowledge or out of which advances in knowledge improved their situation. Instead, increased understanding made possible the conditions for the researcher's desensitization and indifference. And advances in medical knowledge become mechanisms for covering up malnutrition as the cause of most aliments. These are representations of precarious conditions that produce new and different languages for understanding life among the poor ("nervous frenzy" and "madness of hunger"), ones that reconfigure maternal care thought natural to motherhood into a frantic and anxiety ridden love that sometimes ends with mothers taking the life of children so as to end their misery.

Most of the text is organized around the researcher's experiences interacting with participants; the descriptions they offered of their lives; and the roles of church, government, and business in fostering and maintaining their oppression. Yet, rather than present a chronology of stories that build successively in the suffering of the characters, Scheper-Hughes structures the storytellers' offerings to challenge the categories that have come to matter so much in the academy—of maternal and family love, medical knowledge that improves lives, education that increases critical thinking, and a belief that faith can allow for a more peaceful existence. The text offers nuanced descriptions of the lived realities that led to her categorical distinctions, ones that include "Two Feet Under and a Cardboard Coffin" and "The Madness of Nervos." Here the writing offers a sense of time closest to the author's discovery—a researcher finding herself in difficult circumstances and how she is transformed by the experience coupled with a historical overview of the forces that led to current conditions of distress and devastation. Near the end of the text, Scheper-Hughes hopes to find that with the onset of *carnaval* spaces open where roles, statuses, and hierarchies are reversed and the "competing and colliding social worlds" (p. 483) of the rich and poor turn into a social egalitarian utopia, if even just temporarily. Indeed, from community members' descriptions and what cultural anthropologist Victor Turner (1987) offered in his analysis of *carnaval* in Rio de Janeiro, she was warranted in having some hope for a hiatus from the clear divide between the "haves" and "have nots." Her observations dash her optimism, however, and she reflects upon the contradiction between the transformative potential many community members find in *carnaval* as a breach of Brazilian hierarchy and what she observes:

> …what I saw that first evening (and for each subsequent evening) after leaving Biu's house and after catching up with the street dancers was a highly segregated and segmented *carnaval* where the rich and poor, white and black, male and female, adult and child, loose "street" children and pampered "house" children, knew their "proper" places and kept to them. The wealthy families of the big houses played *carnaval* in the privacy of their vacation homes on the coast or in elite social clubs in Recife. They never showed their faces for the duration of the festivities. The middle classes emerged briefly on the street on Friday night, the eve of the official start of the festival. Then they, too, left town. (p. 484)

Given the conflict between images of *carnaval* as a unifying symbol and the class-based reality of what she witnessed provokes Scheper-Hughes to think about her perceptions, the perceptions of the majority of community members, and the conditions that made these multiple and divergent realities possible. She realizes that even as her writing traces her journey, it somehow lacks the capacity to represent the truths of the people she studies, and also lacks any determinability about what the reader might do with such knowledge. This mode of thought, one that attends to the clear race, gender, and class divisions also recognizes the "ambivalences and contradictions" of *carnaval* and that it is both "the opiate of the masses" and "their symbolic Molotov cocktails" (p. 483). That is, rather than repeat efforts to get it right, the author attempts doubled or parallel readings that are heterogeneous and polysemic, ones that when making declarations of truth, fray the edges. The knowledge that will lessen violence against ourselves and the world—of the undecideability over what to say about the contradictions between what is witnessed and the perspective of storytellers and the need to say something—might be "good enough" knowledge. Or, following the work of Lather, knowledge that brings us "to question our own investment in the 'good story' and the 'innocent story' of emancipatory efforts" (p. 155). Here any attempt at dismissing the perspectives of members of the Bom Jesus community or reducing their complexities, contradictions, and novelty of perspectives to caricatures of themselves is discomposed by admitting that the research fails as much as it succeeds—that not even knowledge can save us and so we must begin to ask how the knowledge we have has taken on the significance it has.

In a peculiar way Scheper-Hughes's dilemmas over how to represent the people of the Alto do Cruzeiro region and the City of Bom Jesus da Mata reside in the spaces between teaching and learning, between curriculum and pedagogy. She makes doubled claims about knowledge and about what as of yet remains unknown, understanding the events she witnessed as a montage of disparate stories that also offers the uniformity of experience necessary to underwrite calls for an intervention. Of course, Baker is teaching us that this is the curious state of curriculum studies as well, a crossroads where pressure from the outside and expectations from the inside, much like the stories of Brazilian peasants and the efforts Scheper-Hughes puts forth to think with and through them, are inadequate to what must be thought when thinking of the crisis at hand. What Baker is doing, and what we are suggesting curriculum studies might engage in, is to produce and learn from the failures of our knowledge to lessen violence a state of openness to unsettling questions, where the field can take seriously questions over what curriculum has "marshaled under its umbrella and at what cost it has ignored some key aspects of its 'own' domain formation" (Baker, p. 345).

References

Apple, M. W. (2004). Creating difference: Neo-liberalism, neo-conservatism, and the politics of educational reform. *Educational Policy, 18*(1), 12–44.

Baker, B. (1998). Child-centered teaching, redemption, and educational identities: A history of the present. *Educational Theory, 48*(2), 15–74.

Baker, B. (1999). The dangerous and the good? Developmentalism, progress, and public schooling. *American Educational Research Journal, 36*(4), 797–834.

Baker, B. (2002). The hunt for disability: The new eugenics and the normalization of school children. *Teachers College Record, 104*(4), 663–703.

Baker, B. M., & Heyning, K. E. (2004). *Dangerous coagulations? The uses of Foucault in the study of education.* New York: Lang.

Benjamin, W. (1977). *The origin of German tragic drama* (J. Osborne, Trans.). London: Verso.

Britzman, D. P., & Dippo, D. (2000). On the future of awful thoughts in teacher education. *Teaching Education, 11*(1), 31–37.

Derrida, J. (1990). Force of law: The "mystical foundation of authority." *Cardozo Law Review, 11*(5–6), 919–1039.

Derrida, J. (2006). *Specters of Marx: The state of the debt, the work of mourning and the new international* (Trans. P. Kamuf). New York: Routledge.

Dewey, J. (1997). *Experience and education.* New York: Touchstone. (Original work published in 1938)

Edgerton, S. (1996). *Translating the curriculum: Multiculturalism into cultural studies.* New York: Routledge.

Foucault, M. (1995). *Discipline and punish: The birth of the prison* (2nd ed.). New York: Vintage.

Grumet, M. R. (1988). *Bitter milk: Women and teaching.* Amherst: The University of Massachusetts Press.

Hartman, G. (1999). Benjamin in hope. *Critical Inquiry, 25,* 344–352.

Lather, P. (2000). Reading the image of Rigoberta Menchu: Undecidability and language lessons. *Qualitative Studies in Education, 13*(2), 153–162.

Lather, P. (2002). Applied Derrida: (Mis)reading the work of mourning in educational research. *Educational Philosophy and Theory, 35*(3), 257–270.

Lather, P. (2004, April). *Getting lost: Feminist efforts toward a double(d) science.* Paper presented at the annual meeting of the American Educational Research Association, San Diego, CA.

Miller, J. L. (1992). Shifting the boundaries: Teachers challenge contemporary curriculum thought. *Theory into Practice, 31*(3), 245–251.

Pinar, W. F. (1975). Currere: Toward reconceptualization. In W. F. Pinar (Ed.), *Curriculum theorizing: The reconceptualists* (pp. 396–414). Berkeley, CA: McCutchan.

Pinar, W. F. (1993). Notes on understanding curriculum as racial text. In C. McCarthy & C. Crichlow (Eds.), *Race, identity, and representation in education* (pp. 60–70). New York: Routledge.

Pinar, W. F. (1994). *Autobiography, politics, and sexuality: Essays in curriculum theory 1972–1992.* New York: Lang.

Pinar, W. F. (2004). *What is curriculum theory?* Mahwah, NJ: Erlbaum.

Pinar, W. F., Reynolds, W. M., Slattery, P., & Taubman, P. M. (1995). *Understanding curriculum: An introduction to the study of historical and contemporary curriculum discourses.* New York: Lang.

Scheper-Hughes, N. (1992). *Death without weeping: The violence of everyday life in Brazil.* Berkeley: University of California Press.

Turner, V. (1987). Carnival, ritual, and play in Rio de Janeiro. In A. Falassi (Ed.), *Time out of time: essays on the festival* (pp. 74–90). Albuquerque: University of New Mexico Press.

Watkins, W. H. (1993, Fall). Black curriculum orientations: A preliminary inquiry. *Harvard Educational Review, 63*(3), 321–338.

18 Intimate Revolt and Third Possibilities
Cocreating a Creative Curriculum

Hongyu Wang

Chapter Overview

This chapter offers an alternate understanding of revolt through a parallel reading of Laozi's yin/yang of intimacy and Kristeva's revolt in the search for a third possibility. The author follows Kristeva's exploration of the etymology of revolt and Laozi's notions of change and fluidity and their relationship to multiple notions of return. Next, she notes certain parallels between Kristeva's proposition that both language and psyche are composed of the symbolic and semiotic and Laozi's formation of harmony through the yin and yang relationship. Noting that Kristeva calls for plural singularity in the third generation of feminism and that within the Taoist tradition yin and yang are integrated forces that make possible the transformations of opposites into a third, the author suggests that between the two is the birth of the cocreative. The author then explores the implications of Kristeva's intimacy in revolt before turning to the labyrinth as a bridge between Taoist playfulness and Kristevian intimacy. Finally, the author offers other modes of creativity based on translation and lostness that can account for complexity and polyvalence; ones that confront the recursive nature of human problems.

To discuss post-reconceptualization in curriculum studies implies a position of revolt. The word *revolt* usually refers to a rebellion, a break with the old, a transgression against the limit. Especially under the Western tradition of creation ex nihilo, the birth of the new comes from tearing away from the conventional. In this paper, I intend to offer an alternative understanding of what we are facing in the next (present) moment of curriculum studies through a parallel reading of Kristeva's intimate revolt and Laozi's yin/yang dynamics to generate third possibilities that cannot be confined by a transgressive mode of revolt.

This parallel reading inspires plural visions of revolt in an intercultural, gendered, and intrapsychic space. Although both Kristeva and Laozi valorize the role of the (feminine) flow in creativity, their emphases are not the same. While Julia Kristeva (2000b) asks us "to get back to the intimate wellsprings of revolt" (p. 85) and reconnect with the sensory experience to challenge the paternal, Laozi locates the possibility of renewal and regeneration in a continuum of flow between yin/feminine and yang/masculine, a third possibility that "gives birth to the universe" (*Tao Te Ching*, chapter 42). Both their resonance and their different positioning point us to multiple bridges toward plural singularity and complex interconnectedness in our increasingly transnational and international society. Not necessarily denying the role of transgression, this reading invites us to travel alternative landscapes and open up new possibilities.

The chapter begins with the notion of revolt in its multiple meanings, then moves to the power of intimate revolt and a third possibility, bridged by the notion of play in the labyrinth, and ends with translation as an exemplar for cocreating a creative curriculum as a new generation's task for the next moment in curriculum studies.

What Is Revolt?

Kristeva (2000a, 2000b, 2002) traces the etymology of the word *revolt* and identifies circular movement and temporal return in its Latin verb. She explains that the word's political meaning of revolution and social upheaval did not appear until the modern age. As a psychoanalyst, she points out the occurrences of revolt in both oedipal revolt and the return to the archaic. She further identifies three figures of revolt in the Freudian experience: revolt as the transgression of a prohibition, as repetition/working-through, and as displacement/renewing (Kristeva, 2000a, p. 16). She claims that "understood in these ways, revolt takes on forms that are themselves more complex, less immediately transgressive" (Kristeva, 2000b, p. 85). Facing the failure of rebellious ideologies (to march into a promised land) and the dominance of a consumer culture (in flattening the depth of psychic life) in our contemporary age, she argues that we need to sustain revolt but in a more complex mode. Reconstituting memory along with (self-) questioning through, for instance, literary experience or musical creation, is not confined by any absolute ideal of social contestation but brings back intimacy to renew the psychic space. Revolt is an open, transformative, and creative process that simultaneously involves cultural, political, and psychic working through and renaissance.

Laozi's notions of change and fluidity are also related to the notion of return. He states: "Returning/reversal is the movement of *Tao*" (*Tao Te Ching*, chapter 40). Reversal (反) and return (返) can be used interchangeably in the ancient Chinese language. Here "return" has multiple meanings. First, everything has its opposite, and opposites enable each other. *What is not* makes possible *what is*. Emptiness enables fullness. Second, everything always changes toward its reversal. *Tao Te Ching* is full of teachings about the mutual transformation of opposites. A time of vigor leads to a time of decay; strength comes from holding on to softness; what is worn out will become renewed. Third, returning to the original source of life—Tao as the way of nature—is the direction of movement. This coming back to Tao in its emptiness, quietude, and harmony is a process of constant renewal and regeneration. It is clear here that the multiple meanings of the Taoist return are organically integrated, with one flowing into another.

Reversal, return, and renewal are all embedded in Laozi's notion of movement. This forms an interesting parallel to Kristeva's call for the return to the archaic. A coincidence is that the word *revolt* when translated into Chinese has an element of reversal/return, but its political meaning of revolution is also a modern usage. The psychoanalytic meaning of oedipal revolt is absent in Taoism, at least in its initial formulation. The Taoist notion of change lies in an interconnected sense of the world in which one thing can become something else. In psychoanalysis, the unconscious (or the archaic) is rooted in the unknown, which requires rigorous analysis to become known. By contrast, the Taoist interconnectedness is evident in a myriad of things in the universe, so the demarcation between the repressed and the conscious is difficult to draw. Therefore, the Kristevian return and the Taoist return have different twists and turns. Both offer an understanding of the revolt that is an alternative to the modern Western notion of transgression, but Kristeva retains the edge of questioning in intimacy while Laozi subsumes the sharpness of the reversal into a continuum of movement. As I argue throughout this paper, their differences are generative for enabling both creativity and cocreativity.

Arrested, being afraid to move. Over the edge is darkness. Fear. Fear of what is beyond, beyond what one can cling to. Fear of disappearing into nothingness. Afraid. Afraid of what is within, afraid of the wildness inside, afraid of the inner shadow, one freezes movement. There is a danger in the dark. There is also an intimacy in the dark. Touching the dark edge of fear, one lightens up, no longer afraid. A longing for flow. Mother's singing, father's tears, baby's rhythmic movements, water's playful dancing with rock, the permeating strokes of calligraphy. The past and the future meet in the flow to free the present. Is not curriculum— currere—*about movement, moving out of the frozen state, moving toward what is yet to come?*[1]

Since it is a return, both Kristeva and Laozi emphasize the role of "lowly dwelling." For Kristeva, the return to the irreducible memories of the archaic requires humility on the part of the psychoanalyst, who patiently, calmly, and benevolently enables the analysands to find a home in their own lowly dwelling. Laozi also valorizes the position of the lowly and often uses the metaphor of water to demonstrate its potential (*Tao Te Ching,* chapters 8, 61, 66). Water flows downward to gather strength and to achieve calmness, vastness, and benevolence. While Freud's metaphor of lowly dwelling refers to the unconscious challenging the Western privilege of consciousness, Laozi's metaphor of the lowly position of water refers to the potential of yin questioning the conventional notion of power in a wartime China. Such a positioning has important pedagogical implications. It is not an easy task to provide students with an opportunity to get in touch with their inner worlds, and the pedagogical patience, "watchfulness" (Aoki, 2005), and generosity on the part of the teacher becomes a necessary condition for encouraging such an engagement. I will return to this notion of pedagogical companionship later.

If the return to the archaic is essential to the possibility of revolt, intimacy in revolt becomes a lingering element; if reversal is inherent in the movement of Tao, the third emerging from the mutual transformation of opposites becomes a continuous process. But before we touch the power of intimate revolt and third possibility, we need to detour through the Kristevian dynamics of the semiotic and the symbolic, and the Taoist harmony between yin and yang.

The Semiotic/Symbolic and the Yin/Yang Doublets

Kristeva proposes that both language and the human psyche are composed of two inseparable elements: the semiotic and the symbolic (Wang, 2004). The semiotic refers to tones, rhythms, and traces of language which are characterized by mobility, polyvalence, and instability; in the human psyche, the semiotic is the repressed, unconscious other, which is oriented to the maternal body. The archaic memory is closely associated with the semiotic flow. The symbolic refers to the structure, grammar, or syntax of language, which is characterized by stability and stasis; in the human psyche, the symbolic points to conscious judgment, which is linked to the paternal law. The semiotic has the potential to challenge the symbolic order but the symbolic regulates the semiotic fluidity. These two aspects are always combined and cannot exist without each other.

The word *yang* originally meant the sunshine or light on one side of a mountain and *yin* meant the lack of sunshine or the shaded area on the other side. Later the yin and yang became complementary cosmic forces referring to different aspects of reality and life. Yin signifies darkness, softness, passivity, and femininity while Yang signifies brightness, hardness, activity, and masculinity. The interaction between the two gives birth to all the phenomena of the universe including humanity. It is clear here that the yin/yang polarity is not person-centered but is a cosmological principle, with femininity and masculinity more as a metaphor for the human world.

The Kristevian project is to bring the body back into the language and the human psyche. She privileges the poetic language (to translate the semiotic into words), motherhood (to initiate the child into language and recover the mother's own semiotic relationships), and psychoanalysis (to build bridges between affects and meanings in order to enable psychic rebirth), as the site for getting in touch with the semiotic flow to destabilize and transform the symbolic. She emphasizes that the semiotic and the symbolic form "a sort of dialectic of mutual contradiction" (Kristeva, 1993, p. 183) and that her interest is in the interactive realm between surprise and structure.

While regenerating the maternal body as the site for creativity, however, Kristeva still privileges the paternal function in enabling separation and independence, following the psychoanalytic tradition. In Kristeva's theory, the relationship between the semiotic and the symbolic shifts during different life stages for each individual. In the preoedipal stage, the child is closely in touch with the semiotic, maternal, realm. The oedipal identity declares independence from the maternal to enter into the paternal symbolic realm. Kristeva emphasizes that such separation is a necessary condition for the psychic life. But she also points out that the mother initiates such a move for the child to *desire* knowledge. The postoedipal stage, as Kristeva argues, needs to be marked by the return of the semiotic to sustain the capacity for renewing thinking and life.

In Laozi's formulation of the yin/yang relationship, reaching harmony through interaction is the ultimate purpose, but he privileges the role of the yin/feminine rather than the yang/masculine. While Freud's story is about the father, Laozi's story is about the power of yin. Reading *Tao Te Ching* can be a non-sense experience for many who take the values of strength, activeness, and competition for granted since Laozi teaches otherwise. Laozi is well known for valorizing the sustaining power of softness in preserving the vitality of life and following Tao. There is no demand for fully breaking with the maternal to achieve independence.

Tao Te Ching says, "Knowing the masculine, maintaining the feminine, and being a ravine for all under heaven" (chapter 28). Here Laozi's yin/yang theory is best summarized. Laozi's emphasis on the feminine and softness is against common sense, but as I discussed earlier, his dialectic viewpoint of opposites changing toward the reverse direction makes it necessary to hold on to softness in order to avoid losing strength and to achieve dynamic harmony in Tao. This softness, however, is powerful only when it is linked with a sense of aliveness. The newborn baby's softness is a symbol of energy and possibility because it already incorporates the masculine power but does not yield to this power.

We can see a certain parallel between the Kristevian heterogeneity of the unconscious/ semiotic and the conscious/symbolic and the Taoist polarity of yin/feminine and yang/masculine. However, considering the radical alterity of the unconscious, I doubt whether the Taoist yin can be signified as the repressed other, as *yin/yang* dynamics do not function through repression and resistance but through the movement of nature. The Taoist interaction between yin and yang permeates throughout one's lifetime rather than going through a sequence of original integration with the semiotic, repression of the maternal, and then a regaining of access to the semiotic. The difference in language is also a factor here. As an ideographical language combined with a unique intonation system, the ancient Chinese classical works are usually poetic in both sounds and forms. Chinese art, notably calligraphy and painting, is intimately related to its language. Intellect and aesthetics have seldom been separated in China, so there is no radical difference between thought/intellectual and art/artist in the Chinese mind. Western thought with phonetically oriented languages often lacks such organic integration, so the move into the symbolic realm is more dramatic.

With the ink permeating through the absorbent paper, the intensity of my emotions gradually smoothes out. Under the motion of the brush, each ideograph tells its own story. These stories unfold before my eyes, with the movement of my hands, and the dancing of my intuitive mind, spontaneously, effortlessly. "Love" has a heart in it. "Person" presents a walking posture. "Tao" is a head walking along the way. The moment I write down a word, the meaning of its figure jumps at me. It is a moment when analysis and synthesis operate simultaneously. The edge between my hand and the shape of the ideograph holds the turbulence inside and stretches it out into a flow of energy.

The semiotic/symbolic and yin/yang doublets both value the role of the feminine, but Kristeva, as a contemporary theorist, is more explicit about the status of woman as stranger with her peculiar psychic potential, and credits the feminist movement—despite its ups and downs—for the rehabilitation of "sensory intimacy" (2000, p. 5). At the same time, she argues that the access to the feminine can be more difficult for women. In fact, women encounter double difficulty since turning away from the maternal erotically and socially for independence implies an element of self-denial.[2] But working through this difficulty and negotiating between the maternal and the paternal, women can create "new objects of thought" (Kristeva, 1996, p. 124). If Laozi's metaphor of the feminine embraces harmony, then the Kristeva's semiotic interrupts to create in polyphony.

The Third Possibility

Kristeva (1987) locates the third[3] in Freud's notion of "the father of individual prehistory" (p. 22), the imaginary father, the loving father who combines the functions of both mother and father. The archaic father precedes the oedipal father and serves to enable independence and differentiation from the mother/child dyad, but through incorporating the maternal function of holding. With the introduction of love into the paternal, the negotiation between the maternal and the paternal is already implied in this image of the imaginary father. I prefer to read Kristeva's loving third, following Kelly Oliver's (2002) lead, as moving in the dynamics of the semiotic and the symbolic. At the same time, Kristeva's vigilance against the merging of the maternal and the child is made clear here.

Laozi's third as the source of creating the universe is not ambivalent about the role of the feminine/the maternal. Not excluding the role of yang, Laozi depicts yin as more life-affirming. Even in Laozi's time, this was a radical idea since war, competition, and violence were prevalent. The returning to the way of nature is a movement of the feminine in its interaction with the masculine. The Taoist ecology of harmony loses its power without the affirmation of the feminine. And precisely due to this valorization of the feminine and its waterway flow, the third generated from the yin/yang interaction is generative but not possessive. Just as Tao gives birth to the universe but does not occupy, the third in its continuous emergence nurtures the universe but does not dominate.

If we put Kristeva's vigilance and Laozi's valorization regarding the feminine in a broader intercultural context, it is not difficult to see different orientations. I will focus on one line of departure for illumination: the independence/interdependence axis. Kristeva's vision for a fulfilling postoedipal life is marked by both the return of the repressed semiotic and a spirit of questioning, but it seems to me that the return serves for further contestation. She argues that revolt is indispensable both to psychic life and social bonds, "as long as it remains a live force and resists accommodations" (Kristeva, 2000b, p. 38). Critiquing the first and the second generations of feminist movement, she proposes the third generation for creating "plural singularity" that is infinitely open to the specificity of the feminine other and the specificity of each woman. This follows the long Western tradition of seeking independence, singularity, and originality, although Kristeva acknowledges the necessity for interdependence through introducing the semiotic/maternal flow.

Laozi's world is not the same. As the newborn baby metaphor indicates, the Taoist yin and yang are not mutually exclusive. There is an inherent opening within yin and yang to the other element as the smaller dots in the *Tai-ji* symbol show. Perhaps due to this built-in element of the other in its opposite, opposites are prevented from becoming hostile to each other. Refusing to become enemies, yin and yang are inherently open to and thus connected with each other, which makes possible the mutual transformation of opposites to generate the third. This is the basis for an interconnected worldview. The Taoist notion of unity between humanity and the universe is a dynamic harmony that emerges from the interplay of difference. While the center of the person is displaced, it is in this decentering that the possibility of personal freedom is situated. In proposing both creativity and cocreativity for this paper, I wish to honor both the Kristeva revolt to create plural singularity and the Taoist return to the embrace of interdependence. The polyphony of the semiotic and the symbolic through intimate revolt and the harmony of yin and yang on the watercourse of Tao presents plural possibilities of creation and re-creation. May we envisage a third between the Kristevian third and the Taoist third?

Michel Serres (1997), using the language of the third place, poetically asks us to educate ourselves between two foci: the sun of reason and the shadow of suffering. What is particularly interesting for me here is the echo of Taoist wisdom in Serres's meditation. "Whoever took up too much room loses his place; who had none takes everything; nothing can become everything, which can be drowned in nothingness. The law of transformation through unpredictable bifurcations" (p. 44). While the language of bifurcations resides in contemporary chaos and complexity theory, the principle of transformation between opposites parallels Laozi's thought.

> At dusk, the red, perfectly round, peaceful sun, without dazzling light, is ready to descend, while simultaneously the opaque, aspiring, and full moon quietly rises to be its counterpart. Looking up into the sky from one locus to another, we may have a moment of suspicion: Which one is sun; which one is moon? Can the moon become red while the sun becomes silver? At the moment of transition (a temporal change, perhaps decisively, marking the split of day and night), a third space is born. Being lost in the double of sun and moon, light and dark, a third space weds daylight laughter with nighttime intimacy, bridges words and memories, and connects motion with meditation [italics added]. (Wang, 2004, p. 147)

Between the two foci, the birth of the new is cocreative as it comes from the interaction of doubles, but it is also singular as it generates something unique. A third possibility is about making passages, connecting the land and the sea, the sun and the moon, the light and the dark. Located in the web of interdependence, the third constantly renews its own singular pattern, every time as if it is the first time. The singular and the interdependent enrich, re-create, and sustain each other. It is in this connecting between heterogeneous forces that Kristeva locates the meaning of intimacy.

Intimacy in Revolt

Kristeva traces the Latin root of the word *intimate* as "the most interior," and claims that the liveliest aspect of the intimate "resides precisely in the heterogeneity of the two sensorial/symbolic, affect/thought registers" (Kristeva, 2002, p. 49). To experience this heterogeneous continuity in the cohabitation of sensation and thought is to preserve the intimate in a border region. Intimacy is not reduced to the unconscious and the semiotic, but is claimed at the interstice between contradictory forces. Kristeva (2002) rereads Plato's cave as a sensorial cave. Only when sensory experiences are transformed into words is intimacy in revolt possible. She privileges the poetic language and narrative words in their potential to embody the heterogeneity of the unconscious and the conscious. Perhaps, without a poetic flow, words cannot make peace with the shadows in the cave.

Exhausted but sleepless, I am lying on the sofa. The soft music touches my face gently. Memory of the university lake whispers into my ears through the breeze. Images come and go. Words of books fade away into the shadow. But my own words come back, flowing through the intensity of the body, moving onto a blank sheet of paper. I love ancient Chinese poetry. The sound. The rhythms. The imagery. The mood. Yet I never really write any poetry in Chinese. Is Chinese saturated in the move-ment of English which I am trying to speak? At the crossroads of two languages, the voice of the poetic emerges [italics in original] (Wang, 2004, p. 90).

Intimacy offers a site to experience suffering in a meaningful way. Making passages from the painful affects to words, finding a language to inscribe the unspeakable, we generate our capacity for thinking with compassion to *make sense* of life. The link between pain and representation makes encountering loss and even death more endur-able. Furthermore, intimacy contains the sadomasochism of the unconscious, producing a *jouissance* in "irreconcilable conflictuality" (Kristeva, 2002, p. 237) between desire and prohibition. By formulating and representing such conflictuality in the imaginary and the symbolic, it can be worked out and sublimated for creativity, avoiding its violent or regressive expressions in both personal and social life. This means a process of endless rebirth.

Returning to the memory and inscribing it in thought is copresent with a mode of questioning. Keeping a memory of the past is not enough; one has to question this past in order to make meanings. Kristeva argues that psychoanalytical interpretation is a process of questioning sensory memory first and then thought to open up the unknown in the analysand rather than to offer answers. When necessary, interpretation need not be afraid of being "intrusive" in order to reveal what is behind the screen and the passage between desire and words. She terms this a two-directional "affect-language-request-negation-question trajectory" (2002, p. 151). Kristeva advocates for reading the unknown that students bring and reflecting it back to them rather than looking for the teacher's own ideas in students.

When the unknown of the self is not threatening, permanent questioning in revolt can lead to an opening to the unknown of the other. Intimacy through experiencing pain leads to compassion for others, with pity and tenderness. For Kristeva, social revolt is enabled by psychic revolt. The bridge between the two is our capacity to be with oth-ers in a compassionate relationship. Intimacy in revolt resides in the interior life whose permanent re-creation is dependent upon whether it is "free to internalize the outside, if and only if this outside (to start with, the mother) allows one to play, allows itself to play" (Kristeva, 2002, p. 233). From the mother to the polis, the exterior needs to be ready to be internalized, benevolently. The teacher also belongs to this exterior.

There is no revolt without a certain sense of the limit. The interrogation of the limit does not mean overthrowing the limit once and for all, but bringing more variety and flexibility to the limit. In this sense, the meaning of social revolt is to seek out more spaces for creative activities while at the same time protecting individuals from their inner aggressive drives. Here we can see that the Kristevian intimacy does not follow the line of self against society (Lechte, 1990), but gives it enough of a twist to accommodate the connections between the social and the psychic. Contesting the corporate, techno-logical, entertainment-oriented, consumer culture, Kristeva (2002) does not intend to replace it; instead, she asks us to cultivate another version of culture—culture as revolt—as a parallel space. She proposes a public politics that shows "generosity, recognition or forgiveness" (p. 43). If we approach education as part of such a public politics, a peda-gogical benevolence that gives students freedom to play with the limit rather than being constrained within the limit becomes important.

If intimacy invites the plurality of connections with others as Kristeva argues, it implies a sense of companionship that holds on through confusion and loss to sustain the courage for creativity and rebirth, in the labyrinth.

Labyrinth, Play, and Companionship

Intimacy as recovered from the lost maternal is not Laozi's language, as the maternal is not lost in an oedipal sense. Endurance of suffering and pain is usually accepted as part of being immersed in a nonanthropocentric universe rather than as the site for nurturing the potential for revolt. Instead, the Taoist sense of playfulness with negation parallels the Kristevian intimacy with the repressed sensory experience. The metaphor of labyrinth provides a link between the Taoist playfulness and the Kristevian intimacy.

Sheng Keyong (2004), who is a pioneer in bridging Western psychoanalysis and Chinese cultural tradition, points out that the labyrinth as a feminine space symbolizes death, pregnancy, and rebirth. "Labyrinth" in English is related originally to the house of the double ax (or palace of Knossos on Crete in the Greek myth) whose shape implies the meaning of transformation in the butterfly. Daedalus also made the wings for flying out while creating the Crete underground labyrinth. "Labyrinth" in Chinese is a two-word phrase with the latter word implicated in the meaning of "uterus." Labyrinth is also related to the image of the cave. Interestingly, the literal translation of the Chinese word *insight* is "cave seeing." If we follow Kristeva's reading of the Plato cave as sensory, a labyrinth is a space to nurture insights and wisdom. According to Sheng (2004), a labyrinth also indicates "a test or suffering through which to achieve psychic and spiritual transformation and growth" (p. 297). In undergoing such a test, one needs the support of psychic, emotional, and spiritual resonance from others.

Pedagogically, this need for resonance asks us to accompany our students in their journeys of cultivating wings for flying out of the labyrinth. The teacher's companionship—in refusing to provide direct answers but being together with students' in their struggles—becomes important for students so that they can give birth to their own understandings and insights. The wings of knowledge and the wisdom to work out confusion and to fly out to different worlds cannot emerge without being rooted in the maternal underground, the lowly position of generative potential.

To walk in and through the labyrinth, we need to connect with our childlike state, to play, and to cultivate a sense of humor in order to nurture the capacity to fly and to take responsibility without being crushed by its burden. The childlike quality of our own personhood holds the seed for creative imagining, sensitivity to connectedness, and unanticipated possibilities. For Laozi, being able to regain our childlike state is to find our way back to Tao. What Laozi says here is not to become a child again, but to restore the life force of the child. It is not a simple repetition but a repetition in motion. Returning to the state of infancy is tied to our ability to understand the strength of the feminine, the power of the ravine, and the vitality of the baby. Too often we lose this original state of energy and vitality as we learn the rules of mastery and domination. To grow wings from knowledge, to cultivate wisdom in experiencing life, we need to get in touch with such a childlike state, not in its dependency, but in its endless playful openness. This Taoist play in the labyrinth parallels the Kristevian sensory cave as a dwelling place for recovering vital life energy.

The little girl loves to open doors, doors of different rooms, doors on various toys, doors to dark closets. And close them. And re-open them. She takes great pleasure in what she is doing. Her face glows with excitement and her eyes sparkle with joy. Repetition in motion. As if the mysteries of what holds at the border of the inside/outside and openings to the invisible have an endless appeal. Not yet having mastered the power of language, she uses tones, cries, rhythmic sounds, looks, touches, and the movement of her body to express herself. She speaks with her own language. Her brother, 2 years older, sometimes, is seduced into the rhythm of non-sense sounds, imitates the language of nonlanguage. He loves to play with puzzles. He picks up pieces randomly and puts them together with swift intuition, and takes them apart, and then puts them together again. Repetition in motion. Always finding something fun in iterating the game, he tirelessly performs the formation of the puzzle pattern. In all sorts of games they play, alone or together, they also test and push limits. They risk fear, stretching out to grow.

American culture is usually credited by Chinese people for its humor, a humor full of laughter, performance, and expressiveness. Parody, game, and play also seem to be an important part of the postmodern condition (Doll, 1993) that characterizes our age. However, the sense of humor in Taoism (in Eastern thought in general)[4] is seldom appreciated in Western circles. The playfulness of Laozi is often lost in the sharpness of analysis that attempts to dissect the ambiguity and irony of wisdom. *Tao Te Ching* itself is full of playful wisdom, which does not make sense if one reads it absolutely seriously. "A playful singing in the midst of life" in Ted Aoki's (2005, p. 282) term, "the wheel of comedy" in Mary Doll's (2000) phrase, Taoist humor is essential to a tactful pedagogy. Playing with confusion in the labyrinth, experimenting with dead-ends and passages, making sense of being lost, students stretch out to grow, accompanied by the teacher's watchful and generous guidance. The playfulness is also embedded in the notion of translation, a notion that I will use as a metaphor for cocreating and creating curriculum-in-motion in a transnational and global society.

Translation in Motion: Another Mode of Creativity

Translation is a good example of situating in a third space, marked by attentiveness to the other, the other language, the other horizon. Translation also requires being faithful to oneself so that a transformative space between others' foreign words and one's own native tongue can be cultivated. This play between self and other is difficult yet generative, as translation is inevitably marked by loss, and by the birth of the third from the loss. Derrida (1991) affirms both the necessity and impossibility of translation and clearly understands it as a poetic activity. For a transnational future, a poetics of translation holds out possibilities. Kristeva (2002) asserts that "future humanity will be made up of foreigners trying to understand each other" (p. 257). Here the foreigner is not only literal but also metaphorical, defined as the translator of the sensory universe in its singularity. This multiple sense of translation—linguistic, national, cultural, gendered, psychic—unfolds before us a promise to reenvision curriculum, pedagogy, and curriculum studies as a field.

It was my first time to be an interpreter at an academic conference. To say that I was nervous was an understatement. The British scholar asked me whether I would like him to read from his paper so it would be easier for me to translate. Without any hesitation, I said, "Oh, no, please feel free to say whatever you want to say." I did not want him to feel uncomfortable—in a foreign land—not having the freedom to present in his own way. I had no idea of what I had gotten myself into by this promise. Energetic, expressive, and humorous, he walked all over the place with me following him everywhere. Holding a microphone, I could not write any notes. Side by side I watched him speak and listened to him intensely. Immediately changing his words into my own, I had never been so focused. At the end of the speech, both of us were pleased. It was not the confidence in my own skills but my faithfulness to giving the other a space that made this first translation experience a lingering memory.

Translation in academia here is usually not considered creative. Isn't this notion of linguistic and intellectual purity another form of exclusion? I argue that good translation is an exemplar of another kind of creativity, a creativity marked by cocreativity. One has to know at least two worlds in order to negotiate between the double. Translation is a play and a risk, an interplay with different texts, and a risk of entering different worlds. It is indeed about educating ourselves between two foci, to reiterate Serres's notion. Derrida (1991) also points out that we need to consider "the possibility for languages to be implicated *more than two* [italics in original] in a text" (p. 250). Intralinguistic translation and the complexity of encountering and negotiating the multiplicity of the maternal and the paternal (in a psychoanalytic sense) in different cultures present a multilayered everchanging world in which foci are not only pluralized but also destabilized.

In this broad sense of translation, curriculum and pedagogy become an intricate process of translating among and within teacher, student, and text in such a way that the surprise of the other and of the otherness is welcomed and even encouraged. When the unknown within is opened up through the interaction between and among teacher, student, and text, psychic and social potentialities of curriculum flow out in "revolt." Susan Edgerton's (1996) invitation to translate the curriculum for intertextual, intercultural, and intersubjective transformation requires our attentive listening here. Translating the curriculum depends on whether we are willing to dwell in an intimate realm—a third space—where we take risk translating between the semiotic and the symbolic and negotiate between yin and yang for the possibility of creativity and cocreativity in polyphony and in harmony.

Translation complicates the notion of belonging: one has to both belong and not belong. Making impossible and necessary connections in translation, one needs to be playful about getting lost. Curriculum as "an engagement with the experience of lostness" (Block, 1998, p. 336) defies the current push for standardization, accountability, and conformity in the field of education. Being playful with loss, intimacy, in its embodied touch, requires a pedagogy that leads students out to the unknown but also leads them back to the familiar to respin the wheel of meaning-making while harmony, in its iterative humor, incites the courage to experiment but also gently leads the edge of invention back into the pedagogical circle. Pedagogical tasks lie in revealing what is left unsaid and translating what cannot be represented and further enabling students to cultivate such capacity for illuminating and translation. Without the experience of dislocation, we risk reproducing docile obedience; without the effort to dwell in the shadow, we risk provoking rebellion in its most violent form.

Using this metaphor of translation to look at "the next moment" in curriculum studies, I believe that the "crisis" in the field of education, and in general in this culture, is not (merely) due to the inability to create something new, but due to inadequate understanding of the impacts a network can have on the singular. In other words, it is a symptom of not being able to translate well across difference. The transgressive revolt, without the support of a sustaining interconnected web, can intensify the trauma of creativity and moves further away from the self-organization process of the network. A cultural, gendered, psychic third, as I discuss, however, emphasizes cocreativity—while valorizing singular invention—as a way to soften the edge of giving birth to something new. The newness of the third is not (merely) a singular act of breaking with the old but a cocreative process in which new connections are built across (seeming) disconnection and fragmentation. A labyrinth of complicated interconnections invites us to nurture wings of knowledge, intelligence, and wisdom. When intricate paths are built, we are ready to fly, to play with difficulties, to work with confusions, to reach a new ground.

Discussing the fear of disarray in the U.S. curriculum field, Janet Miller (2005) questions the desire for a seamless unity and argues for the necessity of exchange across differences. To make a certain contestation and conflictuality generative, the simplistic identity politics of a static collective "we" is problematic. Instead, we need to make efforts to translate among different fields of study, among the local, the national, and the international, within localities. Facing "the nightmare that is the present" (Pinar, 2004), which is saturated by the drive for standardization and competitive aggression, I am much less interested in proposing any new version than trying a good translation. Through our collective and individual efforts to translate the curriculum, we may be able to "improvise" (Aoki, 2005) openings and "seek passages" (Martusewicz, 2001), even momentarily, to engage and transform day-to-day educational praxis. The Kristevian return in polyphony and the Taoist humor in harmony are both needed for such a vision of translation in motion for cocreating a creative curriculum.

Translating the curriculum, we need to build intersections not only internally but also externally. The pains of the current moment we confront, I believe, come partially from the denial of our embeddedness in the web of the world—not in the fashionable language of globalization but in a profound sense of interconnectedness—in our national and individual identity. Only when the broken web—the maternal, the human, and the ecological web—is woven back can the singular have a space. While the exterior—the current political condition of freezing any mobility—does not allow us to play, our capacity to crack out a space for such play becomes essential. We cannot replace the exterior condition in which we are situated, but we may attempt to create a parallel space—curriculum as revolt—at the interstice between the exterior and the interior. Listening to dissonant voices outside internationally and cross-disciplinarily while translating across different discourses within, inter/play holds the key to the labyrinth of our present situation. Being able to take attacks from both inside and outside, we need to build connections in the inner world with self and in the outside world with others, carving out passages and loops in intimate revolt and third possibility.

Currere (Pinar & Grumet, 1976) formulated in the reconceptualization movement, as an example of engaging intimate revolt, still remains an educational power that is seldom realized in our teaching. Proposing "post-reconceptualization generation/s," we seem to promise a new response to a new situation. However, for me, if there is a generational problem, the issue is not to highlight the cutting edge of a new generation but to confront the recursive nature of human problems that we are perpetually facing, with their own specific questions and issues contextualized in history, culture, place, and a concrete personhood for our own age. Our specific answers spin from the circle and come back to the circle to spiral in an upward journey. If there is an extra darkness to our generation, a contemporary Chinese poet, Gu Cheng (1979/2001), speaks for us well in "A Generation":

Black night gives me black eyes
I search for light using my black eyes

In darkness lies promise, not the promise for tomorrow, but a "nonbridge bridge" (Aoki, 2005) to the morning light. Searching for dewdrops in the first rays of a breaking dawn, that's our burden, our joy, and our journey along a watercourse of intimacy and thirdness: meandering into our heart, reaching up to dancing stars, flowing toward the distance.

Notes

1. The purpose for using italics is to provide a double text—both in resonance and in contrast to theoretical writing. See Wang (2004, pp. 20, 122–123) for further explanation. With the exception of two quoted italic passages from the previous book, all other italic writings are specific for this essay.
2. Kristeva proposes Oedipal1 and Oedipal2 for women's situation regarding the oedipal complex. Oedipal1 lies in the girl's desire for the mother; later the girl changes the object from the mother to the father to arrive at Oedipal2. For more details, see Kristeva (2000a, pp. 99–103).
3. For the pioneer postcolonial articulation of the third space, see Homi Bhabba (1990). For a poststructural analysis of the third place, see Michel Serres (1997). For educational elaborations of the third space, especially between East and West, see Ted T. Aoki (2005), and David Geoffrey Smith (1996).
4. I would like to acknowledge the discussions I had with Xin Li at California State University-Long Beach regarding this lack of appreciation for the Taoist humor.

References

Bhabha, H. K. (1990). The third space. In J. Rutherford (Ed.), *Identity: Community, culture, difference* (pp. 207–221). London: Lawrence & Wishart.

Block, A. B. (1998). Curriculum as affichiste. In W. F. Pinar (Ed.), *Curriculum: Toward new identities* (pp. 325–342). New York: Garland.

Derrida, J. (1991). *Derrida reader* (P. Kamuf, Ed. & Trans.). New York: Columbia University Press.

Doll, M. A. (2000). *Like letters in running water*. Mahwah, NJ: Erlbaum.

Doll Jr., W. E. (1993). *A post-modern perspective on curriculum*. New York: Teachers College Press.

Edgerton, S. H. (1996). *Translating the curriculum*. New York: Routledge.

Gu, C. (2001). A generation. In Wenxuan Cao (Ed.), *Ershi Shiji Mo Zhongguo Wenxue Zuopin Xuan* [An anthology of Chinese literature at the end of the 20th century]. Beijing: Beijing University Press. (Original work published 1979)

Kristeva, J. (1987). *Tales of love*. (Trans. Leon S. Roudiez). New York: Columbia University Press.

Kristeva, J. (1993). Foreign body. *Transition, 2*, 172–183.

Kristeva, J. (1996). *Julia Kristeva* (R. M. Guberman, Ed.). New York: Columbia University Press.

Kristeva, J. (2000a). *The sense and non-sense of revolt* (J. Herman, Trans.). New York: Columbia University Press.

Kristeva, J. (2000b). *Revolt, she said*. Interview with Philippe Petit (B. O'Keeffe, Trans.; S. Lotringer, Ed.). New York: Columbia University Press.

Kristeva, J. (2002). *Intimate revolt*. (J. Herman, Ed.). New York: Columbia University Press.

Lechte, J. (1990). Art, love, and melancholy in the work of Julia Kristeva. In J. Fletcher & A. Benjamin (Eds.), *Abjection, melancholia, and love* (pp. 24–41). London: Routledge.

Martusewicz, R. A. (2001). *Seeking passage*. New York: Teachers College Press.

Miller, J. (2005). The American curriculum field and its worldly encounters. *Journal of Curriculum Theorizing, 21*(2), 9–24.

Oliver, K. (2002). Psychic space and social melancholy. In K. Oliver & S. Edwin (Eds.), *Between the psyche and the social* (pp. 49–65). Lanham, MD: Rowman & Littlefield.

Pinar, W. F. (2004). *What is curriculum theory?* Mahwah, NJ: Erlbaum.

Pinar, W. F., & Grumet, M. R. (1976). *Toward a poor curriculum*. Dubuque, IA: Kendall/Hunt.

Pinar, W. F., & Irwin, R. L. (Eds.). (2005). *Curriculum in a new key: The collected works of Ted T. Aoki*. Mahwah, NJ: Erlbaum.

Serres, M. (1997). *The troubadour of knowledge*. (S. F. Glaser & W. Paulson, Trans.). Ann Arbor: University of Michigan Press.

Sheng, K. (2004). *Analytical psychology*. Beijing: Life, Reader, and New Knowledge Press.

Smith, D. G. (1996). Identity, self and other in the conduct of pedagogical action. *Journal of Curriculum Theorizing, 12*(3), 6–11.

Wang, H. (2004). *The call from the stranger on a journey home*. New York: Lang.

Suggested Reading Questions

1. How might Kristeva's multiple notions of "intimate revolt" be read as a permanent state of questioning of the cultural, political, and psychological, through the reconstruction of memory and meaning?

2. Laozi's notion of change and renewal suggests both a challenge to conventional norms in education and creates the notion of pedagogical companionship between students and teachers. What pedagogical implications and possibilities might these have for the reconceptualization of curriculum as a creative and transformational experience?

3. The author suggests that a parallel reading of Kristeva's intimate revolt and Laozi's yin/yang dynamics generate third possibilities. How might Kristeva's plural singularity and Taoist interplay of difference within yin/yang inform the process of transgression and transformation to make space for a cocreative understanding of the feminine other?

4. How might the metaphor of labyrinth as a link between Taoist playfulness and Kristevian intimacy allow for a pedagogy that has generative potential without crushing creative imagining and sensitivity to connectedness in the classroom?

5. The author suggests that translation is a third space situated in between the self and the other, the semiotic and symbolic, the yin and yang. How might such a transformed space allow us to reimagine curriculum as an active engagement with lostness.

Response to Hongyu Wang Intersubjective Becoming and Curriculum Creativity as International Text

A Resonance

Xin Li

Resonance often means reverberating sound and voice. Figuratively, it represents echoing images, memories, or emotions. Canadian scholar/writer Northrop Frye (1982) elaborated the figurative use of the term *resonance* and emphasized its capacity for stretching images over time and bridging temporal distance in a manner metaphorically, of flying away from the original as well as maintaining some elements. To illustrate, he used the image of *The Grapes of Wrath* as such a resonance, one that was evoked by a blood-soaked Old Testament deity treading a wine press (Isaiah 63) through the *Battle Hymn of the Republic*. In narrative inquiry, Conle (1996) noticed a similar metaphorical correspondence: one story evokes another, although they may have taken place far apart in time and space, maintaining some aspects of the original and flying away quickly as the resonance carries along from one story to the other. Soon, the emerging stories took a modified or even an entirely new direction. Such resonance is an example of human beings' capacity for metaphorical thinking, which is, as Gadamer (1960/1993) pointed out, omnipresent, necessary, and basic to conceptualization. Conle (1996) concurred with Gadamer and coined the term *resonance* as an important component of narrative inquiry.

As a narrative inquiry researcher, I read Wang's chapter as a story. Within the story, I heard multiple stories: the parallel stories of Kristeva and Lao Tzu, and the third possibility of a cocreation of curriculum conceptualization through the example of translation. They evoked resonance in me. I am offering this resonance in the remaining part of this essay as a theoretical consideration for the moment of post-reconceptualization of curriculum studies.

Intersubjective Becoming

The concept of intersubjectivity is not new to the West. Bruner (1996) identifies intersubjective understanding as sympathy and the basic element of the "human ability to understand the minds of others" (p. 20). Feminist theorist Benjamin (1995) elaborates and develops the psychoanalytic theory of intersubjectivity, challenging us to consider the other as not merely an object of our minds but also a subject in his or her own right, with a center of being equivalent to our own. She found that contrary to the Western logic of subject and object, "intersubjective theory postulates that the other must be recognized as another subject in order for the self to fully experience his or her subjectivity in the other's presence" (p. 31).

As Benjamin noticed here, the concept of intersubjectivity is not considered a Western tradition; rather, many Western thinkers credit it to Taoist philosophy. Capra, in *The Tao of Physics* (1979/1991), presented Taoist intersubjectivity in a way that is accessible to the contemporary English speaking/thinking community. Connecting quantum theory in modern physics to Taoist thinking, Capra noted that opposites are abstract concepts belonging to the realm of thought, and as such they are relative. By the very act of focusing our attention on any one concept we create its opposite. That good and bad, pleasure and pain, life and death, are not absolute experiences belonging to different categories, but merely two sides of the same reality; extreme parts of a single whole. Beyond the relativity and earthly opposites lies the dynamic balance between the opposites—the intersubjective thinking and knowing of the world and the Tao.

Intersubjective reasoning can be found throughout Lao Tzu's *Tao Te Ching*. One example is in its famous chapter 2:

> When people in the world all know beauty as beauty,
> already there arises the recognition of ugliness;
> When people in the world all know goodness as good,
> Already there arises the recognition of badness.
> Therefore:
> The concepts of being and nonbeing give birth to each other,
> Difficult and easy complete each other,
> Long and short form each other,
> High and low fulfill each other,
> Tone and voice harmonize with each other,
>
> Front and behind follow each other. (Lao Tzu, 600 B.C., chapter 2, my translation)

All concepts arise in comparison and contrast. Human understanding about the world of which we are a part is forever partial. Driving directions are not the roads, and a map is not the territory. Capra's interpretation of the Taoist intersubjective worldview seems to be very close to this Taoist script.

Heidegger began to show great interest in Taoism in his 1930 Bremen lecture. Poggeler (1987, p. 52) described how Heidegger asked the audience for the aphorism of Chuang Tzu and was presented with the Buber translation, whereupon Heidegger read aloud the story "Happiness of the Fishes."

Chuang Tzu is believed to have lived 200 years after Lao Tzu. Chuang Tzu developed the philosophy of Lao Tzu in his collections of essays, tales, and anecdotes, all written in a fascinating poetic style. Although Chuang Tzu is less known in the West, except to Sinologists, he has been viewed by many as superior to Lao Tzu both in his philosophical profundity and writing style. He challenges our conventional knowledge and assumption "with a divine sense of humor" (Mair, 1994, p. xiv). "Happiness of Fishes" is one such tale.

It goes like this:

> Master Chuang and Master Hui were walking across the bridge over the Hao River. "The minnows have come out and are swimming so leisurely," said Master Chuang, "This is the joy of fishes."
>
> "You're not a fish," said Master Hui. "How do you know what the joy of fishes is?"
>
> "You're not me," said Master Chuang, "so how do you know that I don't know what the joy of fishes is?"
>
> "I'm not you," said Master Hui, "so I certainly do not know what you do. But you're certainly not a fish, so it is undeniable that you do not know what the joy of fishes is."

"Let's go back to where we started." Said Master Chuang, "When you said, 'How do you know what the joy of fishes is?' you asked me because you already knew that I knew. I know it by walking over the Hao." (Chuang Tzu, Outer Chapters: Happiness 18, my translation)

Like most Taoist tales, the meaning of this story has been interpreted and debated over the years. In agreement with Heidegger and Buber, I understand it as a tale of intersubjectivity. Master Hui questions Master Chuang's intersubjective knowing about the fishes' joy but is caught, humorously, knowing intersubjectively of Master Chuang in Hui's questioning itself.

"Chuang Chou Dreamt of Butterfly" is another story of such inquiry about intersubjective thinking.

Once upon a time Chuang Chou dreamt he was a butterfly, a butterfly flitting about happily enjoying himself, not knowing he was Chuang Tzu. Suddenly he awoke and was palpably Chou. He didn't know if he was Chuang Tzu who had dreamt of being a butterfly or a butterfly dreaming that he was Chuang Tzu. Now there must be a difference between Chou and the butterfly. This is called the transformation of things. (Chuang Tzu, Inner Chapters: Equality 2, my translation)

The story engages us in imagining Chuang Chou and the butterfly—the Taoist master and a usually objectified opposite—as equals. Light-heartedly, the story conveys to us a profound epistemological concept: the commonality as well as the distinction between the two subjects and an imaginary interplay between the two.

Heidegger's notion of friendship in *Being and Time*—let each other be in their ownness and otherness, so that in each the world stands there ready—is believed to be in Chuang Tzu's frame of intersubjectivity (cited by Poggeler, 1987). Such intersubjectivity is not the endless and circular relativism. It is more than sympathy or empathy in modern psychology. It is *Being*.

Martin Buber (1923/1996) depicted characteristics of the twofold attitudes in human relations as *I* and *Thou*, and *I* and *It*. In *I* and *Thou*, there are two equal subjects, whereas in *I* and *It*, there is one subject, *I*, and the other is perceived as an object, *It*, being used to serve the purpose of the *I*. Beyond such two foldedness, he pointed to "the between" as intersubjectivity.

Buber (1951/1965) developed such a beyond into a dialogical two-step movement: setting at a distance and entering into a relation. The primal setting at a distance withdraws the person from the pragmatic needs and wants and sets them as independent opposites. Buber believed that the second movement is to relate to the independent opposite, to that person's specific experiences in connection with time and space. These specific experiences may make present situations in which *I* could imagine what *Thou* experienced as if *I* were *Thou*, who is "becoming a self with me"(Buber, 1951/1965, p. 70). When such self-becoming is known to and recognized by *Thou*, an *I* and *Thou* relation is formed. In his later writings, Buber identified such intersubjectivity as a dialogical ontology (Eisenstadt, 1992).

If we consider us—the curriculum theorists in the United States and the Western tradition—as a collective *I*, and those from outside of the States and the Western tradition as *It*, *I* would understand *It* without sympathy—that basic human ability to understand the minds of other in Bruner's notion. *I* may love *It*, in Benjamin's psychoanalysis, but would never be able to like *It*, because *It* is an object. *I* would mistake *It* for the entire world, as in Capra's quantum physics, excluding the organic totality of an elephant. *I* would see *It* as pure beauty, and miss out *It*'s ugliness, in Lao Tzu's reasoning. *I* would not know the happiness of fishes, nor dream of *I* as a butterfly in Chaung Tzu's epistemological tales. *I* would not be Heidegger's being-in-the-world, nor a being to whom the question of Being is asked. *I* would have only *I* and *It* relations in Buber's theory, without *I* and *Thou* and without *becoming*.

Therefore I propose we consider ourselves as a collective *I* relating to others as *Thou*. Others include those who have been distanced from *I* by cultural boundaries and national borders, and separated by the concept of time—past, present, and future. Such consideration is a choice, an ethnical one as well as a strategic one for surviving. In such a choice, *I* would need to view the distances and separations as only concepts, recognize *It* as equal and different. Recognizing the difference in such a way as what Buber viewed as the first movement in an *I* and *Thou* relation. This vantage point would enable *I* to extend the idea of equality to *It*. Humanize *It*. *I* won't stop here. An intersubjective becoming requires Buber's second movement: relating to *It* as if *It* were *I*. Only then *It* becomes *Thou*, and *I* becomes a self with Thou. That is intersubjective becoming and *splicing* (Li, 2002).

Curriculum Creativity as International Text

In *Understanding Curriculum*, Pinar, Reynolds, Slattery, and Taubman (1995) reviewed the concepts of curriculum at the historical and present state of American curriculum studies, and concluded that the concept is "highly symbolic," a site where "the generations struggle to define themselves and the world" and "it is what the older generation chooses to tell the younger generation" (pp. 847–848). More than a decade has gone by, and we have walked into an era of globalization, which is no longer limited to trades and intercultural exchanges. In this era, as Smith (2003) observed, the global capital is under the pressure of being homogenized, national identities eroded, and indigenous languages and cultures lost. Such a situation calls us to redefine ourselves and the world, and to rechoose what to tell the younger generation. Understanding curriculum as international text "must not be reduced to a scholarly version of American nationalism and neocolonialism. Nor must it be employed only to make domestic political points, as many have done to criticize American schooling" (Pinar et al., 1995, p. 843). Instead, waking up from our own nightmare (Pinar, 2004) as in the method of *currere*, and *splicing* with others as I have worked on in the past decade (Li, 2002, 2005, 2006, in press), appear to be more important than ever before. Interacting with others as Thou in the making of an international *currere* may lead us to a postpostmodern time when intersubjective connectedness is nourished as an important principle in developing diverse and resilient human communities. Such communities sustain by constant self re-creation and cherish creativity as morality—a deep ecology.

The study of creativity had been marginalized until recently (Sternberg & Lubart, 2004). In the Western tradition, "*Creativity* is the interaction among aptitude, process, and environment by which an individual or group produces a perceptible product that is both novel and useful as defined within a social context" (Plucker, Beghetto, & Dow, 2004, p. 90). This product-oriented notion of creativity finds its process-oriented counterpart in the East. Creativity in the Eastern tradition involves a state of personal fulfillment, a connection to a primordial realm, or the expression of an inner essence or ultimate reality (Kuo, 1996). Taoism viewed sympathy, creativity, and peace as interconnected concepts (Chang, 1963). Creativity is a self-realization and an ontological experience of ultimate truth in the interplay between yin and yang. Such an experience "transcends the knowledge which is composed by a system of labels and sees the real reality which is usually blocked by language, tradition, culture, and human needs" (Kuo, 1996, p. 200). To lose one's acculturated self is to be open to creativity.

Intersubjective becoming is a type of self-realization. The moment a self understands another from the other's point of view, a suspension or loss of one's own acculturated self takes place. That moment of loss leads to a moment of the Taoist truth beyond opposites and the door to creativity.

Such creativity resonates with Wang's third possibilities of cocreating a creative curriculum. The product of such creativity in the Western understanding would contain both novel and familiar, past and future, and be recognized as appropriate for the specific present situations. Such a product in the Eastern tradition would be considered as a by-product of creativity—the ontological experience of interplaying between *I* and *Thou* and an intersubjective becoming.

References

Benjamin, J. (1995). *Like subjects, love objects: Essays on recognition and sexual difference.* New Haven, CT: Yale University Press.

Bruner, J. (1996). *The culture of education.* Cambridge, MA: Harvard University Press.

Buber, M. (1965). *The knowledge of man: A philosophy of the interhuman* (M. Friedman, Ed.; M Friedman & R. C. Smith Trans.). New York: Harper & Row. (Original work published 1951)

Buber, M. (1996). *I and Thou.* New York: Touchstone. (Original work published 1923)

Capra, F. (1991). *The Tao of physics* (3rd ed.). Boston: Shambhala. (Original work published 1975)

Chang, C. Y. (1963). *Creativity and Taoism: A study of Chinese philosophy, art, and poetry.* New York: Harper & Row.

Chuang Tzu (400 B.C./1994). *Wandering on the way: Early Taoist tales and parables of Chuang Tzu.* (V. H. Mair, Trans). New York: Bantam Books.

Chuang Tzu (400 B.C.). 庄子·内篇: 齐物论第二 *(Zhuang Zi, Intern Chapters: Equality 2).* Retrieved May 30, 2008, from http://www.cnd.org/Classics/Philosophers/Zhuang_Zi/02.hz8.html

Chuang Tzu (400 B.C.). 庄子·外篇: 至乐第十八 *(Zhaung Zi, Outer Chatpers: Happiness 18).* Retrieved May 30, 2008, from http://www.cnd.org/Classics/Philosophers/Zhuang_Zi/18.hz8.html

Conle, C. (1996). Resonance in preservice teacher inquiry. *American Educational Research Journal, 33*(2), 297–325.

Eisenstadt, S. N. (1992). (Ed.). *Martin Buber on intersubjectivity and cultural creativity.* Chicago: University of Chicago Press.

Frye, N. (1982). *The great code: The Bible and literature.* New York: Harcourt, Brace & Jovanovich.

Gadamer, H. G. (1960/1993). *Truth and method.* New York: The Continuum Publishing.

Kuo, Y. Y. (1996). Taoist psychology of creativity. *The Journal of Creative Behavior, 30*(3), 197–212.

Lao Tzu (600 B.C.). 道德經 *(Tao Te Ching).* Retrieved May 30, 2008, from http://zhongwen.com/dao.htm

Li, X. (2002). *The Tao of life stories: Chinese language, poetry, and culture in education.* New York: Lang.

Li, X. (2005). A Tao of narrative: Dynamic splicing of teacher stories. *Curriculum Inquiry, 34*(3), 339–366.

Li, X. (2006). Becoming Taoist I and Thou: Identity-making of opposite cultures. *Journal of Curriculum and Pedagogy, 3*(2), 193–216.

Li, X. (in press). Black and white may make a rainbow: Cultural creativity from opposites. *Multicultural Perspectives.*

Mair, H. V. (1994). Preface. In Chuang Tzu (Ed.), *Wandering on the way: Early Taoist tales and parables of Chuang Tzu* (pp. xi–xvi). New York: Bantam Books.

Pinar, W. F. (2004). *What is curriculum theory?* Mahwah, NJ: Erlbaum

Pinar, W. F., Reynolds, W. M., Slattery, P., & Taubman, P. M. (1995). *Understanding curriculum: An introduction to the study of historical and contemporary curriculum discourses.* New York: Lang.

Plucker, J. A., Beghetto, R. A., & Dow, G. T. (2004). Why isn't creativity more important to educational psychology? Potentials, pitfalls and future directions in creativity research. *Educational Psychology, 39*(2), 83–96.

Poggeler, O. (1987). West-east dialogue: Heidegger and Lao-tzu. In G. Parkes (Ed.), *Heidegger and Asian thoughts* (pp. 47–78). Honolulu: University of Hawaii Press,

Smith, D. G. (2003). Curriculum and teaching face globalization. In W. F. Pinar (Ed.), *International handbook of curriculum research* (pp 35–52). Mahwah, NJ: Erlbaum,

Sternberg, R. J., & Lubart, R. I. (2004). The concept of creativity: Prospects and paradigms. In R. J. Sternberg (Ed.), *Handbook of creativity* (pp. 1–15). New York: Cambridge University Press.

19 Decolonizing Curriculum

Nina Asher

Chapter Overview

The chapter utilizes postcolonial feminist themes to examine the resilience of an in-group/out-group curriculum in terms of race, class, gender, nation, and so on, in spite of globalization. The author begins this discussion with three vignettes. The first vignette describes a student's refusal to watch Michael Moore's film, *Bowling for Columbine*. The second vignette explores the demographic shift in the U.S. over the last four decades. The third vignette addresses issues of language, culture, power, and categorization. The author uses these stories to illustrate curricula that relies upon static notions of culture, language, and identity, and has a colonial history that attempts to fix the other and under-write contemporary oppressive and anti- intellectual agendas. Describing the ways that colonization occurs on personal, institutional, and cultural registers, the author asks readers to consider how all of us are implicated in and perpetuate colonialism. To decolonize ourselves and our teaching and learning, the author suggests curriculum scholars continue to provide counterdiscourses to that of consumerism and anti-intellectualism. Lastly, the author suggests pedagogy that utilizes self-reflexivity and autobiography might allow students and teachers to engage differences of race, class, and gender and work the struggles that surface with such efforts.

This chapter has evolved from a paper written as an invited keynote talk for the "Articulating the Present (Next) Moment in Curriculum Studies: The Post-Reconceptualization Generation(s)" Conference held at Purdue University in February 2006. As per the theme of the conference, the chapter draws on the tradition—established by the reconceptualists three decades ago—of generating cutting-edge curriculum work (see Miller, 2005; Pinar, 1975), and engages contemporary issues, themes, and theories to interrogate curriculum in a globalized, 21st century context. Specifically, in this chapter, I draw on postcolonial and feminist theories to interrogate how and why the curricula of "us" and "them" (in terms of race, class, gender, nation, and so on) endure in today's globalized and corporatized educational and social contexts.

I launch my discussion of these issues with three illustrative vignettes—two culled from my teaching experiences in Louisiana and one from *The New York Times*—that offer food for thought regarding constructions of identity, culture, and nation, in relation to the curriculum field, in the 21st century United States.

Vignette 1: "Our President"

Some years ago, *before* the much-debated film *Fahrenheit 9/11* (Moore, 2004) was released, while I was teaching the master's level seminar to students in the 5-year Elementary Education program, I mentioned that we might watch Michael Moore's (2002) film, *Bowling for Columbine*. Before I could go any further, one student lashed out that she would not watch it, given that he insulted "our President" (referring here, of course, to George W. Bush). A young, White woman, this student is representative of the typical demographic for elementary education programs in the U.S.

Vignette 2: On being American

A front-page article in *The New York Times*, "Come October, Baby Will Make 300 Million or So," on U.S. demographics, discusses population shifts over the decades (Roberts, 2006).

> In 1967, when the population reached 200 million, *Life* magazine dispatched 23 photographers to locate the baby and devoted a five-page spread to its search....
>
> *Life* immortalized Robert Ken Woo Jr. of Atlanta, whose parents, a computer programmer and a chemical engineer, had immigrated seven years earlier from China. Mr. Woo graduated magna cum laude from Harvard and is a litigator. Now 38, he still lives in Atlanta with his wife, Angie, who is also a lawyer, and their three daughters....
>
> "The 300 millionth will be a Mexican Latino in Los Angeles County with parents who speak Spanish at home and with siblings who are bilingual," said William Frey, a demographer with the University of Michigan Population Studies Center....
>
> Hispanic mothers have higher birth rates, and no state has more births than California, where most newborns are of Hispanic origin. There, Jose ranked fourth in 2004 among the most popular baby names for boys after Daniel, Anthony and Andrew. (pp. A1, 16)

Vignette 3: On Language

A young White teacher, enrolled in my graduate seminar on "Identity, Culture, Curriculum," said, "My boyfriend's last name is Chavez (a pseudonym) and every time he has to go to the hospital, they send him to a Spanish-speaking doctor—and he doesn't even speak Spanish!!"

So, who is the "our" in "our President?" What do such remarks tell us about the curriculum that young American students—or, more accurately, young people in the U.S.—experience, internalize, and re-create? How have their/our minds been colonized, occupied? How have their/our visions been restricted? Why would a future teacher resist the suggestion of taking a critical look at violence in U.S. schools, and that too under the delusion that her resistance is patriotic? How natural is it for "us" to acknowledge that Chavez, Woo, and Jose are "American" names? That bilingualism is at least as "American" as apple pie, and perhaps even as much as Chinese take-out? Indeed, that Mr. Woo is a "Southerner" in a South where race relations are still largely construed in terms of Black and White? And despite four and five generations of Asian American presence in the U.S., why are Asian Americans construed as "strangers from a different shore" (Takaki, 1989)?

Why and how do such curricula of "us" and "them" endure? How do extant discourses and practices of race and gender, class and culture, language and nation, sameness and difference, self and other allow them to regenerate, persist? And, as Fanon (1967) asks, "How do we extricate ourselves?" (p. 10). At the same time, how have those of us—such as the reconceptualists and the "posties"[1]—who do resist, rethink, and work toward social transformation come to do so? This chapter is my effort to think through these questions. To this end, first, I present a brief overview of the relevance of postcolonial and feminist discourses to curriculum work. Next, I interrogate how and why the curricula of "us" and "them" (in terms of race, class, gender, nation, and so on) endure in today's globalized and corporatized educational and social contexts. And, finally, I think through considerations for decolonizing curriculum. To this end, I interweave theoretical analyses with critical reflections on current events as well as pedagogical practice.

Colonization and Curriculum

Generally, colonization refers to the occupation, control, and economic exploitation of one nation by another—as India was by England and Algeria by France (e.g., Chow, 2002; Fanon, 1967; Lorde, 1984; Oliver, 2004; Said, 1978). Furthermore, following such scholars as Edward Said, Gauri Viswanathan, and Dipesh Chakrabarty, among others, we know that colonialism is insinuated with discourse, disciplinary knowledge, and education. For instance, writing about "postcoloniality and the artifice of history" Dipesh Chakrabarty (1995) notes that "'Europe' remains the sovereign theoretical subject of all histories, including the ones we call 'Indian,' 'Chinese,' 'Kenyan,' and so on" (p. 383), and that such disciplinary areas as economics and history contribute to fostering the growth of capitalism and nation states, respectively. Building on this, in this chapter, I argue that curriculum that relies on fixed, essentialist notions of identity and culture is framed and limited by legacies of colonialism as well as the current push toward standardization and corporatization (Pinar, 2004), contributing, ultimately, to an oppressive and anti-intellectual agenda.

Furthermore, as colonization operates at the systemic level, it also operates at the individual level (Fanon, 1967; hooks, 1990; Oliver, 2004; Trinh, 1989). According to Kelly Oliver (2004), "The success of the colonization of a land, a nation, or a people can be measured through the success of the colonization of psychic space. Only through the colonization of psychic space can oppression be truly effective" (p. 26). Thus we see that colonization—the physical and psychic occupation and control of a people, a place, a person—happens at the individual and systemic levels and that the colonized internalize the colonizer.

One issue that I find most troubling, "here," "at home," in the United States, is the slow, poor response to help the South recover from the devastation following Hurricane Katrina, which hit New Orleans and the Mississippi Gulf region on August 29, 2005—the failure to rescue promptly those perched on rooftops and in attics and crammed into the Superdome for days, as New Orleans and the surrounding areas flooded, as well as the ongoing debates about whether or not to rebuild New Orleans, a major, historically significant U.S. port. Questions about whether it was issues of race, class, or location (Deep South versus, say, DC) that led to the slow response have been endlessly discussed in public and private forums (see, for instance, Horne, 2006). The following synthesis affords one example of such:

> What notions of self, place, and identity—at the national level—does this reflect? How can we let ourselves believe that we do not have the wherewithal to take care of our own citizens when we channel unfathomable amounts of resources to wage wars on the pretext of "bringing" democracy to other parts of the world? A number of scholars have noted that the U.S. South has historically been othered, cast as "backward" in contrast to the "progressive" North (Anderson, 1988; Pinar, 1993, 2001). I cannot help but wonder, then, how the response might have been different if a major port in the Northeast or on the West coast had been similarly devastated. Is this then an example of "alienation's double," the "splitting of identity"—our own and not

quite as much our own—that occurs with the frame of colonization (Anzaldúa, 1987; Bhabha, 1994; Fanon, 1967; Oliver, 2004)? Is the Deep South—like the "inner city"— then an example of the fact that the "Third World" exists within the "First?" And, at the national level, then, what sort of oppressive pedagogies are in circulation, so that, due to our inaction, our own citizens and, due to our actions, others elsewhere suffer the loss of home? (Asher, in press)

Of course, the question may be posed that if someone is not from a colonized nation or region, how is the notion of decolonization relevant to her or his narrative or circumstance? While not all of us may have experienced colonialism/imperialist expansion, I argue that we are all implicated in and affected by its effect—the fact of colonization. As Hickling-Hudson, Matthews, and Woods (2004), writing out of Australia, note, "the aftermath of colonialism" (p. 3) pervades both the metropolitan countries that built empires as well as the former colonies, and that postcolonialism offers a "space for moving beyond the negative patterns that persist after colonialism began" (p. 2). Furthermore, postcolonialists (Ashcroft, Griffiths, & Tiffin, 1995; Hickling-Hudson, Matthews, & Woods, 2004) have noted that education itself is deeply implicated in the project of colonialism. Hickling-Hudson et al. (2004) note that, "conflicts rage over the educational implications of race, ethnicity, gender, and degrees of privilege, and not least, over the love–hate relationship between the former colony and the former colonizer" (p. 7). In recent years, a number of scholars (such as Philip Altbach, Dipesh Chakrabarty, Cameron McCarthy, Linda Tuhiwai Smith, Sofia Villenas, Gauri Viswanathan, among others) have critiqued Eurocentrism in education and spoken to the issues of marginalization and loss of indigenous knowledge and ways of knowing, the internalization and reproduction of colonialist structures and practices, and the resultant contradictions and contestations in curriculum frameworks and teaching practices. Critical scholars in the curriculum field argue for the interrogation of relations of power in terms of "race, identity, and representation" (see, for instance, McCarthy, Crichlow, Dimitriadis, & Dolby, 2005) in historical and geographic contexts and leading reconceptualists Janet Miller and Bill Pinar have called for attending to the "necessary worldliness of curriculum studies" (Miller, 2005) and the internationalization of the curriculum field, respectively. Indeed, Hickling-Hudson et al.'s (2004) observation that under contemporary conditions of globalized capitalism, "Many students are unaware of the bloody conflicts and tenuous resolutions that destroyed colonial empires and gave rise to hundreds of post World War 2 nation states" (pp. 7–8), lends ironic emphasis to these calls.

While the issues I have raised above are current, in that they are relevant at the present (next) moment, clearly, they are not "new." Indeed, their very endurance commands the serious attention of curriculum scholars today. How, then, can the "posties" today build on the cutting-edge work of the reconceptualists, which began three decades ago, to continue the work of decolonizing self and curriculum?

Struggling with Implicatedness

As we know, colonization happens at the individual and systemic levels and that the colonized/oppressed internalize the colonizer/oppressor. In his classic, *Black Skin, White Masks*, Frantz Fanon (1967) writes of the experience of meeting the gaze of the White man, of being rendered visible *as* a Negro, "And then the occasion arose when I had to meet the white man's eyes. An unfamiliar weight burdened me" (p. 110). He continues, "On that day, completely dislocated, unable to be abroad with the other, the white man, who unmercifully imprisoned me, I took myself far off from my own presence, far indeed, and made myself an object" (p. 112).

Fanon posits that the Black man having thus been framed, objectified, alienated, and even removed from his own body by the colonizing gaze of the White man, is confronted with the problem of addressing the resultant imbalance in relations of power, *even as* he begins internalizing it. And, as Trinh Minh-ha (1990) has written with great clarity and honesty, "They? Yes, they. But, in the colonial periphery (as in elsewhere), we are often them as well. Colored skins, white masks; colored masks, white skins.... *They* accept the margins; so do *we*" (p. 330).

Certainly, I find myself reflecting on these tensions in relation to my own curricular and pedagogical work. For instance, as I have noted elsewhere (Asher, 2003a, 2005, 2006), my work as a postcolonialist, woman academic of color, born in a former British colony and now teaching in the United States, is shaped by *and* informs these complex, contested tensions. I develop and teach courses on "multicultural education"; "identity, culture, and curriculum"; "gender, race, and nation"; and "globalization, multiculturalism, and education." Situated in the Deep South, where race relations are primarily construed in terms of Black and White even today, I have struggled with the intellectual, personal, and pedagogical challenges of teaching multicultural education courses, ones which are required as part of the elementary education teacher preparation curriculum (e.g., Asher, 2003b, 2005, 2007, in press). I have wondered how I might get White students enrolled in multicultural education classes to see that they are "at the interstices," so that they may begin seeing themselves and their stories *in relation to*—instead of being removed from—differences of race, class, gender, and culture (Asher, 2005).

How, then, do we decolonize curriculum so that it enables us to deconstruct such binaries as self and other, margins and center so that the self unlearns the internalization of the oppressor (Freire, 1970/1982)? Again, in addition to engaging in the work of decolonization at the individual level, we also need to pay attention to such present-day systemic forces as globalization and capitalism, not only in terms of how they are shaped by and reflect legacies of colonialism but also how, in turn, they shape race, gender, culture, and nation, and the related implications for curriculum work.

We know today that "race is gendered and classed and that gender is raced and classed," and that present-day forces of capitalism and globalization have roots in histories of colonialism (Asher, 2007, p. 68). Indeed, as Audre Lorde has noted, "Institutionalized rejection of difference is an absolute necessity in a profit economy which needs outsiders as surplus people. As members of such an economy, we have *all* been programmed to respond to human differences between us with fear and loathing..." (1984, p. 115). Echoing Lorde, Rey Chow (2002) argues that the forces of capitalism, racism, and cross-cultural ethnic relations operate to colonize racial and ethnic minorities "keeping them in their place" in obvious and subtle ways. She writes, "The imperialist agenda for transforming the world into observable and hence manageable units, ...must be seen as inseparable from the historical conditions that repeatedly return the material benefits of such processes to European subjectivities" (p. 2).

Certainly, this agenda is evident in the mantras of standardization and accountability that have been inflicted upon—and now afflict—not only school teachers but also those of us who teach in colleges of education. As Pinar (2004, p. xiv) notes, "citizens (and students) have been reduced to consumers." For instance, in Louisiana, where I teach, schoolteachers are now required to follow the state mandated "Comprehensive Curriculum." My students are always talking about how their mentor teachers are allowed to be ahead of schedule but may not fall behind and how they attempt to be "creative" even as they follow this prescripted curriculum. So, teaching well—teaching from within, owning one's craft—becomes a furtive, guilty act, like smuggling a packet of cigarettes past the prison guards. And forget about pleasure and play. Even teacher education faculty are expected to familiarize themselves with this "Comprehensive Curriculum," so that they may then teach to it in *their* classes. Evidently, in the "nightmare that is the present" (Pinar, 2004), we are to remove ourselves, mind and soul, from our craft. Automatons all. Objects. Dislocated. Fragmented, managed, corporatized, and colonized. Perhaps then we may need to acknowledge that, given our implicatedness, our struggles towards decolonization will be ongoing, recursive, and, at times, even contradictory.

In his brilliant poem in Pinar's (1975) edited volume, *Curriculum Theorizing: The Reconceptualists*, Ross Mooney (1975, p. 173) wrote

> Lost-ness is reality lost;
> reality lost is problem lost;
> problem lost is solution lost;
> solution lost is man lost;
> man lost is life lost;
> life lost is death.
>
> Death sensed
> is source again.

So, then as we find ourselves writing and teaching against the grain in this climate of rampant anti-intellectualism and consumerism, it behooves us to continue the work of "sharing life-in-mind" so that education "comes to life again" (Mooney, 1975, p. 174). To that end, Pinar offers curriculum as "complicated conversation" as the idea that "keeps hope alive" (2004, p. xiii). One of our major tasks then, as this collection indicates, is to ensure that curriculum work, particularly in the realm of practice, does not become posttheory, postthought, post-"life-in-mind."

Decolonization

> We shall see that another solution is possible. It implies a restructuring of the world.
> (Fanon, 1967, p. 82)

As noted earlier, the self, implicated as it is in the colonizer–colonized relationship, is split (e.g., Anzaldúa, 1987; Asher, 2005; Bhabha, 1994; Trinh, 1989). It is by acknowledging one's implicatedness and recognizing that one is "at the interstices" (Asher, 2005), that one can engage in both the intellectual and the psychic/emotional work of decolonization. Witness, for instance, Minnie Bruce Pratt's (1984) emotionally and intellectually powerful essay, "Identity: Skin, Blood, Heart." Writing as a White, Southern, Christian lesbian, Pratt discusses how, in negotiating her own identity and coming out, she found herself becoming increasingly conscious of the oppressions which were present in her seemingly safe hometown. Pratt's efforts to work through the oppressions she encountered as she tried to arrive at a new identity can be construed as "an enactment of careful and constant differentiations which refuses the all-too-easy polemic that opposes victims to perpetrators" (Martin & Mohanty, 1986, p. 209).

Implied in such reworking of the self is also the process of emerging from dehumanization, unlearning repression. As Fanon wrote, "The black man wants to be white. The white man slaves to reach a human level" (p. 9). And, in her essay, "Poetry Is Not a Luxury," Audre Lorde (1984) reminds us, "The white fathers told us: I think, therefore I am. The Black mother within each of us—the poet—whispers in our dreams, I feel therefore I can be free" (p. 39). Kelly Oliver (2004), an attentive student of Fanon's work, suggests that we need to examine critically "our unconscious drives and affects that affect, even govern if not determine" our actions and values, and unlearn repression (p. xxiii). Because, otherwise, "we risk the solidity that prevents fluid, living sublimation and idealization and leaves us with empty and meaningless principles in whose name we kill off otherness and those others who embody it for us" (p. xxiii). Indeed, I find that these analyses apply at least as much to the colonizer as they do to the colonized. Why, in the first place, does the colonizer need focus on controlling an-other? Especially when it diminishes his (I intentionally use the masculine here) inner self? The colonizer's quest for power and control elsewhere, makes me wonder in what ways the colonizer experiences powerlessness, lack of control, inadequacy, and loss of self, right here?

In his analysis of "curriculum as racial text," especially in relation to the South, Pinar has noted that "Not only African Americans have been denied self-understanding.... Institutional racism deforms 'white' students as well" (1993, p. 62). He argues that such deformity occurs almost "unconsciously" for most "Whites" and represents repression. It is the engagement of one's self in relation to one's difference—what one is *not*—that allows one to have fuller, more complete access to the past and the present (Pinar, 1993).

As feminist theorists (see, for instance, Anzaldúa, 1987; hooks, 1990, 1994; Oliver, 2004; Pratt, 1984) remind, we need to think *and* feel our way out of oppression and colonization. bell hooks (1994) has written

> I came to theory because I was hurting—the pain within me was so intense that I could not go on living. I came to theory desperate, wanting to comprehend—to grasp what was happening around and within me.... I saw in theory then a location for healing. (p. 59)

She draws on Thich Nhat Hanh's concept of "engaged Buddhism," which focuses on "practice in conjunction with contemplation" (hooks, 1994, p. 14), to articulate her vision of an "engaged pedagogy." According to hooks (1994), an engaged pedagogy requires teachers to be present fully in the classroom, bringing *both* their intellect *and* their spirit to their practice, so that they may construe their students and themselves as "'whole' human beings, striving not just for knowledge in books, but knowledge about how to live in the world" (pp. 14–15). And, according to Oliver, decolonization entails, along with large-scale resistance movements, "psychic revolts that can take place in the everyday lives of ordinary people who resist domination" (2004, p. 35).

Would not curriculum, then, actually *be* "comprehensive" and more meaningful to both students and teachers, if it emerged from and engaged "life-in-mind" (Mooney, 1975)? If we were (able) to bring theory, thought, and feeling to a self-reflexive engagement with the past and the present, towards envisioning a future in which colonization diminishes and the self thrives in all its multiplicities?

Conclusion: Envisioning Curriculum Work in a Globalized Twenty first Century Context

How do we go about doing this in a United States where the interpretation of freedom has been stretched so far that it has gone (almost) 360 degrees round, to meet fascism? Where scrutiny and surveillance of the quotidian have become the norm? Where even liberal academics and postcolonial scholarship are seen as suspect? For instance, Crary

(2004) posits that institutional responses following the attacks of September 11, 2001 worked to nip the emerging mood of self-reflexivity,

> Carefully soliciting a continuation of habitual routine, of shopping, of work but with just enough sense of crisis and shock to allow state apparatuses and agencies to modify legal restraints on their conduct and to ensure complete non-resistance to any military or security measures undertaken around the world. (p. 425)

According to Crary (2004) and Rajagopal (2004), these intersections of consumerism, capitalism, and repression are not coincidental, rather they are devices to maintain the status quo, to continue to exploit, isolate, contain the "other." As Fanon (1967) reminds us, "Before it can adopt a positive voice, freedom requires an effort at dis-alientation" (p. 231). So, perhaps the curriculum to set ourselves free is one where we acknowledge that White students need to be bussed into neighborhoods that are predominantly African American or populated by Peoples of Color, not just the other way. And, if this feels daunting or may not be a "realistic solution at this time," we need, more persistently than ever, to ask the question "Why?" and to address the issues that emerge in response as we push to continue our progress toward a society where "desegregation" and "integration" become irrelevant terms. This may sound utopian, but abandoning this vision would be the real folly because then we would be giving up hope and resigning ourselves to the alienation that continues to limit, restrict, split us.

Similarly, upper class and upper middle class kids need to be bussed into middle class, working class, and low-income areas, not just the other way. A pedagogy that draws on critical, self-reflexive approaches and autobiography can allow students and teachers to engage differences of race, class, and culture, which they encounter within and without the classroom, and work through the intellectual and emotional struggles that emerge in the process (Asher, 2003b, 2005).

Similarly, instead of homosexuals having to "come out," perhaps heterosexuals can learn that they need to "go in," and reflect honestly on and acknowledge how "normal" the apparent norm actually is even in their own and their family members' stories (Asher, 2007). Similarly, instead of yielding to its perennial preoccupation with penetrating the "mystery" of the East, the West can focus on emerging from its own Cartesian colonization, to break out of divisive and limiting binaries, and reach into its own past for its own stories. Some may say that these are bold, even unrealistic suggestions to make in times of increasing rigidity, scrutiny, fragmentation, and corporatization in both the curriculum and the social field. I argue that it is foolhardy *not to*. While such curricular and pedagogical visions offer no guarantee regarding the transformation of future teachers (Asher, 2005, 2007), they serve as a first step toward decolonization. As long as we continue to practice from theory and theorize from practice, and have the courage and openness to rethink both, we have a chance of passing on *our* "knowledge-skills-and-dispositions" (to borrow from the lexicon of our NCATE colleagues) to future generations—the "post-posties"(?)—so that they, in their turn, may also keep hope alive.

Note

1. The original version of this chapter was presented as an invited, keynote talk at a conference, "Articulating the Present (Next) Moment in Curriculum Studies: The Post-Reconceptualization Generation(s)," at Purdue University, Lafayette, IN, in 2006. Therefore the word *posties* refers to scholars who are engaging the various "posts," such as postmodernism, poststructuralism, post-reconceptualization (of the curriculum field), and so on.

References

Anderson, J. D. (1988). *The education of Blacks in the South, 1860–1935.* Chapel Hill, NC: University of North Carolina Press.

Anzaldúa, G. (1987). *Borderlands/La frontera: The new mestiza.* San Francisco: Spinsters/Aunt Lute.

Ashcroft, B., Griffiths, G., & Tiffin, H. (Eds.). (1995). *The postcolonial studies reader.* New York: Routledge.

Asher, N. (2003a). At the intersections: A postcolonialist woman of color considers Western feminism. *Social Education, 67*(1), 47–50.

Asher, N. (2003b). Engaging difference: Towards a pedagogy of interbeing. *Teaching Education, 14,* 235–247.

Asher, N. (2005). At the interstices: Engaging postcolonial and feminist perspectives for a multicultural education pedagogy in the South. *Teachers College Record, 107*(5), 1079–1106.

Asher, N. (2006). Brown in Black and White: On being a South Asian woman academic. In G. Li & G. H. Beckett (Eds.), *"Strangers" of the academy: Asian women scholars in higher education* (pp. 163–177). Sterling, VA: Stylus.

Asher, N. (2007). Made in the (multicultural) U.S.A.: Unpacking tensions of race, culture, gender, and sexuality in education. *Educational Researcher, 36*(2), 65–73.

Asher, N. (in press). Writing home/decolonizing text(s). *Discourse: Studies in the Cultural Politics of Education, 30*(1).

Bhabha, H. K. (1994). *The location of culture.* New York: Routledge.

Chakrabarty, D. (1995). Postcoloniality and the artifice of history. In B. Ashcroft, G. Griffiths, & H. Tiffin (Eds.), *The postcolonial studies reader* (pp. 383–388). New York: Routledge.

Chow, R. (2002). *The protestant ethnic and the spirit of capitalism.* New York: Columbia University Press.

Crary, J. (2004). Conjurations of security. *Interventions, 6*(3), 424–430.

Fanon, F. (1967). *Black skin, white masks.* New York: Grove Press.

Freire, P. (1982). *Pedagogy of the oppressed.* New York: Continuum. (Original work published 1970)

Hickling-Hudson, A., Matthews, J., & Woods, A. (2004). Education, postcolonialism, and disruptions. In A. Hickling-Hudson, J. Matthews, & A. Woods (Eds.), *Disrupting preconceptions: Postcolonialism and education* (pp. 1–16). Flaxton, Australia: Post Pressed.

hooks, b. (1990). *Yearning: Race, gender, and cultural politics.* Boston: South End.

hooks, b. (1994). *Teaching to transgress: Education as the practice of freedom.* New York: Routledge.

Horne, J. (2006). *Breach of faith: Hurricane Katrina and the near death of a great American city.* New York: Random House.

Lorde, A. (1984). *Sister outsider.* Freedom, CA: Crossing Press.

Martin, B., & Mohanty C. (1986). Feminist politics: What's home got to do with it? In De Lauretis, T. (Ed.), *Feminist studies, critical studies* (pp. 191–211). Bloomington, IN: Indiana University.

McCarthy, C., Crichlow, W., Dimitriadis, G., & Dolby, N. (Eds.). (2005). *Race, identity, and representation in education* (2nd ed.). New York: Routledge.

Miller, J. (2005). *Sounds of silence breaking: Women, autobiography, curriculum.* New York: Lang.

Mooney, R. (1975). Prelude. In W. F. Pinar (Ed.), *Curriculum theorizing: The reconceptualists* (pp. 173–174). Richmond, CA: McCutchan.

Moore, M. (Writer/Producer/Director). (2002). *Bowling for Columbine* [Motion Picture]. United States: United Artists.

Moore, M. (Writer/Producer/Director). (2004). *Fahrenheit 9/11* [Motion Picture]. United States: Lions Gate Films.

Oliver, K. (2004). *The colonization of psychic space: A psychoanalytic social theory of oppression.* Minneapolis: University of Minnesota.

Pinar, W. F. (Ed.). (1975). *Curriculum theorizing: The reconceptualists.* Berkeley, CA: McCutchan.

Pinar, W. F. (1993). Notes on understanding curriculum as racial text. In C. McCarthy & W. Crichlow (Eds.), *Race, identity, and representation in education* (pp. 60–70). New York: Routledge.

Pinar, W. F. (2001). *The gender of racial politics and violence in America: Lynching, prison rape, and the crisis of masculinity.* New York: Lang.

402   *Nina Asher*

Pinar, W. F. (2004). *What is curriculum theory?* Mahwah, NJ: Erlbaum

Pratt, M. B. (1984). Identity: Skin, blood, heart. In E. Bulkin, M. B. Pratt, & B. Smith, *Yours in struggle: Three feminist perspectives on anti-semitism and racism* (pp. 117–129). Brooklyn, NY: Long Haul.

Rajagopal, A. (2004). America and its others: Cosmopolitan terror as globalization? *Interventions, 6*(3), 317–329.

Roberts, S. (2006, January 13). Come October, baby will make 300 million or so. *The New York Times*, pp. A 1, 16.

Said, E. (1978). *Orientalism.* New York: Penguin.

Takaki, R. (1989). *Strangers from a different shore: A history of Asian Americans.* New York: Little, Brown.

Trinh, T. M. (1989). *Woman, native, other: Writing postcoloniality and feminism.* Bloomington: Indiana University.

Trinh, T. M. (1990). Cotton and iron. In R. Ferguson, M. Gever, T. M. Trinh, & C. West (Eds.), *Out there: Marginalization and contemporary cultures* (pp. 327–336). New York/Cambridge, MA: The New Museum of Contemporary Art/MIT Press.

Suggested Reading Questions

1. The author begins the article with three vignettes to illustrate curriculum that relies on static notions of identity, culture, and language. In what ways do these vignettes present oppressive and anti-intellectual agendas in the field of education?

2. According to the author in order to decolonize ourselves and the curriculum, curriculum scholars need to provide a counterdiscourse against practices that reinscribe oppression. How might this be possible in relation to the ways curriculum has been written and practiced as a racial text?

3. How might pedagogy that utilizes self-reflexivity and autobiography allow students and teachers to engage differences of class and negotiate the terms on which such differences are shaped and sustained?

4. Traces of colonial practices are evident in discourse surrounding gendered practices, such as circumcision and female genital mutilation. How might an understanding of the specificities of the social contexts of such discursive practices help in understanding the implication of language in subjugation and oppression of women?

5. Asher suggests that consumerism and capitalism are ways in which colonialism is perpetuated and sustained in the world. How might an awareness of globalization and its influences be understood in terms of curriculum practices and classroom pedagogy?

Response to Nina Asher
Subject Position and Subjectivity in Curriculum Theory

Madeleine R. Grumet

Thirty years ago: That is how long it has been since we published *Toward a Poor Curriculum* (1976/2006). Bill Pinar and I wrote those essays to express our resistance to behavioral objectives, the mind numbing bureaucracy of the accountability trend of the times, and to propose a humanities methodology as an alternative to the social science inquiries that were dominating educational research. Those motives seem contemporary as well as remembered, but rereading our celebrations of individuality in "Mr. Bennet and Mrs. Brown," or "Psychoanalytic Foundations," is somewhat nostalgic, provoking a longing for what we have already relinquished. So what is it that our innocence permitted then and our sophistication inhibits now? It is striking that this collection of essays in *Toward a Poor Curriculum*, put together in the 70s, makes no particular mention of diversity. The questions of equity and multiculturalism that preoccupy our discourse now do not appear in these pages.

Well, then, we were still able to use the individual as the figure for the person of the student. We did not, to our credit, collapse that individual into social, class, race, or ethnic identities, but proposed and tried to practice a way of thinking about educational experience that invited students to think about the way these identifications mediated their experience of school, of texts, of curriculum.

Now what may have been naïve was our reliance on an aesthetic sense of subjectivity, confirmed by our references to Virginia Woolf, Yeats, and Jerzy Grotowski. Their novels, poems, and performances summoned virtual worlds, drawn to reveal the rich profusion of possibilities that lie dormant under the world we live. I am pleased to note that even in our enthusiasm for phenomenology's "suspension of the natural attitude," we took note of Sartre's doubt that Husserl's transcendental ego could think our way out of the biographical and social containers that enclosed our understanding and constrained our imaginations. In the years that followed, our inquiries became more explicitly political, infused with cultural and embodied histories of sexism and racism. In these works we acknowledged postmodernity's expose of individuality as a fiction. Whether we drew on Foucault or Butler, Chodorow or Spivak, we joined our colleagues in engaging these studies of the social and psychological histories of the categories and languages we use when we think about ourselves in the world.

Now it is 2008. We have waded through the fundamentalist and ethnic violence of Bosnia, of Al Qaeda, of Iraq, of Darfur. We don't need deep theory to convince us that humanity is still mired in group identifications that frame desire, fear, and hate. In the face of this rebuke to our fantasies of agency and responsibility, I search for a rationale to turn to curriculum as a source of freedom. I find it in the distinction to be drawn between education and ontology, because the project of education expresses our interest in transforming our state of being. And if our daily existence is simultaneously realized and constrained by the categories of identity that we take into ourselves from place, and family, and history, then curriculum theory provokes questions we may use to lift the ideological drapes that hide these categories from consciousness. What I describe here is the tension that links our subjectivity and our subject position: both sustained, augmented, and transformed dialectically. It can never be a question of one or the other. And so it is this relationship between consciousness on one side, and history/situation on the other that I want to address in response to Nina Asher's paper.[1]

With these caveats, I now welcome back the individual to curriculum. Who else teaches our classes, fights or accedes to the audit culture that has drenched K-12 and higher education, and votes? Politics requires identities, always tied to subject position, but education requires that we imagine their boundaries both flexible and porous, so that we and our students may grow within and outside them.

Nina Asher's questions are located in this passage between subject position and subjectivity. She asks, "How do we deconstruct such binaries as self and other, margins and center? How does the self unlearn the internalization of the oppressor? What are the contradictions inherent in the processes of decolonization for colonizer and colonized?" These are questions that we asked 30 years ago, yet we hear them and answer them differently today.

When we were asking our questions years ago, some of the senior scholars who came to our early reconceptualist conferences would dismiss our urgent arguments by saying, usually to each other, just loud enough to be overheard, "there's nothing new here. This is what Dewey was saying. They should read Harold Rugg. It has all been said before." In recalling their patronizing historicizing of our discourse, I now, having lived through these iterations and reiterations defend what appears to be an obsessive recursion, for the very same question asked in different times can never be the same. What follows is my meditation on the different meanings of the questions and the answers.

So, yes, stripped to their semantic essence, the questions Nina asks repeat education's eternal question: What is the relation of the self to society? But when I think about how that question is different from when we asked it, I realize that we did not use the word *colonization* to stand for oppression. We did use the word *oppression,* and for me, the curriculum theorist who informed that word, bringing it to the heart of teaching and learning was Paulo Freire. I recall his citing of Fanon and Albert Memmi (Freire, 1970/1981, pp. 48–9) and use of the terms *colonizer* and *colonized* in apposition to *oppressor* and *oppressed.* When I was reading *Pedagogy of the Oppressed* (1970/1981) in the 70s, I think we assumed that oppression and colonization were indexes pointing to the specific assaults on humanity suffered by particular groups of people. Then that seemed sufficient. Less satisfied is Stephen Nathan Haymes, whose essay in *Philosophy of Education,* "Race, Pedagogy, and Paulo Freire," addresses the limitations of what he names as Freire's "epistemologically centered conception of pedagogy" (Haymes, 2002, p. 152). Haymes cites Freire, in dialogue with Donaldo Macedo: "[the] over-celebration of one's own location and history eclipses the possibility of engaging the object of knowledge by refusing to struggle directly with readings that involve theory" (p. 155). I suspect that Freire was then reacting to the nominalism of identity politics that proclaimed difference without analyzing it, but Haymes is concerned the theory Freire was calling for was primarily a class analysis, aiming for a universal understanding and offers this Freire citation from his dialogue with Donaldo Macedo in "A Dialogue: Culture, Language and Race."

> The task of epistemological curiosity is to help gain a rigorous understanding of their historical location so they can turn this understanding into knowledge, thus transcending and universalizing it. If one remains stuck in his or her historical loca-

tion, he or she runs the risk of fossilizing his or her world disconnected from other realities. (1996, p. 155)

Sartre (1972) has pointed out that any effort we make to explain our past behavior is speculative, similar to attributions we might make to someone else's experiences. Nevertheless, I am tempted to speculate on what might have led us, in *Toward a Poor Curriculum,* to propose a method of reflection, which Bill Pinar titled *currere* that, made little reference to race or gender, similar to Freire's project of "conscientization." Perhaps the powerful rhetoric of identity politics that evolved in the civil rights and women's movements had created discourses that seemed too particular to be implicated in this approach to educational study that we were advancing.[2] Perhaps we were, despite our commitment to freedom, still stuck on our experiences as a White woman and a White man as a generic or universal consciousness. Perhaps the British Suez crisis in 1956 and the French loss of Algeria in 1962 convinced us that the era of Empire and colonization was ending. Perhaps, we were influenced by Freire, who was not an American, and whose conception of a liberating epistemology and pedagogy was sufficiently universal to influence educators in Africa, the Americas, Asia, and Europe.

Nevertheless, Haymes argues that in this avoidance of race, Freire denied the body as a subject of self-consciousness, thus denying the relation between "racial subjectivity and bodily consciousness" (p. 156), and points out that even though Fanon is a source for the text of *Pedagogy of the Oppressed,* Freire did not include Fanon's account of the experiences of colonized blacks, which effectively denies their subjectivity—arrogating it and their bodies to objects of White consciousness.

I suspect that my own associations with colonization were drawn from literature and cinema: E. M. Forster's *Passage to India*; Tennessee Williams's *Suddenly Last Summer;* Albert Camus's *The Plague.* As a descendent of East European Jews who fled from the tyranny of the Czars I did read my history through the heuristic of colonization, and I think it odd that I did not think of the practice of slavery in the Americas as colonization. So I turn to the *Oxford English Dictionary* to peel back the layers of time and text that made it possible for Freire to write and for me to read about colonization without bodies. The OED provides etymologies that are somewhat contradictory. *Colere* means to till. *Colon* in Latin referred to a serf who was tied to the soil and could not be bought or sold: the epitome of stasis, and of a body that is drawn down into the earth, into its materiality. Ironically, *colonize* also signifies mobility as it refers to those who settle in a new country. The Greek meaning of colonist seemed to retain the backward look, meaning "people from home." The OED indicates that colonists were people who settled in a new place but were bound to their home with religious or spiritual ties. It is interesting to listen to these meanings rattling around in the way we use these words today. The African slaves in this country were tied to the soil that was not theirs. Though rooted in their conditions, they suffered both the stasis of the serf, and the yearnings of the colonizers, the consciousness of those with ties to another place. And the colonizers, having left their own ground are lost and obsessive in trying to determine their position and place. So colonization brings back the ground and in doing this it returns the self of modernity to its psychic history, the bodies we come from, and their relation to the earth and to each other.

Kelly Oliver's text, *The Colonization of Psychic Space,* raises related issues as she reads Hegel, Heidegger, and Sartre (also sources for Paulo Freire's theory of freedom and knowledge), and Lacan through Marx and Fanon to critique their conception of subjectivity as the experience of reflection that results from alienation, that sense of being apart from our labor. In Marx's account, alienation is the experience of refusing to be subsumed in the objects created by one's own labor. Holding the thing one has made, the cart, the hubcap, the dissertation, provokes negation that says, this is not me, I can imagine it/me better, different, other. Oliver finds Marx's distinction between alienation and estrangement significant:

> The difference between alienated and estranged labor is the difference between production that actualizes the human capacities for self-reflection and social relations, and production that undermines those capacities and relations. Marx maintains that it is necessary for human beings to take that which they produce to be outside themselves; they are alienated from their products…. This type of alienation as the distance, or separation that initiates reflection reveals the species being of human beings. In this relationship to labor, human beings eat, sleep, and procreate—stay alive—to maintain themselves so that they can actualize their uniquely human capacity to engage in social production, to be social. In the estranged relationship to labor, on the other hand, human beings work to stay alive; their social production is turned into the means to sleep, eat, and procreate, rather than the other way around. (p. 10)

Referencing Fanon, Oliver rejects the attribution of this alienated subjectivity to slaves who have not had any choice about their labor. Forbidden to claim it, they, she argues, are prevented from the negation that would generate their own sense of possibility and of creative subjectivity. Oliver is critical of the individualism inherent in Hegel's legacy, for she grounds consciousness in relation: before there is an I there is a you. She uses Julia Kristeva's work and draws on psychoanalytic theory to argue that the capacity to make meaning, which she associates with subjectivity, thrives when psychic drives can be sublimated, which means brought into signification and language processes that both enable and express relationships. She brings us back to the body, back to the land. Our embodied, desiring life, pulsing through our unconscious is our grounding, in space, in time, and in other people. Our freedom is enlarged when we are able to bring some of this rich, thick stuff into signification. Drawing on object relations theory, she argues that in order to separate from the maternal body, the child must be connected to a loving, imaginary third that is experienced less somatically though still connected to the fluid, drive dominated semiotic discourse of mother child intimacy. The analogy in social space is the access to this loving third, distorted in the humiliation and abjection of the colonized male in the family relations, and in the language and rational discourses that are withheld from colonized peoples. Denied sublimation the colonized in Oliver's portrayal may not make meaning.

And so we are brought back again to the ineluctable, mutually constituting relation of subjectivity and subject position. For if meaning is made as joy, and fear, as bliss and disgust are drawn up from our bowels and our blood into words, everywhere we see meaningless curriculum that denies the world we live through our bodies. I join with Haymes in insisting that body consciousness is not just consciousness of anyone's body, and often I am dismayed that academic efforts to acknowledge our embodied existences have constructed "the body" as another ideality, as cut off from existence as "the mind."

This persistent tendency to turn the specific into the general haunts Western epistemologies, even colonization, in curriculum discourse. What the contribution scholarship on colonization offers is its specificity. If we agree with Haymes that oppression is not generic, then understanding the educational project requires understanding the specific histories and situations of the communities we work in, exemplified in Willinsky's fine work, *Learning to Divide the World*. We find this specificity in Freire's appreciation for lived experience in his method if not his theory. In the human relationships that he proposes among students and teachers, the curriculum, or the object to be known, is in the center of the table, and it is the responsibility and privilege of everyone present to make his or her relation to this object explicit. Again in the conscientization practices of his literacy workers, Freire requires encodings of community life that transcend language—film, drawings, poems, dances—understanding that these forms are more porous than prose, that they admit feeling and specificity, and so become sublimations accessible to the denied consciousness of oppressed peoples. I confess that although I was very proud to be his friend, I found the contradiction between class based universalism of Paulo Freire's theory, and the relational, and specific character of his pedagogy gendered. His pedagogy and theory were alternating sides of the androgeny that endeared him to me. Even as his postures of class based critical consciousness courted leftist solidarity with "the boys," he extended theory into pedagogy that was attuned to students, respectful of their specificities, and loving. This splitting of theory and pedagogy is, unfortunately all too common to our work, echoed in our theory/ practice discontinuities, in our policy/ pedagogy differences, in our gendered preferences and performances.

In these readings of Haymes's critique of Freire, and of Oliver's use of Fanon to critique negation as the liberating move of human consciousness, I have followed the word *colonization* back to the earth and back to the body, trying to show how subject position and subjectivity are mutually constituting. In *Toward a Poor Curriculum* we invoked the body work of Grotowski's theater and the embodied sensibilities of Virgina Woolf's characters to anchor *currere* in the embodied specificity of lived experience. But we did not extend our body consciousness to imagine seeing one's world always through a body that lived to realize only another's intentions. By now we have adsorbed postmodernism's suspicion of universal themes and truths, and we have seen the embodied hopes and hatreds of generations expressed again and again. Asher invokes the pathos of Katrina to display the racism, regionalism, and classism revealed as the flood waters washed away the neighborhoods that made the good times roll. Her reference to Minnie Bruce Pratt's process of reconceptualization addresses this groundedness as well. There is no detour around libido, around love, around the earth-tied, humid, cluttered, familiar relations that generate our lives. Asher's sociological imagination relocates home as she reverses the routes of the colonizers, bussing White students into schools where people of color have been ghettoized, sending upper and middle class kids to the schools of poor kids.

These sociological moves would have important affects on curriculum. But they are not curriculum. And here I would reclaim the epistemological intention of Freire, for in curriculum we point to the world worth knowing. But we do not only point forward, we also point back to interpret our histories; we do not only point up and out, pursuing the cosmopolitan project of educos; we also point down and in, recognizing the knowledge of our communities and drawing thought and feeling from internal non-ego into their sublimations in expression. We foster the liminal possibilities of curriculum, its capacity to offer itself as the loving third imaginary, offering paths to signification that gather up lived experience into the sublimations that articulate new possibilities. Here I borrow Merleau-Ponty's (1964) paean to sublimation:

> When one goes from the order of events to the order of expression, one does not change the world; the same circumstances which were previously submitted to now become a signifying system. Hollowed out, worked from within, and finally freed from that weight upon us that makes them painful and wounding, they become transparent or even luminous, and capable of clarifying not only aspects of the world that resemble them but others too. (p. 34)

That is very slow work. It means creating the conditions that allow students to speak and to bring wishes, thoughts and feelings into the space of signification. And that also means creating the conditions that allow teachers to speak and to bring wishes, thoughts, and feelings into the space of signification. While I may feel uneasy with an aesthetic sense of subjectivity, I still claim an aesthetic agenda for curriculum, not split off into separate arts classes and experiences, but integrated into the core disciplines, encoding partial thoughts, inclinations, dips and drives into symbols that engage the discourse of the discipline. And even in the structure of the lesson, the unit, the discussion there are possibilities of unraveling the Hegelian binaries, the promise of progress, the myth of resolution.

At the time of writing, it has been 2 years since Nina Asher and I read the papers that have evolved into the essays we write now, in the spring of 2008, as Hillary Clinton and Barack Obama compete to be the Democratic nominee for President. And it is just a few weeks since Barack Obama delivered a speech on race in Philadelphia. For months he had evaded addressing this topic as he presented himself as a candidate for the office responsible to all the people of this country. In that speech he declares his own "hybridity" without presenting it and himself as some totalized ideal of diversity:

> I am the son of a black man from Kenya and a white woman from Kansas. Was raised with the help of a white grandfather who survived a Depression to serve in Patton's Army during World War II and a grandmother who worked in a bomber assembly line at Fort Leavenworth while he was overseas. I've gone to some of the best schools in America and lived in one of the world's poorest nations. I am married to a black American who carries within her the blood of slaves and slaveowners—an inheritance we pass on to our two precious daughters. I have brothers, sisters, nieces, nephews, uncles and cousins, of every race and every hue, scattered across three continents, and for a long as I live, I will never forget that in no other country on Earth is my story even possible. (2008, p. 2)

Subject position and subjectivity: how can one speak of the actual, lived humiliations of generations and still manage to find a song of hope and possibility? The rush to embrace multiculturalism and diversity has silenced our conversations about the various ways that we understand and make sense of our common problems. His response, speaking to both body and spirit, opens a new register for this country's consideration and discussion of our past and future. Because the speech was provoked by the revelation and criticism of the divisive and denigrating views of his pastor, Reverend Jeremiah Wright, he does at the same time recognize the sorrows and despair of Wright's generation and of the hope that Wright brought to his congregation. He names the conditions that provoke the anxiety and resentment of working class and middle class White Americans. He moves back and forth: he names the material conditions and the insults to body and spirit endured by citizens across this country, Black, Brown and White; and then he names the economic, political, educational, health, international and defense policies that promise a better America for all of us. He returns to Reverend Wright, again and again, not letting the theories of history or hope become evasions of this particular moment, in this particular campaign. Most important is this courage that can name injustices and not be overwhelmed by their enormity, that can recognize human aspirations however distorted by power, and sustain the conversation of the next step.

And it is the next step that I worry about. I appreciate the provocation of the 2006 conference on the post-reconceptualist generation that invited this conversation across generations, as the conditions and meanings of the themes and questions that generate our work are compared. I recognize the rhetorical flair of condemning the ideas of the last generation as wrong, misleading, and obsolete, and I also acknowledge the effort, energy, and persistence required to change habits of thought.[3] Nevertheless, affixing the adjective *post* to structuralism, modernism, colonialism, reconceptualization, to me infers an abrupt conclusion to thought, and a repudiation of the lived world that spawns these theories. Let us just say, "to be continued."

Notes

1. As I make this assertion, it sounds familiar, and I remember another paper written in the early 80s, "Song and Situations," published in one of the very early editions of the *Journal of Curriculum Theorizing*, devoted to a similar argument, although the language was somewhat different.
2. In the years that followed we did participate in these discourses more fully. I wrote *Bitter Milk: Women and Teaching*, published in 1988, and Bill Pinar wrote *The Gender of Racial Politics and Violence in America*, published in 2001.
3. See Ernesto Laclau's essay, "Universalism, Particularism and the Question of Identity" (2006) for a critique of the generalizing effect of "post" declarations.

References

Freire, P. (1981). *Pedagogy of the oppressed* (M. B. Ramos, Trans.). New York: Continuum. (Original work published 1970)

Friere, P., & Macedo, D. (1996). A dialogue: Culture, language and race. In P. Leistyna, A. Woodrum, & S. A. Sherbloom (Eds.), *Breaking free: The transformational power of critical pedagogy* (pp. 223–224). Cambridge, MA: Harvard Educational Review.

Grumet, M. R. (1988). *Bitter milk: Women and teaching*. Amherst: University of Massachusetts Press.

Haymes, S. N. (2002). Race, pedagogy, and Paulo Freire. *Philosophy of education yearbook* (pp. 151–160). Champaign: University of Illinois Press.

Husserl, E. (1964). *The Paris lectures* (P. Koestenbaum, Trans.). The Hague, The Netherlands: Martinus Nijoff.

Laclau, E. (2003). Universalism, particularism, and the question of identity. In L. M. Alcoff & E. Mendieta (Eds.), *Identities: Race, class, gender, and nationality* (pp. 360–368). Malden, MA: Blackwell.

Merleau-Ponty, M. (1964). Indirect voices and the language of silence. In *Signs* (R.C. McCleary Trans.; pp. 39–83). Evanston, IL: Northwestern University Press.

Obama, B. (2008, March 18). Barak Obama's speech on race. *New York Times*. Retrieved October 10, 2008, from http://www.nytimes.com/2008/03/18/us/politics/18text-obama.html

Oliver, K. (2004). *The colonization of the self*. Minneapolis: University of Minnesota Press.

Pinar, W. F. (2001). *The gender of racial politics and violence in America: Lynching, prison rape, & the crisis of masculinity*. New York: Lang.

Pinar, W. F., & Grumet, M. R. (2006). *Toward a poor curriculum*. Troy, NY: Educators International Press.

Sartre, J. P. (1972). *The transcendence of the ego* (F. Williams & R. Kirkpatrick, Trans.). New York: Octagon Books.

Songs and Situations: The figure/ground Relation in a case study of currere. (1978). In G. Willis (Ed.), *Qualitative evaluation: Concepts and cases in curriculum criticism* (pp. 274–315). Berkeley: McCutchan.

Willinsky, J. (1998). *Learning to divide the world*. Minneapolis: University of Minnesota Press.

20 Difficult Thoughts, Unspeakable Practices

A Tentative Position Toward Suicide, Policy, and Culture in Contemporary Curriculum Theory

Erik Malewski and Teresa Rishel

Chapter Overview

This chapter employs three counterdiscourses to analyze U.S. state and professional efforts toward suicide prevention through cross cultural international comparisons. More specific, this analysis is taken up via "data-driven" policy making as evidenced in the U.S. Surgeon General's *Call to Action to Prevent Suicide* (1999) and the British Secretary of State for Health's *Saving Lives: Our Healthier Nation* (1999). Against a backdrop of failed state and national policy, the authors offer a discussion of school-based educators who have developed and written about their own experiences with intervention and prevention strategies. The authors discuss the gap between state reasoning and narratives of those who characterize suicide as unpredictable and therefore in excess of reason. Autobiography, Foucaldian analysis, and queer theory are offered as possible alternatives to the narrow instrumental privileged in U.S. and British suicide reduction efforts. Finally, the ongoing use of technically inclined strategies in the face of their failure to produce desired results, even by their own measure of success, is addressed within a context of a youth culture in crisis and of the needs of nation-states for a productive and flexible population amid advancing global capitalism.

In the final analysis, despite many years of experience and hard work, all we can say—and scientifically defend—is that every one of the eight strategies described herein, as currently implemented, may or may not prevent youth suicide. Clearly, this is an unsatisfactory state of affairs. (U.S. Department of Health and Human Services, 1992, p. xi)

Curriculum, in terms of our acculturation to it, has almost always dealt with the life-affirming aspects of teaching and learning: *currere*, the individual experience of the public; phenomenology, events, and objects as they are perceived in human consciousness; and deconstruction, the interrogation of certainty, identity, and truth. Early on, we learned that education was about life—a better quality of life, an improved understanding of our existence, and the creation of a better society in which the pursuit of all this might take place. Even when we were graduate students at the height of the postmodernist era, we were taught to use critical theory to retain the emancipatory aspects of modernist tendencies. Accordingly, we have attempted to address the intersection of curriculum and organizational theory and advocate for reconceptualization of teaching, learning, and social relations and found we have been able to bring unique perspectives to the field thus far. In recent years, however, we found ourselves reconsidering both what curriculum is and what it should be, reading school suicide prevention programs and narratives of survivorship,[1] and have even learned of the 1000 Deaths Writing Project and a support group for parents of children who have committed suicide.[2]

This chapter aims to reason out the state and federal foray into the realm of suicide via an exploration of prevention and intervention strategies, state and national policies, and the ever present and pressing sanity of schooling. While we address some of the efforts to attend to suicide in curriculum, we turn our interest to what Patti Lather (2004b) terms "the structure of the situation" (p. 16). Accordingly, this article addresses the circumstances at work, including shifts in the character of youth culture, curriculum wars over knowledge that will be acknowledged, and nation-states' changing desires for public education among simultaneously advancing neoliberal and neoconservative agendas. Other conditions we found involve technocratic logic, instrumental reason, professional remedies, and a shared desire among many liberals and conservatives to move schools into alignment with efforts to modernize the economy.

By attempting to address suicide and curriculum, we presuppose that accommodations are necessary within the realm of empiricism and instrumentality, those manifestations given evidence in state and national reports, high stakes testing, and the structure of health education curricula. Our goal here is not to revisit the various critiques of scientific methods and instrumental reasoning (Fraser, 1989; Lankshear & Knobel, 2004; Lather, 2005; Lincoln & Guba, 2005), alternative approaches to psychology (Kincheloe & Steinberg, 1993; Sinnott, 1989), or established explorations of the death of curriculum (Britzman, 2002). In their place, we offer three questions regarding curriculum and suicide to get at what we see as extremely debilitating circumstances. First, why do doctoral programs routinely deal with life-affirming and emancipatory aspects of curricular understanding but only occasionally with the dusk of awareness and the uncertainty of what lies beyond? This is not so much a question of which life-affirming approach to take—to carry on with a feminist or cultural studies agenda—but rather to ask, why affirm life at all? Second, what are the curricular implications of the research on suicide, loss, and survivorship? Threading theory with practice, this is the illumination of curriculum's inability to put knowledge to work in the exclusive service of life. Third, how might sparse attention to death be reread as flight from life where good work, under the guise of critical self-examination and comprehension of the conditions of existence, weaves an incapacity, a curricular consciousness too difficult to bear?

What Stevenson (2004) describes as public education's discomfort with "death appearing anywhere in the curriculum" (p. 232) is read as a reaction to the growing number of approaches to teaching and learning that emanate from critical theory, feminist thought, critical policy studies, indigenous knowledge, and cultural studies wherein the call for data-driven lesson and prevention and intervention plans, the everyday symbolic and material practices that induce alienation, trauma, and neglect are ushered in undercover. To put curriculum to work on the issue of suicide might involve coming to terms with public education's own failure to wed teaching and learning with an unfaltering will to carry on with life. As we begin to consider numerous ways this topic might be addressed, we rely upon analyses of knowledge and power by way of Foucault, capacities of autobiography via Pinar, and potentials of queer theory as detailed in the work of Britzman and Villarejo.

A Life and Death Issue: Suicide Engendering Policy or Policy Engendering Suicide?

> This almost reads like our business plan. (Peter Jovanovich, Chief Executive of Pearson Education, in response to President Bush's proposal for increased testing and use of school report cards, Walsh, 2001, p. 8)

> The current push for far greater standardization than we've ever previously attempted is fundamentally misguided. It will not help to develop young minds, contribute to a robust democratic life, or aid the most vulnerable of our fellow citizens. (Deborah Meier, Principal, Mission Hill School in Boston, Massachusetts, 2000, p. 4)

> It's always a concern that professional educators may feel so much pressure that someone might commit suicide. (Charles Larke, Superintendent of schools in east Georgia's Richmond County, in response to the news of an elementary school principal who committed suicide after she found out her school was marked as failing, CNN, 2002)

It is an established convention of curriculum theory that schooling is not to be subsumed under the interests of private business. In one of our first in-depth investigations of this position back when we were doctoral candidates, David Sehr (1997) articulated a strong argument against what he characterized as "privatized democracy," explaining that political theories of the 19th and 20th centuries—utilitarianism and pluralism—have combined with an ideology of mass consumption to greatly influence contemporary conceptions of the role of public education. What we have to add to Sehr's argument is that this position against the corporatization of education is being renegotiated in ways that have far-reaching consequences, from the character of youth culture to the shape of public policy on suicide.

Noting the absence of any in-depth discussion of life and death in schools, Doll's and Gough's (2002) picture of a "curriculum that cannot be found wanting because it cannot be found at all" (p. 89) moved us toward wide-awakeness[3] over the relationship between state and federal efforts to legislate suicide prevention and intervention strategies and "governmentality," wherein calculative rationality acts as a technique for "achieving the subjugation of bodies and the control of populations" (Foucault, 1990, p. 140). Their work is an attempt to locate discourses that counter the prevailing use of "principles and regularities" of the masses to establish "general truths" that enable societal management through predictive surveillance strategies (Deflem, 1997, p. 151). Quite resourcefully, Doll and Gough call for displacement of instrumental visions of education typified by their limited "focus on the future, positive goal orientation, and census" (p. 4) through embodied displays of knowledge and voice that are "produced and mediated by some*body* from some*where*" [italics in original] (p. 5). Insisting on reflective activities (such as journal writing) and negative orientations (such as those informed by critical theory) rather than those "typically found in the overlapping literatures of educational administration, school improvement, and organizational development" (p. 4), their work foregrounds the conflicts between policy making on suicide with appeals to consensus, general principles, model practices, and suicide as it is experienced by suicide survivors, as well as their families, friends, and associates. The latter authors chronicle suicide not as frameworks and typographies but as the breakdown of understanding, failure of categories to uphold, and befuddlement of purpose and direction. Surfacing at the interstices are questions over what the discourse of purpose and procedure locks out in regards to the uncertain and unknown and the very potential trapped beneath the given.

Perplexed over the number of studies that have shown current prevention and intervention efforts have failed to have significant positive effects (Hayden & Lauer, 2000; Mazza, 1997; Shaffer & Craft, 1999; Thompson & Eggert, 1999), have had unwanted effects (Guo & Harstell, 2002; Harden et al., 2001; Vieland, Whittle, Garland, Hicks, & Shaffer, 1991), or have had mixed effects, such as positive short-term impacts on behaviors but not ideations (Aseltine & DeMartino, 2004), we began to read more broadly in an attempt to understand what might be occurring at the intersection of youth culture and public policy that could shed some light on a difficult topic like suicide. David Elkind's (2001) description of the new morbidity in teenagers as a "dramatic postmodern rise" in stress-related dysfunction provided a sign of the current state of things based on recent resolutions via state and federal policies and planning bodies that their knowledge is certain enough to make deep interventions into education. Armed with the unsettling reality that the suicide rate for youth ages 15 to 19 nearly doubled between 1970 and 1990 (U.S. Department of Health and Human Services, 1992),[4] and for each of the 1,773 adolescents in the United States who took their own lives in 2002 another estimated 100 to 200 made an unsuccessful attempt (Kochanek, Murphy, Anderson, & Scott, 2004; McIntosh, 2004), we took seriously Elkind's concern that something has been forgotten in the quick and certain pace at which youth are rushed through 12 years of a curriculum abundant in facts and figures toward a precarious adulthood that offers few easy answers.

Reconfigurations of youth and conceptions of teaching and learning that thrust children and teenagers into situations where they must deal with violence, sexuality, substance abuse, and environmental degradation without having learned skills related to changing their social, economic, or cultural positions (Apple, 2001, 2003; Firestone, Schorr, & Monfils, 2004; Gratz, 2000; McNeil, 2000; Meier & Wood, 2004; Noddings, 2006; Zimmerman, 2002) require dramatic reconceptualization of research methods, knowledge production, and the role of schooling in a participatory democracy. Arguing that educational reforms of the 1980s grounded in modernist control philosophies "misfired," Elkind asks educators to attend to shifts in culture, family, media, and representations of youth, describing forthrightly the heightened tension created by legislation that narrows academic knowledge to what is testable amid increasing demands that schooling help communities understand and cope with the mounting stress of growing up in a postsocialist society.[5] His is an argument for dialogue, deliberation, and exchange rather than circumscribed top-down approaches that fail to provide youth with opportunities to critically think about and reflect on what constitutes a purposeful life. As the latest in a series of attempts by state and federal governments to limit program support to what can be empirically verified, the failures of suicide prevention and intervention strategies represent the problems of a modernist empiricist mode that "operates without variation in every context" (Kincheloe & McLaren, 2005, p. 317) and fails to attend to the "implicate orders of forces that shape what happens in schools" (Kincheloe & Steinberg, 1993, p. 307).

Troubled by the lack of scholarship on the connection between youth culture and suicide and curious about relationships that at first might seem disparate, we began to review the seemingly endless number of safety and prevention plans that have evolved over the last decade. Before long our offices were filled with yellow ribbons, ask for help cards, survivor T-shirts, various awareness campaign materials, and crisis response plans. Their certainty was disconcerting. Most telling was the Light for Life Foundation's Yellow Ribbon Be-A-Link (n.d.) training attempts to "effectively educate youth and adults on suicide" while simultaneously claiming not to "overburden school staff with too much information" or call upon them to "take on too much training or responsibility."[1] Rather than cite the importance of greater engagement, the training maintains that its Be-A-Link protocol is effective in part because it avoids "displacing or replacing professionals already in place" and reduces "the liability issue for teachers, school staff, and community."[7] In spite of efforts by the Yellow Ribbon organization and the S.O.S. Suicide Prevention Program, and the establishment of a National Strategy for Suicide Prevention, the majority of the approaches—including awareness, decreased stigma, and reduced access to lethal materials—seem only to interpolate the ongoing crisis in and among our youth, creating shifts in identities and identifications that many educational theorists have taken into account (Bennett & Kahn-Harris, 2004; Giroux, 2000; Latham, 2002; Mallan & Pearce, 2003; Skelton & Valentine, 1998; Willis, 2003). Where death in the curriculum is not a government priority and prevention programs assume they must not disturb existing structures as the conditions for entering schools, we began to doubt whether prevention and intervention strategies would be able to reason a counterdiscourse of innumerable possibilities regarding life and death that would make it within today's schools.

As we began to map out the various aspects of this article, what became evident were the contradictions between the complicated character of the writing we were doing with all its conjectures, contingencies, and particularities and the official education policies that are being authored and monitored by state and local agencies and actualized on a daily basis through school leadership. Concurrent with our attempts to discompose and deepen the conversation regarding suicide and youth culture there seemed to be another current of state and federal discourses that aims to constrain the character of the discussions we have with youth about life and death, successively standardized practices that function at multiple registers to restrain educational thought and practice. As Fraser and Honneth (2003) describe, these types of affirmative responses to social ills are characterized by overly simplistic aims that attempt to fix the undesirable outcomes of current political, social, and cultural arrangements "without disturbing the underlying social structures that generate them" (p. 74). These are the mandates for programs, policies, and plans that attend to end-state manifestations, such as signs of suicidal behavior, while taking little notice of the need to transform the conditions of possibility, such as the discursive social, economic, and political practices that interplay with the cultural and material terms under which we come to exist in, dwell together, and pass out of this world.

Equal to attempts to intervene on behalf of suicidal youth via the National Strategy for Suicide Prevention U.S. Dept. of Health and Human Services (2001), we attempt to shed some light on the less obvious educational dynamics at work: the ways suicide gets operationalized through discourse contained in state and federal reports and its relationship to a youth culture increasingly shaped by market forces and neoliberal and neoconservative agendas that value heavy-handed policies, increased competition, and the early demarcation of youth as winners and losers over more egalitarian and participatory approaches. When it comes to youth culture, Giroux's (1998) assertion that "self-esteem is being defined within a very narrow standard of autonomy" (p. 41) during an era when "market relations expand their control over the public sphere" and children and youth experience themselves as "consuming subjects and commodities" (p. 45) offers deeper insight into the shifting terrain of youth identities and identifications. As we began to draw relationships across seemingly disparate elements of the situation, we realized counterdiscourses are needed to propel us beyond intervention and prevention protocols that in their attempt to easily fit into existing school structures and practices collude with those elements of public education and curriculum practice that induce alienation.

So how can educators begin to think differently about suicide? Pinar (1992) suggests the notion of an afterlife makes the passing of time comprehensible and moments shared together "worthy of caring, worthy of presence" (p. 99). The predominance of bureaucratic and professional reasoning belies the anxiety death evokes in everyday conversations and school curricula. Detached and stolid, instrumental curriculum strategies might evade discussions of time but not occurrences that, following Derridian deconstructive tactics (see Trifonas & Peters, 2005), leave us clues to what is absent. For each individual, the existence of education is a testament to the finite nature of our time on earth: the birth of children, just as the birth of ideas, enfolds an end. Knowledge that knows only certainty is little more than what Pinar points to as a "tissue of lies" (p. 100) that seeks to transcend human embodiment and the changes that the passage of time brings. What suicide challenges educators to confront is the contradiction between the structures of our teaching and what we know of dwelling in the world as it was experienced in our youth (Grumet, 1988). Avoiding the temptation to name a curriculum model or action plan that allows us to intervene in suicide, we seek to better understand what Foucault (1984) describes as the "forms of rationality" (p. 36) at play. Accordingly, we turn to Colorado as a state on the forefront of issues of suicide intervention, prevention, and public awareness. We recount the strategies in place and the work they do in expanding and contracting curricular certainties. In other words, we address the following: What are the tactics? What do they assume? How do they function?

Reasoning an Unruly Practice: Discourses, Strategies, and Politics

After reading various Colorado documents, news briefs, training guidelines, and reporting system updates, we began to realize that the "Centennial State," with its own office of suicide prevention, has been grappling with these issues for some time. Accordingly, we examine the implications of two seemingly different reports, the State of Colorado *Suicide Prevention and Intervention Plan* (1998) developed by the governor-appointed Suicide Prevention and Advisory Commission (Commission Report) and the *Suicide in Colorado* report produced by The Colorado Trust Foundation (Trust Report).[8] While we focus primarily on the Commission Report, through juxtapositions and intertextual readings we aim to specify some curricular insights about how state and professional bodies make meaning around suicide and how these relate to a youth culture in crisis. Through mapping discourses, strategies, and politics, we attempt to outline representations of intervention and prevention efforts and the ways they enable and constrain intellectual self-reflection. We want to emphasize that we are not attempting to construct either of these reports as necessarily productive or counterproductive. Rather, we suggest that the Commission and Trust reports are exemplary displays of dominant conceptions of suicide and concomitant intervention and prevention efforts and as cultural texts can be taken up curricularly for addressing the inadequacies of recent scholarship on suicide. The following is what we learned.

Two Reports from the State of Colorado: One Before, One After Columbine

The Commission and Trust reports represent a long history of government documents that recount the status of knowledge on suicide, with attention to issues of youth, schooling, and intervention and prevention strategies. Reports, such as the *Youth Suicide Prevention Plan for Washington State*, *Virginia Youth Suicide Prevention Plan*, and *Wisconsin Suicide Prevention Strategy* attend to adolescent struggles and what is at issue for youth who take their own lives. However, the Commission and Trust reports attempt more than a recount of risk factors, methods, nonfatal behaviors, state-by-state comparisons, and types of prevention and intervention efforts, although they examine all of these aspects. The Commission Report functions on at least three registers to chronicle suicide topics addressed by state and professional apparatuses over the spectrum of life. On the first register, the Commission Report represents state and professional bodies as exemplars of reason, objectivity, and proceduralism in the midst of the difficult knowledge and unspeakable practices suicide brings to bear upon the citizenry. On the second register, fringe narratives characterize suicide as unpredictable and therefore capable of "infect-ing" any individual, an ominous and frightening threat to citizens where fear is employed to stabilize reliance upon expert knowledge. On the third register, that requires the first two once an "only the state can save us now" milieu is constructed, bureaucratic and professional discourse is put to work in the buildup of an infrastructure that includes establishing a governmental lead entity, educational awareness, and screening, referral, and follow-up for at-risk individuals. Descriptions of suicide as a contagion that requires governmental intervention are used to manage the paradox of the general citizenry's reliance upon and suspicion of professional and state bodies in what Giddens (1991, 2000) termed posttraditional societies.

Through the interoperation of all three registers, the role of state and professional bodies becomes a referent for rearticulating governmental and professional apparatuses as capable of convincing those who have suffered from alienation and indifference to seek out alternatives to taking their own lives. That is, they do not address the ongoing failure to create for many of its citizens the social, economic, and political conditions for a high quality of life, sense of overall prosperity, and easy access to mental, physical, and spiritual resources necessary to facilitate and maintain the first two. Even as govern-mental and professional remedies have not proven highly effective at reducing suicide ideations and attempts, the larger effect of the technocratic regime of meaning taken up in these two reports is to narrow the organization of knowledge to binary or dialecti-cal logic: a series of affirmative remedies that have proven little by way of establishing a sound response are presented as the only alternative to the irrationality of citizens suf-fering under the weight of attachments to irrecoverable absences.

The Commission Report provisions an allegory for the purpose of government and the politics of state-level strategies within numerous educational settings (medical estab-lishments, public schools, health programs, social services, public venues), masterfully mobilizing prevention and intervention plans as the axis across which it can promote an epistemological structure capable of carrying its ideological communiqué to the people of the state. At-risk citizens, then, contribute the boundary for fabricating the curricular relationships by which bureaucratic reason, possessed by those who have expert knowl-edge, offers strategies that are favored against the incompleteness, particularities, and breakdown emanating from the narratives of those who have actually been confronted with the issue of self-murder. The opposition between common knowledge (personal stories, anecdotes, partial accounts, individual interpretations) and specialized knowl-edge (empirically verifiable, methodologically sound, professionally sanctioned), and the opposition between at-risk populations (sexual minorities, seniors, mentally ill) and those who through their absence are thought to be exempt, are clearly established. Through these binaries the authority of state and professional bodies is confirmed as the best response to the unwieldy nature of storytelling and lived experiences and their defiance of categorization and order. The promise offered in the Commission and Trust reports is one of a Hegelian dialectic where through the recuperation of difference into the same, subjects of the state are promised future arrival at absolute knowledge. The message is that through evidence-based knowledge production, this devastating pursuit of self-destruction can be brought to an end.

The Commission Report starts with a photograph of the National Lifekeepers Quilt followed by a brief narrative of the pain and loss experienced by the survivors of the sui-cide of a friend or family member. Beyond this introduction that claims to put a "picture on suicide" (p. 5) for state citizens who might have difficulty conceptualizing the hun-dreds of Coloradoans who voluntarily take their own lives ever year, the discourse takes a dramatic redirection. Narratives that feature breakdowns in understanding, refusal of closure, and personal trauma are exchanged for official discourse that emphasizes objectivity, empiricism, and rationality in an effort to outline a topography of risk factors divorced from subjective understandings and stories of loss. Built from what little can be generalized about the motivations for taking one's life, the assumption is that the more dimensions within the typography (age; race; gender; sexuality; substance usage; and psychosocial, personality, cognitive, and environmental traits) that apply negatively to individuals (for example, older, single, White, male), the more likely it is that they will attempt self-murder. Even as the Commission Report concedes that "no factor or sets of factors have ever come close to predicting suicide with any accuracy" (p. 9), the intent of the document remains clear: to use uneven, partial, and circumstantial understandings of suicide to develop model practices that are replicable, transferable, and reliable, a totalizing political venture that provides global remedies that homogenize unique place-bound social relations and the importance of culturally relevant solutions.

Both the Commission and Trust reports offer little exploration of the lives of those who have attempted or completed suicide or survived the suicide of someone else, or of the race, class, gender, and sexual identity dynamics that might be at play in the alienation and despondency presented as common precursors to suicidal acts. Decontextualized and dehistoricized, the cultural, economic, and political dimensions of suicide appear marginal to the construction of bureaucratic and professional reason as the organizing principle around which any successful intervention and prevention strategies are believed to be situated. Cultural and material differences in both of these reports are spatially positioned so as to constitute the center and margins, always with the same effect but operationally divergent and contingent upon the dimension under analysis. In the Commission Report, the topic of the role of culture in intervention and prevention strategies is nested deep within instrumental categories that include risk factors and recommendations for change and in appendices that make brief points about the importance of dealing with gender, race, and sexual identity. The Trust Report explicitly recognizes race, gender, and age in detailing who is at risk, although these categories fail to incite deeper analysis or get represented in any significant way in the recommended prevention and intervention strategies. Along the same lines, neither the Commission nor Trust reports examines the relationship between social class and suicide, opting instead for detailed explanations of the indirect and direct economic burdens suicide places on the state and specific mention of unemployment as a key risk factor for suicide.

The ways bureaucratic notions of authority and agency are constructed within a curricular orientation of social service further mask how race, class, gender, and age differences, along with symbolic representation and material distribution disparities, operate within private and public life. The larger effect is that the conflict between cultural and economic differences and the pressure of bureaucratic rationalities for efficiency and homogeneity is resolved through models of prevention and intervention that place the provision of services—including new infrastructure with the ability to provide additional educational programs, screenings, trainings, and resource plans—above attempts to transform the economic, political, and social conditions under which citizens live their everyday lives. The outgrowth of these disciplinary techniques is to offer a body of specialized knowledge that further mystifies the innumerable factors at work in depression, despondency, and alienation and specific practices through which subjectivities are constituted within and through systems of power that might better explain the innumerable interactions where suicide is one of its effects.

Furthermore, by making only passing references to the ways that privileges of race, class, gender, and sexual identity shape perceptions of and access to state and professional resources, both reports assume all citizens have equal authority and ability to negotiate their lives politically, economically, and geographically. Neither report explores the relationship between privilege and state and professional resources. This subtext reinscribes the assumption that even within those most likely to fall victim to suicide there remains intact a U.S. ethic of self-reliance and perseverance that provides the capacity to identify problematic thoughts and behaviors and use such awareness to search out assistance. Within a stratified society where lives are shaped by race, class, gender, and sexual orientation, as well as other determining factors such as social networks, cultural values, and sense of responsibility to others, professional and state perspectives emerge as the rule by which to measure legitimate authority. Through narrow reasoning that suggests state and professional organizations pay scant attention to larger social formations and the complex ways they interact to create conditions where suicide is seen as a viable option, the attempt to offer effective suicide prevention and intervention strategies mystifies state and professional complicity with and culpability for alienating ideologies, disparaging representations, and differing material distributions.

Privilege can also be evidenced in state and professional discourse as near limitless moral and ethical authority over a citizenry constructed as responsible to the state for both their public and private lives. State and professional bodies further guide and correct the perceptions, behaviors, beliefs, and values of citizens who come into contact with one or more of the program categories described in both the Commission and Trust reports. These bodies assume their obligation, even as they struggle to prove their effectiveness, toward saving those who are susceptible to suicidal ideations without questioning assumptions of altruism and benevolence reasoned as the motor force behind their stated goals, procedures, and recommendations. In these reports, authority runs the risk of masking the complex relationships whereby the interaction of incalculable variables of belonging and neglect culminate in psychic–social spaces that share in the formation of attenuated subjectivities.

Cholbi (2002), asserting that suicide is characterized by "nihilistic disenchantment" (p. 245), maintains that self-murder is less an issue of individual conduct than an effect of power's docilizing efforts, a recourse for those foreclosed and atomized by the modalities of their existence. Unfortunately, both the Commission and Trust reports do little to disrupt the classic liberalism that draws focus to the dilemmas surrounding the provision of social services to the less fortunate instead of the actual economic, psychic, and political structures of oppression that shape citizens' everyday life experiences. By attempting to pinpoint a select number of empirically verifiable factors, the reports ignore the immensity and severity of the problems that citizens ideating suicide face, as well as the ways that othering, competition, and disdain for symbolic and material differences are interwoven into the economic, political, and cultural fabric of daily life in and out of schools.

In place of critical consciousness raising, both the Commission and Trust reports focus on the burdens suicide imposes on the economic viability of the state and how these demands can be remedied without calling into question state and professional roles in maintaining oppressive conditions. Through the inversion of accountability, prevention, and intervention plans theorize suicide as individuals' disregard for their duty toward their community and the state. What these reports fail to consider are the regulatory forces of symbolic representation and material distribution that relentlessly countermand all indicators of individual dignity and social arrangements that afford parity of participation, both necessary for creating and maintaining a participatory democracy (Fraser, 2002). Far from isolated acts, the terms for suicide ideation require the eradication of the ability to conceive of intrinsic value and self-worth, the evacuation of all thoughts that validate a reason for existence. As Emile Durkheim (1951/2002) contends, what suicide brings to bear upon education and the state involves, in part, the question of what it means to make sense of social arrangements that regulate to death.

The Commission and Trust reports manage to rewrite the successive dismantling of social safety nets, eclipsing of nation-state sovereignty by multinational corporations, and increasing use of neoliberal logic to formulate public policy within a broader project that rearticulates state and professional bodies as the vanguards of reason, validity, and what Foucault termed "the task of administering life" (Foucault, 1990, p. 139). The representative and distributive politics at work in these documents has a long history in U.S. state and federal policy, particularly when demands upon the government require expenditures that cannot be justified in terms of improving economic and political competitiveness. As Tremain (2005) notes, these historical rearticulations are as much about regulatory schemes of state and federal practices as they are about illuminating opposition to such schemes as proof of ongoing reformation. Regarding the ability of government to recast itself through self-critique, to the extent the counterdiscourses that inform nation-state strategies for change are responses to the subjecting techniques of biopower, the counter demands of suicide prevention and intervention plans are little more than the historical effects of governmentality's polymorphous character. Linked to neoliberal and neoconservative agendas, the ambiguous relationship between methods, knowledge, and recommendations and the affirmative character of remedies thought possible, sheds light on the simultaneous tactics of regulation and reform.

The Commission and Trust reports can be read as a contemporary defense of state and federal authority and expert knowledge reasoned on the grounds that (1) the previous form of governmentality has been abandoned; (2) the current form of governmentality is reasonable and open to reform; and (3) this governmentality is being held accountable through a system of checks and balances that limit the possibilities of abuse (see Foucault, 1997, p. 75). Missing are deeper explorations of state and professional culpability for and complicity with normalizing discourses that succeed in persuading citizens that the bodies they occupy are contemptible or that the only means for affirming their own existence is to end it. Wed Foucault's *no action in life is innocent* to Derrida's *any subjectivity is complicit* and we are confronted with the realization that there is no outside from which to work to develop effective prevention and intervention strategies. The criticisms and efforts toward change levied against and described within the Commission and Trust reports are embedded in the power relations, normalizing tendencies, and discursive practices of the prevailing state system as it functions within particular historical contexts. These are the very discursive formations Foucault (1994) reasoned might be understood through the study of the differences that define the rules of operation.

Alarming if not surprising, then, the urgent questions surrounding how to intervene in the lives of over 30,000 U.S. citizens, on average 700 of them Coloradoans (National Governors Association, 2005), who will commit suicide annually is successively reasoned into a homogenizing solution of 12 program categories that range from school-based programs, suicide prevention centers, and crisis hotlines to limiting access to lethal means, providing programs for suicide survivors, and training community gatekeepers. Rationalizing a discourse of feasibility, expert knowledge as an everyday ritual of truth gives shape to crippling assumptions regarding appropriate policies, correct readings, and acceptable applications. These are the governmental tactics that enable the ongoing redefinition of what is within the state's purview, what Lather (1998) points to as the refusal to disrupt "the horizon of an already prescribed intelligibility" (p. 494) with ways of thinking that exceed binary logic or established practice. Begging a turn toward Derrida's ordeal of undecidability given what little understanding seems to exist, what remains are ominous questions over what can be done lacking the certainty of knowledge or the ability to see the problem clearly.

Considering that contemporary prevention and intervention strategies have had only limited and uneven success, the focus on empirical data analysis and verification through replication on the way toward a workable plan risks becoming a hegemonic activity with dire political and social consequences. Against the Commission and Trust reports, the logic of instrumental reason, objectivity, and proceduralism as the means for establishing recognizable truths languishes given that suicide "operates at the borders and in the interstices of power" (Foucault, 1978/1990, p. 139) which collapse the very categories that structure prevention and intervention programs. The ways in which the disjunctures and discontinuities at work in narratives of the National Lifekeepers Memorial Quilt—a mother who remembers her son Robby, and a number of families who reflect on loved ones who committed suicide—are used to situate as primary numerical representations of reality seems insufficient in light of the interactive complexity of the variables at work in suicide, the very effects of which disrupt the conventional oppositions of state and professional thinking.

Given our emphasis on moving on in the midst of difficult knowledge, what Lather (2004a) points to as the "knowledge that works against security and certainty by inducing breakdowns in representing experience" (p. i), the border crossings that occur between narrative description and bureaucratic and professional reason and the conundrums and contradictions that get written into policy are particularly informative. The prefacing of contradictory findings, struggles to define appropriate ways for professional and state bodies to direct local community organizations, and inability to establish what counts as evidence amount to labored translations between knowledge and policy. There is difficulty in developing effective plans and procedures given the inability to locate innumerable factors at play in suicide. With the complex web of associations involved in the decision to take one's own life and plethora of culturally specific histories (Bhugra, 2004; Bhugra, Baldwin, Desai, & Jacob, 1999; Minois, 2001; Mondesir, 2000), the causal models embraced in both these reports might be poorly suited to understanding the "preponderance of interaction effects" (Lather, 2004b, p. 20) that surface when studying this particular social phenomenon. Herein lie the limitations of professional and bureaucratic reason: the inability to locate nonreductive conceptual maps that meet the promise of producing knowledge that can simultaneously offer strategic direction and operate on shifting ground.

For youth culture and schooling, then, the Commission and Trust reports are a curriculum of diversion, documents that fall short of describing remedies that will provide youth with skills that will help them address the compelling and distressing questions of political, economic, and cultural arrangements that on many fronts have failed to provide for their humanity and well-being. Educational programs on the signs of suicidal behavior and depression, while potentially helpful in the short term (Aseltine & DeMartino, 2004), will not provide the intellectual and material resources necessary to develop youth capable of participating in the creation and maintenance of a public democracy and opposing the antihumane conditions they will encounter both as adolescents and later as adults. Self-actualization and understanding the conditions of their own existence, as part of contributing to the form and operation of nurturing communities, are key curriculum concerns inseparable from the broader question of what it means to live within a nation where public services and projects are under siege (Aronowitz, 2001); market-based reasoning shapes schools, from curriculum and pedagogy to strategic planning and mission statements (Boyles, 2000; Molnar, 2005); and self-help ideologies eclipse a sense of entitlement to symbolic and material resources from the state (Giroux,

2004; Kelley, 1998). The Commission and Trust reports ignore these crucial issues and maintain a near exclusive focus on identifying at-risk groups, methods of suicide, training programs, screening locations, and awareness campaigns. Through these provisions adolescents, just as adults, are constructed within a capitalist political economy as non-participating, consuming objects rather than capable, socially engaged subjects longing for the critical consciousness necessary to negotiate and transform the economic, political, and social contexts in which they live and relate to one another. As Fraser (2002) points out, when it comes to subordinate groups, including those struggling with their own temporality and finding purpose in life, the aim should be "to de-institutionalize patterns of cultural value that impede parity of participation and to replace them with patterns that foster it" (p. 25).

What we propose as a counterapproach to the search for the right strategy involves making commitments to lucidity, transversion, and nonmastery. Here prevention and intervention efforts are continuously under reformation in ways that disable closure, definition, and completion. This is expert knowledge drawn into fractious relationships with lived experience and intuitive understanding on the way toward a praxis of unsurety, wherein interrogations of current prevention and intervention strategies enable the violation of its own reasoning in the search for discourse and language that is more workable and less weighty. Exposing the devices of governmentality as limiting requires analysis capable of revealing the discontinuities within the discourses, procedures, and concepts that provide the conventions of prevention and intervention efforts.

Looking Elsewhere: National Suicide Strategies in Britain and Beyond

The second point we learned was that the United States is not the only country strategizing how to respond to attempts by its citizens to take their own lives. In 1999, the British Department of Health released its national healthcare plan, *Saving Lives: Our Healthier Nation,* and in 2002, as part of the implementation of this plan, established a national strategy for suicide and an institute for mental health featuring suicide prevention as one of its core programs. Britain's national healthcare plan offers a way to understand the place of suicide within national politics, particularly the ways the plan structures the evolution of its rationality around competing storylines. Along the first dimension of reasoning, the plan employs affective narratives that are developed discursively through a number of emotionally driven statements on numerous social issues before settling on the conventional formula of benevolent social service. Along the other dimension, hyperbole and emotive statements introduce professional and bureaucratic discourse rich in appeals to instrumental reason, empirically based practices, and a blend of neoliberal and neoconservative ideologies regarding cultural and material reconfigurations of public space. These dimensions perform in two ways: they provision a logic for locating resources in the private sector and further intervention by experts on behalf of those deemed at risk, particularly the poor, urban, and mentally ill. Similar in function to the Commission Report originating out of the United States, the larger effects of the use of sentiment and reason involve emotive statements, personal narratives, and congeries (for example, "we must match services to the needs of all people" and "we stand on the threshold of the 21st Century") as the devices capable of positioning professional and bureaucratic discourses as primary. Cross-analysis of plans and reports out of Britain and the United States reveals variations on a theme: affective discourse with less epistemological weight and rhetorical complexity provides the discontinuities that formulate weighty bureaucratic and professional discourses rich in appeals to reason and logic as the very language capable of order.

While bureaucratic and professional discourse was deployed similarly across the United States and Britain, the categories of analysis taken up differed between the two countries. One historically important axis for examining social and material difference, social class, has receded in use as a representative force influencing U.S. state and federal policy over the past 3 decades (Clark & Lipset, 2001) and suicide reduction strategies are no exception. Therefore, it is highly significant, but not particularly noted in recent literature on suicide, that the U.S. *National Strategy for Suicide Prevention* and the Colorado Commission and Trust reports examined earlier do not address or in any significant way emphasize the relationship between, for example, suicide and social class, or other factors at play in the social, economic, and political contexts that might give rise to depression or alienation, or inhibit access to resources. Given the triumph of neoliberal free market and neoconservative moral reform strategies within broader efforts toward the globalization of national economies and cultures, attending to social class seems even more integral to understanding changes in the quality of life of a nation's citizenry and the extent to which countries have been able to instill in their people the will to carry on with daily life. Accordingly, reading the class conscious analysis of the current status of health and well-being offered in Britain's healthcare plan was a breath of fresh air; finally we were able to find a government document that spoke explicitly to issues of symbolic representation and material distribution and their connection to issues of quality of life and the probability that individuals might ideate suicide as an option for putting an end to their suffering.

Britain's attention to the relationship between social class, health issues, and quality of life could not come at a more opportune time. Following trends similar to those in the United States, between 1971 and 2002 the gap between richest and poorest households in Britain has more than doubled (Babb, Haezewindt, & Marin, 2005; Shaw, Smith, & Dorling, 2005). Similarly, since 1991 the proportion of wealth controlled by the top 1% increased from 17 to 23% while the proportion controlled by the least wealthy 50% has fallen from 8 to 5% (Babb, Haezewindt, & Marin, 2005). As Britain's health care plan makes clear, social class is an increasingly important dimension for understanding everyday life experiences, not only for the light it sheds on suicide but for its ability to draw together seemingly disparate elements of our social lives, linking globalization, national policy, and access to resources to the desire among different social classes to persist as inhabitants of this earth. At the turn of the century, Britain's healthcare plan underscores the life expectancy for a male as "five years less in the two lowest social classes than in the two highest"; unemployed females have consistently "higher mortality from coronary heart disease and suicide"; and men in manual classes are "40% more likely to report long standing illness that limits their activities than those in non-manual classes" (p. 42). With continued disparities in quality of life among different social classes and the continued dismantling of social services that buffer the underemployed and unemployed from the impact of market forces, Britain's healthcare plan's finding that people "worst off financially and socially, particularly in inner cities" more often commit suicide than those who are well off and "children in the poorest households are three times more likely to suffer from mental illness than children in the best off households" (p. 96) reads like a call to arms. This explanation of differences in cultural and material realities and suffering related to socioeconomic standing further highlights the dearth of research on social class, including in-depth analysis of the relationship among suicide, globalization, and changing socioeconomic realities of various countries.

Given the presence of a Marxist-styled analysis and optimism regarding the government's ability to intervene in contemporary cultural and material practices on the way toward a better future, we wondered if Britain would be able to meet its goal of a 20%

reduction in suicide by the year 2010.[9] In response to the extraordinary way the country's healthcare plan is interposed with a prevention storyline at odds with both its affective appeals and socioeconomic descriptions of difference, we became less optimistic about the prospects. In contrast to the class-conscious analysis of the health and well-being of the population, the suicide intervention and prevention strategies are rooted in market-based philosophies that have the larger effect of tightening the relationship between self-help ideologies and the provisioning of social services. These are the philosophies of presence and agency that underwrite the antistate subjectivities that make it difficult for public services to move beyond the aim of breaking dependency on the government and toward entitlements as citizens of a democratic nation-state. Working from a social and economic logic that equates self-actualization with consumer choices, the focus of Britain's healthcare plan on the "high economic cost" of mental illness, reduced "burdens on business" made possible by a healthier population, decreased depression brought on by employment, and strategic concentration of resources on select programs, such as those emphasizing welfare to work, all naturalize the use of policies that align nicely with privatized, market-driven logic. This is public support going after ways to prop up private business through social service policies that erase the politics of socioeconomic standing outlined elsewhere in the plan.

History, identity, and policy in these documents, then, are dynamic amalgamations. The identity of a potential suicide victim is presented as at least, in part, a social construction that exceeds essentialist frameworks. The next British person to attempt self-murder cannot be identified by any particular set of characteristics, and only through cultural and material reconstruction might a nation mediate this will to die. Even as the outlined prevention efforts fall short of reflecting remedies equal to the problem, a subtext critical of modernist forms of operation informs Britain's healthcare plan and national strategy (and, to a much lesser extent, the Colorado Trust and Commission reports). Here health, well-being, and the will to live become at once markers of race, gender, and class privileges and the susceptibility of privileged subjectivities to despondency, alienation, and self-murder. Working affective statements against bureaucratic and professional storylines, Britain's healthcare plan evokes the potential for an unconventional form of critical awareness that exposes conceptions of human worth and well-being as positioned within the fabric of power relations where it might be possible to establish trends while simultaneously sparing no one of potential susceptibility. This is done not by exceeding dichotomies but through the indeterminacies of frameworks that fail to stabilize knowledge rubbing against the singularity of suicide that, as an event, exceeds the regulatory capacities of state biopolitics.

For the purposes of this article, poststructural persuasions are particularly informative. On many fronts, Britain's intervention and prevention efforts, similar to those of the United States, have fused with business-minded strategies to provision a healthcare model that replaces variegated insights of professionals with data-driven best practices, trainings on promoting the healthcare plan among the general population, and, in the case of suicide, implementing a 12-point risk management program. Absent in improving security at "hot spots" where suicides frequently occur, encouraging mental health among at-risk young men, and training journalists to reduce the glorification of suicide are discussions of the economic, political, and cultural conditions that shape situations where suicide is seen as a viable option. At the end of the day, the intervention and prevention strategies across the United States and Britain are more similar than they are different. Despite the addition of social class analysis, Britain's national healthcare plan and strategy, similar to Colorado's Commission and Trust reports, ends with guarantees of effectiveness through a buildup of government infrastructure and forms of proceduralism that sidestep vital intellectual deliberations regarding symbolic representation and material distribution integral to potentially transformative suicide remedies.

In light of the limitations of prevention and intervention strategies employed by both Britain and the United States, finding ways of combating suicide seems unimaginable. It is precisely these moments when workable alternatives cannot be envisioned within the structure of the current situation that poststructural theory reminds us of opportunities to examine the difficult, intractable knowledge suicide brings to bear upon any efforts at education. Ellsworth (2004) refers to this as "educators coming up against the limits of our theories and practices" that, far from ending in paralysis or retrogression, reveal "concrete instances of how the paradoxes of teaching and learning can be productive" as a way to navigate all that must be rethought in an effort to learn from the failures, omissions, and breakdowns within current regimes of meaning (pp. 99–100). In the search for workable sites, we found in the description of failed efforts the interstices of any knowing where educators might begin to make a difference in how suicide gets constructed. Britain's healthcare plan notes unintended effects and unrealized outcomes tied to cultural and material disparities resulted in situations where "the better off took more notice and changed their behavior faster than others did" (p. 43). Out of the unimaginable in political and bureaucratic discourse here is an opportunity to enact a logic requiring work in actual political, economic, and social contexts while concurrently unsettling assumptions about contending regimes of meaning and the belief that the emergence of one storyline assumes the defeat of another.

We were encouraged by the potential of multiple narratives about the problems with prevention and intervention strategies to interrupt what Czarniawska (1997) describes as "the diagnosis and the cure" trapped in the "same institutional thought structure" that had "originally caused the disease" (p. 152). Convinced by the between space poststructural theory makes conceivable, the possibilities that arise out of the difficult thought suicide evokes involve knowing that knowledge is always partial; this epistemological humility puts in motion a double movement: narratives that appeal to the potential of critical cultural and material remedies that, in the process of outlining their claims to knowledge, chronicle their breakdowns, ambivalences, and failures in the ability to both represent and intervene. Such discourse of modest understanding offers a map of new strategies on the way toward as of yet unknown sites of thinking, strategizing, and planning how to put reports and policies to work. Storylines like the ones we seek attest to the complicity of a Derridian ordeal of undecidability when mobilizing discourses of partial comprehension with the capacity to recoup exclusionary practices, even as efforts are made to leverage truth to power.

Going Back to School: Taking a Lesson on Local Strategies From a Canadian School District

The third point we learned was that in the face of the failures of state and national policy, some educators have developed and written about their own experiences with intervention and prevention strategies. Out of an attempted suicide by a 13-year-old student credited with engendering a crisis that sparked a "new authentic in-service" capable of addressing "difficult subjects" like suicide emerged a 2005 publication in *Social Work Education*. This article, "Schoolyard Conversations: Influencing Suicide Talk in an Elementary School Community," is by Lisa Romano-Dwyer and Glen Carley, both in social work at a Canadian Catholic school district. In the beginning they describe the effects of formalized hierarchies that produced a "shared contagion" (p. 246) of thoughts, fears, and worries that spread along five dimensions of social relations (parent-to-parent, administrator-to-administrator, counselor-to-counselor, student-to-student, and teacher-to-teacher) where "everyone was talking but nobody was talking with each other" (p. 247).

Promising in the article are phrases such as "therapeutic classroom discussion" and "potential knowledge" on the way toward "structured conversations" (p. 247) that linked parallel dimensions and displaced innuendo and myth with "healthy spontaneous" (p. 248) exchanges where "suicide was now talked about" (p. 249). Motivated by six 12-year-old students so affected by the attempted suicide of their peer they "'slashed' their arms and showed the marks as evidence of their despair" (p. 245), their aim was to encourage "discoveries and re-discoveries about certain practice theories" (p. 246) as a way to evaluate the effectiveness of intervention strategies taken up in local communities. Astonished at how quickly within socially differentiated settings "distorted and unhealthy views began to act as a contagion" (p. 246), their work calls for a praxis of dialogue and personalization in excess of formal roles that spill over into fertile conversations concurrent with programming for parents and students focused on the warning signs of depression and suicidal behavior. Intent on creating "a new space to shape the children's reality" (p. 250), as of yet unknown curricular orientations, Romano-Dwyer and Carley document the search for a path through crises of understanding in ways that make it possible to learn from the breakdowns and failures of teaching and learning.

At the core of this article is what can be done for those students who, affected by "poverty, domestic violence, ongoing family conflict, and racism" and harassment by "classmates for being 'gay'" (p. 246), occupy the very subjectivities inscribed on a daily basis—inside as well as outside schools—as not worth living. After a recent suicide crisis, the dangers of schoolyard conversations are evoked through a description of students who began to act as if it were "'cool' to be depressed" and to perceive self-murder as a "'viable' way out of a problem" (p. 246). Foregrounding the difficult, intractable knowledge that suicide elicits as the disease-like spreading of unbearable ideas, they look for ways to "deflate the alarm" with a "'loving response' to children in despair" enacted through suicide talks that also attend to "mental health facts" (p. 248). The aim is the creation of "authentic new models of learning" (p. 250) through the use of new therapeutic structures that operate at the between spaces of conventional knowledge to enable new ways of thinking with the capacity to reshape children's realities. Affective understanding, personal experience, and professional and bureaucratic reason are conjoined in the pursuit of a praxis without guarantees, an orientation toward the stammerings, breakdowns, and ruptures of teaching and learning as a way to carry forward within the intractable, difficult knowledge suicide evokes. Here the very terms for learning to think and do otherwise in regards to curricular practice are not found in reductions, unities, and orders but in connections, multiplicities, and performances.

Counterdiscourses in Curriculum: Policy, Mediation, and New Pragmatism

The fourth point we became aware of was that curriculum theorizing must be put to work in new times. Tracing the ways conservative restoration has fostered an anti-intellectual and antiprofessional common sense among the general citizenry regarding public education, William Pinar (2004) suggests "curriculum theorists work to create conceptual montages for the public-school teacher who understands that positionality as aspiring to create a 'public' space" (p. 33). To engage his point, we suggest these efforts at reconstitution, in what has been termed post-reconceptualization in the moment of our now (Pinar, 2004; Wright, 2005); this attempt involves a policy turn as part of a new pragmatism, with particular attention to the interstices of space, place, identity, and practice as offering compelling laboratories for mapping out counterdiscourses in the field.

Informative in making this move is Elizabeth Ellsworth's *Places of Learning: Media, Architecture, Pedagogy* (2004), where she argues for a shift from circumscribed definitions of pedagogy as already made knowledge toward knowing that focuses on the circumstances, processes, environments, and conditions of meaning in the making. In contrast to the inert bodies of knowledge revealed in state and federal documents that focus on what is known about suicide and turn the singularity of the event into a thing, Ellsworth advocates an effort to think relationally: to explore and discuss the character of innumerable realities in ways that recognize what it means to live in impermanence, as a being invested with a body "continuously and radically in relation with the world, with others, and with what we make of them" (p. 4).

Ellsworth is making a call for a new pragmatism that takes into account transitional spaces and employs affect and sensation to make meaning out of what is felt primordially in the body, understood as "rhythmical experience" (Kennedy, 2000, p. 31) within a "complex set of intersecting forces" (p. 29). Grounding pedagogy in something other than phenomenological accounts, theories are continuously faced with the unintentional and involuntary experiences of what she terms the learning self. In this explication, Ellsworth re-fuses pedagogy in ways where individuals do not have experiences or experience a body, but rather are experiences and bodies whose emotions and sensations are key to understanding material engagements prior to language and subjectivity. Here thinking and doing otherwise is predicated upon circumstances and capacities for confronting the limits of knowing and engaging what cannot through contemporary disciplinary lenses be made into concepts. Emphasizing experimentation in thought and complication of matters, rather than pedagogy that claims to represent knowledge or to save or perfect its students, the intent is not to locate identifiable subjects, objects, and agents. Rather, the will in curriculum and pedagogy might be considered simultaneously as "resonating desires distributed *across the social body* [italics in original]—across different people, practices, and disciplines" (Ellsworth, 2004, p. 28). In such a pragmatism, against the circumscribed practices of state and federal policy making that focus on acquisition of knowledge, teaching and learning involves diffuse and imminent yearning to invent, design, and actualize forms of expression and circumstances for knowing and doing that might engender new understanding.

"Staging pedagogy as the field of emergence of the learning self" (p. 28), Ellsworth envisions thinking, teaching, and learning through Deleuzian notions of affect, sensation, and movement (Massumi, 2002) as experiences before language and subjectivity that might be put to work in curriculum, policy, and education. A focus on the mutant sensibilities and new intensities between people as relations that involve movement, process, and the body but not written word or spoken language, shows the learning self in the making is viewed as possibly more significant to a reconfiguration of self-understanding and perspectives on the world than large-scale political ventures and state and federal interventions. Casting doubt upon the effectiveness of macrolevel policymaking and strategic planning, the aim is to mix up the players and defy the rules so that new concepts can emerge and new problems can be detected. Here is an affirmation of theory and practice made workable in a post-reconceptualization that confronts questions impossible to answer within current regimes of meaning; and failures and breakdowns in experiences craft remedies that the very teaching and learning-in-the-making enables the creation of understanding, reflection, and action. This is research-informed action as something other than experience translated into categorical expressions, then converted into policy, and finally turned over to practice.

Counterdiscourses: Toward Something Other Than What Is

As a last point, we offer three counterdiscourses to the U.S. and British suicide reports and plans that allow us to examine what it might mean to bring curriculum's "fund of doubt" (see Grumet, 1988) to bear upon the conventional storylines of state and federal practice. Working the ruins of state and federal policy under tactical erasure, this is an attempt to think of policy without guarantees after suicide policy has been met with deconstruction.

Deploying Autobiography

According to Pinar (1994), *currere* is an autobiographical method for the study of self-reflexivity taken up in four movements: regressive, progressive, analytic, and synthetic. A first-person iteration of culture, materiality, and historical interpretation, autobiography involves individuals becoming activists in the reformation of their own interior elements. Recognizing the national, regional, and social group identities within each individual, surfacing the stories we tell ourselves, what is at work involves projects of self-awareness where curriculum is reclaimed "as we have lived it" and conceptual frameworks and descriptions are tested "against the evidence of our experience" (Grumet, 1999, p. 25). Self-knowledge, subjective sphere, and collective witnessing all contribute to the sense of satisfaction and completion that once known becomes the measure of which various educational experiences bring us close to a sense of passionate inwardness as the very terms for political engagement. Such knowledge is as much about resisting governmentality by promoting restructured subjectivities as it is "opposition against secrecy, deformation, and mystifying representations imposed on people" (Foucault, 1983, p. 212). Contrary to critics who characterize autobiography as self-indulgent or narcissistic, a politics of ourselves is very much about attending "to social, outer issues addressed by traditional pedagogies with greater, deeper awareness" (Doll, 2000, p. xi).

In *What is Curriculum Theory?* Pinar (2004) focuses his attention on the present political situation of teachers. He explains that to describe the reconceptualized field of curriculum studies as exhibiting signs of flight from practice is to believe in a technocratic rationality that misrepresents how curriculum theorizing concerns "the educational experience, especially (but not only) how that experience is encoded in the school curriculum" (p. 20) as opposed to "an instrumental and calculative concept of intelligence" (p. 29). Positioning curriculum theory as the passage through autobiography and social psychoanalysis, these "provocative conceptual tools" dedicated to a primordial "labor of remembering" (p. 57) are both the perils and potentialities of the field. Critically examining manifest and latent meanings, exploring the content of language for conscious and unconscious significations, and analyzing the political, economic, and social significance of such interpretations, these are the pursuits of educators seeking to understand teaching and learning as human experiences in the making. Rather than lacking in practicality and application, curriculum theory constitutes a "need for continuous reconceptualization of the flow of experience" that includes "theorizing by practicing educators" (Schubert, 1992, p. 238). Here the very ways curriculum studies "folds in, on, and around (in a Deleuzian way) other cultures, knowledges, and identities" (Miller, 2005, p. 250) and the ways in which these elements enfold curriculum content and practice within actual circumstances embody the discursivity appropriate to the field.

The debates over whether this is a "form of praxis" (Pinar, 1999, p. 366) or "flight from the practical" (Wraga & Helbowitsh, 2003, p. 427) lay bare an exhausted rhetoric in the move to discompose the theory–practice gap. The reconceptualized field does not respond to the calls of empiricism, classification, and unification, the traditional measures for appropriate curriculum design, yet the work is inclusive of praxis equal to other historical and contemporary discourses within the field. Curriculum studies is no longer "moribund" (Schwab, 1969, p.1); radicalized notions of autobiography are not "a repetition of old and familiar knowledge in new languages" (p. 4) or departures from "the use of principles and methods to talk about them" (pp. 3–4). This work does not aim to build a repertoire of empirical facts, measure worth by the ability to extend what has been done before, or engineer transferable models for improving students' performance on standardized tests. Eschewing knowledge as transparent, complete, and cohesive, radicalized autobiography enacts "a method for enlarging, occupying, and building the space of mediation" (Pinar, 1994, p. 217) that surfaces the "modes of relation to others our stories imply" (p. 218). Such understanding is about interrogating representative consciousness, the representations that get produced and circulated with claims of their capacity to stand in for the thoughts, ideas, and feelings of others. Here we begin to think differently about the consequences of autobiography in regards to deconstruction of representations. As Deleuze points out, challenges to representative knowledge have been well theorized while there has been a failure to move any further in mapping the implications: "to appreciate the theoretical fact that only those directly concerned can speak in a practical way on their own behalf" (Foucault, 1989/1996, p. 76).

Regarding dominant state and federal reasoning on suicide prevention and intervention strategies, the privileging of "endless derivations of Tylerian curriculum development" (Reynolds & Webber, 2004, p. 6) is based on an ongoing "struggle over the symbolic order, over how the story of 'normal' will be told" (p. 5) wedded to political maneuverings that require and generate these particular forms of discourse. Less about formative ideas on their way to established concepts or the losses suffered under the weight of curriculum design, autobiography is about claims to knowledge and understanding as both non-discursive and discursive occurrences. Here "currere of marginality" with its "(non)categories" and opposition to binary logic and technocratic reasoning becomes a way of "excavating excluded stories" in the search for "alternative meanings and ways of being in the world" (Edgerton, 1996, p. 39). Autobiography emerges as a counterdiscourse that troubles representations within policy reform—particularly oppositional language or discourse that synthesizes difference into the same—through displacement, refusal, and deferral.

Analyzing Power/Knowledge

Revisiting Foucault's work on biopower in preparation for graduate courses we will teach later in the year, we were awed by his framing of suicide as a form of resistance to the proliferating techniques of power that have developed since the 17th century. Upholding this will toward destruction as "difficult to explain as being due to particular circumstances or individual accidents" (Foucault, 1978/1990, p. 139), his interest is in what might be discursively afforded by way of maintaining the singularity of suicide, occurrences thought particularly informative because they operate beyond the "diverse techniques for achieving the subjugation of bodies and the control of populations" (p. 140). Here suicide is a product of the dark underside of governmental attempts to foster the life of the population.

As an effect of biopower, this normalizing society that distributes the living among the realms of worth, utility, and value in the name of evidence and efficiency is linked to conservative political responses toward the reconfigured procedures of power that are a part of innumerable symbolic and material shifts. In what might be termed a reaction to the continuous disruption and redistribution of the order of traditional episteme by way of an affirmation of the right to think differently—postcolonial theory, queer theory, critical race theory, etc.—this is a politics marked by conflation, regulation, and hierarchization in pursuit of a definitive system of rules and procedures. Here suicide policy and intervention and prevention strategies are positioned among struggles between the plentitude of individual possibility and the very systems bent on controlling and rendering human life productive to expanding the capacities of the state. Suicide points to lives that constantly escape techniques of surveillance and administration among the ongoing deployment of tactics aimed at their incorporation.

The risks associated with suicide policy and planning that focuses on "permanent controls, extremely meticulous orderings of space, indeterminate medical or psychological examinations" (Foucault, 1978/1990, p. 145) on the one hand, and "statistical assessments, and interventions aimed at the entire social body" (p. 146) on the other, involve the elimination of opportunities for thinking and doing otherwise in formulating a more workable praxis, one that heeds Foucauldian critical activism where, "If everything is dangerous, then we always have something to do" (Foucault, 1983, pp. 231–232). Against a backdrop composed of challenges to unified theories, grand narratives, and customary hierarchies via work in poststructuralism (Cherryholmes, 1988; Daignault & Gauthier, 1982); feminist theory (Grumet, 1988; Lather, 1991; Miller, 2005); autobiography (Goodson & Walker, 1991; Miller, 1998; Pinar, 2004); and more recently critical geography (Helfenbein, 2006); Black feminism and hip-hop (Guillory, 2006); postcolonialism and feminist theory (Asher, 2006); and poststate explorations (Snaza, 2006), scholarship that has significantly reconfigured the field in which curriculum scholars operate. The epistemological investments used to frame suicide prevention and intervention strategies begin to look like an assault on difference and multiculturalism.

At the nexus of schooling, curriculum, and state and federal policy, the continued privileging of empiricism, positivism, and essentialism for understanding difference despite the proliferation of myriad counterdiscourses only further illustrates Foucault's point that power/knowledge is less a structure, institution, or an individual capacity than "the name one attributes to a complex strategical situation in a particular society" (Foucault, 1978/1990, p. 93). This recycling of decade-old policy models, when confronted with all the variety in the world, can be read as an attack on those who, alienated and suffering, are the very subjects in need of a different course of action. Foucault (1978/1991) points out that strategies capable of challenging governmentality and biopolitics involve "determining problems, unleashing them, revealing them" through frameworks of "such complexity" that they silence the "prophets and legislators" who purport to "speak for others" (p. 159). In the stillness that follows such tactical interventions, "the complexity of the problem" might appear in "connection with people's lives" (p. 159).

Enlivened by debates over what constitutes meritorious work in the field (Hlebowitsh, 1999; Morrison, 2004; Reynolds, 2003; Wraga, 1999), what has transpired in the interaction of Foucauldian thought and curriculum studies has been concepts characterized by ontological stammering, epistemological humility, and the proliferation of possible meaning that brings question to the very rationale that drives prevention and intervention strategies. Governmentality, biopolitics, and technologies of surveillance are the ideas that brought an end to the innocence of any efforts to produce and circulate knowledge neutral in its effects. In response to attempts to transfer a normative model to both research on and strategies to combat suicide, Foucault points to "the dispersion of the points of choice that the discourse leaves free" (1971/1972, p. 36) as a way to move through particular regimes of meaning. Here "reanimating already existing themes" and "arousing opposed strategies" of existing concepts open up possibilities to "play different games" with the professional and bureaucratic discourses we have been given (p. 37).

Martin's (1988) interview with Foucault is particularly instructive in this capacity. As a part of this exchange, Foucault described his own scholarship as a reaction to the "breach between social history and the history of ideas" (p. 14). The former was characterized as intended to describe how humans act without thought while the latter was intended to describe how humans think without action. As Foucault points out, the problem with the division is that "everybody both acts and thinks" (p. 14). Accordingly, his analysis attempts to illustrate the relationship between two seemingly disparate domains of theory and practice where the "ways people act or react" are drawn into association with "a way of thinking" that has its origins in "tradition" (p. 14). In these intellectual investigations into scientific discourse and social sensibility, political action becomes an effort "to show all the factors that interacted and the reactions of people" through methods that surface how a "new way of thinking took place" within a particular historical period (p. 14). Here is a form of praxis that is less about being in the trenches or pontificating in the ivory tower and more about putting ideas to work in illuminating the ways customs and rituals shape our interactions so we might locate practices of opposition that cannot be fixed in one place or settled down.

Using Queer Studies

Against attempts to produce hard-line knowledge about suicide and a reliable, conclusive, and authoritative intervention and prevention plan, queer studies provisions antiessentialist theories where malleability is key and frameworks and strategies are complicated by their own exclusions, gaps, and breakdowns in the ability to represent (Kirsch, 2001). Queer theory is an assemblage of resources deployed in the exploration and interrogation of normative practices with the idea that literal structures can be deranged through highlighting the complexities of relationality and difference. Here intervention is the strange fruit of catachresis: improper metaphors that are obliged to exceed the capacities of an existing referent work to jam the hierarchies of knowledge. As Villarejo (2005) contends, "queer is but one name, hurled back with pride, for social abjection, exclusion, marginalization, and degradation; it provides, by this logic, but one opening toward freedom" (pp. 69–70). Her interest in contemporary efforts "to rewrite queer studies as a discourse about race and class, not simply as a bounded discourse about gender and sexuality" (p. 70) is, in part, based in cultural and material hybridity (Cover, 2004). Villarejo's concern is that heteronormative knowledge regarding African-American life has been so naturalized that we fail to see the ways exclusion and exploitation are configured through as well as dependent upon the categorical values of gender and sexuality. Academic systems of knowledge production are intended to "systematize," methods are "formulated" to provide accurate representations, and pressure is applied to present the meaning taken from investigations into the symbolic and material practices of subjugated groups under "the same terms in which these [practices] have been pathologized" (p. 74). In comparison to this bounded reasoning, the "perverting logic" of nonheteronormative formations, "through the very refusal of subjects to properly normalize themselves" (Britzman, 1995, p. 157), confounds the rationality of state and federal documents "that function as social policy" (Villarejo, 2005, p. 73).

Reason requires ordering discourses, relational hierarchies, and evaluative frameworks within a network of identifications incapable of reading "perversion as agency" (p. 74). What Edelman (2004) terms the "collective fantasy" of "reproductive futurism" highlights the unreasonable and ironic character of queer theory (p. 28). Here the demystification of queerness, and therefore sexuality, in a fashion similar to liberal rationality, dissolves the very investments that give meaning to social order "by doing away with its underlying and sustaining libidinal fantasies" (p. 28). What we are left to work out of the ruins of normativity are antiessentialist theories that offer "ways to fly with language and desire away from homology and continuity" (Villarejo, 2005, p. 75), a series of tactics to avoid enclosure in the "logic of the symptom" (p. 70). The refusal to straighten up disjunctures and transgressions confronts the very conditions for formulating proper policy.

Questions over what constitutes queer studies abound inside as well as outside the academy. Extending Britzman's (1995) inquiry regarding "what is required to refuse the unremarked and obdurately unremarkable straight education curriculum" (p. 151), queer insights into the categorical failures and disruptions the subject of difference produces offer specific techniques of disavowal derived from a twofold gesture: movement toward the continuous resignification of rude subjects and improper theories as a method for challenging propriety alongside the interrogation of the very terms under which identities and theories get constructed. Studying the problem of where thinking stops as a strategy for getting at "the unmarked criteria" that dismiss or valorize a "particular mode of thought" or "insistence upon the real" (p. 156) makes possible the reimagination of the conditions under which policy writes bodies in and out of existence. Queer studies pushes for exceeding the binary oppositions of those positioned at-risk and not at-risk for suicide while retaining historically and contextually specific analyses of culturally and materially relevant differences. Equally telling, these accounts explain how abstract structures of atomization and alienation work in concrete ways, in local instances, as well as on a myriad of social, political, economic, and psychic registers.

Reconcluding: Returning to the Beginning to Think Again, Differently

> It is not surprising that suicide...became, in the course of the nineteenth century, one of the first conducts to enter into the sphere of sociological analysis; it testified to the individual and private right to die, at the borders and in the interstices of power that was exercised over life. (Foucault, 1978/1990, pp. 138–139)

As a way to mark an end, we return to the three questions we used to frame the extremely debilitating circumstances of the present moment: the near exclusive emphasis on life-affirming and emancipatory aspects of understanding; the inability to put research on suicide and survivorship in the service of life; and the continued privileging of modernist perspectives on theory, research, practice, and policy despite their inability to make an impact, even by their own methods of assessment. This is governmentality made possible by "infinitesimal mechanisms," each with its own "history, trajectory, techniques, and tactics" being "invested, colonized, utilized, involuted, transformed, displaced, and extended" by "general mechanisms" and "forms of domination" (Foucault, 1972/1980, p. 99). In suggesting this, we realize we risk total enclosure in the midst of efforts to move past debates over what knowledge is of most worth and calls for disconceptualizing the theory–practice dichotomy (Appelbaum, 2006). Preferable to an Althusserian structuralism that rules out agency (Thompson, 1978), this "swarming effect" (Vincent & Tomlinson, 1997) only strengthens our attraction to what Foucault (2001) termed fearless speech as a way to move toward a "language that tries to speak truth to power" (Said, 1994, p. xvi) by challenging the "stereotypes and reductive categories that are so limiting to human thought and communication" (p. xi). Through conducting an aperçu of the word *parrhesia*, Foucault offered a number of examples of the relationship one might have to danger, criticism, and moral law to allow for voicing the "truth which threatens the majority" (p. 18) in spite of some danger to oneself. The truth-teller, a fearless speaker, has a "critical and pedagogical role to play" that involves the transformation of "the will of citizens" (p. 82) in ways where their desires and interests become the force that cannot be endured by the codes and rituals designed to give continuity and regularity to the processes of the state.

As curriculum theorists bent on shifting the debates over what constitutes theory and practice in the field, we locate in these policy and planning documents the effects of power in a conservative restoration that renounces over 30 years of reconceptualization and critique as a move toward thinking teaching and learning under terms made possible by its very disarticulation. To begin to think about the seemingly disparate relationships among curriculum, policy, youth culture, and suicide, what we have presented here might be viewed as a dimension of Lacanian *jouissance*, the unruly force of pleasure found through forms of resistance in excess of acceptance, affirmation, or inclusion. In this, we "[open] up curriculum to rude bodies" (Taubman, 2004, p. 21) through that which "resists, subverts, and eludes control or domestication or easy analysis. It is, one might say, the life of a rude body" unwilling to surrender to the adoption of communal standards for reason or an attitude of tolerance for other points of view (p. 25). The unreasonable body sees as the primary aim of curriculum theorizing "taking a stand" that "brooks no disagreement" and "comes closer to the Lacanian drive than desire" (p. 27), as opposed to the reasonable body that "tolerates others' views, is courteous in discussion, does not go to extremes, and is modest about the certitude of one's own beliefs" (p. 19). Here disorder, irrationality, and uncontrollability interrupt the logic that often accompanies curriculum development and policy making to pose difficult questions about the politics of yearning in practices toward freedom (Greene, 1995/2000).

In closing, the curriculum debates persist with no less urgency; the tug-of-war between narrow definitions of curriculum development and policy design and increasingly expansive investigations involving curriculum theorizing and critical policy studies remain at the heart of what to do about the very real and pressing problem of suicide. Regarding the appropriate mix of structuralism, formalism, and proceduralism, on the one hand, and criticism, deconstruction, and disavowal, on the other, there is little common ground to be found among government officials, professional agents, health educators, and curriculum scholars except the recognition that all this teaching and learning, like all educational experiences that take place over a lifetime, is the very stuff of making curriculum practice and the practice of curriculum making. Shifting the terms of operation toward the unsurety that any remedy can provide a solution sufficient to the problem does not, however, assume paralysis. Rather, such reconfigurations anticipate the very pertinacity of suicide as an issue and the ongoing failure of efforts to represent it as the very way to move through the structure of the situation and toward different forms of knowledge production so that policy and intervention and prevention strategies might be thought about differently. Foucault (1978/1991) points to this as the "transformation of reality" made possible by those who, "recognizing the relations of power in which they are implicated, have decided to resist or escape them" (p. 174).

Notes

1. For a cogent articulation of the significance of the life stories of suicide survivors, see Sanderson (1998).
2. See the 1000 Deaths Writing Project. Retrieved November 19, 2005 from http://www.1000deaths.com/library/writing/1000deathswriting.html

3. This term refers to Maxine Greene's (1995/2000) premise that human beings define themselves in relation to the projects with which they become involved and, in so doing, can develop heightened consciousness regarding the choice of actions that lend to self-formation and understanding.

4. After remaining stable from 1990 to 1995, the suicide rate decreased slightly by 2000. Suicide remained, however, the third most common cause of death among youth ages 15 to to 19 from 2000 to more recent reporting in 2004.

5. The notion of a postsocialist society captures the current negative public posture toward socialist ideals, including social safety nets and services, and a general loss of the unified capacity for progressive social change (Fraser, 1997).

6. Yellow Ribbon Suicide Prevention Program, Presentation, Workshop, In-Service and Training information (n.d.). *Be-A-Link! Gatekeeper Training.* Retrieved December 2, 2005 from http://www.yellowribbon.org/Presentation_&_Trainings.htm

7. Light for Life Foundation (n.d.).

8. Regardless of whether titled a report, plan, or strategy, many of the various documents represented in this article contain some analysis of contemporary conceptions of suicide, current programs in place, and strategies for future intervention and prevention efforts. For this reason, policy makers, researchers, and educators interchange terms like *reports, plans,* and *strategies.*

9. On September 16, 2002, Britain's Minister of State for Health, Jacqui Smith, released the first ever national suicide prevention strategy as a way to actualize a 20% reduction in the mortality rate from suicide and undetermined injury by 2010, the goal established in the *National Standards, Local Action: Health and Social Care Standards and Planning Framework 2005/06–2007/08.*

References

Appelbaum, P. (2006). Disconceptualizing curriculum: Is there a next in the generational text? *Journal of Curriculum Theorizing, 18*(1), 7–19.

Apple, M. W. (2001). *Educating the "right" way: Markets, standards, god, and inequality.* New York: Routledge.

Apple, M. W. (2003). *The state and the politics of knowledge.* London: Routledge Falmer.

Aronowitz, S. (2001). *The knowledge factory: Dismantling the corporate university and creating true higher learning.* Boston: Beacon.

Aseltine, R. H., & DeMartino, R. (2004). An outcome evaluation of the SOS suicide prevention program. *American Journal of Public Health, 94*(3), 446–451.

Asher, N. (2006, February). *Decolonizing curriculum.* Paper presented at the Articulating the Present (Next) Moments in Curriculum Studies: The Post-Reconceptualization Generation conference, West Lafayette, Indiana.

Babb, P., Haezewindt, P., & Marin, J. (Eds.). (2004). *Focus on social inequalities.* London: Office of National Statistics.

Bennett, A., & Kahn-Harris, K. (2004). *After subculture: Critical studies in contemporary youth culture.* New York: Palgrave Macmillan.

Bhugra, D. (2004). *Culture and self-harm: Attempted suicide in South Asians in London.* New York: Psychology Press.

Bhugra, D., Baldwin, D. S., Desai, M., & Jacob, K. S. (1999). Attempted suicide in West London, II. Inter-group comparisons. *Psychological Medicine, 29*(11), 1131–1139.

Boyles, D. (2000). *American education and corporations: The free market goes to school.* New York: Falmer.

Britzman, D. (2002). The death of curriculum. In W. E. Doll & N. Gough (Eds.), *Curriculum visions* (pp. 92–101). New York: Lang.

Britzman, D. (1995). Is there a queer pedagogy? Or, stop reading straight. *Educational Theory, 45*(2), 151–165.

Cherryholmes, C. (1988). *Power and criticism: Poststructural investigations in education.* New York: Teachers College.

Cholbi, M. J. (2002). Suicide intervention and non-Kantian theory. *Journal of Applied Philosophy, 19*(3), 245–259.

Clark, T. N., & Lipset, S. M. (Eds.). (2001). *The breakdown of class politics: A debate on post-industrial stratification.* Baltimore: Johns Hopkins University.

CNN.com (2002, May 7). Teachers feel stress of high-stakes testing — Results can make or break some educators' careers. Retrieved February 2, 2008, from http://cnnstudentnews.cnn.com/2002/fyi/teachers.ednews/05/07/testing.pressure.ap/index.html

Colorado Department of Public Health and Environment. (1998, November). *Suicide prevention and intervention plan.* Denver, CO: Author.

Colorado Trust. (February, 2002). *Suicide in Colorado.* Denver, CO: Author.

Cover, R. (2004). Material/queer theory: Performativity, subjectivity, and affinity-based struggles in the culture of late capitalism. *Rethinking Marxism, 16*(3), 293–310.

Czarniawska, N. (1997). *Narrating the organization: Dramas of institutional identity.* Chicago: University of Chicago.

Daignault, J., & Gauthier, C. (1982). The indecent curriculum machine: Who's afraid of Sisyphe? *Journal of Curriculum Theorizing, 4*(1), 177–196.

Deflem, M. (1997). Surveillance and criminal statistics: Historical foundations of governmentality. *Studies in Law, Politics and Society, 17,* 149–184.

Doll, M. (2000). *Like letters in running water: A mythopoetics of curriculum.* New York: Lang.

Doll, W. E., & Gough, N. (Eds.). (2002). *Curriculum visions.* New York: Lang.

Durkheim, E. (2002). *Suicide.* New York: Routledge. (Original work published 1951)

Edelman, L. (2004). *No future: Queer theory and the death drive.* Durham, NC: Duke University.

Edgerton, S. H. (1996). *Translating the curriculum: Multiculturalism into cultural studies.* New York: Routledge.

Elkind, D. (2001). *The hurried child: Growing up too fast too soon.* Cambridge, MA: Perseus.

Ellsworth, E. (2004). *Places of learning: Media, architecture, pedagogy.* New York: Routledge.

Firestone, W. A., Schorr, R. Y., & Monfils, L. F. (Eds.). (2004). *The ambiguity of teaching to the test: Standards, assessment, and educational reform.* Mahwah, NJ: Erlbaum.

Foucault, M. (1972). *The archeology of knowledge* (A. M. Sheridan-Smith, Trans.). New York: Routledge. (Original work published 1971)

Foucault, M. (1980). *Power/knowledge: Selected interviews and other writings 1972–1977* (C. Gordon, L. Marshall, J. Mepham, & K. Soper, Trans.). New York: Pantheon Books. (Original work published 1972)

Foucault, M. (1983). On the genealogy of ethics: An overview of work in progress. In H. L. Dreyfus & P. Rabinow (Eds.), *Michel Foucault: Beyond structuralism and hermeneutics* (2nd ed., pp. 229–252). Chicago: University of Chicago.

Foucault, M. (1984). What is enlightenment? In P. Rabinow (Ed.), *The Foucault reader* (pp. 32–50). New York: Pantheon Books.

Foucault, M. (1990). *The history of sexuality: Vol. 1. An introduction* (R. Hurley, Trans.). New York: Vintage Books. (Original work published 1978)

Foucault, M. (1991). Remarks on Marx: Conversations with Duccio Trombadori (R. J. Goldstein & J. Cascaito, Trans.). New York: Semiotext(e). (Original work published 1978)

Foucault, M. (1994). *The order of things: An archaeology of human sciences.* New York: Vintage Books.

Foucault, M. (1996). *Foucault live, interviews, 1961–1984* (S. Lotringer, Ed.; L. Hochroch & J. Johnston, Trans.). New York: Semiotext(e). (Original work published 1989)

Foucault, M. (1997). Security, territory, population. In P. Rabinow (Ed.), *Ethics: Subjectivity and truth* (pp. 67–71). New York: New Press.

Foucault, M. (2001). *Fearless speech.* New York: Semiotext(e).

Fraser, N. (1989). *Unruly practices: Power, discourse, and gender in contemporary social theory.* Minneapolis: University of Minnesota.

Fraser, N. (1997). *Justice interruptus: Critical reflections on the "post-socialist" condition.* New York: Routledge.

Fraser, N. (2002). Recognition without ethics. In S. Lash & M. Featherstone (Eds.), *Recognition and difference: Politics, identity, multiculture* (pp. 21–42). Thousand Oaks, CA: Sage.

Fraser, N., & Honneth, A. (2003). *Redistribution or recognition? A political-philosophical exchange*. London: Verso.

Giddens, A. (1991). *Modernity and self-identity: Self and society in the late modern age*. Cambridge, MA: Polity Press.

Giddens, A. (2000). *The third way and its critics*. Cambridge, MA: Polity Press.

Giroux, H. (1998). Nymphet fantasies: Child beauty pageants and the politics of innocence. *Social Text, 57*, 31–53.

Giroux, H. (2000). *Stealing innocence: Youth, corporate power, and the politics of culture*. New York: Palgrave Macmillan.

Giroux, H. (2004). *The abandoned generation: Democracy beyond the culture of fear*. New York: Palgrave Macmillan.

Goodson, I., & Walker, R. (1991). *Biography, identity, schooling: Episodes in educational research*. Bristol, PA: Falmer.

Gratz, D. (2000). High standards for whom? *Phi Delta Kappa, 81*(9), 681–687.

Greene, M. (2000). *Releasing the imagination: Essays on education, the arts, and social change*. San Francisco: Jossey-Bass. (Original work published in 1995)

Grumet, M. (1988). *Bitter milk: Women and teaching*. Amherst: University of Massachusetts Press.

Grumet, M. (1999). Autobiography and reconceptualization. In W. Pinar (Ed.), *Contemporary curriculum discourses: Twenty years of JCT* (pp. 24–30). New York: Lang. (Original work published in 1980)

Guillory, N. (2006, February). *Schoolin' women: Hip hop pedagogies of Black women rappers*. Paper presented at the Articulating the Present (Next) Moments in Curriculum Studies: The Post-Reconceptualization Generation conference, West Lafayette, Indiana.

Guo, B., & Harstell, C. (2002). *Efficacy of suicide prevention programs for children and youth*. Alberta, Canada: Alberta Heritage Foundation for Medical Research.

Harden, A., Rees, R., Shepherd, J., Brunton, G., Oliver, S., & Oakley, A. (2001). *Young people and mental health: A systematic review of research on barriers and facilitators*. London: Evidence for Policy and Practice Information and Co-ordinating Centre (EPPI-Centre).

Hayden, D. C., & Lauer, P. (2000). Prevalence of suicide programs in schools and roadblocks to implementation. *Suicide and Life Threatening Behavior, 30*(3), 239–251.

Helfenbein, R. (2006). Economies of identity: Cultural studies and curriculum of making place. *Journal of Curriculum Theorizing, 22*(2), 87–100.

Hlebowitsh, P. (1999). The burdens of the new curricularist. *Curriculum Inquiry, 29*(3), 343–354.

Kelley, R. D. G. (1998). *Yo' mama's disfunktional!: Fighting the culture wars in urban America*. Boston: Beacon.

Kennedy, B. M. (2000). *Deleuze and cinema: The aesthetics of sensation*. Edinburgh, Scotland: Edinburgh University Press.

Kincheloe, J., & McLaren, P. (2005). Critical theory and qualitative research. In N. K. Denzin & Y. S. Lincoln (Eds.), *The Sage handbook of qualitative research* (pp. 303–342). New York: Sage.

Kincheloe, J., & Steinberg, S. (1993). A tentative description of post-formal thinking: The critical confrontation with cognitive theory. *Harvard Educational Review, 63*(3), 296–329.

Kirsch, M. H. (2001). *Queer theory and social change*. New York: Routledge.

Kochanek, K. D., Murphy, S. L., Anderson, R. N., & Scott, C. (2004). Deaths: Final data for 2002 (DHHS Publication No. PHS 2005–1120). *National Vital Statistics Reports, 53*(5). Hyattsville, MD: National Center for Health Statistics.

Lankshear, C., & Knobel, M. (2004). *A handbook for teacher research*. New York: Open University.

Latham, R. (2002). *Consuming youth: Vampires, cyborgs, and the culture of consumption*. Chicago: University of Chicago.

Lather, P. (1991). *Getting smart: Feminist research and pedagogy with/in the postmodern*. New York: Routledge.

Lather, P. (1998). Critical pedagogy and its complicities: A praxis of stuck places. *Educational Theory, 48*(4), 487–498.

Lather, P. (2004a, March). *Getting lost: Feminist efforts toward a double(d) science* [abstract]. Paper presented as part of the Women's Studies Feminist Scholar Series, Pennsylvania State University, University Park, PA.

Lather, P. (2004b). This is your father's paradigm: Government intrusion and the case of qualitative research in education. *Qualitative Inquiry, 10*(1), 15–34.

Lather, P. (2005, April). *The foundations/cultural studies nexus: An emerging movement in the education field.* Paper presented at the meeting of the American Educational Research Association, Montreal, Canada.

Light for Life Foundation. (n.d.). *Yellow Ribbon Suicide Prevention Program.* [Brochure]. Westminster, CO: Author.

Lincoln, Y. S., & Guba. E. G. (2005). Paradigmatic controversies, contradictions, and emerging confluence. In N. K. Denzin & Y. K. Lincoln (Eds.), *The Sage handbook of qualitative research* (pp. 191–216). New York: Sage.

Mallan, K., & Pearce, S. (Eds.). (2003). *Youth cultures: Texts, images, and identities.* Westport, CT: Praeger.

Martin, R. (1988). Truth, power, self: An interview with Michel Foucault. In L. H. Martin, H. Gutman, & R. H. Hutton (Eds.), *Technologies of the self: A seminar with Michel Foucault* (pp. 9–15). Amherst, MA: Massachusetts Institute of Technology.

Massumi, B. (2002). *Parables for the virtual: Movement, affect, sensation.* Durham, NC: Duke University.

Mazza, J. J. (1997). School-based suicide prevention programs: Are they effective? *School Psychology Review, 26*, 382–396.

McIntosh, J. L. (2004). *U.S.A. suicide: 2002 official final data* (Report prepared for the American Association of Suicidology). Retrieved April 15, 2005 from http://www.suicidepreventioncenter.org/files/2002datapgvl.pdf

McNeil, L. (2000). *Contradictions of school reform: Educational costs of standardized testing.* London: Routledge Falmer.

Meier, D. (2000). *Will standards save public education?* Boston: Beacon Press

Meier, D., & Wood, G. (Eds.). (2004). *Many children left behind: How the No Child Left Behind Act is damaging our children and our schools.* Boston: Beacon.

Miller, J. L. (1998). Autobiography as a queer curriculum practice. In W. F. Pinar (Ed.), *Queer theory in education* (pp. 365–373). Mahwah, NJ: Erlbaum.

Miller, J. (2005). *Sounds of silence breaking: Women, autobiography, curriculum.* New York: Lang.

Minois, G. (2001). *History of suicide: Voluntary death in western culture* (L. G. Cochrane, Trans.). Baltimore: Johns Hopkins University.

Molnar, A. (2005). *School commercialism: From democratic ideal to market commodity.* New York: Routledge.

Mondesir, D. (2000). *Moderating effects of culture on suicide risk factors.* Bloomington, IN: Authorhouse.

Morrison, K. (2004). The poverty of curriculum theory: A critique of Wraga and Hlebowitsh. *Journal of Curriculum Studies, 36*(4), 487–494.

National Governors Association Center for Best Practices. (2005, April). *Youth suicide prevention: Strengthening state policies and school-based strategies.* Washington, DC: Author.

Noddings, N. (2006). *Critical lessons: What our schools should teach.* New York: Cambridge University.

Pinar, W. (1992). Cries and whispers. In W. Pinar & W. Reynolds (Eds.), *Understanding curriculum as phenomenological and deconstructed text* (pp. 92–102). New York: Teachers College Press.

Pinar, W. (1994). *Autobiography, politics, and sexuality: Essays in curriculum theory, 1972–1992.* New York: Lang.

Pinar, W. (1999). Not burdens—breakthroughs. *Curriculum Inquiry, 29*(3), 365–367.

Pinar, W. (2004). *What is curriculum theory?* Mahwah, NJ: Erlbaum.

Reynolds, W. (2003). Rejoinder: Debate, nostalgia, ressentiment. *Journal of Curriculum Studies, 35*(4), 445–451.

Reynolds, W., & Webber, J. (Eds.). (2004). *Expanding curriculum theory: Dis/positions and lines of flight.* Mahwah, NJ: Erlbaum.

Romano-Dwyer, L., & Carley, G. (2005). Schoolyard conversations: Influencing suicide talk in an elementary school community. *Social Work Education, 24*(2), 245–250.

Said, E. (1996). *Representations of the intellectual: The 1993 Reith lectures.* New York: Vintage.

Sanderson, R. K. (1998). Relational deaths: Narratives of suicide survivorship. In T. Couser & J. Fichtelberg (Eds.), *True relations: Essays on autobiography and the postmodern.* Westport, CT: Greenwood Press.

Schubert, W. (1992). Practitioners influence curriculum theory: Autobiographical reflections. *Theory into Practice, 31*(1), 236–244.

Schwab, J. J. (1969). The practical: A language for curriculum. *School Review, 78*(1), 1–23.

Sehr, D. T. (1997). *Education for a public democracy.* Albany, NY: SUNY Press.

Shaffer, D., & Craft, L. (1999). Methods of adolescent suicide prevention. *Journal of Clinical Psychiatry, 60*(Suppl. 2), 70–74.

Shaw, M., Smith, G. D., & Dorling, D. (2005). Health inequalities and New Labour: How the promises compare with real progress. *British Journal of Medicine, 330*, 1016–1021.

Sinnott, J. D. (1989). A model for solution of ill-structured problems: Implications for everyday and abstract problem solving. In J. D. Sinnott (Ed.), *Everyday problem solving: Theory and applications* (pp. 72–99) New York: Praeger.

Skelton, T., & Valentine, G. (1998). *Cool places: Geographies of youth cultures.* New York: Routledge

Snaza, N. (2006, February). *Thirteen theses on the question of state in curriculum studies.* Paper presented at the Articulating the Present (Next) Moments in Curriculum Studies: The Post-Reconceptualization Generation conference, West Lafayette, Indiana.

Stevenson, R. G. (2004). Where have we come from? Where do we go from here? Thirty years of death education in schools. *Illness, Crisis, & Loss, 12*(3), 231–238.

Taubman, P. (2004). Reasonable bodies. *Journal of Curriculum Theorizing, 20*(2), 15–28.

Thompson, E. A., & Eggert, L. L. (1999). Using the suicide risk screen to identify suicidal adolescents among potential high school dropouts. *Journal of the American Academy of Child & Adolescent Psychiatry, 38*(12), 1506–1514.

Thompson, E. P. (1978). *The poverty of theory and other essays.* New York: Monthly Review.

Tremain, S. (Ed.). (2005). *Foucault and the government of disability.* Ann Arbor, MI: University of Michigan.

Trifonas, P. P., & Peters, M. A. (Eds.). (2005). *Deconstructing Derrida: Tasks for the new humanities.* New York: Palgrave Macmillan.

[UK] Department of Health. (1999). *Saving lives: Our healthier nation.* London: H.M. Stationery Office.

[UK] Department of Health. (2004). *National standards, local action: Health and social care standards and planning framework 2005/06–2007/08.* Quarry Hill, Leeds, England: Author.

U.S. Department of Health and Human Services. (1992). *Youth suicide prevention programs: A resource guide.* Atlanta, GA: Centers for Disease Control.

U.S. Public Health Services. (1999). *Call to action to prevent suicide.* Washington, DC: U.S. Government Printing Office.

Vieland, V., Whittle, B., Garland, A., Hicks, R., & Shaffer, D. (1991). The impact of curriculum-based suicide prevention programs for teenagers: An eighteen-month follow-up. *Journal of the American Academy of Child Adolescent Psychiatry, 30*(5), 811–815.

Villarejo, A. (2005). Tarrying with the normative: Queer theory and black history. *Social Text, 23*(3–4), 69–84.

Vincent, C., & Tomlinson, S. (1997). Home-school relationships: "The swarming of disciplinary mechanisms." *British Educational Research Journal, 23*(3), 361–377.

Walsh, M. (2001, February 21). Pearson hopes to 'widen the definition of education'. *Education Week, 20*(23).

Willis, P. (2003). Foot soldiers of modernity: The dialectics of cultural consumption and the 21st century school. *Harvard Educational Review, 73*(3), 390–415.

Wraga, W. (1999). "Extracting sun-beams out of cucumbers": The retreat from practice in reconceptualized curriculum studies. *Educational Researcher, 28*(1), 4–13.

Wraga, W. G., & Hlebowitsh, P. S. (2003). Toward a renaissance in curriculum theory and development in the USA. *Journal of Curriculum Studies, 35*(4), 425–437.

Wright, H. K. (2005). Does Hlebowitsh improve on curriculum history? Reading a rereading for its political purpose and implications. *Curriculum Inquiry, 35*(1), 103–117.

Zimmerman, J. (2002). *Whose America? Culture wars in public schools.* Cambridge, MA: Harvard University Press.

Suggested Reading Questions

1. The authors offer three questions regarding curriculum and suicide that challenge the life affirming aspect of curriculum theory and practice. How might such an understanding reflect a denial of and violence against the epistemology of uncertainty, loss, and death?

2. The authors map the social, economic, and political discourse around the meanings attributed to suicide and the ways these are operationalized in educational thought. In what ways can autobiographical narratives rupture our scripted notions of suicide and offer a contextual, culturally meaningful understanding of suicidal acts?

3. How might a Foucauldian analysis of discursive practices surrounding suicide discompose the underlying structures of power and knowledge that generate them?

4. The authors suggest history, identity, and culture are essentialized within policies. How might the failures and omissions of such policies give educators a deeper understanding of the relationship between normative assumptions about gender and sexuality and the terms under which they are constructed?

5. Three counter discourses are offered at the end of this chapter as a way to think of suicide prevention and intervention differently. How might these discourses be "put to use" to reconceptualize suicide prevention and intervention within schools?

Response to Erik Malewski and Teresa Rishel "Invisible Loyalty"

Approaching Suicide From a Web of Relations

Alexandra Fidyk

> The dead are invisible, they are not absent.
> —Saint Augustine of Hippo

Erik Malewski and Teresa Rishel's response to U.S. state and professional efforts at suicide prevention and intervention offers critical and thoughtful alternatives through the lens of autobiography, Foucauldian analysis, and queer theory. Through these frameworks, they address the intersection of curriculum and organizational theory and advocate for a reconceptualization of teaching, learning, and social relations. My response to their chapter similarly asks that we step away from the instrumental rationalism that so tightly directs policy and action and become fearless speakers who have roles to play in transformation of what constitutes theory and practice. Their very call to move toward different forms of knowledge asks that we consider an ontological perspective that borrows from the early systems theorist and philosopher Gregory Bateson (1979). Borrowing from his thoughts on ecological patterns in particular "recursive patterns that connect individuals, families, nations, mind to nature, and the mundane to spiritual" (Reynolds, 2005, p. 263), I maintain that ignorance of the interconnectedness of our lives is the greatest error in our thinking today.

When perturbed or injured, living systems not only regenerate but also move to a new balance that sustains the system. However, since the continued development of all living beings occurs through changes in their structure, in every living being there is ambivalence toward influences that are hoped for and those needed to defend the individual. How a system copes cannot be predicted. This aspect is most significant when examining the family, both in parenting and in teaching children, teachers are connected with their families of origin (and with the ideas and rules of the system). Since no system is independent of another system, being part of a "school system" means that school is also part of the family systems that are connected to it and so continues the webbing of systems to youth culture, media, and so on. In failing to appreciate our complex and multiple relationships with the world, our psychological and organizational theories, for example, often ignore the vast social, physical, and other energies and influences within which we live. Might this be another possibility in what Foucault points to as the "transformation of power" (as cited in Malewski & Rishel, this volume, p. 429)?

In keeping with an intergenerational dialogue, I am struck by their question "why affirm life at all?" If one held a perspective of deep interconnectedness, it recognizes the dynamic, simultaneous, and interdependent emergence and existence of all things, where one attends not only to causal relationships but also to synchronistic or acausal relationships. Acausal means that it is not reduced to a simple cause–effect or stimulus–response relationship which undermines most thinking about death, trauma, and suicide. In shifting perspectives, awareness of a universal or transpersonal dimension arises—releasing one from the grip of the modern Western concept of ego consciousness. Herein begins a radical reconceptualization of suicide—which is not about effects (positive or negative), impact, or even the seeable. Collective consciousness and unconsciousness exist along with that of the individual and do not diminish the latter in anyway. In other words, individual consciousness is not a state of "one's own," because within a systemic perspective, people are not perceived as separate individuals but always in the context of relationships. As one's consciousness communicates with that of another, one's unconscious can also communicate with the others' unconscious and so the idea of co-unconscious.

Indeed, there is a form of freedom to be gained in realizing that individual conscious and unconscious mind is always in constant relation to the collective. Such an integrated ontology respects that we are also inescapably connected at a quantum mechanical level: atmosphere, water, or matter. We are codependently arising. With such interconnection, our full self (which includes multiple selves and seeing other as self) extends beyond the boundaries of our skin. In such a collective, individuals may be more attentive to, and less violent toward self and others (human, animal, plant, and systems). Interconnectedness does not exclude individuality. The "one" is not subsumed by the collective as formations are unique, separate, yet fluid, continuously degenerating and regenerating, and not containing or restricting new relationships or formations. Any view of curriculum, then, becomes a possibility of interdiscourse including both visible and invisible, horizontal time and vertical time, known and unknown.

Malewski and Rishel rightly ask: "So how can educators begin to think differently about suicide?" An interconnected view means that we are interdependent, fluid, and boundless both at the physical level and at the level of consciousness (including the unconscious) together in the past, present, and unfolding future. Like Pinar, I wage that we must take heed of an afterlife—if only to position the present. Consider this: in the emerging image of consciousness, it can be understood as a collective consciousness among people, which forms a field of nonlocal intelligence wherein we all dwell. It extends beyond the individual, is spaceless and timeless. Consciousness is an ordering principle that can insert information into disorganized systems, and create higher degrees of order. Consciousness is not the same as awareness. The ordering power of consciousness can occur completely outside awareness, such as in dreams or at the unconscious level. Both individual and group consciousness can insert and withdraw order or information from the world. Coherence among individuals, expressed as love, empathy, caring, oneness, and connectedness, is important in the ordering power of consciousness. Consciousness affects humans and nonhumans alike, for our pets and forests "resonate" with and respond to human consciousness (Fidyk, 2008).

If we imagine consciousness not as some emergent property of life, as mechanistic science and the instrumental rationalism that education typically supposes, but as a primary quality of the universe, then it becomes at least as fundamental as space, time, and matter. With this image of reality our understanding of the physical world would not be altered significantly, but our understanding of mind would be transformed with a fuller realization of this interconnectivity. Our worldview would shift from the intrinsically materialist to the intrinsically interconnected and so affect what it means to teach and learn, and in this context affect how we understand, address, prevent, and accept suicide. In particular, suicide would not only be seen as a case of risk factors to be treated by state and professional bodies as outlined in the Commission and Trust reports, but also might be understood as a case of "free choice" and action where individuals are permitted to choose and be respected for their choices. Keep in mind that such "chosen" action is always bound by the threads of an invisible web marked by the repetitions and coincidences in one's family history, for instance. Paradoxically, then, choice is not a case of individuality; rather, choice is bound by multiple unconscious, unvoiced collectives held in the present by past and future renderings. Thus, individuals choosing suicide—while an "option"—need to consider the consequences for others before they act, as the effects on those left behind are significant. How do we move away from morally judging suicide to more, other, and wider circles of interpretation—to a wider web of relations?

Consider for a moment a weaving with strands that run both horizontally and vertically. Think of the horizontal in terms of families, groups, tribes, communities, and collectives, crossing provincial and national boundaries, and the vertical in terms of the individual (human and nonhuman). We live simultaneously with both strands— nonlocal consciousness, which is not bound by space or time, and local consciousness, which is bound by a particular time and place such as my sitting here writing on a spring day in northwest Chicago. From where I sit, I can see black and white photographs of my ancestors who homesteaded in Canada in the early 1900s. While they are long gone, I am intimately connected to them and their lives and know that they are still forces and energies that influence my life; indeed, we are always deeply connected within our family lines. From a systemic perspective, we are not perceived as separate individuals but always in the context of relationships both alive and dead.

My putting forth a systemic perspective and transgenerational approach stands alongside the important deconstructive and postmodern perspectives offered as approaches that are likely to have a profound affect on the way we conceive of and respond to suicide. This response asks that we consider systemic insights such as orders of love and phenomenological approaches for the classroom, particularly as a healing process, and keep in mind the Roman law, "the dead pass down to the living." Accordingly, we continue the lines of generations and, knowingly or unknowingly, willingly or unwillingly, we pay debts of the past as long as we have not attended its ills, wherein an "invisible loyalty" impels us to repeat and repeat occasions of incredible joy or unbearable sorrow, injustice or tragic death—or its echo (Nice-Hyères in Schützenberger, 1998, p. xii). Acknowledging within our families the individual members and their stories is similar to the first of the four autobiographical moments of *currere* with the first essential movement being historical. If "we must teach what the cover stories hide, exposing and problematizing the 'hidden curriculum'" (Pinar, 2004, p. 39), then this task becomes revolutionary in families, too, recognizing that present conditions carried by one are interrelated to all others of that family.

The laws or orders that govern family systems reflect transgenerational memory and take into consideration justice and fairness within the family. These orders are not like those of a modern paradigm where hierarchy and power rule; rather, the individual may exert influence over the life events if the orders and ills that have been done to the system are acknowledged. It is no easy task to understand the transgenerational ties and the account of "merits and debts" because the process is not simple or straightforward; each family has its own way of defining family loyalty and justice. It is not an objective concept.

To really understand, it is best to do a case study—a transgenerational and horizontal study of a family over at least three generations, preferably five, in order to note how the patterns in place operate (Frank-Gricksch, 2003; Schützenberger, 1998). The family story that develops relies on retrospective information, on memories the living have about the dead, on what the people currently living know about their families and what moves them—even if they do not consciously know what they know. One has to consider what was said and left unsaid, what is conscious and not conscious in the information transmitted, and from the family's point of view (Schützenberger, 1998). In doing so, one comes to see the family narrative which only becomes clear when understanding the system, the composite of mutually interdependent story-lines.

Following Malewski and Rishel's tracks to move on "in the midst of difficult knowledge," I further add to Lather's call to "knowledge that works against security and certainty by inducing breakdowns in representing experience" (p. 420). We are biological, psychological, and social entities whose reactions (at best, responses) are shaped as much by our own psychology as by the rules of our family systems that are shaped by race, class, sexual orientations, values, and so on. In a family system, truly a constellation or "a complex web," one member's psychological position conditions the psychological positions of the other members: "there exists perpetual reciprocal regulation" (Schützenberger, 1998, p. 20). Regulating the way in which the family functions are implicit and explicit rules, although for the most part, they remain implicit and family members are not consciously aware of them. These rules are often taken for granted, unexplained and considered obvious, such as "in our family we do this or that." To a great degree, then, the family—or at least the rules—bind our behaviors and perceptions. Furthermore, families keep a form of accounts wherein each family determines the various individuals' contributions to the family. The underlying family code, then, determines the scale of merits, advantages, obligations, and responsibilities, which are learned reactions, grounded in the family history, in the family's genetic and historic relatedness, and which we can uncover albeit little by little.

Through a phenomenological approach therapists and healers of family constellation work have been able to discern and describe hidden patterns that may either allow or obstruct love to flow in families. Like any phenomenological study, patterns appear that uncover invariant structures about a particular phenomenon. Love, in this context, as well as in a systems view can be likened to the strands or flows of energy that connect all entities; yet, love flourishes when one acts according to its demands and refrains from doing what harms it. While this might sounds trite, it holds veracity.

Not all suffering and illness are caused by disturbances in our relationships, but since we can address the suffering that does arise out of such systemic turbulence, it is worth considering. Offering a systemic and transgenerational approach adds yet another layer to this chapter's calls for counterapproaches that "disable closure, definition, and completion" (p. 26). When we understand the systemic laws that allow love to unfold, we may be able to help suffering families and individuals to find "solutions" and to change their psychological habits. This work, a combination of psychotherapeutic process and energy work, is at the level of the personal and family soul. The nature of the soul lies beyond space and time. Personal soul, or individual consciousness, is always in relation with, affects, and is affected by the family soul, or family consciousness which is in an ongoing relationships with the unconscious. Through ancestral and soul work, one works beyond the scope of the individual and enters into a healing process that can touch many generations of one or more families, and indeed communities. In other words, family constellations work with the events and people of the past in order to effect healing in the present moment. Participants may experience immediate changes in real time or its effects may unwind over time. It is important to note that in addition to working directly on knowing issues, such as intimate relationships and family matters, one may also represent archetypes, concepts, and entities within the field as well. For example, nations, cultural elements such as religion, political movements and groups, plus the "unknown" can enter into a constellation.

Policies or treatments directed at suicide prevention often begin by looking at life circumstances in order to determine the originating cause. Typically, divorce in the family, difficulties at school or in the workplace, unrequited love, rape, incest, continued neglect or abuse, addiction, and low self-esteem are usually identified as the root antecedent. Through a shift in ontological perspective and an approach that derives from this view, family systemic work reveals that something different is at play. Orders of love dictate that what has been forgotten or cast out of the family story will be represented by others in the family system. In particular cases of suicidal tendency, it has been found that the suicidal individual is either drawn directly to a family member who is already dead, or that she or he has taken on the suicidal feelings of other family members. The influence of the dead can span many generations and when their fate is either not accepted or denied, their influence can be detrimental rather than being a healthy support of ancestral energies (Payne, 2005).

Through my own participation in family constellation over the last 5 years, I am repeatedly reminded that nothing is ever truly forgotten or excluded. Someone will always champion another's cause, usually unconsciously, compelled by an inner impulse, however irrational it may seem. The collective soul is inclusive of all things and that which is excluded or denied will be represented as the result of the soul's compulsion to include through representations. A case history that I have witnessed more than once (each with its own particularities) is one where a parent has lost her own mother (or father) at a young age and one of her children has taken on the mother's longing to be with her parent and the child developed suicidal tendencies as a result of deep identification with the dead grandmother. Within this family there is disorder in the flow of love, an "entanglement" (Hellinger & ten Hövel, 1999, p. 3), so the young child acts in ways not accessible to his conscious mind in an attempt to restore order to the family system. Here he is acting on the law "I follow you" wherein he is unconsciously willing to follow the fate of an earlier family member. His actions reveal a deep bond of love and an unconscious desire and a willingness to right the system. Similarly, from a broader transgenerational aspect, tendencies arise amongst children of parents who are descendants of ethnic groups who have lost many family members owing to persecution and war. Holocausts (Ukrainian, Jewish, Rwandan), African slavery, and the pogroms are examples of such transgenerational effects.

The relationships to our parents, siblings, grandparents, uncles, and aunts affect us at a deep and unconscious level. The ways in which we love and serve our families are often unconscious attempts to compensate for debts and needs belonging to our parents or relatives from previous generations. In so doing, we are even willing to take the place of family members who have died tragically or as children, or to compensate for serious losses or deeds carried out by parents or relatives (Franke-Gricksch, 2003). When doing this, people do not live self-determined lives, but instead, feel, consciously or unconsciously, as though they are strangers to themselves, and may feel an urge to die early. To honor the family order, respect and love, as a fundamental attitude and not a feeling, is required. This attitude is, in most cases, unconscious. Shifting people's attitude toward their parents, siblings, or relatives emphasizes their deep interconnectedness, and indicates that our inclusion in a family soul is part of our fate. A change in attitude often has a healing effect.

In the context of a democratic process, dominant thinking believes that a person grows beyond his or her family and becomes an individual. The underlying belief here is that we can reshape reality which is at work in curriculum, policy and education. While this concept is useful, the insights and transformations that I have experienced and witnessed through work based on a systemic and phenomenological approach have come about at a much deeper and more varied level. Acknowledging orders of love and fate, honoring what is incomprehensible, inescapable, invisible, and reliving grief have given me a new sense of belonging and place with respect to family, friends, and world.

Attendance to narratives, transgenerational dialogue, and autobiography situated within several generations contributes to the creation of "'authentic new models of learning'... through the use of new therapeutic structures that operate at the between spaces of conventional knowledge to enable new ways of thinking with the capacity to reshape children's realities" (p. 425). Furthermore, "learning to think and do otherwise in regards to curricular practice" asks for a shift in ontological positioning, one that may permit us to radically redress suicide in our schools.

References

Bateson, G. (1979). *Mind and nature: A necessary unity (advances in systems theory, complexity, and the human sciences)*. Cresskill, NJ: Hampton Press.

Fidyk, A. (2008). Democracy and difference in education: Interconnectedness, identity, and social justice pedagogy. In D. E. Lund & P. R. Carr (Eds.), *Doing democracy: Striving for political literacy and social justice* (pp. 139–158). New York: Lang.

Franke-Gricksch, M. (2003). *You're one of us: Systemic insights and solutions for teachers, students and parents*. Heidelberg, Germany: Carl-Auer-Systeme Verlag.

Hellinger, B., & ten Hövel, G. (1999). *Acknowledging what is: Conversations with Bert Hellinger* (C. Beaumont, Trans.). Phoenix, AZ: Zeig, Tucker.

Payne, J. (2005). *The healing of individuals, families and nations: Transgenerational healing and family constellations* (Vol. 1). Forres, Scotland: Findhorne Press.

Pinar, W. (2004). *What is curriculum theory?* Mahwah, NJ: Erlbaum.

Portalié, E. (1907). Life of St. Augustine of Hippo. In *The Catholic encyclopedia*. New York: Appleton. Retrieved March 7, 2009, from http://www.newadvent.org/cathen/02084a.htm

Reynolds, S. (2005). Patterns that connect: A recursive epistemology. In W. E. Doll, M. J. Fleener, D. Trueit, & J. St. Julien (Eds.), *Chaos, complexity, curriculum, and culture: A conversation* (pp. 263–276). New York: Lang.

Schützenberger, A. A. (1998). *The ancestor syndrome: Transgenerational psychotherapy and the hidden links in the family tree*. London: Routledge.

Part VII

The Creativity of an Intellectual Curriculum

21 How the Politics of Domestication Contribute to the Self-Deintellectualization of Teachers[1]

Alberto J. Rodriguez

Chapter Overview

In this chapter the author discusses the difficult and unsettling contexts in which educators and curriculum scholars expect beginning teachers to become agents of change. He first describes a number of teaching contexts in which a small but vocal group of teacher education students who are resistant to the pedagogical and ideological change necessary to teach for diversity challenge the instructor. He then describes how their resistance can domesticate professors' efforts toward critical awareness by way of negative course evaluations and overt resistance to finishing course assignments offering manifestation of this domestication phenomenon that include a sense of unpreparedness, entitlement, and irrelevance. The author calls for increased emphasis on student voice, curriculum integration, faculty and teacher education student dialogues on accountability issues, and faculty dialogues on the ways domestication impacts parent–teacher processes.

Laying Down Invisible Boundaries

To whom does the "next moment" belong, and who will be responsible for its genesis? Since the reconceptualist movement of the 1970s, the field of curriculum studies has undergone an "intellectual breakthrough" (Pinar, 2004, p. 171); however, the rich insights that have emerged from this postmodern moment continue to fall on the deaf ears of politicians, policy makers, and many others whose position of power enables the ghost of Ralph Tyler (1949) to still animate the lifeless and shallow U.S. curriculum. Even in its more recent reincarnations, the linearity, structuralist, and positivist nature of Tyler's rationale can be easily discerned. Take for instance the widely popular, and poorly named, "backward design" curriculum development program (based on the work of McTighe & Wiggins, 2004), which is arguably Tyler's rationale in reverse.

To interrupt this pervasive cycle, we are going to have to bring to the table topics that are uncomfortable and seldom addressed in curriculum studies. That is, we are going to have to add to our agenda of "complicated conversations" (Pinar, 2004) the contradictory and often untenable contexts in which we expect beginning teachers to become agents of change, and how their reactions to the demands and challenges of these contexts produce negative consequences that truncate their dreams of becoming better teachers than those who discouraged them or those who inspired them. This implies that we must have the courage to implicate ourselves in this process to better understand the *politics of domestication* in which we are all trapped.

In an earlier essay (Rodriguez, 2005), the politics of domestication is defined as a negative process of acculturation by which one's ideals and commitment to work for social justice are tamed and reduced to fit dominant discursive practices. In that paper, I articulate how covert and overt practices are enacted to essentially coerce beginning professors into surrendering their unique professional and individual identities in exchange for the sacred prize—tenure and promotion. In a more recent essay (Rodriguez, 2006), I also use the politics of domestication as a construct to critique the superficial and repetitious nature of the U.S. curriculum and the contradictory national educational policies that sustain it in a self-defeating cycle of punitive accountability. In this chapter, however, I wish to advance these arguments by illustrating how some student teachers engage—either consciously or subconsciously—in a politics of domestication that could end up ultimately serving to deintellectualize their professional development. Again, the goal here is not to add more to the abundant "deficit" literature that often describes teachers and preservice teachers as lacking this or that. As I mentioned earlier, the main goal is to expose this issue and implicate ourselves—as teacher educators and administrators—in the roles that we may inadvertently play as we essentially shoot ourselves in our privileged intellectual foot.

Judging from one of the reviewers' comments on a draft of this chapter, what I propose to do here is obviously not going to be easy and it is bound to be misunderstood. For example, this reviewer stated:

> The issues about the tensions he (Rodriguez) and his students (and we all) face between working within and positioning oneself in opposition to the system...could be taken deeper. The piece reads (primarily) as though Rodriguez is positioning himself and most of his students in opposition to this small band of "resistant" students.... Although Rodriguez seems to appreciate that student resistance often represents divergent understandings or values, I do not see him placing himself in sympathetic relation to those students' realities.

If I could beg the readers' indulgence and request that we move away from traditional deficit models and away from the comforts of dichotomous thinking such as, "we against them," and "sympathetic vs. unsympathetic," I may be able to better draw attention to this difficult and often unexamined phenomenon. Namely, how the politics of domestication serve to deintellectualize the professional development of preservice teachers and the implications this process has on how teacher educators are able to carry out their work. Teachers educators should of course always strive to improve their practice, and we should always pay close attention to our students' needs, but is it not equally important that we also pay close attention to the factors that may obstruct teacher educators' efforts to enact the goals of their teacher education programs in regards to preparing teachers to teach for diversity and for understanding? What if these obstructions are being created consciously or subconsciously by a few student teachers? What if this resistance could have a long-lasting impact on how teacher educators are able to teach for diversity?

It is also critical that readers keep in mind that I am referring to only a small group of preservice teachers here that often seem to be very vocal about their resistance to program goals. While the sources of these students' resistance are complex and rooted in many factors such as lack of pedagogical confidence; lack of subject-matter knowledge; previous negative experiences with various subjects; limited experiences with cultural diversity; and simply just their choice, it is not my intention to discuss these issues here. I and others have written extensively elsewhere on students' resistance to pedagogical[2] and ideological change[3] and the challenges they encounter in their teaching contexts (Rodriguez & Kitchen, 2005). I wish then to focus the conversation here on how the actions of this small group of students who resist learning to teach for diversity and for understanding (for whatever reason) could have significant and long-lasting impact on the effectiveness of teacher educators to carry out the work for which they were hired in the first place.

To this end, I start with a description of the multiple teaching contexts in which I have been fortunate enough to work, followed by a brief explanation of the methodological lens I use in this retrospective and on-going autoethnographical exploration. I also provide an analysis of three examples of how the politics of domestication have taken form in my methods courses in the last 12 years. I close the manuscript with some suggestions for countering the politics of domestication and its detrimental effects on the professional growth of teachers—and of university faculty—as agents of much needed positive change.

Teaching in a Room Full of Ghosts

This is what it often feels like for me during the first day of classes in my science methods course:

> Even though I have taught this class—or a version of it—at three different universities in my three different reincarnations during my journey in academe for the last 12 years, my palms still get sweaty and my heart races. Who could blame me? After all, I'm about to enter a room full of people haunted by *ghosts*.
>
> Usually, up to 26 preservice teachers are inside the classroom—very few smile as I walk in, most look very serious and wide-eyed, and I know their palms are as sweaty as mine if not more. As I greet them in Spanish, some students give me a double take. It is as if they are asking with their eyes, "Are you really our teacher?" I know that look well. I saw it many times when I was a school science teacher, and I also saw it during my first job as a science education professor in the Midwest. At that time, most of the students in my methods courses were Anglo, middle-class, and female—in essence, the mirror image demographics of the majority of the U.S. teaching force. Therefore, seeing a Latino, who was not tending gardens, carrying luggage, cleaning houses, or getting in some kind of trouble—as stereotypes have taught them—gave them reason to pause. As the courses progressed, I came to learn that I was the first Latino professor (or teacher) with whom many of them have ever interacted. Interestingly, the students in the methods classes that I taught in the Southwest, and the ones that I now teach in the Pacific Southwest are more culturally diverse, but one thing most of my students have had in common across the three universities in which I have taught is that they are all haunted by the same ghosts.
>
> Between my students and I, these ghosts always sit. With arms crossed, and with a frown, these ghosts dare me to try to break through their barriers and reach my students. As if being a teacher educator was not difficult enough, I also have to find ways to conduct multiple exorcisms to put to rest my students' ghosts or previous negative experiences in science classrooms or their anxiety about teaching this subject. This anxiety is more pronounced amongst elementary preservice teachers who usually are only required to take three science-related courses before entering the teacher certification program, yet they are expected to be confident and proficient in the teaching of science at the K-6 level.

Sometimes exorcising these ghosts is more challenging than others, and I have never been able to expel all of them in every class. There is always a small group of preservice teachers in my classes whose ghosts prevent me from reaching them. While, we, as teacher educators, for a multitude of reasons, may never be able to reach all of our students, in spite of our best efforts, what is important to emphasize here is the need to deconstruct the implications for teacher educators and teacher education programs that seek to prepare teachers for a pluralistic society. In the next section, I explain how the ongoing autoethnographic study of my practice has enabled me to draw some insights into this phenomenon (the politics of domestication).

Inhabiting the Other in Multiple Spaces

Because I have the (dis)advantage of inhabiting the other in multiple spaces, I have been able to engage in an ongoing autoethnography (Ellis & Bochner, 2000). As a bilingual Latino, with the mestizo physical features that make me both an object of hate and stereotype for some, and an anomaly in academe to others, I can travel between the invisible—yet palpable—cultural boundaries that exist between the haves and have-nots; the researchers and the subjects of study; and the ones in positions of power and those often perceived as powerless.

In these cultural border crossings, the work of Bakhtin (1981, 1986) has made possible for me to navigate through some of the contradictions and expectations that exist in these spaces by providing a framework for making a distinction between acculturation and assimilation. He argues that each community of practice (e.g., lawyers, doctors, teachers, priests, gang members, rappers, etc.) has its specific speech genre (unique discourses) that allows that community to function. In order to become a successful member of a community of practice, one must then undergo a process of acculturation by which the individual becomes more aware of the nuances and discursive practices within the community. However, this does not mean that our unique voices or speaking consciousness (Bakhtin, 1981; Werstch, 1991) must be abandoned to thrive in our chosen community of practice. That would be assimilation instead of positive acculturation, and herein lies the crux of this chapter.

I argue that we need to explore how our voices could be silenced, excluded, or assimilated by the politics of domestication, which in turn end up perpetuating the cycle of contradictions in teacher education programs. In other words, we need to better understand how, for instance, some student teachers' resistance to the cross-cultural goals of their teaching education programs and their professors' efforts to enact these goals in their classes have the potential to "domesticate" their professors' efforts through negative course evaluations and overt resistance to completing course assignments. This is where it is very important that we take a moment to pause and problematize this phenomenon because it exposes the contradictions in which teacher educators are expected to function. That is, while we are supposed to model in our classes the importance of teaching for social justice and of taking pedagogical risks to help our students learn for understanding, the rituals of tenure and promotion also require that we decipher the contradictory messages we receive, such as: be creative but follow the guidelines; be daring but don't rock the boat; be critical but follow the status quo; be yourself but be liked by everyone first, and so on.

While we may agree that curriculum and social changes in our schools are essential and risks are necessary, the halls of academe are haunted by different kinds of ghosts. These ghosts owe their lingering existence to Western aristocratic rituals like the rites of tenure and promotion that add to the increasing stew of contradictions faced by teachers/professors.

Thus, through the autoethnographical enterprise, I am presenting here a reflexive look[4] at my teaching practice in the unique contexts in which student teachers [re]act in response to it (Ellis & Bochner, 2000). In this way, as Anais Nin (1966) exclaims, "we write to taste life twice, in the moment and in retrospection." This retrospection and the transformative choices that arise from it, is what enables us to better connect our espoused beliefs with our beliefs in action and to take the risks necessary to effect change.

Although this autoethnography is a project-in-progress, I present below insights gathered from studying this general question: In what ways do *some* preservice teachers engage in a *politics of domestication* by which they pressure their professors to conform to a culture of low expectations and self-perpetuating contradictions between what teachers need to learn to effect long-lasting change in schools and what they perceive they need to do to just complete their teacher certification?

Three Manifestations of the Politics of Domestication

The politics of domestication that I have observed over the years has taken an amazing variety of forms. Below, I provide only three examples within the context of working with student teachers in the science methods courses I have taught in three different universities.

Walking in Two Worlds [Anxiety and Feelings of Unpreparedness to Teach]

> He knew so much about science that he sometimes intimidated us. (Student Teacher from Bilingual Science Methods Course)

This comment from one of my students on the final course evaluation struck a chord for me. Students' anxiety and feelings of unpreparedness to teach science is so intense that even having a professor who knows the subject was perceived in a negative light. In my methods courses, I often model how to make science lessons more culturally responsive and socially relevant. At the same time, I help students make more meaningful connections between social constructivism (as a theory of learning) and the subject matter being discussed. In this way, I hope that students will realize that it is indeed possible to teach for understanding even complicated topics (e.g., electricity), and still make the lesson culturally responsive and relevant.

This is a tremendous task, however, and in the book I coedited with Richard Kitchen (Rodriguez & Kitchen, 2005), colleagues in mathematics and science education from across the country share the variety of pedagogical strategies they are using to essentially counter the students' resistance to teach for diversity (resistance to ideological change) and for understanding (resistance to pedagogical change). We use the word *resistance* purposely because often some student teachers consciously or subconsciously choose not to use inclusive and student-centered pedagogical strategies even when these strategies are congruent with their own espoused beliefs about what constitutes good teaching. Why? The answer is more complicated than the question, but I have observed that due to their anxiety and feelings of unpreparedness to teach, they opt not to take risks because they fear losing the respect of their students if the lesson does not go well; they fear that they do not know the subject well enough to answer possible questions; or they feel that they "must play the game" in order to "survive" the demands of the student teaching placement.

For example, over the years my students often make statements like these during class discussions, "Yeah, that activity was fun, but I'll have to follow whatever teaching approach my teacher uses in her classroom," or "When I have my own classroom, maybe I'd be able to do more student-centered activities." In essence, these students walk in two worlds. One world is the ideal—the one they hope to inhabit in their own classrooms—a place where they will be able to try what they are learning in their teaching education programs. The other is what they call the "real world"; that is, the one represented by their courses and student teaching placements.

I expand on these notions below, but here it is important to note that it is obvious that many teachers do not reach that ideal world of teaching they hope for when they get their own classrooms—a phenomenon evidenced by the pervasive trend of teacher-centered and transmissive approaches in K-12 classrooms, and by findings from recent surveys and reports. For instance, a survey of almost 6,000 K-12 teachers from 1,200 schools across the United States, by Weiss, Banilower, McMahon, and Smith (2001) found that "while roughly 75% of elementary teachers feel very qualified to teach reading /language arts, approximately 60 percent feel very qualified to teach mathematics and about 25 percent feel very qualified to teach science" (p. 30).

Furthermore, Weiss, Pasley, Smith, Banilower, and Heck (2003) found in another study that after observing 364 lessons taught by K-12 teachers from various parts of the United States, fewer than 1 in 5 lessons were intellectually rigorous. That is, 66% of the teachers observed used inadequate or low level questioning strategies, and in 66% of the classrooms observed, students were engaged in what Weiss and her colleagues called "inadequate sense-making." In other words, teachers were not helping students make relevant connections with the key concepts being covered in the lesson. Only in 16% of the classrooms did the research team find teachers actively engaging students in more meaningful understanding of the subject matter and in high-level questioning. It would be ideal to conduct a similar nationwide survey and include questions regarding how teachers engage their students in critical discussions of the subject matter in terms of how this official knowledge was constructed, who benefits from it, and who is included/excluded in the pursuit of this knowledge. I suspect that the percentage of teachers involved in this kind of socially and culturally relevant pedagogy would be even lower.

So when do preservice teachers get to walk in the ideal world they imagine as they convince themselves that what they are learning in their teacher preparation courses is not for the "real world"? I have been investigating this question through various research projects throughout the years in order to assist students in making better connections between what they learned in my classes and their teaching practice; however, this is not the focus of this manuscript.[5] We need to return then to the politics of domestication. When some students experience various degrees of anxiety and feelings of unpreparedness to teach science, what impact does this have on their professors?

There are of course obvious challenges that come with reaching these students during class, but where their impact is most significant is on their professors' tenure and promotion process. In other words, what do you think members of a tenure and promotion committee or chair of a department would conclude if they read comments like these in the final students' evaluations of a course: "the professor needed to teach more science"; "More science activities and less theory"; "we already get multicultural education in other classes, we should learn science in this class." Colleagues who are not aware of the context I explained might come to different conclusions about a professor's effectiveness in his or her classroom. Thus, my argument is that some students press the professor to deintellectualize their classroom experience by making overt their desire (in class and on course evaluations) that they want more "activities," "more science" (i.e., teacher-centered lectures) and "less theory" and "less multicultural education." While in my classes, as I mentioned earlier, all activities are deconstructed in order to better understand their connections to social constructivism (as a theory of learning) and multicultural education (as a theory of social justice), this approach is not appreciated by some students.

Again to clarify, my course evaluations are rated highly and I believe *most* students benefit from and are deeply engaged in the course. In fact, by the end of the course, many of the students who were anxious about science and felt unprepared to teach the subject comment in the course evaluations that what they learned has better prepared them to teach in culturally diverse classrooms. However, this manuscript is more about that small yet vocal and powerful group of students who I was not able to reach, and thus use their power to deintellectualize their own, their peers', and their future peers' learning experiences and to engage in a politics of domestication. The latter is most powerfully enacted when the professor (or instructor) must make a decision on how to change his or her practice.

We all need to take our students' comments seriously in order to improve our pedagogy. However, how does one reconcile students' demands for more teacher-centered and transmissive content coverage, coupled with more activities disconnected from the research and the learning theories from which they were developed, and at the same time keep the integrity of the course? As a beginning professor in the Midwest, and a single father of two small children, how I chose to answer that question had tremendous implications. Should I allow myself to be in essence domesticated ("don't rock the boat" and "wait 'till you get tenure" as some of my senior colleagues advised me), or should I press forward in developing my own teaching persona as a person of color in academe? These questions are very similar to the kinds of questions our teacher graduates face in their own teaching contexts, and we need to find more effective ways to help them respond to these challenges.

With trepidation, I chose integrity over duplicity and decided that tenure and promotion were not worth getting if that meant becoming someone else and engaging in academic fraudulence. Furthermore, over the years, I have accumulated so many hands-on activities and tricks of the trade that I know that if I wanted to get perfect scores on my students' evaluations I could just simply provide my students with a string of amazing, fun, hands-on science activities without ever having to connect them to current research on multicultural education or learning theories. This approach could have made the walk on broken glass required by the rituals of tenure and promotion less jagged; however, I would have been a fraud to my students and my university by not providing my students with the kind of intellectual engagement, challenges, and professional preparation I know they needed based on my own research and the work of others. Unfortunately, through the politics of domestication, the contexts explained here are not considered in the rituals of tenure and promotion, and I believe that neither our colleagues nor students are aware of the potentially negative consequences their domesticating comments could have in a professor's ability to actually do the job for which they were hired.

A Sense of Entitlement

Another manifestation of the politics of domestication can be observed when some student teachers act on their perceived sense of entitlement by virtue of their privileged positions (i.e., socioeconomic status, membership in the culture of power, etc), or by virtue of their *apprenticeship in teaching*. That is, the notion individuals may have about what constitutes good teaching based on their +/-16 years of observing other people teach during their schooling (Lortie, 1975). I have had, for example, secondary science methods students demand that I show them "the steps of how to teach" a specific concept to diverse students during class discussions. While I do believe that what it is really surfacing here are these students' anxiety over their sense of unpreparedness, their frustration—and sometimes, open hostility—makes it difficult to reach them.

In spite of my best efforts, some students still believe that teaching for understanding and for diversity can be reduced to conform to the positivist frameworks that have worked well for them in their undergraduate science majors. Unfortunately, this situation is not very different for some elementary student teachers who are also plagued by similar concerns. Take for instance the following excerpt from an essay written by one of my Latina elementary science methods students in response to the assigned readings for the class:

> I also believe that is important for educators and teachers, as well as everyone, to embrace diversity and multiculturalism. A few weeks ago, I heard some of my peers discussing multiculturalism, and they were saying that they thought it was so "annoying" that the education department promoted multiculturalism, and that it was stupid, and when they wrote papers they wrote what their professors wanted to hear, not what they really felt. I thought it was sad, and a little scary, that these people are our future teachers and they thought the "whole diversity and multicultural thing was annoying and stupid." It made me think that there are plenty of educators out there who also think like this, and there are even more children who will become the students of these teachers who will suffer because of their ignorance.

One of the main goals of this university's teacher education program, which was serving communities in the Borderlands of the Southwest, was to help student teachers become agents of change in the increasingly culturally diverse and economically disadvantaged schools of the area. Yet, some students objected to this emphasis and appeared to have no problem in sharing this in front of a student of color. They also appeared to demonstrate a sense of entitlement where they knew better what they needed to become professional teachers. I have some students also object in class and in course evaluations to my choice of required readings, such as reports on student achievement trends, or cultural/feminist critiques like Peggy McIntosh's (1988) *White Privilege and Male Privilege*. Other students have made it clear that they were very annoyed when asked to read a research paper I had written, and complained that they were "being brainwashed" by a program that was pushing "multicultural education down their throats."

If it were not by the fact that most students seem to embrace the goals of the teacher education program for which I have worked, and they seemed seriously committed to becoming inclusive teachers, I am certain that I would have left academe a long time ago. Nevertheless, as mentioned earlier, these few disgruntled student teachers plow a path of potential domestication that yields serious consequences long after they walk away with their teacher certification. This is further explained below.

Perceptions of Irrelevance

The third and related example of the politics of domestication I wish to explain here has to do with how some student teachers perceive their teacher education program to be irrelevant and disconnected to the realities of today's schools. I have already described above how some student teachers struggle to walk in two worlds—what they perceive to be the ideal (when they will have control of their own classrooms) and the real (represented by the expectations they need to meet to just complete their teaching certification requirements). I want to expand on this notion because some students engage in a series activities (politics of domestication) that deserve special attention. For example, some students get visibly upset when I have denied their requests to be excused from the methods class in order for them to participate in school-related activities (e.g., parent–

teacher conferences, students' games, fieldtrips, etc.). Even though the policy requiring students not to miss any university class to attend school functions is clearly stated in the department's *Student Teachers' Handbook*, and even though it is a college-wide policy, some students complained about my decision and stated in the final course evaluations that "the professor needs to be more flexible," or "the professor does not understand the demands of students in the program." It is interesting that these students do not complain about, or directly mention the department's policy per se, but make me the target of their frustration instead. What is these students' intention? How would members of a tenure and promotion committee read these comments? How should a professor or instructor react to these comments? Uphold the established policy, or allow students to miss a class that cannot be replicated given the nature of the hands-on, minds-on design of the methods course?

This is where the politics of domestication and the effort of some students to deintellectualize their own teacher preparation need to be better understood by those in charge of evaluating teacher education programs and their faculty. We also need to better understand why some students believe that the classes they take in their teacher preparation programs are somehow less significant than going on a school fieldtrip, watching a school game, or attending a parent–teacher conference. While all of these are worthy endeavors, some student teachers have the mindset that the teacher education program is but an expensive and cumbersome obstacle that gets in the way of their real professional preparation.

I believe that we—faculty and teacher education programs—are partially to blame for these students' negative perceptions because we often place them in contradictory and untenable contexts. For instance, we rarely place student teachers in classrooms where they feel supported to implement the innovative, inquiry-based, and culturally relevant pedagogical strategies they see us model in our classes. In science, this situation is even more desperate because most of my students never get to see their teachers teach science at all in elementary schools if they are placed in grades K-4 or grade 6 classrooms. This is due to the fact that science has only recently begun to be tested in grade 5. Most elementary teachers in our area devote the science and social studies periods for more drill and practice of mathematics and language arts in preparation for the standardized tests (this other form of the politics of domestication is discussed in more detail in Rodriguez, 2006).

In response to this reality—imposed by current educational policies that uphold punitive accountability in higher regard than critical and meaningful learning—I have been engaging my students in more focused discussions on how to create safe spaces during their student teaching placements so they can truly practice teaching in new ways.

Coincidentally, in the midst of writing this chapter, I received this message from one of my last semester science methods students:

> I'm doing my student teaching now…and I have some good news! My teacher is putting me in charge of all the Science instruction, and I am really excited because, up until now, Science has been on the back burner. I'm thrilled because the students are now going to get daily and consistent exposure to Science as long as I am there, and I am looking forward to implementing the concepts I learned from your class into my teaching. Anyway, I just wanted to share my good news with you!

It is exciting that some students are beginning to advocate for themselves and their pupils, but at the same time, it is a bit sad that the "good news" is that she was actually having a chance to do what she was actually paying for—having an opportunity to practice teaching *all* of the curriculum subjects which she will be required to teach in her own classroom after certification.

The Next Moment?

It's better to light a candle than to shout at the darkness (Chinese proverb).

My main goal in this chapter has been to illuminate the complexity and contradictory nature of our work in the current contexts of oppressive and punitive high stakes accountability. In this way, we might be able to better engage our students—and each other—in more metacognitive and transformative dialogic conversations that move away from the dangers of the politics of domestication. To reiterate then, it has been my experience that most of the preservice teachers with whom I have worked have been very committed and open to learning to teach for diversity and understanding. In this chapter, however, I have drawn attention to the politics of domestication enacted by *some* preservice teachers who work against the goals of the teacher education programs to which they belong, and even against their own espoused beliefs to become effective and inclusive teachers. A better understanding of these challenges and how they impact the professional lives of teacher educators is needed so that we can more effectively assist preservice teachers to become cognizant and avoid the detrimental effects of engaging in self-defeating and deintellectualizing politics of domestication. To this end, I provide some suggestions below:

1. We need to assist student teachers in finding their teacher voice so that they can better advocate for themselves and their pupils during their school placements. In this way, they may be able to avoid falling into whatever predominant cycle of despondency is driving the schools in which they are placed or where they may end up finding employment. One way to achieve this goal is by providing student teachers with specific strategies for creating safe spaces for themselves and their pupils so that they can practice and adapt what they are learning in their university context to the school context. This might involve helping student teachers become more aware of their rights (e.g., being able to practice teaching *all* of the subjects for which they are receiving accreditation). Furthermore, this approach may help students to better appreciate the relevance of their methods courses and the importance of becoming agents of change and not just another spoke in the normalcy wheel.

2. Teacher educators should make a more concerted effort to integrate subjects across their curriculum areas. This will enable preservice and beginning teachers to negotiate a better space to effect change in their respective schools as they attempt to manage the pressure to teach less science or social studies. Furthermore, they may not need to sacrifice one curriculum subject area to make more room for more math or language arts drill and practice due to standardized testing. We have been addressing this issue in our current project, Integrating Instructional Technologies with Science Education (I²Tech-SciE) by collaborating with teachers to purposely integrate the language arts curriculum with the science curriculum using learning technologies.[6]

3. Teacher educators and instructors need to take a more active role in creating spaces for their students to connect their methods courses with school practice. Out of frustration with my own Department that continues to ignore my requests to place my methods students in classrooms where they could see and practice science teaching, I recently invited my students to visit the classrooms of two veteran teachers who have worked with me in a science research project. Students were asked to attend these teachers' classrooms as often as they could throughout the semester, and we spent some time

at the beginning of each class discussing the pedagogical strategies they saw and how teachers were integrating learning technologies and other subjects across the curriculum.[7] Although, I cannot require students to visit these teachers' classrooms, they were at least provided with that opportunity.

4. We need to take the risk of engaging students in an honest and metacognitive dialogic conversation about these issues. Perhaps, having students read an article like this one could start this kind of "complicated conversation" where we could all find safe spaces to tackle the contradictory contexts in which we are all working and avoid being trapped in the politics of domestication.

5. Senior faculty and other university faculty and administrators must become more cognizant of the politics of domestication when evaluating faculty for tenure and/or promotion. Given the examples described here, those involved in the evaluation of faculty must pay closer attention to the contradictory and challenging contexts in which we teach. In this way, evaluation committee members would be better prepared to decipher students' comments as indicators that the faculty member being evaluated is actually enacting well the goals of the teacher education program, or where he or she needs professional development support.

To close, I must add that at least for me, the brief autoethnographic tour I have shared here has reinforced the notion that having a disposition to act is not the same as acting on a disposition. I need to do better as a professor to help myself, my students and my colleagues face the lingering ghosts of normalcy that get in the way of creating long-lasting and positive change in our schools. I find comfort in the heteroglossia[8] of the narrative (Bakhtin, 1981, 1986) I have chosen to tell here for it represents a cathartic chorus that—as it has done before—encourages me *not* to give in to the superficial and selfish calmness that mediocrity brings (Rodriguez, 2005). Mediocrity—like a siren's song—is alluring, but complacency takes no courage. I remain optimistic that we can counter the politics of domestication by exposing and better understanding its source(s) and impact, but it will take courage to add this topic to our long and much needed list of complicated conversations in curriculum studies. The second reviewer of a draft of this chapter makes this point clear when he or she states,

> I think it's quite possible that there is less exploration of these issues in our literature than we ought to have because scholars self-consciously tend to avoid the self-exposure involved in writing publicly about such things; so it is to the author's great credit that he has not shied away from doing so.

I believe that by the very nature of the social justice work that some of us do in our university classes, we will always encounter—for one reason or another—that small group of student teachers who resist learning to teach for diversity and for understanding; and in fact resist against the goals of the teacher education programs to which they belong. The question for teacher educators and administrators here is do we allow these voices to domesticate—and consequently—deintellectualize our teacher education programs because of fear of receiving negative course evaluations or having challenging encounters with these students? What roles should senior faculty and administrators play in supporting faculty who are indeed enacting the goals of their teacher education programs and in fact doing the job for which they were hired?

These questions might be better answered if we have the courage to bring these topics to the table after we have taken a moment for reflection, and after we have done all that is possible and obvious, such as exploring ways to improve our own practice, working with colleagues to increase program effectiveness, and so on, and after we are left with nothing less but the politics of domestication's unavoidable and dominating gaze. This may be a good time then to more honestly and purposefully craft that "next moment" in curriculum studies which this volume seeks to instigate.

Notes

1. Some of the work reported in this manuscript was sponsored by a grant from the National Science Foundation (Grant #0306156). The perspectives and findings shared in this manuscript, however, were constructed by the author alone and do not represent the position of the funding agency.
2. Resistance to pedagogical change (or resistance to learning to teach for understanding) has to do with consciously or subconsciously choosing not to implement more student-centered, inquiry-based, and social constructivist pedagogical strategies (Rodriguez, 1998; Rodriguez & Kitchen, 2005).
3. Resistance to ideological change (or resistance to learning to teach for diversity) has to do with consciously or subconsciously choosing not to address equity issues in the classroom (e.g. gender and language inclusion, student ability, sexual orientation, and culturally relevant/responsive curriculum; Rodriguez, 1998; Rodriguez & Kitchen, 2005).
4. These reflexive looks into one's own practice are of course always partial reconstructions. In a previous essay (Rodriguez, 2000), I have argued that in autobiographical studies it is essential for the teller to expose his or her intentionality in whatever chosen version of self he or she chooses to share.
5. Readers interested in this work are encouraged to visit our latest project at http://edweb.sdsu.edu/i2techscie
6. A draft of a manuscript describing our findings can be found at http://edweb.sdsu.edu/i2techscie/conference.htm. Click on "Facilitating the Integration of Multiple Literacies through Science Education and Learning Technologies" to download this paper or review other papers with the same theme that were presented at the Second Institute on Science Research organized by the author.
7. These teachers were participants in our current project, Integrating Instructional Technologies with Science Education (I2TechSciE). Again, for more information on this project visit http://edweb.sdsu.edu/i2techscie
8. Conflicting discourses that imbue the way I write and think as a result of my ongoing cultural and social border crossing.

References

Bakhtin, M. M. (1981). *The dialogic imagination: Four essays by M. M. Bakhtin* (M. Holquist, Ed.). Austin: University of Texas Press.

Bakhtin, M. M. (1986). *Speech genres and other late essays* (C. Emerson & M. Holquist, Eds.). Austin: University of Texas Press.

Ellis, C., & Bochner, A. P. (2000). Autoethnography, personal narrative, reflexivity: Researcher as subject. In N. Denzin & Y. S. Lincoln (Eds.), *The handbook of qualitative research* (2nd ed, pp. 733–768). Thousand Oaks, CA: Sage.

Lortie, D. (1975). *Schoolteacher*. Chicago: University of Chicago Press.

McIntosh, P. (1988). *White privilege and male privilege: A personal account of coming to see correspondences through work in women's studies* (Working Paper 189). Wellesley MA: The Wellesley College Center for Research on Women.

McTighe, J., & Wiggins, G. (2004). *The understanding by design professional development workbook*. Alexandria, VA: Association for Supervision and Curriculum Development.

Nin, A. (1966). *The diary of Anais Nin: Vol. 1 (1931–1934)*. Orlando, FL: Harcourt.

Pinar, W. (2004). *What is curriculum theory?* Mahwah, NJ: Erlbaum.

Rodriguez, A. J. (1998) Strategies for counterresistance: Toward sociotransformative constructivism and learning to teach science for diversity and for understanding. *Journal for Research in Science Teaching, 35*(6), 589–622

Rodriguez, A. J. (2000) Linking Bakhtin with feminist poststructuralism to unravel the allure of auto/biographies. *Research in Science Education, 30*(1), 13–21.

Rodriguez, A. J. (2005). Rejecting mediocrity and the politics of domestication. *Journal of Curriculum Theorizing, 21*(3), 47–59.

Rodriguez, A. J. (2006). The politics of domestication and curriculum as pasture in the United States. *Teaching and Teacher Education, 22*, 804–811.

Rodriguez, A. J., & Kitchen, R. (2005). *Preparing prospective mathematics and science teachers to teach for diversity: Promising strategies for transformative pedagogy.* Mahwah, NJ: Erlbaum.

Tyler, R. W. (1949). *Basic principles of curriculum and instruction.* Chicago: University of Chicago Press.

Weiss, I. R., Banilower, E. R., McMahon, K. C., & Smith, P. S. (2001). *Report of the 2000 national survey of science and mathematics education.* Chapel Hill, NC: Horizon Research.

Weiss, I. R., Pasley, J. D., Smith, P. S., Banilower, E. R., & Heck, D. J. (2003). *A study of K-12 mathematics and science education on the United States: Looking inside the classroom.* Chapel Hill, NC: Horizon Research. Retrieved April 23, 2008, from http://www.horizon-research.com

Wertsch, J. V. (1991). *Voices of the mind: A sociocultural approach to mediated action.* Cambridge, MA: Harvard University Press.

Suggested Reading Questions

1. Lyotard suggests that change agents must avoid reactionary countermoves lest they get caught upon broader systems of discourse where they must always respond to conservative intellectual frameworks. What words, phrases, or ideas within Rodriguez's chapter might help educators exceed their reactionary countermoves?

2. Rodriguez describes how stereotypes frame expectations of instructors by teacher education students—even prior to their meeting—what sorts of counterdiscourses and images might complicate their notions of race, intelligence, and culture?

3. Within teacher education there is an ongoing tension between teaching future teachers to envision alternate possibilities for their classrooms and preparing them to navigate public education in its current incarnation. What are the implications of Rodriguez's chapter for bridging this divide?

4. Teacher education students frequently resist multicultural education and social justice perspectives within claims that they envision themselves as "neutral" teachers who focus on the facts. What kinds of intellectual outlooks act as a pretext for assertions of objectivity and neutrality?

5. The author argues for positive acculturation within rather than assimilation to teaching communities. Given your race, class, and gender, what elements from your cultural background expand and diversify the teaching community in your school?

Response to Alberto J. Rodriguez
Let's Do Lunch

Peter Appelbaum

If Alberto and I were working at the same institution, we would have already discussed the ideas in his chapter over lunch, and we would be planning ways to redesign our teacher education curriculum. In fact, at Arcadia, where I have been for the last 6 years, we did just that. We have initiated a new curriculum, partly instigated by nagging concerns of the faculty that grew out of our recent experiences, and partly justified by the excuse that the state of Pennsylvania was changing the requirements for certification. One might take his chapter as a form of assessment that would be used to rethink the program. For example, if there is a consistent subgroup of students who are not able to take advantage of experiences and assignments, might we not wonder if they are not "prepared" for them by their previous coursework and life experiences? Like Alberto, I do not mean to suggest a deficit discourse here. Instead, I am wondering if a particular analogy is suitable. If I were teaching abstract algebra and my course expected students to apply concepts such as commutability or inverse-functions, and I noticed that the students became anxious and unable to understand the new concepts of groups and rings, might I not wonder whether it is groups and rings that are making things challenging, or whether it is previous work with commutability and inverse functions? If I were expecting students to interact with Shakespeare's plays by performing scenes utilizing alternative notions of staging and character development, might I wonder if students who balk at this have not ever read Shakespeare via staging and character study? Suppose the latter students complained that they are not theater majors, and that they prefer not to perform as actors? Suppose further that these students are not convinced by my gentle request that they trust me, that this approach to Shakespeare can be enjoyable, is based on a great deal of research into the pedagogy of Shakespeare, and that my personal experience is that it is a worthwhile approach to take?

At Arcadia, our redesign of the teacher education program took into consideration the very real concern that education majors were not adequately prepared for student teaching and the beginning of a teaching career, despite extremely positive feedback from local schools regarding our student teachers. We discussed in particular our students' understanding of diversity and difference, and their abilities to apply such understanding in the varying contexts of teaching and learning. It seemed important to us that the early experiences enable students to understand better what their studies would entail if they stuck with education as a career choice. In other words, we were not sure that many of our students were choosing education with a clear notion of what teaching and learning require of the teacher. Does a history major know what historiography is when they start out in their first courses? Does a psychology major know from the beginning that there are controversies over what constitutes legitimate research in their field? No. They instead learn about these things in their early courses, and use these courses to help them determine for themselves what they believe in, what sort of scholar they wish to be within this discipline, and in fact, most of them will probably work in areas not directly related to their major once they obtain their degrees.

In beginning education courses, we often ask, "Why have you chosen to be a teacher?" An overwhelming majority of teacher–wannabees describe long term fantasies of power or control, or a simple, nonreflective love of young children better suited to baby-sitting than teaching. Just as advanced mathematics courses expect a student to have mastered skills of calculus and proof argumentation, I would think advanced education courses would assume a mastery of ideological analysis and intercultural communication skills. One would expect a graduating senior to speak with a different language than a first-year student. Do we see this? At Arcadia we saw this happening, but we wanted more. So our initial courses require students to work in varying educational contexts, including, for example, schools and homeless shelters, in order to introduce ideological and inter-cultural discourses and expectations; and our seniors follow their fall semester student teaching with a thesis semester that includes action research projects in which they are transforming a local educational culture. We have partly flipped the preservice curricu-lum so that it begins with student teaching and ends with foundational courses parallel to postgraduate research. We, too, saw a politics of domestication in action, one which was legitimated by our previous curricular structure; the old program started with university courses, increasingly incorporated the authentic, "real" education of field experiences, and culminated in the only legitimate, deintellectualized period of student teaching, where the accent was on fitting in rather than trying something new that strives for social justice. Like most preservice programs, ours inadvertently taught students to value the authenticity of the field over the theory of the university by leading students from theory to practice, and using the field as the final test of preparedness for teaching. The new structure enables students to move from initial field experiences into a dialogic relation-ship between practice and theory, within a common project of social justice and action.

Why go on at length about a curriculum design at Arcadia? Well, for one thing, as I read Alberto's chapter, I thought about how rare it is for curriculum studies scholars to rethink their own curriculum. This is ironically endemic to the field of curriculum stud-ies. Dewey himself was famous for his tedious lecturing on progressive education. But I am not presenting a simplistic argument that curriculum studies in its reconceptualiza-tion needs to attend more closely to curriculum in its narrowest definition. I see instead in Alberto's chapter a question about why we are not more often working together on common projects. A redesign of a teacher education curriculum is one possible common project. There are many others.

I have presented an analysis elsewhere (Appelbaum, 2002) that the earliest phases of the reconceptual movement in curriculum studies coconstructed a project of conceptual discourse, within which individual scholars are seemingly required to make a name for themselves through the establishment of a concept that is new and original. More recent scholars, the "next generation," I claimed, have sublated the conceptual discourse as they were trained in graduate school to appreciate the commitments and anxieties of postmodern, postcolonial, and transnational theories. Common to both "generations," I claimed, was a tendency to sloppy scholarship where writers do not do their research; that is, where it is OK for a journal article, book, or conference presentation to simply ignore potentially related work that already exists. After all, to be exhaustive in one's reading of the literature might threaten the apparent newness of one's own presentation. Such attention to what already exists makes it harder to invent new concepts. Other con-cepts start to sound a lot like one's own. We tend to work as rugged individualists rather than as collaborators who support each other.

For example, how different is a discussion of resistance within a politics of domestication from my own (Appelbaum, 2002) description of a professional attention deficit hyperactivity disorder in professional discourse, or Mordechai Gordon's (2007) discussion of student uncertainty? Gordon suggested we should not rush to immediately resolve student doubts and concerns, and instead acknowledge them as a "healthy state of mind" (p.52). I think his application of Rilke shifts resistance from a context of social agency toward a psychoanalytic framework (Appelbaum, 2007). Here resistance is seen both as necessary for significant learning to occur (rather than as a problem to overcome), and thus as a sign of powerful learning moments. The forms of resistance that Alberto describes would be recognized as powerful learning opportunities. Students expressing dismay might be in this sense one important sign of a good curriculum.

The critical difference between psychoanalysis and the training curricula in which many teachers and teacher educators operate is that psychoanalysis takes a long time, and training curricula have prescribed boundaries of time and space. Alberto needs to raise the issues because his course is the only point in time when most of his students will ever have the opportunity to explore new alternatives for science education. If we know that some students cannot take advantage of the course at this time, why do we subject them to it in the first place? I am writing this during a sabbatical year in Germany where education for the *Abitur* and eventual university commences for *some, not all* pupils in the 5th grade. What I notice in my work here with teachers at the secondary and university levels is a great expectation that students must be up to the challenge, and fewer expectations that a teacher make it easier for the student to achieve; the burden is on the student, not the teacher. I am not saying this is good or better. But I can't help wondering what it would be like if our teacher education programs demanded upon entry, for example in an application essay, clear evidence that a student has had previous experiences that prepare him or her for work with diverse groups of people. What would happen if some potential teachers were turned away until they could demonstrate that they are prepared for our courses? Until we wrestle with the market economics that require us to increase enrollments with no upper limits (note: there are only a fixed number of places for study of any given field at a university in Germany), we won't be able to consider such prerequisites.

But back to curriculum studies: I read Alberto's chapter as a lone voice working without too much support, except maybe from his colleague and coauthor, Robert Kitchen. My simple reaction is to urge a greater sense of a larger common project in the post-reconceptual age. I know this is challenging in a consumer culture industry that individualizes each of us. But can't we ask why there are not more of "us" on any given campus? Why do we fall into the trap of thinking that there should be a range of ideological and intellectual approaches on every campus, instead of looking for ways to hire people we meet at conferences to be part of our departments? For years, I have tried to get presenters at Bergamo, C&P, and within Division B of AERA to apply for jobs at my university, with little success. It is as if we do not want to blend in. Do we revel in our lone warrior image? By the same token, why do we shy away from hiring others like ourselves when we are members of a search committee? And, why do we not quote or cite articles and books that already exist on the topics at hand? When we review an article for a journal or a conference, do we look to see if the bibliography includes previous articles in the same journal? Without such spadework by the authors, there is no complicated conversation emerging in this article; here is merely narcissism.

Longstanding now is the call by Philip Wexler (1990) for educationists to place their work within larger social movements. Back then, he suggested understanding our work within, say, the environmental movement, or the feminist movement. The point was to see our work within a larger common project, so that we could organize for the cause and build connections along the way. Alberto does this with his application of sociotransformative constructivism to analyze teacher education experiences for understanding teaching in diverse classrooms (Rodriguez & Berryman, 2002). But I would say the overall project of social justice has too much of the character of what Maxine Greene (1973) once called "slogans," phrases repeated warmly and often until they can be agreed upon by most anybody and thus have little specific meaning for action. In Alberto's case, social justice has deep meaning, and clear implications for action. But until his work within the teacher education curriculum is taken as a component of a larger, common social project, rather than dissolved within an amorphous collection of institutional compromises, it can have little educational impact, and more importantly, does little for "the cause."

My final thought has to do with this small group of students. It seems to me that any form of pedagogy fails some small group of students. In a traditional classroom, somebody receives a C- of D on a test; they probably would say the teacher failed to teach them, while the teacher would say they did not study enough for the test. Why in the case of antiracist pedagogy for social justice do we dwell on the small group of students who do not perform well on equivalent measures of success? Well, because we see the ideological complications of blaming the victim. What is analogous to writing a weak argument for the use of time in Chekhov's *Cherry Orchard*? Would it be not being able to describe the way 2nd-grader Nkendra interprets the relationship between number lines and the flow of time on her block on a Saturday night? If preservice teacher Mary can't tell me this after working with NKendra for 5 weeks, twice weekly, should Mary receive a D? If Mary writes on a course evaluation form that I did not teach her what NKendra thinks, have I not done my job? Suppose in fact that we have discussed at minimum 10 different ways to converse with students through which a teacher might learn about NKendra's life, just as an English professor may have discussed time and forms of literary analysis in five other works of literature. If Mary says her teacher did not help her, is this a matter for theoretical analysis, curriculum assessment, teacher evaluation, textbook reconsideration? Surely a post-reconceptual perspective understands that none of these really has much to do with the particular experiences of Mary, NKendra, or Mary's university teacher. What services are provided the student who received a D on the test? Analogous services need to be invented ancillary to our curriculum as well.

References

Appelbaum, P. (2002). Diss-conceptualizing curriculum: Is there a next in the generational text? *Journal of Curriculum Theorizing, 18*(1): 7–19.

Appelbaum, P. (2007). *Children's books for grown-up teachers: Reading and writing curriculum theory.* New York: Routledge.

Gordon, M. (2007). Living the questions: Rilke's challenge to our quest for certainty. *Educational Theory, 57*(1): 37–52.

Greene, M. (1973). *Teachers as stranger: Educational philosophy for the modern age.* Belmont, CA: Wadsworth.

Rodriguez, A., & Berryman, C. (2002). Using sociotransformative constructivism to teach for understanding in diverse classrooms: A beginning teacher's journey. *American Educational Research Journal, 39*(4), 1017–1045.

Wexler, P. (1990). *Social analysis of education.* New York: Routledge.

22 Edward Said and Jean-Paul Sartre
Critical Modes of Intellectual Life

Greg Dimitriadis[1]

Chapter Overview

This chapter explores the growing marriage between corporations and schools and universities. The author demonstrates that as neoliberal economic logic continues to unfold, colleges and universities are actively repositioning themselves within this new terrain and reformulating their dispositions in relation to other non- and for-profit organizations. As a result, the author explains, faculty have experienced hyperprofessionalization and have been cut off from the broader public. The author turns to the work of Sartre and Said to help respond to the pressures of academic capitalism. Both of these scholars critiqued the narrowing of specialties and subspecialties within the academy. Sartre emphasized intellectual work foregrounded in existential choice, human freedom, and the imaginary. Said believed the role of the intellectual is to expand language and discourse in ways that challenge reductive categories and stereotypes. The author concludes that these two intellectuals might help us rethink our roles as curriculum scholars.

Introduction

As Harvard University President Emeritus Derek Bok (2003) points out in his celebrated *Universities in the Marketplace: The Commercialization of Higher Education*, the notion of "commercializing" higher education is an inherently vexed and problematic one. After all, he notes, most people who enter the academy do so to avoid the world of commerce (p. 18). "To commercialize a university," he writes, "is to engage in practices widely regarded in the academy as suspect, if not downright disreputable" (p. 18). These pressures, Bok shows, are not new. Universities have always been commercial enterprises. In fact, he begins his book with a quote from Thorstein Veblen who in 1918 noted that the commercial nature of universities is "one of the unwritten, and commonly unspoken commonplaces lying at the root of modern academic policy" (p. 1). Yet, as Bok argues, the commercialization of higher education has rapidly intensified in recent years—two notable examples being the increasingly high profile investments in athletics as well as scientific research that has clear commercial applications. More and more, universities are expected to operate like any other commercial, profit making enterprise.

These pressures have been met (in the past and present) by liberal defenses of higher education and its goals and purposes—the kind forwarded by Bok, William Tierney (1999), and others. They have also been met my more radical critiques. Indeed, there is a long history of writing on the "corporatization of education" in critical pedagogy and curriculum studies, writing that has powerfully demonstrated the growing marriage between school systems and industry. Among other things, this work has demonstrated how schools are now less concerned with developing citizens who can thoughtfully deliberate the "common good" in the public sphere than with producing workers ready to take their attendant positions in the economic system. From Bowles and Gintis (1976) to

464

Henry Giroux (2005) and beyond, this work has powerfully demonstrated how corporate logics have all but colonized the functions of schools and the language of democracy and democratic possibilities.

This work remains invaluable. All of it underscores the importance of how we as intellectuals navigate the institutions we traverse—as citizens, scholars, and activists. I argue here for the need to rethink and reimagine the role of the modern intellectual. In this chapter, I focus on the work of two scholars who have helped me understand the new roles and responsibilities of contemporary intellectual life—Edward Said and Jean-Paul Sartre. In many ways, both scholars are "big thinkers" capable of thinking across a broad swath of intellectual issues—music, literature, philosophy, among them—while holding fast to evolving sets of political commitments. These commitments located both inside and outside of the university in complex ways.

I locate their work, however, within a slightly different set of arguments about the modern academy than those noted above. In particular, I turn here toward the work of Shelia Slaughter and Gary Rhodes (2004) and their notion of "academic capitalism." As neoliberal economic logics continue to unfold, they argue, universities are *actively positioning* themselves both to survive and prosper in this new terrain. Universities are aggressively competing against one another to attract "high-ability students able to assume high debt loads" (p. 1) while redefining their role as new economy "players." Universities are actively marketing sponsored products (e.g., negotiating exclusive licensing rights for Pepsi, McDonalds, or Apple computers, etc.) to their captive students while aggressively capitalizing on the intellectual work of their faculties (e.g., securing patents and copyrights from ongoing faculty research, etc.). Slaughter and Rhodes open up an important discussion about the ways in which universities are not only responding to external corporate pressures—often an inheritance of the "commercializing" and "corporatization" discourses noted above—but are actively producing institutional dispositions which allow them to compete with a host of other profit-generating businesses. Moreover, they argue, these academic institutions benefit both from public state-sponsorship through their nonprofit status as well as their own private profit making endeavors—a largely unmarked though of course problematic nexus.

Indeed, Slaughter and Rhodes push us in a new if more subtle direction than those of liberal critics such as Bok or radical critics such as Giroux. The particular strength of Slaughter and Rhodes's volume is to highlight the more active role that university administrators and faculty are taking in this regard. As they demonstrate, academia has not been simply "duped" here, nor are they only "acted upon" by outside forces. Following Foucault, they are actively producing these corporate dispositions in new and unpredictable ways as they enter new "circuits of knowledge" which connect them both to other universities and various profit-driven entities. As they write, "The theory of academic capitalism focuses on networks—new circuits of knowledge, interstitial organizational emergence, networks that intermediate between public and private sector, extended managerial capacity—that link institutions as well as faculty, administrators, academic professionals and students to the new economy" (p. 15). While Slaughter and Rhodes are writing out of the U.S. context (as am I), these tendencies are now evidenced in university life worldwide—post-Thatcher Britain and contemporary Australia being perhaps the two most notable examples.

We are all implicated here. While these moves have clearly served to privilege particular areas of research and inquiry—those with grant-getting and profit-making potential—such a discussion does not let any of us "off the hook" as we fashion our own careers and trajectories. Indeed, one pernicious effect of "academic capitalism" is that academics have increasingly come to function as seemingly autonomous individuals who are cut off from broader communities and constituencies. While there have been pushes for "collaboration" in some research circles, it is often narrowly defined, a way to create specialized knowledge in service of funding "niches." A kind of hyperprofessionalization has come to mark much of our work today across any number of fields—even critical ones. Our responsibilities are now increasingly diverted from broader public good toward narrow specialties and subspecialties—along with their attendant journals, presses, conferences, and honors. Of course, the effects have been differential here. As smaller and smaller numbers of academics maneuver and succeed in smaller and smaller corners of the world, large amounts of intellectual labor (adjuncts, part timers) are simply being written off. Survival for the neoliberal subject is now an individual responsibility, not a social one. As Bronwyn Davies writes, "since the individual is responsible for taking care of him or herself and not dependent upon society, such selves, in being cut loose from the social, no longer have the same responsibility to the social" (Davies, 2005, p. 9). The great challenge, it seems, is to reclaim the kinds of academic and institutional dispositions being produced today in new and progressive ways.

Edward Said's work on the "intellectual" is critical here, as is Jean-Paul Sartre's notion of "the project." In this chapter, I bring both these thinkers to bear on the pressures of "academic capitalism" noted above. In one powerful respect, as I will show, Said's work has been an ongoing testament to his continual struggle to look toward the broader social good—as most explicitly realized, perhaps, in his work on Palestine. In an even more profound way, however, Said's particular accomplishment was to do this while always challenging the social, political, and intellectual foundations upon which he stood. Throughout his work, Said again and again called academia "the last utopia"—but it was a utopia that needed to be fought for, to be reinvented again and again. Said continually challenged the tenets of all intellectual and political specialties and orthodoxies—even advocating for the importance of "amateurism" as a guiding disposition. While Said is perhaps best known for his literary insights on "Orientalism," his work on the nature of the intellectual is important—particularly at this moment of political, cultural, and economic retrenchment. I will explore here the contours of Said's work on the intellectual. I will argue that Said gives us a model of intellectual activity at a moment when we have to manage multiple professional and political obligations and responsibilities—all of which are ever-intensifying.

Sartre, I will show, offers us a trenchant example of a morally engaged and committed thinker similarly hard at work, willing to challenge his own ideas to their core as the moment demanded. In the age of the "specific intellectual," Sartre's vision of intellectual work foregrounds existential choice, human freedom, and the imaginary in broad-based ways. It is a disposition that allowed him to think through and across a variety of social, personal, and intellectual issues with a broad range of discursive forms and tools. More than anything, Sartre offers us a strategy that forces us outward, into the problems of the world, with the goal of "interrupting history." Taken together, these two thinkers give us resources for facing our moment and its demands in new and authentic ways.

Edward Said

Edward Said is of course best known as a literary critic. The author of many important texts on a range of subjects, Said's defining work is undoubtedly *Orientalism* (1978/2003). *Orientalism* is an exploration of the ways in which Western scholars have produced a mutually reinforcing distinction between "the Orient" and "the Occident" to understand the Middle East. For Said, Orientalism is a "corporate institution for dealing with the Orient—dealing with it by making statements about it, authorizing views of it, describing it, by teaching it, settling it, ruling over it: in short, Orientalism as a Western style for dominating, restructuring, and having authority over the Orient" (p. 3). Much of this, for Said, is about the production of a self-reinforcing and propelling field of knowledge and inquiry—the production of expertise and authority about "the Orient" and "the Occident."

Said was intimately concerned with how this kind of "authority" gets produced and disseminated. More specifically, he discussed two ways this kind of authority is established. First, he discussed the ways individual writers carved out "strategic locations" in particular texts about the Orient—authoring/authorizing their own place in an ongoing (albeit limited) conversation. Second, he discussed the ways texts become part of a larger "strategic formation" or assemblage of material about the Orient that takes on the veneer of self-evident truth or fact. The point is key. Following Foucault, Said highlighted the cumulative power of these representations, the ways these ongoing conversations developed in specific ways, drawing scholars into certain conversations and lines of thought over and above others. The result is a particular "official" notion of what the Orient "is"—as a body of self-propelling scholarship—cut off from more emergent and heterogeneous realities. The result is the production of "expertise." Often appearing neutral and disinterested, this body of expert knowledge has crafted, for Said, a fantasy about the Orient that has effectively served to underscore and support the dominance of the West.

While Said was primarily concerned with representations of the Middle East, other scholars have found his theoretical framework broadly applicable in other contexts. I recall here, for example, work on aboriginal peoples and representation which has drawn on Said's work (Maxwell, 1999; Meadows, 2001). Said powerfully commented on the uptake of his book in the afterword to the 1994 edition:

> I wanted readers to make use of my work so that they might then produce new studies of their own that would illuminate the historical experience of Arabs and others in a generous, enabling mode. That certainly happened in Europe, the United States, Australia, the Indian subcontinent, the Caribbean, Ireland, and Latin America, and parts of Africa. The invigorated study of Africanist and Indological discourses; the analyses of subaltern history; the reconfiguration of post-colonial anthropology, political science, art history, literary criticism, musicology, in addition to the vast new developments in feminist and minority discourses—to all these, I am pleased and flattered that *Orientalism* often makes a difference. (1978/2003, p. 339)

Clearly, the book has been a foundational text in the metadisciplinary field of postcolonial studies. According to Said, this field is centrally concerned with "studies of domination and control done from the standpoint of either a completed political independence or an incomplete liberationist project"—a fundamentally different orientation from more Eurocentric postmodern work marked by the "decorative weightlessness of history, pastiche, and above all consumerism" (p. 349). Though Said himself locates postcolonialism's origins in the early work of writers and thinkers such as Anwar Abdel Malek, Samir Amin, and C. L. R. James (p. 339), his own work had a critically important "consolidating" effect on the field. With the publication of *Orientalism*, postcolonial studies emerged as a space that others could pick up, extend, or contest in generative ways.

The profound and generous uptake of *Orientalism* has much to do, I believe, with its productive epistemological tension between its poststructural and more traditionally humanist impulses—a tension which marked Said's entire career. On the one hand, this book is indebted to the poststructural work of Michel Foucault. Drawing on *The Archeology of Knowledge* (1982) and *Discipline and Punish* (1979) among others, Said treated Orientalism as a Foucauldian "discourse"—a self-propelling and referential way of representing the other that "produces" the very categories and ideas it represents. On the other, the book evidences a strong faith in more classical notions of humanism. For Said, human beings are not only "produced" by discourse. In some deep sense, we are active agents in our own lives, communities, and cultures, with the potential to transform our circumstances in more humane ways. Said himself commented on this seeming disjuncture:

> Among American and British academics of a decidedly rigorous and unyielding stripe, *Orientalism*, and indeed all of my other work, has come under disapproving attacks because of its "residual" humanism, its theoretical inconsistencies, its insufficient, perhaps even sentimental, treatment of agency. I am glad that it has! *Orientalism* is a partisan book, not a theoretical machine. No one has convincingly shown that individual effort is not at some profoundly unteachable level both eccentric and, in Gerard Manley Hopkins's sense, original. (p. 339)

Indeed, Said looked both to describe and to interrupt this discourse in *Orientalism* and work that followed. Part of the goal here was to disrupt notions of professional competence and control. This move was made most explicit in his volume *Representations of the Intellectual* (1994). In this short book, Said underscored many of the insights of *Orientalism*, crafting them into a meditation on the nature and responsibility of individual intellectual work today. For Said, the intellectual's role was to work against the kind of calcified language that produced concepts like "the Orient" and "the Occident" or "the East" and "the West." The role of the intellectual is to expand language and discourse, to challenge such reductive categories and stereotypes that serve to shut down human thought (p. ix). For Said, such categories and stereotypes most typically served elite interests—and it was the moral duty of the intellectual to always call them into question. The intellectual was always an outsider, on the margins. He writes of the "intellectual as exile and marginal, as amateur, and as author of a language that tries to speak truth to power" (p. xvi).

This is the charge of the contemporary intellectual—to look beyond the deadening effects of official discourse—to struggle toward a new language which champions the disenfranchised. This struggle is highly personal—and it is not only realized on the page, as distant prose. For Said, it was difficult to detach the author's work from his or her personal profile. The true intellectual has a personal signature, one that cannot be contained within the parameters of a particular profession or field, one that resists the easy clichés that preserve the status quo.

How can one separate the relationship, he asks, of Jean-Paul Sartre and Simone de Beauvoir from our understanding of their work? The romantic mythology is constitutive of their intellectual force, the specificity of their voices marked by a moment in time and a particular relationship. The specificity is key to authoring "a language that speaks truth to power" (p. xvi). He continues, "The intellectual does not represent a statuelike icon but an individual vocation, an energy, a stubborn force engaging as a committed and recognizable voice in language and in society with a whole slew of issues, all of them having to do in the end with a combination of enlightenment and emancipation or freedom" (p. 73).

It is precisely this "stubborn force" that we must hold onto as we enter this moment of academic retrenchment—a moment when secure positions that provide living wages and space to think and conduct research are becoming increasingly scare—a moment when the idea of research itself is being constructed in increasingly narrow and functional ways. As resources shrink, we are witnessing ever-accelerating moves toward the hyper-professionalization of areas and fields of study. As individuals are vying for control over their lives and work in these fraught times, the lure of professionalism is increasingly pressing. Here, we see the temptation to operate in increasingly narrow fields and sub-fields, to limit ones audience, to speak an increasingly specific and conscripted language. The temptation is to fight for authority in smaller and smaller corners of the world—a dynamic which helped produce the kinds of hypertheorization which came to mark areas like postmodernism, cultural studies, and (ironically, of course) postcolonialism. Said wrote powerfully on these temptations of professionalism—primary among them, of course, being the material rewards that institutions can offer. With specialization, comes the pressure to narrow one's commitments and audiences.

Of course, it is worth noting that Said spent his entire career at Columbia University, an elite, Ivy League institution. He speaks as someone who has succeeded (quite well) in navigating academic hierarchies, having established himself early on (before he published *Orientalism*) as a fairly traditional literary critic. In many respects, he speaks from a position of comfort and privilege, as someone who has earned the luxury of disdain for arcane academic trappings. Yet, such critiques can easily descend into a series of useless personal or ad hominem attacks which obscure Said's central insights—insights about power, knowledge, and above all else, the so-called expert.

Indeed, from *Orientalism* to *Representation of the Intellectual*, Said continually highlighted the dangers of "professional expertise." The idea of the "expert" implies narrow notions of control and competence. It implies fewer people able to speak from increasingly privileged positions. It implies a broad, wholesale abdication of some of the most important and pressing issues of our times—that certain issues exclusively "belong" to particular groups. With this, of course, comes the "drift" toward consolidated power and authority. Again and again, Said contested these pressures, these moves toward functional and instrumental uses of knowledge in service of the power elites.

In the face of this, Said advocated for the importance of the "amateur." The amateur does not work for the sake of dominant institutions and their rewards. Rather, the amateur operates out of a deep sense of love, affection, and commitment. Amateurism is "the desire to be moved not by profit or reward but by love for and unquenchable interest in the larger picture, in making connections across lines and barriers, in refusing to be tied down to a specialty, in caring for ideas and values despite the restrictions of a profession" (p. 76). This means moving across domains, not beholden to the rewards of different interest groups and their specialty languages. The amateur has always to reinvent his or her language and dispositions, cannot be conscripted by the pull of official discourses.

Here too, one might accuse Said of obscuring his own privilege. After all, being an "amateur" implies a certain kind of freedom from material imperatives and constraints. Said could afford to be an "amateur" across intellectual domains, one might argue, because he had already earned his professional credentials. Yet, we must be careful here as well. While he clearly fought against the idea of academic professionalism, Said did not simply advocate turning away from academic institutions. In fact, Said called them potentially "utopic" spaces many times—but they need always to be called into question. On the one hand, he sharply criticizes those who would simply abdicate their own social, cultural, and political responsibilities for the comfort and security of university life. For example, he highlights the ways in which the Beat poets of the 1960s, with all their "irresponsible" impulses, largely returned to the university to live rarefied and protected lives. On the other, however, he sharply calls into question those who would simply call all academics "sellouts"—"a coarse and finally meaningless charge" (p. 69). Much important work can be done in such spaces, offering one of the last refuges for free thought.

Moreover, work nurtured inside the academy can reach beyond it in important ways, Said reminds us. While he offers Hayden White as an example in the United States, he could have just as easily mentioned himself.

Indeed, Said was perhaps the most visible public intellectual advocating Palestinian self-determination. On TV, in print, and in lectures, he was unequivocal and consistent in his support—even before it became a somewhat fashionable cause. Again and again, he called Israel's occupation of Palestine a crime. Again and again, he highlighted the repressive brutality of its military and policing apparatus. A consistent theme throughout his career, Said's support took on a new urgency in the years leading up to his death—in particular, with the failures of the Oslo process, the attacks of September 11, and the wars against Afghanistan and Iraq (Said, 2004a). While Said was a "professor of terror" for some, however, he was no simple spokesperson for the PLO and its leaders. He was intensely critical of the Palestinian leadership—in particular, Arafat and his circle—for their incompetence and corruption. In the end, he advocated for a "single state solution"—earning him enemies on both sides of the divide. Above all else, Said maintained his singular intellectual and social commitments up until his death—even as a university professor who could have easily rested on his professional laurels.

Ultimately, then, Said asks us always to remain always responsible for how we occupy our positions. We must face up to the realities of contemporary pressures of academia but we must resist them—"not by pretending that they are not there, or denying their influence, but by representing a different set of values and prerogatives" (p. 82). The point is key. The academy is a space that we should neither give ourselves completely over to, nor simply walk away from. We must carve out and find space for our own individual, self-styled voices in our struggles to "speak truth to power." In so doing, we are beholden to multiple audiences—our students, the rigors of our disciplines, and to our own sense of being citizens in the broader world (2002, p. 501). Each of these demands their own attention and autonomy—sometimes coexisting easily with one another, sometimes not. All are worth fighting for. None should provide us respite.

Jean-Paul Sartre

The work of Jean-Paul Sartre is worth revisiting here, as well. While not linked to the academy in the same way as Said, he offers us a complex theorization of the lived life as coconstituted intellectual and political "project." In *Search for a Method* (1963/1996) Sartre discusses the complex intersection between the existential freedoms of the individual and the often encumbering demands of history. In many ways, this volume (a self-professed introduction to his massive two-volume *Critique of Dialectical Reason*) marked Sartre's efforts to come to terms with the ways in which our social circumstances can radically circumvent individual freedom. In this respect, it was an extension of his earlier work which stressed the radical freedom of the individual (e.g., "man [sic] will be what he makes of himself") with perhaps little attention to social context and constraint (2001, p. 28). With *Search for a Method*, Sartre turned to the social and historical. Yet, for Sartre, any social or historical framework which locks actors into prescripted and determining roles is inauthentic. In his discussion of historical materialism, he critiques a deterministic theory of history—"It is *a priori*. It does not derive its concepts from experience—or at least not from the new experiences which it seeks to interpret. It has already formed its concepts; it is already certain of their truth; it will assign to them the role of constitutive schemata" (1963/1996, p. 37). Recourse to deterministic theories of any type is anathema to Sartre, as they look to distance us from our moral and ethical responsibilities and choices.

To move away from this bad faith, for Sartre, is to wrestle with our existential freedoms and choices in a complex world. It is to face the world without recourse to self-imposed illusions that the world cannot be different or that it can be transcended in easy ways by force of human will alone. These are two sides of the same coin for Sartre. If nothing else, Sartre's body of work highlights the ways in which our particular theoretical and practical frameworks cannot fully exhaust an emergent reality that always exceeds our grasp. "Existence," for Sartre, "precedes essence." As Sartre's character Antoine Roquentin writes in the novel *Nausea* (1964) "Existence, everywhere, infinitely, in excess, for ever and everywhere; existence which is limited only by existence" (p. 133). In *Nausea*, Sartre explores Roquentin's efforts to write a historical biography of M. de Rollebon, a minor figure in the French Revolution. He spends many days in the library, combing documents, trying to figure out how to script his life into a coherent narrative. In the end, he abandons the project. He says, "M. de Rollebon was my partner; he needed me in order to exist and I needed him so as not to feel my existence" (p. 98). This notion of history is one that numbs us from reality, distances us from the complexities of life. It is a history marked by bad faith. In the end, Roquentin turns toward something richer. "The essential thing is contingency," he concludes. "I mean that one cannot define existence as necessity. To exist is simply *to be there*" (p. 131).

The challenge is profound—and has only become more pronounced over the past several decades. As Appadurai (2006) has argued, our moment is marked by fundamental conditions of incompleteness and contingency. While Sartre would ask us to face this reality in good faith, many are responding in more limited ways. In particular, the nation-state project itself has become (increasingly) about the latent quest for cultural purity, a quest which often belies the global presence of minority groups. As Appadurai notes, "As a broad fact about the world of the 1990s, the forces of globalization produced conditions for an increase in insecurity and also in the friction of incompleteness" (p. 9). Living in a world where difference and contingency are permanent conditions demands a kind of cosmopolitan disposition often anathema to world leaders and actors. Appadurai continues, "The anxiety of incompleteness (always latent in the project of complete national purity) and the sense of social uncertainty about large-scale ethnoracial categories can produce a runaway form of mutual stimulation, which is the road to genocide" (p. 9).

The impulse is paramount to "be there" as a full participant in this history and its contingencies. For Sartre, this means both facing our specific material and social circumstances while holding fast to a vision of what a better future for all humankind would look like. This is being "for itself," not "in itself." It is to hold on to notions of universal human freedom. Sartre, thus, does not allow us to simply "wallow" in this contingency. While recognizing it as a fundamental, historical condition, he asks us to act ethically within its situation(s). He writes, "The most rudimentary behavior must be determined both in relation to the real and present factors which condition it and in relation to a certain object, still to come, which it is trying to bring into being. This is what we call *the project*" (2001, p. 308). For Sartre, this meant a commitment to Marxism, which defined his moment in addressing its scarcities. But Sartre's Marxism was not one of rigid doctrines or blind faith in leaders—he came to be one of the Soviet Union's greatest critics, in fact. It was a Marxism that provided "coordinates" for imagining a future of freedom for all, a future where human beings could realize their full potentials, free from the pull of material scarcity. For Sartre, Marxism was a way of facing our ethical responsibility to become more human as we acknowledge the humanity of others in all their particularities. Facing one's historical moment with a radical imagination and a profound sense of responsibility for unavoidable, existential choice, was paramount.

This commitment to Marxism forced Sartre and others in his circle to wrestle with the brutal realities of Stalin and the USSR. Most famously, his friendship with Albert Camus ended over their respective commitments to Marxism. While Sartre remained committed to Marxism in spite of its perversions, Camus passionately turned away from it (Aronson, 2004). The debate was fierce and divisive. In *Humanism and Terror: An Essay on the Communist Problem* (1947), Sartre's mentor, the phenomenologist Maurice Merleau-Ponty, tried to pull apart and deconstruct the binary which largely came to define the moment (i.e., that one could be either "pro-communist/USSR" or "pro-capitalist/USA"). As a committed French Marxist, he argued that other positions were possible, that one could hold onto the tenets of Marxism without wholly supporting the USSR. According to Merleau-Ponty, the Left faced an "intractable situation"—the Marxist critique of capitalism was critical but the proletariat's authentic revolution in the USSR had come to a halt (p. xxi). Importantly, he refused the stark distinction that many anticommunists deployed—that one was either an "innocent" or a "murderer" (p. xxxvii). For Merleau-Ponty, Sartre, and others, the Marxist humanist ideal defined the moment, though it did not demand toeing "the party line" or deterministic thinking. It demanded, rather, a passionate engagement with their historical moment and all its messy complexities.

While a sense of class inequality often marked his work—what he sometimes called a "socialism of abundance" (Flynn, 1997, p. 227)—Sartre was remarkably wide-ranging in the issues he took on. Perhaps most notably, Sartre became a spokesperson for a broad condemnation of colonialism in all its forms—a key point of overlap with Said of course (Sartre, 1964/2006). He was a particularly fierce critic of his government's role in colonizing Algeria. He said clearly that there are no "good" or "bad" colonizers, there are only colonizers. For Sartre, colonization turns other people into "things," often accomplished by scripting, mobilizing, and naturalizing racial categories. Authentic dialogue and engagement is precluded by these ossified racial categories which reproduce debilitating binaries between Whites and Blacks, self and other, civilized and primitive, among others.

In addition, Sartre took a very public stance on his country's involvement in torture—in many ways, a practice which naturally emerges from the logics of colonization. In a classic Sartrean gesture, he declared that torture dehumanizes the torturer as well as the tortured; a point made by Caribbean poet Aimé Césaire in his *Discourse on Colonialism* (1953), as well. One cannot debase another without debasing oneself, cannot deny another's freedom and humanity without denying one's own. The effort to do so here, to justify torture, is often accomplished through the kinds of "bad faith" discussed above. As Sartre writes, the popular media in France often reached out and painted its audience as innocent and good, absolving them of their complicity in their nation's policies. In particular, he discussed a TV show called "You Are Wonderful!" where callers helped downtrodden individuals featured on the show (pp. 63–71). This show perpetrated France's sense of "purity" and "innocence" in the face of its atrocities in Algeria. This is a quintessential gesture of "bad faith" for Sartre. It is an abdication of collective, national responsibility. It is a lesson, of course, the United States should have learned before the horrors of Abu Ghraib and Guantanamo Bay—and their attendant political containments.

Indeed, while Sartre's notion of history was linked to Marxism and historical dialecticism, it was not rigid or prescriptive. It allowed him to "move," to see his work as always "in progress." More than anything, he reflected in his later years, Marxism "existed in a milieu, an intellectual and emotional atmosphere that was broader than the theory itself and in certain ways was disappointed by the theory. The environment was the left" (Sartre & Levy, 1996, p. 77). This community—and its personal, intellectual, and political projects—could not be exhausted by Marxist theory.

For Sartre, a commitment to human freedom can never be atomistic or parochial. One can only be free when one commits oneself to freedom for all. One cannot use one's freedom to enslave another. This reads today like a radically ecumenical (if anachronistic) gesture, particularly as political commitments on the left seem increasingly fractured and local. But its implications for intellectual work are nevertheless profound. Committed, creative work cannot have any other goal but human freedom. Sartre writes, "whether he is an essayist, a pamphleteer, a satirist, or a novelist, whether he speaks only of individual passions or whether he attacks the social order, the writer, a free man addressing free men has only one subject—freedom" (2001, p. 276). One's commitment to these ideals seems paramount here, moving across work that is both personal (those that take "individual passions" as their subject) as well as explicitly political.

The implications for thinking through history—and interrupting it—are broad ranging. According to Thomas Flynn, Sartre's "concept of a 'science' of history is that of a committed thinker whose reading-interpretation of the ambiguities of history will occur from the valuative perspective of maximizing the condition of freedom for all" (1997, p. 96). For Sartre, understandings of the past are open to multiple and varied readings. The committed thinker and writer will take a "valuative" position in narrating them. Flynn highlights the aesthetic impulse behind much of Sartre's perspective on historical work, "Like the person who connects the dots in a puzzle, the existentialist historian must imaginatively link the actions, events, facts, and states of affairs so as to yield the desired forms of intelligibility" (p. 148). He continues, "Sartre likens the intelligibility of history to that of an artwork because he considers the former as much the product of creative freedom as the later" (p. 214). This notion of the imagination—of the ability to think toward a different kind of future—is at the heart of Sartre's notion of history. Neither inherently progressive nor regressive, the imaginary is necessary for political engagement and transformation. Flynn sums up, noting that for Sartre, "historical 'facts' are ambiguous, allowing for a multiplicity of readings." It becomes the responsibility of the historical to read these facts from a position that "gives hope for the oppressed of the world." All of this, Flynn notes, becomes "Sartre's guide for writing histories and biographies that totalize one another. The ideal which inspires these efforts is variously called the 'city of ends,' a 'socialism of abundance,' or simply 'freedom'" (p. 227).

Yet, to echo the discussion above, this interpretive disposition toward intellectual work does not justify what Sartre calls "ignorance"—the willful turning away from an emergent reality that always challenges us to our core. There is thus a critical difference between what Sartre calls "truth" and "opinion." The latter is nonverifiable. It does not imply a deep responsibility for justifying one's commitments. This is the problem, as well, with positivism. It defines us only in relation to what we know, what we see in front of us, precluding an imaginative encounter with the "not yet." For Sartre, our relationship to reality is oriented by the imagination and (later) the "totalizations" of Marxism. He writes, "every concrete and real situation of consciousness in the world is pregnant with imagination in as much as it always presents itself as withdrawing from the real" (2001, p. 101). Sartre advocated what he called a "project of discovery" (1992, p. 15)—an ongoing mode of inquiry that pushes us out into the world in good faith. He contrasts this with the "empty intensions" of many simple polemicists—"We are replacing the empty intension by the project of discovery. The richness of for-itself is measured by the multiplicity of its projects, and these constitute exactly the quantity of being that is given it to reveal" (p. 15). Sartre resists the lure of determined and determining end-states. We are, in this sense, constituted as the sum total of our projects in the world.

If nothing else, then, we see a morally engaged and committed thinker at hard work—willing to challenge his own ideas to their core as the moment demanded. In the age of the "specific intellectual," Sartre's vision of intellectual work foregrounds existential choice, human freedom, and the imaginary. It is a disposition that allowed him to think through and across a variety of social, personal, and intellectual issues with a broad range of discursive forms and tools. This has become profoundly unfashionable—one reason, perhaps, the left has wed itself more closely to the university and its professional pull and away from the public sphere. Indeed, I would argue that the rise of the "specific intellectual" has perhaps been co-opted perhaps too easily into our contemporary university logics. As Foucault writes,

> A new mode of "connection between theory and practice" has been established. Intellectuals have become used to working not in the modality of the "universal," the "exemplary," the "just-and-true-for-all," but within specific sectors, at the precise points where their own conditions of life and work situate them (housing, the hospital, the asylum, the laboratory, the university, family, and sexual relations). This has undoubtedly given them a much more immediate and concrete awareness of struggles. (Chomsky & Foucault, 2006, p. 162)

This seems to be the best hope for the "specific intellectual." Yet, I am not sure that the work of specific intellectuals has put us much closer to the lived realities of individual struggle. I argue that such a disposition has perhaps dovetailed too nicely with the professionalizing, specializing imperatives of the academy. At the very least, even taken on its own terms, such work has not allowed academics to think in "big ways" about the connections between and among disparate phenomena. Such work has had a perhaps debilitating effect on the efficacy of the left in its ability to look across a wide swath of reality, girded by a vision of what a better future would look like.

Conclusions

Sartre himself noted this in a remarkably prescient passage, written before his death, "What with the third world war that can break out any day, and the wretched mess our planet has become, despair has come back to tempt me with the idea that there can be no end to it all, that there is no goal, that there are only small, individual objectives that we fight for" (Sartre & Levy, 1996, p. 109). The stress on "small, individual objectives," has indeed come to mark our moment—a perhaps unfortunate inheritance of Foucault's notion of the "specific intellectual." On one level, we see this is the narrowing of specialties and subspecialties within the academy. As Edward Said (1994) made so clear, the idea of the "expert" implies narrow notions of control and competence. It implies fewer people able to speak from increasingly privileged positions. It implies a broad, wholesale abdication of some of the most important and pressing issues of our times—that certain issues exclusively "belong" to particular groups. With this, of course, comes the "drift" toward consolidated power and authority—a key danger, even among progressives.

More broadly, we see this in the often disconnected and even fractious relationships among progressive groups. Jean Anyon points out, for example, that there is a no shortage of progressive activism today—just few common goals linking groups together. In her important book, *Radical Possibilities: Public Policy, Urban Education, and a New Social Movement* (2005), Anyon discusses five important community-based movements of the past two decades—the broad, organized press for "economic justice" in urban centers; the organization of urban parent groups around educational issues; the activism of immigrant and other minority groups for labor rights; the "living wage" movements in different municipalities across the country; and the organization of urban youth around issues such as rising incarceration rates (p. 154). These important movements, she notes, have largely operated and been prosecuted independently. Yet, as she writes, "For maximum power, the various movements today…need to unite, and acknowledge that the problems they tackle can be best resolved if they are tackled as intimately interrelated issues" (p. 175). This, it seems, demands a profound, even "totalizing" at times, "radical imagination."

Turning to these figures, I argue, is an important step in realizing such an "imagination," authentically rooted in our roles as intellectuals and academics. Such a move is imperative as the ground beneath us in the academy is reconfiguring itself in new and often dangerous ways—in the ways discussed at the outset of this essay. It becomes the paramount struggle of our time to claim the ground that's left as we contest these forces, rethinking and imagining our roles as intellectuals.

Note

1. Portions of this chapter appeared in *Discourse: Studies in the Cultural Politics of Education* (2006), On the production of expert knowledge: Revisiting Edward Said's work on the intellectual, *27*(3), 369–382 and in *Cultural Studies/Critical Methodologies,* (2009), Jean-Paul Sartre and the moral authority of the intellectual. *9*(1), 3–13.

References

Anyon, J. (2005). *Radical possibilities: Public policy, urban education, and a new social movement.* New York: Routledge.

Appadurai, A. (2006). *Fear of small numbers: An essay on the geography of anger.* Durham, NC: Duke University Press.

Aronson, R. (2004). *Camus and Sartre: The story of a friendship and the quarrel that ended it.* Chicago: University of Chicago Press.

Bok, D. (2003). *Universities in the marketplace: The commercialization of higher education.* Princeton, NJ: Princeton University Press.

Bowles, S., & Gintis, H. (1976). *Schooling in capitalist America.* New York: Basic Books.

Cesaire, A. (1953). *Discourse on colonialism.* New York: Monthy Review Press.

Chomsky, N., & Foucault, M. (2006). *The Chomsky-Foucault debate: On human nature.* New York: New Press.

Davies, B. (2005). The (im)possibility of intellectual work in neoliberal regimes. *Discourse: Studies in the Cultural Politics of Education, 26*(1), 1–14.

Foucault, M. (1979). *Discipline and punish.* New York: Vintage.

Foucault, M. (1982). *Archeology of knowledge.* New York: Pantheon.

Flynn, T. (1997). *Sartre, Foucault, and historical reason: Towards a theory of history* (Vol. 1). Chicago: University of Chicago Press.

Giroux, H. (2005). *Border crossings: Cultural workers and the politics of education* (2nd ed.). New York: Routledge.

Maxwell, A. (1999). *Colonial representation and exhibitions: Representations of the "native" and the making of European identities.* London: Leicester Press.

Meadows, M. (2001). *Voices in the wilderness: Images of Aboriginal people in the Australian media.* Westport, CT: Greenwood.

Merleau-Ponty, M. (1947). *Humanism and terror: An essay on the Communist problem.* Boston: Beacon Press.

Said, E. (1994). *Representations of the intellectual.* New York: Vintage Books.

Said, E. (2002). *Reflections on exile and other essays.* Cambridge, MA: Harvard University Press.

Said, E. (2003). *Orientalism.* New York: Vintage Books. (Original work published 1978)

Said, E. (2004a). *From Oslo to Iraq and the roadmap.* New York: Pantheon.

Said, E. (2004b). *Humanism and democratic criticism.* New York: Columbia University Press.

Sartre, J. (1963). *Search for a method.* New York: Vintage. (Original work published 1963)

Sartre, J. (1964). *Nausea.* New York: New Directions.

Sartre, J. (1992). *Truth and existence.* Chicago: University of Chicago Press.

Sartre, J. (2001). *Basic writing* (S. Priest, Ed.). New York: Routledge.

Sartre, J. (2006). *Colonialism and neocolonialism.* New York: Routledge. (Original work published 1964)

Sartre, J. & Levy, B. (1996). *Hope now: The 1980 interviews.* Chicago: University of Chicago Press.

Slaughter, S., & Rhodes, G. (2004). *Academic capitalism and the new economy: Markets, state, and higher education.* Baltimore: Johns Hopkins University.

Tierney, W. (1999). *Building the responsive campus.* Thousand Oaks: Sage.

Suggested Reading Questions

1. What sort of discourses need to be produced and circulated to counter the increasing dominance of academic capitalism within colleges and universities and other historically key sites for debating the public good?

2. According to the author, Said's work suggests that the role of teacher intellectuals is to describe and intercept discourses that alienate curriculum from lived experience. In what ways are these alienating discourses also desirous of enticing?

3. According to the author, Sartre's work suggests educators must grapple with the ways our theoretical and practical frameworks cannot fully exhaust an emerging reality that always exceeds our grasp. In what ways have our problem solving—in successive regimes of meaning—led to disillusionment with educational reform efforts?

4. The author suggests that increased specialization within academic disciplines is related to hyperpersonalization and heightened capitalistic impulses within colleges and universities. How might these phenomena also be related to educators' investment in modernist notions of progress and intellectual advancement?

5. The author suggests intellectuals must reclaim the ground of the academy. In what ways might this reduction of the academy to capitalist concerns require a return to the study and reconceptualization of institutional discourses within curriculum studies?

Response to Greg Dimitriadis
The Curriculum Scholar as Socially Committed Provocateur
Extending the Ideas of Said, Sartre, and Dimitriadis

Thomas Barone

My response to the paper by Professor Dimitriadis consists mainly of an endorsement, and an attempt at extension, of the ideas of its author, and the two scholarly giants whose work he explores. I resonate strongly with the hopes of Dimitriadis for reclaiming and enhancing, "in new and progressive ways," our space as curriculum scholars in our "hyperprofessionalized milieu." Indeed, since the 1990s, I have struggled with issues related to the manner in which we professors of curriculum might reinvent ourselves as public-minded scholars who aim to transform that milieu and thereby rescue from an ever-increasing marginalization a field that rightfully lies at the heart of education.

Like Dimitriadis, I too have found inspiration in the works of Sartre and Said. Indeed, my own suggestions are for complementing the kinds of scholarly projects that currently dominate our field with others, less often practiced, that resemble a blending of ideas from these scholars.

This brand of inquiry requires a particular sort of socially committed provocateur, a citizen-scholar who, in caring for progressive ideas and values, moves outward from their field of study and familiar audience of colleagues, to confront orthodoxy and dogma by posing within the public domain "embarrassing questions" (Said, 1994, p. 1). This provocation, moreover, is promoted within a modified version of Sartre's (1992) "project of discovery." These are projects both personal and socially committed, and aimed at "interrupting history" (Sartre, 1988, p. 102).

I will highlight five dimensions of this sort of project. The first is that of a *dual focus*. Dimitriadis recalls the objections of Sartre (and Foucault) to the compartmentalization and fragmentation of knowledge through academic specialization, a phenomenon not unfamiliar to students of curriculum. Indeed, fractious relationships exist among progressive groups both within and outside of our field. Dimitriadis, however, suggests that the work of Sartre and Said may serve as important sources for realizing a "radical imagination" that is fundamental to understanding the *commonalities* among all progressive intellectuals. That commonality, I propose, is partially located within points of intersection between two "authoritative" metanarratives, one field-specific (in our case, to education) and the other general to the culture at large.

Within the first—a quite familiar educational metanarrative—nearly everyone involved with public schooling is maligned. Children are stereotyped as lazy and undisciplined, and in turn, seen as miseducated by K-12 teachers who are in need of constant surveillance and accountability. Low standardized test scores serve as primary evidence of the failure. The lowest scorers tend to be children of poverty who are caricatured within the metanarrative *both* as unredeemable perpetrators of social crimes *and* as victims of a system of competition-free "government" schools. Finally, professors of education are portrayed as detached pseudo-intellectuals, apologists for a self-serving educational establishment and responsible for the purported ineptitude of the nation's corps of public schoolteachers. Such apologists—especially those who appear as activists—are viewed as highly expendable.

This field-specific educational narrative may be seen as operating within a more inclusive cultural narrative that tends to constrain the work of activists in many fields. This second metanarrative, also familiar, is likewise thematized around race, gender, social class, the nature of childhood, private (and corporate) initiative versus public good, and other issues. Thematically intertwined, these two metanarratives share other features. Both are transparent but totalizing, invisible in their pervasiveness, residing beyond critique in the privileged realm of the "commonsensical." And both arise more out of the reigning mass culture industry than from academia. Nevertheless, in both cases, scholarly "expertise" is tainted with colonialism in an avoidance of real interrogations of the "cumulative power of these representations" to distort reality (Dimitiriadis, p. 467). Each metanarrative refuses to valorize the activist intellectual, and what Said (1994) insists is their "moral duty...to call into question the reductive categories and stereotypes that serve to shut down human thought" (p. ix).

A "specific-but-transcendent" progressivist educational scholar, however, may indeed find it their moral duty to problematize these overlapping narratives simultaneously. They may contest the crude caricatures of school people, moving to reinscribe these exiled, demonized "others" as familiar human beings, as students, for example, who are worldly aware, diversely capable, more personally complex than could ever be imagined from test scores. Through such a project embarrassing connections may be revealed between "concrete...struggles" (Dimitriadis, citing Chomsky & Foucault, 2006, p. 162) and larger debilitating social forces.

Within works of art a dual focus encompassing the general and the specific operates within the metaphor—a point that serves to introduce the second dimension of our "project of discovery": *the modes by which this dual focus is communicated*. Here we honor Said's recommendations to stray, as amateurs, outside comfortable paradigms and limits, while also accepting a Sartrean notion of literacy, by employing a "broad range of discursive forms and tools" (Dimitriadis, p. 474) with their underemployed premises, procedures, protocols, and modes of representation.

This might imply an extension of the revelations of curriculum reconceptualists regarding the centrality of autobiography ("the personal") in the inquiry process. It could also demand further navigations of the narrative turns in our field. It could suggest additional "amateurish" experimentations with a myriad of methodologies, communications media, and forms of disclosure that include the postmodernist, the poststructuralist, and others as yet unimagined. And it might represent (channeling Said here more than Sartre) postcolonialist extensions of the largely humanist ideas of Eisner (1991) and Greene (1995) regarding the role of the arts in calling attention to otherwise unnoticed cultural phenomena.

These and other educationists have imagined new modes of scholarship with a potential for disrupting a settled state of affairs. But of these, those associated with the arts may offer special promise for simultaneously challenging the dual metanarratives, which are, after all, largely conveyed through stories and images, representational forms that are central to the arts.

James Baldwin (1962) noted that the fundamental purpose of art is the "unearthing of questions that have been long buried by answers." Moreover, while all good art may raise questions about that which the prevailing narratives obscure, some art more specifically addresses cultural politics. As if they had read Said, many recent activist artists have operated out of an *outlaw culture*, one that, writes bell hooks (1994), promotes "engagements with...practices and...icons that are defined as on the edge, as pushing the limits, disturbing the conventional, acceptable politics of representation" (pp. 4–5). As if they had read Sartre, many socially conscientious literati throughout history have produced what he called *literature engagée*, a kind of literature that uses aesthetic power to "contest the established values of the regime." Understanding how art both shapes and is shaped by the Zeitgeist, Sartre, the amateur, moved beyond his familiar professional landscape of argument through philosophy and theory, into the composition of novels, plays, radio scripts, and literary essays.

In my own ideal scenario, this aesthetic power serves to interrupt history by shedding light through and beyond the portraits of schoolchildren onto hidden power arrangements that account for the current deplorable state of sociopolitical affairs. Our twin narratives, with their rhetoric of crisis and personal blame, would be, simultaneously, harshly interrogated at the least, and at best, abandoned.

For such a project to succeed, however, a third dimension would need attention, that of *audience blending*. What sorts of people might progressive curricularists aim to provoke? In addition to fellow educationists, candidates might include our research collaborators, parents, other noneducators, and school practitioners. Nowadays, however, the professional autonomy of the latter is (even more than ours) considerably curtailed by policymakers operating under the spell of the dominant metanarratives. And while these policy makers may themselves represent an important audience, they comprise only a minor segment of the polity from whom they, at least theoretically, derive their own authority.

A gesture of inclusion in the style of either Said or Sartre might blend all constituencies within the polity into a general audience for our work that consists of the publics-at-large. Said was, after all, a highly visible public intellectual, whose work "inside the academy…reach[ed] beyond it in important ways" (Dimitriadis, p. 470). And Sartre was a privileged author who nevertheless worked toward a decolonization of the imaginations of a self-satisfied populace through the mass media.

We are all, indeed, as Dimitriadis notes, complicit. We are all part of that populace, under the sway of metanarratives that offer a degree of coherence in a jarring and bewildering world, that resemble, not catalysts for deep reflection about complex educational and social issues, but murky, toxic pools of presumptions from within which most public deliberations emerge.

The power of the arts to persuade us to reconsider these presumptions may indeed be greater than that possessed by the prosaic, discursive forms of theory and argumentation. But a cautionary note is in order here: Our fourth dimension is an *attitude of epistemological humility*. An epistemologically humble stance implies a reluctance to replace prevailing metanarratives with others just as arrogantly totalizing. Rather, it is evidenced within the production of small local stories that are partial, incomplete, and tentative. Indeed, the artist may avoid the narrow, dogmatic, and even propagandistic, by offering essays, novels, poems, literary ethnographies, biographies, films, plays, that bring its audience members to experience what Lyotard (1979/1984) called *differends*—disputes between incommensurable local stories. This is the socially committed amateur as vulnerable observer, or as Said has noted, as a "fallible human being, not a dreary and moralistic preacher" (1994, p. 140).

But where are some examples of the progressivist artist-provocateur whose ability to significantly alter dominant metanarratives in the U.S. culture has offered inspiration and hope in troubled times? A search might lead us to the final dimension of our proposed projects: a consideration of its *heroic versus collaborative/collective nature*.

Following Said and Sartre, we might imagine the promethean efforts of singular individuals working on behalf of others who have been malportrayed within the dominant metanarrative. Their well-intentioned hopes are for altering mass consciousness by publishing within today's nearly impenetrable culture industry. But while they should not be dismissed, singularly heroic, widely disseminated "cultural events" of the sort that produce a "tipping point" in the dislodging of an entrenched metanarrative are quite rare.

With smaller audiences in mind, some relatively recent cultural outlaws of the last few decades have in a spirit both Saidian and Sartrean, moved out of the sacred, circumscribed locations of the studio and academy to enact their art in public places. They have rebelled against the notion of the socially engaged artist as control-oriented "auteur," in favor of a public pedagogy that adopts a humble stance of amateurish collaboration with members of local communities. Some researchers identified as "arts-based" have already begun to explore what such a notion of artistry might look like.

Another example suggests a public pedagogy operating within a collectivity of artists. Consider the politically committed U.S. artists of the 1930s—including photographers, painters, cartoonists, and playwrights—whose work, as Edelman (1995) notes, successfully coalesced to subvert the prevailing metanarrative about poverty. After their artwork allowed the American public to vicariously experience the miseries of being poor, the needy were no longer blamed for their own unfortunate circumstances. The truly artistic, never totalizing evocations and provocations within this collective artistic effort, insists Edelman (1995), helped make possible the policy initiatives of the New Deal.

How might curriculum scholars as socially committed provocateurs emulate these history makers, or others unmentioned here in moving to save our schools, ourselves, and our profession in today's hard times? An adequate response to this difficult question demands, I believe, an acquisition of precisely the rare sort of radical social imagination that, as Dimitriadis, to his great credit, reminds us, is promoted in the work of Sartre and Said. Such an imagination might also guide curriculum scholars toward a greater appreciation of the potential of the arts for interrupting history.

References

Baldwin, J. (1962). *Creative process*. New York: Ridge Press.
Edelman, M. (1995). *From art to politics: How artistic creations shape political conceptions*. Chicago: University of Chicago Press.
Eisner, E. (1991). *The enlightened eye*. New York: Macmillan.
Greene, M. (1995). *Releasing the imagination*. San Francisco: Jossey-Bass.
hooks, b. (1994). *Outlaw culture: Resisting representations*. New York: Routledge.
Lyotard, J-P. (1979/1984). *The postmodern condition: A report on knowledge*. Minneapolis: University of Minnesota Press.
Said, E. W. (1994). *Representations of the intellectual*. New York: Vintage Books.
Sartre, J-P. (1988). *What is literature? and other essays*. Cambridge, MA: Harvard University Press.

Part VIII

Self, Subjectivity, and Subject Position

23 In Ellisonian Eyes, What is Curriculum Theory?

Denise Taliaferro-Baszile

Chapter Overview

This chapter discusses self-understanding and self-knowledge as critical social justice projects. The author focuses upon the significance of "voice" and "self" in relation to work as the only counterforce for transferring our problems to other sites. Her specific project in this chapter is to understand the racial subject as a curricular construction. To engage in this understanding the author first explores the lack of critical Black perspectives within curricular history. Next, she turns toward performative writing to draw the reader into the present moment of the paradoxes and complexities of a Black female self. Describing the ways that Ellison's *The Invisible Man* conveys the plight of the subperson who is both invisible and hypervisible, she describes how the dilemma Ellison presents is onto-epistemological. She relates this dilemma to colonization, imperialization, and White supremacy and scientific rationality and the effect they have on the ontological resistance of the Black (female) subject. Using performative writing as a pretext, the author explains that liberation of the Ellisonian self is only possible through onto-epistemological projects that interrogate sites that incite the dilemma. To engage in these projects, she turns toward critical race currere.

Prologue

> Our credibility in the white-male run intellectual establishment is constantly in question and rises and falls in direct proportion to the degree to which we continue to act and think like our black female selves, rejecting the modes of bankrupt white-male Western thought. Intellectual passing is a dangerous and limiting solution for black women, a nonsolution that makes us invisible women. (Hull & Smith, 1982, p. xviii)

All work is autobiographical. That is, we all bring our sorted histories, hopes, and desires to the project of curriculum theory, hooking onto familiar stories and creating new ones. And to the extent we are in dialogue, in conversation about these stories and the histories in which they are forever entangled, we produce, perform, and engage the "complicated conversations" that are curriculum theory. I have never been one for the debates that plague the field, the ones about what exactly curriculum theory is or should be, about categories, labels, and allegiances (see Marshall, Sears, & Shubert, 2000/2007 for discussion of these issues), primarily because my attraction to it has been its emphasis on the self as important to all meanings and manifestations of curriculum. Pinar notes (2004), that curriculum theory is about "discovering for one's self and with others, the educational significance of school subjects for self and society in the ever-changing historical moment" (p. 16). Within this context, self-knowledge and self-understanding are in and of themselves critical social justice projects, which work to develop a sense of agency in an increasingly endangered democracy (Giroux & Giroux, 2004; Marable, 2002). And if we are to take seriously—in the course of our scholarly and pedagogical work—the significance of the self in the understanding and production of curriculum, then it makes sense to also acknowledge the same for the field of curriculum theory, which is just as much about self-making as the curricula about which and through which we theorize. In this vein, to acknowledge the significance of our voices, our selves in the production of our work is the only way—it seems to me—to make a faithful attempt at avoiding "transreferentiality" or the extent to which the very problems we attempt to displace show up rather un-self-consciously as our work (Gutierrez-Jones, 2001). From this perspective, I know that any conversation about curriculum theory must begin not so much with the question of *what it is*, but rather *what is my* curriculum theory project, how do I engage the complicated conversation?

This question, for me, is an overwhelming one, which I always struggle to answer in coherent and meaningful ways. There are many layers of complexity, which I myself do not claim to understand in any complete sense, but which I keep trying to interject into a conversation that has been going on for sometime, and which historically has not included the likes of me. The conversation has been dominated primarily by the concerns of the White male psyche. And although some of these voices offer important perspectives on issues of race and gender (Castenell & Pinar, 1993; Kincheloe, 1993; Pinar, 2000; Taubman, 1993) that challenge Whiteness and maleness, they remain—of course—concerns of the White male psyche. While the explicit goal of much of this work is to understand curriculum as racial text, my project, in contrast, is more specifically about understanding the racial subject as a curricular construction. To this end, much of my work is consumed with one major concern: the lack of Black voices, of Black selves within the historical and contemporary discourses of curriculum theory.

Setting the Stage: Blackness Invisible

> True, I am a woman and I am Black. I ask you to take a painful journey with me. The waters are high and the treasures are buried deep. What are these precious treasures that I long to find and labor for in the walls of ivory institutions? They are the forgotten achievements of Black women. (Payton, 1981, p. 223)

Arguably, before the reconceptualization of the field, the marginalization of racially diverse perspectives was indicative of the fact that the education of Black and Brown children, for instance, was seen as a separate question, a separate concern from the ones that dominated the field at the time (Tyack, 1974). Thus, as Watkins (1993) demonstrates in "Black Curriculum Orientations," instead of engaging within dominant discourse of curriculum, critical Black perspectives emerge in the shadows, revealing different responses if not a different set of questions altogether. As a result, the perspectives of such scholars as Alexander Crumwell, W. E. B. DuBois, Carter G. Woodson, Anna J. Cooper, Horace Mann Bond, Fannie Jackson Coppin, Mary McLeod Bethune, and many others are not considered critical voices within mainstream curriculum history.

Since the reconceptualization of the curriculum field, however, the shift from development to understanding has created a much more critical and open space, which acknowledges the significance of race and gender, among other marked subjectivities in the production of curriculum (Pinar, Reynolds, Slattery, & Taubman, 1995). Understanding curriculum theory as dialogic has offered a vital space for not only speaking to the ways race and gender politics shape curriculum as an object of study and also curriculum theory as the lens through which we engage these dynamics; it is also a space through which and upon which multiple and varied voices can intervene, and yet—at least in terms of racial difference—they remain few.

Why does it matter? Well I suppose it doesn't if we assume that once people reach a certain intellectual level, they rise above their racial distinctiveness. This is not all that likely however, since it is obvious that some of the foremost Black intellectuals have become more rather than less racially conscious, and as such have struggled to theorize within and against the paternalistic structure of academic discourse (Collins, 1998; Cruse, 1967; DuBois, 1940/1975). When I was a graduate student I had this "crazy" idea that I would make a concerted effort not to cite White male theorists in my work, which was fundamentally about African-American education and identity. My desire to do this was not because I thought these theories lacked efficacy, it was instead an activist intention and political project through which I was trying to resist multiple practices that, from my perspective, epistemologically reproduced White hegemony. I had to wrangle, of course, with more than a few people with respect to my choice, because many thought my concern or my allegiance should have been to the integrity of the theories, and not who produced or wrote said theories. For me, however, to not acknowledge the role of the self—as raced, gendered, and more—in the production of theories is to refuse difference, to refuse the extent to which one's experience is intimately, even if tacitly, implicated in one's process of theorizing. And to suggest that the racial background of the theorist should be insignificant in a study that is primarily about the racial self is to ignore the fact of racial difference, and to again subsume the racial other in the White psyche.

I realized early on that for my project to be even remotely possible, I had to begin my studies almost from scratch, so to speak. Because I wanted to begin in the space of the Black psyche, I knew I would have to start searching for those voices I believed—but did not know for sure—existed in the theoretical landscape. I wanted to reach beyond the acceptable voices and search for those who had been systematically marginalized or simply ignored. I was and still am convinced that the failure to study the perspectives of Black folks renders an inadequate understanding of the complex and crucial role that the African-American struggle for education has played in shaping American democracy. For instance, how can we claim to understand the fight for public education without acknowledging DuBois's (1935) contention that public education in the South largely emerges out of Black folks' quest for education during Reconstruction? How can we claim to understand multiculturalism without acknowledging the work of Woodson (1933) and his insistence on the importance of cultural context and knowledge in the quest for education? How can we truly interrogate the feminization of the American teaching force without considering the efforts of Anna J. Cooper (1988), Fannie Jackson Coppin (1913), Mary Church Terrell (1968) and many other Black women who taught under very different conditions than White teachers?

At some point, I realized the enormity of the task at hand, particularly when it came to searching for the historical voices of Black women. And in the course of trying to accomplish it and failing miserably to remain true to my political project, I realized that what I wanted to accomplish in one dissertation was actually meant to be a lifetime project. Although, I am not so much committed anymore to the idea of a piece of work that does not cite White scholars, I am still quite fascinated with the racial self and its production of and as knowledge. To this end, my curriculum theory project, as mentioned earlier, is not only to understand curriculum as racial text but more to the point, to understand the racial self as a curricular construction.

This is messy work, particularly since it requires that I interrogate it as part of me and not me at the same time. What I do know for sure is that the arduous work of not only trying to understand it but to articulate it has compelled me, really required me to do things differently, to take more serious risks in both my teaching and my scholarly endeavors. The remainder of this essay will be one of those risks, as I attempt to get at the heart of the Black (female) self's dilemma by troubling its curricular construction and confinement. The question of what to do with the very breakdowns and failures in logic that come from my attempts to reason my way through a traditional academic analysis is the point of the chapter. Instead, I turn toward the performative as a way to resist the rational and to intervene in the complicated conversation as difference. Performative writing, argues Anna Pollack, "evokes worlds that are other-wise intangible, unlocatable: worlds of memory, pleasure, sensation, imagination, affect, and in-sight" (quoted in Madison, 2005, p. 194). Thus, performative writing allows me to draw you into just one moment in the lived curriculum of the Black (female) self, where paradoxes abound.

Performing the Dialogue

> Reclaiming Black feminist intellectual traditions requires more than just doing analyses of Black women's realities with a traditional epistemological criteria. It requires challenging the very terms of intellectual discourse. (Collins, 2000, p. 15)

It was Sunday morning and I was camped out at a small table in the corner coffee shop, looking no doubt like death on a stick. This is always the way I look when I am trying to write, trying to put on the page all of the things running ramped in my head. I've never had the kind of writer's block that is indicative of having nothing to say. I have lots to say, perhaps too much to say. And yet writing is always a slow torturous process for me. I really don't remember, quite frankly, the last time I truly enjoyed it. Sitting there crouched over the table, I had not figured it out yet, my trouble with getting it out in a way that moves beyond the basic requirement of being informative, contributing something thoughtful to the field. After an hour or so, the word that I have erased several times now comes out again, it refuses—it seems—to go away, to be silenced. The word is *I*. I erase it again for the millionth time and force another word on to the page. This time, I follow it with another. Yes! Two words: "Research shows…."

Just then, I catch a glimpse of this woman in the corner of my eye. She's searching for a place to sit. I keep my head down because she seems to me a little uptight looking, very organized, a rule follower. Not my kind of person at all or so I thought. The material, around the buttons on her tweed suit jacket, is pulled too tight, and her skirt is definitely reconstructing her walk. One piece of unruly hair keeps falling out of place and she keeps diligently pushing it back, as her eyes self-consciously roam the room. When she looks in my direction, I think I recognize her from somewhere, but I don't know where. Instead of lingering, I quickly avert my eyes back to my paper. She might ask to sit in the empty chair across from me, and since she came in with no books or bags, she would have nothing to do but sip coffee and talk and I would be obliged to chat. I tried to meditate her away; you know, redirect my energy so as not to inadvertently call her into my space. I guess I did not have the process down, because she came anyway right in the middle of my redirecting efforts. She politely asks if she may sit in the chair. I hesitate for a moment, trying to muster up the courage to say no or tell a lie, but instead I hear myself say cheerfully "sure!" I can't ever seem to find a good lie when I need one.

When I look up to acknowledge her, I catch a glimpse of her eyes. They seem to me like jealous hurricanes. They were too wild for a woman who stuffed herself in a suit and came out to have a cup of coffee. Just as I suspected, she took one sip and began chatting away. She wanted to know what I was writing about. Frustrated at the fact that after two hours, I still only had two words on the page, I did not want to entertain this strange woman's curiosity. So I responded curtly, "The Ellisonian Self," hoping that divulging so little information would give her a clue that I wanted to be left alone to write.

The Ellisonian Self

In *Blackness Visible*, Charles Mills (1998) notes that the traditional Western notion of personhood is premised on the modern European sense of self, the Cartesian self. In this respect, identity is singular and stable; the individual's plight is to know the world, to ask —What can I know?—and to seek the answers that will allow him to know, to develop, to control his world. In contrast to this sense of self, Mills conceptualizes what he calls "subpersonhood." A (racial) subperson, he explains, is

> Not an inanimate object, like a stone, which has…zero moral status. Nor is it simply a nonhuman animal, which…would have been regarded…as outside the moral community altogether…. Rather the peculiar status of a subperson is that it is an entity which, because of phenotype, seems…human in some respects but not others. It is a human who, though adult, is not fully a person. And the tensions and internal contradictions in this concept capture the tensions and internal contradictions of the black experience in white-supremacist society. (pp. 6–7)

Mills goes on to describe how the narrator of Ralph Ellison's classic, *The Invisible Man*, epitomizes the plight of the (racial) subperson. Ostensibly, the narrator—a representation of a subjugated and marginalized person—does not engage the same philosophical predicament as the Cartesian self; he is not pondering the existence of the world or of those who impose their reality on him. Instead,

> His problem is his "invisibility," the fact that whites do not see him, take no notice of him, not because of physiological deficiency but because of the psychological "construction of their inner eyes," which conceptually erases his existence…. So his problem is to convince them that he exists, not as a physical object, a lower life form, a thing to be instrumentally treated, but as a person in the same sense that they are, not as a means to their ends. Moreover because of the intellectual domination these beings have over his world, he may also be frequently assailed by self-doubts, doubts about whether he is a real person who deserves their respect or perhaps, an inferior being, who deserves the treatment he has received. (pp. 8–9)

But it's more than being invisible. In "The Fact of Blackness," Frantz Fanon provides a rather thick description of corporeal malediction as the hyperconscious awareness of one's Black body caused primarily by being fixed in the gaze of the White other. He writes that in the instant he must meet the eyes of a White man, he bears an immediate burden: "The body is surrounded by an atmosphere of certain uncertainty…. A slow composition of my self as a body in the middle of a spatial and temporal world" (1967, p. 111). Fanon, then, further complicates the dilemma of the Ellisonian self, suggesting that one's invisibility also gives way to hypervisibility, or becoming visible to one's self as not one's self. His major contention is that the Black man [sic] has no ontological resistance in the presence of Whiteness.

"Ahhh…yes," the woman says, "It's also reflected in the question DuBois (1903/1973) raises at the very beginning of *Souls of Black Folk*: How does it feel to be a problem? It's the question that leads him to theorize the double-consciousness. In my line of work I deal with that question a lot in trying to get people to talk about their feelings, the things that hurt them mostly."

Oh God, she's a therapist, just what I need—a bunch of talk about feelings when I am trying to write a serious academic paper. But I was surprised that she knew enough to carry on the conversation. When I tuned back in, I heard her ask, "So does this Ellisonian self have a gendered dimension? What about the Black female self?"

"Yes" I contend, "I suppose." And I go on to make the point that while the Black female self certainly faces the same dilemma of invisibility/hypervisibility in the presence of Whiteness, she also must contend with the fact of her femaleness and the different ways in which it makes her either invisible or especially visible to various groups in differing ways.

"So it's a real ontological dilemma," she says as if she still not satisfied with my response.

"It is," I respond, "but it is also an epistemological construction as well." I hesitate a moment because I am now thinking she might be a philosopher and not a therapist, or maybe both. Although I am always philosophizing, I don't want to sound as crazy as I must look at the moment. But she nudges me on, hmmm—just like a therapist. I manage to explain to her that one's sense of Being, of reality, cannot be anything other than an epistemological re/construction. If the self is not singular, complete, and intact at birth, if it is negotiated, performed, created, or even searched for then we must continually come to know it, to construct it through our systems of knowledge. "So the dilemma of the Ellisonian self is an onto-epistemological one."

She just looked at me, contemplating her next question or comment perhaps. Suddenly suspicious, I was not sure now if she was trying to pull something out of me or put something into me. Is she a therapist or a philosopher? She turned up the corner of her mouth in a half smile as if she already knew what I was thinking. "So tell me more about the construction of these inner eyes," she said. Where were her questions leading me? I pushed the nagging feeling aside, scratched my head, and shared with her my thoughts about how I felt that academia was largely responsible for the re/construction of those inner eyes and their signification of the Ellisonian self.

Academia's Inner Eyes

Knowledge is power! With this refrain, many see and seek academia as the place where an unknowing soul can become liberated. It is my contention, however, that academia's liberatory possibilities lie in our ability to see and to resist its unrelenting commitment to epistemic violence. Academia's dominant epistemological paradigm is elitist and exclusionary, embracing and reflecting a notion of rationality which has defined the Euro-American quest to know as a quest to "define, distance and dominate" the other (Ladson-Billings, 2000). A point well articulated in Mirimba Ani's (1994) erudite analysis of European cultural thought and behavior, where she identifies Plato's epistemology as a relative beginning to the social construction of difference that has consumed and carried the West to world domination. She contends that by separating the human into distinct and conflicting parts (i.e., "reason" and "appetite" or emotion) Plato lays the groundwork for one of the most destructive and pervasive aspects of Euro-American epistemology—the dichotomization between reason and emotion, with reason, the superior faculty being the pursuit of self-mastery and control. Plato's epistemology is, as Ani surmises, evident in European (Euro-American) theories of universe, state, and human nature, where

The person is constantly at war within himself and is not properly human until his reason controls his emotion, i.e. men were to control women.... Plato has already described what for Europe becomes the "Ideal State" one in which the human being who has gained control of himself in turn controls those who haven't (women, of course, were perceived as not having the necessary control). It would follow that the universe then is put in order by the nation of people who are "higher" (controlled by reason).... The group that has the power to enforce its definition of "reason" so that it becomes the most "reasonable" consequently has a mandate to control those whose reasoning abilities are judged to be less (and so there is a need to measure intellectual ability. Enter I.Q. mythology). (p. 36).

Ani goes on to argue that the Academy is, in fact, Plato's legacy, as it embodies at its core the transformation of Plato's epistemology to ideological apparatus central to the projects of imperialism, colonization, and White supremacy.

Plato's epistemology is the basis of what we have come to know as (scientific) rationality, and as E. Frances White (2002) points out, in *The Dark Continent of Our Bodies,* it is indicative of the ways in which race, gender, and science have become inextricably linked in the production of legitimate knowledge. White's analysis teaches us that Enlightenment scientists often used constructions of gender to justify racial domination and vice versa and in the process bolstered its own legitimacy:

Although science did not create racism, it legitimated and helped solidify a new kind of racism for the industrial age. At the same time and in dialectical fashion racism contributed to the growth of science as a privileged worldview because scientists' beliefs were largely congruent with dominant ideology. The same can be said of the relationship between science and sexism. (p. 84)

Although there have been many challenges to it—as we have come to know it—scientific rationality continues to be the cornerstone of academia's dominant epistemological project, most deeply embedded within those practices considered normal, neutral, and necessary to sustaining academic integrity, rigor, and elitism. The linchpin is objectivity or rather the pathological distance we must maintain in order to know something not fully, but legitimately. In *A Curriculum of Repression,* Haroon Kharem speaks to what such a commitment entails:

The academy hopes to detach a person from his or her emotions or control them by placing "reason" in control of emotions. Yet the ultimate goal is to cause disorder or a self-hate in the nonwhite student, disconnecting him or her from his or her histories, spaces, language, culture, cognition, emotions, and way of interaction with others. (2006, p. 12)

The distance, the separations circulate as curriculum on all levels of schooling. Even when educators manage to incorporate the subjugated histories, we do so in ways that deny the different ways a non-Cartesian self might come to know the world and one's existence within it. Herein lies the ontological dilemma of the Ellisonian self. Academia's inner eyes cannot see her, but the heart of her dilemma is that they affect her ability to see her self as well, hence her lack of ontological resistance. Their inner eyes are now her inner eyes and yet these eyes distort and refract much like a funhouse mirror.

With her right leg crossed over the left one, she begins shaking her foot. I am watching it as I talk, I know this means something, but I can't figure out what. Is she tuning out? Is she mad? What? "Okay you referred to this Ellisonian self as 'her,' is there a Black female specificity?" Her tone suggests that she is annoyed at the way I continue to let this question of gender go without explicit articulation.

I am annoyed as well, because I know what she means, what she's trying to get at. Yet, I have no words really to explain. I think gender is absolutely, if implicitly, influencing my process of theorizing. I cannot think as anyone other than a Black woman, a self that I am perhaps projecting onto my analysis in a way that actually subsumes the question of maleness. The problem, I think, is that I often find my rage in the words of men and my healing in the words of women.

When I look at the woman in the too tight suit, I can tell that her mood has shifted. She's getting emotional. She must be a therapist. "It's sad really," she mutters while pulling the bobby pins from her hair. I guess she's given up on tucking that one wild hair back into her crop.

"What?" I ask anxiously, "What is so sad?"

She was clearly mortified at that question, but manages to pose one of her own, "Is liberation possible for the Ellisonian self?"

"Yes…no…well, not exactly" I sputter, "it depends on how one imagines liberation."

Liberating the Ellisonian Self

If we understand the Ellisonian self as an onto-epistemological construction that emerges at the site of curriculum as a cultural and political practice, then liberation is itself an onto-epistemological project that must actively interrogate those sites of curriculum that define the dilemma of the Ellisonian self. By denying its existence she is thus left to doubt her realness and to reinscribe her invisibility. This, it seems to me, is what Patricia Hill Collins (1990, 1998), for example, struggles with in her valiant attempt to make visible and valuable a Black feminist epistemology. She describes it and yet feels compelled to operate primarily outside of its scope, and within the purview of academia's dominant epistemological paradigm. Admittedly and paradoxically, Collins's effort is caught up in a process that is simultaneously legitimizing and delegitimizing; as Black feminist epistemology is made visible and invisible at the same time. Is it ever possible to escape, or is negotiation the only leverage an Ellisonian self might ever have? In Ellisonian eyes, liberation is never an outcome of struggle, it is embedded within the struggle; it is not attached purely or permanently to people, places and ideas. What is liberating can simultaneously be or suddenly become not liberating at all. In this sense, liberation is always a negotiation between what was, what is and what will be.

The woman looks flush. Maybe that too tight suit is finally squeezing the life out of her. It looks even more ridiculous than it did before. Her hair matches her eyes now. They are both wild. She tries to unbutton the top button of her too tight tweed suit and the button flies off, hitting me in the eye. Damn. She does not even apologize, she just shouts out like a crazy woman, "So what are you doing for this Ellisonian self? Are you just writing, keeping your intellectual distance or what?" The tone in her voice made me feel like I was in some new version of Amiri Baraka's *Dutchman*. But I answered her calmly.

Toward a Critical Race Currere

There is some hope, I think, for the Ellisonian self. It lies, of course, at the intersection of two of academia's more radical discourses—curriculum theory and critical race theory. In *What Is Curriculum Theory?* Pinar (2004) reiterates his call for autobiography in education: "What would the curriculum look like if we centered the school subjects in the autobiographical histories and reflections of those who undergo them? The 'subjects' in school subjects would refer to human subjects as well as academic ones" (p. 16). Specifically he discusses the method of currere, which works to reconceptualize curriculum "from course objectives to complicated conversation with one's self (as private intellectual), an ongoing project of self-understanding in which one becomes mobilized for engaged pedagogical action as private and public intellectual—with others in the social reconstruction of the public sphere" (p. 37). Currere "seeks to understand the contribution academic studies makes to one's understanding of his or her life (and vice versa) and how both are imbricated in society, politics and culture" (p. 35). It involves moving across and within four moments: the regressive, progressive, analytical, and synthetical. In the regressive moment, we call up our past lived experiences, for they are our source of data. The progressive moment is an opportunity to consider what is hoped for but not yet present. In the analytical moment, we attempt to make sense of the ways in which the past and the future impend upon the present moment. Finally, in the synthetical moment, having put together the past and the future, we return to the present moment, fully conscious of our selves in the historical and natural world.

Pinar (2004 insists that, "cultural politics cannot be conducted at this time, in this place without a politics of the individual, and within this subjective sphere the individual himself or herself must be an activist working to democratize one's interiority" (p. 38). To this extent, currere works to legitimize a space where the Ellisonian self can, at least, engage the question of her ontological dilemma. Yet, within this understanding of currere, the Ellisonian self still must struggle with the stories academic knowledge hides and how such hiding shapes what kind of conversation she is able to have with herself much less engage in with others. Thus, unless the epistemological shift away from the hidden I is significant, the Ellisonian self remains arrested and assailed by the ways in which the structure of the academic subjects continue to reproduce a conversation about her invisibility. Hence, the ontological is held hostage by the epistemological.

Perhaps this is what DuBois (1935) understood when he noted in *Black Reconstruction* that the problem of race in America defies logical argument. Over his lifetime he had grown increasingly disillusioned with the idea that scientific rationality was the way to deal effectively with racism (Oatts, 2006). As such he made an avid practice of writing within and against the dominant epistemological paradigm, regularly inserting his "I" into essays, autobiographies, novels, poems, and theater. This epistemological challenge has played out—to some extent—in Black feminist theory, most notably in the work of bell hooks (1994) who explicitly and even aggressively at times inserts her "I," acknowledging her experiences of pain as the beginning of her process of theorizing. For the Ellisonian self, it is critical race theory (CRT) that has strongly reasserted the importance of interrogating race at the epistemological level. Critical race theory's break—certainly not a clean or unnegotiated one—with traditional academic forms of expression acknowledges that, at least in part, the Ellisonian self's ontological dilemma is an epistemological challenge. Patricia Williams, for instance, speaks poignantly to the challenge:

> I think, though, that one of the most important results of reconceptualizing from "objective truth" to rhetorical event will be a more nuanced sense of legal and social responsibility. This will be so because much of what is spoken in so called objective, unmediated voices is in fact mired in hidden subjectivities and unexamined claims that make property of others beyond the self, all the while denying such connections. (1991, p. 11)

To this end CRT, as Derrick Bell surmises (1995), uses "unorthodox structure, language, and form to make sense of the senseless" (p. 910). Following Bell's lead, many CRT scholars engage conversations with alter egos, fantasies, testimonies, and poetry in their/in our search for ontological resistance in the presence of Whiteness, which has settled even deeper into the American psyche. I am particularly interested in CRT's use of the Black autobiographical voice as counterstoryteller, and thus as onto-epistemological intervention.

Critical race currere, as I am imagining it then, is not in opposition to currere but a particular kind of currere. In looking back at my dissertation, *Education for Liberation as (An) African American Folk Theory* (Taliaferro, 1998), this project—in its earliest stages—began as a currere of marginality, which Susan Edgerton (1996) describes as an infusion of the margins and the center where the "margin 'must know' the center in order to survive" (p. 38). Back then, I was trying to negotiate the many tensions that circulate around self and other—within one self and across different selves—the emphasis on deconstructing the multiple layers of marginality was helpful. However, in this current project—this critical race currere—I am looking specifically to understand and to signify the production of the racialized extended-self and the meanings it makes of education for liberation. Wade Nobles (1999) contends that the Black self symbolizes what he has called the extended-self, "that is the conception of self transcends and extends into the collective consciousness of one's people" (p. 129). Thus to discover one's self is to understand one's connection to and significance in the group. And although, as Edgerton (1999) points out, there is no such thing as not paying attention to the center, my emphasis is on the educational significance of the Black autobiographical voice/s for the intellectual development of the Black self.

In this sense, critical race currere emphasizes the significance of race—and to some extent as it intersects with class, gender, sexuality and other subjectivities—in shaping one's self and one's educational experiences. But to the extent that the focus of such work is to bear witness to racial trauma, the significance of other identities may be repressed. In essence, it builds on critical race theory's mission of placing conventional race studies, "in a broader perspective that includes economics, history, context, group and self interest, and even feelings and the unconscious" (Delgado & Stephancic, 2001, p. 3). Second, it is done in relationship to the stories academic knowledge hides. In this case, it's the subjugated knowledge interjected by the Black autobiographical voice. In this way it builds on CRT's strategy of counterstorytelling and its revival and reassertion of the Black, Latino, Asian, Native autobiographical voices as a means of intervening on the epistemological dominance of 'deracialized" rationalist discourse (Baszile, i2008. Third, while "currere" as Pinar (2004) sees it, is largely a private intellectual activity that is—nevertheless—vital to the re/construction of the public intellectual self, critical race currere is simultaneously private/public autobiographical excavation for the good of the self and the group in one signifying move. It works to cultivate, in this case, a radical Black intersubjectivity. This is where my project is suspended at the moment.

Slumped back in her chair, the woman looks exhausted now. I'm not sure why. It seems as though I have been doing all the talking. She must be a therapist.

"What's the problem, why are you having such a hard time writing about it?" she manages.

"I'm not sure. I've been working on it pedagogically for some time. It started with a student, Steven. He kept coming to my office, wanting to borrow and read my books, wanting to talk, but he never once turned in an assignment. He said that writing depressed him. I understood what he meant, but I never got to the point of not being able to write.

And yet I find myself there now." I go on to explain that I believe I have crossed over into somewhere else. I know too much and that too much does not allow me to write comfortably or unproblematically in the "proper" academic prose. When I write without my "I" or despite my "I," it feels to me very much like a reproduction of invisibility, not simply of my invisibility, but the invisibility of the collective history in which and because of which I stand.

Although I am talking and talking, I don't think I am talking to the woman anymore. I'm just talking myself through something. In fact, I don't even realize that the woman is nearly passed out on the floor. Her too tight suit jacket is wide open and so are her jealous hurricanes. As I kneel down on the floor next to her, for the first time since she walked into the coffee shop, I can't resist the urge to look into her wild green eyes. So I do. A little panicked about her condition, I prop her up against the table and run off to the bathroom to make a cool compress out of paper towel. Yet when I leaned over the bathroom sink, I suddenly felt faint. Splashing water onto my face, I glanced in the mirror as I dried the sweat-tinged water from my brow and then patted gently around my somber green eyes. And suddenly I knew why she seemed so familiar, yet strange.

I quickly wet another sheet of the brown paper towel and dashed back out to the table. I was surprised to see the woman up on her feet, brushing back her hair with one hand, carrying her shoes in the other and heading for the door, suit coat unbuttoned. I wanted to yell wait, but I stood there unable to speak. After a few minutes of trying to put all the pieces of the last hour or so together, I could see clearly, beyond those inner eyes I have been trained to use; those eyes that did not allow me to see the moment she entered the coffee shop; to see that she had wanted nothing more than to let down her wild hair and to shed the too tight suit; to see who she really was. At that moment, I knew that we would talk again and again and again. I picked my pen, scratched out "research shows" and wrote "I" and committed to follow it "somewhere in advance of nowhere" (Cortez quoted in Kelley, 2002).

Epilogue

People irrationally believe they are rational beings. (Simmons, 2001, p. 56)

Thinking toward a post-reconceptualist curriculum theory requires, I believe, that we more explicitly address the epistemological possibilities and limitations of our work. If we acknowledge that a primary focus of our project/s is to "educate the public" (Pinar, 2003), then we must (continue to) shake up the logic through which we attempt to carry out this task, and find more ways to reach beyond our appeals to intellect as *the* site where reason trumps emotion, where the "I" must remain invisible. We must do this, of course, with the realization that again liberation from such logic, is never a clean break from it, but only a serious negotiation with it.

References

Ani, M. (1994). *Yurugu: An African-centered critique of European cultural thought and behavior.* Trenton, NJ: Africa World Press.

Baszile, D. T. (2008). Beyond all reason indeed. *Race Ethnicity, and Education, v11*(3), 251–265.

Bell, D. (1995). Who's afraid of critical race theory? *University of Illinois Law Review, 4*, 893–910.

Castenell, L. A., & Pinar, W. (1993). *Understanding curriculum as racial text: Representations of identity and difference in education.* Albany, NY: SUNY Press.

Collins, P. H. (1990). *Black feminist thought: Knowledge, consciousness, and the politics of empowerment.* Boston: Unwin Hyman.

Collins, P. H. (1998). *Fighting words: Black women and the search for justice.* Minneapolis: University of Minnesota Press.

Cooper, A. J. (1988). *A voice from the south.* New York: Oxford University Press.

Coppin, F. J. (1913). *Reminiscences of school life, and hints on teaching.* Philadelphia: African Methodist Episcopal Book Concern.

Cruse, H. (1967). *The crisis of the Negro intellectual.* New York: Morrow.

Delgado, R., & Stephancic, J. (2001). *Critical race theory: An introduction.* New York: New York University Press.

DuBois, W. E. B. (1935). *Black reconstruction.* Millwood, NY: Kraus-Thomson.

DuBois, W. E. B. (1973). *The souls of blackfolk.* Millwood, NY: Kraus-Thomson. (Original work published 1903)

DuBois, W. E. B. (1975). *Dusk of dawn.* Millwood, NY: Kraus-Thomson. (Original work published 1940)

Edgerton, S. H. (1996). *Translating the curriculum: Multiculturalism into cultural studies.* New York: Routledge.

Fanon, F. (1967). *Black skin, white masks.* New York: Grove Press.

Giroux, H. A., & Giroux, S. S. (2004). *Take back higher education: Race, youth, and the crisis of democracy in the post-civil rights era.* New York: Palgrave Macmillan.

Gutierrez-Jones, C. S. (2001). *Critical race narratives: A study of race, rhetoric, and injury.* New York: New York University Press.

hooks, b. (1994). *Teaching to transgress: Education as the practice of freedom.* New York: Routledge.

Hull, G.T., & Smith, B. (1982). Introduction: The politics of Black women's studies. In G. T. Hull, P. B. Scott, & B. Smith (Eds.), *All the women are white, all the blacks are men, but some of us are brave: Black women's studies* (pp. xvii-xxxi). Old Westbury, NY: Feminist Press.

Kelley, R. D. G. (2002). *Freedom dreams: The Black radical imagination.* Boston: Beacon Press.

Kharem, H. (2006). *A curriculum of repression: A pedagogy of racial history in the United States.* New York: Lang.

Kincheloe, J. (1993). The politics of race, history, and curriculum. In L. A. Castenell & W. Pinar (Eds.), *Understanding curriculum as racial text: Representations of identity and difference in education* (pp. 294–262). Albany, NY: SUNY Press.

Ladson-Billings, G. (2000). Racialized discourse and ethnic epistemologies. In N. Denzin & Y. Lincoln (Eds.), *Handbook of qualitative research* (pp. 257–278). Thousand Oaks, CA: Sage.

Mabokela, R. O., & Green, A. L. (2001). *Sisters of the academy: Emergent black women scholars in higher education.* Sterling, VA: Stylus.

Madison, D. S. (2005). *Critical ethnography: Method, ethics, and performance.* Thousand Oaks, CA: Sage.

Marable, M. (2002). *The great wells of democracy: The meaning of race in American life.* New York: Basic Civitas Books.

Marshall, J. D., Sears, J. T., & Shubert, W. H. (2007). *Turning points in curriculum: A contemporary American memoir.* Upper Saddle River, NJ: Merrill. (Original work published 2000)

Mills, C. W. (1998). *Blackness visible: Essays on philosophy and race.* Ithaca, NY: Cornell University Press.

Nobles, W. W. (2006). *Seeking the sakhu: Foundational writings for an African psychology.* Chicago: Third World Press.

Oatts, T. (2006). *W. E. B. DuBois and critical race theory.* Atlanta, GA: Exceptional.

Payton, L. R. (1981). Black women in higher education: Power, commitment and leadership. In G.L. Mims (Ed.), *The minority administrator in higher education* (pp. 223–230). Cambridge, MA: Schenkman Publishing Co.

Pinar, W. (2004). *What is curriculum theory?* Mahwah, NJ: Erlbaum.

Pinar, W. F., Reynolds, W. M., Slattery, P., & Taubman, P. M. (1995). *Understanding curriculum: An introduction to historical and contemporary curriculum discourses.* New York: Lang.

Simmons, A. (2001). *The story factor: Inspiration, influence and persuasion through the art of storytelling.* New York: Basic Books.

Taliaferro, D. (1998). *Education for liberation as African American folk theory.* Unpublished dissertation.

Taubman, P. (1993). Separate identity, separate lives: Diversity in the curriculum. In L. A. Castenell & W. Pinar (Eds.), *Understanding curriculum as racial text: Representations of identity and difference in education* (pp. 287–306). Albany, NY: SUNY Press.

Terrell, M. C. (1968). *A colored woman in a white world.* Washington, DC: National Association of Colored Women's Clubs.

Tyack, D. B. (1974). *The one best system: A history of American urban education.* Cambridge, MA: Harvard University Press.

Watkins, W. (1993). Black curriculum orientations. *Harvard Educational Review, 63*, 321–338.

Williams, P. J. (1991). *The alchemy of race and rights.* Cambridge, MA: Harvard University Press.

Woodson, C. G. (1996). *Miseducation of the Negro.* Lawrenceville, NJ: Africa World Press. (Original work published 1933)

Suggested Reading Questions

1. The author suggests that while in the past the focus has been upon understanding curricular as a racial text, her focus is upon understanding the racial subject as a curricular construction. What is the significance of the difference between reading race as a text and constructing a racial subject?

2. If being is never merely ontological or epistemological construction, in what ways do academic or disciplinary bodies incite the invisibility of and violence toward real bodies?

3. In what ways is locating the Black voices of history (regressive) fundamental to envisioning and actualizing a participatory democracy?

4. The Cartesian self is premised upon the question "What can I know" while the plight of the (racial) subperson is to convince the White Cartesian self that he or she is a "person in the same sense they are." Given the author's focus upon the relationship between ontology and epistemology, what might be required for the subperson to see her- or himself as a real person who deserves respect and not a subjugated person who receives inferior treatment?

5. The author suggests critical race currere utilizes counterstory telling through Black, Latino, Asian, and Native autobiographical voices as a vehicle for intervening in the epistemological dominance of nonracialized rational discourse. How might autobiographical Whiteness studies function as an intellectual site within critical race currere?

Response to Denise Taliaferro-Baszile
The Self

A Bricolage of Curricular Absence

Petra Munro Hendry

"We are what we know." We are, however, also what we do not know. If what we know about ourselves—our history, our culture, our national identity—is deformed by absences, denials, and incompleteness, then our identity—both as individuals and as Americans is fractured. (Castenell & Pinar, 1993, p. 4)

I imagine Denise sitting in the coffee shop hunched over her computer, staring at the blank screen waiting for words to appear. The self is waiting to be written into existence. This self is a product of language—language that does not speak "I," language that resists desire, and language that falls short of words. How do we access this curricular absence? The "absence" which is present is the curricular gap that sits across from Denise. It is the woman with wild hair, green eyes, and too tight jacket. She is beautiful, brilliant, and radical. She is revolutionary. She is the Sensuous Sapphire Spirit. She resists being written into existence. She is illusive. She is the gaze of the other. She is the absent presence.

I struggled to understand who was sitting across from Denise in that coffee shop. I had to read and reread to try to get it: Was she a real stranger? Was she an illusion? Was she representative of the "existential" self or the "imaginary" self, or the "double consciousness" self; or, perhaps the "repressed" self or the "reinscribed" colonized self? A-ha. The clue came on page 2, she was the "transreferential" self, the unconscious self that shows up when we displace our problems. Is she the displaced "I" that Denise struggles to write? I am still not absolutely sure who the person sitting across from Denise is, but I have a *sense* of who she is and I know that it matters that she is there. Her presence is the invisible "I" or inner "eyes" that brings into conversation the "racial self as a curricular construction." This dialogue creates a profound shift in normative understanding of curriculum theory. As Denise suggests, her project is "not only to understand curriculum as racial text but more to the point, to understand the racial self as a curricular construction." This inversion radically resituates the relation of curriculum to the project of the "self." While I might never know for sure "who" is sitting across from Denise, I do know that she was invoked to bring into existence the *absent presence*.

This essay provokes me to ask once again "What is identity?" Identity politics has been a critical issue within the field of curriculum theory. In fact, one might argue that the field emerged as a consequence of shifts in understanding the relationship between the self and knowledge. While I am often quite comfortable to remain within my own feminist, poststructural understandings of identity as nonunitary, situated, and always in flux (Munro, 1998), it is the concept of "invisibility" or absence that stuns me. Not that I haven't ever thought of the "invisibility" of persons of color, women or children as they are continually constituted as "objects." But, as Denise makes clear, it is not just about being invisible. It is in fact a "hypervisibility, or becoming visible to one's self as not one's self." Is the green eyed, wild haired woman across from Denise the "ontological resistance" to absence?

Identity politics is often constituted through the binary construction of either the modernist self (unitary) versus the postmodernist (nonunitary). We are left with either the whole or the fractured self. Nevertheless, we have a self, and more importantly an understanding of a self that presumes an identity. However, neither of these tidy descriptions contains the relationship of invisibility or absence that Denise addresses in her essay. Consequently, it is the space of absence that becomes present in Denise's essay. This absence is not a void. It is sitting across from Denise. And, she must engage with it. My reading of the essay elicits layers (or a bricolage) of absence. Absence is not nothingness, Blackness or emptiness, it is rich with meaning.

It is the "fiction" of the self that has become the hallmark of postmodern identity politics. This fiction takes on multiple meanings: Denise embraces "fiction" to write the self into existence. She turns to the performative as a way to resist the rational and to intervene in "complicated conversation as difference." This is not the self of endless deferral; it is the self that continues to be problematic to the project of liberation. Liberation has traditionally been understood as freeing the self from the imposition of the "gaze." Liberation in "Ellisonian Eyes" is the refracting of the "White" gaze. Ironically, this deflection constitutes Whiteness through looking back. Radical, Black intersubjectivity it is implied by Denise, requires resistance to looking back through developing an extended self. This is a self embedded in counternarratives that "talk back" to reason, logic, and rationality in order to deconstruct the "self" that has been contained, bound, regulated, and disciplined. The flying button from the "too tight" suit hits Denise in the "eye/I."

Peter Taubman (1993) refers to the "fictional" register of identity as the site in which identity emerges as a construct of language and as an artifact imposed on the individual. Within this register identity is seen as objectifying and alienating the individual or as a violence done to the ineffable (1993, p. 288). Here attempts are made to endlessly evoke and utter the unutterable, to map the uttered and to expose the absence under the fading presence of the word. Like Ellison, Denise is writing against a fiction, an identity not of her own making. This opposition can lead to alienation, with the consequence of imprisoning the subject. Is this the woman across from Denise with wild hair imprisoned in her too tight jacket? The "fictional" self is constructed through the split constituted in the imposition of an identity by the other. This gaze of the other in which the fragmented self (Denise and her table mate) congeals both freezes the subject as object and becomes itself the object of desire. Yes, Denise's desire is to understand the woman across from her. Although she attempts to ignore her, to not see her, to make her invisible, make her absent, she engages with her. They do not become one, they do not even understand each other. But the other (acting as imposed self) is kept in dialectical tension. There is no repression or reconciliation but an ongoing conversation that has not as it purpose liberation but dialogue.

"Maybe we are all exiles in a dehumanizing educational process" (McCarthy, 1998, p. 261). I am not Black. I am a White woman. I will not make caveats regarding how I cannot speak from a Black perspective. However, I will not speak as a deracialized White woman. While my physical features identify me as White, if Blackness is a construction of Whiteness then perhaps I am more Black than White? This is the il(logic) of the binary. The continual reification of Blackness and Whiteness as somehow real rather than as constructions is embedded in a long history of "othering," which begins with Plato's epistemology, Descartes mind–body dualism, and colonialism's center-periphery. This "othering" is the Western curriculum writ large. It is an ontological, epistemological instruction that is deeply embedded in the psyche. We are all subject to this curriculum.

Dominant theories of curriculum, ones that don't allow for understanding, have functioned to construct identities, which are stuffed into suits that are too tight, that contain, that hold us in, that don't allow excess, and which will bind us. This is a theory of repression. It is no coincidence that this theorizing of control began ironically in the age of "Enlightenment," at the same time that the project of colonization began, as well as the very notion of "schooling." That these projects intersect is significant. I would argue that the "Enlightenment" is no less than a project to show the "lighter" the better. According to Ruth Frankenberg (1993), colonization occasioned the reformulation of European selves. Central to colonial discourses is the notion of the colonized subject as irreducibly other from the standpoint of a White "self." This means that the Western self and the non-Western other are coconstructed as discursive products, both of whose "realness" stands in extremely complex relationships to the production of knowledge, and to the material violence to which "epistemic violence" is intimately linked (p. 17). The Western White self is itself produced as the effect of the Western discursive production of its Others.

Postcolonial theorists like McCarthy (1998), Asher (2002), Trin Minh-ha (1991) and Fanon (1967) maintain that identity politics must be conceptualized in ways that resist the imposition of subject identities which privilege the binary of a subject–object duality through male/female, self/other, Black/White, and colonizer/colonized. These colonial binaries continue to be produced through contemporary educational discourses such as multiculturalism, and thus, schools continue colonizing students by imposing subject identities (at-risk, gifted, in the gap) that are not of their own making. Postcolonial education seeks ways in which we can unlearn this binary by thinking in more "hybrid" ways that allow us to understand the other in relation to, rather than apart from ourselves and vice versa (Asher, 2002, p. 82). Denise's chapter is just such an unlearning. The curriculum of subjugation is one of control and fear—fear of absence. It is the absence we must embrace. To live with the ambiguity of no-self as one that is continually constituted through a web of relations in which there are no points of reference. This is an unlearning that requires us to loosen the grip of control as the site of learning, and to enter the absent presence of fear-fear of the other sitting across from us, fear from an identity that is not constrained by the fantasy of liberation, and fear of an identity that is invisible.

The knowledge of self/other, Western/non-Western, White/Black, female/male, has constituted the theory of curriculum as one of colonization for the past 500 years. It is this history of the relationship between history, identity, and culture that is the absence in curriculum. For Denise this absence or invisibility is critically present in the ongoing marginalization of Black intellectual scholarship that theorizes curriculum history. When curriculum has been understood as neutral, ahistorical, and objective it functions to maintain identity as static and unitary. The history of curriculum theory itself is conceptualized as a field that emerged at the turn of the century, was solidified after 40 years of struggle with Tyler's (1949) *Basic Principles of Curriculum*, and then reconceptualized as political, cultural, social, and autobiographical and is now being re-reconceptualized. This tidy conceptualization in essence dehistoricizes the field and constructs a narrative of identity in which there is a natural progression of evolution in which our identity as curriculum theorists can be clearly defined. As Ann Winfield (2007) has eloquently articulated in her recent book *Eugenics and Education*, it is the "long history of historical misrepresentation" that has obscured the complex relationship of the past and present. Current notions of an "achievement gap," "standardization," "testing," and "tracking" are all implicated ironically in progressive historical discourses that emerged in and through the eugenics movement. The lack of historical context and historicity has denied us a theory of identity in which past and present are in dialogue with each other. This historical gap is a curricular absence that seeks not to "rewrite" history or get it "right" but instead to ask what makes this history possible, what identities does it make available?

Thus identity politics is deeply embedded in historical consciousness. As Denise suggests these gaps or absences are many. This is not an identity politics of recuperation. Identity is understood as embedded in history. Sankofa, the West African understanding of the past, present and future as one moment, is the disruption of identity, culture or liberation as progress. The stories of Carter G. Woodson (Brandon-Taylor, 2001), Sojourner Truth (Dar Saleem, 2003), Anna Julia Cooper, Ida B. Wells, Septima Clark, Marion Wright, Maria Stewart (Lathon, 2005), and Henriette Delille (Porche-Frilot, 2005) are invoked as way to construct a counternarrative to identity *as* history.

Curriculum of Absence

Rather than seek emancipation or liberation I would suggest that we engage in a curriculum of absence, one in which we embrace "ironic scholarship" (Rorty, 1989, p. 7). This is a scholarship that resists explanation. It does not tidy up, provide a vision, condemn, or redeem. According to McWilliam (2004), ironic research is instead "self-referential knowledge, that is, knowledge that cuts across traditional consensus to create distance from our most familiar categories, treating them as contingent and strange" (p. 144). Thus, self-referential knowledge asks not "who am I?" but what are the taken-for-granted knowledges through which we produce our selves as works of art. Clearly, Denise's conversation is a work of art.

References

Asher, N. (2002). (En)gendering a hybrid consciousness. *Journal of Curriculum Theorizing, 18*(4), 81–92.

Brandon-Taylor, L (2001). *Navigating knowledge/complicating truth: African American learners experiencing oral history as real education*. Baton Rouge, LA: Louisiana State University, Department of Curriculum and Instruction, unpublished PhD dissertation.

Castenell, L. A., & Pinar, W. F. (1993). *Understanding curriculum as racial text*. Albany, NY: SUNY Press.

Dar Salaam, T. (2003). *So-journeying: Creating sacred space in education*. Unpublished PhD dissertation, Baton Rouge, LA: Louisiana State University, Department of Curriculum and Instruction.

Fanon, F. (1967). *Black skin, white masks*. New York: Grove.

Frankenberg, R. (1993). *White women, race matters: The social construction of whiteness*. Minneapolis: University of Minnesota Press.

McCarthy, C. (1998). The uses of culture: Canon formation, postcolonial literature and the multicultural project. In W. F. Pinar (Ed.), *Curriculum: Toward new identities* (pp. 253–263). New York: Garland.

McWilliam, E. (2004). Feeling like teaching. In B. Baker & K. Heyning (Eds.), *Dangerous coagulations* (pp. 135–152). New York: Peter Lang..

Minh-ha, Trin (1991). *When the moon waxes red*. New York: Routledge.

Munro, P. (1998). *Subject to fiction: Women teachers' life history narratives and the cultural politics of resistance*. Buckingham, England: Open University Press.

Porche-Frilot, D. (2005). *Propelled by faith: Henriette Delille and the literacy practices of black women religious in antebellum New Orleans*. Unpublished PhD dissertation, Baton Rouge: Louisiana State University, Department of Curriculum and Instruction,

Rorty, R. (1989). *Contingency, irony and solidarity*. New York: Cambridge University Press.

Taubman, P. (1993). Separate identities, separate lives: Diversity in the curriculum. In L. A. Castenell & W. F. Pinar (Eds.), *Understanding curriculum as racial text* (pp. 287–306). Albany, NY: SUNY Press.

Tyler, R. (1949). *Basic principles of curriculum and instruction*. Chicago: University of Chicago.

Winnfield, A. (2007). *Eugenics and education*. New York: Peter Lang.

24 Critical Pedagogy and Despair
A Move toward Kierkegaard's Passionate Inwardness

Douglas McKnight

Chapter Overview

This chapter explores how Kierkegaard's notion of passionate inwardness is crucial to critical pedagogy and curriculum studies. The author discusses the key principles and corresponding problematic assumptions of critical pedagogy. Noting the emphasis on the critical pedagogue to facilitate awareness among students on the ways knowledge and schooling is used to sustain power and privilege, the author notes such scholarship does not translate well within colleges and universities that prepare teachers and teacher educators. Instead, critical awareness sometimes produces paralysis and despair when the precepts cannot be used within contemporary classroom settings focused on accountability and assessment. The author then turns toward Kierkegaard's exploration of the ways institutional discourse, with its emphasis on predetermined ends, dislocates individual's interiority from their existential becoming. Next, the author explains that within Kierkegaard's three spheres of existence (aesthetic, ethical, and religious) there is the possibility for realizing a proper relation between the infinite and finite conditions that constitute the human self. The author closes with the suggestion that passionate inwardness provides the existential turn necessary to cope with the despair that critical pedagogy illuminates and also might provide the tools to act in the world.

> The crucial thing is to find a truth which is truth for me, to find the ideas for which I am willing to live and die…. What is truth but to live and die for an idea? (Kierkegaard, 1835/1967c, p. 5100)

During more than a year-long dialogue with several public high school teachers returning to the university for graduate work, much was spoken about aspirations to appropriate and apply the theories of critical pedagogy in the tradition theorized by Paulo Freire (1970/1994). However, in time, their words, tone, and even body language indicated frustration and hopelessness over what many came to consider a practical impossibility—aligning their pedagogical existence with the critical theories they learned about. I came to identify this phenomenon not as burnout from the weight of external burdens placed upon them in the classroom, a common interpretive misconception (McKnight, 2004), but as a distinctive existential condition of despair.

These graduate students, many of whom I had taught as undergraduates, spoke of their desire to engage in critical pedagogical and curricular practices by exploring, alongside their students, issues of race, class, gender, and power as each related to the discipline being taught and the overall institution of school in relation to society. However, just as quickly, these same graduate students asserted that institutional peer expectations, administrative techniques of governing the individual, and curriculum constraints tied to technical standards and assessments focused on measurable achievement prohibited anything but superficial forays outside the "official knowledge" (Apple, 1999). They became caught within a condition that 19th century Danish philosopher Søren Kierkegaard (1849/1980) called the "despair of necessity."

This form of despair drapes over and appears to block any point of departure, despite one being conscious of and sensitive to what is perceived as external causes of this condition. This consequence generally leads to a decision: either the decision to leave teaching (which, according to various national reports, is occurring at an alarming rate); or the decision to give up a critical existence and surrender to institutional, technocratic rule-based demands that are presented as the exclusive *ethical* actions. These teachers speak of having no other choices. They want to remain in teaching but they also want to diminish the despair.

However, it is a mistake to assume that the despair of necessity, simply defined as performing in a manner that is counter to one's own existential charge of becoming, is an externally initiated burden to be lifted. Instead, Kierkegaard provides a lesson here: despair should be an indispensable existential condition in a teacher's journey toward becoming a critical pedagogue. In other words, the way of being in the classroom within the tradition of critical pedagogy and curriculum theorizing should embrace this form of despair as a potential trajectory out of the either/or choice and toward a life of critical resoluteness. This path was given a name by Kierkegaard (1835/1967 a,b,c,d; 1844/1992; 1849/1980), *passionate inwardness*, which has not received attention nor been part of the vocabulary of critical theorists concerned with education (e.g. Freire, 1970/1994; Giroux, 1983; McLaren, 1989).

In fact, Kierkegaard has not been situated as a social thinker and so is not considered applicable to critical theory concerns. For most of the 20th century, Kierkegaard was dismissed by critical theorists as a thinker merely interested in the singularity and pure subjectivity of the individual and of that individual's internal relation to the Christian God. Unfortunately, Kierkegaard was interpreted as having little to comment upon in terms of social theory—and hence, critical theory—and as such was not believed to reference the historical and political conditions that shape an individual (Adorno, 1989; Levinas, 1998). Recent scholarship has reevaluated that interpretation, however. Scholars (e.g., Dooley, 2001; Marsh, 2001) have begun to find linkages between Kierkegaard's existential theory and the philosophical underpinnings of critical theory. More specifically, in terms of this essay, Kierkegaard provides some crucial existential components that can serve the principles and goals of critical pedagogy.

An example is that critical pedagogy theories have tended to operate from the belief that individual transformation occurs as a cognitive act in which the teacher or student rationally changes her or his behavior once conscious of a school's institutional oppressiveness and marginalization of certain groups. However, this critical notion of dispassionate reasoning and understanding fails to produce the desired embodied dispositions necessary for such a transformation to occur: "To seek cognitive understanding without an earnest existential response is mistaken" (Beaufort, 1996, p. 78). Most teachers, once exposed to the theories of critical pedagogy and curriculum, understand the damage done, to themselves as well as the students, when they align their teaching existence with institutional demands. However, upon returning to the concrete conditions of the school setting, they are rarely able to perform and exist critically, and so retreat to the either/or: give in and accept the ethics of the institution; or leave in an effort to escape such ethical demands.[1]

It is my intent to articulate how Kierkegaard's notion of "passionate inwardness" is crucial for those engaging in critical pedagogy and curriculum theorizing—an activity identified and described, but not fully theorized by Maxine Greene (1986/2003, 1988). Passionate inwardness will not only intensify one's experience of the despair of necessity over the federal and state government policies that create institutional restrictions on curriculum and pedagogy, but will also provide a reflexive means, beyond rational awareness, to exist within and even move beyond such enclosures. A teacher with critical pedagogical beliefs may then be able to fulfill his or her existential obligation of self-becoming along with the students. In other words, passionate inwardness affords a means to surmount the despair of necessity that settles in and gives the impression of no way out. It is my contention that this activity is crucial to any kind of success for an existing individual who represents herself or himself as a critical pedagogue and theorizer.

Some General Precepts of Critical Pedagogy

The basic tenets of critical pedagogy have been thoroughly described, discussed and critiqued (e.g. Darder, Baltodano, & Torres, 2009; Ellsworth, 1989; Freire, 1970/1994; Giroux, 1983, 1988; Glass, 2001; Gore, 1993; Greene, 1986/2003; Kincheloe, 2004; Shor, 1987; Weiler, 1988). However, I want to frame this discussion of despair by providing a brief sketch of a few significant principles and problematic issues within critical pedagogy that have their philosophical roots in the Frankfurt School of critical theory. Critical pedagogy in America was first introduced by Ira Shor (1987) through his work with Freire, and then appropriated by Giroux (1988) and Peter McLaren (1998), each producing a legacy that continues to operate. Though many theoretical variations of critical pedagogy exist, all begin with the conviction that schools are institutionalized mechanisms that produce and reproduce the inequities between the powerful and the marginalized, hence sorting out who can experience freedom and who cannot. For many critical theorists who address pedagogical issues, race, class, and gender are reproduced through the ritual of schooling (McLaren, 1998), but at the same time human beings are not merely passive receptors easily controlled and manipulated by the rule of the hegemony. Such constructions are never complete due to humanity's possession of consciousness and the inherent drive toward freedom. Simply, agency does exist and so resistance and change are always possible (Giroux, 1983).

Following Gramsci's (1971) social theories of education and hegemonic control, humans are capable of critically reflecting upon their condition (Mayo, 1999). Freire, probably the most celebrated and studied critical pedagogy theorist in the world, declared that his philosophy rested upon teachers' and students' capacity to recognize their historically created oppressed condition. The proposed effect of this awareness, a type of raised consciousness, was social action to transform oppression into freedom for all, not just for one small segment of society. For Freire (1970/1994), social action was defined as a critical praxis of dialogue and the decoding of the cultural practices and literatures that constituted hegemonic control. Hence, resistance and change would be possible through the recognition that history is not a linear, predetermined force that carries us along in a wave. Instead, history is created through choices. Many critical pedagogues perceive school as a site of selves being produced through resistance to the school's attempt to normalize certain social conventions (Giroux, 1983). If one accepts this critical perspective, a unique burden is attached to the pedagogue: to facilitate each student's awareness that knowledge is a social construction claimed as the property of certain groups in society, and who utilize the knowledge to sustain power and privilege; that schooling as a function of the desires of the dominant class seeks to "sort" students into particular societal roles (Spring, 1976 in order to protect and reproduce itself; and therefore, embedded in the institution is the tendency to foreclose on self-transformation and the search for freedom that is believed to be inherent in a democratic society (Greene, 1988).

One forceful critique delivered against critical pedagogy is that this line of sociopoliti-cal work is unable to translate well within institutions that prepare teachers and teacher educators. This is due to several, possibly irresolvable, issues: (1) the language of critical theory and pedagogy is found by most would-be teachers to be foreboding, obscure, and difficult to convert into daily classroom practices, especially given the types of behav-iors privileged in school settings; (2) along the same lines, critical pedagogy is theoreti-cally visionary but lacks the practical tools to accompany it (Kanpol, 1998); and (3) most teachers are trained to see themselves as politically neutral professionals operating as if "best practices" is not an ideological strategy. However, this ideology of "best practices" positions the teacher as a kind of knowledge delivery mechanism, research tested and guaranteed to secure student mastery of information deemed appropriate to a given subject field. In other words, to engage in critical pedagogy is considered unethical by such notions of professional standards and expectations. There is no practical sense of a pedagogue as a cultural/political worker and intellectual critically examining demo-cratic communities and opening up spaces for themselves and others to become free democratic agents who can theorize and create curriculum.

Over the last 5 years, I have found undergraduate preservice teachers unable to cap-ture the possible concrete effects that an approach from a critical pedagogy perspec-tive can have on their daily classroom existence. As teacher education has moved to the clinical approach, in which university students spend most of their academic hours "apprenticing" in the field, it has become more difficult for these students to achieve the kind of conceptual distance needed from the classroom to fully apprehend the social cri-tique supplied by critical theory. Most of their time is spent in the technical activities of emulating teachers generally uninterested in any sort of "critical pedagogy" language or lesson plans, or who are also frustrated and exhausted from the ever restrictive nature of teaching and the bureaucratic, legalistic demands to cover the material for the next stan-dardized test. However, for those who have taught in public schools and have returned for graduate work,[2] once they become somewhat more comfortable with the underlying claims and language of critical pedagogy, they recognize the critiques as having concrete reality in their own lives (that is, unless they immediately dismiss the critical appraisal as having nothing to do with education/schooling). As the critical scholarship alters their interpretative lens and reveals the various forms and effects of classroom politics, many report a new reality and an escalating discomfort. My students speak of recognizing an ethic of teaching that contradicts the conventional form of institutional ethics that privilege the bureaucratic needs of the administration or some professional organiza-tion. In other words, these newly "radicalized" pedagogues realize that they must take responsibility in how their existence in the classroom perpetuates the very oppressive institutional rituals they had just spent a full year coming to understand.

It is not uncommon for most of these teachers to lose the sharpness and clarity pro-vided by the newly acquired critical lens when they return to their own classroom. Mundane life and more than a decade of training to function at school by way of a technocratic and peer–teacher ethic can quickly reassert claims and privileges on the individual teacher. However, a few cannot seem to shake the insights of critical pedagogy theory and its charge to engage in social transformation, to reveal and analyze how his-torical inequities are perpetuated through the institution of school, and to move toward a more democratic philosophy of education for their students. As one graduate student/ teacher, who retained the insights after being exposed to critical pedagogy readings, explained in one of many interviews over the course of a year, there is a moment of real-ization that is quite disconcerting and reveals the onset of despair:

> Reading Freire, at least once I made sense of what he was saying, because I am still trying to understand his language, though I get it that I was (still am, I guess) in his banking education mode…. But reading him made me realize how much I was doing the same things he was criticizing. I went back to my classroom and it really began to bother me. It seemed every day I would see something else going on at school that I had never noticed before that our books [in critical pedagogy] pointed out. At first I didn't see myself as part of that, you know, because I never considered myself as part of the, what is the word? Hegemony. But then I started looking at the curriculum I was using and how I stood up in front of those kids and went right into the official speak, you know, what [Michael] Apple [1998] called it? "Official knowledge." That began to really bother me. I'm wondering what the hell I am doing with my life…. I mean, I can't seem to find a way out. Just because you see something and, well, you know it doesn't mean you can change it. I've got standardized tests coming up in April that our principal said we have to stop what we're doing and "prepare"… drill…the kids for those tests. (December 2005, interview with graduate student 2B; McKnight, 2005–2006)

This experience of confusion, uncertainty, and awareness of an emerging despair reveals tension and conflict within a deep belief embraced by both traditional and critical pedagogy: "knowledge is power." In traditional pedagogical theory, this phrase assumes that power is a kind of control situated within individuals. If an individual is able to achieve mastery over the "knowledge" of a discipline, meaning that he or she is able to understand the idea as well as observe the effects of that idea on others, then the next logical step is that he or she is empowered to control those effects—or in the official discourse of educational policy, those performance outcomes. This form of rationality operates powerfully in the teaching research that seeks to justify the current federal education policies, which positions the teacher as wholly "accountable" for each student's achievement, no matter the condition of the student's life outside of school or how a school's institutional practices perpetuate cultural inequities. However, a similar trajectory of belief functions within critical pedagogy.

A convention within critical pedagogy has been the act of dialogue as a transforming activity that empowers the teacher and student. The teacher is taught that through dialogue, differences can be transcended; power inequities between teacher and student can be flattened and all can come to a communal understanding or at least tolerance which, in practice, means an environment controllable for the teacher. Burbules (2000) critiqued the underlying beliefs of this form of dialogue at work in critical pedagogy, especially in terms of how the use of dialogue as a tool of emancipation and transformation of the student at times actually serves to normalize and co-opt.

Ellsworth (1989) problematized how critical pedagogy forms of dialogue as constructed by Freire and others fail to recognize the issues of power (and the irony of that when democratic agency and social transformation are tenets of critical theory). Ellsworth (1989) found her attempts to put such theories of dialogue and democratization into practice dissipated into confusion—power struggles between teacher and student and even the same sort of authoritarian oppression that conventional schooling often creates. In fact, for the teacher, sometimes knowledge brings paralysis, disruption, and recognition that she or he actually does not possess the kind of professional self-efficacy previously thought. Understanding the knowledge produced by critical theory and pedagogy, such as the inequitable and often oppressive conditions that occur in the practice of schooling, is difficult and challenging enough. Finding the tools to navigate through the institution in an effort to transform both self and students becomes more than a daunting task. A teacher may adhere to the tenets of critical pedagogy and so believe in personal autonomy, just as many current traditional teacher education agencies (i.e., National Council for Accreditation of Teacher Education [NCATE]) advocate for "professionalized" autonomy. However, each teacher must come face to face with a force that is operating against either one of these possibilities—deskilling:

> Deskilling is at its peak when teachers lack autonomy over [the] teaching and decision making process. By making teachers accountable for state-mandated curriculum (such as basal reading materials) and by promoting competency-based education, system management, and employing rigid and dehumanizing forms of evaluation along with numerical rating scales, teacher are controlled and simply march to the tune of the state. (Kanpol, 1998, p. 6)

These well-documented institutional constraints have intensified over the last decade due to federal legislation (and possibly more important, how state departments of education have interpreted and implemented the legislation) emphasizing performance outcomes as assessed by standardized tests and rubrics. As pointed out above, a corresponding political shift was to saddle the teacher with blame if a student failed to "achieve." This occurred without reference to a mountain of critical scholarship that reveals the degree to which a student's cultural capital (Bourdieu & Passeron, 2000), passed on heavily through child raising practices (Lareau, 2003), upon entering school equates into academic achievement due to the type of discourse privileged in school.

Such cultural capital is outside the control of a teacher, yet the discourse of accountability does not allow for the critique to gain any traction in educational policy. This shift toward placing all accountability on the teacher has created an impoverished social ethic that: normalizes a "good" teacher as one who follows the stated rules of accountability and assessment; takes on the dispositions of one willing to accept mandates even when those mandates counter what is believed to be good and true about the vocation of teaching; and one who accepts the so-called disposition of professionalization that supports the testing regime (McKnight, 2004).

This creates a whole new set of tensions for the teacher who desires to engage in critical pedagogy, yet, at the same time, perform the tasks deemed ethical and necessary by an institution with a hierarchical, patriarchal administrative history (Labaree, 1992; McKnight, 2004). Often these same teachers acknowledge that they retreat and accept the institutional constraints that make their teaching homogenous, politically neutral, and inoffensive in the eyes of school administrators.[3] Kierkegaard worked through many of the same issues in his attack on the institutional church in Denmark during the 1800s, which he claimed represented itself as the true ethical arbiter of what it meant to be a Christian and, hence, would accept no other interpretation. Kierkegaard asserted that the individual who doubted, disagreed, and even despised what the institution was demanding would usually still surrender to the institutional leveling of the individual, creating a despair of necessity, or despair of the "mass man."

Necessity and the Leveling of Ethics: Creating the Mass Man

In his book, *Two Ages* (1845/1978), Kierkegaard, by way of a literary review of two novels published in Denmark in the 1840s, critiqued the state's move to ontologically condition each individual to accept abstract reflection, dependent upon detachment and acceptance of universals or necessities determined by the dominant institutions, as the best sort of deliberation. This form of deciding was a powerful means to govern the "mass man." Elrod (1984) elaborates upon Kierkegaard's point:

> The "web of reflection," then, enfolds the individual in a set of philosophical, political, and economic rationalistic abstractions that cause him to appear in a form that is tirelessly replicated…. Viewed through the institutional lenses of nineteenth-century Denmark, each individual sees in himself only what he sees in the other. As the fabrication of the modern state, this universalized human form is capable of including the particular in only a quantitative sense…, and this quantification of the particular is the direct consequence of the institutional embodiment of the reflective and rationalistic conception of the individual in the modern-national state. (p. 9)

However, this is not to say that Kierkegaard dismissed reflection and celebrated the other end of the register, irrational disconnection from any interest in human activity in favor of some pure subjective connection to an ideal and an experience of pure emotion. There exist many forms of reflection. Kierkegaard writes in *Two Ages* (1845/1978) "Reflection is not the evil" (p. 96). Deliberation as something we all do everyday as a means to think through an action is not the problem. The issue for Kierkegaard is when deliberation becomes a strategy for diversion away from action based upon a passionate articulation of deliberation. It is then that "reflection is a snare in which one is trapped" (Kierkegaard, 1845/1978, p. 89). In terms of the pedagogical existence, Maxine Greene (1988) captured the same predicament:

> The problem with this highly cognitive [objective rationality] focus in the classroom has in part to do with what it excludes. Also, it has to do with whether or not reasoning is enough when it comes to acting in a resistant world, or opening fields of possibilities among which people may choose to choose. (p. 119)

This snare represents a form of social inertia in which an institutional ethos claims to be reforming or even engaged in a revolutionary change, such as that which No Child Left Behind (NCLB) claims to completely redo public education by creating mechanisms to secure, through quantification and technical reflection, some outcome based on managing individual thought and action. Decisions become disinterested, dispassionate and the reform meaningless:

> An age that is revolutionary but also reflecting and devoid of passion changes the expression of power into a dialectical tour de force: it lets everything remain but subtly drains the meaning out of it; rather than culminating in an uprising, it exhausts the inner actuality of relations in a tension of reflection that lets everything remain and yet has transformed the whole of existence into an equivocation that in its facticity is…that it is *not*. (Kierkegaard, 1845/1978, p. 77)

In terms of contemporary schooling institutions, ethical discourse or deliberation has become a type of dispassionate engagement in technocratic reasoning in which the answer to any question or problem is determined before the questioning begins. This is represented in the popular instructional decision making model that claims to give power to the teacher to make appropriate changes in pedagogy, but that is entrenched in technocratic reasoning that predetermines the outcomes. The only concern left is how to go about reaching that technocratic end, which usually involves a kind of evidence that quantification of existence provides. This web of reflection, also known in teacher education circles as "reflective practitioner" (Schön, 1983), encourages stagnation and a turning away from the kind of existential ethical reflection that is willing to risk paralysis when confronted with the complexity of even a homogenous classroom: [T]he state of reflection, stagnation in reflection, is the abuse and corruption that occasion retrogression by transforming prerequisites into evasion" (Kierkegaard, 1845/1978, p. 96).

Hence, for many teachers existing in the present age under the burden of so-called revolutionary national reform that celebrates standardization and homogenization (despite rhetoric of diversity and social justice), the point of deliberation is not whether the curriculum (presented as politically neutral information of a subject field) or the assessment tools (rooted in the tenets of quantifiable, technocratic outcomes) are acceptable or not as ways of understanding one's existence in the classroom. The issue becomes simply to what degree all students conform to the standards prescribed beforehand and how the teacher can increase the percentages mastering those standards so that school administrators and politicians can claim success. While such outcomes or performance-based assessments inherent to the logic of standards appears on the surface to supply a teacher with the power to make certain technical, pedagogical decisions, the detrimental effects have been identified by Keesing-Styles (2003): "...the more I have used this style of assessment, the more convinced I am that it dictates what students learn and how they learn it, it focuses students' attention on assessment rather than on learning, and it creates a degree of conformity."

This sort of curricular approach assumes the ethical questions are reduced to finding the best means to most quickly achieve this goal, either in fear of being reprimanded by administrators or in belief that such decisions actually improve the educational existence of students. Institutional necessity is sometimes subtle, as in creating rituals of school that appear benign but are actually tools of governance (e.g., desks in rows, teachers separated from each other in different classrooms, grade levels, textbooks, PowerPoint as technological teaching tool, etc.). But more often than not, subtle forms of rule are set aside and administrative power imposes explicitly institutional necessity under the guise of serving its community. As one graduate student, also a teacher at the time at a high school in the northern portion of Alabama and who was one of the three graduates that I extensively interviewed, reported:

> Our principal instituted a script that is supposed to, well, at least if you followed it perfectly, supposed to raise standardized test scores for reading and math. He comes around and checks to make sure we're following it. I feel like making a video of myself and just sitting back and showing it, you know, using a clicker to click on and off at the correct times when a question has to be asked. At the same time, I'm expected to research my class, you know, find out what works best at getting the correct responses.... And we've go total inclusion...several who are just learning English, a bunch of special needs students hardly able to do anything. How do I respond to their needs when I'm forced to into mastery and achievement mode? I'm not even able to look at them like human beings because they are more like percentage points on the test. (Interview 2c, October, 2005; McKnight, 2005–2006)

In other words, this form of institutional ethics is articulated not just in rule-based listings of do's and don'ts for teachers, but in the very discourse of rationalization and its accompanying rituals that generates the conditions (Haberman, 1991) in which a teacher has two choices: become a "mass man" by embodying the dispositions to value and operate from the abstractions set forth by the ethos of the institution and, hence, not call into question the assumptions and claims of the ethos; or leave, which, according to Kierkegaard, does not diminish the despair.

In terms of "a becoming self," this institutional necessity, with its promise of professional autonomy for each individual as long as he or she embraces the institutional discourse that predetermines ends and means and dislocates the individual from the particular, creates a misrelation within the individual. The individual may perceive himself or herself as quite capable, affable and able to move through the rules quite easily with the use of the dispassionate form of reasoning. Yet, despair will settle in as the becoming self grows ever diffused:

> Surrounded by hordes of men, absorbed in all sorts of secular matters, more and more shrewd about the ways of the world—such a person forgets himself, forgets his name, divinely understood, does not dare to believe in himself, finds it too hazardous to be himself and far easier and safer to be like the others, to become a copy, a number, a mass man. Now this form of despair goes practically unnoticed in the world. Just by losing himself this way, such a man has gained an increasing capacity for going along superbly in business and social life, indeed, for making a great success in the world…. He is so far from being regarded as a person in despair that he is just what a human being is supposed to be. (Kierkegaard, 1849/1980, pp. 33–34)

Such an individual has learned how to function well within institutions by understanding what values and thoughts are deemed appropriate. In terms of teaching, the "mass man" is the professional whose mastery of subject matter and fluency in the instructional decision-maker model is directly tied to standards that are quantifiably assessed. The model ethically binds the teacher to perform tasks that are believed to result in student achievement. A teacher does not even have to believe the model to be sound. A teacher just has to be fearful enough that if the model is not followed and student proficiency not attained, then he or she will be at fault, causing the student to fail and not proceed through the various institutional hurdles and legitimating processes as defined by standards, outcomes, and standardized testing. In fact, the model is so powerful that despite gaining a more informed understanding of the critical pedagogy's critique of the ethic of standards and teaching, the overwhelming response by my graduate students who have taught for a year or more is one of great apprehension that such alternative practices would be unfair to the student:

> If I don't follow the rules, you know, the written and unwritten rules that we all learn as teachers of what is considered acceptable by my peer teachers and by my administration, then I'm just asking for trouble, even though I have tenure…. Everyone will question why I'm failing to give the student what they need to move on to the next grade, next class, you know, on and on. It's like I'm hurting the kids. How do I explain to them or justify to my administration that the child is being hurt more by what is already happening? (Interview 3b, May 2006; McKnight, 2005–2006)

Practical reality dictates a kind of survival ethic. These teachers perceive their actions as ethical because they respond to students' supposed needs, which are about moving through the institution rather than journeying toward "a becoming self." This is the despair of necessity in which a misrelation emerges between one's ethical obligation of existential becoming and the ethical demands of institutional schooling. In other words, when one's identity is consumed and produced by the institution, then responsibility is wholly defined by the needs of that institution, which is about survival and perpetuation of the institution and not about the individuals within that environment having the freedom to be becoming selves. For Kierkegaard, identity is an unfinished project. However, for such interested institutions as schools, his philosophy runs counter to the impulse toward sustaining "what is" rather than "what should be." This condition relates well to

Kierkegaard's complaint that when the "established order continues to stand...[as] passionless reflection is reassured" (1845/1978, p. 80).

This misrelation may or may not be a conscious condition for the individual teacher within school, but it will occur, according to Kierkegaard's framing of life as an institutional practice. Often an individual misinterprets the misrelation (a condition in which one's interiority is not in proper alignment with the principles of existential becoming and, hence, acts in ways that block this becoming) and considers it a form of burnout (McKnight,2004). However, once awareness occurs, despair becomes a very real condition for them. The three graduate students/teachers interviewed, all of whom were already familiar with the basic foundational philosophy of critical pedagogy, reported this conscious sense that they were being split in two. Once they began to manage the general and then the more subtle and sophisticated concepts of critical theory and pedagogy, upon returning to the classroom they quickly identified institutional rituals and practices that prohibited both teacher and student from truly engaging in critical practices necessary for a thriving democratic society. These same institutional conditions they had just months before considered natural and common sense.

However, to know and understand does not necessarily mean to change. The graduate students return generally disturbed and bothered by what they see, and speak of the realization that they had not "seen" it before. Many experience the misrelation of the self and become steeped in despair over the belief that nothing can be done about it. They seem paralyzed and unable to muster the will to change due to the social ethos and values naturalized for them by others.

Passionate Inwardness: No Exit from Ethics

Despair, to reiterate, is a misrelation of the self that occurs within each of what Kierkegaard theorized as the three basic spheres of existences: the aesthetic, the ethical, and the religious. These spheres are not part of a linear, stair-step system of transcendence to ideal selfhood, though each holds the promise for a kind of purposeful form of existence depending upon one's choices. Important for this discussion is that within each sphere resides the potential of realizing a proper relation between the infinite (eternal, "spiritual," potential) and the finite (temporal, material, mundane existence) conditions that constitute a possible human self. However, this relation tends to collapse into conflict when beliefs come into contact with the material demands of a daily existence that normalizes certain acts as the only ethical ones. As indicated above, with such certain conflict comes choice and with choice comes despair: "The self in despair experiences a total loss of hope as the threat of nothingness...becomes overwhelming.... Despair is a disruption, disrelationship or disproportion of the elements which structure the interior of the self" (Schrag, 1987, p. 88). This misrelation is a fundamental condition of humanity with which each individual struggles throughout life, especially if one is concerned with creating a meaningful existence through the activity of becoming. However, just because the misrelation exists does not mean all willingly embrace it, and in fact, most attempt to deny it. A becoming self, though, has the existential project of understanding the misrelation by bringing it into consciousness (Kierkegaard, 1849/1980).

What critical pedagogy theory does quite powerfully for the individual teacher is to press this despair into the open and reveal it as a condition of others who have experienced and continue to experience oppression and marginalization, which greatly prohibit any drive toward becoming and freedom. The teacher also realizes that the same despair constrains herself or himself as an agent of a state institution that has historically reproduced the inequities that sustain oppression. Freire (1970/1994) indicated as much when he warned the middle class that all the efforts to protect their material wealth would never secure their freedom but instead guarantee unfreedom if they failed to join the oppressed in the fight against hegemonic forces of the state.

An example would be the unconscious despair of the teacher who sees him- or herself as a professional following the normative written and unwritten ethical rules represented within the institution of schooling without any sort of interrogation of who the rules serve and toward what purpose. The teacher, in unconscious despair, assumes that he or she performs morally good or even politically neutral acts of instruction. His or her identity becomes overly determined by the finite institutional attributes, and less by the subjective reflection upon the infinite possibilities of "what could be" that always call into question any such claims or privileges of those individuals and discourses that dictate the "real" of material existence. The misrelation is intensified when a teacher surrenders to the normalizing tendencies of the finite instead of remaining in the tension of the finite and infinite that generates a becoming self capable of keeping the conversation going through critical questioning.

Even though a teacher may seem content to identify the institution as good and virtuous, despair continues to function in ways that further foreclose upon the teacher's existence within and without the classroom. However, with an engagement with critical pedagogy comes a potential awareness of this foreclosure. Only at this point of consciousness is it possible to begin to shift the misrelation into its proper relation. However, while critical pedagogical theory can make one aware of this misrelation, that in itself is not enough to overcome the despair and realign the self into a proper relation to one of the spheres of existence. A proper relation would mean that a teacher develops a disposition to create an ironic distance from institutional conventions that claim reality. Such a disposition is necessary to navigate and alter the landscape in subtle ways that begin to favor the principles of critical pedagogy and existential becoming. This disposition is a passionate inwardness that existentially removes one from the ethos of the institution, always presented as universal, normative, and common sense, in an effort to confront the concrete particularities of the existing world (Kierkegaard, 1844/1992).

This notion of passion indicates that such a move is existential rather than cognitive (Beaufort, 1996; Elrod, 1984). While the move may be reasoned and well thought out, the actual shift, the actual willingness to thrust one's self back into a tension that will certainly include a struggle with despair, can never be a "rational" choice. Instead, it is purely in the realm of an "existential leap" (Kierkegaard, 1849/1980). Such a double move—a reasoned madness—creates possible spaces for the individual to advance criticality and generate a new, proper relation that dissipates that specific form of despair. For the individual to first make the inward turn seems at odds with the kind of social theory that critical pedagogy historically adheres to. However, in order to challenge the conventions of an institution that has participated in the parsing out of students into cultural and economic categories that are either rewarded by society or marginalized, one must first scrutinize his or her moral stance and existential place within society (Kierkegaard, 1844/1992). Simply, one must first turn away from the "other" in order to eventually hear and see the "other," to hear and see the truth of the existing particularity of the present.

Kierkegaard theorizes his notion of passionate inwardness as an intensification of one's focus on the particularity of his or her life that calls into question universal codes and conventions presented as true and good by any community:

> At its highest, inwardness in an existing subject is passion; truth as a paradox corresponds to passion, and that truth becomes a paradox is grounded precisely in

its relations to an existing subject. In this way the one corresponds to the other. In forgetting that one is an existing subject, one loses passion, and in return, truth does not become a paradox; but the knowing subject shifts from being human to being a fantastical something, and truth becomes a fantastical object for its knowing. (1844/1992, p. 199)

This notion of passionate inwardness, in terms of modern theoretical trajectories, resembles the curriculum theory work of William Pinar, who developed what could be called a method of passionate inwardness otherwise known as *currere*. As Pinar writes, "[C]urrere refers to my existential experience of external structures. The method of currere is a strategy devised to disclose this experience, so that we may see more of it and see more clearly. With such seeing can come deepened understanding of the running, and with this, can come deepened agency" (Pinar & Grumet, 1976, p. vii). Much like currere, passionate inwardness also seeks to begin with the principle that one must interrogate any claim to universal ethics upon the individual.[4] In other words, passionate inwardness does not indicate a blind repudiation and permanent exit from institutional ethics (Dooley, 2001). Instead, passionate inwardness is an activity, an engagement in a critical dialectic between one's particularity—and eventually the particularity of the other—and the institutional claim to abstract universality as evidenced by the impulse to measure and quantify. In other words, one cannot just accept the institutional ethos as universal or despair will be the *only* condition of one's existence.

For instance, Kierkegaard critiqued modern institutions, specifically the church, for universalizing a discourse that asserted that life could be approached as if time could be stopped and absolutes maintained. This enabled the institution to impose an arbitrary ethic of behavior that served the power of the institution and the power of those who controlled the institution. However, Kierkegaard's writing illustrated existence as fluid, complex, and ambiguous. To set over some universal framework of ethical behavior is to believe that laws and norms unfold according to a plan that is outside of time and existence. Kierkegaard recognized that human beings are situated in time, embedded in historicity and, hence, any truth ascertained by one is contingent. There may exist something outside of time, but humans have no access to it for the very fact that they are human: "Everything that becomes historical is contingent...inasmuch as precisely by coming into existence, by becoming historical, it has elements of contingency, inasmuch as contingency is precisely the one factor in all coming into existence" (Kierkegaard, 1844/1992, p. 98).

As existence is contingent, then one easily falls into a misrelation of the self when attempting to accept any universal claims (even common sense, practical claims) set forth through an institutional ethos. The existing individual then only makes matters worse, existentially, when attempting to employ the so-called professional, rational discourse of decision making while functioning within the classroom. One becomes, according to Kierkegaard, a "ghost at a feast" (1843/1987, p. 197). This thin, airy existence leads to a kind of transparency in which more and more is known, but less and less is connected to concrete life except as a life conditioned by and dictated by the institutional ethos. Such universal abstraction creates a condition in which what one knows becomes more important than how one knows (Kierkegaard, 1843/1987).

This type of "objective" research-based pedagogy depends upon a type of empiricism that claims success as determined by quantitative measurement of the student. The teacher, if her or his pedagogy is not producing desired results, must then make an "instructional decision" based upon some other form of research-proven pedagogy that will supposedly work on the type of student that he or she has in the classroom. Ethical behavior, then, is to operate as a disinterested self that believes the best for the student in terms of quantitative outcome. That is the prevailing norm. In other words, the more one engages in such objective reflection, which fails to take the individual particularity of existential self and other into consideration (a move made by the *reflective practitioner*, see Schön, 1983), the more the misrelation of the self intensifies and widens, even as a teacher believes he or she is doing quite well by being a good professional.

However, instead of rejecting the institutional ethos, according to Kierkegaard, to bring the self into relation one must make an inward turn. This does not mean to reject the conventions out of hand and run away, but to make a passionate, concentrated turn toward subjectivity that in no way resembles the old dismissive quip that such a move is nothing but "navel gazing." For Kierkegaard, passion is not a romanticist's sensibility of escaping so-called reality into a "feel good" place. Instead, passion is most aligned with a sense of investment, of being interested (Latin, *inter esse*, translates as being caught between, to be in the middle of), a movement that leads to paradox and suffering. What follows is intensive questioning of the institutional ethos and one's place within it:

> "Inwardness" [Kierkegaard, 1844/1992, p. 73], is the movement the individual makes while becoming subjective; that is, in order to transform impersonal objective reflection into engaged and passionate subjective reflection, the individual is required to adopt a critical distance from the prevailing ethical, political, and religious truths governing his or her reality, with the object of responding to the claims of singularity. (Dooley, 2001, p. 5)

In other words, according to Dooley's (2001) interpretation of Kierkegaard's passionate inwardness, the task of the individual is to balance between finite demands of sociopolitical milieu and that which is eternal within us: "We are always/already inside socio-political structures and yet we all have the propensity to take up a critical distance in relation to them, to momentarily suspend our affiliation with such frameworks so as to render them more applicable to the demands of the age" (Dooley, 2001, p.11). The passionate move inward is fleeting, but nonetheless an essential activity that generates the possible healing of the misrelation between the finite and infinite: "An existing person cannot be in two places at the same time, cannot be subject-object. When he is closest to being in two places at the same time, he is in passion; but passion in only momentary, and passion is the highest pitch of subjectivity" (Kierkegaard, 1844/1992, p. 199).

As discussed above, the existing individual must deliberate upon existential becoming within this particular time and place, which translates into an analysis of the degree to which one participates as an actor within the sociocultural milieu. Passionate inwardness produces questions: Who do the rules serve? Who and what do the rules protect? How do the rules discriminate and what inequities are embedded? And, to what degree do I as a moral agent existing within this institution embody, reflect, and participate in the maintaining of those ethical constraints presented by the institution as universal good? How can I engage in a meaningful act of becoming alongside other existing individuals within this institution? These are not ethereal, abstract. or academic questions that have little or no import on how one may exist within the institution of school.

Such questions open up what Kierkegaard called "fear and trembling," the suffering and despair of suspending one's own security within the community for a moment of "hidden inwardness" that enables him or her to understand the paradoxes of existence and the limitations of the ethical conventions. To begin to ask and give tentative answers to such questions, one must carefully tend to one's own subjective existence and particular thoughts and acts within the given concrete reality not bound by institutional conventions. In turn, one then recognizes the despair as a misrelation that can be lived in a way generates new possible choices. This relation is not only between aspects of the self, but between the self and others. In other words, passionate inwardness not only provides the needed existential turn that enables one to handle the recognition of despair that critical pedagogy can press to the surface, but it also can give one the tools by which to act in the world. A powerful persona that often returns from the inward turn is that of Kierkegaard's notion of the ironic stranger, the "hidden knight of hidden inwardness" (1844/1992) who looks like everyone else but exists within the tension between the finite and infinite, where contradiction and paradox play freely:

> He lives in the finite, but he does not have his life in it. His life, like the life of another, has the diverse predicates of a human existence, but he is within them like the person who walks in a stranger's borrowed clothes. He is a stranger in the world of finitude, but he does not define his difference from worldliness by foreign dress (this is a contradiction, since with that he defines himself in a worldly way); he is incognito, but his incognito consists in looking just like everyone else. (1844/1992, p. 410)

This stranger, who looks like everyone else, however, sees the concrete world and its powerful claims toward objective reality with an ironic eye. The stranger refuses to deify the universal claims of institutional ethics, yet is passionate in her or his ethical concerns of acting in the world: "Irony is the unity of ethical passion, which in inwardness infinitely accentuates the private self, and of development, which in outwardness (in association with people) infinitely abstracts from the privatizing self. The effect of the second is that no one notices the first; therein lies the art, and the true infinitizing of the first is conditioned thereby" (1835/1967b, entry 1745, p. 267). Such ironic positioning acknowledges and embraces the acts that press despair to the surface so that this human condition can become a part of a curriculum that does not deny the "official knowledge" of textbook curriculum that currently rules the institution of schooling, but thinks through it critically and with an eye toward how such knowledge affects each student and teacher as existential beings in the world.

To situate one's self in this way opens more spaces within the institution that point toward a "smaller," more attentive, more subtle existence within the classroom that does not mean wholesale repudiation of the institution, or wholesale radical calls for implosion and destruction of the institution due to its participation in oppression of students and teachers alike. Instead, the institution for the teacher becomes a place where all differences come together and allows the individual to engage in a different kind of education, a different kind of dialogue that exist alongside the ethos of the institution, one that helps others engage in passionate inwardness. Within that comes change, for teachers will begin to ask: "What of the ethos of this institution forecloses on my own existential becoming as one of a community of others existing as individuals? How do I fight such inequities in which I can truly choose to change?"

Notes

1. At this writing, the three graduate students with whom I was involved, and excerpts from whose case studies are presented in this paper, have all left or are in the process of leaving the classroom. One went into administration, one left public school to become a full time graduate student, and the third has graduated and moved to a university to work as a professor. Of the other teachers whom I have interviewed as part of my graduate level teacher

education class, most continue to struggle, but admit that one of the reasons they came back to graduate school was to somehow find a way out of what they believed was "burnout," a condition that over time most admit is something much deeper— despair.

2. This assertion, of course, applies to those teachers who have come into my proximity of interpretation and as such presents no universal generalization.

3. A recent example of this phenomenon comes from one of the interviewees, who decided to teach Howard Zinn's *A People's History of the United States* (1980/2005). A parent complained to the principal and school board that the teacher was being anti-American. The superintendent's response was to order the teacher to stop using the materials and stop providing a voice for those marginalized within American history. This teacher, one of many graduate students deciding to leave the public school classroom, now complains of a feeling of paralysis in his teaching and is looking for ways out of the classroom.

4. The difference between Pinar and Kierkegaard is within the actual development of a method by which to approach these existential and institutional issues. While space does not permit here to parse out this important thread, I can offer a brief generalization on the difference: Whereas Pinar attempts to lay out a transparent means by which to approach these issues in an almost empirical, linear maneuver (McKnight, 2006), Kierkegaard operates through deception. By deception I mean that Kierkegaard never claimed to be the author of any of the books he wrote, but instead used pseudonyms that allowed him to play with various ideas that could conflict with previous ideas he put forth. Whereas Pinar was interested in much of his earlier writings to find a way to "lay bare" the self, Kierkegaard was seeking to find multiple selves that would exist within tension and play off each other depending upon what sphere of existence he or she resided within.

References

Adorno, T. (1989). *Kierkegaard: construction of the aesthetic* (R. Hullot-Kentor, Trans.). Minneapolis: University of Minnesota Press.

Apple, M. (1999). *Official knowledge: Democratic education in a conservative age*. New York: Routledge.

Beaufort, G. (1996). *Freedom and its misuses: Kierkegaard on anxiety and despair*. Milwaukee: Marquette University Press.

Bourdieu, P., & Passeron, J. (2000). *Reproduction in education, society, and culture*. London: Sage.

Burbules, N. (2000). The limits of dialogue as a critical pedagogy. In P. Trifonas (Ed.), *Revolutionary pedagogies* (pp. 251–273). New York: Routledge.

Darder, A., Baltodano. M., & Torres, R. (Eds). (2009). *The critical pedagogy reader* (2nd ed.). New York: Routledge.

Dooley, M. (2001). *The politics of exodus: Kierkegaard's ethics of responsibility*. New York: Fordham University Press.

Ellsworth, E. (1989) Why doesn't this feel empowering? Working through the repressive myths of critical pedagogy. *Harvard Education Review, 59*(3), 297–324.

Elrod, J. (1984). Passion, reflection and particularity. In R. L. Perkins (Ed), *International Kierkegaard commentary: Two ages* (pp. 1–19). Macon, GA: Mercer University Press.

Freire, P. (1994). *Pedagogy of the oppressed*. New York: Continuum. (Original work published 1970)

Giroux, H. (1983). *Theory and resistance in education*. Westport, CT: Greenwood.

Giroux, H. (1988). *Teachers as intellectuals: Toward a critical pedagogy of learning*. South Hadley, MA: Bergin & Garvey.

Glass, R. (2001). On Paulo Freire's philosophy of praxis and the foundations of liberation Education. *Educational Researcher, 30*(2), 15–25.

Gore, J. (1993).*The struggle for pedagogies: Critical and feminist discourses as regimes of truth*. New York: Routledge.

Gramsci, A. (1971). *Selections from the prison notebooks*. (Q. Hoare & G. N. Smith, Ed. & Trans.). New York: International.

Greene, M. (1988). *Dialectic of freedom*. New York: Teachers College Press.

Greene, M. (2003). In search of a critical pedagogy. *Harvard Educational Review, 56*(4), 427–441. (Original work published 1986)

Haberman, M. (1991). Pedagogy of poverty versus good teaching. *Phi Delta Kappan, 73*(4), 290–294.

Kanpol, B. (1998). Critical pedagogy for beginning teachers: the movement from despair to hope. Retrieved April 15, 2006, from http://www.lib.umwestern.edu/pub/jcp/issueII-1/kanpol.html

Keesing-Styles, L. (2003). The relationship between critical pedagogy and assessment in teacher education. *Radical Pedagogy, 5*(1). Retrieved February 1, 2006, from http://radicalpedagogy.icaap.org/content/issue5_1/

Kierkegaard, S. (1967a). *Søren Kierkegaard's journals and papers* (Vol. 1, H. V. Hong & E. H. Hong, Ed. & Trans.). Bloomington, In.: Indiana University Press. (Original work published 1835)

Kierkegaard, S. (1967b). *Søren Kierkegaard's journals and papers* (Vol. 2, H. V. Hong & E. H. Hong, Ed. & Trans.). Bloomington: Indiana University Press. (Original work published 1835)

Kierkegaard, S. (1967c). *Søren Kierkegaard's journals and papers* (Vol.5, H. V. Hong & E. H. Hong, Ed. & Trans.). Bloomington: Indiana University Press. (Original work published 1835)

Kierkegaard, S. (1967d). *Søren Kierkegaard's journals and papers* (Vol. 6, H. V. Hong & E. H. Hong, Ed. & Trans.). Bloomington.: Indiana University Press. (Original work published 1835)

Kierkegaard, S. (1978). *Two ages: The age of revolution and the present age. A literary review* (H. V. Hong & E. H. Hong, Ed. & Trans.). Bloomington: Indiana University Press. (Original work published 1845)

Kierkegaard, S. (1980). *Sickness unto death* (H. V. Hong & E. H. Hong, Ed. & Trans.). Princeton, NJ: Princeton University Press. (Original work published 1849)

Kierkegaard, S. (1983). *Fear and trembling/repetition* (H.V. Hong & E. H. Hong, Ed. & Trans.). Princeton, NJ: Princeton University Press. (Original work published 1843)

Kierkegaard, S. (1987). *Either/or Part 1 and 2* (H. V. Hong & E. H. Hong, Ed. & Trans.). Princeton, NJ: Princeton University Press. (Original work published 1843)

Kierkegaard, S. (1992). *Concluding unscientific postscript to philosophical fragments* (Vol. 1, H. V. Hong & E. H. Hong, Ed. & Trans.). Princeton, NJ: Princeton University Press. (Original work published 1844)

Kincheloe, J. L. (2004). *Critical pedagogy primer.* New York: Lang.

Labaree, D. (1992). Power, knowledge, and the rationalization of teaching: A genealogy of the movement to professionalize teaching. *Harvard Educational Review, 62*(2), 123–154.

Lareau, A. (2003). *Unequal childhoods: Class, race and family life.* Berkeley: University of California Press.

Levinas, E. (1998). Existence and ethics. In J. Ree & J. Chamberlain (Eds.), *Kierkegaard: A critical reader* (pp. 26–38). Oxford: Blackwell.

Liston, D. (2000). Love and despair in teaching. *Educational Theory, 50*(1), 81–102.

Marsh, J. (2001). Kierkegaard and critical theory. In M. J. Matustik & M. Westphal (Eds.), *Kierkegaard in post/modernity* (pp. 199–215). Bloomington: Indiana University Press.

Mayo, P. (1999). *Gramsci, Freire and adult education: Possibilities for transformation action.* London: Zed Books.

McKnight, D. (2004). Kierkegaard and the despair of the aesthetic existence in teaching. *Journal of Curriculum Theorizing, 29*(1), 59–79.

McKnight, D. (2005, August–2006, December). Interviews by author of curriculum and instruction graduate students. (Transcribed June 2006)

McKnight, D. (2006). The gift of a curriculum method: Beginning notes on William F. Pinar. *Curriculum and Teaching Dialogue, 8*(2), 171–183.

McLaren, P. (1998). *Life in Schools: An introduction to critical pedagogy in the foundations of education* (3rd ed.). New York: Allyn & Bacon.

Pinar, W. F. (1994). *Autobiography, politics and sexuality: Essays in curriculum theory, 1972–1992.* New York: Lang

Pinar, W. F., & Grumet, M. (1976). *Toward a poor curriculum.* Dubuque, IA: Kendall/Hunt.

Schön, D. (1983). *The reflective practitioner: How professionals think in action.* New York: Basic Books.

Schrag, C. O. (1987). *Existence and freedom: Towards and ontology of human finitude.* Chicago: North-western University Press

Shor, I. (1987). *Critical teaching and everyday life* (3rd ed.). Chicago: University of Chicago Press.

Spring, J. (1976). *The sorting machine: national educational policy since 1945.* New York: Longman.

Weiler, K. (1988). *Women teaching for change: Gender, class and power.* New York: Bergin & Garvey.

Zinn, H. (2005). *A people's history of the United States.* New York: HarperCollins. (Original work published 1980)

Suggested Reading Questions

1. The author suggests that passionate inwardness might provide the reflexive means beyond rational awareness to exist and move beyond finite institutional discourses. Critical pedagogues have indicated that a passionate turn outward is necessary to change inequitable social conditions under which we live. How might one resolve the author's call for passionate inwardness with critical pedagogy's historical call to focus on systemic transformation?

2. There is a clear difference between the becoming self with its emphasis on ongoing meaning making practices and institutional self with its emphasis on stable concepts. How might these two divergent selves be drawn together to remake pedagogy to help meet the promise of education for a participating democracy?

3. What is the responsibility of curriculum theorists to craft and articulate discourses that can be translated into classroom practice in contemporary public education?

4. In what ways has the deskilling of teachers and the intensification of work changed the relationship between deliberation and action for teachers?

5. The author suggests teachers should create "ironic" distance between their subjective and institutional realities. How might teachers who return from the passionate turn inward discussed by the author relate to their students and other teachers differently?

Response to Douglas McKnight
Deep in My Heart

Alan A. Block

In her autobiography, *A Life in School: What the Teacher Learned* (1996), Jane Tompkins (1996) narrates her struggle to break the bonds holding the teacher to curriculum so that she might fulfill her desire to practice currere, though she cannot name that attempt because she proudly announces at the very beginning of her book that "I had no desire to pick up a book on teaching—in fact, I had a positive aversion to doing so— and I couldn't even muster the energy to feel guilt about it…. It was to my own experience that I needed to turn for enlightenment" (p. xii). I think Tompkins addresses here a mythology that pervades our society and one that especially permeates the schools: that teaching can only be learned in experience and has no theoretical or philosophical support. Philosophy of education exists, but it is an intellectual tradition though hardly a practical one. In tightly structured accreditation programs for teacher licensure, classroom management often replaces philosophy of education as a required course. This is a misunderstanding so serious that I cannot begin to address it here, though this belief and practice sits at the center of too many teacher education programs. Teachers, they hold, are *not* intellectuals! Try to imagine the last representation of a teacher anywhere in American culture that focuses on her intelligence and critical acumen. The field is overrun by practitioners but no scholars, and the propaganda announces that teaching can be learned merely by practice and in the absence of ideas. We even hire people who have never taken an education class to practice in the classrooms where sit our children! As if there is nothing to teaching but management of the classroom for the purpose of efficiently transmitting the subject matter; as if education *is* subject matter. As if Tompkins' book itself is not itself filled with ideas she would have the educator-reader accept, but which, had Tompkins read just a bit in education, she might have recognized as ideas already constituting a significant field occupied by an impressive array of scholars and practitioners. She would also have discovered a field with a long and deep history. Then, she might have considered joining the movement rather than imagining that she had discovered it. She says,

> What I would like to see emerge in this country is a more holistic way of conceiving education—by which I mean a way of teaching and learning that is not just task-oriented but always looking over its shoulder at everything that is going on around. Such a method would never fail to take into account that students and teachers have bodies that are mortal, hearts that can be broken, spirits that need to be fed. It would be interested in experience as much as in book knowledge, and its responsibility would be the growth of whole human beings, in harmony with the planet and with one another. (p. xiii)

Tompkins pronounces this as if John Dewey had not written a word, and that the reconceptualization—which for me, at least, has its more recent roots in Joseph Schwab (1969)—had never occurred. Tompkins would certainly have done well to delve into the extensive literature concerning curriculum studies that has been written during the years when she studied and taught, and, as she said, mightily suffered. Tompkins' complaint, however, is a real one: she describes schooling as an environment permeated by fear and insecurity, alienation and despair. For many, this is an accurate characterization of the their lives in school, some of them writing eloquently in this text. Along with many of us, Tompkins would prefer that it were not so. She writes, "Yet I believe that school should be a safe place, the way home is supposed to be. A place where you belong, where you can grow and express yourself freely…" (p. 127). Dewey had argued this almost one hundred years before Tompkins, but, of course, she didn't read John Dewey when she studied the classroom. Interestingly enough, it would seem that Tompkins's own home was hardly the idyllic haven she would have the school model. She describes a Christmas dinner in 1958. Responding to a question about her studies, she quotes a line from Eliot's *The Family Reunion,* a poet for whom she expresses affinity: "You are the consciousness of your unhappy family, its bird sent flying through the purgatorial flame" (p. 127). Not unaware of the irony of this moment, Tompkins comments: "That moment can stand as well as any other for the lesson I'm trying to teach myself. It is the moment I want most to avoid: unconsciously enacting on a public stage an inward drama of which I have no knowledge" (p. 128). So, for Tompkins, life in school can be understood as an acting out in the classroom of an inner reality, a stance at once very personal and intimate and yet very much public. Unfortunately, nothing in the pedagogy she experienced and didn't study helped her understand this. The position at which Tompkins finally arrives makes clear that "All along I'd known in the abstract that I taught from places inside me that needed healing" (p. 177). That is, her life in the classroom *as a teacher* was an attempt to heal the damages that derived not merely from her life in school, but from her life compleat.

Of course, as McKnight suggests in his chapter, "Critical Pedagogy and Despair: A Move toward Kierkegaard's Passionate Inwardness," Tompkins could have turned to philosophy as a resource for her learning in school. Indeed, McKnight addresses in his essay the very condition which oppresses Tompkins: fatigue, depression, and alienation. McKnight notes that in the schools this condition refers to "teacher burnout." He speaks of the complaint of his own graduate students: "I came to identify this phenomenon not as burnout from the weight of external burdens, placed upon them in the classroom, a common interpretive misconception, but as a distinctive existential condition of despair." McKnight associates this particular state with Danish philosopher Sören Kierkegaard's concept, the "despair of necessity," a condition caused by having to act in a manner counter to one's own existential charge of becoming. McKnight suggests that Kierkegaard, rather than simply understanding this despair as paralysis, posits a use for this despair of necessity. Kierkegaard argues that if the despair derives from the paralysis which arises out of the essential contradiction between the desire to function honestly in the world in an existential sense, and the objective demands of the social strictures, then a passionate inwardness is a focus on exactly those personal conflicts raised by the contradictions. McKnight writes, "Passionate inwardness is an activity, an engagement in a critical dialectic between one's particularity—and eventually the particularity of the other—and the institutional claim to abstract universality as evidence by the impulse [today] to measure and quantify." Passionate inwardness seems to be a forerunner of the talking cure, of psychoanalysis, and of currere. If passionate inwardness is not, as McKnight says, "to reject the conventions out of hand and run away, but to make a passionate, concentrated turn toward subjectivity," then currere, says McKnight, is an identical turn. McKnight quotes Pinar: "[C]urrere refers to my existential experience of external structures. The method of currere is a strategy devised to disclose this experience, so that we may see more of it and see more clearly. With such seeing can come deepened understanding of the running, and with this, can come deepened agency." Out of the despair of necessity might come the necessity of self.

Sometimes I think we would all like to get back to the Garden. I am myself inclined to arise and go to Innisfree. Everything was present in the garden, and Adam and Eve had nothing to really to do there except to eat and to mate, though apparently without the worry of pregnancy. In the Garden, there must have been no disconnect between self and world, the objective and the subjective. Every desire was met instantly. But when the two lone humans eat of the Tree of Knowledge of Good and Evil, the peace of their lives in Eden is forever gone. They become aware of themselves; nothing in the Garden has changed, but Adam and Eve may no longer live there. They know too much.

Now, I am not here concerned with the exact nature of the knowledge of good and evil so much as I am interested in the consequences of that knowing. Clearly, though the serpent seems to understand the consequences of eating the fruit, this knowledge is particular only to human beings; the serpent had apparently never eaten of the tree. And that knowledge, once acquired, is irrevocable; once learned, it may not be unlearned. And though the Garden may yet remain paradisaical, Adam and Eve no longer maintain an unadulterated vision of the Garden as the whole of the pure world. In an interesting way, whether or not they were allowed to remain in the Garden after their sampling from the tree, their lives were forever altered by the knowledge of good and evil. The awareness of evil would make them wary—their first response is to put on clothes—and they would have become aware of the presence of evil *outside* of the Garden; they would have come to understand that they must protect the Garden from that which threatens it from without. Out there in the world is where the work is necessary, but this belief assumes a world in need of repair. And that repair requires that we dirty ourselves in the work, that we bear our children in pain, that we must work for our bread, and that we live with the sense of our mortality.

We teachers often speak as if there was once a Golden Age of Education, a Garden where education required no effort, and everyone happily and successfully learned what we taught. In this vision, we teachers were like the angels, aware of the knowledge of good and evil but untainted by that knowledge. Alas, we teachers do not live in the Garden; thank goodness for that, for in there I would not need to study. We teachers do not live in the Garden; thank goodness, there is much work to do. I think that teaching stands at this paradox: we would love to invent the classroom as Eden having long been banished from it. And like for most Edens, each of us has our vision of an impossible Paradise. We suffer alienation, exile, and despair. We work in the world. The despair of necessity leads us out of despair.We live in troubled times in education. Pinar (2004) writes, "The present historical moment is … for public-school teachers and for those of us in the university who work with them, a nightmare." (p. 3). I have written (Block, in press),

> We read regularly of the ineffectiveness of teachers and curriculum; we hear regularly the politicians' rhetoric bemoaning the horrid state of our educational institutions and the impending national doom which must inevitably follow from this failure. We hear regularly about the necessity of repairing these institutions immediately. And in the educational communities, we have come to accept these accusations as true. We accept the criticisms of us and our work, and we deny the effectiveness we know we possess; we accept their descriptions of our incompetence, and agree to their retributive measures of correction; we accept their judgment concerning our failures and relinquish our authority to function as we know best. We give up our faith in ourselves and our work, suppress our love and awareness of the children,

and cower in the undercrowded teachers' rooms from the overcrowded classrooms in fear of the political bureaucracies. We subsist in a constant state of crisis. We cease to do our work.

Jane Tompkins (1996) bemoans "an educational process that infantilizes students, takes away their initiative, and teaches them to be sophisticated rule followers. Of course, as professors we don't see the ways in which what we do as teachers narrows and limits our students: for we ourselves have been narrowed and limited by the same process." (p. 209). And McKnight writes that "Most teachers, once exposed to the theories of critical pedagogy and curriculum, understand the damage done, to themselves as well as the students, when they align their teaching existence with institutional demands" (p. 501). There is a certain unanimity to these views; our despairs are real, and for us, have legitimacy. We each mean to begin in our teaching the healing that our world and our spirits require. It is what we know must be done.

Rabbi Moshe Leib (in Buber, 1975) said, "The way in this world is like the edge of a blade. On this side is the netherworld, and on that side is the netherworld, and the way of life lies in between" (p. 93). McKnight's Kierkegaard thought that we must keep on keeping on, but that finally, we must all come to the abyss and there make our leap of faith. There is nothing to convince us that there is anything to believe in, but we engage nonetheless because we personally have faith that there is purpose and meaning. Personally, I like Moshe Leib's metaphor, because it promises not escape from the demons chasing us, nor even some blind leap into we know not what. Rather, Leib insists that our effort in this world is not to leap over the chasm, but to maintain ourselves on the substantive path though the chasm lies on either side. We continue in our work. But it is no matter, really. McKnight's Sorën Kierkegaard, like my Rabbi Moshe Leib, offers us a way out of despair. Better to light a candle than to curse the darkness, though too often we must light our candles in the rain.

Lately, I have been listening almost daily to Dylan's composition, "Mississippi," the second composition on the *Love and Theft* (2001) collection. It is a narrative of aging, of pain and regret, and yet one of promise and hope. It gives me great comfort. Dylan (2001) writes,

> Well, my ship's been split to splinters and its sinking fast/I'm drownin' in the poison, got no future, got no past/But my heart is not weary, it is proud and it is free/I've got nothing but affection for all those who've sailed with me.

We live in troubled times, and I am concerned for our children. I have spent my entire life in schools, and I suffer too many moments of despair. Yet, for all of my spleen, when I read through this wonderful collection, my heart is not weary, its light and its free. I've got nothing but affection for all those who've sailed with me.

References

Block, A. A. (In press). *Ethics and teacher: Religious perspective on revitalizing education.* New York: Palgrave Macmillan.
Buber, M. (1975). *Tales of the Hasidim.* New York: Schocken.
Dylan, B. (2001). On *Mississippi.* Love and theft. New York: Special Rider Music.
Pinar, W. F. (2004). *What is curriculum theory.* Mahwah, NJ: Erlbaum.
Schwab, J. J. (1969). The practical: A language for curriculum. *School Review, 78,* 1–23.
Tompkins, J. (1996). *A life in school: What the teacher learned.* Reading, MA: Addison-Wesley.

Part IX

An Unusual Epilogue

A Tripartite Reading on Next
Moments in the Field

And They'll Say That It's a Movement

Alan A. Block

This is a book of many voices. These voices are eloquent, erudite, and always engaged with events and the world. These voices are also often in tension. Though it has its common use as a mode of complaint, I would like to think of tension as a potentially generative state. In physics, tension refers to "a constrained condition of the particles of a body when subjected to forces acting in opposite directions away from each, thus tending to draw them apart, balanced by forces of cohesion holding them together" (*Oxford English Dictionary,* 2nd, p. 188). Tension derives from an opposition between two *balanced* forces each vainly vying for prominence or for dominance. I push against the wall and the wall resists my pressure: tension is created. As long as the wall continues to resist my insistence, it remains standing, and I continue to push against it. Myself and the wall are in tension. We achieve a stasis until something happens, and while we are in tension, nothing changes.[1] The conflict between candidates Clinton and Obama was experienced as a tension by the electorate,[2] and this tension was relieved when Obama won the nomination and the struggle ended. Alternatively, the tension could have achieved resolution when both candidates agreed that each held viable but differing positions, and perhaps, they might cooperate. In either case, the tension resolves when the move is not toward consensus but toward consonance. In the resolution of tension, movement becomes possible, and that movement can be productive, glorious, and resplendent. Harmony occurs when the various voices achieve together the same key in which the piece is scored, though each voice may sing a different note. I think that in our field we would want to resolve tension and move toward harmony.

This is a book filled with tensions. No doubt our intellectual diversity strengthens the field; the resulting tensions give assurance of our continued viability. But left alone, tension results in stasis, and as we desire to move forward, we must somehow learn to resolve these tensions into some triumphant and glorious harmony. Marion Milner (1987, p. 10) writes that

> Conflict is essential to human life, whether between different aspects of oneself, between oneself and the environment, between different individuals or between different groups. It follows that healthy living is not the direct elimination of conflict which is possible only by forcible suppression of one or other of its antagonistic components, but the toleration of it—the capacity to bear the tensions of doubt and of unsatisfied need and the willingness to hold judgment in suspense until finer and finer solutions can be discovered which integrate more and more the claims of both sides. Thus it is the psychologist's job to make possible the acceptance of such an idea so that the richness of the varieties of experience whether within the unit of the single personality or in the wider unit of the group can come to expression. (1987, p. 10)

What Milner refers to as conflicts are, I think, equivalent to my notion of tensions, and I am pleased to discover that, for Milner, healthy conflict leads through intellectual activity to positions of greater and greater tolerance and inclusivity. The end of tension should result not in victory but in some consonance.

Milner argues that the psychologist's effort is not to end tension, but to make it acceptable, tolerable, and productive. Perhaps this might be true for the curriculum studies scholar. Individually, we resolve our personal tensions in our writings; we might in some like manner learn to resolve the tensions between us. To end tension is to achieve some repose; how wonderful that this condition might be accomplished in jubilance. And the resolution to which I refer is not a capitulation, but a majestic and exultant affirmation. Milner advocates conflict not for winning, nor even for compromise, but for self-control and growth. Conflict is to be encouraged, but its end must be harmony and concert. If, as Milner asserts, we cannot do without tension and conflict, and if tensions are endemic to growth, then perhaps we must think how to more productively orchestrate our tensions: the notes that we write out of the key signature, and the rhythms we produce that are uneven. Productive uses of tension can lead to new and glorious possibilities. A productive tension offers a hope for a joyous resolution and delight. Tension, perhaps, is an excellent way to describe the nature of the field of curriculum studies. We thrive in perpetual tension. Though we argue that the nature of conflict is hidden in the schools (Apple, 1975/2000), we have never hidden our tensions with or from each other. From Schwab's accusation that the field of curriculum is moribund, to the vituperative accusations of exclusionary discourse at the 2006 Articulating the Present (Next) Moment Conference, held at Purdue University, we continue to censure each other for behaviors, we accuse, which do not yet achieve what we singly hold as a perfect standard. Perhaps this tension is valuable, but I wonder when and how we are to resolve these tensions. We are a diverse group, as a cursory perusal of the table of contents will attest, and we are a concerned and engaged community holding a variety of perspectives on a wide array of issues, as the study of these chapters will attest. I think that as a group, as we discover in these essays, we thrive on tension; we even require tension for our work. We inspire tensions in others to inspire their stimulation and growth. But I wonder if we seem to lack the ability to work with our tensions and conflicts to achieve some harmony and productive pleasure. Sometimes I think we have abandoned the field for the territory, and opted for perpetual tension and stasis.

I am reminded of Korach's argument with Moses in the wilderness. Korach complained that despite his own illustrious ancestry, and despite his good standing in the community, he has been passed over for positions of leadership in the wilderness-wandering community. Korach means to oppose Moshe and nullify everything he said, and thereby raise his own standing in the community. In this attempt, the Rabbis say, Korach went out and gathered 250 heads of Sanhedrin, and he dressed them in clothes made completely of *techeilet*. Now, *techeilet* is a specific blue dye which would be used for a fringe bound to the corner of the garment which Jews are commanded to wear to remind the wearer to perform the *mitzvot*. Korach asks Moses if a man dressed in a garment dyed completely in *techeilet* yet requires a *techeilet-dyed* fringe on the piece of clothing. Moshe argues yes, that the directive in *Deuteronomy* requires the fringe dyed in *techeilet* be attached to the garment, even a garment dyed entirely in *techeilet* requires a fringe. Korach and his colleagues scoff. Then, Korach asks Moses if a house filled with Torah scrolls yet requires a *mezuzah* on the door. Since a Torah has all the parts of a *mezuzah* already in it, why is a *mezuzah* on the doorposts necessary? Again, Moshe judges that the commandment in Deuteronomy which insists that the words of study be on the doorposts of the house, even a house filled with Torah scrolls, requires a *mezuzah* on the door. Again, Korach and his cohorts scoff.

What Korach is doing, however, is subtle and devious: he is engaging in specious practices which cannot further life in the desert wanderings, but rather, merely promote his own grandstanding. In Tanhuma, a midrash collection named for Rabbi Tanhuma, from which this story derives, the Rabbis portray Korach as picking a fight—engaging in *pilpul*—inventing an absurd situation for which no actual answer is possible, and then arguing with whatever answer Moses offers, already aware what that answer must be. Or, Korach asks questions that display his knowledge, but that don't really require an answer. The purpose of the question is to place the one who must answer it in an untenable situation. Korach's effort is to *prevent* Moses from responding at all. It is to create a tension from which no resolution is possible; only conflict and destruction results. I think we must be careful of the questions we pose each other, and the questions to which we demand response.

I would like here to reinscribe (a word apt here, for I mean to address our writings in my writing) the idea of tension and conflict, and see if from this attempt at a reconceptualization I might offer some understanding of our efforts. I would like to redefine what have traditionally been our conflicts, as rather the developments of tensions: differing lines of thoughts and words pulling at us with equal force from opposite directions. This condition of tension is characterized by unsettledness, unresolvedness, ultimate discomfiture, and stasis. But, the experience of this tension might impel us toward some ultimate resolution which leads to harmony and consonance. How we might achieve this satisfaction, I think, determines our pedagogies and our lives.

The coda at the end of the first movement of Beethoven's 7th Symphony works via this idea of tensions and resolutions. I think it offers a way to consider our own positions in the field of curriculum studies. I do not mean to analyze thematically this magnificent work, but I would like to describe the means by which Beethoven creates a magnificent tension, and the means by which he resolves that tension into a glorious and intoxicating homecoming, as it were. By placing the various voices each individually singing beautifully, though not necessarily where a listener might expect to hear those voices; by placing voices singing not in harmony, but in opposition; by establishing uneven and unbalanced rhythms, Beethoven develops a tension in the coda which demands and receives resolution. The end of the first movement is a glorious arrival at harmony and resplendency.

Now, a coda is traditionally an addition to the sonata form for a movement, and functions as a place where the composer can add to the form within the form; the coda itself, then, derives from a conflict between expression and form, and represents a place for personal expression within the form. Though codas existed prior to Beethoven's Eroica Symphony, his codas were almost always long: I think he was working out complex ideas and feelings.

Interestingly enough, this coda begins not with sound, but with silence. For two whole measures, Nos. 387–388, Beethoven institutes a rest. It is as if the entire symphony has come to an abrupt halt. Then, in measure 389, the flutes, clarinets, violins, violas, cellos, and basses sing a single note, but this note is not in the key of A major; rather, it sounds in A^b, a step down from the original key signature, as if to suggest that the whole foundation is falling apart, even crumbling. Tension between the entire first movement and the coda is instituted. Next, Beethoven writes another two full measures of silence. This is a halting beginning, a hesitancy to speak. The silence itself represents a tension. It does not know what to say. It exists in no key. The music begins, as it were, in silence. And if the key of A in which the symphony is written represents a bright sound, then the A^b key which musically begins the coda moves away from that brightness. Indeed, in measure 391, the bass and cello begin a line which Michael Steinberg (1995, 42) refers to as "obsessive," and these voices, too, are written in the key of A minor, a mournful and even tragic sound. The composer adds a sense of sadness, doubt, or disappointment in these opening lines. And this line of basses and cellos descends in half step notes which again do not belong to the A major key signature. Beethoven has created a multiplicity of tensions here: there is the halting willingness to speak, the descending notes out of key, until measure 399 when the bass and cellos finally arrive at notes in the A major key. It is an unsettling mood, one that aspires to resolution and arrival, but which is continually frustrated by the orchestration. As I have noted, in measure 399 the basses and cellos briefly arrive home, only to quickly leave it again, singing notes which again do not belong to the key signature, circling home, sometimes voicing notes in the A major key, but somehow unable to sustain it; they hover about home without the ability to attain it, singing notes that do not belong. There is the desire to arrive home, but none of the comfort of arrival.

The tension continues as the basses and cellos play notes not in the key signature, while the upper voices, the flutes and clarinets, begin to sing in key. Furthermore, the rhythms remain unbalanced, with the notes in unequal time, producing on the whole a driving, relentless movement. The rhythms continue unbalanced through the next several measures; the whole effect establishes a tension and unsettledness, as the basses and cellos struggle to join the upper voices. Nor is this conventional: traditionally, it would be the lower voices, the basses and violincellos, which would serve as foundation, and the upper voices which would seek their security. Here, it is as if the foundation, which should be strong and solid, was itself trying to find the structure which it should undergird; it is as if the foundation itself sought some grounding. And then, in the upper voices at measure 400, the rhythms become regular, and the basses and cellos begin to ascend to the Tonic, finally arriving at notes belonging to the A major signature. Finally, at measure 423, the rising bass and cello, and all of the orchestral voices return home, and the symphony explodes in a sound that is magisterial, resplendent, and glorious. The rhythms which until now were unbalanced, become regular, and all the tensions are resolved in jubilancy. And so the coda and the movement close: all the instruments are in the major key, grounded in the tonic; there are no uneven rhythms, and the sound is bold, ecstatic, and heartening. This joyfulness and expectancy derive from the resolution of a created tension.

So, too, of the voices in this book: they create a tension even as they derive from it. The references which appear at the end of each chapter speak to the complicated conversations which each chapter represents, and speak of the tensions which provoke and arise out of these conversations. In our field, tension develops out of the voices we put in opposition; we are often to ourselves voices in opposition. And I would urge us to consider how we might resolve those tensions and arrive *together* back in the home key and in harmony. It is a glorious sound. As the movement of Beethoven's coda develops from and because of these tensions to a final resolution of majestic and glorious declaration of harmony and power, so might we resolve our tensions and bring our voices together in majesty and jubilance. It is this movement which seems to me to be necessary in the next moment for curriculum studies.

No doubt, our words are powerful though imperfect entities. In Milan Kundera's *The Unbearable Lightness of Being* (1984, p. 94), Franz, the university professor thinks:

> Noise has one advantage. It drowns out words. And suddenly he realized that all his life he had done nothing but talk, write, lecture, concoct sentences, search for formulations and amend them, so in the end no words were precise, their meanings were obliterated, their content lost, they turned into trash, chaff, dust, sand; prowling through his brain, tearing at his head, they were his insomnia, his illness. And

what he yearned for at that moment, vaguely but with all his might, was unbounded music, absolute sound, a pleasant and happy all-encompassing, over powering, window-rattling din to engulf, once and for all, the pain, the futility, the vanity of words. Music was the negation of sentences, music was the anti-word! (p. 94)

But we might, I think, by acknowledging the tensions our words contain, learn to resolve those tensions even in those words. We need not drown out our words, but acknowledge the tensions within them, and then to work to resolve those tensions. We might work in the codas of our first movements to jubilance and joy.

References

Apple, M. W. (2000). The hidden curriculum and the nature of conflict. In W. Pinar (Ed.), *Curriculum studies: The reconceptualization* (pp. 171–184). Troy, NY: Educator's International Press. (Original work published 1975)

Kundera, M. (1984). *The unbearable lightness of being* (M. H. Heim, Trans.). San Francisco: Harper & Row.

Milner, M. (1987). *The suppressed madness of sane men*. New York: Tavistock.

Steinberg, M. (1995). *The symphony*. New York: Oxford University Press.

The Next Moment

William F. Pinar

> Through what acts of repudiation, forgetting, and violence will this generation con-
> stitute itself? (Jennifer Gilbert, this volume, p. 65)

This collection began as the proceedings of the 2006 Purdue University Conference
chaired by Professor Erik Malewski.[1] This expanded volume remains faithful to the project of that meeting, which was to delineate the "next moment" in curriculum studies by
representing a broad range of contemporary scholarship. Malewski had asked senior
scholars to reply to the conference keynote addresses, all given by younger scholars, at
Purdue in February 2006. Generational tensions had been loud during the 1970s reconceptualization of the field (Pinar, Reynolds, Slattery, & Taubman, 1995, pp. 230–238),
but if these seem muted today perhaps it is because they have been usurped by identity
politics, a prominent feature of the Purdue conference.

It was the 1973 University of Rochester conference (Pinar, 1974; Pinar et al., 1995,
pp. 218–219) that inaugurated the reconceptualization of U.S. curriculum studies, and
Malewski viewed the Purdue meeting as possibly playing a similarly stimulating role.[2]
My PhD mentor, Paul R. Klohr, and I had planned the 1973 Rochester conference as a
"state-of-the-field" meeting; we did not foresee that it would initiate a decade of dispute
that would result in the field mapped in *Understanding Curriculum* (Pinar et al., 1995).
While the concept of "moment" overstates the temporal cohesion of lived time— not
everyone is living in the same present nor regards the past as past (Hlebowitsh, 2005;
Wraga, 1999; Wraga & Hlebowitsh, 2003)—it is a useful device to enable us to focus on
present circumstances.[3]

In fine postmodern fashion, the "next moment" splinters into, not fragments of
a whole,[4] but separate and not obviously related domains, some of which recall (and
extend) the discourses we identified over a decade ago (understanding curriculum historically, internationally), others appearing since (postcolonialism, Southern studies), or
those becoming even more prominent (understanding curriculum aesthetically, ecologically, racially, technologically, psychoanalytically). The present state of the field seems
sufficiently variegated to conclude that what we curriculum studies scholars have in common is not the present but the past. Perhaps that is why curriculum history has emerged
as a key specialization (Pinar, 2008a, p. 493).[5]

Despite its centrality in efforts to understand the present, curriculum history remains
underdeveloped in a field traumatized by malevolent politicians and undermined by
opportunistic colleagues.[6] The present field is not entirely ahistorical (as evident in this
collection); it remains, however, plagued by an ameliorative orientation (Kliebard, cited
in Pinar, 2000, pp. 41–43). The educational left's obsession with "social justice" reiterates
the right wing's claim that schools— not government—are responsible for redressing the
inequities of the present.[7]

In no area is that claim expressed more stridently than in contemporary identity politics. I myself have participated in the identity politics phenomenon with the publication of *Queer Theory in Education* (1998). I employed identity categories in my 2001 study of racial politics and violence in the United States (distinguishing between men's and women's participation in lynching events and antilynching campaigns). Five years later I had shifted my focus from identity categories to the problem of "Whiteness" (2006a), providing a genealogy of phenomena no longer linked literally to anatomy. In the interim I situated school "deform" historically and psychoanalytically, again invoking categories of identity (2004).[8] Self-consciously working within and from the academic field of curriculum studies I replied to the reality of that fractious moment.[9]

The excess of contemporary identity politics—Patchen Markell (2003) characterizes the problem as one of being "bound by recognition"—was performed at the Purdue conference. Serving as one of Erik's consultants, I supported his preoccupation with identity politics. At every stage of the year-long preparation for the conference, Malewski focused on two equally important criteria for selecting keynoters (and they blurred into each other): (1) diversity of identity, specifically as these represented (2) those intellectual formations constitutive of the present moment in curriculum studies. Ever after a Black African immigrant (whose expertise is cultural studies) withdrew at the last minute, the conference program was unusual for the extent of its diversity: the eight keynoters included an African-American woman, a Puerto Rican man working in Canada, one woman from China and another from India (both working in the U.S.), and three lesbians. (Even without knowing these speakers as persons, as I do, these identity categories are crude, echoing my critique of identity politics as misrepresenting identity: see Pinar, in press).

At one point during the conference, acting as if the event were a demographic exercise, a Latina audience member complained *she* was not represented. A senior African-American scholar (herself on the program as a discussant) followed suit, complaining that in racial terms curriculum studies had not changed in 30 years, a fantastical claim given the centrality race and antiracism obviously occupy in the field (see Pinar et al. 1995, pp. 315–357).[10] Other testimonies of victimization followed, including that of a keynoter, who glosses the episode as "generative" (Gaztambide-Fernández, 2006, p. 63). What the event generated was the excess of contemporary identity politics: self-indulgent indignation substituting for scholarship and dialogical encounter. In an especially memorable enactment of what I call strategically dysfunctional essentialism, self-segregating identity politicians constructed a new hierarchy in the conference room that day, relegating listeners of European descent to the status of supplicants. Maurizio Viano (1993) observes that, "The denial of hierarchy becomes a hierarchy itself. As such, it is more dangerous, because it is not subjected to constant verifications" (p. 311).

Plagued externally by politicians determined to silence the education professoriate[11] and internally by the excesses of contemporary identity politics and the ameliorative posture it self-destructively reproduces, contemporary curriculum studies is intellectually vibrant as it is threatened.[12] The problem of the present is intensified by the field's historic preoccupation with "the school," too often severed from material specificity. Now an abstraction without concrete referents, "the school" functions as free-floating signifier of fantasy. In one version, it is a site of corruption (schools are failing our children) and in another, it is a site of redemption (schools will save a nation at risk). Emptied of concrete content (material or intellectual), the "school" devolves into a business, the "bottom line" of which is student "outcomes." The reduction of academic achievement to standardized test scores functions to obliterate the reality of individual teachers and students in actual schools. Knowledge is traded for "skills," another concept without content.[13] Even prominent education professors appear to accept the grift and make claims about teachers and schools without empirical verification or even scholarly reference (e.g., Darling-Hammond, 1997, p. 213). Why U.S. teachers' unions have not sued for libel escapes me; that is, until I remind myself of the unions' record of utter incompetence in contesting decades of assault upon the profession (Pinar, 2004, p. 177).

It is long past time to speak of schools sparingly (Pinar, 2004, p. 175). Generalization without empirical verification (or at least scholarly reference) is not only unprofessional, in the nightmare that is the present it reproduces politicians' self-serving distortions of locally distinctive institutions occupied by particular individuals at specific times. It is long past time to speak to (not past) each other, by which I mean to the ideas advanced in the field.[14] It is through sustained engagement with the scholarly production of the field that the field can be advanced intellectually. For students and scholars alike, this collection provides a compelling opportunity.

Notes

1. http://www.education.purdue.edu/thenextmoment/
2. University-affiliated conferences punctuated that decade in which the founding paradigm of the field shifted from "curriculum development" to "understanding curriculum." In the *Sage Handbook* chapter (Pinar, 2008a, p. 501), I proposed a possibly paradigmatic moment after "understanding": "internationalization." That remains only a suggestion, as—despite calls to attend to the "worldliness" of the field (Miller, 2005, p. 250)—U.S. curriculum studies remains as narcissistically self-involved as ever. During the calamity that was the Bush Administration, the field recoiled inward, not in a cool-calm-and-collected way, as I hoped "internationalization" would provoke, but in an "in-fighting" way, intensifying a hallucinatory flight from reality—as in the Hlebowitsh and Kridel and Bullough efforts to rehabilitate Tyler: see Kridel and Bullough (2007, p. 96). Hlebowitsh (2005, p. xiv) had to go to Bulgaria to peddle Tyler's wares! This present collection, which represents yet another moment past Tyler, underscores how removed from the reality of the present such scholars are. I begrudge no one removing oneself from the nightmare that is the present—I'm working on doing so myself—but "critical distance" (Anderson, 2006, p. 1) should enable the apprehension of reality, not its denial.
3. Efforts to understand the relations between the discipline's intellectual production and its present historical circumstances I designate as its horizontal structure (Pinar, 2007).
4. Partly to contradict the presentism that accompanies such splintering, at the 2007 annual meeting of the American Association for the Advancement of Curriculum Studies I advocated, and the General Membership accepted, a Canon Project, enabling us to structure a scholarly field self-conscious of its historic concerns. Given its hijacking by opponents at the 2008 meeting, the Canon Project appears blocked, at least for the moment. Perhaps in countries where the field is less threatened externally by the right wing and undermined internally by identity politics and political correctness, these ideas will meet a different fate. In Canada, for instance, the May 2008 reissuing of George Tomkins' canonical history of Canadian curriculum, *A Common Countenance* (1986/2008), and a national conference scheduled for February 2009 at the University of Ottawa (devoted to the state of the field) may contribute to the Canadian field's horizontality and verticality.
5. Historicity translates as verticality (Pinar, 2007).
6. The Bush Administration mandated "opportunities" to conduct "scientific" research on "what works": for one example of this Sisyphean nonsense see Slavin (2008). Even for those who refused to collaborate with the Bush Administration, frustration builds, as Dollard and his colleagues (1939) might have appreciated (see Pinar, 2001, pp. 189–191). Identity politics may be intensified now due to such displaced frustration.
7. Certainly the curriculum can be organized according to commitments to social justice. To illustrate how, I offered teachers two synoptic texts from which they can devise classes

focused on racial politics and violence (2001) and their gendered antecedents in European culture (2006a). Having separated instruction (or teaching or pedagogy) and learning from the curriculum, there are, evidently, education professors who assume they can "*teach* for social justice." Such a phrase reiterates the arrogance of social engineering and raises the specter of indoctrination while concentrating social responsibility in the classroom. (For all its potential, the classroom is no Archimedes' lever.) Speaking of indoctrination, Counts' slightly more considered assertion that "a transformed curriculum *could* [italics added] reshape national ideals and democratize America's collective future" (cited in Perlstein, 2000, p. 55) overstates still what teachers can expect. Today we realize that the scale and complexity of social justice requires not only its study in schools, but legislative action undertaken by government at all levels. (There is as well a secondary role for churches and other organizations and groups, local and national.) Social justice is also a matter of restructuring subjectivity (Pinar, 2004, pp. 4, 38).

8. *What Is Curriculum Theory?* (2004) was not only about identity, however; there and in *Race, Religion, and a Curriculum of Reparation* (2006a) and in *The Synoptic Text and Other Essays: Curriculum Development after the Reconceptualization* (2006b), I was demonstrating curriculum development as the composition of synoptic texts for teachers, an intellectual rather bureaucratic (i.e., Tylerian) undertaking that employs juxtaposition as a method (see Pinar, in press).

9. However unfashionable certain strands of postmodernism have made the concept, I refuse to relinquish reality. "As the idea of an objective 'out there' crumbles," Viano (1993, p. 177) notes, "the subject comes to the fore, inextricably implicated in the making of the object." The object—indeed, reality—remains. "The subject should not, however, be intimidated by the lack of universality in her/his judgment" Viano (1993, 213) continues, as the individual's "truth unveils the reality of difference"; that truth forefronts the alterity that is actuality.

10. By the "logic" of identity politics, in which utterances are reduced to their identity politics subtexts, the fact that this event followed a speech by a lesbian and a response by a homosexual man (*c'est moi*), it was "obviously" a homophobic repudiation of sexual minorities disguised in racial drag. (Given that the other discussant was Jewish, the event "must" be decoded as anti-Semitic as well.) There is no acknowledgment of Jews or lesbians (or women generally: we "must" add misogyny to the list of identity transgressions) or gay men in Gaztambide-Fernández's (2006, p. 63) praise of the conference program: he calls it "unusual" and "impressive" due to "the fact" that "four of the 10 keynote addresses were written by people of color." Despite his acknowledgment that he "may sound reductive," he complains that curriculum studies "sounds White" when he reads it. Whatever sound "White" makes when he reads, here the concept functions to efface ethnicity, gender, sexuality, and class, as does his discovery that the field is "grounded in the work of white scholars" (2006, p. 61). While the prominent participants in early 20th century curriculum studies (as in practically every other academic discipline) were male and of European descent, women and African Americans were not entirely absent nor are these historic figures invisible today (see, for instance, Brandon this volume; Crocco, Munro, & Weiler, 1999; Urban, 1992). That "White" scholars work on race—including on DuBois (e.g., Blum 2007), the ignorance of whose work Gaztambide-Fernández decries (2006, p. 61)—contradicts Gaztambide-Fernández's segregation of the field. Painted over in Gaztambide-Fernández's whitewash of the conference are Jews, women, and sexual minorities.

11. While education scholars have long been aware of progressivism's demise (see Cremin, 1961; Pilder, 1974), the paranoid (see Hofstadter, 1965/1996) right wing regards the education professoriate as a political threat, presumably because we still teach Dewey's *Democracy and Education*, listed as the fifth most "harmful" book published in the last 200 years: Retrieved May 9, 2008, from http://www.humanevents.com/article.php?id=7591

12. Certainly the political situation in the United States differs dramatically from that in, for instance, China, where the recent national curriculum reform has fostered a "boom" in curriculum studies (see Zhang & Zhong, 2003), characterized by the establishment of numerous institutes, an increase in scholarly production, and the translation into Chinese

of curriculum scholarship worldwide. Curriculum studies fields are nationally distinctive—even when grappling with global neoliberal school deform initiatives—and require sustained attention to the specific imperatives of national culture and history, especially as these are reproduced and contested within the discipline.

13. "As an instrument of domination," Viano (1993; parenthetical concepts added) notes, "culture can dispense with content [curriculum] and exist as mere form [skills]" (p. 301). Even in Canada, the curriculum becomes a casualty of test mania (Mahoney & Peritz, 2008). In educational terms the two countries share much, except, historically, the U.S. obsession with standardized test scores (Pinar, 2008b). Now even that difference disappears, as the above news item indicates.

14. The journal of the professional association dedicated to the field's advancement features such scholarship: Retrieved May 12, 2008, from http://www.uwstout.edu/soe/jaaacs/ In *Intellectual Advancement through Disciplinarity* (2007) I illustrated this idea through my engagement with the work of Janet L. Miller and of other key figures past and present. Because this engagement took the form of introductions to books, criticism is absent, but of course intellectual engagement requires criticism on occasion (see Pinar, 2006b, pp. 135–148).

References

Anderson, A. (2006). *The way we argue now: A study in the cultures of theory.* Princeton, NJ: Princeton University Press.

Blum, E. J. (2007). *W. E. B. Du Bois, American prophet.* Philadelphia: University of Pennsylvania Press.

Cremin, L. A. (1961). *The transformation of the school: Progressivism in American education, 1876–1957.* New York: Knopf.

Crocco, M. S., Munro, P., & Weiler, K. (1999). *Pedagogies of resistance: Women educator activists, 1880–1960.* New York: Teachers College Press.

Darling-Hammond, L. (1997). *The right to learn: A blueprint for creating schools that work.* San Francisco: Jossey-Bass.

Dollard, J., Miller, N., Doob, L., Mower, O., Sears, R., Ford, C., et al. (1939). *Frustration and aggression.* New Haven, CT: Yale University Press.

Gaztambide-Fernández, R. A. (2006). Regarding race: The necessary browning of our curriculum and pedagogy public project. *Journal of Curriculum and Pedagogy, 3*(1), 60–65.

Hlebowitsh, P. S. (2005). *Designing the school curriculum.* Boston: Pearson.

Hofstadter, R. (1996). *The paranoid style in American politics and other essays.* Cambridge, MA: Harvard University Press. (Original work published 1965)

Kridel, C., & Bullough, Jr., R.V. (2007). *Stories of the eight-year study: Reexamining secondary education in America.* Albany, NY: SUNY Press.

Mahoney, J., & Peritz, I. (2008, April 30). Quebec students' top rank tied to course reform. *Toronto Globe and Mail* . Retrieved May 7, 2008, from http://www.theglobeandmail.com/servlet/story/RTGAM.20080430.wscores30/EmailBNStory/National/Quebec

Markell, P. (2003). *Bound by recognition.* Princeton, NJ: Princeton University Press.

Perlstein, D. (2000). "There is no escape...from the ogre of indoctrination": George Counts and the civic dilemmas of democratic educators. In L. Cuban & D. Shipps (Eds.), *Reconstructing the common good in education: Coping with intractable dilemmas* (pp. 51–67). Stanford, CA: Stanford University Press.

Pilder, W. J. (1974). In the stillness is the dancing. In W. F. Pinar (Ed.), *Heightened consciousness, cultural revolution, and curriculum theory: The Proceedings of the Rochester Conference* (pp. 117–129). Berkeley, CA: McCutchan.

Pinar, W. F. (Ed.). (1974). *Heightened consciousness, cultural revolution and curriculum theory: The proceedings of the Rochester conference.* Berkeley, CA: McCutchan.

Pinar, W. F. (Ed.) (1998). *Queer theory in education.* Mahwah, NJ: Erlbaum.

Pinar, W. F. (Ed.) (2000). *Curriculum theorizing: The reconceptualization.* Berkeley, CA: McCutchan.

Pinar, W. F. (2001). *The gender of racial politics and violence in America: Lynching, prison rape, and the crisis of masculinity.* New York: Lang.

Pinar, W. F. (2004). *What is curriculum theory?* Mahwah, NJ: Erlbaum.

Pinar, W. F. (2006a). *Race, religion and a curriculum of reparation.* New York: Palgrave Macmillan.

Pinar, W. F. (2006b). *The synoptic text today and other essays: Curriculum development after the Reconceptualization.* New York: Lang.

Pinar, W. F. (2007). *Intellectual advancement through disciplinarity: Verticality and horizontality in curriculum studies.* Rotterdam, The Netherlands: Sense.

Pinar, W. F. (2008a). Curriculum theory since 1950: Crisis, reconceptualization, internationalization. In F. M. Connelly, M. F. He, & J. Phillion (Eds.), *The Sage handbook of curriculum and instruction* (pp. 491–513). Los Angeles: Sage.

Pinar, W. F. (2008b). Introduction. In George S. Tomkins, *A common countenance: Stability and change in the Canadian curriculum.* Vancouver, Canada: Pacific Educational Press.

Pinar, W. F. (in press). *The worldliness of a cosmopolitan education: Passionate lives in public service.* New York: Routledge.

Pinar, W. F., Reynolds, W. M., Slattery, P., & Taubman, P. M. (1995). *Understanding curriculum: An introduction to historical and contemporary curriculum discourses.* New York: Lang.

Slavin, R. E. (2008). What works? Issues in synthesizing education program evaluations. *Educational Researcher, 37*(1), 5–14.

Tomkins, G. S. (2008). *A common countenance: Stability and change in the Canadian curriculum.* Vancouver, Canada: Pacific Educational Press. (Original work published 1986)

Urban, W. J. (1992). *Black scholar: Horace Mann Bond, 1904–1972.* Athens, GA: University of Georgia Press.

Viano, M. (1993). *A certain realism: Making use of Pasolini's film theory and practice.* Berkeley: University of California Press.

Wraga, W. G. (1999, January–February). Extracting sun-beams out of cucumbers: The retreat from practice in reconceptualized curriculum studies. *Educational Researcher, 28*(1), 4–13.

Wraga, W. G., & Hlebowitsh, P. S. (2003). Toward a renaissance in curriculum theory and development in the U.S.A. *Journal of Curriculum Studies, 35*(4), 425–437.

Zhang, H., & Zhong, Q. (2003). Curriculum studies in China: Retrospect and prospect. In W. F. Pinar (Ed.), *International Handbook of Curriculum Research* (pp. 253–270). Mahwah, NJ: Erlbaum.

The Unknown

A Way of Knowing in the Future of Curriculum Studies

Erik Malewski

> How does the deconstruction of the sign, the emphasis on indeterminism in cultural and political judgment, transform our sense of the subject of culture and the historical agent of change? If we contest the grand, continuist narratives, then what alternative temporalities do we create to articulate the contrapuntal (Said) or interruptive (Spivak) formations of race, gender, class, and nation within a transnational world culture? (Bhabha, 1992, p. 49)

Attempting to bring together a collection of essays on the state of the field that exceeds and works against being subsumed under the discourse of progress and advancement, there has been a desire within me to close with multiple voices and in essence to avoid a comforting conclusion to this text. To such unconventional ends, I invited Alan Block and Bill Pinar to also craft an epilogue in hopes that a tripartite reading might work more in translations and proliferations than in declarative rhetoric about what stage we are at on the way toward absolute or contamination-free understanding. Part of me wanted to end the book with the detailed description of the breakdown at the 2006 Purdue conference that is now just a short reflection at the end of this essay. The above quote from Bhabha, however, seemed too perfect given the identity politics that marked the Purdue conference (see the preface and acknowledgments and Pinar's epilogue in this collection) and their onto-epistemological implications for present and next moments in the field. It brought to the surface concerns over how we might make doubled claims about knowledge and what remains as-of-yet unknown, disjunctive readings that contest continuist narratives while also offering the terms for a "good enough" solidarity or network of relations necessary to underwrite calls for action within the world (see Gaztambide-Fernández, this volume). Is this not the site we occupy after postdiscourses cast doubt on the centrality of consciousness and transparency of language? How to work strategically out of our canonical knowledge to make interventions while upholding doubt and uncertainty as ways of knowing? How to think with and through complicated conversations in terms of our demands for theorizing with more to which we must ethically commit by way of the intricacies of languages, cultures, and societies?

After reading this collection, the reader might find the intention to be something other than a conventional representation of the state of an academic field in light of the effect postdiscourses have had on the study of curriculum and pedagogy. Holding traits of success and failure simultaneously, the purpose behind this collection's intergenerational structure is to discompose the hold "the state" has over the terms by which we self-reflect as a field and in so doing allow for alternative and as-of-yet unknown representations and ideas. The reader might also find as a collection—and while acknowledging the themes prevalent in these essays—this is not a search for a clean synthesis, break from the past, or the realization of the ultimate purpose or design for curriculum studies. Situated at the crossroads of various clusters of theorizing, as well as more recent hybridization of theories in the field and imports from other fields, this collective more closely resembles a discipline-based movement that attempts to maneuver curriculum thought beyond the current horizons of its own representations.

Similar to Lather's (2007) recent work on a doubled science as a strategy for negotiating difference and resisting categorization, the purpose here is to offer doubled readings on multiple registers, to deploy ambiguity to induce breakdowns in discourses that impede the study of experiences in, with, and through education alongside efforts to locate through-lines around which we might organize our reading and intervening practices. Across the chapters and response essays the reader folds forward (chapter speculations on the next moments) to fold back (reflective essays on such speculations) to think of the field to come, what Derrida describes as thinking "...toward the operations of childbearing...the as yet unnamable which is proclaiming itself" (Derrida, 1980, p. 293). Lather teaches us that to fold back—to revisit former texts and readings—is common, "But to fold forward, to speculate about an as-yet-not-produced text, showing a work in the making, would be new ground, a sort of dialogue across texts, time, and researching selves" (p. ix). Birthing next moments in the field, this collection attempts to break new ground through intra-/intergenerational dialogues that create a sense of movement between time and space, between past and future.

In a field where numerous theoretical perspectives have been brought to bear upon the question of curriculum, this is an exercise in reading and understanding that attempts to locate and get a handle on itself. A field shaped by functionalist logic and instrumental rationality has clearly been established as inadequate to our present condition, one where technical operatives and the frantic search for epistemological certainties in a sea of crises eclipse understanding, reading, and intervening in the world. Ironically, it is this urgent pursuit of knowledge that inhibits our thinking (see my response essay in this collection). The development/understanding binary that was at one time necessary to our work is now part of this dangerous situation and new development-understanding-reading-intervening interactions are in movement across the field of curriculum studies (see Eppert & Wang, 2007; Jardine, Clifford, & Friesen, 2002; Slattery, 2006; Whitlock, 2007).[1] The exact character of such interactions and their implications for curriculum studies are for the most part too new to tell (although as I suggest in the introduction it seems understanding and interpreting have been joined by reading and intervening). Nevertheless, the complexity of contemporary work and the lack of definition within curriculum studies are symptomatic of a field inherently contested, political, and in a state of flux, a field with foci that range from "embodied ways of knowing" (Riley-Taylor, this volume) and "existential despair within critical pedagogy" (McKnight, this volume) to "eugenics ideologies and curriculum history" (Winfield, this volume) and "social class, schooling, and identity" (Howard & Tappan, this volume).

In terms of lessening violence toward ourselves and others, what difference does curriculum theorizing make to education and to the world? Texts that function as a political intervention have the capacity to spur people to think in excess of common thoughts and practices. They account for the unknowability that resides at the crossroads of discursive challenges (within a particular episteme that cannot fully reveal itself) and the need to take action informed by our doubts and uncertainties. Here our not knowing becomes a way of knowing. In an attempt to move curriculum's discourse outside the range of the known, I have located my intervention at the site of our investments in the current state of things as revealed in the organization of this book: the canon, technology, the body, place, cross-cultural perspectives, creativity, and the disjunctive character of self, subjectivity, and the subject position, and so on. Questioning how our concepts and objects have come to matter so much, curriculum is a site where we can address the forces of change at the specificity of language and experience rather than in more exclusionary ways at the levels of transcendence and salvation found in concepts that include *advancement* and *progress*, both of which forgo complicated conversations with their emphasis on totalizing intentionality. Working in next moments to discompose theorizing done in the name of merely interpreting the world, this is repositioning curriculum scholarship that claims to advance understanding in its present state so as "to change terrain...by brutally placing oneself outside"—to induce "a radical trembling" by looking at long-standing grounds from the viewpoint of a new site (Derrida, 1985, p. 134).

In an era of post-reconceptualization, how might we discern between concepts that have come to matter so much to the field and concepts that might allow us to see more clearly what has come to matter? Such a question remains at the heart of debates in the curriculum field with various clusters of theorizing privileging one or more of the following: social, cultural, and political forces; the forces of subjectivity and existential experience, or "being in the world"; or the capacity of language to map realities and the possible. Working the ruins toward what remains available after postdiscourses became all the rage, the reconceptualist practice of getting to work within particular discourses (outlined well in Pinar, Reynolds, Slattery, & Taubman, 1995) is being extended, reconfigured, and transposed. If currere privileged subjectivity and the unconscious over empiricism, structuralism privileged processes and frameworks over subjectivity and agency; and poststructuralism foregrounds uses of language toward alternative logics in which structure, language, and the unconscious are not opposing but interrelated, then in the next moments historical and contemporary discourses are being put to use in peculiar ways to offer highly stylized and disjunctive readings.

"The reconstruction of the public sphere cannot proceed without the reconstruction of the private sphere" (2004, p. 21) Pinar asserted in his autobiographically focused challenge to the tendency toward "the formulation of principles of curriculum development applicable anytime and anywhere" (p. 94) as the motor force of education. Here developmentalism with its premise of growth and change outside the subject and emphasis on formal, institutional frameworks is thwarted by existential, self-reflexive, and place-based theories that feature experience, context, and lived history for explaining the interplay of knowledge and power in meaning making processes. Once again within the contested site of post-reconceptualization curriculum theorizing is being remade. The subject-centered interior-focused theories that are the hallmark of reconceptualization (although by no means exclusive) have been interrelated with critical cultural practices that include, for example, critical race theories. Similarly, postdiscourses of Derrida and Foucault, which have been criticized for their use of obtuse language and inapplicability, have been put to work on issues that range from policy and classroom practice to local histories and global identities and used as tools for discomposing and rearticulating the theories and practices that set the terms for post-reconceptualization. Here what our theories rail against and remake in the image of different generations in conversation—toward a different state—is what we ourselves are both a part of and supplement to, what Derrida describes as that which is ultimately undecidable in terms of whether it is an addition or a replacement (Derrida, 1998, p. 200).

Post-reconceptualization, rather than being a break or a shift in the terms for curriculum studies scholarship, seems to foreground new sensibilities within the field: (1) flux and change; (2) hybrid spaces; (3) reading differently; (4) divergent perspectives; (5) different contexts; (6) status questions; and (7) understudied histories (see Introduction) which might be read as a middle way against the parts of the book. Such work necessitates understanding what I have termed elsewhere "a post-reconceptualist bricolage, clusters of montages that—suspicious of each other and caught in juxtaposition—read one another both intracluster and intercluster as incomplete" (Malewski, 2007); it has a tendency to account for the limits of consciousness and intentionality, and relay an unavoidable and indeterminable will to power in any efforts at curriculum theorizing, one that necessitates doubled readings that challenge the terms by which the other makes claims to truth alongside third readings that mark through-lines around which to rethink theories and practices that might meet the promise of democracy. Termed the "getting to work" of postdiscourses, what has been challenged across the range of chapters and response essays presented here are frameworks for producing knowledge that are assumed to provide the oppressed with access to language, ideas, and realities crafted by curriculum scholars who take on the role of the ones who are "in the know," well reasoned subjects with the capacity to surface truths and advocate practices for those who are "out of the know" or thought to possess a false consciousness.

Working out of the uncertainty and ambivalence created through critiques of theories that privilege consciousness and assume interventions are made possible through critical practices that hope to locate justice on behalf of others positioned as without a voice and adequate capacities for understanding, the sorts of strategies at work in present and next moments are not exclusively mechanisms for mastery or transcendence. These tactics are more complicated, partial, and often read against themselves in making their theoretical claims. Taking serious the call to have complicated conversations, they are more likely to marry deconstructive and dialectical discourses (what might be terms for various forms of essentializing and discomposing discourses) as a technique to check and situate their own stated truths, or subsume self-critique as a part of the theorizing process. Here post-reconceptualization is in part an attempt to produce and learn out of the failures and breakdowns induced by postdiscourses new and different positions for theorizing and practicing curriculum.

As the work in this edited collection illustrates, the efforts of curriculum studies scholars toward social, economic, political, and educational transformation takes place within a nexus of symbolic and material forces that have launched and sustained neoliberal, neoconservative "empire" building efforts around the globe. Accordingly, we have been confronted with the limitation of our own theories and practices to "get to work" in the ways we had imagined. For example, Baker notes that the events that led to the "apparent discovery" of the objects that are the repetitive focus of curriculum history have been understudied. Wang senses that engaging in an intimate style of revolt (as opposed to transgressive) remains an educational power seldom recognized in education. Snaza suggests that what we might need involves the production of posthumanistic concepts related to education. Curriculum theorizing in post-reconceptual times then is caught up at the crossroads of a certain undecidability as to what to do so as to engage in political mediations and remain flexible enough to accommodate nuance and ambivalence. Here the question is how to offer strategically essentialist readings to the point necessary to make symbolic and material interventions and also remain in flux and dynamic to the point necessary to keep from falling into rigid, orthodox positions in spite of our recent focus on embodiment and personal experiences within education and public spheres. Baker calls for an investigation into the discursive thresholds that had to be crossed in order for our concepts to come into view. Wang suggests that rather than something new what we need is to better translate across difference. Snaza turns to what the question of love offers in terms of a space for posthuman dwelling.

Post-reconceptualization has been described as the next phase in the progression of the field, a shift in the style of theorizing, the move to see the lack of definition that characterizes the field as a healthy state, and the inevitable generational change over as one generation heads center stage and another contemplates the last phases of their careers or retirement. Clearly, competing views on post-reconceptualization abound. As something other than a sign that we are in need of more synthesis, this rivalry might be the very terms by which the field refrains from dualisms whether they be individual/social, justice/law, interpreting/intervening, empirical/conceptual, understanding/development, singular/network as well as from reductionistic claims about cause and effect relationships. Addressing the impasse between theorizing significant to curriculum studies and historical conditions that have led to the objects and concepts most dear to the field, post-reconceptualization functions as a reminder that the next wave of scholarship might be characterized by purposeful theoretical juxtapositioning that spurs as of yet known ways of thinking by inciting breakdowns in continuity: onto-epistemological, existential–poststructural, autobiographical–critical, queer–phenomenological, humanist–feminist–Marxist theories, and so on. This fractious theorizing assists in simultaneous analysis of the mechanisms of power and knowledge across a spectrum of levels and disjunctive affirmations of multiple ways of theorizing in terms of entering into less comfortable terms for curriculum scholarship.

Focusing on contextual and experiential understandings of power-in-use in curriculum and pedagogy and the social conditions that elicit such understandings, what becomes possible is the study of locating, theorizing, and naming difference; marking through-lines and themes in our findings; and outlining possibilities for struggling materially and symbolically against those economic, political, and educational formations we least respect. As this edited collection illustrates, there is work being done in (1) overcoming philosophical–conceptual categories that separate epistemology from being-in-the-world, autobiographical complexities from structural abstractions, and understanding and reflection from action; (2) asking questions about alterity, otherness, and how language uses and intellectual practices in the field make and unmake room for historically excluded concepts and peoples; and (3) challenging the field to rethink our theories and practices in light of changing economic, political, cultural, and economic circumstances that include grassroots movements, internationalization of curriculum scholarship, technological innovations, and ecological sustainability, among other events and issues.

Within such a context, post-reconceptualization might help us ask questions that we as a field have not thought to ask until now: about understudied and unstudied histories that have led to our most deeply invested concepts and practices; about what in the name of understanding, reading, and intervening we have difficulty acknowledging, failed to account for, and consciously excluded from the field; and about what becoming posthuman means for learning to live aesthetically. Exploring post-reconceptualization—not to nail down the right strategy for next moments in the field—but from the perspective of proliferation and multiplicity might offer the uniformity of experience and understanding necessary to underwrite calls for an intervention. This is the next moment in curriculum studies. Here we (1) continue to make and unmake our meaning making strategies in regards to the political commitments embedded in the various clusters of theorizing that mark the field and (2) move in the direction of understanding the limitations of our theorizing and practices in our efforts to meet the promise of a democracy that is yet to come. What we have is not more transcendent understanding, less contaminated theories, or successor regimes more capable of guiding us toward truth; rather, in present and next moments in the field we are left with figuring out how to produce and learn out of the failures and breakdowns in our efforts toward political, economic, social, and, of course, educational transformation.

It is the night after the conference and I wonder, what am I to make of things that don't go as planned? If the conference had stayed on task and followed the prescribed agenda, what would we as curriculum scholars have missed? I am left to wonder—and not to know—but somehow I feel like there was something productive and powerful in the very dissolution of the frameworks that were in place, as careful as I was to create what I thought were "open" and "dialogic" rap group discussions that paralleled formal keynote addresses. Maybe this conference is a signal about what we will have to face in our theories and practices in the "next moments" in curriculum studies. Maybe what we will have to confront is not simply the dissensus and dispersals brought on by the posts, but how to work out of difference to name and enact communities where differences are neither subsumed nor become so tyrannical that they bring us to sever our relationships with each other. Here I am thinking, how do our differences become the very terms by which we mark through-lines and intersections—and therefore the conditions for trust and reciprocity—without falling under the lure of synthesis and salvation?

Note

1. What I refer to as a dangerous situation involves what has been and is being addressed in the contemporary field. That is, the need to simultaneously challenge uncritical developmental discourses while also reinventing it in new and unforeseen ways. A wonderful example of such work, one which is cited above, is Patrick Slattery's (2006) *Curriculum Development in the Postmodern Era*. There are also clear examples of the reconceptualization of curriculum development discourse in the Commission on the Status of Curriculum Studies and The Canon Project. Given these examples, it might be that development is not so much dead as being read differently and intervened upon so as to rearticulate the concept. That is, to rearticulate what gets thought when one thinks about development, the work being done dissolves to binaries between understanding and development.

References

Bhabha, H. K. (1992). Freedom's basis in the indeterminate. *October, 61*, 46–57.

Derrida, J. (1980). *Writing and difference* (A. Bass, Trans.). Chicago: University of Chicago Press.

Derrida, J. (1985). *Margins of philosophy* (A. Bass, Trans.). Chicago: University of Chicago Press.

Derrida, J. (1998). *Of grammatology* (G. Spivak, Trans.). Baltimore, MD: Johns Hopkins University Press.

Eppert, C., & Wang, H. (Eds.). (2007). *Cross-cultural studies in curriculum: Eastern thought, educational insights*. Mahwah, NJ: Erlbaum.

Jardine, D., Clifford, P., & Friesen, S. (2002). *Back to the basics of teaching and learning: Thinking the world together*. Mahwah, NJ: Erlbaum.

Lather, P. (2007). *Getting lost: Feminist efforts toward a double(d) science*. Albany, NY: SUNY Press.

Malewski, E. (2007). A reading on four registers: Educational reforms, democratic cultures, research methodologies, and the question of the posts. *Journal of the American Association for the Advancement of Curriculum Studies, 3*. Retrieved August 4, 2008, from http://www.uwstout.edu/soe/jaaacs/vol3/malewski.htm

Pinar, W. F. (2004). *What is curriculum theory?* Mahwah, NJ: Erlbaum.

Pinar, W. F., Reynolds, W. M., Slattery, P., & Taubman, P. M. (1995). *Understanding curriculum: An introduction to historical and contemporary curriculum discourses*. New York: Lang.

Slattery, P. (2006). *Curriculum development in the postmodern era* (2nd ed.). New York: Routledge.

Whitlock, R. U. (2007). *This corner of Canaan: Curriculum studies of place and the reconstruction of the South*. New York: Lang.

About the Contributors

Peter Appelbaum teaches at Arcadia University in Philadelphia, where he is Coordinator of Mathematics Education and Curriculum Studies Programs, Director-at-Large of General Education, and Director of the Strangely Familiar Music Group. His publications include *Embracing Mathematics: On Becoming a Teacher and Changing with Mathematics*; *Children's Books for Grown-up Teachers: Reading and Writing Curriculum Theory*; *Multicultural and Diversity Education*; *(Post) Modern Science (Education)*; and *Popular Culture, Educational Discourse and Mathematics*.

Nina Asher is Associate Professor and the J. Franklin Bayhi Endowed Professor of Education in the Department of Educational Theory, Policy, & Practice at Louisiana State University. She is the Co-Director of the Department's Curriculum Theory Project and is also on the faculty of LSU's Women's & Gender Studies Program. She writes in the areas of postcolonial and feminist theory, critical perspectives on multiculturalism, and Asian American studies in relation to education. Her work has appeared in such journals as the *Educational Researcher, Teachers College Record,* the *Journal of Curriculum Theorizing,* and the *International Journal of Qualitative Studies in Education* (QSE), among others. She currently serves as Book Review Editor for the *National Women's Studies Association Journal* and the *QSE.*

Bernadette Baker is a Professor at the University of Wisconsin in the Center for Global Studies, The Holtz Center for the Social Studies of Science and Technology, and the Department of Curriculum and Instruction. Her research interests lie in philosophy, history, and sociology of education, science, and cosmology, transnational curriculum studies, and "post" literatures. In addition to her book, *In Perpetual Motion: Theories of Power, Educational History, and the Child* (Lang, 2001), she coedited with Katharina E. Heyning, *Dangerous Coagulations? The Uses of Foucault in the Study of Education* (Lang, 2004).

Thomas Barone is Professor of Education at Arizona State University. Nearly 30 years ago, Barone's dissertation at Stanford University investigated the possibilities of literary non-fiction for researching and writing about educational matters. Since then he has explored, conceptually and through examples, a variety of narrative and arts-based approaches to contextualizing and theorizing about significant educational, especially curricular, issues. He continues to advocate consideration by curriculum scholars of additional (especially artistically oriented) means for reaching a broader readership for our work. He is the author of *Aesthetics, Politics, and Educational Inquiry: Essays and Examples and Touching Eternity: The Enduring Outcomes of Teaching.* He currently teaches courses in curriculum studies and qualitative research methods in the ASU Mary Lou Fulton College of Education.

Theodorea Regina Berry, is the Assistant Chair, Curriculum and Instruction for the American College of Education, Chicago. She completed a 3-year AERA postdoctoral research fellowship at the University of Illinois-Chicago. Berry's scholarship focuses on the intersections of curriculum theory, critical race feminism, and urban teacher education. Her early work focuses on the use of educational memoir integrated with bell hooks's notion of engaged pedagogy for African-American female preservice teachers. Berry's scholarship continues to examine the connections between curriculum theory, critical race feminism, teacher education, and teacher leadership. She currently serves as the Program Chair, Critical Examination of Race, Ethnicity, Class, and Gender Special Interest Group, AERA. She has published several articles and book chapters and is lead editor and contributing author of *From Oppression to Grace: Women of Color and their Dilemmas Within the Academy* (Stylus, 2006). She is also coediting *Living, Learning, and Teaching Race* (Hampton Press, in press).

Alan A. Block has taught for 36 years in classrooms of the public schools and universities. He is presently a Professor in the School of Education at the University of Wisconsin-Stout. He has published extensively on matters of curriculum, ethics, and teaching, and teacher education. His previous work includes *Talmud, Curriculum, and the Practical: Joseph Schwab and the Rabbis* (2004) and *Pedagogy, Religion, and Practice: Reflections on Ethics and Teaching* (2007). His newest book, to be published by Palgrave-Macmillan in 2009, is titled *Ethics and Teaching*. Currently, he is studying how teachers tell their stories (yes, yes, yes, he will write on this topic) and trying not to act old. He is having great fun in the former, but not a great deal of success in the latter.

LaVada Brandon is Acting Head of the Department of Teacher Preparation, Purdue University, Calumet. In addition to her administrative responsibilities she teaches courses in social studies methods and diversity and education. A 17-year veteran in education, she began her teaching career in 1991 in New Orleans public schools. A curriculum theorist, she earned her PhD from Louisiana State University in curriculum and instruction. Her current research interests focus on postmodern notions of race, class, gender, and language and how these elements of identity enable and impede academic success for historically marginalized learners, as well as the use of oral history as culturally relevant pedagogy with urban African-American learners.

Ellen Brantlinger retired from the Department of Curriculum and Instruction at Indiana University in May 2004. She has written four books: *Politics of Social Class in Secondary Schools, Fighting for Darla, Sterilization of People with Mental Disabilities*, and *Dividing Classes: How the Middle Class Negotiates and Rationalizes School Advantage*, and edited a multiauthor volume titled, *Who Benefits from Special Education? Remediating (Fixing) Other People's Children*. As a critical theorist, she has always been interested in understanding and overcoming oppressive power differentials among individuals and groups. She has become a strong advocate for qualitative inquiry and has published articles on that research design in recent years. She is perhaps best known for (and most proud of) her article, "Using Ideology: Cases of Nonrecognition of the Politics of Research and Practice in Special Education," published in the *Review of Educational Research* in 1997.

Nancy J. Brooks is an Assistant Professor in the Department of Educational Studies at Ball State University where she teaches graduate and undergraduate courses in curriculum and social foundations. After teaching at the elementary and secondary levels for 18 years, she received her EdD in curriculum studies from Oklahoma State University, where her dissertation research focused on the early works of scholars credited with inspiring the reconceptualization: Maxine Greene, Dwayne Huebner, Paul Klohr, and James Macdonald. Her current research interests lie in the possibilities for philosophical hermeneutics as curriculum and pedagogical theory, curriculum history, and emerging curriculum trends. She has served on the Governing Council of the Curriculum and Pedagogy Group and is currently a member of the Technology Committee for the American Association for the Advancement of Curriculum Studies.

Dennis Carlson is a Professor of Curriculum and the Cultural Studies of Education at Miami University, Oxford, Ohio. He is the author of *Teachers and Crisis: Urban School Reform and Teachers' Work Culture* (1992), *Making Progress: Education and Culture in New Times* (1997), and *Leaving Safe Harbors: Toward a New Progressivism in American Education and Public Life* (2002). He has coedited a number of volumes, including most recently with C. P. Gause, *Keeping the Promise: Essays on Leadership, Democracy, and Education* (2007). He has published in major educational journals on topics related to the formulation of a democratic cultural politics of education attuned to changing times.

B. Stephen Carpenter II is Associate Professor of Art Education and Visual Culture at Texas A&M University and teaches courses in curriculum development, curriculum theory, cultural foundations of education, art education, and visual culture. His scholarly writing has appeared in numerous publications including *Art Education*, *Ceramics: Art and Perception*, *Educational Leadership*, *The Journal of Aesthetic Education*, *The Journal of Cultural Research in Art Education*, *The Journal of Curriculum and Pedagogy*, *The Journal of Educational Multimedia and Hypermedia*, *Studies in Art Education*, and *Visual Arts Research*. He is co-author of *Interdisciplinary Approaches to Teaching Art in High School* (with Pamela G. Taylor, Christine Ballengee-Morris, and Billie Sessions) and co-editor of *Curriculum for a Progressive, Provocative, Poetic, and Public Pedagogy* (with Jennifer Milam, Stephanie Springgay, and Kris Sloan). Carpenter is past editor of *Art Education*, the journal of the National Art Education Association and co-associate editor and co-editor elect of the *Journal of Curriculum and Pedagogy*.

Greg Dimitriadis is Professor of Sociology of Education at the University at Buffalo, The State University of New York. He is interested in new ways of thinking about urban education and the policies that serve urban youth. More specifically, he is interested in the potential value and importance of nontraditional educational curricula (e.g., popular culture), programs (e.g., arts-based initiatives), and institutions (e.g., community centers) in the lives of disenfranchised young people. His most recent work has dealt with the contemporary complexities of qualitative inquiry, including its history and philosophical and theoretical underpinnings, as well as the ways "theory" generated outside of the field of education can be brought to bear on the questions and concerns facing educational researchers and practitioners today.

Karen Ferneding, an independent scholar published in the areas of curriculum studies and the social foundations of education, draws from a broad cross-disciplinary scope that includes the critical theory of technology, communication and media studies, cultural studies, and art and aesthetics, to examine the postmodern context of education. She seeks to understand the reflexive nature of sociotechnological systems, or how such systems articulate political and institutional power, and thus has analyzed educational reform political discourse in relation to the convergence of technoscience, global capitalism and the ethos of techno-utopianism. She is interested in examining how the amalgamation of commercial society and technoculture, a cultural sphere dominated by virtual realities created by electronic media, may inculcate an aesthetic sensibility and way of being in the world. She asks how this condition impacts youth culture, moral development and the meaning of democratic social values, and ultimately curriculum, learning and teaching.

Alexandra Fidyk's life and work has been deeply shaped by movement—internally in the soulful tracking of Hermes; externally as lived in Japan, Colombia, Egypt, and South Africa. She recently joined the Department of Depth Psychology at Pacifica Graduate Institute, as Core Faculty and Research Coordinator. Trained in philosophy and hermeneutics and as a Jungian psychotherapist, her transdisciplinary approach weaves the imaginal and pedagogic, the creative and philosophic. Her work tends the realms of ontological splendor, ethics, and the poetic; her writing addresses questions about silence, Eros, identity, and place. Forthcoming is her book, *Silence and Eros: Beckoning the Background Forward*, and recent publications include chapters in *Epistemologies of Ignorance in Education*, *Doing Democracy*, as well as *Educational Insights* and other educational and Jungian journals.

Debra Freedman is an independent scholar living in Guelph, Ontario, Canada. Her research and teaching interests include curriculum theory, cultural studies, and teacher education. Her research foci with respect to curriculum studies include teacher identity and beliefs in relation to classroom practices, pedagogy, and curriculum, and the development of curriculum and pedagogical practices that sustain democratic communities. She is coeditor, with Stephanie Springgay, of *Curriculum and the Cultural Body* (2007, Lang). Currently she teaches curriculum courses online, as contract faculty, for Ball State University and The Pennsylvania State University. In her previous career, she was an Associate Professor of Educational Leadership at The Pennsylvania State University.

Rubén A. Gaztambide-Fernández is an Assistant Professor in the Department of Curriculum, Teaching and Learning at the Ontario Institute for Studies in Education of the University of Toronto. He teaches courses in curriculum theory, cultural studies, and the arts in education. His articles have been published in education journals like the *Harvard Educational Review*, *Curriculum Inquiry*, *The Review of Education/Pedagogy/Cultural Studies*, and the *Journal of Curriculum and Pedagogy*. He is coeditor of the collections *Cultural Studies and Education: Perspectives on Theory, Methodology, and Practice* (Harvard Education Press) and *Curriculum Work as a Public Moral Enterprise* (Rowman & Littlefield). His forthcoming book, tentatively titled *Educating Elites* (Harvard University Press), is based on 2 years of ethnographic research at an elite boarding school in the United States. His current research focuses on the experiences of young artists attending urban arts high schools in North America.

Jennifer Gilbert is an Associate Professor of Education at York University in Toronto, Canada. Her research interests include adolescent development, theories of sex education, and the use of literature and film in teacher education. She has published articles on sex education in the journals *Sex Education*, *Teaching Education*, *Changing English*, and *Journal of Curriculum and Pedagogy*. She is currently working on a project that investigates the meanings of "abstinence" for adults and youth in sex education and is completing a book manuscript, *Between Curiosity and Human Rights: Sexuality, Human Development and Education*.

Madeleine R. Grumet is a Professor of Education and Communication Studies and Dean Emerita at the University of North Carolina at Chapel Hill. Previously she served as dean of the School of Education and Brooklyn College, City University of New York, and as professor at Hobart and William Smith Colleges. Her published work includes a study of gender and education, *Bitter Milk: Women and Teaching*, and *Toward a Poor Curriculum*, with William Pinar, and numerous essays addressing curriculum theory and arts and humanities education.

Nichole A. Guillory, who earned her PhD in curriculum theory at Louisiana State University in 2005, is currently an Assistant Professor of Adolescent Education in the Department of Secondary and Middle Grades Education at Kennesaw State University. Her research interests include social justice education, Black feminism, and cultural studies. She teaches courses on the social foundations of education and multicultural education. As an affiliated faculty member in the Gender and Women's Studies Program at KSU, she teaches a course in hip-hop feminism, which she developed as an extension of her dissertation study. Her published work on contemporary black women rappers includes "Readin', Writin', Rappin'" in the *Journal of Curriculum & Pedagogy*.

Robert J. Helfenbein is Assistant Professor of Teacher Education at Indiana University-Indianapolis and Associate Director of the Center for Urban and Multicultural Education (CUME). He earned his PhD and BA from the University of North Carolina at Chapel Hill. A former middle and high school social studies teacher, Dr. Helfenbein offers courses in middle school methods, teaching secondary social studies, and graduate level courses in curriculum theory and social foundations of education. Dr. Helfenbein has published and edited numerous research articles and book chapters about teacher education and contemporary education analysis in urban contexts. His current research interests include curriculum theorizing in urban contexts, cultural studies of education, and the impact of globalization on the lived experience of schools.

James Henderson is a Professor in the Curriculum & Instruction Program at Kent State University where he has taught graduate courses in curriculum fundamentals and advanced curriculum studies for 18 years. His research focuses on practicing the artistry and fidelity of democratic education. He has individually or collaboratively published four books and over 50 essays on this subject. His book, *Reflective Teaching: Professional Artistry through Inquiry*, introduces teachers to reflective practice informed by diversified inquiry. His coauthored book, *Transformative Curriculum Leadership*, provides guidance for inspiring and nurturing elevated curriculum deliberations; and his coauthored book, *Curriculum Wisdom: Educational Decisions in Democratic Societies*, explores the arts of curriculum inquiry that are inspired by a love of democratic wisdom. He has served as leader of the Professors of Curriculum honorary society and is currently coeditor of the *Journal of Curriculum and Pedagogy*.

Petra Munro Hendry is a Professor in the Department of Educational Theory, Policy and Practice at Louisiana State University where she serves as the St. Bernard Parish Alumni Endowed Professor. She is codirector of the Curriculum Theory Project and a member of the women's and gender faculty. Her research interests are the narrative analysis of women educators' life histories, curriculum history, and discourses of qualitative research. Hendry is the author of Subject of Fiction: Women Teachers' Life History Narratives and the Cultural Politics of Resistance (Open University, 1998) and coauthor of Pedagogies of Resistance: Women Educator Activists 1880–1960 (Teachers College

Press, 1999). Her book *Engendering Curriculum History* (Teachers College Press, 2009). Her work has also appeared in such journals as JCT: Journal of Curriculum Theorizing; QSE: International Journal of Qualitative Studies in Education and Qualitative Inquiry.

Adam Howard is Associate Professor of Education at Colby College. He has held faculty positions at Antioch College and Hanover College. He also served as Associate Dean of Faculty and Director of Teacher Education at Antioch. Prior to teaching at the college level, he taught high school English and history and directed a nonprofit organization. His research interests include social class issues in education, privilege, service learning, and curriculum theory. He is author of Learning Privilege: Lessons of Power and Identity in Affluent Schooling. He is chair of the Bergamo Conference on Curriculum Theory and Classroom Practice and coeditor of Journal of Curriculum Theorizing.

Nathalia Jaramillo is an Assistant Professor of Cultural Foundations and affiliated faculty member of American Studies at Purdue University. She has authored and coauthored a number of publications in the field of critical pedagogy, sociopolitical critique, and feminist studies. She is currently working on a coedited text titled *Epistemologies of Ignorance and the Study of Limits in Education* and a coauthored book, "Essays in Critical Pedagogy." Nathalia's scholarship is transdisciplinary and she is interested in examining the connection between local spaces of transformation and broader socioeconomic and political relations characteristic of global capitalism. Social movements in Latin America inform much of this work.

Patti Lather is a Professor in the Cultural Foundations in Education Program, School of Educational Policy and Leadership at Ohio State University where she teaches qualitative research in education, feminist methodology and gender and education. She has held visiting positions at the University of British Columbia, Goteborg University, and the Danish Pedagogy University as well as a 1995 sabbatical appointment at Humanities Research Institute, University of California-Irvine, seminar on feminist research methodology. She is the author of three books, *Getting Smart: Feminist Research and Pedagogy With/in the Postmodern* (1991 Critics Choice Award) and *Troubling Angels: Women Living With HIV/AIDS,* coauthored with Chris Smithies (One of CHOICE's Outstanding Academic Titles for 1998), and *Getting Lost: Feminist Efforts Toward a Double(d) Science* (2007). Her hobby aspirations include learning to play the accordion and bridge.

Xin Li is a Professor in the College of Education at California State University–Long Beach. Her research interests include narrative inquiry of cross-cultural experiences. She approaches Taoism as a philosophy that provides guidance for surviving social–cultural vicissitudes, living meaningful lives in interruption, and cultivating cultural creativity in diversity. Her recent publications on the topic include *The Tao of Life Stories: Chinese Language, Poetry, and Culture in Education* (Lang, 2002), and the articles "A Tao of Narrative: Dynamic Splicing of Teacher Stories" (*Curriculum Inquiry,* 2005), "Becoming Taoist I and Thou: Identity-Making of Opposite Cultures" (*Journal of Curriculum and Pedagogy,* 2006), and a book chapter "My Lived Stories of Poetic Thinking and Taoist Knowing" (In Eppert & Wang, *Cross-Cultural Studies in Curriculum: Eastern Thoughts, Educational Insights,* 2008). She teaches graduate courses in cross-cultural education and literacy, and credential courses in cultural and linguistic diversity.

Erik Malewski is an Assistant Professor of Curriculum Studies at Purdue University. His research interests include curriculum theory, state of the field studies, internationalization by way of study abroad, and difficult knowledge and ignorance within education, including not knowing as a way of knowing. He has had articles appear in various peer-reviewed journals, such as *Teaching and Teacher Education*, and published book chapters in numerous edited collections, including *The Praeger Handbook of Latino Education in the U.S.* He is currently working on a coedited collection with Nathalia Jaramillo entitled, *Epistemologies of Ignorance in Education.* He also serves on the Publications Committee for the American Association for the Advancement of Curriculum Studies and is coguest editor with JoAnn Phillion on an upcoming special issue of the *Journal of Curriculum Theorizing* focused on the internationalization of curriculum and studying abroad.

Douglas McKnight is an Associate Professor of curriculum studies at The University of Alabama. His areas of research include curriculum theory, history, and the social theory of technology. He brought these different interests together in his book, *Schooling, the Puritan Moral Imperative and the Molding of an American Identity: Education's "Errand into the Wilderness"* (Erlbaum, 2003). He is currently working on a series of articles focused on curriculum and critical theory's relationship to the existential condition of the educator as read through a Kierkegaardian theory of despair. When he is not "despairing" over the state of educational affairs in America, he is driving his son to various soccer tournaments.

Janet L. Miller is Professor and Director of Research in the Department of Arts & Humanities, Teachers College, Columbia University. She was elected AERA Vice-President for Division B (Curriculum Studies) for the 1997–1999 term, and elected Secretary of Division B for the 1990–1992 term. She served as Managing Editor of *The Journal of Curriculum Theorizing* (JCT) from 1978 through 1998, and as Chair of JCT's Bergamo Curriculum Theorizing Conferences during that time frame. She also was elected President of the American Association for the Advancement of Curriculum Studies (AAACS) for two consecutive terms, from 2001 through 2007. She is the author of *Creating Spaces and Finding Voices: Teachers Collaborating for Empowerment* (SUNY Press, 1990), *Sounds of Silence Breaking: Women, Autobiography, Curriculum* (Lang, 2005), and Coeditor, with William C. Ayers, of *A Light in Dark Times: Maxine Greene and the Unfinished Conversation.* At the 2008 AERA Annual Conference, Janet received the AERA Division B (Curriculum Studies) Lifetime Achievement Award.

Stuart J. Murray is Assistant Professor of Rhetoric & Writing in the Department of English at Ryerson University in Toronto, Canada. He received his PhD (2004) in rhetoric from the University of California at Berkeley, after which he completed a 2-year SSHRC postdoctoral fellowship in philosophy at the University of Toronto. His work is concerned with the constitution of human subjectivity and the links between rhetoric, politics, and ethics. Current research includes a book-length project on the rhetorical dimensions of biopolitics and bioethics after Foucault, a collaborative study on the politics of death (thanatopolitics), and a collected volume edited with Dave Holmes, titled, *Critical Interventions in the Ethics of Healthcare* (Ashgate, 2008).

JoAnn Phillion is Associate Professor of Curriculum Studies at Purdue University Indiana. Her research interests are in narrative inquiry in cross-cultural immigrant education issues in Hong Kong, the United States, and Canada; preservice teacher development in field experiences in international contexts; and study abroad in Honduras. She is Associate Editor of *The Sage Handbook of Curriculum and Instruction* (Sage, 2008), Coeditor of *Narrative and Experience in Multicultural Education* (Sage, 2005), Coeditor of the book series *Research for Social Justice* (Information Age, in press), and has published extensively on narrative inquiry in curriculum journals. She teaches courses in multiculturalism and curriculum and teacher development in the United States and Hong Kong.

William F. Pinar moved to the University of British Columbia in 2005, where he holds a Canada Research Chair and directs the Centre for the Study of the Internationalization of Curriculum Studies. Previously he taught curriculum theory at Louisiana State University, where he served as the St. Bernard Parish Alumni Endowed Professor. He has also served as the Frank Talbott Professor at the University of Virginia and the A. Lindsay O'Connor Professor of American Institutions at Colgate University. He has lectured widely, including Harvard University, McGill University, the University of Wisconsin-Madison, as well as the Universities of Chicago, Oslo, and Tokyo. He is the author, most recently, of Intellectual *Advancement Through Disciplinarity*: *Verticality and Horizontality in Curriculum Studies*.

Molly Quinn is Associate Professor in the Curriculum & Teaching Department at Teachers College, Columbia University. She enjoys teaching graduate courses in arts-based pedagogies, elementary social studies, and curriculum theory—engaging students dialogically, philosophically, autobiographically, aesthetically, experientially, critically, in the study of curriculum and art of teaching. Molly also serves on the journal editorial boards of *Journal of Curriculum Theorizing, C&P, Encounter,* and *Taboo*; and enjoys active membership and participation in Professors of Curriculum, AERA, *JCT, C&P,* and AAACS (with IAACS), for which she currently serves as a conference committee member, and last year served as conference site codirector. The author of *Going Out, Not Knowing Whither: Education, the Upward Journey and the Faith of Reason* (2001), much of her scholarship in curriculum studies—drawing principally upon the traditions of existentialism, phenomenology, hermeneutics and poststructuralism—engages "spiritual" and philosophical criticism toward embracing a vision of education that cultivates wholeness, beauty, compassion and social action.

Elaine Riley-Taylor is an Assistant Professor at the University of Louisiana at Lafayette where her focus on language and cultural diversity impassions her teaching and her writing. Growing up in the southern United States, she spent six years at Northern Arizona University in Flagstaff before coming "home" to her native Louisiana. Dr. Riley-Taylor's scholarly work foregrounds the critical nature of diversity as a common denominator underlying the health and long-term viability of, both, human cultures and ecological systems. In her book *Ecology, Spirituality, and Education: Curriculum for Relational Knowing* (Lang, 2002), she uses the power of storytelling and creative theoretical integration to highlight the importance of human "diversity" and "relationality" toward learning to live sustainably with one another and with the planet.

Teresa Rishel is an Assistant Professor in Curriculum and Instruction and Middle Childhood Education at Kent State University. Her educational experience includes serving as an elementary principal and teaching elementary and middle level grades. At Kent State, she teaches undergraduate and graduate courses in methods, pedagogy, multicultural education and educational theory. Her research focuses on adolescent suicide and schooling in terms of sociocultural relationships, the hidden curriculum, leadership, and affective education. Her research and teaching are based on her interests in reflective thinking, curriculum theory, multicultural issues of education and social justice.

Alberto J. Rodriguez is Co-Director of the Center for Equity and Biliteracy Education Research and Professor of Science Education in the Department of Policy Studies in Language and Cross-Cultural Education at San Diego State University. He teaches bilingual science methods courses in undergraduate and graduate courses. His research focuses on the use of sociotransformative constructivism (sTc). Dr. Rodriguez's work has been published in several journals such as, *The American Educational Research Journal, the Journal of Research in Science Teaching, Research in Science Education, The Journal of Teacher Education,* and others. Dr. Rodriguez Received the Kappa Delta Pi—Teaching and Teacher Education Research Award from the American Educational Research Association in 2000, and the New Mexico State University Award for Exceptional Achievements in Creative Scholarly Activity in 2002. He published a coedited book with Rick Kitchen (math education) titled, *Preparing Prospective Mathematics and Science Teachers to Teach for Diversity: Promising Strategies for Transformative Action* (2005).

William H. Schubert is Professor and University Scholar at the University of Illinois—Chicago, where he coordinates the PhD Program in Curriculum Studies, and was chair of Curriculum and Instruction for 7 years. Author or editor of 16 books and over 150 articles and chapters, Schubert has served as vice president of AERA, president of the Society of Professors of Education, the John Dewey Society, and the Society for the Study of Curriculum History. He is recipient of the 2007 Mary Ann Raywid Award and the 2004 AERA Lifetime Achievement Award in Curriculum Studies. Currently, he is senior consulting editor of the *Encyclopedia of Curriculum Studies* and has completed a book entitled *Love, Justice, and Education: John Dewey and the Utopians.*

Suniti Sharma is a doctoral student in the Department of Curriculum and Instruction, Purdue University and currently a teaching assistant within the teacher education program. She earned her MA in English Literature from the University of Delhi, India. She taught high school English in India for 12 years and has been teaching as an English instructor at a detention facility for young women. Her research and teaching interests focus on curriculum and feminist theories, understanding student subjectivities in relation to school reform, research efforts in detention classrooms, and autobiography as a poststructural feminist form of qualitative inquiry. She plans to finish her PhD in 2009.

Patrick Slattery is Professor and Regents Scholar in the College of Education and Human Development at Texas A&M University where he teaches courses in Philosophy of Education, Curriculum Theory, and Arts-Based Research. His most recent book is "Curriculum Development in the Postmodern Era" (Routledge, 2006). He has published research articles in *Harvard Educational Review, Journal of Curriculum Studies, Educational Theory, Qualitative Inquiry,* and *Curriculum Inquiry.* He is the coeditor of *The Journal of Curriculum and Pedagogy* and President of the American Association for the Advancement of Curriculum Studies. He is also an artist, lecturer, and activist for social justice issues in his current hometown of Austin, Texas. The central theme of his work is the promotion of a just, compassionate, and ecologically sustainable global culture through holistic and reconceptualized approaches to curriculum, constructive postmodern understandings of education, queer studies in gender and sexuality, and process philosophical visions of creativity and change.

Nathan Snaza is a doctoral student in the department of Cultural Studies and Comparative Literature at the University of Minnesota, where he received an MEd in English education. He has presented work on the ghosts of U.S. curriculum studies, the concept of "voice" in radical writing pedagogy, and the lessons teacher education might learn from critical studies of blackface minstrelsy. His writings have appeared in *Bad Subjects*, *Animal Liberation Philosophy and Policy Journal*, and *InterActions: UCLA Journal of Education and Information Studies*. His current research interests include the figuration of teaching in literary texts, the function of "hope" in literary and cultural studies, and the possible uses of Hardt and Negri's theory of empire for conceptualizing education today.

Celeste Snowber, a dancer, writer and educator, is an Associate Professor in the Faculty of Education at Simon Fraser University, Burnaby, BC, Canada. She has focused her work in the area of embodiment, spirituality, ecology and arts-based inquiry. She has written numerous essays and poetry in journals and chapters in books in the areas of the arts, holistic education, and curriculum studies as well as being the author of *Embodied Prayer*, which is in its second edition. Her most recent work has been exploring a poetics of embodiment through her essays, performance, and poetry. Much of her poetry explores the connections between the inner and outer landscapes of the natural world. She has published these poems in various journals as well as created site-specific performances outside which include dance and poetry in sites near the ocean. Celeste lives outside Vancouver raising three lively sons.

Stephanie Springgay is an Assistant Professor of Art Education and Women's Studies at Penn State University. Her research and artistic explorations focus on issues of *relationality* and *an ethics of embodiment*. In addition, as a multidisciplinary artist working with installation and video-based art, she investigates the relationship between artistic practices and methodologies of educational research through a/r/tography. She is the coeditor of *Curriculum and the Cultural Body* (Lang, 2007) with Debra Freedman and author of *Body Knowledge and Curriculum: Pedagogies of touch in youth and visual culture* (Lang, 2008).

Denise Taliaferro-Baszile received her MEd in Secondary English Education and her PhD in Curriculum Theory at Louisiana State University. Currently she is an assistant professor in the Department of Educational Leadership at Miami University, where she teaches courses on curriculum theory, critical race theory, and critical media literacy. Her research interests are in the historical, political, and philosophical foundations of race and its relationship to curriculum and pedagogy. She has published several articles and book chapters on the pedagogical challenges of teaching race in predominately White Universities, the importance of considering radical leadership for educational change, the significance of the Black autobiographical voice in curriculum studies and critical race testimony, and the curriculum of hip-hop culture.

Mark Tappan is Professor of Education and Human Development and Chair of the Education Program at Colby College in Waterville, Maine. He received his AB in religion from Oberlin College, his MA in education from the Ohio State University, and his EdD in human development from Harvard University. He has also taught at the University of Massachusetts/Boston, Trinity College, Clark University, and the Harvard Graduate School of Education. His research and teaching interests include moral development and moral education, identity development, boys' development and education, risk and resilience in childhood and adolescence, and social justice. He is coeditor (with Martin Packer) of *Narrative and Storytelling: Implications for Understanding Moral Development* (Jossey-Bass, 1991), and *Cultural and Critical Perspectives on Human Development* (SUNY Press, 2001), and coauthor (with Lyn Mikel Brown and Sharon Lamb) of *Packaging Boyhood* (St. Martins, forthcoming).

Kevin Tavin is an Associate Professor in the Department of Art Education at The Ohio State University in the United States. He holds a BFA, MEd, and a PhD in art education and has taught K-12 and postsecondary courses since 1990. Tavin's research focuses on visual culture, critical pedagogy, psychoanalytic theory, and art education. His work is published in *Art Education; InSEA News, The Journal of Cultural Research in Art Education; The Journal of Social Theory in Art Education; NAEA News, Studies in Art Education; and Visual Arts Research*. Tavin has presented keynotes and research papers at various international, national, and regional conferences and symposia, in Sweden, Germany, South Korea, Japan, Brazil, Finland, Denmark, the Czech Republic, and the United States. In fall 2008, Tavin worked at the University of Art and Design in Helsinki, Finland as a Fulbright Senior Specialist.

Hongyu Wang is an Associate Professor in Curriculum Studies at Oklahoma State University . She has authored books and published numerous articles both in Chinese and in English. Author of The Call *from the Stranger on a Journey Home: Curriculum in a Third Space* (Lang, 2004), she is coeditor, with Donna Trueit, William E. Doll, Jr., and William F. Pinar, of *The Internationalization of Curriculum Studies* (Lang, 2003), and coeditor with Claudia Eppert of *Cross-cultural Studies in Curriculum: Eastern Thought, Educational Insights* (Erlbaum, 2008). She received the Regents Distinguished Research Award at Oklahoma State University in 2006. Cofounder with Xin Li of the Special Interest Group in Confucianism, Taoism, and Education at the American Educational Research Association in 2007, she is currently a coeditor for the *Journal of Curriculum Theorizing*.

William H. Watkins was born in Harlem, New York and raised in South Central Los Angeles. A former high school teacher, he completed his PhD in 1986 at the University of Illinois at Chicago. Bill served on the College of Education and Black Studies faculties at the University of Utah before returning to the College of Education at the University of Illinois at Chicago in 1995. Bill is the author of *The White Architects of Black Education* (2001), lead editor/contributor to *Race and Education* (2001), and editor/contributor to the book, *Black Protest Thought and Education* (2005). His numerous articles, chapters, essays, and reviews have appeared in scholarly journals, books, encyclopedias, and the popular press. Bill has presented papers, lectured, and traveled widely throughout the world. He has served on numerous editorial boards and held leadership positions in professional organizations. His life's work is dedicated to equality, social justice, and peace.

John A. Weaver is Professor of Curriculum Studies at Georgia Southern University. He is the author of *Rethinking Academic Politics in Reunified Germany and the United States* and *Popular Culture: A Primer*. He coedited with Marla Morris and Peter Appelbaum, *(Post) Modern Science (Fiction)*, and with Karen Anijar and Toby Daspit, *SF Curriculum, Cyborg Teachers, and Youth Cultures*. John is currently writing a book titled *Educating the Posthuman*.

Ugena Whitlock holds a PhD in Curriculum and Instruction from Louisiana State University (2005). She is currently Assistant Professor of Education and Gender Studies and Associate Coordinator of the Gender and Women's Studies Program at Kennesaw State University in Georgia. Her research interests include curriculum theory, gender and sexuality, race, class, popular culture, and Southern studies. Ugena's book, *This Corner of Canaan: Curriculum Studies of Place and the Reconstruction of the South,* was published in 2007. She has had articles appear in various peer-reviewed journals. She serves as Secretary on the Executive Council of the American Association for the Advancement of Curriculum Studies.

Ann G. Winfield is an Assistant Professor of Philosophical and Social Foundations of Education at Roger Williams University in Bristol, Rhode Island. Subsequent to a BA in Cultural Anthropology and years of work in the nonprofit sector, Winfield received her PhD in educational goundations, research and policy analysis with a concentration in curriculum studies from North Carolina State University. Growing up during the 1960s and the 1970s in Canada and on both coasts of the United States prompted an early interest in root causes. This interest has focused, of late, on the machinations of ideological residue in the present, collective memory as the mode of transport, and the use of history as both a weapon of oppression and a wellspring of possibility.

Index